2ND EDITION

MUSIC
OF THE
PEOPLES
OF THE
WORLD

WILLIAM ALVES

Harvey Mudd College

SCHIRMER
CENGAGE Learning™

Australia • Brazil • Japan • Korea • Mexico • Singapore • Spain • United Kingdom • United States

Music of the Peoples of the World, Second Edition
William Alves, Harvey Mudd College

Publisher: Clark Baxter

Senior Development Editor: Sue Gleason

Assistant Editor: Kimberly Apfelbaum

Editorial Assistant: Nell Pepper

Senior Media Editor: Wendy Constantine

Marketing Manager: Christina Shea

Marketing Assistant: Jillian D'Urso

Marketing Communications Manager: Heather Baxley

Content Project Manager: Georgia Young

Art Director: Cate Barr

Print Buyer: Karen Hunt

Permissions Editor, Text: Sarah d'Stair

Permissions Editor, Image: Deanna Ettinger

Production Service: Charu Khanna, Macmillan Publishing Solutions

Text Designer: Marsha Cohen, Parallelogram Graphics

Photo Researcher: Eric Schrader

Copy Editor: Julie McNamee

Cover Designer: May Liang

Cover Image: Wendy Stone/CORBIS

Compositor: Macmillan Publishing Solutions

For product information and technology assistance, contact us at
Cengage Learning Academic Resource Center, 1-800-423-0563
For permission to use material from this text or product,
submit all requests online at **www.cengage.com/permissions**.
Further permissions questions can be e-mailed to
permissionrequest@cengage.com.

Library of Congress Control Number: 2008935836

ISBN-13: 978-0-495-50384-2

ISBN-10: 0-495-50384-3

Schirmer Cengage Learning
25 Thomson Place
Boston, MA 02210
USA

Cengage Learning products are represented in Canada by Nelson Education, Ltd.

For your course and learning solutions, visit **academic.cengage.com**.

Purchase any of our products at your local college store or at our preferred online store **www.ichapters.com**.

Dedication
For Lou Harrison and Gilbert Blount

Printed in Canada
1 2 3 4 5 6 7 12 11 10 09 08

CONTENTS IN BRIEF

CHAPTER 1 ◆ WORLD MUSIC CULTURES: AN INTRODUCTION   1

The Round Continuum of Music   2
Sound and Cultural Conventions   4

CHAPTER 2 ◆ PITCH AND MELODY   7

What is Pitch?   7
Melody   11
Ornamentation   14
Motives and Themes   14
Structure   15

CHAPTER 3 ◆ RHYTHM AND LOUDNESS   17

Organizing Time   17
The Beat   18
Tempo   19
Meter   19
Metrical Stress and Syncopation   21

CHAPTER 4 ◆ TEXTURE   23

Texture   23

CHAPTER 5 ◆ TIMBRE AND MUSICAL INSTRUMENTS   29

Timbre   29
Musical Instruments   30
Classification   31
Chordophones   32
Aerophones   36
Membranophones   38
Idiophones   41
Musical Style   41

CHAPTER 6 ◆ SUB-SAHARAN AFRICA   45

Elements of Traditional African Music   46
Traditional African Instruments   48
Drumming in West Africa   53
Music of the Jali   56

Mbira Music   61
African Popular Music   67

CHAPTER 7 ◆ THE MIDDLE EAST AND NORTH AFRICA   77

Elements of Middle Eastern Music   78
The Instruments of the Region   81
Arabic Music Theory   85
Arabic Music Performance   89
Popular Music in the Arab World   93
Music in Iran   94
Jewish Music   96

CHAPTER 8 ◆ CENTRAL ASIA   107

Elements of Central Asian Music   109
Tibetan Music   109
Mongolian Music   116

CHAPTER 9 ◆ INDIA   125

Elements of Indian Classical Music   127
Indian Instruments and Their Functions   129
Raga—The Melodic Dimension of Indian Music   134
Tala—The Rhythmic Dimension of Indian Music   139
A Performance of Raga Khamaj   141
Vocal Music in India   142
The Influence of Indian Music on Contemporary Western Music   159

CHAPTER 10 ◆ CHINA   163

Elements of Traditional Chinese Music   165
Traditional Chinese Instruments   169
Guqin Music   174
Folk and Contemporary Music   177
Chinese Dramatic Music   181
Popular Music   187

CHAPTER 11 ◆ JAPAN   191

Elements of Japanese Music   192
Gagaku: Ancient Court Orchestral Music   196

Japanese Instrumental Music 199
Music of the Japanese Theater 208
Popular Music and Influences from the West 211

CHAPTER 12 ◆ INDONESIA   215

Elements of Gamelan Music 217
Java, Its Gamelan and Instruments 218
Javanese Composition 223
Bali, Its Gamelan and Instruments 232
Balinese Composition and Performance 237
Popular Music in Indonesia 242
New Gamelan Music 244

CHAPTER 13 ◆ EASTERN EUROPE   247

Elements of Eastern European Folk Music 249
Hungarian Folk Music 253
Bulgarian Folk Music 258
Russian Folk Music 262

CHAPTER 14 ◆ WESTERN EUROPE   269

Elements of Western European Music 271
Music in Austria 276
Traditional Music of Ireland 280
Spain 288

CHAPTER 15 ◆ LATIN AMERICA   297

Elements of Traditional Latin American Music 298
Music in Mexico 302
Music in Brazil 309
Music in Andean Countries 316

CHAPTER 16 ◆ NORTH AMERICA   321

Elements of European and African Musical Traditions in North America 324
Early European American Music 325
Music of Indigenous Americans 333
African-American Music 340
Popular Music in America 351

CONTENTS

PREFACE   XII

CHAPTER 1 ◆ WORLD MUSIC CULTURES: AN INTRODUCTION   1

THE ROUND CONTINUUM OF MUSIC   2
The Graceland Controversy 2
Music and Culture 4

SOUND AND CULTURAL CONVENTIONS   4
The Functions of Music 5
Listening 6

CHAPTER 2 ◆ PITCH AND MELODY   7

WHAT IS PITCH?   7
The Octave 8
Tuning Systems 8
Tonality 9
Modes 10
A Complete Definition of Mode 11
Keys and the Relativity of Pitch Perception 11

MELODY   11
Melodic Contour and Motion 12
Melodic Range and Tessitura 13
Cadences and Phrases 13

ORNAMENTATION   14

MOTIVES AND THEMES   14

STRUCTURE   15
Phrases and Hierarchical Structures 15
Repeating Structures 15
Variation 16

CHAPTER 3 ◆ RHYTHM AND LOUDNESS   17

ORGANIZING TIME   17

THE BEAT   18

TEMPO   19

METER   19

METRICAL STRESS AND SYNCOPATION   21
Loudness in Music 22

CHAPTER 4 ◆ TEXTURE   23

TEXTURE   23
Monophony 23
Homophony 24
Polyphony 25

Heterophony 25
Other Textures 26
The Drone 26
Drums 26

CHAPTER 5 ◆ TIMBRE AND MUSICAL INSTRUMENTS   29

TIMBRE   29

MUSICAL INSTRUMENTS   30

Resonance 30

CLASSIFICATION   31

CHORDOPHONES   32

Zithers 34
Lutes 34
Lyres 35
Harps 35

AEROPHONES   36

Flutes 36
Double Reeds 38
Single Reeds 38
Buzzed-Lip Instruments 38

MEMBRANOPHONES   38

IDIOPHONES   41

MUSICAL STYLE   41

CHAPTER 6 ◆ SUB-SAHARAN AFRICA   45

◆ SOUNDS: *Atsia* Suite 45

ELEMENTS OF TRADITIONAL AFRICAN MUSIC 46

Polyrhythm 47

Music and Language 48

TRADITIONAL AFRICAN INSTRUMENTS   48

Membranophones 49

Idiophones 50

Aerophones 50

Chordophones 51

DRUMMING IN WEST AFRICA   53

A Drumming Orchestra Performance 56

MUSIC OF THE *JALI*   56

◆ LISTENING GUIDE: *Atsia* Suite 57

◆ LISTENING EXERCISE 1: *Atsia* Suite 60

MBIRA MUSIC   61

◆ LISTENING GUIDE: *Yundum Nko* (Man from Yundum) 62

An *Mbira* Performance 64

◆ LISTENING GUIDE: *Nyamaropa* (excerpt) 66

AFRICAN POPULAR MUSIC   67

Popular Forms in West Africa 68

Popular Forms in South Africa 69

◆ LISTENING GUIDE: *"No Buredi"* ("No Bread") 70

◆ LISTENING EXERCISE 2: *"No Buredi"* 74

CHAPTER 7 ◆ THE MIDDLE EAST AND NORTH AFRICA   77

◆ SOUNDS: *Dastgah Mahur* 77

ELEMENTS OF MIDDLE EASTERN MUSIC   78

The Middle East and Religion 79

Islam and Music 80

THE INSTRUMENTS OF THE REGION   81

ARABIC MUSIC THEORY   85

The *Maqam* Scale 85

Other Characteristics of a *Maqam* 87

Rhythm in Arabic Music 88

ARABIC MUSIC PERFORMANCE   89

Music Forms and Practice in Arabic Music 89

A *Takht* Performance 90

◆ LISTENING GUIDE: *Waslah* in *Maqam Huzam* (excerpt) 91

◆ LISTENING EXERCISE 3: *Waslah* in *Maqam Huzam* 93

POPULAR MUSIC IN THE ARAB WORLD   93

MUSIC IN IRAN   94

Iranian Classical Music 95

A Performance of an Iranian *Dastgah* 96

JEWISH MUSIC   96

◆ LISTENING GUIDE: *Dastgah Mahur* 97

Religious Music 99

Klezmer 100

Modern Israeli Music 101

◆ LISTENING GUIDE: *A Rumenisher Doyne* 102

◆ LISTENING EXERCISE 4: *A Rumenisher Doyne* 104

CHAPTER 8 ◆ CENTRAL ASIA   107

◆ SOUNDS: *Mahakala Puja* 107

ELEMENTS OF CENTRAL ASIAN MUSIC   109

TIBETAN MUSIC   109

Ritual Music and Its Instruments in Tibet 110

A Tibetan Music Performance 113

Folk and Art Music in Tibet 113

◆ LISTENING GUIDE: Invocation from *Mahakala Puja* (excerpt) 114

MONGOLIAN MUSIC   116

Traditional Songs 117

Höömii Singing 118

Instruments 119

◆ LISTENING GUIDE: *"Hoyor Bor"* 120

A Mongolian Music Performance 121

◆ LISTENING EXERCISE 5: *"Hoyor Bor"* 122

CHAPTER 9 ◆ INDIA   125

◆ SOUNDS: Raga *Khamaj* 125

ELEMENTS OF INDIAN CLASSICAL MUSIC   127

The Nature of Improvisation in Indian Music 128

Training for Performance of Indian Music 128

INDIAN INSTRUMENTS AND THEIR FUNCTIONS   129

The Soloist 129

The Drummer 132

The Drone 133

Chordophones in Indian Music 133

RAGA—THE MELODIC DIMENSION OF INDIAN MUSIC   134

The Tuning of Ragas 134

The Scales of Ragas 135

Arohana/Avarohana (Ascending/Descending Scale) 135

The Hierarchy of Pitches 137

Gamak (Ornamentation) 138

Pakar—Important Motives in Indian Music 138

Extramusical Associations 138

TALA—THE RHYTHMIC DIMENSION OF INDIAN MUSIC   139

Patterns of Beats in the *Tala* 140

A PERFORMANCE OF RAGA *KHAMAJ*   141

VOCAL MUSIC IN INDIA   142

◆ LISTENING GUIDE: Raga *Khamaj* 143

◆ **LISTENING EXERCISE 6: Raga *Khamaj* 146**

North Indian Vocal Music 146

South Indian Vocal Music 147

Performance of the *Kriti "Ninnada Nela"* 148

◆ **LISTENING GUIDE: *"Ninnada Nela"* ("Why Should I Blame You?") 149**

Folk Song in India 151

◆ **LISTENING EXERCISE 7: *"Ninnada Nela"* 152**

    Baul Music 152

Filmi Popular Music 153

    Performance of *"Dil Cheez Kya Hai"* 154

◆ **LISTENING GUIDE: "Dil Cheez Kya Hai" ("What Is a Heart?") 155**

THE INFLUENCE OF INDIAN MUSIC ON CONTEMPORARY WESTERN MUSIC   159

CHAPTER 10 ◆ CHINA
163

◆ **SOUNDS: *"Ping sha lo yen"* ("Wild Geese Descending onto the Sandbank") 163**

ELEMENTS OF TRADITIONAL CHINESE MUSIC 165

Religion and Music in China 165

Traditional Music Theory in China 167

TRADITIONAL CHINESE INSTRUMENTS   169

Chordophones 169

Wind Instruments 173

Percussion 173

GUQIN MUSIC   174

A *Guqin* Performance 175

◆ **LISTENING GUIDE: *"Ping sha lo yen"* (excerpt) 176**

FOLK AND CONTEMPORARY MUSIC   177

Instrumental Folk Ensembles 177

Sizhu 178

A *Sizhu* Performance: *Fan Instead of Gong* 178

◆ **LISTENING GUIDE: *Fan Instead of Gong* 179**

◆ **LISTENING EXERCISE 8: *Fan Instead of Gong* 180**

Reform Music 180

CHINESE DRAMATIC MUSIC   181

Narrative Song and Folk Dramas 181

Regional Opera 182

Jingxi—Beijing Opera 182

A *Jingxi* Performance: *The Drunken Concubine* 184

◆ **LISTENING GUIDE: "An Island in the Sea," *The Drunken Concubine* 185**

POPULAR MUSIC   187

CHAPTER 11 ◆ JAPAN
191

◆ **SOUNDS: *Daiwa gaku* 191**

ELEMENTS OF JAPANESE MUSIC   192

Kagura: Shinto Music 193

Shomyo: Buddhist Chants 194

Modes in Japanese Music 195

GAGAKU: ANCIENT COURT ORCHESTRAL MUSIC   196

A *Gagaku* Performance 198

JAPANESE INSTRUMENTAL MUSIC   199

Music for the *Shamisen* 199

◆ LISTENING GUIDE: *Etenraku Nokorigaku Sanben* (excerpt) 200

◆ LISTENING EXERCISE 9: *Etenraku* 202

Music for the *Shakuhachi* 203

A *Shakuhachi* Performance 204

Music for the *Koto* 204

◆ LISTENING GUIDE: *Daiwa gaku* 205

A *Koto* Performance 206

◆ LISTENING GUIDE: *Rokudan no shirabe* (excerpt) 207

MUSIC OF THE JAPANESE THEATER   208

Noh Classical Theater 208

Kabuki Classical Theater 209

POPULAR MUSIC AND INFLUENCES FROM THE WEST   211

CHAPTER 12 ◆ INDONESIA   215

◆ SOUNDS: *Ladrang Pangkur* 215

ELEMENTS OF GAMELAN MUSIC   217

JAVA, ITS GAMELAN AND INSTRUMENTS   218

Javanese Culture 218

The Javanese Gamelan 219

Javanese Gamelan Instruments 219

JAVANESE COMPOSITION   223

The *Balungan* 223

The *Kembangan* 223

Patet (Mode) 224

Colotomic Structure 224

Irama and Stratification of Rhythm 225

A Javanese Gamelan Performance 227

◆ LISTENING GUIDE: *Ladrang Pangkur* 229

◆ LISTENING EXERCISE 10: *Ladrang Pangkur* 232

BALI, ITS GAMELAN AND INSTRUMENTS   232

Characteristics of the Balinese Gamelan 233

The *Gamelan Gong Kebyar* 234

The *Kebyar* Instruments 235

BALINESE COMPOSITION AND PERFORMANCE   237

Topeng (Mask Dance) and *Kebyar* 237

Kecak 238

Interlocking Patterns 238

   Kotekan 239

A Balinese Gamelan Performance 239

◆ LISTENING GUIDE: *Gending Pengalang Bebarongan* 240

◆ LISTENING EXERCISE 11: *Gending Pengalang Bebarongan* 242

POPULAR MUSIC IN INDONESIA   242

NEW GAMELAN MUSIC   244

CHAPTER 13 ◆ EASTERN EUROPE   247

◆ SOUNDS: *Dilmano, Dilbero* 247

ELEMENTS OF EASTERN EUROPEAN FOLK MUSIC   249

Epic Songs 250

Asymmetrical Meters 251

Socialist Realism 251

Professional Folk Ensembles 252

HUNGARIAN FOLK MUSIC   253

Historical Background 253

The Characteristics of Hungarian Folk Song 254

Representative Hungarian Instruments 254

Dance House Music 255

Romani Folk Song 255

◆ LISTENING GUIDE: *Téglaporos a kalapom* 256

A Performance of a Romani *Szájbögö*—Mouth Bass Song 257

BULGARIAN FOLK MUSIC   258

Historical Background 258

Bulgarian Folk Songs 258

Bulgarian Rhythm 259

Representative Bulgarian Instruments and Their Performance 259

A Performance of a Bulgarian Folk Song 260

◆ LISTENING GUIDE: *Dilmano, Dilbero* 261

◆ LISTENING EXERCISE 12: *Dilmano, Dilbero* 262

RUSSIAN FOLK MUSIC   262

Folk Songs and Genres 262

Russian Instruments 263

A Performance of a Russian Folk Song 264

◆ LISTENING GUIDE: "Play, Skomoroshek" 265

CHAPTER 14 ◆ WESTERN EUROPE   269

◆ SOUNDS: *Die lustige Bäurin* 269

ELEMENTS OF WESTERN EUROPEAN MUSIC   271

European Harmony and Notation 272

Folk Music 274

The Rise of Popular Music 275

MUSIC IN AUSTRIA   276

◆ LISTENING GUIDE: *"Die lustige Bäurin"* 278

TRADITIONAL MUSIC OF IRELAND   280

Historical Background 280

Irish Genres 282

Singing 282

Dance Music 284

An Irish Instrumental Performance 284

◆ LISTENING GUIDE: *"Bean An Fhir Rua/O'Farrell's Welcome to Limerick"* 285

SPAIN   288

Spain's Folk Traditions 288

Flamenco 289

A Flamenco Performance 291

◆ LISTENING GUIDE: *Fuente de Piyaya (The Fountain of Piyaya)* 292

◆ LISTENING EXERCISE 13: *Fuente de Piyaya* 295

CHAPTER 15 ◆ LATIN AMERICA   297

◆ SOUNDS: *Ritmo* 297

ELEMENTS OF TRADITIONAL LATIN AMERICAN MUSIC   298

Latin American Dance Rhythms 299

Harmony 300

Latin American Musical Instruments 301

MUSIC IN MEXICO   302

The *Son* and Other *Mestizo* Forms 302

Folk Bands in Mexico 303

A Performance of a *Son Jarocho* 303

Conjunto 304

◆ LISTENING GUIDE: *Siquisirí* 305

◆ LISTENING EXERCISE 14: *Siquisirí* 308

Art Music in Mexico 308

MUSIC IN BRAZIL   309

The Afro-Brazilian Heritage 309

The Samba 310

A Performance of a Samba *Batucada* 312

◆ LISTENING GUIDE: *Ritmo* 313

MPB—*Música Popular Brasileira* 315

Art Music in Brazil 315

MUSIC IN ANDEAN COUNTRIES   316

CHAPTER 16 ◆ NORTH AMERICA   321

◆ SOUNDS: *Weeping Mary* 321

ELEMENTS OF EUROPEAN AND AFRICAN MUSICAL TRADITIONS IN NORTH AMERICA 324

EARLY EUROPEAN AMERICAN MUSIC   325

A Shape Note Hymn Performance 328

◆ LISTENING GUIDE: "Weeping Mary" 329

Anglo-American Folk Music 331

Country Music 332

The Folk Music Revival 333

MUSIC OF INDIGENOUS AMERICANS   333

Elements of Indigenous American Traditional Music 334

Indigenous American Regions 336

   Arctic North America 336

   Northwest Coast 337

   California and the Great Basin 337

   Southwest 337

   Pueblo 337

   Plains and Subarctic 338

   Eastern 338

Pan-Indian Music 338

Contemporary Indigenous American Music 339

AFRICAN-AMERICAN MUSIC   340

Wind Bands and Ragtime 341

Early Jazz 342

Blues 344

Gospel Music 345

Big Band to Bebop 346

A Bebop Performance: "Koko" by Charlie Parker 347

◆ LISTENING GUIDE: "*Koko,*" 348

◆ LISTENING EXERCISE 15: "*Koko*" 351

POPULAR MUSIC IN AMERICA   351

Rock and Roll 351

From Soul to Rap 354

Electronica 355

The Shrinking Musical Planet 356

BIBLIOGRAPHY   358

INDEX AND GLOSSARY   362

PREFACE

In 1934, American composer Henry Cowell began teaching his groundbreaking course, Music of the Peoples of the World. At the time, the class was a great rarity. Today, seemingly every imaginable type of music is just a few mouse clicks away, but Cowell's call for a deep and sensitive understanding of the music and its place in culture to guide our open-minded listening remains just as important. This book emphasizes the necessity of this understanding to truly appreciate the profoundly beautiful worlds of music available to us, drawing on diverse perspectives to guide the student, including music theory (the analysis of music and musical systems), musicology (the history of music), and ethnomusicology (the study of music in culture).

To help us accomplish this goal, *Music of the Peoples of the World, Second Edition,* offers distinctive and unique features.

ORGANIZATION AND CONTENT

The text's first five chapters focus on an introduction to world music cultures and the elements of music, introducing the basic terms and listening skills that we will use throughout the book. This section allows students with no background in music theory to appreciate, interpret, and discuss knowledgeably the music we survey. This section makes every effort to avoid presenting these principles from a particular cultural perspective, although nothing in this approach should prevent instructors from describing music in whatever way makes it clearest to their students.

Each of the eleven musical cultures in the book is the subject of a chapter that encompasses the music of a specific region. Within each chapter is an overview of the elements of that music culture, the region's history and musical life, and individual works that represent the musical variety of that culture. This format should make it easy for instructors to focus on, and students to review, the aspects of any musical culture that deserve special attention.

Although the sequence of regions presented reflects one logical ordering of these interconnected cultures (so that pentatonic modes introduced in the China chapter may be referred to in the Japan chapter, for example), for the most part, the regional chapters are organized so that an instructor may reorder or skip chapters according to the needs of a particular course. Depending on the depth in which an instructor wants to pursue a particular culture's music, it may not be possible to cover all eleven musical cultures in a single semester or quarter. Therefore, the chapters have been designed to make it as easy as possible for instructors to choose only those cultures that they want to present.

WHAT'S NEW IN THE SECOND EDITION

In response to feedback from instructors, the second edition incorporates many significant changes to make it more flexible and useful as a teaching and learning tool.

◆ Two new chapters have been added to the book—Chapter 14 on Western Europe, incorporating coverage of Austria, Ireland, and Spain, and Chapter 16 on North America, which includes coverage of European-American, indigenous, African-American, and popular music.

◆ Expanded and new sections on contemporary popular and fusion music now conclude many chapters or sections within chapters, such as those on Africa, the Middle East, India, China, Japan, Indonesia, Western Europe, Latin America, and North America.

◆ The book now offers 50 percent more musical selections, with more than twice as many Listening Guides. The CD set has expanded to three CDs. A complete list of all musical selections in the text appears on the inside front and back covers.

◆ Each musical culture is now organized as a single chapter, making assignments and text references more straightforward.

PEDAGOGICAL FEATURES

◆ **NEW** Each chapter on a musical culture now opens with a series of iconic signposts—Place, Times, Setting, and Sounds—to further emphasize the importance of listening to music in its cultural context.

  ◆ *Place* presents a map of the region, often accompanied by a side note on the significance of the area's geography.
  ◆ *Times* provides a chronological overview of the region's history.
  ◆ *Setting,* as its name implies, is a scene-setting introduction to the chapter's region, where the reader is immediately immersed in its sights, smells, and sounds.
  ◆ *Sounds* is a marginal key to the typical music of the region on the text's CD set—an initial experience for the chapter's scene-setting.

◆ The many full-color photographs in the book illustrate the amazing variety of every culture's instruments, the people who make music with these instruments, and the kinds of venues in which these people play.

◆ Instrument Galleries throughout display and describe the instruments of a culture in special photo essays. Each Instrument Gallery concludes with a reminder that these instruments may be seen and heard in the text's Active Listening Tools (as described later).

◆ Boldface terms help the student key on and review unfamiliar material.

◆ Listening Guides keyed to the audio selections and displaying thumbnail photographs of the performing instruments lead the student from the initiate's first listen through a thoughtful discussion of representative works. Schematic diagrams often visually represent the contours of a musical idea or characteristic. Each Listening Guide concludes with a reminder that the piece may be viewed in the text's Active Listening Tools.

- ◆ **NEW** Listening Exercises follow one or more Listening Guides in each regional chapter, allowing students to test themselves on their listening experience. The text's fifteen Listening Exercises are also available, in interactive form, in the text's World Music Resource Center, where answers may be emailed to the instructor.
- ◆ **NEW** The end of each chapter provides a reminder that students may find a wealth of materials to help them succeed in the course, at the text's Companion Website.

ANCILLARIES

- ◆ **CDs.** A three-CD set of all the audio selections we examine in the text is available for purchase. The CD set includes forty-four selections that correspond to thirty Listening Guides in the text and work in conjunction with the downloadable Active Listening Tools.
- ◆ **World Music Resource Center.** The World Music Resource Center provides a wealth of tools.
  - ◆ Downloadable Active Listening Tools, which include photographs and illustrations of instruments; detailed background information on each featured instrument; numerous video clips of musical performances from various cultures; and animated "Active Listening Guides" that work in conjunction with each of the Listening Guides in the text and the audio selections on the CD set
  - ◆ Electronic flashcards of instruments used in other cultures
  - ◆ Interactive versions of the text's Listening Exercises
  - ◆ A collection of YouTube videos

  Students can access the Resource Center by using the card packaged with this textbook. Instructors may register for an instructor account at *academic.cengage .com/login.*
- ◆ **Companion Website.** The companion website, at *http://academic.cengage. com/music/alves*, provides access to helpful study resources, including flashcards, glossary, tutorial quizzes, and instructors' PowerPoint presentations.
- ◆ **PowerLecture.** PowerLecture is an Instructor's CD-ROM containing Instructor's Manual, Test Bank with Examview, and PowerPoint presentations.

MUSIC NOTATION AND REPRESENTATION

Representing music visually, as we will do in this book, is a tricky business. Notation inevitably involves simplifications and choices about what to emphasize about the sound and how to depict it. Such decisions can introduce cultural bias, a problem that can be especially acute when adapting a notational scheme developed for one kind of music to represent another, very different tradition. Western notation, for example, is useful for showing diatonic melodies, but when pressed into service to represent music of very different scales and tuning systems, it becomes potentially confusing or misleading.

Yet visual representation of music can be a very powerful tool for understanding what is otherwise a time-based art that disappears as we experience it. Even professional musicians with highly trained ears often rely on some kind of notation to analyze the frequently complex listening experience at a glance.

This book adopts certain conventions of displaying music schematically (sounds shown as lines with pitch down to up, time left to right). Like all such schemes, this one involves simplifications and other assumptions, but its easily understood principles allow us to visually analyze some aspects of many different types of music with consistent conventions. For those who prefer Western notation even as they understand its potential shortcomings, we have made available Western notation of many of the examples in the text on the text's Companion Website as well as the Resource Center.

LANGUAGES AND ORTHOGRAPHY

The multiplicity of foreign terms from many languages creates many challenges for a text such as this. Sometimes competing transliteration or spelling standards may create unavoidable inconsistencies between different publications. At other times, the same musical term may exist in related languages with different spellings. I have endeavored to be as clear and consistent as possible in my choices.

A particular problem involves the use of plurals. Plurals are handled very differently in various languages, sometimes creating words quite dissimilar from the singular versions. Some languages handle plurals by context or reduplication. Meticulously following this multiplicity of rules potentially means that the number of foreign terms the student faces effectively doubles. Therefore, I have adopted the expedient convention of using the singular form of the word for both the singular and plural (with a few exceptions, notably terms that have become English words). Although this convention risks confusing native speakers of the languages, I believe it is a reasonable approach for the large majority of students.

THE WHOLE ROUND WORLD OF MUSIC

Henry Cowell's approach strongly influenced his student, my dear friend and inspiration, Lou Harrison. Before his death in 2003, Lou, who had gone on to teach his own course on Music of the Peoples of the World, enthusiastically supported my first drafts of this project. He has expressed to me a belief that dedication to arts from around the world can be a pacifying force in an otherwise troubled planet. Echoing a well-known saying of Cowell's, Harrison wrote, "When you grow up and leave home, there is a wonderful Whole Round World of Music."[1] It is my hope that you, the student, will come to share this sense of exhilaration from the exploration of music around the world.

---

[1]Lou Harrison. *Lou Harrison's Music Primer*. New York: Peters, 1971, p. 47.

ACKNOWLEDGMENTS

Cowell's own like-minded teacher, Charles Seeger, together with Mantle Hood, influenced another crucial teacher, mentor, and friend, Gilbert Blount. Gil helped shape my ears and mind and introduced me to many of these wonderful worlds of human expression.

As a generalist, I am greatly indebted to the many intrepid specialists who defined their fields and upon whose work mine depends. I would especially like to thank those who generously provided direct help with *Music of the Peoples of the World,* including Lydia Ayers, Isabel Balseiro, Robert Brown, Lina Doo, Janet Farrar-Royce, John Gilbert, David Hagedorn, Katherine Hagedorn, Yao Hong, Margaret Hontos, Deen Ipaye, Maria Johnson, Roderic Knight, Katalin Kovalcsik, Alfred Ladzekpo, Danlee Mitchell, N. Muralikrishnan, Kathleen Noss, Leonard Pronko, Jihad Racy, George Ruckert, Melinda Russell, David Schmalenberger, Schott Warfield, Albi Wethli, and particularly Bill Shozan Schultz.

I would also like to thank my own teachers in the performance areas covered in this book; they include Kobla Ladzekpo, Philip Schmidt, David Trashoff, Trustho, Wayne Vitale, and I Nyoman Wenten. Among the many people who supported the writing of this book, I would especially like to acknowledge the efforts of Brett Campbell. I also thank Clark Baxter, my publisher at Schirmer Cengage Learning, as well as my development editors Sue Gleason and Beth Hoeppner. And I thank the students at Harvey Mudd College, Claremont Graduate University, and the Massachusetts Institute of Technology who provided early and valuable feedback on this text.

Among the instructors whose comments have informed changes both significant and small in this edition are James M. Burns, Binghamton University; Kenneth S. Habib, California Polytechnic University; Ronald Horner, Frostburg State University; Damascus Kafumbe, Florida State University; Michael Kaloyanides, University of New Haven; Barbara Rose Lange, University of Houston; Hafez Modirzadeh, San Francisco State University; Charles Sharp, Fullerton College; Robert Stephens, University of Connecticut; and Lindsay Weightman, Penn State Abington.

And I owe particular thanks to Ed Ward, rock historian for NPR's Fresh Air with Terry Gross and coauthor of *Rock of Ages: The Rolling Stone History of Rock & Roll,* for his guidance on the new Chapter 16, "North America."

Last but not least, I extend special thanks to my wife, Lynn Burrows, in part for her remarkable forbearance during this project, and to my family as well as to all those students, fellow performers, and colleagues who continue to inspire me.

MUSIC
OF THE
PEOPLES
OF THE
WORLD

WORLD MUSIC CULTURES:
AN INTRODUCTION

THE ROUND CONTINUUM OF MUSIC

In 1987, a group of independent record label owners met in a pub in Islington, England, to discuss the increasing number of albums that did not fit into established record store categories. The beats and singing styles of these CDs—specifically those in languages other than English—struck many listeners as novel, even exotic. For years, the few such recordings to appear in record stores were either lost in the sea of general pop albums or dumped behind an "International" bin divider alongside collections of the world's national anthems and field recordings of Pygmy chants.

Rock icon Peter Gabriel had been among the first in his field to explore this music beyond early experiments with psychedelic *sitar* tracks. In 1982, the former Genesis singer and songwriter had begun the World of Music, Arts, and Dance (WOMAD) Festival as a way to bring together great bands from around the world. But despite an enthusiastic reception, the bands still found distribution of their CDs in the Euro-American market difficult. As a solution, the independent labels proposed a publicity campaign to popularize a new category—their choice for its name was "World Music."

FIGURE 1.1

Peter Gabriel performing at the World of Music, Arts, and Dance Festival.

© Reuters/CORBIS

The label "World Music" had popped up frequently before, sometimes to describe New Age and jazz groups that drew inspiration and techniques from Indian or African music. But during the 1970s, a growing access to audio technology (first radio, then cassettes) in developing countries had produced the inevitable cross-influences that led to an internationalization of the music business—and made it increasingly clear that musical appeal was not limited to North American and European music. Rhythms from Africa and South America soon found their way into popular music (Peter Gabriel's own songs among them) and, increasingly, musicians looked to the world's traditional and classical musics that lay at the root of these pop hits. This text is an introduction to many of those traditions.

THE GRACELAND CONTROVERSY

The World Music label began popping up in record store bins in 1987, the same year of the most influential album to date spotlighting international musics—Paul Simon's *Graceland*. Like Gabriel, Simon was open to diverse sources and musical collaborations. In 1984, he first heard *mbaqanga* music from South Africa, also known as "township jive." This music, bubbling with the fizz of early rock and roll, featured characteristically African elements that you will learn about in a later chapter.

Simon was intrigued enough to explore other South African styles, including the choral style known as *iscathamiya* and the energetic dances of mine workers called *gumboot.* These and other influences came together in the immensely successful *Graceland* album, where they emerged in the form of songs such as "Diamonds on the Soles of Her Shoes" and "Gumboots." Intended as a tribute to the musicians and musical styles of the black South African culture then suffering under apartheid, the album soon became a center of controversy—precisely because of those very goals.

At the time, the United Nations had enacted a cultural boycott to exert economic pressure on South Africa's minority white regime. Some thought Simon had broken that boycott. Furthermore, they considered foreign white liberals condescendingly presumptive, even exploitative, in their borrowing from black South Africa's repressed culture. The debate boiled over at a talk Simon gave at the predominantly black Howard University in Washington, DC. There a student asked, "How can you justify taking over this music? For too long artists have stolen African music. It happened with jazz. You're telling me the Gershwin story of Africa".[1] (George Gershwin was a hugely successful white songwriter whose compositions frequently drew upon his experience of African-American jazz.)

Like other pop musicians, Simon had assimilated South African musical influences in the same way that he had absorbed the music of American blues and R&B artists. "I went as a musician, and I interacted with other musicians," Simon responded.

By emphasizing the essential unity of musical cultures over geopolitical boundaries, Simon was echoing a tradition of twentieth-century classical composers. One of the first composers to advocate non-Western music as a source of enrichment rather than novelty was the American composer Henry Cowell (1897–1965). He applied his careful study of the music of India, Java, and other regions to his own modern compositions in the same way that he learned lessons from Bach and Beethoven.

His student, Lou Harrison, whose cross-cultural explorations are discussed in Chapter 12, commented on Cowell's approach:

> During a conference in Tokyo in 1961, Henry Cowell made a plea on behalf of hybrid musics, pointing out that combinations of the kind have often proved new and stimulating. Out of my respect for him, I took his remarks at face value (and "on faith" as it were) until a little while later when I realized that the full idea was: "don't underrate hybrid musics BECAUSE THAT'S ALL THERE IS." It is as though the world is a round continuum of music. Perhaps here a particular kind of expression is at its most intense and perfect. Then by gradual and geographic degrees, we move to some other center with a special expression. Anywhere on the planet we may do this—always by insensible degrees the music changes, and always the music is a compound, a hybrid of collected virtues.[2]

Against a history of colonialist exploitation, it is perhaps not surprising that some might view these universalist sentiments with some suspicion. To incorporate another culture's music in one's own, Western music was seen as potentially threatening the authenticity of the other culture's music to benefit its own. As Paul Simon himself said, the Howard University students saw the

---

[1]"Singer Paul Simon Strikes Sour Chord . . ." *Jet* 71 Feb. 2, 1987: 59.
[2]Harrison, Lou. *Lou Harrison's Music Primer.* New York: C. F. Peters, 1971.

music of *Graceland* as "neither Zulu, Xhosa, Shangaan, or American [but as] . . . a dilution of cultures".[3]

MUSIC AND CULTURE

"I *hate* world music," wrote rock star David Byrne, a stunning statement from someone who is known as a pioneer in that very category.

> In my experience, the use of the term *world music* is a way of dismissing artists or their music as irrelevant to one's own life. It's a way of relegating this "thing" into the realm of something exotic and therefore cute, weird but safe, because exotica are beautiful but irrelevant; they are, by definition, not like us. . . . It's a none too subtle way of reasserting the hegemony of Western pop culture. It ghettoizes most of the world's music. A bold and audacious move, White Man![4]

From nineteenth-century operas to contemporary techno tracks, Euro-American music has a history of adopting the sounds of other cultures for the sake of simple novelty, or **exoticism**. Although everyone always has his or her own cultural perspective, reducing music to an exotic status can be **ethnocentrism**, that is, judging music by its relationship to our own cultural experience.

In this text, we will endeavor to understand music cultures on their own terms. Such new listening experiences can challenge and enrich the perspectives you've grown up with. To achieve a deeper understanding of music, musicians use a variety of disciplines that overlap considerably. **Musicologists** study the history of music; **music theorists** analyze composition and musical systems; and **ethnomusicologists** study music as a part of people's way of life.

SOUND AND CULTURAL CONVENTIONS

The mind has a remarkable facility for categorizing new experiences into learned patterns. It is a process that transforms the new into the familiar and allows us to make sense of the new sounds and images we encounter every day. So, no matter how musically open-minded we try to be, our experiences can lead us to expect music to exhibit certain common elements in certain contexts.

For example, a person growing up in the United States is inclined to expect harmony as a standard musical trait. **Harmony**, several notes occurring at the same time to form a chord, is found in virtually everything we hear on the

[3]Simon, Paul. "Highbrows and Hits: A Fertile Compound." *The New York Times,* 30 Aug. 1998, Section 2, page 1.

[4]Byrne, David. "Crossing Music's Borders in Search of identity." *The New York Times,* 3 Oct. 1999, section 2, page 1.

radio and in music videos, film scores, classical music concerts, and church choirs. But this musical element, at least in the familiar chords of the West, is a European invention. Thus, we may find music without harmony strangely thin and find ourselves missing what's *not* there instead of listening to what *is* there—to other dimensions of sound, to nuances of melodic variation and pitch, for example.

Furthermore, sound is not the only dimension that shapes our musical expectations. We also understand musical experiences through their place in our social lives, through their context. Much of the music-making that we hear in Western culture comes from professionals who are paid to entertain. At a party, few nonprofessionals would feel comfortable singing a song for others. But in many areas of traditional Africa, where not singing is like not talking, everybody sings as a natural social function. Musicians who specialize in the area called **ethnomusicology** study this particular aspect of music, as it is part of people's way of life.

THE FUNCTIONS OF MUSIC

Think for a moment about the contexts in which you hear music—on headphones, at parties and concerts, in films, and on TV. Music as entertainment is such a pervasive function in the West and in popular music around the world that we might consider it a standard function of music in all society, but that is not always the case.

Certainly we can think of other functions of music—to inspire religious dedication, to express political protest, to coordinate work, to lull a baby to sleep, and so on. In these examples, participation in the music is at least as important as its sound. Through such functions, music can reinforce family ties or strengthen communities; it can also provide a path to meditation, exhibit devotion, or act as an inseparable component of rituals. And music may not be directed to human listeners at all. In some cultures, music is performed as entertainment for, or communication with, the divine.

In these cases, the conventional three-part division of musical participants into composer/performer/listener may not be the most helpful model for understanding the musical process. In the case of improvisation, for example, the composer may be one and the same as the performer, and the composition may be a communal effort. The composer of folk music may be a skilled artisan rather than a tortured songwriter, but he or she challenges the conventional dismissal of folk music as lacking an individual composer. This example brings up a conventional classification of traditions as folk music, art music, and popular music. **Folk music** is created by amateurs for their own community's enjoyment. **Popular music**, on the other hand, is created by professionals for mass audiences, usually with the intention of selling it as a commodity. **Art music** or classical music is also created by professionals, but selling it to large audiences is less important than depth of expression, which can be very complex and sophisticated. These categories are useful in some cultures, but they can also be problematic: popular and folk music can be very sophisticated, sometimes in ways different from art music; folk songs can be performed by professionals; and so on. Nevertheless, we will frequently find it useful to refer to this general division.

LISTENING

The focus of this text is on listening. In addition to the cultural and historical backgrounds in each unit, Listening Guides closely examine the recordings on the CD set. Your investment in careful listening will not only open worlds of deep enjoyment and appreciation but also offer a listening approach that you can apply to your future CD purchases. The next chapters on the essential elements of music will give us a basic vocabulary for discussing the music we hear.

If cultural and social context are as crucial to a real understanding of non-Western music as we claim, a novice might despair of ever fully appreciating it. True, you may never understand the music of the Ashanti people of West Africa the way Ashantis do, but as long as you make the effort to listen with an open mind and ears, you will be able to enjoy the music as music. And just as important, you may see your own culture and music from a new and deeper perspective.

BOOK COMPANION WEBSITE

You will find flashcards, a glossary, and tutorial quizzes, as well as other materials that will help you succeed in this course, at the *Music of the Peoples of the World, 2nd Edition,* Companion Website at www.cengage.com/music/alves/world2e.

PITCH AND MELODY

WHAT IS PITCH?

Musicians describe **pitch** as the quality of a note that distinguishes a high note from a low one. So commonly do people in Western culture speak of "high" versus "low" notes that they sometimes forget that these terms are metaphors. Other cultures may use different metaphors, such as "big" versus "small" pitches (reflecting the sizes of xylophone bars), or a culture might reverse "high" and "low" to reflect hand position on a string instrument. This text will indicate pitch schematically by showing high pitches toward the top of diagrams and low ones toward the bottom (see Graphic 2.1 on page 14).

Pitch relates to the physical property that scientists call **frequency**—that is, the number of sound waves per second, with a higher frequency producing a higher note and a lower frequency producing a lower one. Frequency is measured in **hertz**, named after a nineteenth-century physicist, and abbreviated Hz. For example, the frequency of 261.6 Hz (261.6 sound waves per second) corresponds to the pitch known as "middle C" in the West.

Pitch is one of the most important elements in music all over the world. Variation in pitch (along with rhythm) gives us **melody**, discussed later in this chapter, and playing different pitches simultaneously creates **harmony**. Because it is a natural part of the human voice, pitch is found in all musical systems the world over.

This is not to say that all instruments have definite pitch. Many drums can be tuned to a pitch, but it is often difficult to hear a pitch from a drum. Instead we hear a "thump," and although we may be able to describe it as relatively low or high, it lacks the specific pitch of, say, a string instrument. Likewise, a cymbal does not seem to have any pitch at all. Bells and triangles have pitches,

© Wendy Stone/CORBIS

FIGURE 2.1

The human experience of pitch and its place in musical systems is universal, probably because pitch is a natural part of the human voice and all peoples of the world sing. Here a group of Masai people from Kenya sing along with a cassette machine.

William Alves

FIGURE 2.2

Musical instruments may have varying degrees of definability of pitch. Whereas it is usually easy to hear the pitch of a string or wind instrument, bells such as this Japanese *densho* temple bell seem to have a less-defined pitch or perhaps several perceptible pitches at once.

but they are sometimes difficult to hear precisely (see Figure 2.2). They are on the borderline of what we would call the *definability of pitch.*

THE OCTAVE

An **interval** is the distance in pitch between any two notes, and the octave is the most fundamental interval in music. It is one of the few musical phenomena found in virtually all cultures in the world. (Although different cultures have different words for this interval, we will use the Western term *octave,* even though the interval doesn't necessarily encompass eight pitches.) A possible reason for its fundamental nature is that, aside from a unison (two notes that are exactly the same in a 1:1 ratio), the **octave** is defined by the next-simplest possible ratio between two different frequencies, 2:1. For example, a pitch of 200 Hz is exactly one octave lower than a pitch of 400 Hz. Although a ratio like this may seem like a mathematical abstraction, there is a distinctive quality to pitches an octave apart. The fact that, in musical systems around the world, the names of pitches an octave apart are often the same reflects this perception that the pitches are somehow equivalent.

Two pitches an octave apart sound so much alike that sometimes we hardly recognize them as distinct. When men and women sing together, for example, they are often singing melodies an octave apart from each other, but because the notes an octave apart blend so well, we scarcely consider it any different from singing in unison (that is, all on the same pitch). Two otherwise identical melodies sung simultaneously an octave apart are said to be in **parallel octaves**.

TUNING SYSTEMS

If all musical systems include octaves, which *other* pitches and intervals should be included? A **tuning system** is the method by which musicians decide which frequencies will be represented on instruments or in a musical system. The tuning system now standardized in the Americas and Europe, as well as in virtually all music derived from those cultures, is called **twelve-tone equal temperament** (see Figure 2.3). This standardization of tuning enables Western musicians to notate music and easily recombine their instruments into different ensembles.

Some cultures have multiple or flexible tuning systems because the instruments may be more flexible and more easily tuned than, for example, the piano. With such instruments, the fine points of a tuning system can be left largely up to the players on a particular occasion. For example, in India, although some theorists recognize a tuning system of twenty-two pitches per octave, in practice, a solo *sitar* player may decide the precise tuning system; if other musicians are present, they tune their instruments to match the *sitar*. This process is relatively easy with instruments that take the performer just minutes to tune, as opposed to instruments such as the piano, which may take a specialist much longer to tune.

The musical cultures of the islands of Java and Bali often use orchestras of bronze instruments that can take hours to tune. For this reason, their tuning system is fixed, usually when the instruments are built. However, because a particular group of instruments is built to be played only with one another, the tuning system for one orchestra may not match that of the orchestra in the next village. In the classical European orchestra, the players own their instruments and may play in several ensemble groups. This is not the case in Bali, where a school, club, or village often collectively owns an orchestra of instruments (see Figure 2.4). The idea of removing one instrument from the orchestra and taking it to play with another group is unthinkable.

TONALITY

In many melodies, one pitch within the octave has a special significance—it functions as a gravitational center to which the melody always returns at the end or other points of rest. Try singing a familiar melody leaving out the last note. Your feeling of dissatisfaction arises not only because the lyrics may be interrupted but also because the truncation leaves the melody sounding almost painfully unfinished.

This "home base" pitch is called the **tonic** or sometimes the **tonal center** or **key center**. This isn't to say that the tonic is the most common or even the most important pitch. Much of the interest and even drama in many types of music result from the artful play of tension between withholding and then returning to this central pitch. The feeling that a melody revolves around this pitch is called **tonality**, and we call music that uses tonality **tonal**.

In this very general sense, the phenomenon of tonality is found in virtually every musical culture on earth. However, not *every* piece is necessarily tonal. Some Western classical composers have sought ways to evade a sense of tonality, creating so-called **atonal** music. There are many pieces around the world that may also seem to have ambiguous or nonexistent tonal centers. Some of the music of Thailand, for example, may seem to defy the identification of a tonal center (see Figure 2.5). Whether one should call these

William Alves

FIGURE 2.3

Twelve-tone equal temperament, the tuning system developed in the West, is reflected in the configuration of a piano keyboard. Each octave of the keyboard repeats the same pattern of twelve keys, seven white and five black.

William Alves

FIGURE 2.4

Each Balinese orchestra, such as this ceremonial *gamelan selonding*, is tuned to its own tuning system, although they share general characteristics. Therefore, each orchestra has its own distinctive sound.

FIGURE 2.5

The tuning system of classical Thai ensembles divides the octave into seven roughly equal parts, making identification of a tonal center sometimes difficult.

pieces "atonal" is perhaps debatable (the term *nontonal* is sometimes preferred); often the feeling of tonality is highly subjective and learned within a culture.

MODES

Not every piece of music uses all the pitches available within the tuning system at all times. Pieces often use only a select subset of pitches in the tuning system. Western classical and popular music usually uses only seven of the available twelve pitches at a time. This particular subset, represented in one form by the white keys of the piano keyboard, is called the **diatonic** set. One Javanese tuning system has seven tones, but typically only five are used at a time.

After we have identified one of these pitches as a tonic, we have the basic material that defines a **mode**. Modes with five, six, or seven pitches are known as **pentatonic**, **hexatonic**, and **heptatonic**, respectively. If we arrange the pitches of the mode in one octave to start on the tonic and end on the tonic in the next octave, we have defined a **scale**. A scale is therefore a convenient construction for illustrating the tonic and pitch set used in a piece of music.

Chinese theorists identify a tuning system of twelve pitches per octave, but traditional Chinese music generally uses only five of those pitches at a time. Any of those pitches in the subset may serve as the tonic, meaning that there are then five possible pentatonic modes. Each of the scales of the five modes has its own characteristic sequence of intervals, and melodies in each of the different modes therefore have their own distinctive characteristics. Because of these distinctions, many cultures consider that different modes impart distinct emotional or expressive characteristics to melodies. Whereas many listeners in the West associate the **major mode** with happy melodies and the **minor mode** with sad melodies, modal associations elsewhere in the world may be much more complex and powerful. The ancient Greek philosopher Plato proposed that the government should ban modes believed to make people prone to drunkenness and licentiousness. Classical musicians from India, who have dozens of modes to choose from, associate very specific emotions, as well as times of day, with different modes (see Figure 2.6).

Although a subset of the pitches of a tuning system and a tonic within that subset are the two most basic necessities for the definition of a mode, many other musical qualities may distinguish modes in some cultures. For example, certain melodic practices may be appropriate to one mode but not to other modes, even though they may share the same scale. A certain **motive**, or melodic fragment, may be characteristic of a certain mode but not others. Specific **ornaments** or embellishments might occur on some notes in one mode but elsewhere in others. One pitch may be used in ascending passages, but a different one may be used when the melody is descending. Sometimes the range of a melody may be a part of a mode's defining characteristics. In India, the melodic implications of different modes are immensely complex, and students spend years learning them. Representing such modes with a simple scale would be totally inadequate.

A COMPLETE DEFINITION OF MODE

Depending on the culture, then, the definition of a mode may include any of the following criteria:

◆ The pattern of intervals in the scale, that is, the subset of tones from the tuning system used

◆ The tonic or starting point within the pattern

◆ Certain motives, ornaments, and other melodic practices

◆ Melodic range

Through all of these characteristics, the mode becomes the basis for melody, often with specific emotional associations. Modes can help us to characterize and categorize melodies in a particular culture.

KEYS AND THE RELATIVITY OF PITCH PERCEPTION

One of the fundamental principles of our musical hearing is that we recognize melodies not by the absolute pitch, or frequency, of each note, but by the relative relationship of one pitch to another—that is, by the intervals between successive notes in the melody. We can easily recognize a familiar tune no matter what pitch it starts on. The song "Happy Birthday" is "Happy Birthday" no matter whether it starts on the frequency 260 or 320 or 440 Hz. Intervals and relative pitches, not a sequence of absolute pitches, define melodies.

A mode in music is also defined relatively—by its tonic within the tuning system. We can derive a minor scale by starting on any pitch in the tuning system and using the set of intervals that define the minor mode. All of these scales will sound "minor," and we would recognize a minor mode melody in any one. We distinguish these different minor scales—that is, the minor that starts on one pitch from the minor that starts on another pitch—as different **keys**. We said earlier that Chinese theorists recognize a tuning system of twelve pitches per octave and five possible pentatonic modes. This means that there are twelve possible keys for each mode, for a total of sixty possible pentatonic keys.

British Library

FIGURE 2.6

In North India, modes known as *ragas* have such specific associations that painters and poets can depict these modes according to certain conventions. In this painting's depiction of a raga, a girl worships Brahma, who sits between two fires on a terrace.

MELODY

Many people think of **melody**, a sequence of pitches in rhythm, as the most important element of music. It's what you whistle after hearing a piece that has made an impression on you. Virtually all cultures have melodic music of some kind, perhaps because all cultures have singing. However, melody may not be important or even present in some types of music. Also, the concept of what makes a beautiful melody differs considerably from culture to culture, and, of course, from person to person.

What makes a melody distinctive and memorable is far more than a particular sequence of pitches. Rhythm or other elements may contribute to making a melody memorable because all dimensions of a piece of music work together toward a single effect on the listener.

MELODIC CONTOUR AND MOTION

If we adopt the conventions of showing pitch relative to its height on the page and of time moving from left to right across the page, then we can graph a melody such as the one here, a simple excerpt from the popular round "Row, Row, Row Your Boat" (see Graphic 2.1). Although such a representation cannot clearly show all important characteristics of melody, we will show many examples in this text this way.

GRAPHIC 2.1

Graph of melody

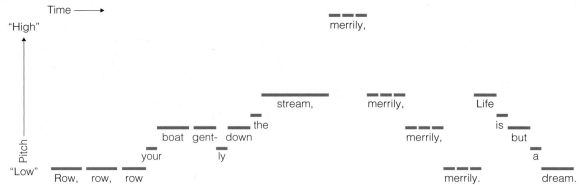

It is easy, then, to abstract a *general direction or shape of a melody over time*, a characteristic called the melody's **contour**. Despite momentary changes in direction, we can hear the melody of Graphic 2.1 as having the general contour shown in Graphic 2.2. In many melodies, the contour may be more complex and

GRAPHIC 2.2

Contour

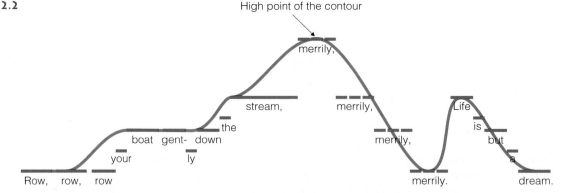

can often be exploited for expressive purposes. For example, the peak of a contour is often the most expressive or dramatic point in a song (see Graphic 2.2).

A related musical characteristic is called **melodic motion**. The sizes of the intervals between adjacent notes in the melody define the steepness of the curves of the contour. The motion of melodies with relatively small intervals between adjacent notes is called **conjunct motion**, and the motion of melodies with relatively large intervals between adjacent notes is called **disjunct motion**. Conjunct motion is by far the most common type of motion throughout the world, although most melodies are an artful mixture of both.

MELODIC RANGE AND TESSITURA

Where a melody lies in relation to the absolute pitch system is described by two characteristics: range and tessitura. **Range** refers to the difference between the highest and lowest notes of a melody and can be relatively wide or narrow. Most folk songs have relatively narrow ranges, often less than an octave. Other songs may have a range of two or more octaves, as in European opera or Mongolian "long" songs.

The **tessitura** of a melody is where the melody lies in relation to the possible range of the singer or instrument. For example, Tibetan ritual melodies are known for lying at the very bottom of the singer's range, that is, having a low tessitura. Some roles in Chinese opera are sung in a very high tessitura.

CADENCES AND PHRASES

Melodies commonly have points of "rest," where the music momentarily pauses or gives the feeling of having momentarily "arrived." When speaking, people take breaths at logical stopping points, such as the ends of sentences or clauses. Singers and players of melodies must take breaths as well, both literally (when playing wind instruments) and figuratively. Such points of momentary rest or arrival are called **cadences**. Cadences of some kind are found in almost all melodies, and they often fall on the tonal center or another important pitch. The section of the melody from one cadence to another is called a **phrase** (see Graphic 2.3). The obvious analogy is language, in which natural pauses also occur to set off sections of speech.

Cadences and phrases are found throughout the world. In many songs, the cadence serves as a literal breathing point for the voice, and, in fact, some phrase lengths seem to be determined by the natural length of time that a person can sing in a single breath. However, the rhythm does not always have to come to a momentary halt for us to feel the cadence. Other elements of the music, including relative importance of pitches, the contour, the harmony, and so on, can influence our sense of rest or arrival. A recurring melodic fragment, called a **cadential motive**, may also signal cadences.

The resoluteness or finality associated with a cadence may also vary. There are some cadences that create a resting point in relation to what immediately precedes but could not be used to end the piece. Sometimes these cadences are called **half-cadences** or **semi-cadences**. In Javanese music, composers put together phrases with cadences of varying levels of finality into large-scale hierarchical structures so that the most final cadence comes at the end of the section or piece, the next most final often at the halfway point, and so on.

GRAPHIC 2.3

Phrases and cadences in "Amazing Grace"

Amazing grace, how sweet the sound   cadence
|◄——— Phrase ———►|

That saved a wretch like me   cadence
|◄——— Phrase ———►|

I once was lost, but now I'm found   cadence
|◄——— Phrase ———►|

Was blind, but now I see.   final cadence
|◄——— Phrase ———►|

ORNAMENTATION

One very common cadential motive in eighteenth-century European music was a rapid alternation between two notes a step apart, called a **trill**. The duration and even number of notes in this alternation may vary according to the wishes of the performer, although the performer does not have this latitude in varying the other notes of the melody. In other words, one performer may sing or play more and faster notes in the trill than another performer, and yet they would both be correct.

To indicate this freedom, the Western composer does not write down each separate note in a trill, but instead indicates this ornament with a special symbol consisting of the letters *tr* followed by a wavy line above the affected note. Another reason for this shorthand notation is that in a trill, we don't really perceive a melody with many notes as much as we perceive a single note (the one written) with a kind of flourish added to it, in this case to draw the listener through to the cadence.

The trill is an example of a musical device called an **ornament**—added notes or other small changes in pitch or loudness that don't change the overall character of the melody as much as they enhance or embellish it. The composer may compose only the bare, unornamented melody, leaving the inclusion and execution of ornaments up to the performer or, as in the preceding example, notate obligatory ornaments with special symbols.

Although the name "ornament" connotes a nonessential decoration, certain ornaments are expected or even required, given a certain style, mode, or melodic situation. Very strict rules often govern when a certain ornament is or is not appropriate. A performer on the Chinese *guqin* zither, for example, will bend the pitch only on certain tones and never on the cadence note. Folk singers in regions of Romania and Bulgaria have a distinctive ornament of a sudden leap up in pitch, but it occurs only at cadences in certain types of songs.

In general, music of the West—at least that of the past two centuries—is relatively bare of ornamentation when compared to some of the rich melodic traditions elsewhere in the world, especially in Asia and the Middle East.

MOTIVES AND THEMES

One of the most important ways of unifying a melody is through repetition. The recognition of previous musical materials serves to form a structure, a coherent whole, in the mind of the listener. Repetition often occurs on many levels in a melody, from just a few notes to repetitions of whole sections several minutes long.

A short melodic fragment that is repeated at certain points is called a **motive**. A motive is usually only a handful of notes and is often used as a "cell" or "building block" from which composers can construct larger melodies. We have already seen how musicians often use motives to indicate important **cadences**.

A **theme** is an entire melody recognizable as a discrete entity and may be anywhere from the length of one phrase to over a minute in length. The listener's recognition of these repeated melodies is one of the most important ways by which performers and composers structure a piece of music, a topic to which we return in more depth in Chapter 4.

STRUCTURE

Structure or **form** is the name given to the very largest levels of musical architecture. Structure is what guides our listening experience—the expectations and surprises that come from following repetitions and contrasts, sectional changes, and variations. If we don't perceive the structure of a piece of music, it will soon become boring, like reading a book of unrelated pages. However, if we are aware of the immense drama being worked out in an intricate and artful performance, we will often be entranced.

What exactly is it that tells our mind that one section is ending and another beginning or how one section is related to another? There are many methods to articulate these important signposts. At the low level, there is the cadence, or resting point in a melody.

At higher levels, there are contrasts—in loudness, harmony, tempo, the instruments playing, and so on. In Japanese *gagaku* music and Javanese *gamelan* music, certain instruments periodically punctuate the musical texture, creating clear delineations.

PHRASES AND HIERARCHICAL STRUCTURES

At the lower level of structural building blocks are melodic phrases. To extend the metaphor of a melodic phrase, phrases may join together to form the "sentences" or "paragraphs" of a large musical composition. Using this analogy, we can relate a chapter to the musical term **movement**. Movements are set apart by actually stopping the music between each one, but still they are large sections within a single composition.

Another metaphor that comes to mind is musical structure as architecture. As in architecture, pieces of music have small parts that add up to larger and larger parts, structures within structures, eventually resulting in a large building. Although hierarchical structures such as this are common, in some types of music, phrases may simply be strung together one after another with no implication of a higher grouping level.

REPEATING STRUCTURES

Repetition as an important structural element exists not only in the recurrence of melodic motives and themes but also on many different levels. In writing about these structures, it is sometimes convenient to use letters to represent the different melodic phrases: *A* the first phrase, *B* the next unique phrase, *C* the third, and so on. Repetition in simple songs creates forms we diagram as *AAB, AABC,* or *AABA,* for example.

Letters can be used at levels higher than the phrase as well. Each letter may stand for a group of phrases (sentence or paragraph). A song that repeats a group of melodic phrases over and over but with different words is called **strophic**. Each repetition is called a verse, a stanza, or a strophe. Modern Christian hymns are often strophic, as are many folk songs. The form of the music of such a hymn would be simply *AAAA*. Sometimes, if the music is varied slightly from one repetition to another, prime marks are added to distinguish the different versions: *A, A', A'', A'''*, and so on, pronounced *A, A prime, A double prime,* and so on.

An even more common variation of this form is to repeat a section with the *same* words, called a **refrain**, after every strophe. Such a form, nearly ubiquitous in modern popular songs, is called **verse–refrain** or stanza–refrain form. In this form, the stanza may be constructed so that the verse does not end on a final cadence, thus helping to propel us into the refrain.

VARIATION

In some musical contexts, repetition by itself is perceived as dull. Therefore, composers or performers introduce variation to increase interest while maintaining elements of repetition. One of the most fundamental ways in which a melody can be varied is by playing it at a different pitch level, that is, by **transposition**. Hungarian folk songs often repeat a phrase but start it at a different pitch. If we perceive the tonic to have temporarily changed to this new pitch, or, to put it another way, the melody to have changed key, then the melody is said to have **modulated**. Modulation can also mean temporarily changing modes, even if the tonic does not change.

There are innumerable ways to vary a repetition, but some common ones include the following:

- Transposition
- Increased or different ornamentation
- Different mode
- Different tonal center
- Different tempo or rhythmic density (number of notes per beat)
- Different instruments used
- Different texture (see Chapter 4)

In fact, the possibilities are so numerous that many composers have written pieces that are artful studies of these possibilities called **theme and variations form**. This form is common in the West, in China, in Africa, and elsewhere. In this structure, a melody (theme) is introduced and then played many times in different variations. These variations are often arranged to articulate a larger form with a beginning, middle, and end, with rising tension in one variation giving rise to resolution in another and final resolution at the end, and so on.

 BOOK COMPANION WEBSITE

You will find flashcards, a glossary, and tutorial quizzes, as well as other materials that will help you succeed in this course, at the *Music of the Peoples of the World, 2nd Edition,* Companion Website at www.cengage.com/music/alves/world2e.

RHYTHM AND LOUDNESS

Rhythm is the term that describes how music is organized in time. Because different people and different cultures perceive time in very different ways, it becomes important to distinguish **psychological time** from **clock time**.

Our psychological-time perception of the organization of events in music may vary considerably over the course of a piece or different performances. For example, we might estimate that a particularly boring piece of music lasted twice as long in clock time than it actually did. But after we learn how to discern events in the music to which we were not formerly attuned, suddenly our interest grows, and the sense of time changes remarkably.

Cultures may profoundly influence perceptions and thought processes that affect both the ways in which people organize the sounds in music and the ways that they perceive sound in time. For example, psychologists have found evidence that time sense in highly goal-oriented societies tends toward shorter and shorter intervals.

ORGANIZING TIME

If we were to look at a graph of a piece of, say, piano music that showed loudness versus time, we would see not only the gradual rise and fall of overall volume but, on a smaller scale, a series of sudden jumps corresponding to the beginning of each note. Graphic 3.1 shows an actual amplitude (loudness) plot of a melody played in the introduction to a Javanese *gamelan* orchestra composition. The beginnings of each of the notes are clear from the sudden jumps in loudness.

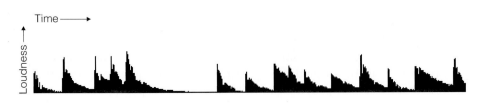

GRAPHIC 3.1

Amplitude plot

A brain trying to make sense of this information has certain obvious ways of dividing the music into discrete events. In particular, at certain places, the loudness changes suddenly—so does the pitch, if we were to look at that dimension. We call these discrete events **notes**, and our listening process delineates them so clearly that we hardly even think about it. To see how these notes are organized by time, let's look at the pattern formed by their beginnings—that is, the sudden changes in loudness (Graphic 3.2). If we mark the time each note begins in Graphic 3.1, it is apparent that many of the note durations are the same or nearly the same and that others are two or three (or some other whole number) times the length of the shortest durations.

GRAPHIC 3.2

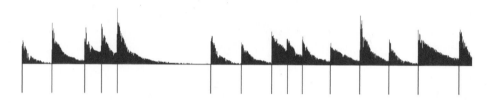

That greatest of pattern finders, the human brain, also notices that many of these lengths of time are the same and that the longer lengths are pretty consistently two or three times the smaller lengths. Even though the spacing isn't always exactly even, the brain forgives slight deviations and interprets others as speeding up or slowing down. This suggests that the whole piece could be put on a fairly consistent time grid (Graphic 3.3). Every note now begins on one of these lines marking a constant interval of time.

GRAPHIC 3.3

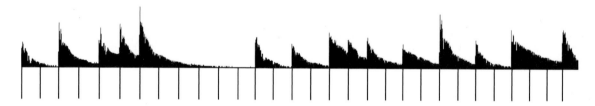

Most music can easily fit into such a grid, so that all of its notes fall on one of these equally spaced periods of time or even divisions of time. This is such a natural part of our listening process that we don't need any training to find this grid—even in relatively complicated pieces of music, we often find our feet tapping out these regular pulses. This regular division of time is called the **beat**.

THE BEAT

Most of us know intuitively what a beat is—we find ourselves tapping our feet, clapping, or otherwise moving our bodies along with music. But does all music have a beat? If the timing of notes cannot be interpreted as falling into a periodic pattern, or if the music defies our ear's attempt to find events that can be identified as notes at all, then we may not be able to clap, tap, or move along.

Such music is called **nonpulsatile**. Still other music we might call **quasi-pulsatile**; that is, notes of more or less the same length follow each other, but the rhythm is so free that it is hard to pin down a constant pulse.

Nonpulsatile music is sometimes called **nonmetric** music, but it is *not* correct to say that it "has no rhythm." Because all music somehow organizes time, all music has some kind of rhythm. What people probably mean by "has no rhythm" is that familiar landmarks in time organization, such as a steady beat, are missing. Such music nevertheless organizes the notes in time—which is rhythm—and this organization may, in fact, be very complex.

TEMPO

In a pulsatile piece, the *rate* at which the beat passes is called the **tempo**. To specify an absolute tempo, musicians indicate the number of beats per minute. For example, a tempo of 120 beats per minute means that every beat lasts exactly one-half second. Most popular music has a tempo of between about 90 and 140 beats per minute, whereas the tempos of Western classical music can vary widely, from about 50 to 180 beats per minute. Some Japanese traditional music may unfold very slowly, sometimes as slowly as 30 beats per minute; at this tempo, unaccustomed ears might not at first detect any beat at all.

Because our impression of the passage of time is based on a variety of psychological factors, specifying tempos relative to absolute clock time has limited usefulness. Often musicians express tempos with more subjective terms and may vary tempos according to the circumstances of a particular performance. Of course, tempo may change over the course of a piece. A tempo may change suddenly or gradually. A gradual speedup of tempo is called an **accelerando**, and a gradual slowing down is a **ritardando** or **rallentando**.

METER

In the graphic showing the beginnings of notes (Graphic 3.2), it is clear that there does not need to be a note on every pulse for the beat to be perceived. As long as the notes that are there fit into the steady grid of time divisions, our brain can still find the beat, even though some notes are two or three beats long. Sometimes notes may last less than a beat in time, but in those cases, the note is often either one-half or one-third of a beat. The ways in which the beat can be divided into smaller periods or grouped into larger ones tends to be consistent through a piece of music. The way in which beats are organized in a piece of music is called the *meter*.

Meter is an organization of beats, divisions of beats, and groupings of beats into distinct levels of the passage of time. If you ask someone to clap along with a piece with a tempo of 120 beats per minute, chances are they hear that beat and clap every half-second. However, some people might clap along at half that rate—that is, at a tempo of 60, or 1 beat per second. Both are correct—they just demonstrate different perspectives. One person hears the beats at 120 and faster notes as divisions of beats. The other hears notes faster than 60 as divisions of the beat. In fact, it may also be possible to identify a plausible pulse at 240 beats per minute or even other speeds. The beginnings of notes nearly always coincide with one of these divisions (Graphic 3.4). The same rhythm outlined in Graphic 3.2 here is shown not only against a grid of short durations extending in time left to right, as in Graphic 3.3, but also as a hierarchy of groupings of those pulses. When you tap your foot to a song, you are unconsciously identifying one of these levels in the hierarchy as the beat.

GRAPHIC 3.4

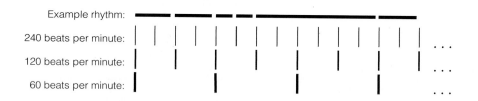

Because in this example each division or grouping of pulses is by twos, we might write the relative hierarchy from long to short as 2:2, that is, one of the longest pulses (60 bpm) equals 2 beats, each of which equal 2 divisions of beats. Keep in mind, however, that in a metrical system like this, we could mark any number of levels of subdivisions or groupings, but in a practical sense, we are concerned mainly with the groupings and divisions of the beat.

Meters with hierarchies of two are very common in music around the world, but beats may be grouped and divided in different ways. In Graphic 3.4, they are grouped into twos. The most common grouping other than two is three. In Graphic 3.5, beats are grouped in threes. In this example, the beat is grouped into threes but divided into twos.

GRAPHIC 3.5

Simple triple meter

Subdivisions of the beat:

The beat:

Groupings of beats:

In this case, the hierarchy is 3:2—that is, the beats are grouped in threes but still divided by two. A meter in which the beats are grouped in threes is called a **triple meter**, whereas a meter in which beats are grouped in twos is called a **duple meter**. The beat itself may also be divided into two or three.

A meter in which the beat is divided into three is called a **compound meter**, whereas a meter in which the beat is divided into two is called a **simple meter**. The meter shown in Graphic 3.5 is called *simple triple* and is well known as the meter for the European waltz. Graphic 3.6 shows a compound duple meter, that is,

GRAPHIC 3.6

Compound duple meter

Subdivisions of the beat:

The beat:

Groupings of beats:

beat groupings in twos and divisions in threes. Graphic 3.7 shows a compound triple meter in which the beat is both divided by and grouped into threes. Although uncommon, this is the meter of the Irish dance called a slip jig.

How does this grid of beats and beat groupings relate to rhythm? Very simply, a rhythm that exists in a certain meter nearly always has notes that begin on a beat or its subdivision, although they may last any number of beats.

The hierarchy of beat levels can be extended in both directions—that is, the beats may be grouped into larger segments, and the divisions of beats may themselves be subdivided. In cultures such as India or Java, large-scale groupings of beats may grow to very large structures of 256 or more beats. Following such an expansive meter can take intense concentration.

METRICAL STRESS AND SYNCOPATION

Musicians often speak of the point in time that coincides with the beginning of a whole group of beats, such as the lines in the highest levels of Graphics 3.4 through 3.8, as "stressed" beats. This term does not mean that notes on those beats are necessarily played more loudly nor that they are somehow more important. All beats, groupings, and subdivisions are important because they represent the organization of time in a pulsatile piece of music. Rather, the amount of stress associated with a beat refers to a sense of expectation of a new beginning, which that level of organization can articulate. In some pieces of music, such a beat might be emphasized or associated with a hearty stamp in a dance, but sometimes such emphasis may be deliberately withheld to give the music a floating quality or a sense of surprise.

Syncopation is a term for rhythm in which the metrical stress of a note is displaced in the meter so that the emphasis occurs on normally unstressed beats. This type of rhythm is especially characteristic of ragtime, jazz, and some Latin American dances.

The shifting of stress normally occurs one of two ways. The first and most common way is for a note that begins on a normally unstressed beat to extend through the next stressed beat (Graphic 3.8). In this example showing the simple

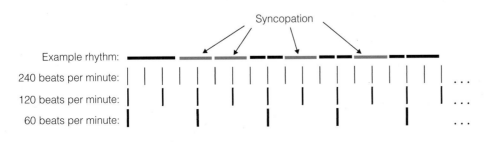

duple meter from Graphic 3.4 with the rhythm of a Brazilian *maxixe*, a note starting on an unstressed division (a point with only one vertical bar below it) extends through a following stressed beat (a point with more than one vertical bar aligned). The note seems to get more stress than it otherwise would because the rhythm temporarily shifts metrical stress and creates a syncopation. Notes that begin on an unstressed division but do not extend through the following stressed beat do not have the same sense of shifting stress and are therefore not syncopated (such as the fourth and fifth notes in this example).

The other way that a composer or performer can shift stress is to emphasize notes on normally unstressed beats by playing them more loudly or giving them a harder attack. Such an emphasis given to a single note is called an **accent**.

LOUDNESS IN MUSIC

Although **loudness** is an important part of much music, it is usually treated with much less precision in theory and notation than are pitch or rhythm. The use of loudness as a musical element is called **dynamics**. A gradual increase in loudness is called a **crescendo**, and a gradual decrease in loudness is called a **decrescendo**.

Although composers of Western classical music frequently notate such changes in dynamics or levels of relative loudness, the performers in most cultures control loudness, as well as choices of instrumentation, as an expressive element. The lack of notation or even a precise language to indicate dynamics does not mean that the music does not change in loudness nor that those changes are unimportant, just that the musician does not need the aid of notation or precise terminology.

As you might expect, loud dynamics are often used for sections of music that are highly dramatic, joyful, celebratory, or in some way climactic. However, sometimes very soft sections can portray just as much drama and intensity. It is more often the artful contrasts of loud and soft that make for effective musical expression.

BOOK COMPANION WEBSITE

You will find flashcards, a glossary, and tutorial quizzes, as well as other materials that will help you succeed in this course, at the *Music of the Peoples of the World, 2nd Edition*, Companion Website at www.cengage.com/music/alves/world2e.

TEXTURE

When two or more instruments or singers play together, they often have different roles. For example, a guitar may play a supporting role to a singer who sings the main melody. We call the guitarist's part the accompaniment. When a choir sings, the members may all sing the same melody together, they may sing in harmony (different pitches sung simultaneously), or they may sing accompaniment to a single singer (the soloist). These are all examples of different *textures*.

Texture is the musical characteristic that describes the relative importance and distribution of various instrumental or vocal parts. Each single melody is called a line, a part, or a voice (even when it's played by an instrument). Just as in the cloth metaphor from which the term "texture" comes, these lines can be woven like threads loosely, tightly, and in many other different ways. Texture is an important musical characteristic in ensemble music, in which changes in texture over the course of a piece often articulate important sectional divisions and make them obvious to the ear.

Musicologists generally divide textures into four large categories, but there is a great amount of overlap, and many textures may not seem to fit neatly into any of the categories.

MONOPHONY

The first type of texture is **monophony**, meaning *one sound*. It is simply that—a single melody (Graphic 4.1). When an instrument plays only one note at a time, or a singer sings a melody, that is monophony. Even when a number of voices or instruments are playing, if they are all playing the same melody together, it is still monophony. Monophony is extremely common throughout

Time⟶

Pitch⟶

GRAPHIC 4.1

Monophony

the world, much more than those who are accustomed to harmony accompanying melodies might think. Graphic 4.1 shows a monophonic texture of a song from Lebanon.

Although the definition and identification of monophony may seem fairly straightforward, many situations blur the distinction between monophony and other textures. For example, when men and women sing together, they do so in **parallel octaves** (Graphic 4.2). Even though, strictly speaking, there are two different melodies, they are not really distinct to the ear. Singing in parallel octaves sounds virtually the same as a single melody to us; therefore, we still call it monophony.

GRAPHIC 4.2

Parallel octaves

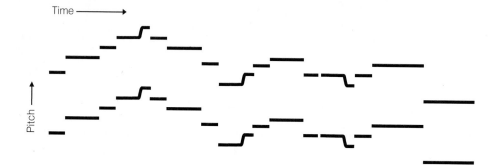

When other types of music have melodies in parallel but are separated by intervals other than the octave, our ear more readily discerns separate melodies. Such textures begin to blur the line between our impression of monophony (one melody) and polyphony (more than one independent simultaneous melody).

HOMOPHONY

A single melody accompanied by supporting harmony is called **homophony**. Virtually all popular music and much Western classical music has a homophonic texture, also known as melody and accompaniment. Homophony is sometimes described as a melody accompanied by other tones of lesser importance, but perhaps *focus* is the better way to think about it. None of the parts is more "important" than any other nor can any be omitted without harming the music, but our attention is *focused* on the melody—in the spotlight, so to speak. In Graphic 4.3, of a homophonic texture from a Mexican folksong, the melody

GRAPHIC 4.3

Homophony

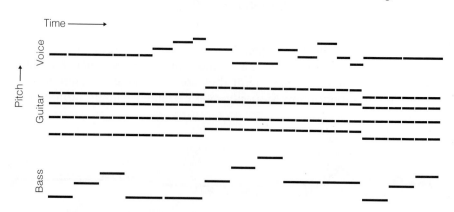

that the voice sings is the principal melody we associate with the song. The parts played by the guitar and bass support and accompany it.

Although most of the accompaniment in much popular music consists of strummed guitar chords, accompaniment may also consist of several melodies combined into harmony, as is often the case when a choir sings. Each section of singers has its own melody, but only one of those melodies (generally the highest) has the focus in a homophonic texture. Although elements such as drums and drones are also accompaniment in a sense, they are not usually perceived as separate melodies and thus are treated differently, as we will explain shortly.

POLYPHONY

Although it is common for one melody to dominate our attention in a texture with multiple melodies (homophony), sometimes a texture divides our focus between several simultaneous melodies. When there are several melodies of more or less equal focus at the same time, the texture is called **polyphony**. In Graphic 4.4, which depicts a polyphonic texture from a choral piece by the medieval English composer John Dunstable, there are three different melodies (indicated by the different colors), no single one of which always has the focus.

GRAPHIC 4.4

Polyphony

One of the most familiar forms of Western polyphony is the **round** or **canon**, such as "Row, Row, Row Your Boat," in which singers sing the same melody at staggered time intervals. Even though there is just one melody, this is considered polyphony because we perceive two different things happening at the same time. More specifically, it is an example of **imitative polyphony**, in which one line plays the same melody as in another line but starts later in time, so that the melody overlaps with itself. In a polyphonic texture, no one line can be said to be any more important than another in the way the melody in homophony is more important than the accompaniment.

Imitative polyphony is found in Western classical music, Indian vocal music (in which an instrumentalist sometimes imitates the singer), and elsewhere. However, nonimitative polyphony is more common elsewhere, as in the intricate textures of Javanese *gamelan* orchestras, West African ensembles, or traditional Thai ensembles. In these cases, many different melodies, guided by common structural principles, weave around one another.

HETEROPHONY

In some cultures, musicians playing together would consider it dull to play the same melody in exactly the same way. Instead, each musician enriches the texture by adding his own ornamentation and variations to the melody.

Although we would perceive a single basic melody, the texture is not monophony because each rendition is somewhat different. At the same time, it cannot be polyphony because there is only one basic melody. This texture of simultaneous variations is therefore separately classified as **heterophony**. Heterophony is common in many cultures around the world, although not in the West. Graphic 4.5 of a heterophonic texture shows the performances by a south Indian singer (blue lines) and violinist (red lines). Although they sing and play the same basic melody, their slight differences in notes and ornamentation create simultaneous variations.

GRAPHIC 4.5

Heterophony

OTHER TEXTURES

Many textures are hybrids. One example of a hybrid texture is a homophonic piece in which the melody is played heterophonically by two instruments or singers. This texture would not fit easily into either the homophonic or the heterophonic category; therefore, it would be best to simply describe it as what it is.

THE DRONE

A **drone** is a long, constant pitch played throughout all or part of a composition. The ear does not recognize a drone as an independent melody but as kind of a background scrim of sound, which, in the case of Indian classical music, for example, serves as a foundation and point of reference over which the soloist improvises. Although the drone in such a texture is in one sense an accompaniment, it makes more sense to describe this texture as monophony with a drone than as homophony because the drone is not a melodic or harmonic accompaniment.

DRUMS

Drums are very important to texture in some musical cultures, such as those of Africa, the Middle East, India, Japan, Korea, and Western popular music. At some point in an Indian classical performance, the drone and melody are joined by a drummer, but drums and other nonpitched percussion instruments do not fit neatly into the general classification scheme for texture. Although it is possible for drums to be tuned to give an impression of pitch so that a set of such drums *could* play a melody, a drum more often provides rhythmic punctuation to the melody.

The Indian texture is best described as a melody and drone with drum accompaniment. Because the accompaniment isn't harmony, it would be stretching the definition to call this texture homophony. Besides, some-times the drummer takes the leading role, and the melodic soloist takes the subordinate role.

The great drum ensembles of West Africa often have only a single sung melody or sometimes no melody at all. Instead, most of the focus is on the complicated polyrhythmic drum lines. It would not be out of place to compare these performances with polyphony because each individual drum has a line all its own, but the "melodies" of the drums are very limited, if they can be called melodies at all. This type of texture has been called **drum polyphony**, which is as good a name as any. With a single sung melody, the texture might be described as "a melody with polyphonic drum accompaniment."

 BOOK COMPANION WEBSITE

You will find flashcards, a glossary, and tutorial quizzes, as well as other materials that will help you succeed in this course, at the *Music of the Peoples of the World, 2nd Edition,* Companion Website at www.cengage.com/music/alves/world2e.

TIMBRE AND MUSICAL INSTRUMENTS

TIMBRE

Timbre (pronounced TAM-ber) is a French word that means "tone color"—that is, the quality of an instrument's sound that distinguishes an oboe from a flute or a voice or a trumpet. Musicians have a fuzzy vocabulary for describing the differences between timbres, using such general metaphors as "bright" or "dark." Instead, musicians typically describe the timbre of one instrument by comparing it to the timbre of another. Care should be taken in making comparisons this way, however, because it may reinforce an attitude that the instruments of a particular culture form the standard to which all other music is compared.

In most music, timbre is controlled through instrumentation and orchestration. **Instrumentation** refers to the choice of instruments that play a certain piece. **Orchestration** is the art of combining the instruments in different ways for musical effect. The term *orchestration*, by the way, does not necessarily apply only to the orchestra; it can just as well refer to any combination of instruments. A good orchestrator knows, for example, that certain instruments make a good musical "foreground" for solos when combined with certain other instruments that serve as "background."

Ensembles may have **heterogeneous** (all different) or **homogeneous** (all similar) instrumentation. The *gagaku* orchestra of Japan, for example, has a well-balanced heterogeneous instrumentation consisting of plucked strings, flutes, reed instruments, a metal gong, and drums. The *sho* mouth organs form a constant background against which the solo double reeds and flutes are easily heard. The plucked string and percussion timbres fill in the slow melody with occasional punctuations.

The Western string quartet is an example of a homogeneous ensemble (Figure 5.1). It is made up of two violins, a viola, and a cello, all string instruments of the violin family. This choice of instruments enables them to achieve great variety of sound and yet blend beautifully when necessary.

Tokyo String Quartet

FIGURE 5.1

The European string quartet consists of four instruments of the violin family including, from left to right, violin, another violin, cello, and viola. Although these instruments differ in range, they are all of very similar construction, and so this group is classified as a homogeneous ensemble.

MUSICAL INSTRUMENTS

Musical instruments are important not just for the sounds that they make but often for the ways in which they reflect a musician's personality, expression, and culture. They can be rudimentary or extremely expensive, simple or technologically sophisticated, mass-produced to a standard or unique. The fact that some musicians give names to their instruments reflects the bond they feel with them, for an instrument can become a direct extension of a musician's expressive thought. In some cultures, musicians may personify their instruments in other ways or consider them spiritually charged. The respect that they give them goes far beyond their monetary value.

RESONANCE

Instrument makers can change an instrument's tone quality and loudness by building in hollow chambers or solid pieces called **resonators**, which work by filtering and amplifying the sound waves in specific ways. A resonator may be a solid board, such as the soundboard of a piano, an open box, or some other open or closed cavity. Some instruments have a resonator for each pitch, such as the marimba or the Indonesian *gendér* (Figure 5.2).

Not only are sound waves caused by moving objects but also sound waves can cause other objects to move. For example, plucking a string on a *sitar*, an Indian string instrument, can cause another nearby string tuned to the same pitch to vibrate softly even though the second string was untouched. If you put your ear next to this string, you hear its "ghost" sound, as if it were played very softly, because of a phenomenon called **sympathetic vibration**. The air is being pushed and pulled by the first string, and the air slightly pushes and pulls the second string. However, only the string tuned to the same note vibrates; the others are silent because they are not designed to move at that frequency. Each string has its own vibrating frequency, which depends on the string's length and tension. This frequency is called the *resonant frequency* of that string. All physical objects have at least one resonant frequency and sometimes a range of frequencies. When a wave in the air around them matches this frequency, the object vibrates in sympathy, making the original sound seem louder. For example, a violin maker constructs the body of the instrument to have roughly equal resonant frequencies throughout the violin's range. However, certain frequencies resonate better than others, and the precise loudness of these frequencies is largely responsible for the violin's distinctive sound.

William Alves

FIGURE 5.2

The Balinese *gendér wayang* has a separate bamboo tube resonator for each bar. The inside of each tube is stopped at different points (marked by the hearts on the tubes) to tune them to the correct resonant frequency.

CLASSIFICATION

Musical instruments around the world come in an astounding variety, and there are equally various ways of classifying them. Instruments are classified by their musical function, their range, their construction, their method of producing a sound, and so on.

One common method of classification organizes instruments into three categories: string instruments (instruments whose strings are the sounding body), wind instruments (instruments that are blown through), and percussion instruments (instruments that are struck). Like any classification scheme, there are problems with this one. Strings and winds are classified by what makes the sound, whereas percussion instruments are classified by how a sound is made. The piano, for example, is an instrument whose strings are struck. Is it a string instrument or a percussion instrument? (It has been classified both ways.) Although this classification works well for Western orchestras, for which it was developed, it is not as useful for other types of ensembles. In Korea, instruments are classified by the principal material of their construction—wood, metal, stone, skin, and so on—but, again, this scheme is less useful outside a Korean orchestra.

Two early researchers of musical instruments from around the world, Erich von Hornbostel and Curt Sachs, drew up a similar but more consistent classification scheme that ethnomusicologists commonly adopt today. At the highest level, they arrange the instruments by precisely what makes the sound:

1. **Chordophones** (string instruments). A vibrating string, whether plucked, bowed, or struck, makes the sound.

2. **Aerophones** (wind instruments). A column of air within the instrument makes the sound.

3. **Membranophones** (drums). A membrane (skin) stretched over a resonator or frame makes the sound.

4. **Idiophones**. The entire instrument vibrates to make the sound.

5. **Electrophones**. The instrument makes sound through a loudspeaker.

Note that this classification scheme is very similar to the strings/winds/percussion organization scheme, except that it divides conventional percussion instruments into two groups. Not only does this division make the method more consistent, it is also less ethnocentric because in many cultures, percussion instruments are the majority, not the minority. Because of this consistency, the piano is now more clearly classified as a chordophone. There are still gray areas and hybrids, of course, although not as many.

CHORDOPHONES

Chordophones share many general characteristics. First, the strings have to be stretched somehow. They must be secured at both ends but allowed to move freely in between. Usually a construction known as a **bridge** is used to lift the string up over the body of the instrument so that it vibrates freely (Figure 5.3). A string instrument often has two bridges, one at each end, although one may be higher than the other. In instruments such as the violin and guitar, the higher piece is usually called the bridge. A single bridge may serve for several strings,

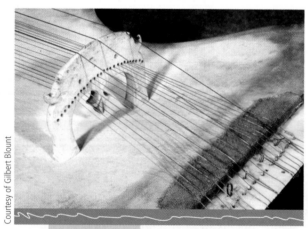

Courtesy of Gilbert Blount

FIGURE 5.3

A string instrument bridge lifts the string above the instrument and forms an edge for the vibration of the string. This bridge on a *dilruba* from India has a main set of strings that cross over its top and another set of strings that are threaded through holes in the middle.

© Keren Su/CORBIS

FIGURE 5.4

Frets on a *ty ba*, a lute-type chordophone from Vietnam. Pressing down behind the fret stops the string at that point.

or each string may have its own bridges. The Hungarian *cimbalom* and Iranian *santur* often have a bridge in the middle of each string, so that it is possible to play different pitches on each side of a center bridge.

There are several methods for obtaining different pitches on a string instrument. First, one may have a different string for each pitch, as in a piano. On other chordophones, the pitch of a string may be varied by pressing the string down at a certain point and therefore shortening its vibrating length. In this case, the finger can determine the vibrating length, or the finger can push the string down so that it is stopped by an intermediate bridge, called a **fret** (Figure 5.4). Guitars and mandolins are examples of string instruments with frets, whereas violins and *sarods* are examples of instruments without frets.

There are several reasons to use frets: they make the task of finding the pitch easier and thus make it more practical to finger several strings simultaneously, as is common on the guitar. Because the fret creates a sharp, hard point, the string vibrates longer and more loudly than it does when stopped by the flesh of the finger. But frets lock the player into a certain tuning and generally make it impossible to change pitch by sliding the finger along the string. However, 1930s blues guitarists in the United States began to use the tops of soft-drink bottles to obtain **glissando** (sliding pitch) effects. This technique evolved into the slide guitar, an example of a movable bridge.

Adjusting the tension of the string can also vary its pitch, and in this way, players of fretted instruments can create small changes in pitch, such as a **vibrato**, a continuous wavering of pitch often used on the classical guitar or the Indian *sitar*. On zithers such as the Chinese *zheng* or Japanese *koto*, the player may press down on the string behind a tall bridge to create pitch slides or vibrato (Figure 5.5). The **whammy bar** is a modern innovation used on electric guitars to slide the pitch up and down by varying string tension.

FIGURE 5.5

When playing the Korean *kayagum* curved-board zither, the player plucks with the right hand and then presses down behind the bridge with the left hand to bend the pitch.

Some kinds of chordophones may have more than one string tuned to a certain pitch. For example, some guitars have two adjacent strings per pitch, in the configuration known as a twelve-string guitar. The collection of adjacent strings associated with a particular pitch is called a **course**; when there are two strings in a course, it is a double course; three strings, a triple course; and so on (Figure 5.6). There may be several reasons for having multiple courses, but the most common is that they provide extra volume. When describing a chordophone, it is common to refer to it as a "six-course" rather than a "six-string" instrument, for example.

Let's look at some ways in which chordophones are divided even further.

FIGURE 5.6

The Iranian *santur* uses multiple courses for each pitch to increase volume. This *santur* uses quadruple courses (four strings for each pitch).

ZITHERS

Chordophones in which the strings are parallel to a resonator that extends their entire length.

◆ **Stick zithers**. Those in which the sounding board is relatively narrow and round, like a stick. The similar bar zither has a string attached to a curved stick (see Figure 6.6, p. 52).

◆ **Tube and curved zithers**. Strings attached around the outside of a tube that serves as a resonator (Figure 5.7). When a part of the tube is cut away to form a surface for the instrument, it is known as a half-tube or curved-board zither (Figure 5.5).

◆ **Raft zithers**. Those with a flat sounding board parallel to the strings (see Figure 6.9, p. 53).

◆ **Flat box zithers**. Those with a hollow box resonator (Figure 5.8).

◆ **Trough zithers**. Zithers with a trough carved in their sounding boards for resonance (see Figure 6.9, p. 53).

LUTES

Chordophones in which the strings are parallel to the body that holds them, with a resonator at one end.

◆ **Spike lute**. Mostly bowed and hence also known as a "spike fiddle." The neck is a round stick that extends through the resonator and forms the spike (Figure 5.9).

◆ **Fingerboard lute**. The neck is a flat surface that the fingers press the strings down to. A fingerboard may have frets (Figure 5.11) or be fretless (Figure 5.10).

William Alves

FIGURE 5.7

The *valiha* from Madagascar is an example of a tube zither.

William Alves

FIGURE 5.8

The *kecapi* from West Java, Indonesia, is a zither with a box resonator.

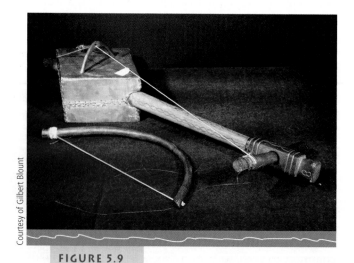

Courtesy of Gilbert Blount

FIGURE 5.9

The *masingo* is a spike lute chordophone from Ethiopia. Also known as a spike fiddle, the string is supported on a single stick that extends through a resonator at the bottom end.

LYRES

Sometimes considered a form of lute, but in these chordophones, the strings are attached to a crossbar held up by two posts with a resonator at the bottom (Figure 5.12).

HARPS

Chordophones in which the strings are roughly perpendicular to a resonator.

♦ **Angle harps**. The strings are stretched between two pieces of wood joined at an angle (Figure 5.13).

♦ **Bow harps**. The strings are stretched between the sides of a single piece of wood shaped like a curved bow (Figure 6.8, p. 54).

William Alves

FIGURE 5.11
The European cello or violoncello is a lute instrument with a flat neck but no frets.

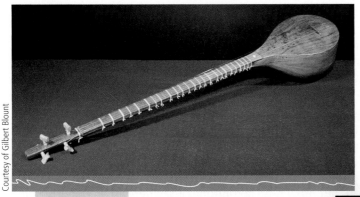

Courtesy of Gilbert Blount

FIGURE 5.10
The Iranian *sehtar*, an example of a fretted lute chordophone.

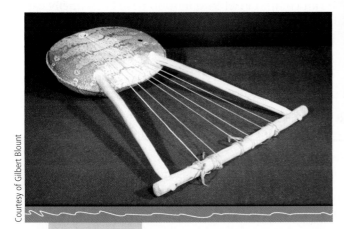

Courtesy of Gilbert Blount

FIGURE 5.12
The *seron* is a lyre from Uganda.

Courtesy of Gilbert Blount

FIGURE 5.13
A harp, like this one from Jalisco, Mexico, has strings attached more or less perpendicularly to the resonator rather than parallel to it. In this photograph, the resonator is on the bottom, although in performance, it would lean against the player's shoulder. In an angle harp, like this one, the other end of the string is attached to a bar (on the right in this picture) attached at an angle to the resonator.

AEROPHONES

In aerophones, it is not the physical instrument or string that vibrates but the air itself, inside a vessel such as a tube. This air is called an **air column**, even though the tube it is in may be wrapped around many times, as in a trumpet. Just as a string vibrates only at certain frequencies when stopped at a certain length and tension, air inside a tube vibrates only at certain frequencies.

These frequencies correspond to the **harmonic series**. The player can make the instrument vibrate in different frequencies in this series by increasing the air pressure, a technique called **overblowing**. For the pitches in between the notes of the harmonic series, the player varies the length of the tubing through the use of **valves** (European trumpets), holes (*zurna*, clarinet), or **slides** (trombone).

The aerophone player may set the air into motion in a number of different ways. In flutes, the player blows over a sharp opening or notch. When the angle is just right, the stream of air oscillates over and under the opening, causing the air inside to vibrate. In double reed instruments, the player ties two flat pieces of wood, plant, or plastic (the **reed**, often actually made of reed) tightly together and fixes them in the end of the tube (Figure 5.14).

When under air pressure, the reeds quickly open and close, creating the vibration of the air column. In single reed instruments, the reed is attached tightly to the end of the instrument itself (Figure 5.15).

The aerophone player may also buzz her lips into the end of the tube. In the West, such instruments are called brass instruments because of the material of their construction, but buzzed-lip aerophones elsewhere are frequently made of wood or other materials.

The tone may be varied also by the shape of the tubing, called the **bore**. For example, the European trumpet's tubing varies very little in diameter over the vast majority of its length. Only the bell at the end is flared. Thus we say that overall it has a **cylindrical bore**. However, the bore of the French horn gets gradually larger over its length; thus we say that it has a **conical bore**.

The ways in which the air column is set into motion have been briefly categorized, but let's break it down even further.

FLUTES

Aerophones in which a stream of air is focused on a sharp edge.

- ◆ **End-blown notch flute.** The player holds the tube straight away from the mouth but blows over the rim of the hole of the tube (Figure 5.16).

- ◆ **Transverse or side-blown flute.** The player holds the tube perpendicular to his head and blows over an open hole (Figure 5.17).

- ◆ **Duct flute.** The player blows directly into a hole (the duct) that directs the air stream to another hole with a sharp ramp, called a *fipple* (Figure 5.18).

- ◆ **Globular flute.** The sound body is a roughly spherical chamber rather than a tube (Figure 5.19).

FIGURE 5.14

A double reed like this one from an Iranian *zurna* consists of two flat pieces of cane or other material tied tightly together and inserted into the end of a tube. This instrument has a small metal disc at the bottom of the reed for the lips to rest on.

Courtesy of Gilbert Blount

FIGURE 5.15

A single reed, like this one attached to the mouthpiece of a saxophone from the United States, is a flat piece of wood or some similar material that vibrates on top of the end of the tube when blown.

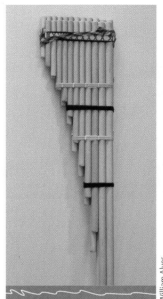

FIGURE 5.16

Panpipes, such as this *zampoña* from Bolivia, are collections of end-blown flutes. The player blows over the edge of each pipe to create the vibration.

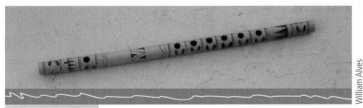

FIGURE 5.17

A transverse flute, like this *bansi* transverse flute from Sulawesi, Indonesia, is held out perpendicular to the player's head. The player focuses a stream of air over the hole on the left.

FIGURE 5.19

An ocarina globular flute from Mexico.

FIGURE 5.18

A duct flute, like this *suling* from Indonesia, directs an air stream over a sharp notch in an opening. In this case, there is a small opening between the ring around the top of the instrument and the stopped end of the tube. When the player blows into this opening, the air stream is automatically directed over the notch in the opening below.

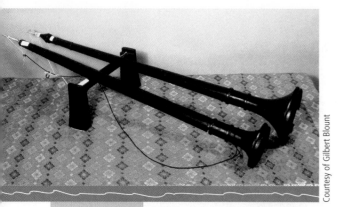

Courtesy of Gilbert Blount

FIGURE 5.20

Here are two slightly different sizes of *shahnai*, a double-reed instrument from India.

William Alves

FIGURE 5.22

Despite its name, the *gong bambu* of the Banyumas region of Indonesia is really a buzzed-lip aerophone. Its deep tones are used to imitate the tolling of large gongs.

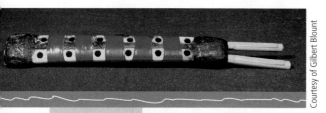

Courtesy of Gilbert Blount

FIGURE 5.21

The *duzele* is a single-reed instrument from Azerbaijan and related regions. This one is actually two single-reed instruments bound together so that the same player can play two tones at once.

DOUBLE REEDS

Aerophones in which two pieces of reed or other material are tied tightly together at the end of a tube, and when put under enough air pressure, begin to vibrate against each other. The tube may have a cylindrical bore or a conical bore (Figure 5.20).

SINGLE REEDS

Aerophones in which a flat piece of wood is tied to the mouthpiece of a tube and blown over, causing it to vibrate. The tube may have a cylindrical bore or a conical bore (Figure 5.21).

BUZZED-LIP INSTRUMENTS

Aerophones, also known as brass, in which the player buzzes his lips into the end of a tube. The tube may have a cylindrical bore or a conical bore (Figure 5.22).

MEMBRANOPHONES

Membranophones, or drums, have some kind of skin or thin plastic stretched tightly over a frame or resonator. The side with the skin is called the **head** and may be played with the hands or with sticks. There are several methods for stretching the head tightly over the resonator. It may be attached with rivets (Figure 5.23); with strings threaded through its edges and tied to the drum (Figure 5.24); with a hoop tightly pressed on top of the head and over the drum resonator (Figure 5.25); or with glue or other methods.

Resonators come in a variety of shapes for a variety of different types of sound. They form the basis for the most basic classification of most membranophones:

◆ **bowl** (Figure 5.26)

◆ **cylindrical** (Figure 5.27)

◆ **barrel or waisted** (Figure 5.28)

◆ **hourglass** (Figure 5.29)

◆ **conical** (Figure 5.30)

◆ **goblet** (Figure 5.31)

◆ **frame drum** (Figure 5.32)

Drums are sometimes provided with rattles or other secondary sources that vibrate sympathetically with the drum. The tambourine, for example, has small cymbals inserted in its frame, and the snare drum is named for small wires that rattle inside the drum. Such instruments are actually combination membranophones and idiophones.

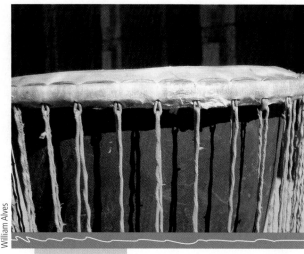

William Alves

FIGURE 5.24

In this *donno* drum from West Africa, the head is kept at tension with string threaded through the edges of the drum head.

William Alves

FIGURE 5.23

The skin of the *bedug* drum from Java, Indonesia, is attached with rivets around the edges of each head.

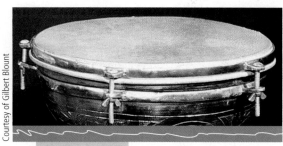

Courtesy of Gilbert Blount

FIGURE 5.25

In this head of a *doumbak* drum from North Africa, the skin is kept taut under a hoop that is fastened onto the drum body with bolts.

FIGURE 5.26

Drums with bowl-shaped resonators are found in Europe, the Middle East, and South Asia, such as these *dukar-tikar* drums from Jammu and Kashmir, India. (Two musicians are playing *shahnai* double reeds at the left.)

FIGURE 5.27

The *tupan* bass drum from Bulgaria has a cylindrical resonator.

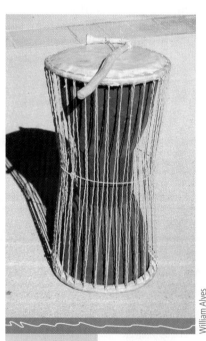

FIGURE 5.28

Many drums have a barrel-shaped resonator, that is, one that bulges outward in the middle. This *petia* drum of the Ashanti people of West Africa is covered in leopard skin.

FIGURE 5.29

The *donno* drum from Ghana has an hourglass-shaped resonator.

FIGURE 5.30

The *mpuunyi* drum from Uganda has a conical resonator.

Courtesy of Gilbert Blount

FIGURE 5.31

The *zarb* or *tombak* is a goblet-shaped drum from Iran.

© Kevin Schafer/CORBIS

FIGURE 5.32

Frame drums are simply skins stretched over hoops or frames so shallow that there is effectively no resonator. Frame drums are common in the Middle East as well as among indigenous people of North America and the Arctic, such as these Koryak people from Ossora, Russia.

IDIOPHONES

Idiophones are instruments in which the entire body of the instrument vibrates when struck or (more rarely) rubbed or otherwise set in motion. They include all sorts of bells, cymbals, wood blocks, gongs, and so on. Almost anything can be made an idiophone if you hit it. Because of this variety, idiophones classification can be difficult. For the purposes of this book, we will classify idiophones not by their construction but by the identifiability of their pitch, even though that characteristic can be a spectrum more than definite categories:

- **instruments of definite pitch** (Figure 5.33)

- **instruments of semi-definite pitch** (Figure 5.34)

- **instruments of no definite pitch** (Figure 5.35)

MUSICAL STYLE

The choices a culture makes in its construction and selection of musical instruments contribute to that culture's expression of **musical style**—the complex and fluid combinations of all the elements we've discussed in this

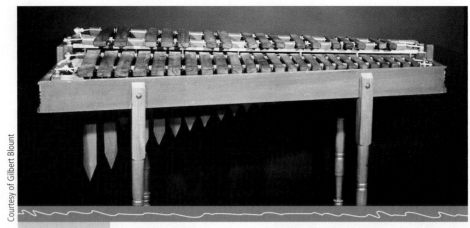

Courtesy of Gilbert Blount

FIGURE 5.33
Idiophones of definite pitch are often collected into sets played with mallets, such as this marimba from Mexico.

William Alves

FIGURE 5.34
Gongs, such as this *gong cina* from Java, Indonesia, often have a semi-definite pitch.

Courtesy of Gilbert Blount

FIGURE 5.35
Unpitched idiophones include rattles, such as these seed rattles from Africa.

section that help us generalize about related musical compositions and performances. In the beginning chapters of this book, we have looked at many ways we can describe and analyze the sound of a piece of music and how that sound is created. However, we should never lose sight of the fact that musical style cannot exist independently of the culture and society that produce it. In the following chapters, we will focus on paths toward understanding musical style within its social context and enriching the listening experience.

 ## BOOK COMPANION WEBSITE

You will find flashcards, a glossary, and tutorial quizzes, as well as other materials that will help you succeed in this course, at the *Music of the Peoples of the World, 2nd Edition,* Companion Website at www.cengage.com/music/alves/world2e.

WESTERN SAHARA (Occupied by Morocco)

TUNISIA

MOROCCO

ALGERIA

LIBYA

EGYPT

Aswan (Dam) •

SAHARA

MAURITANIA

MALI

NIGER

CHAD

SUDAN

ERITREA

DJIBOUTI

SENEGAL
• Dakar

GAMBIA

GUINEA BISSAU

GUINEA

SIERRA LEONE

LIBERIA

BURKINA FASO

BENIN

TOGO

IVORY COAST

GHANA

NIGERIA

• Lagos

CAMEROON

CENTRAL AFRICAN REPUBLIC

Addis Ababa •
ETHIOPIA

SOMALIA

EQUATORIAL GUINEA

GABON

CONGO

UGANDA

KENYA
• Nairobi

RWANDA

DEMOCRATIC REPUBLIC OF CONGO

BURUNDI

CABINDA

• Brazzaville

TANZANIA

ANGOLA

MALAWI

COMOROS

ZAMBIA

MOZAMBIQUE

ZIMBABWE

MADAGASCAR

NAMIBIA

Walvis Bay •

BOTSWANA

Johannesburg •

SWAZILAND

LESOTHO

SOUTH AFRICA
• Cape Town

Notice not only the contemporary political boundaries but the geographical divisions that we use in this unit: West Africa, East Africa, Central Africa, and Southern Africa. (We cover North Africa in Chapter 7.)

c. 400 BCE

Iron forging begins in the Sudan, creating new weapons and musical instruments.

c. 100 BCE

Trade with Arabia, India, and Indonesia. Some musicologists argue that Asian musical influences followed these routes as well.

c. 0 CE–1000 CE

Crops and other trade enable Bantu-speaking cultures of West and Central Africa to sustain denser populations and migrate south. As they occupy most of Central and Southern Africa, they displace indigenous Central African Pygmy and South African Khoikhoin and San ("Bushmen") populations.

c. 400–1076

Kingdom of Ghana, one of the first powerful West African kingdoms that became rich largely through trans-Sahara trade in gold. Royal retinues patronize sophisticated drumming orchestras in West Africa as well as praise-singers, reciters, and musical storytellers. Later kingdoms include Mali, Benin, Songhai.

SUB-SAHARAN AFRICA

SETTING

Listening to this first recording, you may find the intensity of the many drums exciting, even overwhelming. You may find yourself moving with the music, perhaps tapping your foot. Certainly you would find many onlookers in a Ghanaian village dancing and clapping when this drumming orchestra played. Still, as engaging as this sound is, the real story lies below the surface in a nuanced web of relationships, such as community and family, the most basic social structures in Africa.

SOUNDS

CD 1:1

Atsia Suite, Kobla Ladzekpo leading Ewe drumming orchestra

Many Africans reckon the bonds of family not only laterally, that is, as a relationship between siblings, cousins, and so on, but linearly back in time, sometimes far back. Thus, an entire village may trace its genealogy back to a common ancestor. In some cultures, one of which we meet later, in "Music of the *Jali*," it is the job of a professional caste of musicians to memorize these genealogies and recite them in song. Scholar and musician C. K. Ladzekpo quotes the African proverb "A dead animal cries louder than a live one," referring not only to the dead animal skin of the drum head but also to the voice of the player's ancestor that speaks through the music.

c. 1000	1502–1865	1652	1880–1900	

c. 1000	1502–1865	1652	1880–1900
Islam arrives immediately south of Sahara. Kingdoms that depend on trans-Saharan or East African coastal trade adopt Islam and many Arabic musical instruments, such as the *rabab* fiddle. Key trade centers, such as Timbuktu and Gao, bring Islamic scholarship to mosques there.	Period of Atlantic slave trade, depopulating large areas of West Africa and disrupting nations and cultures. Millions of Africans are taken to the Americas, bringing with them their music and other aspects of their cultures.	Dutch settle Capetown, South Africa. During the Napoleonic wars, the British take over the colony, which becomes the nation of South Africa.	Advanced firearms, as well as depopulation and interethnic warfare caused by slave trade, enable Europeans to claim vast territories as colonies, often with artificial borders that ignore traditional ethnic boundaries. These political expedients led to significant interethnic strife within modern African nations.

Courtesy of C. K. Ladzekpo

FIGURE 6.1

Togbui Adeladza II, Paramount Chief of the Anlo-Ewe, and his entourage enter the Durbar grounds of the Hogbetsotso festival at Anloga, Ghana. The drum orchestras (just visible on the left) that accompany them reflect the hierarchy and interconnectedness of society symbolized in such ceremonies.

The Ewe drumming ensemble that we hear in the first recording reflects the structure of the family. The lead drum is the metaphorical father of the ensemble, guiding the other drums by means of musical signals—when to start, stop, move to the next section, and so on. Likewise, mother and brother drums engage in a musical conversation, often in an almost literal way. Because certain syllables represent different drum strokes, each drumming pattern is not only a rhythm but also a melody and a linguistic phrase. The lead drum and a timekeeper instrument, in this case an iron bell, unify the many layers of sound. They keep the lively and complex conversation from dissolving into an un-African chaos that would represent the dissolution of the order of the family and the forces of nature.

Yet this tight cooperation still allows for individuality, for different points of view, through the most distinctive of traditional African musical characteristics—polyrhythm. **Polyrhythm** means different meters or metrical starting points going on at once. Like the disparate dynamic forces of the spiritual world that ideally find equilibrium, so the polyphony and polyrhythm of the drums are tied together in an exhilarating affirmation of life.

ELEMENTS OF TRADITIONAL AFRICAN MUSIC

The many languages and distinct cultures of the huge area of Sub-Saharan Africa clearly demonstrate its diversity. In addition to industrial economies in the growing urban areas, many traditional ways of life are still vital: farming, nomadic herding, hunting, and gathering. Despite the difficulties of generalizations, several musical characteristics are common throughout Sub-Saharan Africa. For the most part, these characteristics apply to the music of traditional cultures, although their influence is felt even in popular music.

◆ **Polyrhythm.** Rhythms that occur simultaneously in two different meters, or with different starting points. Polyrhythm can be very difficult and, in traditional African music, extremely complex.

▶ 1960–1980   1993

African countries gain independence. Governmental support for traditional art forms sometimes accompanies growth of African nationalism. African popular music becomes widespread and influential within and outside the continent.

Apartheid ends in South Africa.

- **Responsorial forms.** These forms feature an exchange between a single performer's vocal or instrumental call and a group response. Often simply called call-and-response, this practice is very common in African music, sometimes in very subtle ways.

- **Ostinato.** A short pattern that repeats over and over; ostinato most often refers to a repeating melody but can also refer to a repeating rhythm. In Africa, ostinatos often form foundations for improvisation, variation, or the addition of other patterns.

- **Use of percussion.** This characteristic reflects the Sub-Saharan emphasis on making music with drums, rattles, bells, xylophones, and *mbiras*. (We will discuss these instruments later.) Some orchestras include only percussion instruments, and nonpercussion instruments are sometimes played in a percussive manner. Nevertheless, such instruments as harps, lyres, horns, and flutes are equally important in many areas.

- **Background shimmer.** African musicians often attach beads, coins, or other small objects to their instruments to create a constant buzzing or rattling sound in the background of a performance.

- **Close connection between music and language.** Drums executing a combination of rhythm and pitch that represent spoken syllables and form a kind of speech illustrate the close association between music and words. Nearly all traditional African music involves song. Even purely instrumental pieces are considered songs without words—that is, pieces in which melody and rhythm imply words.

- **The participatory nature of the arts.** Most traditional cultures in Sub-Saharan Africa share the expectation that music is something everyone does. Although many societies have professional musicians, and some musicians are recognized as having more talent than others, no Western-style gulf separates musician from audience.

- **A close connection between the performing arts.** Many African languages have no separate word for "music," and although a word for "song" often exists, it may also imply poetry and dance. Thus, most African cultures share the expectation that a musical performance will involve singing and dancing. Music without dance is rare. Even in solo performance, the musician may also dance or move while he plays, remembering the physicality of the performance as much its sound.

POLYRHYTHM

Despite its literal translation, "many rhythms," polyrhythm more specifically means two distinct rhythmic patterns in different meters or with different starting points superimposed on one another. Although many pieces may have different rhythms in different simultaneous parts, they are rarely polyrhythmic because they all align to the same meter. One of the simplest examples of polyrhythm is mixing a meter that is two groups of three pulses (compound duple) with a meter that is three groups of two pulses (simple triple). Both meters take the same amount of time—they are just different groupings of the same six pulses.

GRAPHIC 6.1

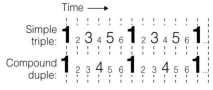

GRAPHIC 6.2

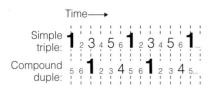

Although the superimposition of different meters in this example is very common in traditional African music, displacement of one of these layers can also create polyrhythm. In this case, two or more parts may have different **downbeats** (the stressed beginning of the metrical cycle). Sometimes these two effects are combined. Here we see polyrhythm formed by combining simple triple with compound duple but offset by two pulses.

MUSIC AND LANGUAGE

Many languages of Sub-Saharan Africa are **tonal**, that is, words may have different meanings depending on their **inflection**, the relative pitch at which they are spoken. Whereas inflection may carry meaning in European languages as well, a word in tonal languages may have three or more different meanings depending on its being spoken at a high, medium, or low pitch. In addition, accent or emphasis on a word or syllable is indicated more by long or short duration than a louder sound. Thus many African languages have a very musical quality to them.

More than other cultures with tonal languages (such as those of China and Southeast Asia), many African cultures have connected the tonal nature of their language to their music. An example is the so-called **talking drum**—a drum that can imitate the rhythm and most common pitch levels of speech. A skilled player of such a drum can imitate speech so well that listeners can understand what is being said.

Because the sounds of drums can carry over long distances, this ability has been used as a signaling device. Although some drums or idiophones are built especially for this purpose, *all* drums can "talk." A player in an African drumming orchestra is always thinking of the words or special drum syllables that he will make the drum "say." The carefully controlled pitches of the different strokes are as important as the rhythm, and drum parts are literally melodies—melodies of just a few pitches, but melodies nevertheless. We hear these qualities in the drumming orchestra performance on our first African recording (CD 1:1). The following is a graphic of musical instrument language transcribed from a portion of a recording of the Ndokpa people in the Central African Republic.[1] Graphic 6.3 demonstrates how a xylophone (black rectangles) can imitate the rhythm (shown left to right) and three pitch levels of speech so that listeners can understand what is being said without spoken words. The sentence here means, "It rained just now; it will be fine tomorrow."

GRAPHIC 6.3

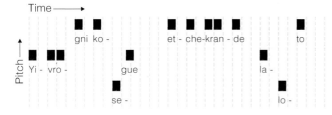

TRADITIONAL AFRICAN INSTRUMENTS

In addition to drums, African musicians play a wide variety of traditional instruments, including lyres, harps, zithers, lutes, flutes, and trumpets. The linguistic diversity of Africa compounds the difficulty of cataloguing the many

[1]Recorded by Charles Duvelle on *Musique centrafricaine*, rerelaesed on *Musique banda*, France: Prophet 22 CD 468448–2, 2004.

instrument types. A single instrument type may have dozens of different names across the continent. Therefore, this section gives only representative names or general descriptions.

Rough-hewn construction from readily available materials characterizes many of Africa's instruments. Although professional instrument makers produce beautiful instruments, almost anyone can make various types of African instruments, a feature that facilitates the general population's participation in music. Some musicians consider each musical instrument to have a spirit of its own, which the player must respect.

MEMBRANOPHONES

Drums are, of course, the most famous instruments of Africa, and they come in a staggering variety of forms—cylindrical, conical, goblet-shaped, hourglass-shaped, or barrel-shaped. Hemispherical drums (such as the European timpani) are not as common, and the shallow frame drum is mostly associated with Islamic areas where it has been introduced from the Middle East.

Drummers use either their hands or sticks (sometimes one of each) to hit the drum head. One distinctively African stick is the **elbow stick** (Figure 6.2).

Courtesy of Danlee Mitchell

FIGURE 6.2

African drums may be closed at the bottom or open for greater resonance. If open, the drum may be held at an angle between the legs to allow the sound to escape, or, if the drum is too large, it may be mounted at an angle on a frame (above) or (right) constructed on feet that raise the bottom and allow the sound to escape. The image above shows a group of drummers from Ghana, West Africa. Notice that their sticks are L-shaped, a shape that allows the performers to stand behind the drums and hit the heads with a perpendicular impact. The image on the right shows royal drummers playing footed drums in Ho, Ghana. Notice the laces and pegs on the sides of the drums. The laces attach the edges of the hide to the drum heads and tighten around pegs hammered diagonally into the drum's body. The drummer may periodically hammer at these pegs to keep the skin taut and the drum in tune.

Courtesy of Danlee Mitchell

Made of two sticks attached at an angle or carved from a single piece of wood, the elbow stick allows the player to stand behind the drum and strike the head with a solid, straight impact.

IDIOPHONES

Prominent in Africa, idiophones sounded by shaking, hitting, or rubbing the entire instrument range from a dancer's tiny jingles to large multiplayer xylophones. Some instruments known as "drums" are actually idiophones, such as log drums, slit drums, and pottery drums. The slit drum consists of a box or hollowed-out log resonator with slits cut in the surface to form wooden tines of different pitches.

A xylophone may be very large or small enough to suspend from the neck and carry in procession. It consists of wooden keys suspended over tuned resonator boxes, gourds, or a simple pit in the ground (Figure 6.3) and played with mallets. Occasionally played as a solo instrument, more often, the xylophone is an ensemble instrument with several instruments playing at once or multiple players on a single instrument. As with drums, xylophones can imitate speech and are sometimes used in narrative musical forms.

African slaves brought the xylophone to the Americas, where one variety has retained its African name—the marimba. "Marimba" is a variant of *mbira*, a term in Southern Africa for an instrument that consists of metal tines fixed to a resonator and plucked with the player's thumbs. Variations of this instrument, a kind of personal xylophone, are common throughout Central and Southern Africa under a variety of names. We discuss the *mbira* in detail later in this chapter.

Rattles can be made of baskets, gourds, seed pods, or other materials, and their beads may be contained inside or wrapped around the outside in a net. Bells, jingles, and other idiophones made from forged iron are common, although cymbals of the type found in the Middle East are not.

Courtesy of David Schmalenberger

FIGURE 6.3

The **balafon** or *bala*, an instrument common to the *jali* musicians (see later in this chapter) of West Africa, is a wooden xylophone with gourd resonators under each rough-hewn bar. Sometimes pebbles are placed inside the gourds to add a rattle to the sound.

AEROPHONES

As in most cultures, the human voice is a fundamental musical instrument, and its use in Africa is as diverse as the region's cultures. Open-throated sounds distinguish much of Sub-Saharan singing from the more "husky" or nasal tones preferred in many Islamic cultures of the North. Other distinctive kinds of African singing include **whisper singing**, a soft, breathy, almost growling tone, and **yodeling**, well known among the Pygmies of Central Africa.

© CORBIS

FIGURE 6.4

The *endere*, an end-blown flute from Uganda, appears in a historical photograph, which, according to ethnomusicologist Peter Cooke, represents the royal flute ensemble in use among the Kiganda people in the early twentieth century.

Whereas reed instruments are generally found only in areas with Arabic influence, flutes occur in virtually every form on the African continent: vertical and horizontal, with and without notches, with a wide or limited range, and so on (Figure 6.4).

Buzzed-lip or trumpet-type instruments are widespread and often made from animal horns into which a hole has been bored at the small end (Figure 6.5). In some cases, trumpets have large gourds attached to one end for greater resonance.

Although trumpets and flutes may have a limited range, even just a single note, a large group can create a melody by dividing the notes up among the different players, a practice called **alternation playing**. Thus, one player plays the first note, another the second, another the third, and so on. The alternating parts may also be polyrhythmic ostinatos, becoming rather like pitched versions of drumming ensembles.

Courtesy of Danlee Mitchell

FIGURE 6.5

A group of horn trumpet players in Ho, Ghana. Generally, mouth holes are bored on the side of the horn, making these instruments transverse trumpets.

CHORDOPHONES

String instruments are popular in Africa often because a single player can create polyrhythmic ostinatos by plucking in different patterns. The simplest type of chordophone is the **musical bow** (Figure 6.6), which consists of a single string attached to two ends of a curved stick, like the bow archers use. As in other African chordophones, the string may be vegetable matter (such as a vine), animal gut, or (more recently) nylon cord, which is plucked or struck with

© Peter Johnson/CORBIS

FIGURE 6.6

By resonating different harmonics, the player of the musical bow can create a melody, rather like a jaw's harp.

Courtesy of Face Music

FIGURE 6.7

The *endongo* is a bridged lyre of Uganda, where there is an especially large variety of harps and lyres. The strings are made of ox tendons attached to metal rings that can be slid along the crossbar for fine tuning.

Courtesy of Face Music

FIGURE 6.8

The *adungu* bow harp from Uganda is played by Bukenya Richard, Zaake Nathan, and Ntambi Abbey of the Ensemble Akadinda.

a stick. The instrument frequently has a half-gourd in the middle of the bow that serves as a resonator or may be placed next to the player's mouth for resonance, like a jaw's harp. Even though the musical bow usually produces only a single pitch, the player can resonate various harmonics in his mouth, in effect creating a second melody above the monotone sound of the bow string.

Harps and lyres are common in many parts of Africa, especially in Central Africa, where they are thought to have come from ancient Egypt via the upper Nile. The lyre consists of a symmetrical frame with several strings in the middle and often a resonator at the bottom. The strings may go over a bridge set on the resonator or may be attached directly to the resonator or the bottom of the frame (Figure 6.7).

The most common type of harp in Sub-Saharan Africa is the **bow harp** (Figure 6.8), which is similar to the musical bow, except that it has several strings instead of just one strung across a curved stick.

The **triangular harp** consists of a wooden frame of two or three parts with strings strung between them. This type of harp is more commonly found in North Africa, although one particularly African variant is the bridged harp or harp-lute, a hybrid of the two forms. We will discuss the *kora* harp-lute in "Music of the *Jali*."

Courtesy of Gilbert Blount

Courtesy of Face Music

FIGURE 6.9

The *inanga* from Uganda (right) is called a trough zither because of the carved wooden trough over which the strings are strung, thus eliminating the need for separate bridges. Alternatively, the *totombito* from the Congo (above) has a bridge and is called a raft zither because its simple flat sound board acts as a resonator.

Zithers come in many different forms as well (Figure 6.9), including tube zithers, bar zithers, raft zithers, trough zithers, and box zithers. Lutes are not as common in Sub-Saharan Africa as in North Africa and the Middle East. Except for the harp-lute, most instruments of the lute type in Sub-Saharan Africa appear in Islamic areas where the influence from the Middle East is the strongest.

DRUMMING IN WEST AFRICA

In the cold pre-dawn hours on the outskirts of a village of the Ewe people of Southeastern Ghana (see map), a music and dance club of costumed young men and women have gathered under a large tree.[2] Several months earlier, they paid a local composer to create a new piece for them, and their leader has also taught the group related compositions that they have been practicing at night, after work, ever since. Today, they have assembled early to surprise the town with their inaugural performance.

The leader pours a libation on the ground and intones an invocation to ancestors for a successful performance. After one last dress rehearsal, the group assembles in a parade and enters the town's main street, playing the drums, rattles, and bell, and dancing as the sun rises. Most people who hear the music rush out and follow, clapping along and moving to the music. The parade may stop at the house of a mayor or other town official to encourage celebrity participation. The group comes to a halt in the community's outdoor dance arena, and

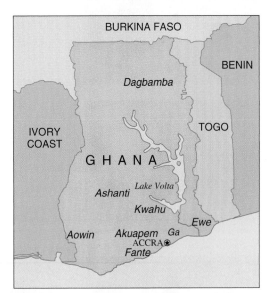

Map of Ghana. Notice the locations of the Ewe and other ethnic groups.

[2]Much of the following description is adapted from Kobla Ladzekpo, "The Social Mechanics of Good Music: A Description of Dance Clubs among the *Anlo* Ewe-Speaking People of Ghana," *African Music Society Journal* 5/1 (1971): 6–21; and A. M. Jones, *Studies in African Music* (New York: Oxford University Press, 1959).

the large crowd of onlookers, although they are participants as well, form a semi-circle around the troupe (Figure 6.10).

After another libation and prayer, the singers begin their signature song. The bell player accompanies in a characteristic rhythm, and the lead drummer plays a loud signal to bring in the rest of the ensemble and dancers. Throughout the performance, the lead drummer not only sets the tempo but also directs the other drums and the dancers. By playing certain audible patterns, the lead drummer signals the others to start, stop, or go on to the next section. These same patterns also signal the dancers to change their steps. Unlike a performance of European orchestral music in which a conductor gives visual cues, here the cues are built into the music. This performance will continue for some hours as the club plays the different pieces in their repertory. At times, they will play a *hatsiatsia*, or bell piece, during which the dancers rest.

These West African forests and grasslands were the home of powerful ancient kingdoms made wealthy largely through the lucrative trans-Sahara trade,

INSTRUMENT GALLERY

The Instruments That We Hear in the *Atsia* Suite

William Alves

ATOKE

The *atoke* is a small circular piece of iron folded in half, thus resembling a boat or (to some) a banana. It is held loosely on the palm and hit with a small metal stick.

William Alves

GANKOGUI

The *gankogui* double iron bell is the indispensable timekeeper of the group. The two bells welded together give two different pitches. Similar instruments are common throughout West Africa and as far away as Brazil, where the *agogo* performs a comparable function in the African-derived samba.

Courtesy of Danlee Mitchell

AXATSE

Instead of having beads or pebbles inside the gourd, as in most rattles (such as maracas), the *axatse* has a loose net of beads woven together around its outside. The player can shake the *axatse*, lightly hit it against a palm or leg, or twist it to give a swishing sound. On our recording, the performer alternately brings the rattle upward to the other hand and downward to the knee. Similar rattles are common throughout West Africa, and, depending on the variety of gourds grown in the area, can be quite large.

the same trade that brought the influences of Islam and Christianity to this region. The kings and other feudal lords often kept retinues of drumming orchestras and other musicians. Drumming ensembles were and still are crucial components in religious societies, in which particular deities and rituals have specific, often secret repertories of music. Similar musical religious practices are also found among African cultures in the Caribbean and South America. Although this chapter focuses on the specific practices of drumming among the Ewe people, traditional drumming orchestras are common throughout this region.

Although today the modern nation-state has replaced the political power of the kings, and people today drum as much for recreation as for ritual, orchestras such as this still represent the interconnected bonds of the family that is this community.

Kobla Ladzekpo

FIGURE 6.10

A traditional music and dance ensemble performs in an Ewe village.

ATSIMEWU

William Alves

In performance, the *atsimewu,* shown here with Ewe drummer Alfred Ladzekpo, is the so-called master or lead drum, played by the leader of the orchestra with a combination of sticks and hands. It is a large, long drum, usually about five feet tall and roughly cylindrical, but thicker in the middle and smaller on bottom than on top. The bottom is open, and the drum skin is attached to the top by a series of straps attached to pegs, which are hammered into the side of the drum at an angle. (All the Ewe drums have similar heads.) Because of its height, the *astimewu* is supported on a stand at an incline.

EWE DRUMMING ENSEMBLE

Danlee Mitchell

This photo shows an Ewe drumming ensemble in Kpata, Ghana, similar to the one heard in our *Atsia* recording. From left to right in the front row, the drums are *kaganu, kidi, sogo,* and *boba* (a cylindrical drum not heard in *Atsia*). The lead drummer stands behind them. The *kaganu* player holds the drum between his knees and plays with long sticks. The *kidi* drum is slightly larger and rests on the ground. The *sogo* is larger yet and is played with either hands or sticks. In smaller ensembles, it can function as the lead drum.

Hear and see the instruments of *Atsia* Suite in your downloadable **ACTIVE LISTENING TOOLS,** available at the World Music Resource Center.

A DRUMMING ORCHESTRA PERFORMANCE

Some Ewe music clubs specialize in the drumming orchestra piece *Atsia*, which is several hundred years old, according to the Ewe. Like most traditional Ewe pieces, new song melodies may be added to the core rhythms, and the drumming itself may vary according to the tastes of the performers. Thus, although some characteristics always identify what an *Atsia* club plays as *Atsia*, the piece may vary considerably from one club to the next. Thus, *Atsia* itself is somewhere between an individual work and a genre. A full performance, which could last for several hours, is a suite of different songs and dances that are all related versions of *Atsia*.

The name *Atsia* means simply "display" or "style," referring to the musicians and dancers showing off their performance. The song lyrics speak directly of the music itself and the club, sometimes bragging about the performance. This suite begins with a bell song, a *hatsiatsia*, accompanied in a beautiful polyrhythm by two types of iron idiophones: the **atoke**, a folded piece of iron , and **gankogui**, a clapperless double iron bell. In this *hatsiatsia*, two performers play each instrument.

Like many *Atsia* songs, the lyric simply refers to the piece itself. Here is a paraphrased translation of the lyrics.[3] Dzokoto is a revered historical figure to the Ewe, so the lyric "Dzokoto's music" is intended to indicate how great the music is. "Coming outside" means that the club is coming out to start the piece.

LEADER:	*Atsia dogbe lo*	Atsia is speaking!
	Mekawoe nye huna miya yawoda	Go and get the drummers.
CHORUS:	*Atsia dogbe loo*	Atsia is speaking!
	Mekawoe nye huna miya yawoda	Go and get the drummers.
	(Leader and chorus repeat.)	
LEADER:	*Dzokotovua digo*	Dzokoto's music is coming outside.
CHORUS:	*Todeme ha*	In our community circle,
	Dzokotovua digo	Dzokoto's music is coming outside.
	Mile wage	We will perform it.
	(Leader and chorus repeat.)	
CHORUS:	*Atsia dogbe loo…*	Atsia is speaking!…

MUSIC OF THE *JALI*

The function of musicians in the kingdoms of ancient West Africa was only partly entertainment. In societies without a written language, the history of a people and the stories of their ancestors must be committed to memory. In West Africa, musicians often specialized in these mnemonic feats, and, because their

[3]These lyrics are adapted from the translation and explanation in Dan Gorlin, *Songs of West Africa* (Forest Knolls, CA: Alokli West African Dance, 2000). © 2000 Dan Gorlin, alokli.com, reprinted by permission.

CD 1:1. *Atsia* Suite, Kobla Ladzekpo leading Ewe drummimg orchestra

Hatsiatsia—played entirely on iron bells

0:00

A single *atoke* (bell) sounds the timekeeping pattern.

Pulse:	1	2	3	4	5	6	7	8	9	10	11	12	1...
Atoke 1:	X		X		X	X		X		X		X	X
	long		long		short	long		long		long		short	long

The long notes are twice the length of the short notes, leading to a characteristic rhythm in a metrical cycle of twelve pulses. Many Ewe pieces use this standard pattern, and its asymmetrical rhythm helps orient the other players.

0:02

The second *atoke*, and two *gankogui* enter, creating an intricate polyrhythmic web.

Any latitude in these parts would ruin the carefully crafted conversation; therefore, the players do not improvise. Each *gankogui* has two different pitches that players refer to by syllables. The precise pitches of these instruments are not as important as the overall texture of interrelated, polyrhythmic bell sounds. Notice that the second *gankogui* part has the same rhythm as the second *atoke* part but offset in time.

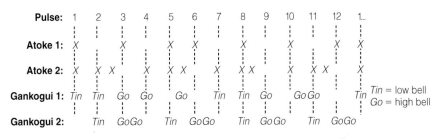

Pulse:	1	2	3	4	5	6	7	8	9	10	11	12	1...
Atoke 1:	X		X		X	X		X		X		X	X
Atoke 2:	X	X	X		X	X	X		X	X		X	X		X
Gankogui 1:	Tin	Tin	Go	Go		Go		Tin	Tin	Go		Go Go		Tin	X
Gankogui 2:		Tin	Go Go		Tin	Go Go		Tin	Go Go		Tin	Go Go	

Tin = low bell
Go = high bell

First Song—call-and-response between the lead singer (usually the lead drummer) and the chorus (who may be the dancers, other drummers, or even onlookers)

Second Piece —"Circle" *Atsia*, a round dance

1:53

One *gankogui* player takes over the timekeeping pattern, playing the first note on the lower bell and the other notes on the higher bell.

The *axatse* rattle enters with a standard *axatse* pattern that is a simple variation of the *gankogui* pattern and links the two instruments in texture.

Lead singer begins the next song.

1:59

Chorus answers the lead singer.

The lead drummer on the *atsimewu* mirrors the timekeeping melody by striking the side of his drum with a stick.

2:04

The *atsimewu* drummer sounds a distinctive call, a signaling pattern to the drums and dancers, who respond by whirling around and moving on to a new repetitive movement pattern.

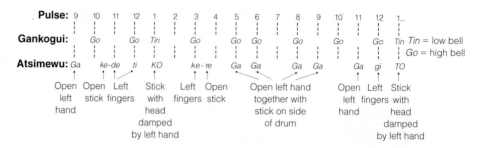

Whenever this signaling pattern comes from the lead drum, the dancers respond. The lead drummer therefore acts as a conductor for the performance, giving cues in his drumming patterns. There are many different call patterns for a particular piece, each signaling a different change in the choreography. The syllables that guide the drummer are a kind of drumming language known as *wu-gbe*. Different syllables are associated with different types of strokes, although they may also vary according to the context of the pattern.

2:08

The *kaganu*, *sogo*, and *kidi* drums respond to the lead drummer's *atsimewu* pattern and begin the first section of the circle dance.

The timeline that follows shows the ostinato patterns from the circle dance section *Atsia*. As each drummer plays, he thinks of certain syllables, each of which corresponds to a particular stroke and therefore often a different pitch. Players repeat these patterns (only the *kidi* and *sogo* may introduce slight variations) until the lead drum signals a move to the next section. (The *atsimewu* is not in this timeline because it does not play a constant ostinato pattern.)

These patterns overlap different meters. The *gankogui* bell and *axatse* rattle repeat an asymmetrical pattern of long and short beats, while the claps and the low-pitched *sogo* divide the cycle into four groups of three. (The second and fourth beats are played damped with the open hand rather than a stick. The hand comes down on the head of the drum but presses there rather than bouncing up; it thus damps the vibration, giving the note a higher pitch and a dryer sound.) The high-pitched *kaganu* plays a pattern of short-long four times in the span of the *gankogui* cycle but offset in relation to the *sogo*. The *kidi* drum plays two sets of six notes with each

languages have an inherent musical quality, it is a small step to make words into songs. Just as blacksmiths of this period achieved powerful status as the artisans of weapons, these musicians were the "artisans of the word"[4]—keepers

[4]This description is from Eric Charry's *Mande Music* (Chicago: University of Chicago Press, 2000), an excellent survey of the music and musicians of this region.

set arranged in patterns of four plus two. (The group of four notes is distinguished from the other two because they are played as damped strokes.) The *kidi's* pattern thus forms an almost literal dialogue with the *sogo*. Many Ewe compositions contain such interplay between the parts. This diagram does not show the dancer's movements, which add another layer of rhythm to this polyrhythmic web.

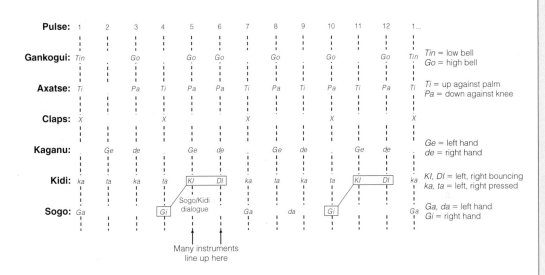

The lead drummer on the *atsimewu* plays a warning pattern, a signal for the drummers and dancers to prepare for a change, and then a new call.

2:25

The drummers respond by varying their patterns, and the dancers twirl around and begin a new step.

3:03

Another warning signal from the *atsimewu* leads to a variation on the first pattern.

Alternations between different patterns in the drums and dance steps continue throughout the Circle *Atsia* section. Listen for more warning signals and pattern changes at 4:05, 5:18, and 7:04.

8:12

The lead drummer on the *atsimewu* gives a loud warning signal that the piece is about to end. The warning signal is followed by a pattern that signals to the other players that this is the last metrical cycle, and everyone ends together.

Hear and see the instruments of *Atsia* **SUITE** in your downloadable **ACTIVE LISTENING TOOLS,** available at the World Music Resource Center. *f*
CD 1:2, *Hatsiatsia* examples; CD 1:3, Circle *Atsia* examples; CD 1:4, *Atsimewu* part

of a people's history, of legendary stories, of royal genealogies, and singers of praise songs of kings, religious leaders, and patrons.

One of the most important traditions in West Africa is the specialized caste of musicians the French called *griots*, who have different names in each of the languages of the region. Among the Mande people of Gambia, Senegal, and

Listening Exercise 1	CD 1:1. *Atsia* Suite

1. What is the texture through most of the piece?
   a   monophonic vocal melody
   b. heterophonic instruments and voices
   c. polyphonic with vocal melody

2. The underlying structure of the piece depends mainly on
   a. short repeating patterns in most of the instruments.
   b. sections in which different instruments alternately solo.
   c. sequences of harmonies.

3. When the chorus answers the lead singer (at 0:08),
   a. they repeat the same melody that the lead singer has introduced.
   b. they sing a different melody that completes the phrase.

4. How would you characterize the timbre of the singers?
   a. nasal, high tessitura
   b. husky, loud, "brassy"
   c. open-throated, medium tessitura

5. At 1:53, the audible signal to go on to the next section is given by the
   a. atsimewu (lead drum).
   b. gankogui (double iron bell).
   c. lead singer.

6. Responsorial form is found in
   a. the ways in which a chorus of singers answers the lead singer.
   b. the ways in which the instruments change their parts in response to signals from the lead drummer.
   c. both of the above.

You can take this Listening Exercise online and receive feedback or e-mail answers to your instructor at the World Music Resource Center.

Mali, such a musician is called a **jali** or *jeli*. Not anyone can become a *jali*—normally one must be born into the profession, and many of these musicians trace their musical lineage back to a time when their ancestors were important members of the royal retinues of West Africa's historical kingdoms. Today, however, a *jali* is more likely to find patronage singing at a market, at a festival, or, increasingly, as a part of a popular music band.

The *jali*'s principal instrument is the **kora**, a large chordophone that has been described as a hybrid harp-lute (Figures 6.11, 6.12). Because its twenty-one strings are stretched on two sides of the bridge, the performer's left hand plays the eleven strings on the left side of the bridge and the right hand plays the ten strings on the right side. Such an arrangement, common among African chordophones, makes possible intricate polyrhythmic patterns between the hands.

Kora pieces are based mostly on standard ostinato patterns called *kumbengo*. A characteristic sequence of core tones defines *kumbengo*, but musicians weave many elaborate variations of these basic outlines. Contrasting embellishments called *birimintingo* periodically interrupt the constant cycle of *kumbengo*. Although *kora* pieces may be entirely instrumental, more commonly, the performer sings a song on top of the set of variations.

Singers may also polyrhythmically clap, snap their fingers, tap on the *kora* resonator, or play small iron bells. Songs are commonly praise songs for ancestors, patrons, or Islamic leaders but may also be historical stories, mythic tales, or improvised verse. Whereas kora players are traditionally men, both men and women sing.

Youri Lenquette

FIGURE 6.11

Musician and singer Mory Kanté plays the *kora*, a hybrid lute-harp from West Africa. The resonator of the *kora* is a very large hemispherical gourd covered with antelope or other animal hide. The long neck extends up vertically from the gourd and opposite the player. A small, flat piece of metal is loosely attached to the bridge and serves as a jingle that provides the background buzz so common in this region. Traditionally, the twenty-one strings were made of leather, but today nylon is more common.

Courtesy of Gilbert Blount

FIGURE 6.12

In a close-up of the *kora* bridge, notice that the strings stretch over the sides of the bridge, not the top, so that the fingers of each hand can reach half the strings. The sticks parallel to and below the strings stretched under the resonator cover are hand posts used to hold the instrument while playing.

Another instrument of jali musicians is the ***balafon*** or *bala*, a wooden xylophone with gourd resonators under each rough-hewn bar (refer to Figure 6.3). Both the *balafon* and the *kora* are heptatonic (seven tones per octave), although the intervals of the *kora* may vary considerably depending on the player and the song. The *kora* player may tune to the *balafon* so that the two may be played together, an especially popular ensemble today.

Some *jali* musicians also rely on popular concerts and recordings as a new source of patronage. Several, including Mory Kanté from Senegal, have produced rock-fusion albums. One of the most famous in this popular style is Foday Musa Suso, who moved to the United States and founded the Mandingo Griot Society in America in 1978. Since then, he has produced his own albums and collaborated with American composers Herbie Hancock and Philip Glass.

MBIRA MUSIC

Along the dirt roads of Southern Africa, it is not uncommon to hear buzzing, metallic sounds ringing from within a large hollow gourd held by a dusty traveler. Inside is an instrument consisting of rows of metal tines stretched over a series of bars so that the ends can be plucked with the player's thumbs. The gourd serves as a resonator and may also have shells or bottle caps attached to it to create the buzzing background players consider indispensable. Known as

CD 1:5. *Yundum Nko* (Man from Yundum), Jali Nyama Suso*

Nyama Suso comes from a long line of *jali*, the professional traditional musicians of the Mande people of the Gambia river area of West Africa, and is a specialist in songs for the *kora*, such as this one.

0:00

Yundum Nko begins with a series of flourishes that set the tonality. The tuning system for this piece is known as *tomoraba*, one of four commonly in use among *kora* players. It is a diatonic scale, roughly equivalent to the Western major mode.

0:11

This is the first of contrasting sequences of repeated motives, in this case, a series of three descending pitches repeated at progressively lower scale tones. Such patterns are idiomatic to the *kora* because the pitches of the strings alternate between the left and right side of the bridge. That is, if the player plays a scale, first the left hand will pluck, then the right, then the left, and so on.

0:19

At this point, the introduction ends, and an ostinato alternating between pitches 1 and 5 is set up in the bass (played by the left thumb). Despite occasional variations, this pattern will continue throughout the rest of the song. Meanwhile, the forefingers play a series of downward scales, again alternating between the hands. These quick scalar passages above the ostinato are called *birimintingo* and are mostly improvised whenever the voice is silent.

0:33

The quick notes of the *birimintingo* stop, and a new ostinato called the *kumbengo* begins in its place. The *kumbengo* is the standard repeating pattern that accompanies the song, although it too is frequently varied. The meter is polyrhythmic, and the twelve pulses of the ostinato can be heard in six groups of two or in four groups of three. The graphic shows the version of the *kumbengo* that begins here.

Note that, aside from the bass ostinato played by the thumbs (in black), certain pitches occur on certain beats. During the first of the 12 pulses (shown by the vertical lines), as well as pulses 6, 7, 10, and 12, only pitches 2, 4, 5, and 7 are heard (shown in red). On pulses 2, 5, 8, and 11, the player plays only pitches 1, 3, and 5 (shown in blue). Although the player may create many variations, this pattern of pitches associated with particular beats primarily defines the *kumbengo*, and, more than anything else, the song *Yundum Nko* itself.

*For the translation of the lyrics and background to the song, I am indebted to Roderick Knight, *Mandinka Jaliya: Professional Music of The Gambia* (diss. UCLA: 1973) and notes to Jali Nyama Suso, *Gambie: L'art de la kora*, CD audio (Paris: Ocora C 580027).

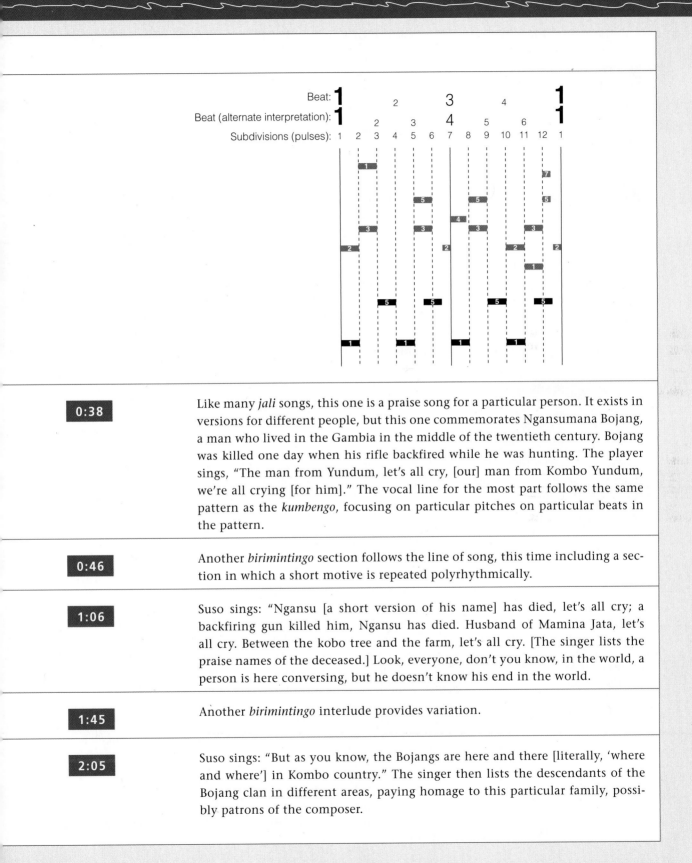

| 0:38 | Like many *jali* songs, this one is a praise song for a particular person. It exists in versions for different people, but this one commemorates Ngansumana Bojang, a man who lived in the Gambia in the middle of the twentieth century. Bojang was killed one day when his rifle backfired while he was hunting. The player sings, "The man from Yundum, let's all cry, [our] man from Kombo Yundum, we're all crying [for him]." The vocal line for the most part follows the same pattern as the *kumbengo*, focusing on particular pitches on particular beats in the pattern. |

| 0:46 | Another *birimintingo* section follows the line of song, this time including a section in which a short motive is repeated polyrhythmically. |

| 1:06 | Suso sings: "Ngansu [a short version of his name] has died, let's all cry; a backfiring gun killed him, Ngansu has died. Husband of Mamina Jata, let's all cry. Between the kobo tree and the farm, let's all cry. [The singer lists the praise names of the deceased.] Look, everyone, don't you know, in the world, a person is here conversing, but he doesn't know his end in the world. |

| 1:45 | Another *birimintingo* interlude provides variation. |

| 2:05 | Suso sings: "But as you know, the Bojangs are here and there [literally, 'where and where'] in Kombo country." The singer then lists the descendants of the Bojang clan in different areas, paying homage to this particular family, possibly patrons of the composer. |

2:42	The player sings: "His own gun killed him, let's all cry for Ngansu; a betraying gun killed him, Ngansumana from Yundum."
2:52	As the tempo and volume increase somewhat, Suso plays another *birimintingo* variation.
3:49	Suso plays an even faster and more virtuosic *birimintingo*.
4:25	Suso closes the song with a variation of the opening lines, followed by a gradual decrease in loudness (fade out).

Hear and see the instruments of *Yundum Nko* in your downloadable **ACTIVE LISTENING TOOLS**, available at the World Music Resource Center.

William Alves

FIGURE 6.13

The large traditional *mbira* of the Shona is the *mbira dzavadzimu*. It consists of twenty-two metal tines arranged in three rows. When the player plucks the keys with his or her thumbs and right index finger, the bottle caps lightly attached to the metal plate on the bottom provide a constant background buzz. The player usually puts the instrument inside a large hollow gourd (not shown here) for further resonance.

the **mbira** to the Shona people of Zimbabwe, this instrument has a number of names for its many variations across the continent. It is often a traveler's personal pastime instrument (Figure 6.13).

The instrument also has a deep spiritual significance among the Shona, for it has the crucial function of calling to the ancestors in a ritual called the *bira*. As Paul Berliner described in his landmark 1978 study *The Soul of Mbira*, at all-night ceremonies, people call upon the spirits to answer crucial questions; the constant variations in the *mbira* performance aid the participants in going into a trance in which spirits take over the participant's body. Although the *mbira* has become an important national symbol and even taken over the function of the guitar in so-called "mbira pop" bands of the region, the Shona never forget these spiritual connections.

Despite the instrument's popularity as a personal recreational instrument, the Shona usually consider a solo performance incomplete. There must be at least one other *mbira* to form the community of the ensemble—that is, to play interlocking polyrhythms with the first player. A kind of rattle called a *hosho* and sometimes a small drum called a *ngoma* are also common additions to the ensemble, and, of course, singing and dancing are often just as important.

A Shona *mbira* piece is really a framework for a short ostinato melody. However, the flexibility of this framework allows for nearly endless variations on the basic melody and can continue for hours. On top of these complex yet infectious intertwining parts, the *mbira* player sings, at times in a near-whisper and at other times with emotional cries. These songs may be composed or improvised but always draw their melody out of the fabric of the gently cycling *mbira* parts.

AN *MBIRA* PERFORMANCE

The Shona consider *Nyamaropa* to be among the oldest and most representative traditional pieces in the standard repertoire. It can be played for rituals as well as for entertainment.

The *mbira* part consists of a basic melody repeated over and over with variations. The basic melody, which lasts forty-eight pulses, goes by quickly—about every eight seconds for each repetition in this recording. Graphic 6.4 shows a representation of the notes as small rectangles arranged so that time is represented horizontally and pitch vertically.

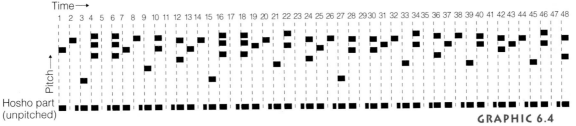

GRAPHIC 6.4

The basic *mbira* part for *Nyamaropa* (after Berliner 1978).

Although such a graph may be helpful, the notes are as yet undifferentiated. The experience of listening to the piece is much different, sounding to the ear like multiple melodies—because indeed there are. In fact, a single musician is playing three distinct melodies *polyrhythmically*. Graphic 6.5 shows the same graph, but now with the notes of the three melodies distinguished by color. Though unified by the forty-eight-pulse cycle, each melody exists in its own meter, made clear when they are separated in Graphic 6.6.

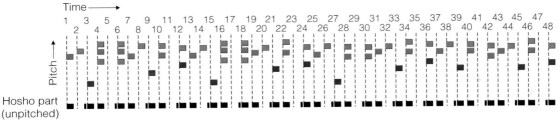

GRAPHIC 6.5

Here, the three melodies that make up the *mbira* part are colored red for the high melody, green for the middle melody, and blue for the low melody, demonstrating the different layers that the *mbira* player creates.

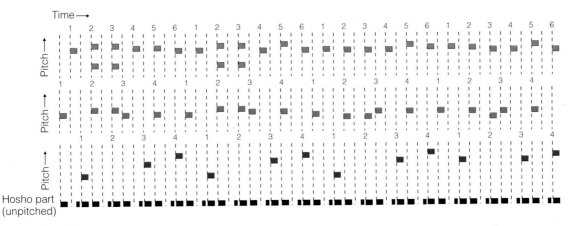

GRAPHIC 6.6

Each of the different layers has its own meter and start time. Here the three melodies are separated and their pulses numbered to show the metrical cycle for each one.

LISTENING GUIDE

CD 1:6–7. *Nyamaropa* (excerpt), Hakurotwi Mude, voice and *mbira*; Cosmas Magaya, *mbira*; Ephraim Mutemasango, *hosho*.

0:00	Listen to the low tones of the *mbira* to orient yourself to the basic melody cycle (refer to Graphic 6.6).
0:10	Singer enters in the *huro* style, loud cries improvised at the top of the singer's range, frequently ornamented with glissandi (sliding pitches) and yodeling (quick jumps between vibrational modes in the vocal cords).
0:31	Singer makes a sliding transition into the *mahon'era* style, a soft breathy voice at the bottom of the singer's range, also improvised with vocables. The singer spontaneously creates the melody by picking out notes in the *mbira* part.
0:54	Singer returns to the *huro* style.

Hear and see the instruments of *Nyamaropa* in your downloadable **ACTIVE LISTENING TOOLS,** available at the World Music Resource Center.

In the recording, we hear two *mbira* performers. Neither performer plays the above basic melody all the time. Each plays a separate variation of the melody, interlocking in such a way as to create yet another polyrhythmic level in the piece. In all the repetitions on this recording, the players create variations that diverge significantly from the bare version yet remain true to the structure that makes this piece recognizable as *Nyamaropa*. This structure is crucial to understanding this music.

Shona *mbira* pieces use only a certain subset of pitches at a given time during the basic melody. This rhythmic progression of pitch sets is as much a defining feature of a particular piece of music as its melodies because while the melodic contours and rhythmic interactions may change considerably throughout all the variations in a performance, the sequence of available pitches remains the same. They create a sense of gentle back-and-forth motion, rocking with the participants of the *bira*.

What most distinguishes *Nyamaropa* from other *mbira* pieces is not the melodies themselves, but the sequence of available pitches during the cycle. For example, as we see in Graphic 6.7, for the first four pulses (counting from the point shown), only the tonic (pitch 1) and the fifth note of the scale (shown above as 5) are allowed. In the next three pulses, only pitches 3 and 7 are allowed, and so on.

This structure gives *Nyamaropa* a certain distinctive sequence of pitches similar to Western harmonic progressions but without Western chords. The number of pulses for each of the pitch sets is also important because it adds a

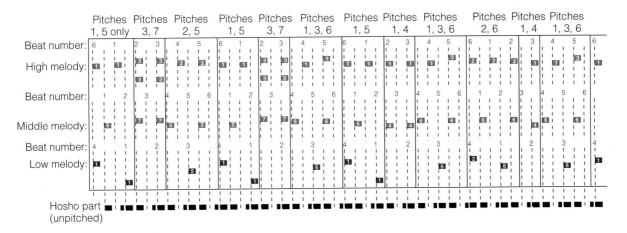

characteristically asymmetrical harmonic rhythm—4 + 3 + 5 pulses for the first three quarters with a contrasting 5 + 2 + 5 phrase at the end.

The *mbira* part is only part of the performance. At least as important is the vocal part, which is usually sung by the lead *mbira* player in different singing styles appropriate for the words. Pieces may include a precomposed song with poetic lyrics, perhaps a short allegorical poem or a longer epic narrative. The singer may improvise poetry about the specific occasion, people in the audience, politics, and so on. On our listening selection, we hear alternating *huro* and *mahon'era* singing styles—sung on **vocables**, syllables chosen for their expressive qualities but without any other meaning. This recording is excerpted from a long performance.

AFRICAN POPULAR MUSIC

In the mid-1970s, entering the famous club Afrika Shrine in Lagos, Nigeria was like opening the doors to a blast furnace of sound. A half-dozen percussionists, three or four trumpet and saxophone players, several guitarists, and six or seven singers fed a dense wall of rhythm with an ostinato-based groove that could go on for more than half an hour on a single song. Alternately playing saxophone and keyboards or singing was the lean, shirtless, face-painted leader of this band, a madman or hero, depending on your perspective, named Fela Kuti.

Fela (as millions familiarly called him) was the son of a pastor father who was also a musician and a mother who was a pioneering activist for social justice and women's rights. He built his own career in equal measure around music and social justice. As a youth, jazz, traditional African music, and the urban popular music styles known as highlife and juju formed his musical world. When given support by his parents to study medicine, he went to London but enrolled in a music school instead. Returning to a newly independent Nigeria in 1963, he started his own highlife band with a unique blend of European jazz, African beats, and American rhythm and blues.

A tour to the United States in 1969 brought a life-changing exposure to the African-American militancy of Malcolm X and the Black Panthers. Fela's music

© PIUS UTOMI EKPEI/Getty Images, Inc.

FIGURE 6.14

Fela Kuti performs at the Afrika Shrine.

became a forum for protests against Africa's military dictatorships, the oppression of the poor, Western imperialism, and corruption. To reflect the pan-African identity he sought in his music as well as his politics, he dubbed his unique sound "Afro-Beat" and sang in pidgin English (a hybridized language spoken in much of West Africa) rather than his native Yoruba.

The successive military governments of Nigeria took notice, and at various times, Fela was beaten and imprisoned, his residence burned to the ground. Soldiers even threw his then eighty-two-year-old mother out a second-story window. Such incidents only seemed to make his songs and the legendary harangues against political evils that he delivered between sets during his four-hour concerts all the more caustic. For his willingness to stand up for these principles, he became a hero to millions of Nigerians and a powerful symbol of popular music as a social force in modern Africa.

Popular music in Africa has often reflected the continent's uneasy struggle with issues of identity and nationalism, tradition and modernity. Even while adopting Western harmonies, instruments, and song forms, Fela and others also enriched it, self-consciously or not, with ostinatos, emphasis on percussion, responsorial forms, and layered textures (though not, in general, polyrhythm), all derived from their traditional African heritage. Still other influences, while ostensibly American, originated in or were influenced by the African diaspora (the scattering of Africans throughout the Americas because of slavery)—the horn sections from swing bands and rhythm and blues; the rhythms of Caribbean dances, especially the Cuban rumba; American funk and soul, especially that of James Brown; and reggae, to name a few.

When Fela died in 1997 from AIDS-related illness, more than a million people attended his funeral procession down the streets of Lagos. His son Femi Kuti is a very popular performer in his own right who carries on the Afro-Beat legacy at the Afrika Shrine and through tours and recordings.

POPULAR FORMS IN WEST AFRICA

Fela's Afro-Beat had its roots in the coastal and urban areas of West Africa, where there is a long history of Africans adapting European popular forms and instruments to their own expression. Originally known as palm-wine music, after the favorite beverage drunk where these entertainers played, this lively guitar music was by the 1920s known as **highlife**. Popular dance bands in the 1950s known for their large horn sections took over the name and style. *Juju* was a similar popular band music in Nigeria. Beginning in 1966, civil war and political instability in Ghana and Nigeria led to the dispersion of these styles, spreading them to other African countries and also to Europe.

Some highlife and juju artists, such as "King" Sunny Ade, became multi-millionaire pop stars and attained success in Europe and the United States. The same Africanist impulses that influenced Fela around the 1970s also fed into a new Nigerian style known as *fuji*. Drawing from a tradition of Islamic praise songs, traditional talking-drum music called *apala*, and popular dance music, *fuji* featured huge percussion sections but no guitars. The style known as **mbalax** in Senegal also popularized innovative connections to traditional instruments, styles, and forms.

Sometimes the most impressive characteristic of bands in each of these styles is their sheer size, often numbering more than two dozen performers, all contributing to a powerful groove. Despite the lack of polyrhythms, this multilayered groove is the amplified version of the traditional ostinato, and the bands still reflect the African sense of community.

POPULAR FORMS IN SOUTH AFRICA

The ethnic diversity of South Africa, combined with its economic development and creative responses to apartheid, make it arguably the most creatively active country on the continent in the area of popular music. An early example is **gumboot** music or **isicathulo**, a style of dance performed by workers at the diamond mines, who wear long waterproof boots. To the accompaniment of a guitar, they clap and slap their boots, creating their own percussion.

In the 1920s and 1930s, tightly improvised folk harmonies (developed from the Western chords introduced in missionary schools and the polyphony found in traditional African music) sung by a cappella groups (consisting entirely of singers without instrumental accompaniment) became very popular in Zulu areas. In 1939, one of these groups, the Original Evening Birds, recorded chorus leader Solomon Linda's "The Lion" ("*Mbube*"), which became such a hit that the style itself became known as **mbube**. After this song found its way across the Atlantic, it eventually became the 1961 doo-wop hit "The Lion Sleeps Tonight," although at first Linda was not credited.

Although American jazz influenced many South African bands, most disbanded following the forced removal of black South Africans to townships and "tribal homelands" in the 1950s. An exception were the homemade bands of cheap tin whistles and one-string basses who played music known as **tin whistles jive** or **kwela**, which was also related to British "skiffle" music. From such humble groups, larger and very popular bands developed in the 1950s.

By the 1960s, saxophones and electric guitars replaced the tin whistles and acoustic strings. Together with the influence of American rhythm and blues, traditional ostinatos, and gumboot music, these bands originated a style known as **sax jive** or **mbaqanga**. They soon added female choruses reminiscent of mbube's tight harmonies, although often with a contrasting male "groaner" voice. A cappella music, often now called **iscathamiya**, continued to be popular, although white authorities frequently banned many of these groups.

Sax jive and *iscathamiya* eventually caught the attention of American pop composer Paul Simon. Simon collaborated with some township jive musicians and the a cappella group Ladysmith Black Mambazo in his African-influenced album *Graceland* of 1986. The album was a huge hit and exposed Ladysmith Black Mambazo and others to a wide international audience (Figure 6.15).

Leon Morris/Redferns Music Picture Library

FIGURE 6.15

Ladysmith Black Mambazo in concert.

CD 1:8. *"No Buredi"* ("No Bread"), excerpt, Fela Anikulapo Kuti and Africa 70*

In 1975, the Nigerian government released a windfall of oil revenues in the form of huge salary increases for government workers. These Udoji payments, so named for the Justice Jerome Udoji, who headed the panel that recommended them, fueled massive inflation that hit the poorest the hardest and inspired Fela Kuti to create this song, a blistering attack on government corruption and its effect on poverty. One of Fela Kuti's most important influences was the American form of rhythm and blues known as **funk**, which came to prominence in the early 1970s, especially through the work of James Brown. This music did away with the typical harmonic progressions of popular music (see Chapter 16), instead layering different ostinato rhythms in a single mode, very similar to composition in traditional African music.

0:00

"No Buredi" has three melodic ostinatos that continue throughout the fourteen-minute song (of which we hear only an excerpt here), played by two electric guitars and an electric bass guitar (see graphic). In addition, a drum set, two congas (large vertical drums played with the hands), and maracas add to what critics have called Fela's "endless groove."

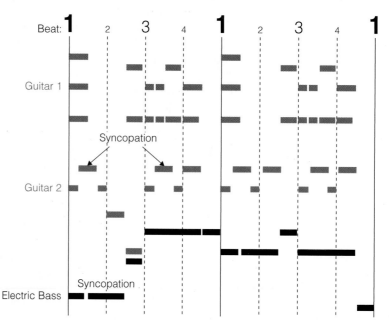

0:05

Fela begins singing in pidgin English, answered by a group of female singers in a responsorial form:

Look-u you, wellu-wellu-well (looku you!)   Look at you, well, well, well!

You stand-e for ground, your leg-e dey shake (looku you!)   You are standing but your legs are shaking

* The transcription, translation, and interpretation of the lyrics of *"No Buredi"* in this listening guide are by Deen Ipaye. (deencatt@yahoo.com) Reprinted by permission.

Nah your leg whey keep ground noh dey shake (looku you!)	Or is it your legs that are keeping the ground from shaking?
Your face look like you don reach-e gbee (looku you!)	Your face looks like you have reached the end
You si(t)down for chair like e you don reach-e gbee (looku you!)	You sit down in a chair like you have reached the end

In this first section, Fela addresses the poor, asking them in doing so to take a look at themselves. Their legs are shaking (like their shaky standing in society), but perhaps it's the ground itself that is shaking. They feel like they have reached the end (gbee is a letter in the Yoruba alphabet whose percussive sound implies an ending).

`0:29`

The next contrasting section continues:

Your head dey ache, welle-welle	Your head aches,
Mouth dey dry, welle-welle	Your mouth is dry,
Stomach dey turn, welle-welle	Your stomach is churning (empty),
Hungry dey show him power,	You are overpowered by hunger,
[4 lines repeat]	
You noh get-e power to fight (No Buredi)	You don't have the power to fight, (No bread)

Fela addresses the distressed poor, saying that they face those with power, and they don't have the power to fight back. The chorus and the title of the song, "No buredi," literally means "no bread," but also "no money."

`1:11`

The melody returns to the first section with new lyrics:

Look-u you, looku wellu-wellu-well (looku you!)	Look at you, well, well, well!
On the day or the night or the afternoon (looku you)	During the day, the night, or the afternoon
The trouble of the world e catch you for road (looku you!)	All the problems of the world meet you wherever you go

Man must wack nah him put you for the road (looku you!)	You are on the road [looking for work] because you must eat
You noh fit make the thing now for your wack (looku you!)	You can't even earn enough to afford a meal
You start to find excuse for your fault (looku you)	You start to find excuses for your predicament
You mouth dey shake, welle-welle,	You start to stutter,
Music noh dey, welle-welle	There's no music in your world,
Eye dey roll, welle-welle,	Your eyes are rolling in their sockets
Like thief-u eye, welle-welle,	Like a thief's eyes
(A beg, nah so e dey do you everytime, abi? henh?)	(That's what always happens, isn't it?)
Problem dey show him power,	The problem is manifested—they show you power,
You noh get-e power to fight (No Buredi)	You don't have the power to fight.

1:57

Wind instruments enter in the next section (including trumpet, tenor saxophone, and baritone saxophone) in repeating interjections relating to the frequent use of wind instrument "hits" common in funk music. However, in this case, they may also be related to traditional ensembles of buzzed-lip horns (refer to Figure 6.5).

2:04

Fela continues:

For Africa here e be home (No Buredi)	For Africa is our home,
Land-e boku-boku from north to south (No Buredi)	There is plenty of space,
Food-u boku-boku from top to down (No Buredi)	There is plenty of food,
Gold dey underground like water... (No Buredi)	Underground gold is abundant as water,

Diamond dey underground like san-san...(No Buredi)	Diamonds are as abundant underground as sand on a beach,
Oil dey flow underground like-e river...(No Buredi)	Oil flows underground like a river,
Everything for overseas, nah here e dey goooo (No Buredi)	But all these riches are exported,
Na for here, man-e still dey carry s**t-e for head...(No Buredi)	Here people have to cart around human waste in pails
Na for here we know the thing dem dey call...(No Buredi)	Only here do they have this thing called, "no bread,"
Me I tire for the thing dem dey call (No Buredi)	I am tired of this thing called, "no bread."

2:49

In the next section, Fela uses a play on words to refer to the increasing "Udoji" payments. "Eji" is Yoruba for two (thus, the name could be rendered as "Udo-two"). "Eta" is three, creating Udota, then Udorin for four, Udarun for five, and so on. Fela is saying that whether they double salaries, triple them, quadruple, and so on, it doesn't matter to the poor because they will see none of this money.

Udota I don tire e (No Buredi)	Udo-three, I have tired of it.
Udorin I don tire e (No Buredi)	Udo-four, I have tired of it.
Udarun I don tire e (No Buredi)	Udo-five, I have tired of it.
Udofa I don tire e (No Buredi)	Udo-six, I have tired of it.
Udoje I don tire e (No Buredi)	Udo-seven, I have tired of it.
Me I tire for the thing dem dey call (No Buredi)	I am tired of this thing called, "no bread."

3:04

Although most of the layering is not polyrhythmic, Fela, at this point, introduces a piano part in a new meter that he plays while continuing to sing.

Hear and see the instruments of "*No Buredi*" in your downloadable **ACTIVE LISTENING TOOLS**, available at the World Music Resource Center.

| Listening Exercise 2 | CD 1:8, *"No Buredi"* |

1. What is the texture?
   a. monophonic
   b. heterophonic
   c. homophonic

2. What is the meter?
   a. simple duple
   b. simple triple
   c. compound duple
   d. compound triple

3. During the first verse (about 0:13 - 0:30), how would you characterize the sung melody?
   a. wide range (significantly more than an octave), mostly disjunct motion
   b. mostly narrow range (less than an octave), medium tessitura
   c. short motives that alternate between just two pitches
   d. medium range concentrating on very high tessitura

4. The four sung lines of this verse consist of
   a. four short variations of a single melody (AA'A''A''').
   b. two short melodies repeated (ABAB).
   c. four distinct phrases (ABCD).

5. Beginning at 1:52, how often does the backup chorus sing "no buredi?"
   a. every four beats
   b. every six beats
   c. every eight beats
   d. every sixteen beats

6. At 3:45, a sudden "hit" signals the end of the section. This hit is played on
   a. a trumpet.
   b. a conga drum.
   c. an iron bell.
   d. an electric bass.

You can take this Listening Exercise online and receive feedback or e-mail answers to your instructor at the World Music Resource Center.

REFERENCES

DISCOGRAPHY

DRUMMING IN WEST AFRICA

The Dzigbordi Group. *Ewe Drumming from Ghana.* London: Topic Records TSCD924, 2004.

Various artists. *Ghana: Ancient Ceremonies, Songs, and Dance Music.* New York/Los Angeles: Elektra/Nonesuch 9 72082-2, 1979/1991.

Various artists. *Rhythms of Life, Songs of Wisdom: Akan Music from Ghana, West Africa.* Smithsonian Folkways SFCD40463, 1996.

MUSIC OF THE JALI

Kanté, Mory. *Sabou.* London: Riverboat Records/World Music Network TUGCD1034, 2004.

Konte, Dembo, Kausu Kuyateh and Mawdo Suso. *Jaliology.* Danbury, CT: Green Linnet Records XEN 4036, 1995. Mandingo Griot Society.

Mandingo Griot Society. Chicago: Flying Fish FF70076, 1979/1992.

Suso, Jali Nyama. *Gambie: L'art de la kora.* Paris: Ocora C 580027, 1972/1996.

Various Artists. *Mali: Cordes Anciennes.* Paris: Buda Records 1977822, 2001.

MBIRA MUSIC

Mujuru, Ephat and Dumisani Maraire. *Masters of the Africa Mbira*. Clearwater FL: ARC Music EUCD 1549, 1999.

Various artists. *Zimbabwe: The Soul of Mbira*. New York/Los Angeles: Elektra/Nonesuch 9 72054-2, 1973/1995.

OTHER TRADITIONAL MUSIC

Adzido Pan-African Dance Ensemble. *Traditional Songs and Dances from Africa*. East Grinstead, UK: ARC Music EUCD 1590, 2000.

Various artists. *Africa—Drum Chant & Instrumental Music*. New York: Elektra/Nonesuch, 9 72073-2, 1976/1988.

Various artists. *African Tribal Music and Dances*. Beverly Hills, CA: Legacy International CD 328; also Santa Monica, CA: Laserlight/Tradition Records 12 179, 1993.

Various artists. *Echoes of the Forest: Music of the Central African Pygmies*. Roslyn, NY: Ellipsis Arts 4020, 1995.

Various artists. *Kenya and Tanzania: Witchcraft and Ritual Music*. New York/Los Angeles: Elektra/Nonesuch 9 72066-2, 1975/1991.

Various artists. *Musique centrafricaine*. Paris: Ocora OCR 43, 1962, 1983; re-released on *Musique banda*, France: Prophet 22 CD 468448-2, 2004.

Various artists. *Sierra Leone: Musiques traditionnelles*. Paris: Ocora C 580036, 1992.

AFRICAN POPULAR MUSIC

Acquaye, Saka. *Ghana: High-Life and Other Popular Music*. New York/Los Angeles: Elektra/Nonesuch 79701-2, 1969/2002. (Highlife)

Ade, King Sunny. *Juju Music*. New York: Mango CCD 9712, 1982. (Juju)

Ayinde, Sikiru "Barrister." *New Fuji Garbage*. London: Ace Records/Globe Style CDORBD 067. (Fuji)

Kuti, Fela. *The Best of Fela Kuti*. Universal City, CA: MCA Records 314 543 197-2, 2000. (Afro-Beat)

Ladysmith Black Mambazo. *Shaka Zulu*. Los Angeles: Warner Bros. 25582-2, 1987. (Iscathamiya)

Maal, Baaba. *Djam Leelii*. London: Rogue Records: FMSD 5014, 1989. (Mbalax)

Mapfumo, Thomas. *The Best of Thomas Mapfumo*. Culver City, CA: Hemisphere 7243 8 35582 2, 1995.

Touré, Ali Farka. *Niafunké*. Salem, MA: Hannibal HNCD 1443, 1999.

Various artists. *The Rough Guide to the Music of South Africa*. London: World Music Network RGNET 1020, 1998.

 BOOK COMPANION WEBSITE

You will find flashcards, a glossary, and tutorial quizzes, as well as other materials that will help you succeed in this course, at the *Music of the Peoples of the World, 2nd Edition,* Companion Website at www.cengage.com/music/alves/world2e.

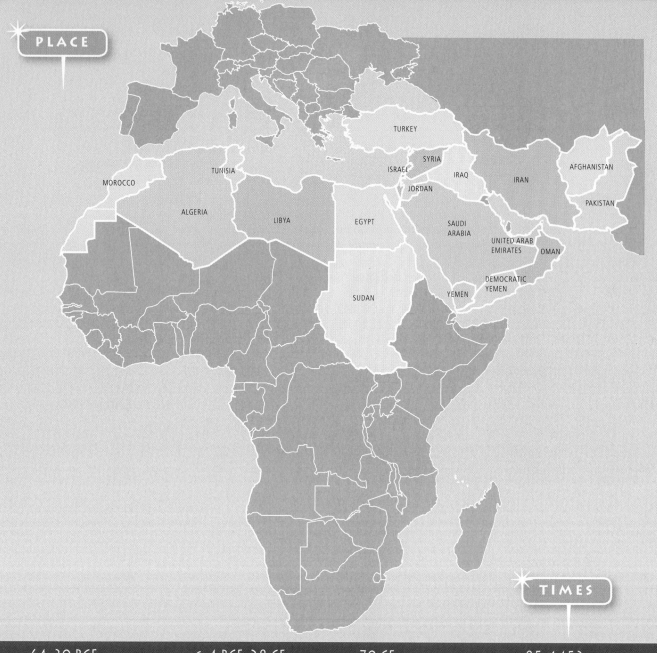

TURKEY

SYRIA

ISRAEL

JORDAN

IRAQ

IRAN

AFGHANISTAN

PAKISTAN

MOROCCO

TUNISIA

ALGERIA

LIBYA

EGYPT

SAUDI
ARABIA

UNITED ARAB
EMIRATES

OMAN

SUDAN

YEMEN

DEMOCRATIC
YEMEN

64–30 BCE

Middle East and Egypt come under Roman rule.

c. 4 BCE–28 CE

Lifetime of Jesus. Early Christian chant is apparently based on Jewish models.

70 CE

Romans destroy Jewish Temple in Jerusalem. The musical practice of Levites is ultimately lost and replaced by regional practices in synagogues led by cantors. In centuries after the destruction of the Temple, many Jewish people leave Palestine to settle in North Africa, Europe, and elsewhere.

95–1453

Byzantine Empire with capital at Constantinople (Istanbul). Byzantine music is based on modes called *echoi,* which implied not only a particular scale but also appropriate melodic patterns for each. Names of what seem to be modes are also recorded in early Iranian music, possibly the early basis for modal systems of *dastgah* (Iranian) and *maqam* (Arabic).

THE MIDDLE EAST AND NORTH AFRICA

SETTING

As you enter the cool marble monument surrounding the tomb of Hafiz (c.1325–c.1389), one of Iran's most famous poets, your gaze is drawn, not down onto the tomb itself but upward to a beautiful example of pattern in Islamic art (Figure 7.1). Every space in the swirling design is filled with intricate figures and lines that weave elaborate paths.

These visual patterns find a counterpart in the ornate melodic paths of classical Iranian solo improvisation, where every space also seems to overflow with gracefully fluid ornamentation. Classical improvisation in Iran is based on linear melodies assembled, like mosaic tiles, one after the other and decorated with tiny motives and ornaments.

SOUNDS

CD 1:10

Dastgah Mahur. Hussein Ali Zodeh, *tar.*

c. 570–632	632–736	9TH–13TH C.	1096–1187	▶▶▶
Lifetime of Muhammad, founder of Islam.	Period of Islamic conquest, spreading Islam from the Middle East through North Africa, Spain, Iran, and India. Arabic musical influences and instruments follow through these areas and into much of Europe. Arabic language and scholarship becomes a unifying element throughout Islamic areas. Establishment of affluent courts forms a basis for secular patronage of art music.	Golden age of Islamic scholarship at Baghdad. Many works of ancient Greece, including works of music theory, are translated. Period of great Islamic music theorists: al-Kindi, al-Farabi, Ibn Sina, Safi al-Din.	European crusaders invade and occupy Palestine, including Jerusalem.	

FIGURE 7.1

The ceiling of the tomb of Hafiz at Shiraz, Iran, shows elaborate mosaic patterns. These patterns reflect the intricacy also found in Islamic art music, as well as its preoccupation with mathematics in music theory.

In mosques and other holy places, visual patterns draw one into contemplation, perhaps of the **Qur'an**, the holy book of Islam. Its eternal message is reflected in the ever-repeating and circular patterns found in mosaics, carpets, calligraphy, and architecture in the Middle East. Just as the radial symmetry of the Hafiz tomb mosaic draws the eye ever inward, so does the elaborate music of Iranian improvisation invite thoughtful reflection. Still, this introspection can find surprisingly passionate, emotional expression as well, a feeling of transcendence that is at once deeply spiritual and profoundly human, as expressed in this poem by Hafiz himself:

> O keep squeezing drops of the Sun
> From your prayers and work and music
> And from your companions' beautiful laughter
>
> And from the most insignificant movements
> Of your own holy body.
>
> Now, sweet one,
> Be wise,
> Cast all your votes for Dancing!
>
> —From "Cast All Your Votes for Dancing!"
> by Hafiz of Shiraz[1]

ELEMENTS OF MIDDLE EASTERN MUSIC

As you would expect from its expansive geography and diverse traditions, generalizations about Middle Eastern music are difficult. Nevertheless, here are some of the most distinctive qualities characteristic of much of the music of this region.

[1]From *I Heard the God Laughing,* Renderings of Hafiz by Daniel Ladinsky. Published by Penguin Books. Copyright © 1996 and 2005 Daniel Ladinsky and used with his permission.

▶ 1483–1918	1798–1918	1948	1949–1962
Period of Turkish Ottoman Empire, to eventually include much of Eastern Europe, Syria, Armenia, Egypt, Mesopotamia.	Napoleon's entry into Egypt begins period of European colonization of North Africa and Middle East. Cultural influences from Europe sometimes prompt backlash. Many national universities and music schools adopt Western-style pedagogy, and the use of Western harmony is common, especially in popular and light classical music.	Israel established as independent Jewish state.	North African states become independent. In some countries, nationalism produces a revival of indigenous art music, often government-sponsored, as well as distinctive popular music.

© CORBIS

- ◆ **Elaborate melodies and melismas.** Middle Eastern melodies are often ornate and filled with intricate figurations. Elaborate **melismas**, sung melodies with many notes to a syllable, are common.

- ◆ **Improvisation based on basic tones or melodies.** In the Middle East, improvisations are based on either elaborations around the traversal of a series of core pitches or, as in Iran, more explicit melodies.

- ◆ **Heterophony.** Because Middle Eastern classical music focuses on melody, the melodic instruments in ensemble usually create a characteristic texture of heterophony, the simultaneous performance of different elaborations of the same melody.

- ◆ **Rhythms based on beat patterns.** Rhythms are often elaborations of a specific beat pattern or basic rhythm inside the meter.

- ◆ **The use of quarter-tones.** Modes in the Middle East have a wide variety of scales, some of which feature intervals that lie in the middle between the tones on a Western piano keyboard. These distinctive divisions are called quarter-tones.

THE MIDDLE EAST AND RELIGION

Judaism is one of the oldest continuously practiced religions in the world, and, unlike Islam or Christianity, can imply not only a set of beliefs but also an ethnic identity. That ethnicity has largely remained through the centuries, in spite of the Jewish **diaspora**, the scattering of Jews from their ancestral homeland in Palestine to many areas throughout the world. In the twentieth century, the phenomenon of Zionism encouraged the return of hundreds of thousands of Jews back to this region, now the nation of Israel. They have brought influences from many different areas around the world but have retained many distinctively Jewish cultural and musical traits, especially in their sacred music. Very old Jewish minorities also exist in areas such as Yemen, Ethiopia, and Morocco. Although the center of Christianity moved from the Middle East to Europe in the early centuries of the modern era, important Christian traditions also remain in countries such as Lebanon, Egypt, and Ethiopia.

Islam is a religion founded by Muhammad (c. 570–632), who, unlike Jesus to the Christians, was a prophet, not a deity. Like Christianity and Judaism, Islam is a monotheistic religion descended from the biblical Abraham/Ibrahim.

1979

Iran becomes a fundamentalist Islamic state and restricts practice of some music.

The Five Pillars of Islamic faith include a confession of faith, prayer five times daily, almsgiving, fasting during the month of Ramadan, and making at least one pilgrimage to Mecca (in Saudi Arabia), the birthplace of Islam. Followers of Islam are also called Muslims.

Islam was founded on the Arabian peninsula and, after Muhammad's death, spread with amazing swiftness through Arabic military conquest from Spain to Central Asia and eventually India and Indonesia. With the spread of Islam came Arabic culture and language, especially because Muhammad decreed that the *Qur'an* should only be read in Arabic. This rule had the brilliant effect (at least in theory) of binding together all Muslims of the world with a single language and so helped the spread of Arabic music and music theory throughout the Islamic world.

ISLAM AND MUSIC

Even after centuries of debate, the tension between the pious contemplation of the next world idealized by Islam and the celebration of life as found in Hafiz's poetry continues to provide a backdrop of controversy to music and dance in Islamic countries. In Egypt, the **ghawazi**, women who dance for entertainment, are often in conflict with conservative factions who seek to allow only religious genres of music. According to those conservatives, even classical music, such as the solo improvisation that we will hear, can distract the senses that should be focused on spiritual existence.

Some conservative Islamic scholars have interpreted certain Islamic texts as forbidding most music, although the Arabic word *musiqa* is never used in a religious context, for example, to describe the chanting of *Qur'anic* verses and the call to prayer. In other words, there is no such thing as Islamic religious "music," and therefore these practices are excepted from this ban, as are certain types of folk music. Even in less conservative Islamic societies, music never found a patron in religious institutions as it did in Europe. The vast majority of music was and is performed in secular contexts, and many scholars interpret Islamic texts as supporting music as a secular art form. On the other hand, music in nightclubs, music for dancing, and music where men and women sing together is suspect in many Islamic societies.

At certain times and places under especially reactionary Islamic rule, nonreligious music has been banned. After the revolution in Iran in 1979, Western music as well as classical Iranian music, if heard at all, was performed only in private homes. However, just before his death in 1989, the supreme Iranian religious leader Ruhollah Khomeini issued an edict that generally accepted music, with some restrictions. More recently, the Taliban government of Afghanistan (1995–2002) banned virtually all nonreligious music and punished those caught with cassette tapes, videos, or even musical instruments. Although these extremist views are certainly not representative of the majority of Islam, they do highlight the controversy surrounding the legitimacy of certain kinds of music in Islamic history.

One of the most revered forms of Islamic religious music is the chanting of *Qur'an* verses, known as **qira'ah** or **tilawah**. Although very strict rules govern pronunciation, articulation, placement of pauses, and so on, these prescriptions still leave open many possibilities for musical interpretation. Lay chanters learn very simple syllabic settings based on fixed melodic formulas, but in many countries, particularly Egypt, venerated traditions of exceptionally florid *Qur'anic* chant have developed. These artful styles have greatly influenced many secular song styles as well.

The **adhan**, call to prayer, is a familiar sound in most Islamic countries. Today, the **mu'adhdhin**, the singers of the adhan, chant over loudspeakers placed in the minarets of mosques and often over radio and television as well. These florid two- or three-minute songs float through the streets of most Islamic cities five times a day, and the faithful are expected to pray in response. Allowing for regional variations, *adhan* styles, like *Qur'anic* chanting, are unaccompanied and nonpulsatile, and often include melismas.

Sufism is a mystical form of Islam that is more accepting of music in a religious context than the more orthodox branches of the religion. In the Sufi ceremony known as **dhikr** ("remembrance"), cyclic rhythmic figures accompany repetitive chanting of scriptural text and sometimes dance, eventually inducing a joyful union with God or even an ecstatic trance.

One famous Sufi dance tradition is that of the *Mevlevi* order of Turkey, better known as the **dervishes**, dancers who whirl around and around to achieve this spiritual union. The dervishes are accompanied by a large ensemble of *nay* flutes, *daff* drums, other instruments, and a chorus, often singing the words of the thirteenth-century mystical poet Jalal al-Din Rumi. Although the music of these ceremonies has influenced drum patterns and other elements of secular Arabic music, perhaps the most important connection between Sufism and secular Arabic music lies in their shared awareness of music's capability to awaken and express spiritual ecstasy, as described in this medieval Sufi treatise:

> Music is in the coming to rest of all thoughts from the burdens of the human state. It excites the temperament of men. It is the stimulant of divine mysteries. To some, it is a temptation because they are imperfect. For others, it is a sign, for they have reached perfection.
>
> –Ruzbihan Baqli (d. 1209), *The Treatise on Holiness*[2]

THE INSTRUMENTS OF THE REGION

Many of the most important musical instruments in the world apparently originated in the Middle East. Countries as far apart as Latin America to the west and China to the east have instruments with a common origin in the Middle East. Very few European instruments are *not* descended, at least indirectly, from Middle Eastern sources.

Plucked chordophones are especially important throughout the region, both in the variety known as the **'ud** and in the long-necked variety known generally as the **tanbur**. Both are played monophonically (one note at a time), although drone strings are often intermittently strummed. There are many types of bowed fiddles, and, since the colonial period, the European violin (also known as the **kaman**) has become a popular instrument. Other European instruments commonly used in classical or semi-classical repertories include the clarinet, cello, and double bass. Harps and lyres have an ancient history in the region, although today they are chiefly found in Africa.

[2]Adapted from the translation by Seyyed Hossein Nasr in "Islam and Music: The Views of Ruzbahan Baqli, the Patron Saint of Shiraz," *Studies in Comparative Religion* 10 (1976): 37–41.

INSTRUMENT GALLERY

INSTRUMENTS OF THE MIDDLE EAST AND NORTH AFRICA

© Dave Bartruff/CORBIS

'UD

Historically, the *'ud*, shown here, is the most important art music instrument of the Islamic region. A fretless, pear-shaped lute with five or six courses (sets of strings) and a distinctively angled peg box (where the strings are attached to the tuning pegs), it has elaborately carved latticework on the sound hole and is traditionally played with an eagle-feather plectrum (pick). Although at different times in its history, it has had frets, the modern *'ud* has no frets. A highly respected classical instrument, today it is less common than the long-necked lute. After being introduced to Spain, it acquired frets and additional strings and became the lute (from *al-'ud*) of Renaissance Europe. The *'ud* is found throughout the Arab world and also in Turkey, Iran, Greece, and East Africa, where it is of secondary importance.

© Wolfgang Kaehler/CORBIS

TANBUR

Long-necked fretted lutes come in many sizes and varieties, sometimes in a single country. Closely related versions of the long-necked lute in this region include the *tanbur* (Arabic countries), *sehtar* (Iran), *buzuq* (Syria and Iraq), *buzuki* (Greece), *tambura* (Bulgaria), and *saz* or *baglama* (Turkey), the form shown here. In general, this instrument has a teardrop-shaped body and three or four strings, the lowest of which may be a drone string. It often uses metal strings and has a much brighter timbre than the *'ud*. Players extend notes by repeatedly strumming them (known as tremolo in the West). In between melody notes, players also often strum drone pitches tuned to the tonic or tonic and the fifth scale degree above.

Courtesy of Gilbert Blount

TAR

The respected classical plucked lute of Iran, the **tar** is a distinctive variation of the long-necked lute with an hourglass-shaped sound body (resonator) covered in sheepskin.

© Dean Conger/CORBIS

RABAB

The **rabab** is a spike fiddle, that is, a bowed chordophone with a spike on the bottom. It is held vertically with its spike resting on the ground or ankle. This version has a roughly hemispherical resonator and cylindrical neck but no fingerboard. It may have from one to four strings. Instead of firmly pressing the string down on the neck, the finger stops the string by sliding along it. A common folk instrument with a variety of sizes and types of resonators, the *rabab* is sometimes used as a classical instrument in Morocco and Iraq. Known as the *rabab* in most Arabic countries, the instrument is also known as the *joza* (Iraq), *kamancheh* (Iran), *gijak* (Central Asia), and *k'yamancha* (Armenia), the form shown here.

© Chris Lisle/CORBIS

KAMANCHE

The various forms and names of the **kamanche**—a short-necked fiddle usually with a fingerboard and a pear-shaped body—may overlap with those of the *rabab*. The *kamanche* is known as the *rabab* in North Africa, the *k'aman* in Armenia, the *gadulka* in Bulgaria, and the *kemençe* in Turkey.

© Hideo Haga/HAGA/The Image Works

SANTUR

The **santur** is a trapezoidal hammered dulcimer (zither). The strings are stretched over bridges in multiple courses (multiple strings per note) and struck with small wooden mallets. Some varieties are fitted with a damping mechanism. Known as the *santur* in Iran, Iraq, and Turkey, and as the *santuri* in India, the instrument is also found in Europe, China, and Korea.

Sami Asmar, Courtesy of A. J. Racy

QANUN

The **qanun**, here played by Antoíne Harb, is a plucked zither shaped like a rectangle with one corner cut off. It is similar to the European psaltery but is plucked with ring-plectra attached to the fingers of both hands. A series of levers and intermediate bridges for each string allow quick changes of tunings for different *maqam*. Elaborate tremolos (repeated notes) and glissandos (scale sweeps) are common. The instrument is also found in Southeast Europe and in Turkey, where it is called the *kanun*.

© Craig Aurness/CORBIS

NAY

The **nay** is an end-blown notch flute found in Iran, Turkey, and Arabic countries. Note that it is played from the side of the mouth and held at an oblique angle. It is the only aerophone commonly found in classical ensembles.

INSTRUMENT GALLERY

INSTRUMENTS OF THE MIDDLE EAST AND NORTH AFRICA *(continued)*

Courtesy of Gilbert Blount

ZURNA

The **zurna** is a loud double-reed with a bell flare at the end. There may be a metal disc that the lips rest on. The thick reeds are taken entirely into the mouth, which forms an air chamber in which the reeds vibrate. The *zurna* migrated to medieval Europe, where it became the shawm, ancestor of the modern oboe. Known as the *zurna* in East Arabic countries, Turkey, and the Caucasus, the instrument is also known as the *surnay* (Central Asia), *sornay* (Iran), *gaita* (North Africa), and *mizmar* (Egypt).

Courtesy of Barbara Racy

ARGHUL

The Egyptian **arghul** is a single-reed aerophone with two cylindrical pipes tied together and blown at the same time, in effect a double clarinet. One pipe plays the melody, and the other is a drone pipe without fingerholes. In another single-reed instrument with double pipes—the *mijwiz* or *zumarrah*—the two pipes are played together but slightly detuned, creating a beating effect. In Mediterranean countries, cow horns may attach to the ends of the pipes. Single-pipe, single-reed instruments came to Europe in the form of the chalumeau, the ancestor of the clarinet. Instruments similar to the *arghul* include the *mizwij* in Iraq, the *jifti* in the Gulf states, the *dozal* among the Kurds, and the *magruna* in North Africa.

© Peter Turnley/CORBIS

DAFF

The **daff** (or *def*) is a shallow frame drum played with hands and fingers. Although used in many ways throughout Islamic areas, it is often associated with religious contexts, such as accompaniment to Islamic chant and Sufi rituals. Small cymbals may be added to the frame to create the familiar form of the tambourine to accompany folk songs and dances. With cymbals, the instrument is known as the *riqq*, *bendir*, or *tar*, depending on the size.

Courtesy of Gilbert Blount

DARABUKKAH

Known as the **darabukkah** in most Arabic countries, this instrument is a goblet-shaped drum of various sizes made of ceramic, wood, or metal, and played with the fingers. The bottom is open. Especially popular in North Africa, this instrument is held under the player's arm or on the player's knee. It is also known as the *dumbuk* (Iraq), *zarb* or *tombak* (Iran), and the *darbuka* (Turkey).

Hear and see the instruments of the Middle East and North Africa in your downloadable **ACTIVE LISTENING TOOLS,** available at the World Music Resource Center.

Elaborate traditions of singing are common throughout the Middle East. Low, husky tones or rich, reedy timbres are common. Ornamentation is extensive, and vibrato (wavering pitch) may be wholly absent or present in an exaggerated form as an ornament. Melismas are especially characteristic of Middle Eastern singing. A distinctive folk practice associated with the women of North Africa is the **zagharit**, a ululation (high cry rapidly trilled with the tongue) that accompanies celebrations. In fast folk dances or other festive pieces, aerophones sometimes imitate the *zagharit*. To play long continuous melodies, players of aerophones such as the double-reed zurna practice **circular breathing**—a difficult technique in which the player blows out while simultaneously breathing in through his nose to achieve an uninterrupted air stream.

ARABIC MUSIC THEORY

At a concert of Arabic classical music, you might notice, even more than the music itself, the transported state of the singer, as if expressing the poetry was at once creating a sense of inward ecstasy as well as an outward connection with the audience. This is the feeling of **tarab**, the transcendent emotional experience that comes from the combination of highly expressive music and poetry. The importance of the word in Arabic art reflects the importance of the *Qur'an*, which is a single unified work Muslims believe to be the literal word of God.

Vocal music, therefore, from art music to folk music, is paramount in Arabic musical culture. From pre-Islamic sources, we learn of the long tradition of caravan songs, songs of women, entertainers, and other folk songs on the Arabian peninsula. Diverse folk traditions continue to thrive throughout the Arabic world. The traditions of **responsorial** (alternating leader/group singing) and **antiphonal** (two alternating groups singing) choral music in Saudi Arabia are similar to the poetic forms recorded in the Bible.

Following the expansion of the early Islamic world, a new internationalism brought rich art music traditions from other regions, especially Byzantium (modern Turkey), which had a history of improvisation and composition based on modes known as **echoi**. This tradition, which extended back to the ancient Greeks and probably long before, plus early Greek manuscripts, formed the foundation of a golden age of scholarship centered in Baghdad, where writers such as al-Farabi (d. 950) wrote extensively on the construction of scales and rhythmic modes in music.

Following the fall of Baghdad to the Mongols (1258) and the later rise of the Ottoman empire (especially 1512–1520), however, this sophisticated and unique art music tradition represented by al-Farabi and other Arab theorists, musicians, and poets largely declined. Arabic classical traditions distinct from those of Turkey made a resurgence in the late nineteenth century and early twentieth century, when the modal construct known as the **maqam** acquired its modern form.

THE MAQAM SCALE

Writers usually introduce the *maqam* by its tuning theory, which forms a crucial link not just to the great medieval theorists who wrote about it, such as al-Farabi, but also to ancient Greece and Byzantium. Theorists at that time built up scales from segments of four notes (**tetrachords**) related to one another by the mathematics of vibrating string ratios. For example, they represented the interval known in Europe as the perfect fifth by the simple ratio 3:2. Successive applications of this ratio created other intervals from which scales derived. This tuning system, known in Europe as "Pythagorean" after its supposed Greek inventor, is also the basis for ancient music theory in China and probably India.

Much more than a mathematical abstraction to the Greeks or to al-Farabi, this process was a way of making perceptible the beautiful mathematical relationships of God's creation. The mystical importance of numerical ratios is also the basis for the geometrical abstractions of Islamic art (refer to Figure 7.1). Although this tuning system led to the twelve-tone system of Europe, Arabic musicians took it further, creating a theoretical system of twenty-four notes per octave. This tuning system therefore has intervals that are about half the size of the smallest European interval (the semitone) and so are called **quarter-tones**. The question of whether the quarter-tones should be precisely equal, such as semitones in modern European tuning, or if they vary slightly to maintain traditional ratios is still controversial. Although fretted chordophones reflect this tuning system, in practice, the pitches are varied with subtle inflections to contribute to the ecstatic feeling evoked by the music.

Whatever the details of the tuning system used, each quarter-tone pitch in a two-octave scale has its own name, although many modern writers prefer to use the European alphabetic system, in which the first seven letters of the alphabet represent the basic diatonic pitches, with additional symbols called accidentals. In addition to the sharp (♯) and flat (♭) used in Europe to indicate the displacement of a scale degree by a semitone up or down, respectively, Arabic theorists have added accidentals representing a lowering of a pitch by a quarter-tone (♭̸) and raising it by a quarter-tone sharp (♯̸). (Iranians use different symbols.) In this section, we will use the letter system.

Like their Greek and Byzantine predecessors, Arabic theorists build up scales from smaller segments, called **jins**, which are usually tetrachords but may also be trichords or pentachords. Some theorists give the scales of *maqam* in versions extending more than an octave and with different pitches ascending and descending. Nevertheless, the central ascending octave of seven pitches is the most characteristic part of this scale, as we see here in one version of the scale *maqam nahawand* (Graphic 7.1). The bold letters indicate the tonic of the scale—G in this case, although it can be transposed to fit any instrument or vocal range. Note that the pitch B exists in two versions: natural when the melodic line is ascending and flat when descending. The brackets show the tetrachords from which this scale is constructed.

Although quarter-tones are not used between adjacent scale steps, steps of ¾ of a tone or 1¼ tone (intervals quite unfamiliar to the Western ear) commonly occur, as we see in Graphic 7.2, in a *maqam huzam*. In Graphic 7.2, the flat with a slash through it (♭̸) indicates that the note is lowered a quarter-tone. Therefore, in this scale, the interval between D and E (♭̸) (E half-flat) is ¾ of a tone, and between E (♭̸) and F is also ¾ of a tone.

Note how this scale indicates that the pitches B and A are sometimes treated differently in ascending and descending versions.

GRAPHIC 7.1

Maqam nahawand

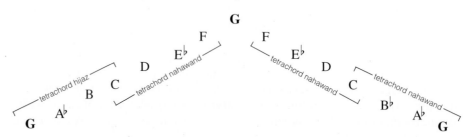

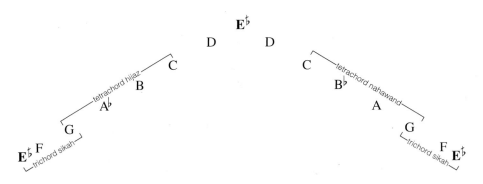

OTHER CHARACTERISTICS OF A MAQAM

The scale is just part of the definition of a *maqam*. Some *maqam* may share the same characteristic scale and yet be treated differently in improvisation, resulting in a distinct emotional experience for each. The *maqam* is therefore represented in its purest form in nonpulsatile improvisations, known as **taqsim** if played by a solo instrument. **Layali** is a similar vocal form that uses melismas on the syllables "*ya layl, ya 'ayn*" ("oh night, oh eyes") with one or more instrumentalists following the singer's improvisations. Such abstractions, rather like the abstractions of Islamic decorative art, serve as introductions or interludes to extended songs based on classical or colloquial poetry sung by a soloist and accompanied by an ensemble.

The performance of the *taqsim* is a journey through a sequence of emphasized pitches, the principal tones of the *maqam* scale, a form known as the **sayr** (path) of the *maqam*. In Graphic 7.3's schematic representation from a performance of a *taqsim* in *maqam hijaz* on the *'ud*, Sultan Hamid of Bahrain exposes the nature of the *maqam* by playing around pitches that are temporary focal points. In the first line, his melody undulates around the principal pitch represented by the letter D (indicated by the red dotted line), but by the second line, he shifts his attention to the pitch G.

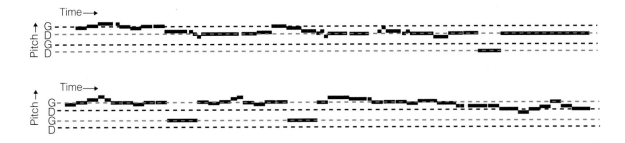

Each of these pitches will in turn form a point of focus around which the performer weaves supple elaborations of the melodic line. Just as Arabic calligraphy has no sharp corners, the improvisations of the *taqsim* consists of graceful arabesques connecting one tone to another.

Unlike performances of Indian ragas or other modal types around the world, traditional Arabic performances commonly use **modulation**, temporary shifts to a related *maqam*, and certain modulations are characteristic of different *maqam.* A tetrachord or other *jin,* which is the same in two *maqam* scales, can serve as a common point to help smooth a modulation from one to the other.

RHYTHM IN ARABIC MUSIC

As you might expect in a tradition so closely bound to the art of the poetic song and the importance of the word, the complex meters of classical Arabic poetry have served as a framework for rhythm in classical music. Known by a variety of names, here as **iqa'**, these meters are defined not only by durations and accents but also by levels of accents, so that different beats may have characteristic sounds. An *iqa'* is defined more as a characteristic rhythmic pattern than as a hierarchy of beat divisions, and different *iqa'* may share the same meter. The *iqa'* rhythmic pattern called **maqsum**, a simple quadruple pattern, is commonly used in Egyptian folk music, among other repertories. The right hand in the center of the drum makes the low drum stroke "dumm," and the higher tone "takk" is made toward the edge of the drum.

GRAPHIC 7.4

Iqá maqsum

The *iqa'* pattern in Graphic 7.5, called **wahdah**, is also contained in a simple quadruple meter like *maqsum* but has a very different sound. "Mah" is a low left-hand stroke on the drum.

GRAPHIC 7.5

Iqá wahdah

The primary carrier of the *iqa'* is often the *riqq* (tambourine) player in the classical ensemble or the *darrabukka* (goblet drum) player in folk and dance ensembles, although they rarely play the *iqa'* pattern in its most basic form. Graphic 7.6 shows an example of one possible interpretation of the *iqa'* maqsum by a *darrabukha* drummer. *Keh* is a high left-hand drum stroke.

GRAPHIC 7.6

A realization of *Iqa' maqsum*

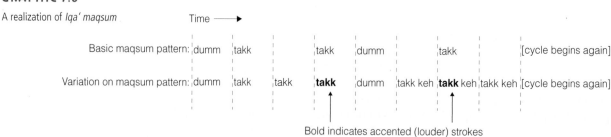

In any case, drummers' mnemonic syllables define the beats of the cycle. For example, as you have seen, the onomatopeic syllable *dumm* refers to the low sound that comes from the middle of the drumhead, whereas *takk* comes from near the edge of the head.

Iqa' can be considerably more complex than the preceding examples, especially in the classical tradition. Graphic 7.7 shows the *iqa' murassa' shami*, which consists of nineteen beats divided into groups of 4 5 4 6. These groups within the cycle are shown by darker dotted lines.

Time →

| dumm | takk | takk | dumm | dumm | takk | dumm | takk | keh | dumm | takk | takk | takk | takk | [cycle begins again] |

Although surveys differ, some have enumerated 111 different *iqa'* patterns in eastern Arab countries, lasting from just a few to 176 beats, although only a fraction of those are in common use. The very long *iqa'* in particular are attempted only by the most learned and virtuosic musicians.

ARABIC MUSIC PERFORMANCE

MUSIC FORMS AND PRACTICE IN ARABIC MUSIC

The classic expression of the traditional urban Arabic performance is the **suite**, a series of songs and instrumental pieces unified by their reference to a single *maqam*, despite temporary modulations. These suites artfully contrast metered and unmetered, sung and instrumental, and fast and slow genres of songs and instrumental pieces in set formats. These suites have different forms and names in different countries—***nuba*** in Morocco, ***fasil*** in Turkey and Syria, ***waslah*** in Egypt, ***nawbah*** in some North African countries, and *maqam* in Iraq—although some are rarely heard today. All these forms can excite *tarab*, a passionate emotional state, among the connoisseurs who patronize this art.

The most traditional medium for the Arabic suite is an ensemble of about five musicians called a ***takht*** (Figure 7.2). A *takht* might include a *qanun* (zither), *'ud* (lute), *nay* (flute), *riqq* (tambourine), violin, a solo singer, and perhaps a chorus, or the instrumentalists may act as a chorus. The texture is primarily heterophonic.

© Nidaa Abou Mrad

FIGURE 7.2

The *takht* is the classical Arabic ensemble. The one pictured here is the Ensemble of Classical Arab Music, with, left to right, violin, singer, *qanun*, singer, *'ud*, and *riqq*. A *takht* also frequently includes a *nay*.

An Arabic suite often begins with a *taqsim*, an instrumental improvisation to introduce the mood of the *maqam* in its purest form. Some of the other genres that may form movements of the suite or independent forms include the following:

◆ **Mawwal.** A partly improvised song in colloquial (not classical) Arabic that usually follows a *layali* (nonpulsatile vocal introduction).

◆ **Qasida.** A song that sets a poem in classical Arabic language. The singer may render the text melodically in modal improvisation or interpolate improvisatory extensions of a composed setting of the poetic lines. Thus, an extended song may result from just a few lines of poetry.

◆ **Sama'i.** An instrumental piece with a refrain that begins in a ten-beat *iqa'*, moves to a lively triple meter, and ends in the original ten-beat pattern.

◆ **Tahmilah.** An instrumental piece in which the various instruments take turns playing solo improvisations, alternating with a refrain, somewhat as in jazz.

A *TAKHT* PERFORMANCE

A *waslah* is a classical suite of songs and instrumental pieces played by a small ensemble (*takht*) in Egypt. In its original form, the *waslah* died out early in the twentieth century, but in this recording, Nidaa Abou Mrad and the Ensemble of Classical Arab Music have applied this title to a modern suite. In this example, the movements are somewhat abbreviated; a full performance could easily last an hour. This excerpt includes four short movements: *bashraf, taqsim, dulab,* and *muwashshah.* The *maqam* is *huzam,* and its distinctive sound comes partly from the fact that the tonic is flattened by a quarter-tone (refer to Graphic 7.2). Instead of the fifth scale degree forming a secondary point of stability in the scale, the third scale degree is a point of focus.

This suite begins with a short excerpt from "Qarah Bitaq Sikah" by Khi'dr Agha al-kamani, a piece in the form of a *bashraf,* an instrumental genre adapted from Turkish Sufi music. The *riqq* (tambourine) and the melody articulate the *iqa'*, which is *sama'i thaqil,* a distinctive pattern in a ten-beat meter:

GRAPHIC 7.8

Iqa' sama'i thaqil

The *muwashah* (at 2:10 in the Listening Guide) is a song form that developed in the opulent courts of Muslim Spain; thus its text is in classical Arabic and concerns the courtly ideal of a woman's beauty and her love. Like the ornate patterns that cover the walls of the palaces at Alhambra and Granada, this heterophonic texture is so densely ornamented that every crevice is filled in with graceful lines. Although a *muwashshah* typically has an AABA form, this performance leaves out the contrasting section.

CD 1:9. **Waslah** in **Maqam Huzam** (excerpt). Nidaa Abou Mrad (violin), Mohamad Ayache (voice and **'ud**), Maria Makhoul (**qanun**), Ali Wehbé (**riqq**).

The *bashraf*—instrumental form with a refrain (*taslim*) that recurs before and after a series of contrasting phrases (*khana*). Heterophonic.

0:00

Taslim (refrain), violin and 'ud.

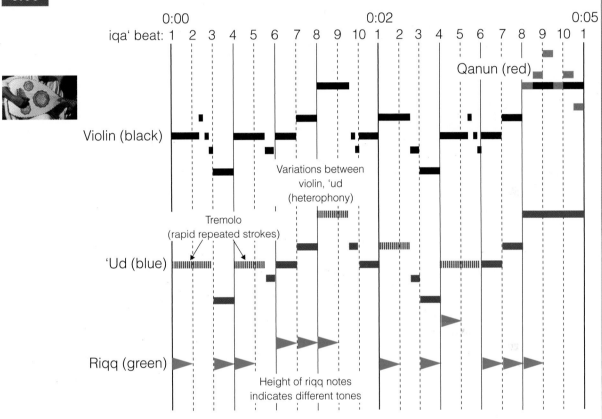

0:14

Khana phrase; the *qanun* takes over the melody from the violin.

0:25

Khana repeats.

0:37

Taslim repeats.

The *taqsim*—unmetered interlude that clearly establishes the *maqam* and mood of the following performance. The *sayr*, or path, of central tones creates the melodic structure of the *taqsim*.

0:51 Violin, the leader of this ensemble, goes directly into the *taqsim's* first phrase.

Centers on the tonic, although it touches in turn on each of the other important tones. This journey through different focal pitches is an interpretation of the *sayr* of the *maqam*.

Violin shifts the focus to another pitch.

1:07  *Qanun* (zither) strums a drone, gradually becoming more prominent.

1:16 Pitch focus shifts, and the violin part becomes more active and elaborate.

For variety, the violin often mixes the different pitches that occur in ascending and descending versions of the *huzam* scale even when the contour of the melody is not clear.

Dulab—metered instrumental form—brief heterophonic introduction to the next song.

1:48 Violin leads a new *iqa'* with 16 beats per cycle.

Muwashshah—"You, with the slender waist"—strophic form.

2:10 First verse, sung by the *'ud* player who stops playing.

Rhythmic cycle returns to *iqa' sama'i thaqil*.

Dense heterophonic texture.

2:42 Instrumental repeat with variations.

3:14 Second verse.

3:48  The *qanun* plays a nonpulsatile *taqsim*.

Violin plays a drone.

Notice the *qanun's* highly melodic, characteristic techniques: quickly alternating notes between octaves, glissandos (fast strumming up or down several strings), and very fast strums circulating up and down several adjacent strings.

Hear and see the instruments of *Waslah in Maqam Huzam* in your downloadable **ACTIVE LISTENING TOOLS,** available at the World Music Resource Center.

Listening Exercise 3

CD 1:9. *Waslah* in *Maqam Huzam*

1. When the *taslim* returns at 0:37, the tempo
   a. gets faster.
   b. gradually slows down (ritardando).
   c. doubles.

2. At 0:41, during the cadence of the main melody, an instrument inserts a brief countermelody of six notes by itself. This instrument is a(n)
   a. *'ud.*
   b. *qanun.*
   c. violin.
   d. *nay.*

3. During the *dulab* section beginning at 1:52, the *riqq* is playing.
   a. True
   b. False

4. The vocal part during the *muwashshah* section beginning at 2:10 is mostly
   a. syllabic.
   b. melismatic.

You can take this Listening Exercise online and receive feedback or e-mail answers to your instructor at the World Music Resource Center.

POPULAR MUSIC IN THE ARAB WORLD

In the twentieth century, several important changes occurred in ensembles of the classical tradition. With the growth in popularity of the singers as soloists, shorter forms, such as a *layali-muwwal*, became more popular than extended suites. Under the influence of European orchestras, the *takht* grew into a large ensemble of twenty or more musicians, known as a **firqa** in Egypt, which combined both Arabic and European instruments, including a large section of the violin family.

Because of the size of the ensemble and the popularity of large concert venues, microphones became necessary for singers. Singers such as the Egyptian Umm Kulthum (1904–1975) achieved superstar status through concerts, recordings, radio, and film (Figure 7.3). Instead of performing long and complex suites, such singers often extracted a single form such as the *qasida* for performances. A performance of a single *qasida* by Kulthum could easily last twenty-five minutes, for she lovingly repeated each line of poetry several times, each with its own subtle melodic variations.

Composers increasingly adopted European practices such as the use of notation, the avoidance of scales involving quarter-tones, and, by the 1960s, electric instruments. These innovations caused some controversy, especially among the connoisseurs who continue to patronize the now marginalized classical ensemble of the *takht*.

Despite the immense popularity of singers such as Umm Kulthum, the streets of Cairo still rang with the sounds of folk bands, especially at weddings, and songs without the very extended and intricate phrases of Kulthum. By the early 1970s, street-corner shops in Egypt were filled with cassettes of a new sound associated with underclass youth: **sha'bi**. This music retained the propulsive rhythmic patterns of folk dances (such as *iqa' maqsum*), together with monophonic or heterophonic

FIGURE 7.3

Umm Kulthum.

© Bettman/CORBIS

melodies, and sometimes the nonpulsatile vocal improvisations (*mawwal*) of traditional music. However, this working-class music also adopted the short phrases, clear refrains, and syllabic text-setting of popular music elsewhere in the world. The lyrics' frank sexuality and provocative social commentary often shocked Egyptians who idolized the refined poetry sung by Kulthum and sometimes caused government authorities to ban songs. One of the most enduring singers of the genre is Hakim.

A similar style associated with the restive youth of the underclass was **raï** music from Algeria. It originated in the 1920s and 1930s in Algeria's coastal cafes, where female singers dared to broach subjects of sexuality, colonialism, and poverty. By the 1960s, *raï* folk instruments such as *rebab*, *guellal* (a cylindrical drum made from ceramic or metal pipe), and *gaspah* (an end-blown flute), as well as *'ud*, began to give way to European instruments such as the accordion, saxophone, drum set, and guitar, and male singers began to take up the form (in part because of a ban on women singers at that time). In the 1970s, the sound became popular throughout the Arab world and Europe.

However, *raï*'s roots are still clear in many of its distinctive traits: its use of repeating rhythmic patterns sometimes derived from folk dance (often with indigenous drums such as the *darabukka*), occasional nonpulsatile melismatic interludes, and above all its unflinching willingness to confront controversial subject matter, especially sexuality and governmental and fundamentalist repression. In the 1980s and later, *raï* was the protest music of the young, and many of its singers added the title *cheb* or *cheba* ("youth") to their names, including Cheb Mami and Cheb Khaled. Unfortunately, its subject matter put those singers on a collision course with the rise of Islamic fundamentalism, especially during the period of the Algerian civil war (1992–1999) when several prominent *raï* artists were assassinated or exiled.

In addition to *sha'bi* and *raï*, you are likely to hear a wide spectrum of popular music in Arab cities, radio, and television. Mainstream pop music, in some countries called **al-jil**, often smoothes out the rough edges of earlier underground genres, adding synthesizers, European harmonies, and sometimes influences from the high melismatic singing of film music from India. It is nevertheless distinctively Arabic, especially because of its driving percussion, although today those rhythm tracks may be electronic in origin. Whereas *al-jil* songs frequently have the same sorts of innocuous lyrics found in pop genres elsewhere in the world, the style known as **nashid** has explicitly Islamic lyrics.

MUSIC IN IRAN

In Arabic classical music, the intricate interactions of the classical ensemble help to create the distinctive expression of *tarab*, or musical ecstasy. In Iran, solo performances epitomize the classical tradition, and musical expression may be correspondingly introverted and contemplative. This is not to say the music is without the feeling of joy that *tarab* represents, but it is an inward joy, perhaps even expressing the musician's connection with the divine. "We are as the flute," said the famous Iranian poet Rumi (1207–1273), "and the music within us is from thee."[3]

Because Iran sits between India and the Orient on one side and the Middle East and Europe on the other (see map, p. 76), opposing influences have operated at different times in its history—as seen in its names. Persia, its early name, came from the name that the Greeks gave it, *Pars*. In 1935, the country's name officially changed from Persia to Iran, a native term derived from Aryan-based languages (such as those in India). Expatriates opposed to the current Iranian government sometimes prefer to call themselves and their music Persian.

IRANIAN CLASSICAL MUSIC

Just as the basis for melodic composition and improvisation in Arabic countries is the *maqam*, in Iran, classical improvisation is based on the **dastgah**. Like the *maqam*, each *dastgah* has a characteristic heptatonic scale, called the **maye**, which may include steps of ¾ of a tone and 1¼ tone.

Unlike the *maqam*, however, a *dastgah* is defined more as a collection or system of many short, related melodies called **gusheh**. The *gusheh* within each *dastgah* are all related by their melodic character, mood, and home scale, although modulation to related scales is common. To construct an improvisation, the performer selects a number of *gusheh* from a single *dastgah* and improvises on them one after another. The *gusheh* is simply a guide to improvisation, the essence behind the player's melody; only a beginning student would play it in its original form (see the first graphic in the Listening Guide).

Because the number of *dastgah* is limited—there are only twelve—and the number of *gusheh* in each *dastgah* is generally standardized, from ten to thirty per *dastgah*, it should be possible to publish a **radif**—the entire corpus of *gusheh*. In fact, several twentieth-century musicians have done just that, producing large books of several hundred melodies transcribed into Western notation, even though it is difficult to find two musicians who agree on the exact form of any given *gusheh*.

The selection and order of the *gusheh* within a performance is mostly up to the performer, but the performer does not select the *gusheh* randomly. Because they are grouped within the *dastgah* according to their range and the notes that they emphasize, the *gusheh* are generally played in ascending order of pitch so that the excitement within the performance builds.

Like the Arabic *taqsim*, a *dastgah* is played by a single musician on one of a wide variety of instruments, most commonly the *tar* (hourglass lute), the *sehtar* (long-neck lute), the *santur* (dulcimer), the violin, or the voice. Singers' improvisations on the *gusheh* are generally without words, although a verse of a precomposed song often separates each *gusheh*. A performance typically lasts between ten and thirty minutes. A dastgah performance is mostly nonpulsatile but may include contrasting quasi-pulsatile *gusheh* and others, called **chahar mezrab**, which are strongly rhythmic.

---

[3]This translation by Reynold A. Nicholson comes from Maulana Jalál al-Dín Rúmí, *The Mathwnawí of Jalálu'ddín Rúmí* (London: Luzac, 1982).

Although there are other genres of Iranian classical music, these solo improvisations have come to epitomize the mood and essence of the *dastgah*. Nevertheless, through Arabic and European influences, ensemble music has also become important. Genres of ensemble music may be arranged in suites, as in Arabic countries, or interspersed with solo movements, such as a *chehar mezrab* performed independently. Other genres include the following:

- ◆ **pishdaramad.** An introductory piece for ensemble in duple or triple meter. Although the piece is mostly precomposed, the texture is heterophonic, with the different instruments offering variations of phrases derived from the *dastgah*.

- ◆ **tasnif.** A composed song in a fixed meter accompanied by a soloist or ensemble. Whereas these songs traditionally set words in classical poetic meters, modern ballads, also called *tasnif*, do not.

- ◆ **reng.** Ensemble music in a dance rhythm. Such music may feature the *tombak* (goblet drum), which is otherwise mainly a folk or light classical instrument.

Musicians known as **motreb** perform light classical, dance, and traditional entertainment music, although restrictions by the Iranian government since the 1979 revolution have made this music rare today. Popular music, and female performers in particular, are also severely restricted, although a thriving music industry exists among expatriate communities in cities such as Los Angeles.

A PERFORMANCE OF AN IRANIAN *DASTGAH*

A popular *dastgah* is **mahur**, marked by a characteristic optimistic mood that is unusual for much of Iranian classical improvisation. Some authors have commented that the name even sounds similar to the Western word "major," and indeed, the home scale of *mahur* is similar to the Western major scale, also associated with happy moods. Like all performances of the classical *dastgah*, this performance consists of a sequence of improvisations based on *gusheh* melodies of different character, but all having a unifying *mahur* sound. A full performance might include extended improvisations on ten to fifteen *gusheh* and last up to an hour. This short recording by Hussein Ali Zodeh playing the *tar* consists of just a few *gusheh* but preserves the overall form of a larger piece. Zodeh begins with a *daramad*, a *gusheh* with the specific function of starting a performance. He chooses subsequent *gusheh* for their contrasts in rhythm, mode, and character, and to achieve a gradual increase in tessitura. The final tone, or tonic, of *mahur* is called **ist** in Iran. The *tar*'s topmost string carries the melody, and the other three strings are used for drones and rhythmic ostinatos.

JEWISH MUSIC

It is difficult to generalize about Jewish music because of the diaspora that scattered the Jews from their original Middle Eastern home to other areas of the Middle East as well as North Africa, Europe, Russia, the United States, and elsewhere. Still, although Jewish musicians adopted many musical characteristics

CD 1:10. *Dastgah Mahur*, Hussein Ali Zodeh, *tar*

First *gusheh*—*daramad*, nonpulsatile.

0:00

Relatively slow, gradually revealing the essence of the *dastgah*.

The main functions of the *daramad*, the few *gusheh* used to open a performance, are to establish the *ist* (tonic), scale, basic mood of *mahur*, and to explore the lower tetrachord (the tonic and the three notes below it).

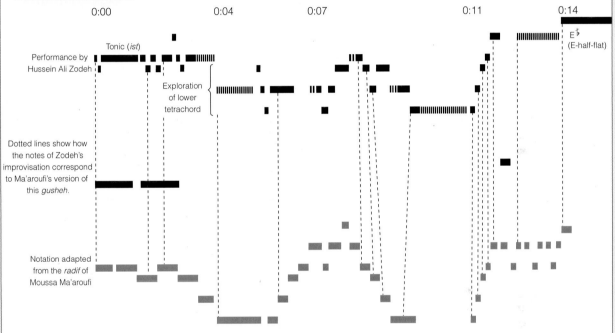

0:14

Suddenly, an accidental, or note outside of the scale is introduced. Its distinctive sound comes from the fact that the third pitch has been lowered by a quarter-tone. While the performer allows us to savor this delicious pitch, not found in Western tuning systems, momentarily we are back in the home scale. The *daramad* concludes with a firm cadence on the tonic.

Second *gusheh*—*kereshmeh* (literally "nod" or "wink"), nonpulsatile.

0:31

Now that the *daramad* has established the tonic, scale, and basic mood of *mahur*, the performer moves onto the next *gusheh*. This *gusheh* moves for the first time to new high pitches and some distinctively quasi-pulsatile sections.

Chahar mezrab section

1:40

Frequent rhythmic strums on the drone strings establish a compound duple meter.

1:45

The melody enters, but in a simple duple meter, creating a lively polyrhythm with the drone accompaniment.

The focus in this section is on the dynamic rhythms and patterns; the melodies are fairly simple and are typically developed by means of sequences—that is, the same melodic fragment repeats at successively higher or lower starting points.

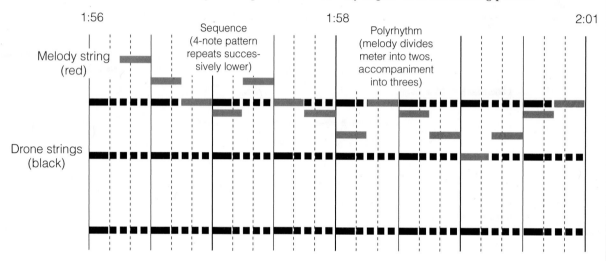

2:55

Comes to an end with a simple phrase that takes us back to the nonpulsatile rhythm and introduces a new pitch, a lowered seventh scale step that will be prominent in the next section.

Third *gusheh—shekasteh* (literally "broken" or "doleful").

3:05

Introduces a new scale, creating a sense of modulation, a temporary journey to a different landscape.

Emotional high point of performance emphasizes the scale's highest pitches.

New scale includes the lowered seventh step and the third step lowered by a quarter-tone. Centered not on the ist but on the fifth scale step, called by some theorists the **shahed** (stressed pitch) in *mahur*.

4:34

A short coda (ending section), descending gently from the fifth scale step to the tonic, brings us back home to the *mahur* scale.

Hear and see the instruments of *Dastgah Mahur* in your downloadable **ACTIVE LISTENING TOOLS**, available at the World Music Resource Center.

of their new countries, the segregation of Jewish communities in some areas helped to keep their culture and music distinct. Comparative studies have shown striking musical similarities between communities far removed in time and geography. Even though Jewish musicians have absorbed influences from these various areas, including attributes such as harmony as discussed in Chapter 14, we'll discuss their music here, including genres such as klezmer, which originated in Europe and the United States.

RELIGIOUS MUSIC

Sing to God our strength: make a joyful noise to the God of Jacob.
Raise a song and bring the drums, the harp, and the lyre.
Blow the trumpet at the new moon; at the full moon, and on our feast day.

—Psalm 81[4]

The Bible records many such references to music, including folk songs and praise songs, many of which were apparently sung antiphonally (by alternating groups) or responsorially (by a leader alternating with the group). Especially important was the sacred music of the Temple, where a hereditary caste of professional musicians, the **Levites**, performed. The Bible mentions a variety of instruments that have since been found in archeological sites. Of these, the most important is the *shofar*, a ram's horn trumpet still used as a ritual instrument in Jewish ceremonies (Figure 7.4).

By about the fifth century BCE, **cantillation**, a standard method of chanting Biblical texts, had evolved. To sing these texts, which may vary widely in line length and meter, ancient Jewish singers used nonmetrical melodic formulas, similar to those used by epic singers in Eastern Europe and the Near East. Lay singers, rather than Levites, sang the texts in small local places of worship known as synagogues. The many different melodic formulas for cantillation are indicated by signs called *ta'amim*, the first extant examples of which date from the ninth century. Later translations of these signs to European notation show remarkably consistent interpretations, even between widely separated traditions.

© Richard T. Nowitz/CORBIS

FIGURE 7.4

The shofar, the ancient ram's horn trumpet, is still used as a ritual instrument in Jewish religious ceremonies.

Political uprisings led to the destruction of the Temple by the Romans in 70 CE. Within a short time, as many of the Jewish people gradually dispersed to other countries, the synagogue tradition replaced that of sacred music of the Temple. Today, a single singer called the **cantor** performs most cantillation in public services. Developing into professional singers, the cantors were soon entrusted with preserving the cantillation melodies through oral tradition.

The split of the Roman Empire into western and eastern states in 395 CE is reflected in the differing traditions of the diaspora communities. The Jews of the **Sephardic** tradition initially settled in Spain and Portugal, and after their expulsion in 1492 and 1497, respectively, they scattered throughout the Mediterranean region. The Jews of the **Ashkenazi** tradition eventually settled in Central and Eastern Europe, although they retained many of the nondiatonic modes of the Middle East.

[4]Translation adapted from the American Standard Version Bible.

The Ashkenazi Jews also retained a tradition of modal improvisation through sung prayers known as **hazzanut**, nonpulsatile songs based on certain scales and collections of melodic motives. The Jews had a system of modes, each of which had certain mystical associations, like the ancient Byzantine and Greek modes. The medieval Ashkenazim also composed metrically fixed, non-improvised chants, many influenced by European music. Some of these have become famous Jewish melodies, including the *Kol Nidre*.

The modes of the Ashkenazi cantoral traditions, called **shteygers**, are complex and include characteristic motives and tonal relationships used in *hazzanut* improvisations. Scales in Eastern Europe often included an augmented second, an interval consisting of three semitones, not found in the diatonic scales of Western Europe but common in Arabic *maqam*. This distinctive interval is common in klezmer music as well as popular folk melodies such as the famous *Hava nagila*.

One distinctive tradition of this region was the Hasidic movement, a mystical sect that arose in the eighteenth century and for whom music, even borrowed from folk sources, could represent an ecstatic union with the divine. Feeling that words limit the ineffable feeling of this joy, their songs, known as **nigun**, have only abstract syllables.

KLEZMER

Although ensembles of Jewish musicians have been common throughout the diaspora, those of the Ashkenazi tradition, particularly in Russia and Eastern Europe, became known for a distinctive style that distinguished them from non-Jewish bands. These folk musicians, known as **klezmorim** (the singular form is **klezmer**), typically played vigorous dance music for weddings and other events in small Jewish communities. The music of these ensembles featured characteristic syncopation (shifting of metrical accents) and nondiatonic scales. The ensembles typically included a pair of violins, a bass, a *cimbalom* (hammered dulcimer), and, later, a famously expressive clarinet. By the early twentieth century, bands sometimes added brass (buzzed lip) instruments and an accordion, although the instrumentation was never fixed.

Aside from dance music, klezmer bands sometimes accompanied popular songs or highly expressive unmetered introductions related to the Middle Eastern *taqsim* and the Eastern European *parlando rubato* tradition (see Chapter 13). By the end of the nineteenth century, many of these musicians were professionals who included European harmonies in their accompaniments. However, pogroms—systematic persecutions of Jews—in this region caused many of these musicians to emigrate, largely to the United States, between about 1880 and 1920.

Once in the United States, these groups absorbed influences from jazz and American musical theater, but retained their distinctive sound. The use of the term "klezmer" to refer specifically to this music and the recognition of this music as a distinct tradition is a relatively recent phenomenon, associated mostly with the United States and, through further immigration, Israel. Since the 1970s, this music has undergone a revival in the United States with the popularity of such groups as the Klezmatics (Figure 7.5).

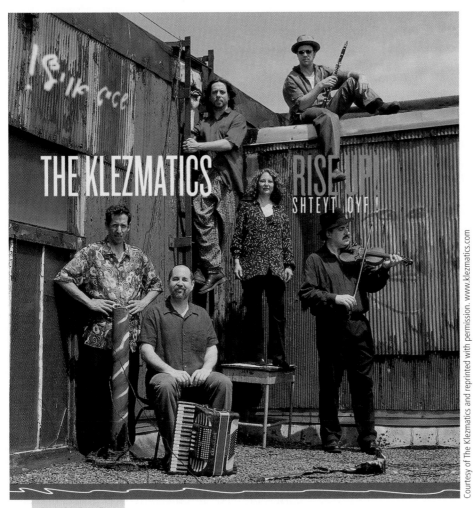

FIGURE 7.5

The Klezmatics, an American klezmer band.

Courtesy of The Klezmatics and reprinted with permission. www.klezmatics.com

MODERN ISRAELI MUSIC

The modern state of Israel is home to immigrants from every extant Jewish musical tradition in the world. Since 1915, self-conscious attempts to create a national music and to encourage the use of the national language (Hebrew) in song lyrics have met with rather mixed success. Nevertheless, the diversity of these musical traditions, from Yemenite folk song to American jazz, creates an exciting mix.

One of the most popular genres among the Jews of the Sephardic (Mediterranean) tradition is the ***romance*** or ***romancero***, which has its origins in Renaissance Spain. Like other songs of this tradition, it is sung in the Sephardic language, Ladino. These ballad-type folk songs were originally sung without accompaniment by women, although modern Ladino musicians often sing with guitar accompaniment.

CD 1:11. *A Rumenisher Doyne,* Klezmer Conservatory Band with Don Byron, clarinet

First section: *doina*

0:00

A *doina* or *doyne* is a nonpulsatile klezmer form that features an improvisatory soloist, in this case, on clarinet. The *doina* emerged from Romania at a time when it was under Ottoman rule, and spread among klezmer musicians of areas around the Ukraine who then brought the form to the United States. It shows the influence of improvisation found in such Middle Eastern forms as the Turkish *taksim* but also reflects the related art of cantoral singing in Eastern European synagogues. Unlike those predecessors, though, this *doina* is not monophonic but is accompanied by extended chords (simultaneous collections of pitches) based on European harmony. The instrumentation of a klezmer band can vary, but this recording includes cornets and trombones (European buzzed-lip aerophones), saxophones, accordion, violins, double bass, and (later) drums.

0:12

The clarinet plays a **portamento** (sliding pitch), which is especially characteristic of the klezmer style. This semitone slide and skip down also outlines the distinctive mode used in this piece, called *mi sheberach* after a cantor prayer that uses it (see graphic.).

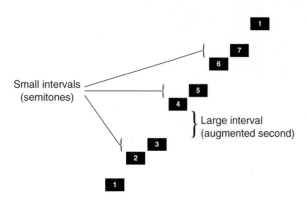

Like several of the most common klezmer *shteygerim* (modes), this one has a distinctively large interval between pitches three and four in the scale. This interval, called an augmented second, is not found in diatonic European modes but is common in both Jewish and Arabic music and gives klezmer music one of its most distinctive qualities. In this piece, pitches outside the mode are often introduced, sometimes as passing ornaments and sometimes to accommodate European harmonies. After the initial sliding pitch here, the clarinetist ornaments individual notes with short slides down, sometimes known among American klezmer musicians as "chirps."

0:30

As Middle Eastern nonpulsatile sections are structured by their exploration of the mode (thus called modal improvisation), the structure of this *doina* is also determined by the sequence of accompanying chords. The chord changes here for the first time, and the soloist must respond, in part by incorporating pitches that are outside the mode.

0:34

The harmony changes again to the lowered fourth scale degree, temporarily altering the mode to allow this harmony, which is common in European songs. The chords continue to change on cues from the soloist, until:

Second section: *terkish*

2:13

The band launches into a moderate tempo dance known as a *terkish*, presumably a form originating in Ottoman influence in Eastern Europe. Its characteristic rhythm of 3 + 1 + 2 + 2 in a quadruple meter is superficially similar to the Latin American *habañera* rhythm, but they have different origins.

Third section: *doina*

2:34

The band returns to the nonpulsatile *doina*.

Fourth section: *freylekhs*

3:02

The performance is rounded out with a lively duple meter dance known as a *bulgar* or *freylekhs*. This form is one of the most common in the klezmer repertory. The phrases are eight beats long, which the drummer sometimes divides into a pattern of 3 + 3 + 2 while the bass and harmony instruments emphasize a constant beat (see graphic). The first four phrases here are each a variation of the same melody (A).

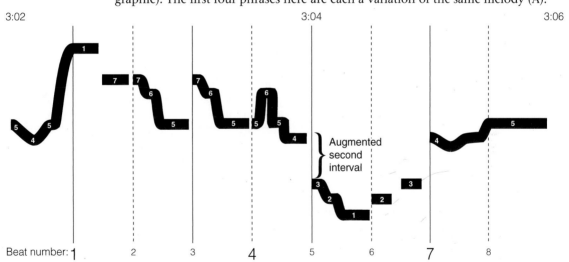

3:15

This contrasting section introduces a new tune (B), although still with the same rhythm.

3:27

The return to the A section is emphasized by cymbal crashes.

3:39

The B melody returns.

3:50

The clarinet runs up the scale to the tonic, and the band plays unison ending notes on scale tone five followed by the tonic. This is a stereotypical ending for a klezmer dance.

Hear and see the instruments of *A Rumenisher Doyne* in your downloadable **ACTIVE LISTENING TOOLS,** available at the World Music Resource Center.

Listening Exercise 4   **CD 1:11.** *A Rumenisher Doyne*

1. When the clarinet comes in at 0:04, it plays
   a. portamentos (sliding pitches).
   b. trills (rapid alternations between adjacent pitches).
   c. chirps.

2. When the beat appears in the *terkish* section at 2:13, it is articulated by the drum set.
   a. True
   b. False

3. The meter of the *terkish* section is
   a. simple triple.
   b. simple duple.
   c. compound duple.

4. The texture of the *freylekhs* section at 2:34 is
   a. heterophonic with drums.
   b. monophonic with drone and drums.
   c. homophonic with drums.

You can take this Listening Exercise online and receive feedback or e-mail answers to your instructor at the World Music Resource Center.

Minority communities of Jews living in the Middle East have often been known for their distinctive music, but at the same time, they have absorbed many attributes of Arabic culture. Israeli bands such as Bustan Abraham feature accompaniments by the *'ud, qanun, darrabukka*, and other Arabic or Turkish instruments.

REFERENCES

DISCOGRAPHY

ARABIC MUSIC   Racy, Ali Jihad. *Mystical Legacies*. New York: Lyrichord 7437, 1997.
Ensemble of Classical Arabic Music. *A Concert in the Nahda Style*. Beirut: Byblos BLCD 1023, 2002.
Hakim. *Yaho*. Sherman Oaks CA: Mondo Melodia 186 850 017 2, 2000.
Kalthoum, Oum [Umm Kulthum]. *El Sett [The Lady]*. Paris: Buda 82244-2, 2002.
Various artists. *Egypte: Les Musiciens du Nil*. Paris: Ocora HM CD83, 1987.
Various artists. *Music in the World of Islam* (3 CDs). London: Topic Records TSCD901-903, 1976/1994.

MUSIC OF IRAN   Payvar, Faramarz. *Iran: Persian Classical Music*. New York: Elektra/Nonesuch 9 72060-2, 1974/1991.
Various artists. *Iran: The Masters of Traditional Music* (3 CDs). Paris: Ocora C 560024/25/26, 1979–1991.

JEWISH MUSIC   Bustan Abraham. *Ashra*. Haifa, Israel: Nada 18, 2000.
Klezmer Conservatory Band. *Yiddishe Renaissance*. New York: Vanguard VCD 79450, 1981/1991.

Various artists. *Cantares y romances tradicionales Sefardíes de Marruecos y Oriente [Traditional Sephardic songs and ballads from Morocco and the Balkans].* Madrid: Saga KPD(2)-10.202, 1994.
Various artists. *Israeli Songs and Dances.* Paris: Buda 82495, n. d.

Erguner, Kudsi and Soleyman Erguner. *Sufi Music of Turkey.* New York: CMP Records CMP 3005, 1990.
The Erkose ensemble. *Tzigane: The Gypsy Music of Turkey.* New York: CMP Records CMP 3010, 1991.

MUSIC OF TURKEY

 BOOK COMPANION WEBSITE

You will find flashcards, a glossary, and tutorial quizzes, as well as other materials that will help you succeed in this course, at the *Music of the Peoples of the World, 2nd Edition,* Companion Website at www.cengage.com/music/alves/world2e.

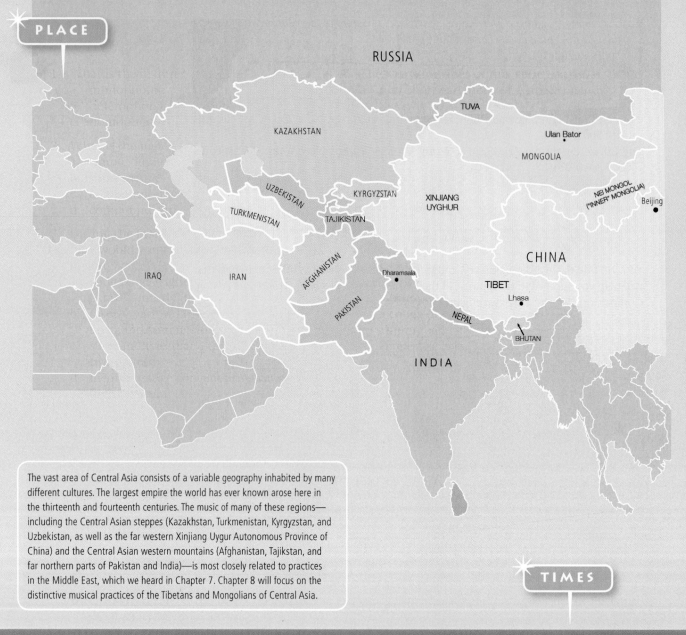

PLACE

RUSSIA

TUVA

KAZAKHSTAN

Ulan Bator •

MONGOLIA

UZBEKISTAN

KYRGYZSTAN

XINJIANG
UYGHUR

NEI MONGOL
("INNER" MONGOLIA)

Beijing •

TURKMENISTAN

TAJIKISTAN

CHINA

IRAQ

IRAN

AFGHANISTAN

Dharamsala •

TIBET

Lhasa •

PAKISTAN

NEPAL

BHUTAN

INDIA

The vast area of Central Asia consists of a variable geography inhabited by many
different cultures. The largest empire the world has ever known arose here in
the thirteenth and fourteenth centuries. The music of many of these regions—
including the Central Asian steppes (Kazakhstan, Turkmenistan, Kyrgyzstan, and
Uzbekistan, as well as the far western Xinjiang Uygur Autonomous Province of
China) and the Central Asian western mountains (Afghanistan, Tajikistan, and
far northern parts of Pakistan and India)—is most closely related to practices
in the Middle East, which we heard in Chapter 7. Chapter 8 will focus on the
distinctive musical practices of the Tibetans and Mongolians of Central Asia.

TIMES

c. 200 BCE–1000 CE	661–750	7TH–9TH C	1208–1242
Height of Silk Road, trade route that carries commerce and cultural influences between East and West. Through this trade, musical influences reach Central Asia, and Central Asian music influences other cultures, including the famous Tang dynasty in China.	Introduction of Islam brings Arabic and Iranian musical influences into large areas of Central Asia as far as Uighur (modern west China). Islamic courts patronize advanced traditions of art music.	Buddhism becomes dominant religion in Tibet, which becomes an influential empire in the region. Despite later isolationism, musical influences enter Tibet from China, India, and elsewhere.	Mongolian Empire spreads across China, Russia, Central Asia, and the Middle East. Reopening of the Silk Road allows Marco Polo to travel from Europe to China in thirteenth century. Tibetan form of Buddhism introduced to Mongolia, where it is firmly established by the sixteenth century.

CENTRAL ASIA

SETTING

The awe-inspiring view from a Buddhist monastery on a Himalayan mountainside in Tibet, the "rooftop of the world," seems to extend forever (Figure 8.1). Many of the musical arts of Central Asia reflect this vastness, from the epic songs sung by horseback nomads on the steppes (flat grasslands) to the very slow "long songs" of the Mongols, whose long melodic lines and elaborate vocal ornamentation seem to be in no hurry.

In the Tibetan monastery, sound is expansive in another way. The elaborate symmetrical paintings called ***mandalas***, which serve as objects of contemplation for the monks, depict multitudes of Buddhas, each representing a different deified manifestation of the transcendent truth (Figure 8.2). Associated with each manifestation is a particular sound that can become a part of this world through the chanting of those cosmic tones in ritual formulas called ***mantra***.

SOUNDS

CD 1:12

Invocation from *Mahakala Puja*, The Monks of Sherab Ling Monastery, Tibet

1365–1500	1731–1876	1917–1991	1924–1992	
Timur's empire, establishing a golden age of scholarship, including music scholarship, centers at Samarkand (in modern Uzbekistan).	Russian annexation of Central Asian states brings new musical influences to these regions.	Soviet Union dominates region. Soviet government largely ends nomadism and organizes people into collective farms or moves them to urban industrial areas. The socialist state controls much musical expression and establishes professionalized "folk" ensembles. Similar state control and support of music occurs in communist China and Mongolia.	Mongolia becomes independent communist state. Buddhism and Buddhist music are suppressed. After transition to democracy in 1992, some traditional musical and religious practices return.	

© Ric Ergenbright/CORBIS

FIGURE 8.1

Tibetan monks look out over a vast Himalayan valley from their monastery in the Zanskar Valley, Ladakh, India. They play *kungling*, a buzzed-lip instrument traditionally constructed of human femurs to remind us of the brevity of human existence. *Kungling* may also be constructed from metal and played in groups.

© Alen MacWeeney/CORBIS

FIGURE 8.2

Here we see a *tanka*, a Tibetan painting of a mandala, a symbolic representation of the Buddhist spiritual universe. These paintings are hung in monasteries as objects of meditation.

To Westerners who may picture meditative music as quiet and relaxing, the crashing cymbals, raucous double reeds, and deep trumpets that accompany Tibetan Buddhist rituals may be startling. The most remarkable sound, however, comes from the deep-voiced chants themselves. Instead of melodies that traverse discrete pitches of a scale in a distinct beat, the melodies of some of these chants consist of slowly sliding pitches, gradually changing timbres, and beats that never stay constant. Some of these chants are sung in a special style that allows a single singer with a growl-like tone to create simultaneously two or three identifiable pitches, helping to create an overwhelming atmosphere filled

▶ 1950

Tibet annexed by China, which, especially during 1959–1978, suppresses the practice and music of Buddhism.

with the luminescent sound of the cosmos. To the Tibetan Buddhists, music is both a means to understanding and enlightenment as well as a reflection of the ultimate truth made briefly audible in this transitory world.

ELEMENTS OF CENTRAL ASIAN MUSIC

Ethnic Mongolian people live not only in Mongolia proper (long ago known as "Outer" Mongolia) but also in neighboring regions of China ("Inner" Mongolia) and Russia. Tibet is currently an autonomous region within China, which claimed sovereignty over it in 1950. Many Tibetans live in expatriate communities in India, Nepal, Bhutan, and elsewhere. Whereas Tibet is dominated by the Himalayan mountain range, Mongolia consists largely of immense plains through which herders have traditionally moved their animals from season to season. The musical instruments of nomads must be portable, and long treks provide excellent opportunities to develop long songs and sophisticated performance practices.

Characteristics of traditional Central Asian music include the following:

- **Epic songs.** Sung by specially trained bards, these narrations of grand mythic poems may last from hours to days. Related to similar traditions throughout Eurasia and perhaps introduced to China by the great Mongol conquerors, this ancient practice is dying out in many areas. (We will discuss epic singing from Eastern Europe in Chapter 13.)

- **Multiphonic singing.** This is a remarkable vocal technique in which a single singer can produce two or even three tones at once. By growling very low tones and adjusting their vocal cavities in very specific ways, a singer can resonate certain overtones or **partials** to sound like a separate whistling sound. Although this practice is found in different forms throughout Tibet and Mongolia, the Western Mongols and neighboring Russian groups such as those from the Tuva region are especially known for this technique.

- **Tone-contour melodies.** Lacking a conventional melody made up of discrete variations in pitch, tone-contour melodies of chants follow subtle and continuous fluctuations of timbre, loudness, and slides between tiny pitch differences. Although this remarkable type of singing is only one type of Tibetan Buddhist chant, other Central Asian forms, such as the "long songs" of Mongolia, also focus attention on subtleties of pitch slides and shifts in timbre.

TIBETAN MUSIC

In mid-winter, stinging winds gust down the steep faces of the sky-kissing Himalayan peaks that rise above Dharamsala, India. The winds carry the sounds of prayers that are inscribed on hundreds of small flags hanging from ropes strung above the Buddhist temple. The winds also carry the sounds of

© Earl & Nazima Kowall/CORBIS

FIGURE 8.3

A *dung-chen* is a metal, straight, buzzed-lip instrument that creates a very low pitch. These highly revered objects are sometimes constructed in telescope fashion and may extend to fifteen feet. Often two or more play together in ritual contexts. Each plays a very low, sustained pitch, although, like the singers of low *dbyangs* chant, the player can vary the pitch slightly.

enormous ten-to fifteen-foot metal ***dung-chen*** trumpets (Figure 8.3). These trumpets play profound, rumbling tones that the Buddhist monks of this famous monastery associate with the natural force of the winds. Music for these monks has two components: an external music, which is what we hear, and an internal music that accompanies the external in the musician's soul. In the same way, the *tantras*, books of esoteric religious teachings central to Tibetan Buddhism, speak of the external winds of nature and the *lung*, winds of the inner spirit that are the basis for consciousness.

Humanity's harmonious relationship to natural forces and the earth is a focus of Tibet's indigenous religion, known as *Bön*, and its practitioners, sometimes called **shamans**, often use music to help mediate between the spiritual forces of the earth and people. This tradition of shaman music is found in many areas of Central Asia, north to Mongolia, Siberia, and Korea, although these practices are extinct or increasingly rare in some regions. Around the seventh century, when Tibet became a powerful kingdom controlling trade routes, Buddhism entered from India. Although *Bön* and Buddhism have at times competed, today they peacefully coexist, Buddhism mediating the individual's relationship to the spiritual world's cycles of life and rebirth, and *Bön* his connection to the natural world.

In Tibet, Buddhism developed into a unique form emphasizing monasticism, an esoteric knowledge of the spiritual world, and elaborate rituals in which music plays a vital role. Despite important influences from China, India, and elsewhere, for centuries Tibet remained a kingdom isolated in the Himalayas and developed its own distinctive arts and traditions.

The Dharamsala monastery is the home of the Dalai Lama, the spiritual leader of Tibetan Buddhists, now the Tibetan leader in exile. In 1950, Communist Chinese troops suddenly invaded Tibet, but Chinese suppression of the indigenous culture and religion precipitated an uprising in 1959. The even more severe crackdown that followed led to the escape of the Dalai Lama and ultimately thousands of his followers to the neighboring countries of India, Nepal, and Bhutan. In the period that followed, especially during the Chinese Cultural Revolution of 1966–1976, Tibetan Buddhism and its musical traditions, virtually eliminated from Tibet, survived only in expatriate communities such as Dharamsala in India. Since the liberalization of religious tolerance in 1978, some Buddhist practices have returned to Tibet, although especially since a 1989 uprising, the Chinese authorities still strictly control them.

RITUAL MUSIC AND ITS INSTRUMENTS IN TIBET

The tuba-like tones of the enormous *dung-chen* trumpets announce the evening prayers at the monastery. As the monks gather in an incense-filled hall, butter lamps dimly illuminate sacred images, including mandalas. Like the mandala paintings, the music of the prayer ritual also serves to focus the mind for meditation but lacks so many of the elements of conventional music we might expect—melody and beat, for example—that some writers have described it as "ritual sound" rather than music. Yet this powerful, otherworldly sound of deep trumpets, loud double reeds, clattering cymbals, and drums is as precisely organized as the detailed mandala images, creating (in the term of ethnomusicologist Ter Ellingson) a "mandala of sound."

Tradition so precisely prescribes the music that virtually no improvisation is allowed. The rhythm, controlled by cymbals called **rul-mo** (Figure 8.4), is often neither pulsatile nor non-pulsatile in the usual sense. Instead of beats represented as regularly spaced articulations in the sound, they are arranged in sections in which they gradually accelerate but are rarely static. Monks hold these bulbous brass cymbals in careful balance so that slight movements cause them to sizzle or strike together with precise control.

© Craig Lovell/CORBIS

FIGURE 8.4

Rul-mo, large metal cymbals with a prominent central boss (raised portion), are the leaders of the instrumental section of the rituals. These cymbals are carefully balanced in two hands so that the players can strike them along the edges in a variety of ways, ranging from a resounding crash to a delicate sizzle.

Tibetan ritual chant may take the form of conventional melodies (*rta*) or repetitive recitation (*'don*), but the most astonishing sounds come from a specialized style called **dbyangs**, chants where the "melodies" consist of subtle changes in timbre, loudness, and sliding pitches. Different monasteries often write down these small slides and changes in pitch, although the details of the notational systems vary from one monastic tradition to another (Figure 8.5). The monks read from these sacred chant notations and use them to preserve ancient performing practices.

To produce differences in timbre, musicians have developed a wide repertory of techniques for achieving relatively bright, nasal, deep, or other vocal timbres. The monks may also interpolate vocables (syllables without literal meaning) between the words of the chant for the sake of tone color variation.

The most remarkable vocal effect, though, is multiphonic singing, the singing of more than one pitch at a time. We will hear a related type of multiphonic singing from Mongolia, a region with strong historical ties to Tibet.

Copyright © 1975 by Indiana University Press. Reprinted by permission. From Kaufman, Walter, *Tibetan Buddhist Chant.*

FIGURE 8.5

Mahakala chant notation.

© Christine Kolisch/CORBIS

FIGURE 8.6

The *nga chin* is a cylindrical bass drum with two heads, often struck with a mallet shaped something like a question mark. Drums come in different sizes with specific names appropriate to specific rituals and traditions.

Only cymbals and **nga chin**, a kind of double-headed bass drum (Figure 8.6) accompany the ritual chant. But the chant often alternates with a larger ensemble of instruments that may include the *dung-chen* trumpets, *rgya-gling* double reeds (Figure 8.7), and smaller *kungling* trumpets. These latter trumpets are traditionally made of a human leg bone, which remind us of the transitory nature of human existence. The *kungling* we will hear are made of metal. Like the *dung-chen*, they play long extended tones that vary only slightly, though quite deliberately, in pitch and volume. This music, known as **rul-mo** (the same name as the cymbals) is filled with elements of special symbolic significance. The fact that this music rarely repeats may remind listeners of the Buddhas who have escaped from the cycles of death and rebirth. In one piece, ethnomusicologist Ter Ellingson showed how the placement of strikes and lines along which the two cymbals clatter against one another symbolically create a mandala image (Figure 8.8).

© David Samuel Robbins/CORBIS

FIGURE 8.7

Rgya-gling are large, very loud, conical double reeds, with a metal disc on which the lips rest and a flared bell. There are seven equidistant holes. The players practice circular breathing, a technique that allows for continuous sound. Two or more play elaborately ornamented melodies based on a few core tones.

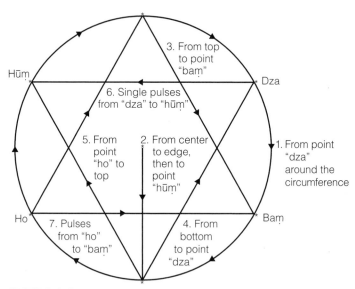

FIGURE 8.8

This schematic drawing shows how a succession of strikes between two *rul-mo* cymbals can symbolically create a mandala image. Four points along the rims of the cymbals are given Sanskrit syllables as names: *dza, bam, ho,* and *hūm.* At the beginning of the section, the player creates a series of accelerating pulses around the rims (1). During each succeeding *brdung* (lit. beat), a series of accelerating strikes on the cymbal, the player follows the pattern shown (single strikes and an accelerating series of strikes) to create a six-pointed mandala inscribed in a circle.

Chant and *rul-mo* instrumental music are not the only expressions of the spiritual mathematics of the mandala image. In the sacred dance known as *'cham*, each of the dancers assumes the identity of one of the deities of the mandala. Performed to the accompaniment of an ensemble similar to the *rul-mo*, *'cham* choreography is a highly stylized movement of high-stepping knees and precise hand gestures of symbolic significance, known as *mudra*.

A TIBETAN MUSIC PERFORMANCE

At the end of each day, monks in the Kagyu tradition of Tibetan monasticism gather in a large incense-filled hall and chant an invocation and offering to their tradition's protector deity, Mahakala. Although depicted as a terrifying being surrounded by fire, this deity is an emanation of the compassionate Buddha Vajradhara; Mahakala directs his wrath towards obstacles to compassion and enlightenment (Figure 8.9). This ritual of chant, instruments, and offerings is called a *puja*, during which time the monks pray for the benefit of all sentient beings.

Our audio selection is an excerpt from a Mahakala invocation in an hour-long *puja*. Here, as in other accompanied chants, the *rul-mo* cymbals carefully control the music's time dimension. The cymbals clatter with a gradually accelerating beat. This whole series of accelerating strikes on the cymbal is called a **brdung** (literally "beat"), and the *brdung* themselves are arranged in a set pattern for each section of this piece. Generally, in each pattern, the time between the *brdung* gradually shortens, creating an acceleration of the groups of beats, which themselves accelerate.

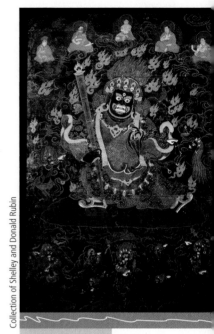

Collection of Shelley and Donald Rubin

FIGURE 8.9

A *tanka* painting of Mahakala, the protector deity of Tibetan Buddhism, from the Kagyu tradition.

FOLK AND ART MUSIC IN TIBET

As elsewhere in Central Asia, Tibetans have a rich repertory of folk songs associated with activities of daily life—nomadic or pastoral songs, agricultural work songs, love songs, and so on—that seem very different from the otherworldly sounds of religious ritual music. Although many songs have conventional pentatonic (five-tone) scales like those of China (see Chapter 10), Tibetan modes and melody types are often quite different, and some songs may use six- or seven-tone (heptatonic) scales, like those in India. Pastoral or nomadic songs are known for their elaborate **melismas** (many notes to a single syllable), which are common in Iran and Mongolia but are not as common in China. The **sgra-snyan** is a lute with a long, unfretted neck that sometimes accompanies folk songs (Figure 8.10). Folk songs are otherwise usually unaccompanied, although singers and other participants often dance.

© David Samuel Robbins/CORBIS

FIGURE 8.10

The *sgra-snyan* is a fretless long-necked lute with three to seven strings played with a plectrum (pick). Its resonator is often covered in snake skin. The number of strings depends on the geographical region.

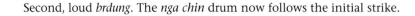

CD 1:12. Invocation from *Mahakala Puja* (excerpt), The Monks of Sherab Ling Monastery

First Section

0:00

Dung-chen trumpets begin an interlude in the ritual. *Rul-mo* cymbals begin a series of accelerating strikes called a *brdung* (beat).

0:13

Second, loud *brdung*. The *nga chin* drum now follows the initial strike.

0:22

A softer intermediate strike without the drum follows 9 seconds after the last strike, which began 13 seconds after the first one, creating the effect of accelerating placement of the *brdung*.

0:30

Another pair of loud and short *brdung* repeat this pattern.

This larger structure—introductory *brdung* followed by pairs of generally accelerating *brdung* and a concluding *brdung*—is a standard pattern used in the Mahakala *puja* in this tradition.

0:55

A special type of *brdung*, called a *bzhag rol*, announces the end of the pair structure with a much longer acceleration ending in a prolonged sizzle as the cymbals become so close as to rattle against each other until the player finally settles them in his lap. At this point, *kungling*, the smaller trumpets, take over the wind instrument part. Like the *dung-chen*, they play long extended tones that vary only slightly, although quite deliberately, in pitch and volume.

Second Section
A pattern called *dgu brdung* (nine beats), referring to the number of *brdung*, not counting the introductory beat or the long, concluding, accelerating series.

1:17

A new pattern on the cymbals signals a new series of *brdungs*. A single drum beat announces each *brdung*, and the time between each *brdung* gradually shortens—first 11 seconds, then 9, then 7, then 5, 4, 3, and so on.

The *kungling* trumpets play dramatic crescendos (swelling of volume), often swooping down in pitch at the end of each crescendo, between *brdungs* 2 and 3, 5 and 6, 8 and 9, and during the concluding section.

1:51

By this time, the cymbal strikes happen every 2 seconds or so.

2:00	The time interval between cymbal strikes becomes so short that the line dividing the acceleration between *brdung* and the acceleration of strikes within the *brdung* gradually blurs.

Cymbals and drums fade out. |

Third Section

2:14	*Rul-mo* cymbals introduce a third section and a lower-pitched *dung-chen* trumpet joins the texture.

Nga chin drum plays along with the accelerating strikes of the cymbals (rather than just once, signaling a new *brdung* series).

Again the sequence of *brdung* accelerates, with 20 seconds between the first two, then 13 seconds, then 7, and then 4. Another accelerating sequence follows. |

3:27 	The low *dung-chen* trumpets enter again to accompany the long accelerating *bzhag rol* that concludes this instrumental section.

***Dbyangs* chant** |

3:39	Tone contour melody with subtle sliding pitches at the very bottom of the vocal range (see contour below) as well as shifts in timbre and loudness.

Semi-regular cymbal and drum interjections, called *tshig rnga*, articulate and precisely control the timing. Each cymbal and drum strike corresponds to a change in syllables, so that the words unfold at a very slow pace, allowing the participants to meditate on them. |

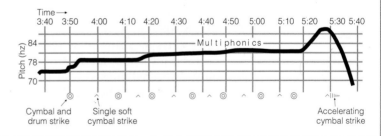

4:30	Listen closely here for multiphonic singing—a single singer producing the effect of two or more simultaneous pitches. Above the growling bass note that the singer chants (called the fundamental), you may hear a quiet whistling sound that moves up and down before the next cymbal strike. That pure sound is a partial (overtone) resonated by special treatment of the vocal tract. These changes in timbre are as important to the chant as the changes in pitch.

Hear and see the instruments of Invocation from *Mahakala Puja* in your downloadable **ACTIVE LISTENING TOOLS**, available at the World Music Resource Center.

In Tibet, as in Mongolia, there is an ancient tradition of extremely long epic songs. Tibetan epic songs are based on the mythic story of the ancient Tibetan king Gesar and his battles against evil. The lead performer narrates in stylized, heightened speech, while the characters sing from a repertory of stock melodies. Amateur troupes also perform stories from the Gesar epic in a form of theater known as **lhamo**, performances of which may last for a full day or more. In *lhamo* performances, narration in heightened speech alternates with action and songs, frequently accompanied only by cymbals and drums. Although the stories often include Buddhist elements and the form sometimes borrows from sacred dance (*'cham*), *lhamo's* purpose is secular entertainment and celebration. Banned during the Cultural Revolution, *lhamo* was preserved mostly in expatriate communities, although new *lhamo* troupes have resumed performances in China since the 1980s.

Nangma and the related genre of **töshe** are sometimes called the art music of Tibet. Small instrumental ensembles prominently including a *yangqin*, the hammered dulcimer of China (see "Traditional Chinese Instruments" in Chapter 10), accompany singers heterophonically. Because of its associations with the elite classes of old Tibet, the Chinese suppressed *nangma* in the 1960s, although groups such as the Tibetan Institute of Performing Arts in Dharamsala, India, preserved it as an art form. Since the liberalization of the 1980s, the Chinese have allowed *nangma* to return, but its traditional melodies now collide with popular music forms influenced by Chinese pentatonic songs, Indian film music, and Western pop. In contemporary Lhasa, the capital of Tibet, *nangma* clubs with disco lights and beer are as common as karaoke bars elsewhere. In these venues electric guitars have often replaced Tibetan and Chinese instruments, but traditional melodies still find a place, and many Tibetans view this new *nangma* with some pride as one of the unique cultural expressions of their country that Chinese authorities still allow.

MONGOLIAN MUSIC

A Mongolian hosting a celebration (a *nair*) ritually greets visitors and conducts each to a special area in the **ger**, the large round felt-covered tent that is the traditional home of Mongolians (Figure 8.11). Every point inside the *ger* has meaning in symbolic social and spiritual space—the entrance is on the south side, men sit on the left (the west), women on the right. The most respected guests sit at the northern-most end, next to what in earlier times would have been a Buddhist shrine, but today is more likely a table of keepsakes and family photographs. At the center of the *nair* celebration is the performance of the *urtyn duu*, a Mongolian long song, whose expansive, nonpulsatile melodic elaborations recall the fenceless vastness of the Central Asian steppes.

Although most Mongolians now live in urban areas, many are still pastoral herders. In the spring, they move their herds of sheep or cattle to fertile mountain valleys, and in the winter, they move to the lower grasslands. As their ancestors have done for centuries, they carry their *ger* homes with them. Long songs and portable instruments are well-suited to this semi-nomadic way of life, but celebrations and travel are not the only occasions for music. Men sing to move their herds, to coax animals to nurse, to calm animals, to accompany hunts, and so on. Songs are important accompaniments to traditional wrestling or archery contests at festivals. Herders also control their animals through whistling, a sophisticated musical art that symbolically connects the herders with the winds that gust over these immense plains and valleys. So closely is whistling identified with the spirit of the wind that it is considered bad luck to whistle indoors. In addition to the wind, the sounds of rivers and birds also serve as musical connections to the spirit world and inspire singing.

Courtesy of Face Music

FIGURE 8.11

The professional Mongolian ensemble Tumbash sits in front of a Mongolian *ger* (round tent). From left to right, the instruments are the *yoochin* (a hammered dulcimer similar to the Chinese *yangqin*), the *morin huur* (the horsehead fiddle), the *limba* (transverse flute), and the *kuuchir* (spike fiddle, similar to the Chinese *hu*).

The subjects of Mongolian songs reflect the importance of animals and nature in the lives of the people, and songs about love for a horse are as common as songs about romantic love in other cultures. The point in a long song when a mythological horse sacrifices himself still brings tears to the eyes of those attending the *nair* celebration. Although practices of Buddhism have been gradually returning to Mongolian culture since the 1990s, spiritual beliefs known as shamanism still permeate traditional life, and music creates a symbolic opening to that supernatural world.

TRADITIONAL SONGS

Like music in other nomadic cultures, the great majority of Mongolian music is vocal, and songs tend to share the same pentatonic modes that we hear in many other regions in Central Asia and in China. The **urtyn duu**, literally long songs, are so named not necessarily for their duration, but for their free, expansive rhythms, which the singer may draw out to any length. These highly expressive songs have wide ranges (up to three octaves) and melismas with highly developed ornamentation, especially pitch slides, wide vibratos (wavering pitches), and falsetto (a male high vocal tone).

Long song subjects may be heroes, myths, praise of nature, or praise of one's community; these songs are always serious and deeply felt. In some areas, instruments heterophonically accompany the long song singers, whereas elsewhere they are always unaccompanied. Sometimes, other celebrants or singers join in a refrain. Traditionally, only men perform *urtyn duu*, although this has changed somewhat in recent times.

Short songs, **bogino duu**, may in fact be rather long, but they differ from the long songs in their fixed meter and limited ornamentation. Whereas the long songs are associated with formal celebrations and rituals, short songs are often sung informally for different everyday situations. Also unlike the long songs, short songs tend to be lively and syllabic (one note per syllable), with relatively simple tunes that repeat (strophic form). A distinctive type of short song is the satirical song, which often pokes fun at drunk or rude people. However, the communist government effectively ended the tradition of such songs commenting on politics. Some short songs represent a dialogue between two speakers, and performers often dramatically act out the parts of those speakers in their voice, manner, and facial expressions. One is reminded of the similar Chinese *drum song* (see Chapter 10), a dramatic narrative said to have been introduced to China by the Mongols.

Also associated with the Mongols from a very early date are *epic songs*, generally known as **tuul'**, traditional performances of which could last hours or days. Such narrative songs entertained the courts of the great Khans, and they were frequently performed for special *nair* celebrations among the nomadic communities. Although some of the epic stories are also found in Tibet, such as the Gesar story and its many derivative episodes, many epics are particular to a certain regional identity.

Each section of an epic is set **strophically** (that is, with a repeating melody for the verses) with pentatonic melodies of fixed types that the singer freely chooses from a traditional repertory. In some traditions, the singer usually accompanies himself heterophonically on an instrument, typically the **morin huur** fiddle. Between each section, the singer may insert dramatic spoken or nonpulsatile sung improvisations.

The specially trained singers of epics, sometimes called *bards* in the West, often belonged to families that traced their patrilineal heritage of training in this art back to the time of the Khans. Years of training often culminated in the young bard's examination by an expert panel. Although modern urban industrialization and communist-era censorship have threatened this tradition, there remains a great interest in epic singing among many communities and state-sponsored folk art groups.

HÖÖMII SINGING

Earlier, we saw how Tibetan monks produce more than one pitch simultaneously in **multiphonic singing**. In Tibet, the high, pure tones produced by this remarkable technique create a subtle shifting of timbre that is a part of the tone-contour melody. Some Mongolian groups have refined this technique, called **höömii** or "throat singing" in the West, to create extraordinary, clear melodies.

As in Tibetan *dbyangs*, the singer sings a low and timbrally rich, sometimes growling, tone while contorting the vocal cavities to resonate certain partials or 'overtones.' These partials are normally present in a sound but not heard as separate tones. Through the *höömii* technique, the partials become so loud that they emerge as a kind of whistle. As the singer further adjusts the shape of his mouth, different partials become prominent and create a melody even as the low-sung pitch remains constant.

Different traditions identify different kinds of multiphonic singing, each distinguished by the timbre of the voice, the relative range of the sung pitch, the method of creating the partials, and other criteria. Traditionally, it was taboo for women to perform *höömii*, ostensibly because some forms take great strength to perform, and incorrect practices could lead to physical damage. Nevertheless, some women have taken up the practice in recent times.

Although it is not possible to sing words on these tones, *höömii* may be inserted into songs, especially at the ends of phrases or verses. In some versions of *höömii*, the sounds are onomatopoeic, evoking the whistling winds of the steppes, the rushing sounds of rivers, and the songs of birds.

INSTRUMENTS

Although there are important instruments that require advanced techniques and virtuoso players, their traditional role is to provide accompaniment. Instrumental orchestras were found at the courts of the Mongolian empire, and, although these groups influenced ensembles in China and vice versa, they died out with the disappearance of the courts. Today, purely instrumental music is not as common as songs, but there is a repertory of **programmatic or representational music** for solo instruments. In these works, the music may describe part of an epic legend, such as the story of a mythological horse or the origin of the instrument itself. Often these stories are so well known to the audience that they can recognize the story purely through the virtuoso performance. Modern conservatories and professional music groups have also reintroduced instrumental ensemble music as an independent art.

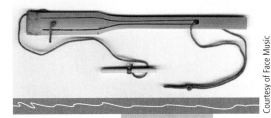

Courtesy of Face Music

FIGURE 8.12

The *khomuz*, the Mongolian jaw's harp, has a stiff tongue of metal or wood that is plucked and resonated in the player's mouth.

An important instrument in some regions is the ***khomuz***, a type of jaw's harp, a stiff tongue of metal or wood that is plucked and resonated in the player's mouth (Figure 8.12). By changing the shape of the mouth, different partials can be resonated, just as in *höömii*.

String instruments, relatively portable and useful for accompanying oneself when singing, are the most important Mongolian instruments. The ***morin huur*** or *hil huur* is a large, bowed instrument of the lute type. With a top carved in the shape of a horse's head, it is sometimes known as the horse-head fiddle (Figure 8.13). Although it is traditionally associated with Central and Eastern Mongolian groups, the government has elevated it to a national instrument. It is unfretted, with two horsehair strings and a large trapezoidal resonator usually covered with goat skin. The player changes the pitch with the unusual technique of pressing against the string laterally with the first knuckle of the index finger. Traditionally used to accompany epics and long songs in some regions, it also plays solo melodies at times.

In other areas, such as Western Mongolia, the primary string instrument for accompaniments is the ***topshuur***, also a two-string unfretted lute, but held laterally and plucked (Figure 8.14). The resonator may

© Viviane Moos/CORBIS

FIGURE 8.13

Amarjargal of the Ensemble Temuzhin in Mongolia plays the *morin huur*, a lute-type instrument— the national instrument of Mongolia. A horse head carved on the top gives it its alternate name, the "horse-head fiddle."

Courtesy of Face Music

FIGURE 8.14

The *topshuur* is a two-string unfretted lute held laterally and plucked.

CD 1:13. "*Hoyor Bor*" ["Two Dark Horses"], Ganbold, Yavgaan, and Tubsinjargal.

0:00 	The *morin huur* player begins by bowing the two open strings of the instrument, sounding the tonic and the fourth pitch in the pentatonic scale.

0:07	The *urdyn duu* singer and the *höömii* singer enter. You will hear the *höömii* singer first sing a low pitch, the second pitch of the scale, and then create a whistling sound—the resonated partial—above it. A single singer produces both sounds. The two singers and instrument play the first phrase in a heterophonic texture.

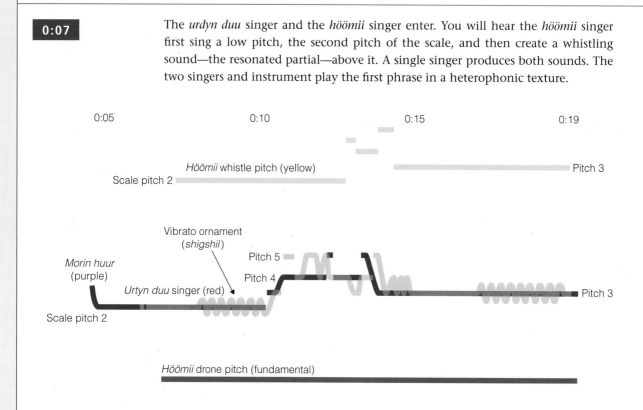

be oblong or circular and is also covered with skin. The **limba**, a small, portable, transverse bamboo flute, may also accompany long songs (Figure 8.11).

Since the liberalization of the 1990s, Buddhists have reintroduced Tibetan ritual instruments to Mongolia. These buzzed-lip instruments, double reeds, and cymbals are otherwise uncommon. Many other instruments are direct counterparts of those found in China, where the name for fiddle, *hu*, may be related to the Mongolian word *huur*.

0:19	As in the first phrase, the melody of the second phrase moves first up before descending again to the cadence tone. Some writers have compared this typical up-and-down contour of Mongolian phrases to the mountains of the Western Mongolian landscape. The *urtyn duu* singer's melody is elaborately ornamented, often using a pronounced vibrato (rapidly fluctuating pitch), a technique known as *shigshil*.
0:42	As the pitch settles on the tonic in the middle of the next phrase, the *urtyn duu* singer ornaments the held tone with glottal repetitions, known as *tsohil*. Because this pitch is not exactly represented by a partial of the drone pitch initially sung by the *höömii* singer, he has to adjust the drone pitch down so that the "whistle" note will match those of the other singer and the *morin huur*.
1:13	The *urtyn duu* singer ascends to a very high pitch in the climactic phrase of this section. Like many *urtyn duu* songs, this one has a very wide range of about two octaves.
1:32	Each of the phrases so far has had a cadence pitch of 1, 3, or 4—the most important structural pitches of the pentatonic scale. Now the same sequence of cadence pitches repeats, even if the phrases themselves are not exactly the same. This phrase thus mirrors the first phrase in its cadence pitch and contour.
2:38	This phrase is nearly a repetition of the high tessitura phrase at 1:13, before descending down the mountain slope and taking us back to the tonic.

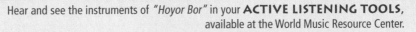

Hear and see the instruments of *"Hoyor Bor"* in your **ACTIVE LISTENING TOOLS,**
available at the World Music Resource Center.

A MONGOLIAN MUSIC PERFORMANCE

Hoyor Bor is a brief excerpt from an *urtyn duu* (long song) about horses, but here, it is combined with a second singer singing *höömii* as well as the traditional *morin huur*. Among the people of the Chandman region of Mongolia, including these performers, *höömii* embodies the sounds of birds and mountain winds, and it is said that when an ancient virtuoso of the form sang, the spirits of the land and water emerged to listen.[1]

[1] Much of this information comes from Carole Pegg, *Mongolian Music, Dance, and Oral Narrative* (Seattle: University of Washington Press, 2001).

Listening Exercise 5 | **CD 1:13** *"Hoyor Bor"* ["Two Dark Horses"]

1. The rhythm for this song is
   a. in triple meter.
   b. mostly nonpulsatile.
   c. made up of gradually accelerating beats.

2. The whistling *höömii* melody
   a. forms harmony (chords) with the *urtyn duu* melody.
   b. has the same basic tones as the *urtyn duu* melody but two octaves higher.
   c. is a distinct tune polyphonically combined with the other two melodies.

3. Which musician starts the phrase at 0:55?
   a. The *morin huur* player
   b. The *urtyn duu* singer
   c. The *höömii* singer

4. At 1:57, the *urtyn duu* singer creates what kind of ornament?
   a. Slow portamento (sliding pitch)
   b. Ululation (singing with fluttering tongue)
   c. Vibrato (fluctuating pitch)

 You can take this Listening Exercise online and receive feedback or e-mail answers to your instructor at the World Music Resource Center.

REFERENCES

DISCOGRAPHY

TIBET

Monks of Sherab Ling Monastery. *Sacred Tibetan Chant*. Franklin, TN: Naxos 76044-2, 2003.

Monks of Gyütö Tantric College, Dalhousie. *Tibetan Buddhism: Tantras of Gyütö: Sangwa Düpa*. New York/Los Angeles: Elektra/Nonesuch 9 79224-2, 1989.

Tibetan Institute of Performing Arts. *Nangma Toshey: Classical Music of Tibet*. Auckland, NZ: Voyager 1466, 1994.

MONGOLIA

Ganbold, Yavgaan and Tubsinjargal. *Mongolia: Höömii and Urtin Duu*. Tokyo: JVC VICG 5211, 1992.

Various artists. *Tuva: Voice from the Center of Asia*. Washington DC: Smithsonian Folkways CD SF 40017, 1990.

ELSEWHERE IN CENTRAL ASIA

Khushnawaz, Mohammad Rahim. *Afghanistan: The Rebab of Hérat*. Geneva: AIMP XXV/VDE 699, 1974/1993.

Various artists. *Instrumental Music of the Uighurs*. Tokyo: King Records KICC 5138, 1991.

Various artists. *Central Asia: Masters of the Dotar*. Geneva: AIMP XXVI/VDE 735, 1993.

BOOK COMPANION WEBSITE

You will find flashcards, a glossary, and tutorial quizzes, as well as other materials that will help you succeed in this course, at the *Music of the Peoples of the World, 2nd Edition, Companion Website* at www.cengage.com/music/alves/world2e.

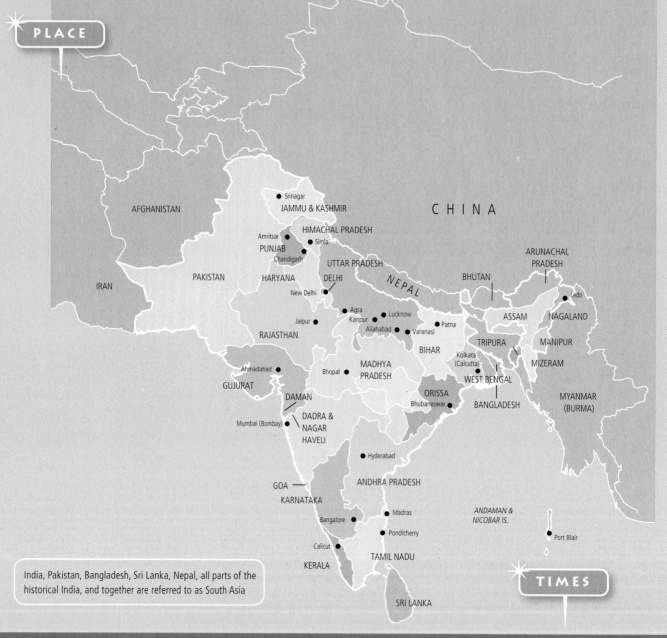

India, Pakistan, Bangladesh, Sri Lanka, Nepal, all parts of the historical India, and together are referred to as South Asia

c. 1800–c. 1200 BCE

Migration of Aryan-language peoples into India; development of caste system. The highest of classes was priests, so-called Brahmins. Today, castes have become a complex system indicating not only relative social placement but also occupation and one's place in religious rituals.

? 1500–1200 BCE

Development of early Hinduism and composition of *Vedic* hymns, a series of holy books of rituals, prayers, and incantations that form the earliest literary basis for the Hindu religion. Brahmin priests chanted the oldest of *Vedic* texts, the *Rig-Veda*, in a kind of heightened speech associated with the pitch levels given by certain diacritical marks. The *Sama-Veda* includes notation for chants, which now span octave scales.

563–483 BCE

Lifetime of Gautama Siddhartha, founder of Buddhism. By emphasizing personal enlightenment and inner peace, Buddhism has had a lasting influence on Indian culture, even though the practice of Buddhism mostly disappeared from its country of origin by 600 CE.

c. 100 BCE

Composition of *Mahabharata*, the long Hindu epic revered as a spiritual text of religious and moral lessons in its long tales of gods and ancient battles between good and evil. The stories of the *Mahabharata* have become the source for much drama and dance in India as well as areas touched by Hinduism, including Indonesia.

INDIA

SETTING

The dusty streets of Varanasi in northern India resonate daily with the sounds of loudspeakers playing hits from the latest Hindi-language films, wedding bands, pop songs, and a collage of many other sounds. But this ancient city is also known as the traditional center of a **gharana**, a particular school of vocal or instrumental performance in India's classical music traditions, which extend back to the times of the great medieval courts. Connoisseurs of Indian classical music still frequent the concerts and festivals of this very sophisticated art music tradition (Figure 9.1).

SOUNDS

CD 2:1

Raga *Khamaj. Sarod*, Ali Akbar Khan; *tabla*, Pandit Mahapurush Misra.

One of these performances, generally featuring a vocal or instrumental soloist and a drummer, begins very quietly, almost reverently, with an assistant playing a soft **drone** (extended pitch). Very slowly, without any perceptible beat, the melodic soloist, but not the drummer, starts to gradually expose the various notes of the mode and the characteristic melodic motives that will be used for the piece. Slowly the entire range of the instrument or voice unfolds. Moments of great beauty and passion emerge as the soloist withholds, then finally plays, important notes of

5TH C?	c. 1100–1400	1520–1590	1660	▶▶▶
Natyasastra, first important treatise on the arts, including music; some date it much earlier. Established many important premises of Indian music, including devotional nature, connections to other arts, and perhaps the basis of its scales.	Iranian influence and introduction of Islam in north. Eventually courts of North India adopt the new religion, becoming sultanates, while southern peninsular areas retain Hinduism as the official religion. Although court music in the north retains a spiritual or devotional personal component, its context becomes secular.	Lifetime of Miyam Tansen, most famous *Mughal* (Hindustani court) composer. Beginning of golden age of arts patronage in rich *Mughal* courts of North India.	*Chaturdandi Prakasika* by Venkatamakhi establishes theory of Karnatic *melakarta* scale system.	

© Michael Freeman/CORBIS

FIGURE 9.1

A performance on the *sitar* (left) and *tabla* (right). The drone instrument is not visible in this photograph.

the scale. After twenty minutes or more of this improvisation enveloping the audience in the mood of the piece, the drums dramatically enter for the first time. The rest of the performance, which may last an hour or more, consists of improvisations by the soloist and the drummer on the mode, the meter, the original melody (if there is one), or other standard melodic fragments.

Indian musicians trace the origins of these complex practices to holy traditions thousands of years old, the echoes of which can still be heard in chants greeting the first rays of sunrise on the steps down to the Ganges River in Varanasi. These chants are known as **mantras**, repeated scriptures, prayers, or phonetic formulas that, through repetition, enhance one's karma or predisposition to goodness. Mantras also represent the audible manifestation of the divine. This sonic dimension of the spiritual in life is apparent not only in the ritual chants that accompany the daily activities of Hindus of this area but also in the sounds of nature, from the songs of birds to the thunder of the monsoons.

While lay people chant mantras every day to enhance their spirituality, in another part of the city, highly trained specialists sing the fluid chants of the *Sama-Veda* that also celebrate the divine nature of the sun and the cyclic rebirth of the morning. The ***Vedas*** are unmetered songs of devotion and ritual that form the oldest books of the Hindu religion (Figure 9.2). These chants center around a core tone that serves as an earthly foundation. Priests assemble the chants in mosaic fashion from carefully learned fragments, creating melodies that, while modest in their range, are stunning in their ornate elaborations. Pauses for breathing clearly separate the phrases, just as the careful discipline of breathing structures yoga meditation.

Vedic chants demonstrate several elements that may have become the basis of India's modern classical traditions: a fixed foundation tone and other core tones, elaborate but highly codified melodic ornamentation practices, characteristic motives, and, above all, a devotional attitude toward art. Although this part of our text will focus mainly on this classical tradition, it represents

▶ 1764–1948	c. 1780–1847	19TH C	1920s
British colonial rule. Certain Western instruments and musical concepts are adopted during this period, such as violin and harmonium, a portable reed organ. British military bands inspired tradition of bands of Western buzzed-lip instruments (trumpets, trombones, tubas) now common in wedding processions.	Period of the trinity of great composers in South India, including Tyagaraja.	Gradual acceptance of purely instrumental classical performances in North India and rise to prominence of *sitar*, *sarod*, and *tabla*. Because of association of classical music with courts, it becomes largely an urban art.	Shift of patronage to public concerts, radio, and film. Although this trend has resulted in the decline of very complex, long, and refined forms favored at courts, it has brought Indian classical music to much wider audiences.

a small fraction of the region's day-to-day musical culture, which extends from diverse folk traditions to popular film music to wedding bands to the mantras that echo daily across the Ganges River.

We will use "India" to refer to the entire region of South Asia, including the modern nation of India, but also Pakistan, Nepal, Bangladesh, and Sri Lanka. India is often divided into two large cultural regions that reflect different classical music traditions: North India or **Hindustani** India, and South India or **Karnatic** India. The country of India has several distinct languages and dialects, including Hindu, Urdu, Bengali, Tamil, and Telugu. The traditional language of scholarly and classical literature is Sanskrit, whereas English has become a common language of the government and national media. Although the large population of the country India is 80 percent Hindu, other important religions flourish, especially Islam, which is the majority religion in Pakistan and Bangladesh.

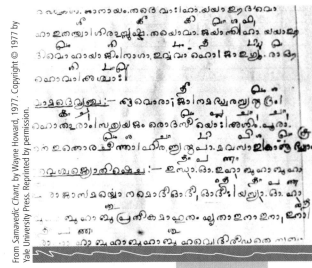

From *Samavedic Chant*, by Wayne Howard, 1977. Copyright © 1977 by Yale University Press. Reprinted by permission.

FIGURE 9.2

In this notation of *Vedic* chant, the figures above the lines of Sanskrit text indicate melodic formulas that are the basis for the chant.

ELEMENTS OF INDIAN CLASSICAL MUSIC

The civilization of the subcontinent of India is one of the oldest in the world. Its huge population represents a great deal of diversity in culture and musical practice. The two classical music traditions known as Hindustani in the North and Karnatic in the South represent many differences in music theory, practice, and terminology, although both traditions have in common the following elements:

◆ **Melodic improvisation by a soloist.** Classical performances always feature improvisations by a single soloist, who may sing or play a melodic instrument.

1910–1932	1947–1948	1950–1980
V. N. Bhatkhande's *Hindustani-sangitapaddhati* music theory treatise establishes the *that* system of North Indian scales. He and other Indian scholars sought to create a unified theoretical basis for North Indian music.	Independence from British rule and partitioning of India into mostly Islamic Pakistan and Bangladesh and mostly Hindu India.	Golden age of popular film music (*filmi*).

◆ **Accompaniment by a drummer.** A single drummer using palms and fingers (no sticks) plays elaborate patterns to accompany classical performances.

◆ **Improvisation based on raga.** The collection of guidelines for a particular melodic improvisation is called a **raga**, which includes aspects of tuning, scales, functions of pitches, melodic motives, and ornamentation.

◆ **Cyclic conception of meter.** Meter is made up of cycles of beat groups in systems called ***tala***.

◆ **Drone.** A string instrument, such as a *tambura*, plays a **drone** (constantly sounding pitch) of the tonic and one other pitch. The drone accompanies performances and creates a tonal foundation for the raga.

THE NATURE OF IMPROVISATION IN INDIAN MUSIC

Some people associate the word *improvisation* with music that is without rules and left entirely up to the whims of the performer. In fact, improvisation rarely means that. The performance of any piece of music entails hundreds of decisions. A composer may determine such elements as the form, meter, tonality, on down to the individual notes of the melody and rhythm. For those elements that the composer has not determined, the performers use tradition and their sense of style to make decisions before the performance about how to play the precomposed elements. During the performance, a performer makes further decisions about the improvised elements. But these choices will be constrained by harmony, meter, tonality, and other complex and strict guidelines about what is and is not appropriate.

Some Indian musicians bristle at the term improvisation; they believe that what they do is so closely bound by rules and tradition that the term overstates the performer's ability to make spontaneous changes. An Indian musician makes decisions based on the form, the **raga**, the melodic basis of the piece, and the ***tala***, the metrical basis of the piece.

Students of Indian music begin not by learning rules for improvisation but by learning a raga's precomposed songs or themes, called ***bandish*** in the North and ***gitam*** in the South. Eventually, students will learn enough of a particular raga's themes to get an intuitive sense for the melodic characteristics of that raga. After presenting the *bandish* or a precomposed song more or less in its original form, students begin to weave its phrases together in new ways, perhaps with characteristic phrases learned from other songs in that raga. More advanced players are able to spontaneously compose new phrases in the same style as those songs but only after truly internalizing the conventions, traditions, and spirit of that raga.

TRAINING FOR PERFORMANCE OF INDIAN MUSIC

As in many cultures, students of Indian music are traditionally taught not in schools but by a **guru**, an individual teacher. Before the modern era of public schools and public concerts, young musicians were apprenticed to a guru, lived with him, and, in between intensive music instruction, did chores like a member of the family. The decision to become a musician is not taken lightly, and the choice may not rest with the student. Family associations and caste still sometimes determine a person's role in society, and families of musicians commonly extend back many generations. Especially in North India, the guru most often is an exponent of a **gharana**, a particular school of vocal or instrumental performance, and the secrets of a *gharana's* instruction and compositions are kept within a literal or symbolic family of musicians.

Although this form of exclusive apprenticeship from a young age is no longer common, the devotion of dedicated students to a particular guru and *gharana* remains. A *gharana* may no longer be associated with a family of blood relatives, but it is still strongly connected to a particular style and region. Dedicated students still proudly associate themselves with a particular guru, but they may also seek lessons from other teachers and study the recordings and public performances of musicians from other traditions. Some students may study an instrument without intending to become professionals.

The institutionalized educational system of the British colonialists was the basis of India's modern system of schools and universities, where traditional music is often taught as well. Classical Indian music at universities is largely independent of any particular *gharana*, and instruction there may emphasize scholarship and the articulation of music theory.

INDIAN INSTRUMENTS AND THEIR FUNCTIONS

Indian classical music performances generally include a small number of players; orchestral music is rare. Indian classical music generally comprises at least three elements: one or more soloists (singers or instrumentalists), drums, and a drone. Although other parts may be added to these three elements (a second melodic instrument, for example), all three are necessary for a traditional music performance.

THE SOLOIST

The focus of an Indian classical performance is the melodic soloist, who may play an instrument or sing. The most common of the many diverse melodic instruments are the **sitar** (a plucked lute with frets), the **sarod** (a plucked lute without frets), the **sarangi** (a bowed lute), the **bansuri** (a transverse flute), the **bin** (an ancient and venerated plucked stick-zither), and the violin (borrowed from the West). (See Instrument Gallery.) The violin is commonly used in accompaniment and as a solo instrument in the Karnatic music of South India, although it is tuned and held differently from the way it is in the West. A seated performer holds the body of the violin on his left shoulder and the other end (the "scroll") against his ankle.

Although each of these instruments has its own idiomatic qualities, including its own melodic characteristics, ornamentation, and so on, their roles in the course of a piece are roughly the same. The exception is the voice, which has the further complication of incorporating precomposed lyrics or improvised text or syllables.

INSTRUMENT GALLERY

TRADITIONAL INSTRUMENTS OF INDIA

Courtesy Ravi Shankar Foundation, photo by Vincent Limongelli

William Alves

SITAR

The famous Indian musician Ravi Shankar (left) plays the *sitar* (an instrument of North India), a plucked lute with a large neck and tall, metal, hoop-shaped frets; five metal melody strings; and two *chikari* or drone strings. The strings are plucked with a metal plectrum (pick) attached to the index finger of the right hand. Approximately thirteen sympathetic strings (*taraf*) run underneath the frets and over a second, smaller bridge.

Courtesy of Alam Madina Music Productions

SAROD

Ali Akbar Khan is one of the most famous masters of the *sarod*, a plucked lute with no frets but a metal-covered, tapered fingerboard, four metal melody strings, and *chikari* (drone) strings. The strings are plucked with a single hand-held plectrum and are pressed to the slick metal fingerboard with the nails of the left hand, making long slides possible. The resonator is covered with skin, rather than wood, which helps give the instrument its highly reverberant timbre. The *sarod* has about fifteen sympathetic strings.

© Sophie Bassouls/CORBIS SYGMA

BIN

The **bin** or *rudra vina* (left) is a highly revered and plucked stick-zither with frets, associated with the *dhrupad* and other old court forms. It has two large gourds attached to the bottom of the soundboard that act as secondary resonators. The performer pictured here is the famous French ethnomusicologist Alain Danielou. The South Indian equivalent is the **vina** (below), which is more common today than the North Indian variety.

Courtesy of Gilbert Blount

SARANGI

The **sarangi** of North India is a bowed fiddle with three gut melody strings, stopped with the upper fingernails of the left hand, and about thirty-five sympathetic strings. Traditionally a secondary melodic instrument that accompanies singing, the *sarangi* has recently become recognized as a solo instrument in its own right.

TAMBURA

The **tambura** (*tanpura* in North India) is a plucked chordophone whose only function is to provide a drone. Although shaped like a lute, it is more of a hybrid lute-zither because the resonator extends through the neck. The four open strings are lightly strummed with the flesh of the finger to provide a constant background drone.

BANSURI

The **bansuri** (*venu* in South India) is a transverse bamboo flute. Although still more common in folk music, the *bansuri* has become a classical instrument as well. A type of transverse flute known as the *murali* has been associated with the god Krishna since ancient times.

HARMONIUM

The **harmonium** is a portable, hand-pumped, reed organ with a small keyboard played by the right hand and a bellows operated by the left. Adapted from the organs that European missionaries imported during British rule, this instrument has been controversial, partly because of its fixed tuning. It is nevertheless a popular instrument for accompanying singing. In India, the harmonium is normally played monophonically—that is, one note at a time.

NAGASVARAM

The **nagasvaram** is a loud, conical double reed in South India that can be up to a meter long. Related to the *zurna* of the Middle East, these instruments are often played in ensembles at weddings and religious processions. The North Indian version, the **shahnai** (Figure 5.26, p. 40), has recently been used as a classical solo instrument, although it is also traditionally a folk instrument.

INSTRUMENT GALLERY

TRADITIONAL INSTRUMENTS OF INDIA

Courtesy of Gilbert Blount

TABLA

The **tabla** is a pair of drums used in North India—the wooden cylindrical *daya* or *tabla* (right) and the rounder metal *baya* (left). The centers of several layers of drum heads are cut out in concentric circles to provide different playing surfaces. Leather straps along the slide of the body secure the heads. The drummer tunes the right drum to the tonic pitch by hammering cylinders under the straps to tighten or loosen them and by the careful application of black paste in the middle of the drum head. The left drum is lower but has an indefinite pitch.

Courtesy of Gilbert Blount

MRDANGAM

The **mrdangam** or *mrdang*, a double-headed cylindrical drum held on the lap, is the standard classical drum of South India. The North Indian equivalent, the *pakhavaj*, is used only in old court repertories.

Hear and see the instruments of India in your downloadable **ACTIVE LISTENING TOOLS**, available at the World Music Resource Center.

Many performances include more than one melody instrument. A singer, for example, is often paired with a harmonium (a portable reed organ) or a *sarangi*. In these cases, the singer is the primary soloist, while the instrument plays a secondary melody that complements or imitates the singer's line. Although the harmonium is a keyboard instrument, it generally plays one pitch at a time.

In the North, the emergence of instrumentalists as primary soloists, especially on the *sitar* and the *sarod*, has occurred mostly in the past century or two. Instruments that were primarily associated with vocal accompaniment, such as the *sarangi*, or folk or religious music, such as the *shahnai*, have found champions in the twentieth century who have promoted them as solo instruments in the classical tradition. In South India, all performances are based on composed songs, even those played by instruments alone.

THE DRUMMER

Drumming is an indispensable part of an Indian classical music performance. Although the melodic soloist is clearly the focus of the performance, the drummer is considered the soloist's equal as a musician. The drummer plays solos at times and, because his different strokes sound clearly identifiable pitches, even imitates the soloist's melodic phrases. In North India, the drummer usually plays the **tabla** (a pair of small drums) with palms and fingers. South Indian drummers play the **mrdangam**, a single drum with two heads. (See Instrument Gallery.)

From among a repertory of patterns, the drummer chooses those that fit into the meter and rhythmic scheme of the performance. The drummer's interaction with the soloist also determines the selection of patterns and the variations the drummer plays on them. A good soloist and drummer can be almost telepathic in their ability to improvise together and anticipate each other's music.

THE DRONE

A **drone** is a very long or unchanging note. In Indian music, a string instrument, the **tambura** (**tanpura** in North India), normally plays the drone. The *tambura* player actually strums the strings continuously but so gently that it sounds like a constant drone. The sound of the *tambura* is the familiar softly shifting background in Indian classical music. Because of its characteristic sound, some people mistake it for the more famous and similar-sounding *sitar*, but the *sitar* is a solo instrument with a very different function.

The drone functions as more than a background—it is a point of reference, the musical foundation on which the soloist's intricate melodies stand. The drone consists of two different pitches, usually the tonic pitch and another pitch five scale steps above. In certain ragas, the tonic pitch and the pitch a semitone lower may be used. This more dissonant interval gives the performance an aura of mystery that may be especially appropriate for evening ragas. The *tambura* player is often an apprentice and is not necessarily even acknowledged in the program. The soloist and drummer are the featured musicians. Sometimes singers play the *tambura* as they sing.

In South India, a **sruti box**, a specialized reed organ, sometimes substitutes for the *tambura*. Modern musicians sometimes use an electronic version that continuously emits a tone like a *tambura* or a CD recording of a *tambura*. Such electronic substitutes can be very convenient for the working musician.

CHORDOPHONES IN INDIAN MUSIC

Chordophones—string instruments—have an ancient history in India and play a central role in classical music. Pitch-bending ornamentation, for example, is very important to the music. Thus, the bridges of some chordophones are broad and flat, a shape that enables the player to move a string side to side and change the pitch significantly. This type of bridge also helps create a characteristic slow timbral shift, a sort of "owowo" sound, as the end of the string buzzes along the top of the bridge. Most chordophones use metal strings, in part because the brighter tone helps to create this timbre.

Many chordophones in India also retain a feature called **taraf**, meaning sympathetic strings. A performer can set a string in motion not only by playing it directly but also by exposing it to the sound of the same pitch. Vibrations in the air corresponding to the pitch of the *taraf* string will cause it to vibrate very softly, a phenomenon known as **sympathetic vibration**. Sympathetic strings ring continually in response to the pitches played on the main strings. The player carefully tunes each of the perhaps dozens of sympathetic strings to the pitches of the scale being played, so that the notes of the raga are a constant presence in the music. This vibration sets up a subtle but unmistakable reverberation in the instrument that adds to the constant strumming of the tambura.

RAGA—THE MELODIC DIMENSION OF INDIAN MUSIC

The most important guiding principle for melody in India is the concept known as **raga**. (*Raga* or *ragam* is the Sanskrit form of the word, and *rag* is the Hindi form of the word.) Raga includes the concept of mode as broadly defined in Chapter 2, but it implies much more than the usual Western use of the term. So complex a subject that some Indian musicians despair of ever arriving at a complete and accurate definition, the concept of raga includes at least the following components:

◆ A tuning system, which may vary slightly among ragas that otherwise share the same scale

◆ A scale system, which may be different in ascending and descending forms

◆ A tonic, or starting point, within the scale as well as defined roles for some of the other pitches within the scale

◆ Certain melodic motives that are associated with a particular raga or are especially appropriate

◆ Certain ornamentation practices, although these may also vary according to the instrument playing

◆ Extramusical associations, such as the appropriateness of a particular raga for a particular time of day or for its ability to express certain emotions

Raga is sometimes broadly spoken of as the melodic dimension of Indian classical music, and, it is true that in performances that are entirely improvisational, raga is the ever-present force that guides the melodic instrument. Although the bulk of a performance, often over an hour, is devoted to the metered section with the drum, the core of the feeling of the raga is best encapsulated in the nonpulsatile introduction, the **_alap_**, which we will discuss shortly.

THE TUNING OF RAGAS

The history of ragas and their tuning has created a great deal of controversy among musicians and scholars. It seems that the theory, at least, of raga has developed considerably over time, although many writers have attempted to reconcile current theory with revered ancient sources such as the *Natyasastra*. The *Natyasastra* mentions a tuning system in which each octave is divided into twenty-two *sruti*; in this context, **_sruti_** means microtone, that is, a very small interval. The intervals of each scale were constructed from different numbers of *sruti*. Although some writers have attempted to apply this tuning concept to modern practice, in reality, musicians today use twelve pitches per octave.

The intervals between adjacent pitches are not necessarily the same, and the tuning of these intervals is neither fixed nor standardized, except in the case of the harmonium and string instruments with fixed frets. For other instruments playing twelve pitches per octave, the intervals between the pitches may vary slightly (but significantly) for different players and for different ragas. These differences can give different ragas a noticeably different flavor even when they share the same nominal pitches.

THE SCALES OF RAGAS

A raga most often uses seven out of the twelve possible pitches (**svara**). Some ragas, however, use as few as five pitches or as many as nine, and may use yet more pitches as auxiliary tones. Also, although there is a genre of performance in which ragas are mixed, musicians never modulate between keys in the Western sense.

Just as Western musicians may use solfege syllables—*do, re, mi, fa, sol, la,* and *ti*—to refer to the seven notes of a Western scale, the seven *svara* of Indian scales have names as well: *sa, re* (in the South *ri*), *ga, ma, pa, dha,* and *ni*. **Sa** (*do*) is the tonic or home pitch, although not necessarily the most important pitch. Pitches in different octaves can be indicated by placing a dot under the syllable indicating an octave down or by placing a dot over it for an octave up.

The seventeenth-century theorist Venkatamakhi was the first to create a system to enumerate all the possible seven-note scales that ragas could use, scales known as **melakarta**. Each of the different pitches in the scale, except for the tonic (the first pitch), may be altered by raising or lowering it by one semitone. We use the Western term *semitone* here as a convenience to indicate the interval between any two adjacent notes in the complete twelve-tone per octave tuning system. A lowered tone is called **komal** (the Western flat), and a raised tone is called **tivra** (the Western sharp). When it is necessary to distinguish an unaltered tone (neither *komal* nor *tivra*), it is referred to as **shuddh** (the Western natural). Venkatamakhi showed that there are seventy-two possible *melakarta* scales. The *melakarta* system is used mainly in South India, although only about twenty-four of the possible seventy-two scales are commonly used.

Classification of scale types became important in North India when Indian scholars in the early twentieth century sought to establish a theoretical basis for North Indian classical music. Influenced by the South Indian *melakarta* system, the theorist Vishnu Narayan Bhatkhande sought to classify the possible scale types in Hindustani music. He devised a system of thirty-two possible heptatonic (seven-tone) scales he called **that**. Of these, he found that the overwhelming majority of the hundreds of known ragas could be classified under just ten that (Table 9.1).

Many musicians, however, never fully accepted these scale systems because of the simplifications and ambiguities they present when ragas are classified within them. First, in practice, many ragas have more than or fewer than seven *svara*. A raised version of the scale step may be used in ascent, and a lowered version may be used in descent. To classify the raga, it is necessary to decide which version of that pitch is most characteristic. These classifications have resulted in many seemingly dissimilar ragas being grouped into the same category. To summarize more clearly the pitch material of a raga, musicians rely on a more complex demonstration of the pitches in a melodic context, called **arohana/avarohana**.

AROHANA/AVAROHANA (ASCENDING/DESCENDING SCALE)

Although the *that* and *melakarta* are useful for classifying ragas, they do not describe the musical use of pitches. A pitch in the raga may occur only when the melody is descending. The melody may never descend from a certain pitch

Table 9.1		THE TEN *THAT* OF BHATKANDE						
Kalyan that:	sa	re	ga	ma-tivra	pa	dha	ni	sa
Western equivalents:	C	D	E	F♯	G	A	B	C
Bilaval that:	sa	re	ga	ma	pa	dha	ni	sa
Western equivalents:	C	D	E	F	G	A	B	C
Khamaj that:	sa	re	ga	ma	pa	dha	ni-komal	sa
Western equivalents:	C	D	E	F	G	A	B♭	C
Bhairav that:	sa	re-komal	ga	ma-tivra	pa	dha-komal	ni	sa
Western equivalents:	C	D♭	E	F♯	G	A♭	B	C
Purvi that:	sa	re-komal	ga	ma-tivra	pa	dha-komal	ni	sa
Western equivalents:	C	D♭	E	F♯	G	A♭	B	C
Marva that:	sa	re-komal	ga	ma	pa	dha	ni	sa
Western equivalents:	C	D♭	E	F	G	A	B	C
Kafi that:	sa	re	ga-komal	ma	pa	dha	ni-komal	sa
Western equivalents:	C	D	E♭	F	G	A	B♭	C
Asavri that:	sa	re	ga-komal	ma	pa	dha-komal	ni-komal	sa
Western equivalents:	C	D	E♭	F	G	A♭	B♭	C
Bhairvi that:	sa	re-komal	ga-komal	ma	pa	dha-komal	ni-komal	sa
Western equivalents:	C	D♭	E♭	F	G	A♭	B♭	C
Tori that:	sa	re-komal	ga-komal	ma-tivra	pa	dha-komal	ni	sa
Western equivalents:	C	D♭	E♭	F♯	G	A♭	B	C

without immediately going up again. These factors are integral characteristics of the raga—as important as the scale itself. The construction called the **arohana/avarohana**, the ascending/descending scale, shows the characteristics of the melody line.

For example, Bhatkande classified the raga *Desh* under the *that* (scale) *Khamaj*, even though it typically uses the *ni-komal* (lowered seventh scale step) found in *Khamaj* when descending, but *ni-shuddh* (unaltered *ni*) when ascending. Also, the simple scale by itself fails to demonstrate that *ga* and *dha*, the third and sixth pitches of the scale, are usually omitted in ascent, whereas *sa*, the tonic, is usually approached from *ni-shuddh*. Descending lines in *Desh* typically also have momentary changes of direction in them. The *arohana/avarohana* shows these elements. In Graphic 9.1's version of the *arohana/avarohana* of raga *Desh*, the syllables representing the pitches are arranged approximately proportional to their pitch.

CD 2:3 Raga *Desh* examples: *(that, arohana/avarohana, chalan)*

GRAPHIC 9.1

The *arohana/avarohana* of raga *Desh*. The tonic pitch, *sa*, is in boldface. A dot above or below the pitch name indicates an octave displacement.

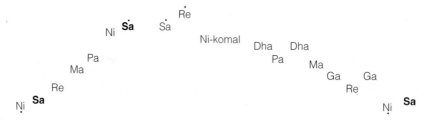

Bhatkande classified the raga *Khamaj* under the same *that*—in fact, he named the *that* scale for this raga. Like raga *Desh*, it uses both forms of pitch *ni*, but its *arohana* and *avarohana* are quite distinct and give the raga *Khamaj* a character very different from the character of *Desh*. In Graphic 9.2, the pitch *re* (second scale degree) is absent in the ascent, but the descending scales can be direct, without the momentary changes of direction of raga *Desh*.

GRAPHIC 9.2

The *arohana/avarohana* for raga *Khamaj*

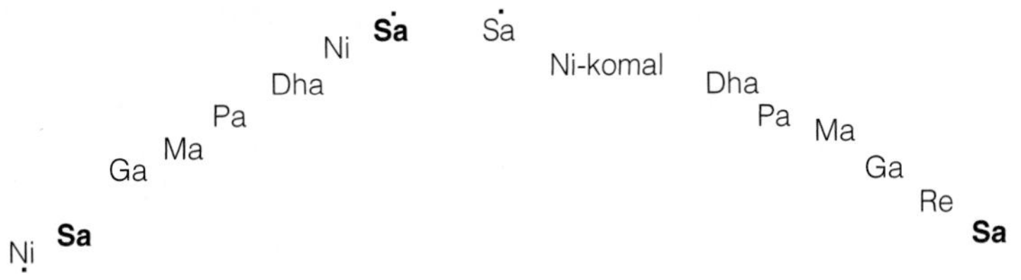

The details of the *arohana/avarohana* may vary from musician to musician, and especially between schools of performers and different instruments. Nevertheless, in the ear of the educated listener, the *arohana/avarohana* creates the unmistakable sound of a particular raga. The **chalan** is a yet more expanded representation of a raga's characteristic rising and falling melody that includes its characteristic motives. A *chalan*, such as that in Graphic 9.3, for raga *Khamaj*, begins to resemble a musical phrase more than a scale and is used as a basis for improvisation.

CD 2:4 Raga *Khamaj* examples (*that*, *arohana/ avarohana*, *chalan*)

GRAPHIC 9.3

The *chalan* for raga *Khamaj*

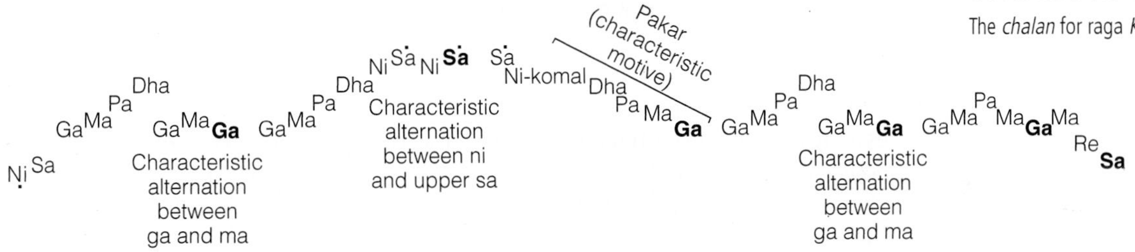

THE HIERARCHY OF PITCHES

In tonal music, the tonic, or home pitch, is often spoken of as being the most important of the pitches, but such a statement may be misleading. It is often the relationships among all of the pitches that are really important, and none could really be dropped. The tonic is best described as the pitch that provides the foundation, the home base, for the melody. Usually, the melody comes to rest on the tonic at the end, although not always.

In addition to the tonic, *sa*, Indian theory also specifies a principal tone (which might, with more justification, be called the most important tone) called the **vadi**, and a secondary principal tone called the **samvadi**. Neither corresponds to the tonic *sa*. Instead, they are pitches on which the musician is likely to dwell in a performance of a raga, and differences between them can give very different sounds to ragas that otherwise share the same basic scale.

The *samvadi* is normally three or four *svara* (scale steps) above the *vadi*. Although not emphasized as much as the *vadi*, the *samvadi* is relatively prominent and is often used as a cadence pitch, that is, the pitch on which the melody comes to rest at the ends of phrases. Given differences in performance practice and interpretation, *vadi* and *samvadi* are not universally agreed upon for all ragas. Indeed, many different scale degrees are emphasized during the course of a performance, and it is sometimes difficult to assign them all to a consistent hierarchy.

GAMAK (ORNAMENTATION)

Another characteristic that helps distinguish one raga from another is the characteristic ornamentation, called **gamak** or **gamaka**. Ornamentation and embellishment may be misleading terms because they imply that these melodic figures are optional and may be played or not according to the player's will. But in Indian classical music, *gamak* are the life of the melodic line. They provide graceful and smooth transitions from one core pitch to another, creating interest in the nuanced character they give to the melody, just as subtle shading and filled-in curves give life to much Indian art.

Certain *gamak* are as indispensable as the notes of the raga scale. Not only do they help give a raga a characteristic sound, but also their absence at specific points would disturb listeners or even suggest another raga. Many *gamak* are idiomatic to a particular instrument, and pitch bends, slides, and occasional wide vibratos are characteristic of most prominent solo instruments in India. The lack of the capability to produce these continuous changes in pitch has relegated to secondary status such instruments as the *santuri* zither and the harmonium.

PAKAR—IMPORTANT MOTIVES IN INDIAN MUSIC

One of the first ways that an experienced listener of Indian classical music recognizes a raga is not through its scale, which many ragas share, nor even through the *arohana/avarohana*, which may not be immediately apparent, but through certain motives (short melodies) called **pakar**, which are uniquely associated with certain ragas. Frequently, the *pakar* is represented in the *chalan*, the concise summary of the melodic material of a raga. A performer often features the *pakar* prominently at the beginning of a **gat** (metered section) and returns to it in many different forms throughout the performance, particularly at the ends of phrases (cadences).

A performance of a raga will, of course, include many motives, but most will be inventions of the performer. Each of these motives is developed in sophisticated ways throughout the piece, especially in the metered section.

EXTRAMUSICAL ASSOCIATIONS

Musicians often quote an old Sanskrit saying: "Raga is that which colors the mind." That is, musicians first think of raga not as a scale, a characteristic melodic contour, or a set of motives, but as the emotional effect that this combination of attributes produces.

Writers as far back as the *Natyasastra* codified a set of specific feelings that art can express—the **rasa**. By tradition, the basic rasa are nine in number: tragic, romantic/joyful, heroic, comic, furious, fearful, odious, surprising, and peaceful. But the nine basic *rasa* are only starting points for the much more complex emotional associations and symbolism of a raga. In addition to expressing more specific emotions than can the general *rasa* categories, a performance of a raga may take the listener on an emotional journey through different *rasas* characteristically associated with the raga. The characteristics became so specific, especially in the North, that schools of painting and poetry arose to symbolically represent various ragas. These paintings, known as **ragamala**, traditionally depict certain scenes that illustrate the mood of a raga and provide insights into its emotional and symbolic associations (see Figure 2.6 in Chapter 2).

One of the best known of a raga's extramusical associations is the time of day that is appropriate to the raga's performance. Even though the practice is not always observed today, now that concerts take place mostly in the evening, and radio broadcasts and recording sessions take place at unalterable times, knowledge of this association is important to truly understanding a raga. Although South Indian ragas no longer are associated with time of day, they still carry specific connotations of mood and tradition.

For example, the name raga *Darbari Kanada* means "of the court of Kanada," and it is one of the most majestic and grand of all ragas. It is a nighttime raga, meant to be performed around midnight. In the *ragamala* painting tradition, the raga *Darbari Kanada* symbolizes strength, heroism, and nobility and is usually portrayed as a victorious king who has killed an elephant.

The North Indian raga *Desh* literally means "of the country," which indicates its origin as a regional or folk raga. Therefore, most musicians do not treat it with the same weightiness as, for example, raga *Darbari Kanada*. Raga *Desh* is a late night raga, and *ragamala* paintings illustrate it as two lovers lying on a bed underneath an awning at night, the woman watching her sleeping mate.

TALA—THE RHYTHMIC DIMENSION OF INDIAN MUSIC

Mantra are textual formulas chanted over and over. Their repetition creates not only a sense of spiritual quietude and goodness but also captures the cyclic nature of time, an important attribute of Hindu cosmology. Whereas other traditions may treat time as an inexorable progression, Hinduism sees existence as bound up in cycles of death and rebirth, not only of individuals but also of days, seasons, and civilizations. The careful periodic breathing of **yoga** (spiritual discipline) also reflects these wheels within wheels, as well as the breathing between the lines of *Vedic* chant, which is otherwise unmeasured.

The meters of classical Sanskrit poetry are also built on repeating patterns, and their rhythmic nature is emphasized by the fact that the words have **quantitative accents**, that is, syllables are accented not through loudness (as in English) but by holding them twice as long as unaccented syllables. Therefore, the elaborate and subtle rhythms of this poetry already give it a very musical sound.

These cycling rhythms eventually came to define the repeating meters of all classical music as the concept of **tala** (*tal* in Hindi). In the same way that the concept of raga governs the melodic dimension of Indian music, so *tala* governs the rhythmic dimension. *Tala* includes the concept of meter discussed in Chapter 3, but it may also imply the way beats lie within this framework.

Tala has a hierarchy of pulses, that is, ways of grouping and subdividing beats. It has a system of subdivisions of beats, beats themselves, groupings of beats (called *vibhag* in the North or *anga* in the South), groupings of groupings of beats (called *avarta* or *avritti*, or, more informally, the *tala* cycle).

The numbers by which beats and groups may be grouped is sometimes considerably complex in the Indian system. In addition to groupings of twos and threes, groupings of fours, fives, and even one-and-a-half occur. Sometimes different sizes of groupings are mixed in asymmetrical patterns. For example, in the North Indian *tala* called *Jhampa*, each *avarta* or large cycle has four *vibhag*, the first and third *vibhag* consisting of two beats each, and the second and fourth consisting of three beats. A shorthand way of writing this meter would be 2 + 3 + 2 + 3. An even more complex meter is the *tala* called *Upatal Jhampak*, which is 2 + 3 + 2 + 1½. In this case, the last *vibhag* contains one-and-a-half beats—unusual, but still possible.

Traditions elsewhere in the world occasionally use complex meters. However, assuming that Indian metrical concepts are the same as those of the West, for example, would cause us to overlook subtle but crucial differences in the ways that musicians in the two cultures think about meter, especially in the ways that drummers and melodic soloists establish and treat patterns of beats.

PATTERNS OF BEATS IN THE *TALA*

In a *tala*, stress is usually placed on the first beat (**sam**) of the cycle. However, this doesn't necessarily mean that any note falling on that beat is automatically louder. Rather than thinking about the *sam* in terms of loudness, it is better to think of it as the rhythmic equivalent of *sa*, the tonal center in the melodic dimension of music. In the same way that the listener expects a return to *sa*, so we anticipate the completion of the *tala* cycle on *sam*. However, just as it is common for the melodic player to withhold *sa* to create tension, the drummer may deemphasize *sam* for the same reason. Its structural importance remains in the performers' minds, and presumably in the minds of the audience, or else this artful play of expectations would have no effect.

On the other hand, the polar opposite to the *sam* beat is the deemphasized beat of the cycle, called **khali**, meaning "empty." It often comes about halfway through the cycle. Normally, low or loud beats are avoided on *khali* beats, but this, too, may be changed for musical effects. Both *sam* and *khali* normally occur at the beginnings of *vibhag*, and, on a higher level, these *vibhag* are also considered emphasized or deemphasized, respectively. The first beats of *vibhag* that are neither *sam* nor *khali* are called **tali**.

When musicians, or often audience members, count along with the *tala*, they use special hand signs. *Sam* and *tali* beats are indicated by a hand clap or a hand beating on the thigh; the word *tala* itself refers to this clapping. *Khali* (empty) beats are indicated by waving the right hand away from the left or by beating the back of the hand on the palm or thigh. The remaining beats are counted off on the fingers by touching fingers to the thumb. In notation now commonly used, X stands for a clap, O for *khali*, and numbers for the beat within the *vibhag*.

The *tala tintal* is the most frequently used *tala* today; more than three-quarters of all performances are in *tintal*. It consists of a cycle containing sixteen beats divided 4 4 4 4. The first beat of the third *vibhag*, beat nine, is *khali*. It would thus be notated like this:

Table 9.1	*TINTAL TALA*		
Vibhag number	*1*	*2*	*3*	*4*
Beat number	1 2 3 4	5 6 7 8	9 10 11 12	13 14 15 16
Notation	*X 2 3 4*	*X 2 3 4*	*O 2 3 4*	*X 2 3 4*
Action	clap (count)	clap (count)	wave (count)	clap (count)

At a further level of detail, musicians assign different characteristic *tabla* strokes to each beat. These strokes are useful as a guide to the different characteristics and importance of each of the individual beats but do not represent the actual part the drummer plays. Each of the different types of strokes is known by syllables called **bols**. The use of mnemonic syllables is common in complex drumming in music around the world—in Africa, Indonesia, Japan, and so on. The four most basic beats are *dha, dhin, ta,* and *tin*; their names are onomatopoeic. *Dha* and *dhin* are played with both drums and are thus lower and more resonant, whereas *ta* and *tin* are played by the smaller drum alone. Different *bols* may represent many other types of strokes. The *bols* assigned to the beats of *tintal tala* are as follows:

Table 9.2	TINTAL TALA															
Vibhag number	1				2				3				4			
Beat number	1	2	3	4	5	6	7	8	9	10	11	12	13	14	15	16
Notation	X	2	3	4	X	2	3	4	O	2	3	4	X	2	3	4
Action	clap (count)				clap (count)				wave (count)				clap (count)			
Bols	dha	dhin	dhin	dha	dha	dhin	dhin	dha	dha	tin	tin	ta	ta	dhin	dhin	dha

A pattern of *bols* is called a **theka** (North) or **sokattu** (South). The *theka* for *tintal* shows that the *tala* is far more than a simple foursquare pattern. The predominance of the higher *bols* that begin with the T sound toward the end of the pattern creates a sense of expectation for the resolution of *sam* that is reflected in the drumming patterns in a performance.

For performances, students memorize complex *theka* patterns, and, just as the melodic soloists create variations on known phrases and motives in a raga improvisation, a drummer improvises variations based on a wide variety of such patterns. Of course, the musical situation, the interaction with the soloist, and the player's personal taste will always guide such improvisations. The Indian musician feels syllables cycling around as though strung together like beads on a necklace.

A PERFORMANCE OF RAGA *KHAMAJ*

In the **alap**, the nonpulsatile section that begins a classical Indian performance, the melodic soloist gradually reveals the characteristics of the raga as if folding back the petals of a flower. A skilled performer, such as Ali Akbar Khan in this recording, creates moments of delight or great drama as he slowly builds this melodic world by withholding, and then artfully exposing, the raga's tones, motives, and ornaments. Thus, the *alap* is the section in which we can hear the characteristics of the raga in their purest form.

Raga *khamaj* is traditionally associated with sensuality and feminine beauty. *Ragamala* paintings depict *khamaj* in different ways, but most include a beautiful woman (Figure 9.3). Romantic songs in light classical genres thus often use this raga, although it can also express deep emotions. It is a late night raga, meant to be performed between about midnight and 3:00 A.M.

Raga *khamaj* uses an unaltered seventh scale step (*ni-shuddh* or simply *ni*) in ascent and lowered seventh step (*ni-komal*) in descent and avoids the second scale step (*re*) in ascent (see Graphic 9.2). The *vadi*, or stressed tone, in *khamaj* is

British Library [nhil 021 0001546, Add.Or.28]

FIGURE 9.3

This *ragamala* painting illustrates raga *Kambhavati*, an earlier form of the raga *Khamaj* that we hear on CD 1:10. It depicts a beautiful woman making an offering of fire to the god Brahma.

ni, the seventh scale step. Because it lies just a semitone below the tonic, it often seems to be striving to resolve to the tonic (*sa*). By stressing this tone, the musician creates a sense of yearning or striving that is part of the mood of *khamaj*. The *samvadi* (secondary stressed tone) is the third scale step (*ga*), which is a semitone below scale step four (*ma*). Characteristic of *khamaj* is the way in which players create mirror-like motives of moving up and back the semitone from *ni* to *sa* and down and back the semitone from *ga* to *ma*. These patterns are prominent in the more extended melodic outline called the *chalan* (see Graphic 9.3).

The *alap* is generally divided into at least two parts, called the **sthai** and the **antara**. In each part, the player gradually explores different parts of the scale, often beginning with the four notes below *sa*, then the notes below that, and then gradually the octave above *sa*, increasing excitement and tension as he does. In a full performance, in which the *alap* could last half an hour, these sections are followed by sections called the **jor** and **jhala**, which are quasi-pulsatile, although still without the accompaniment of the drums.

This performance, like many recordings, is rather abbreviated, with the *alap* lasting less than three minutes. Therefore, there are no *jor* or *jhala* sections, and the unfolding of the raga is somewhat compressed. In addition, the famous *sarod* virtuoso Ali Akbar Khan inverts the usual practice of moving from the lowest part of the scale up and instead exposes the upper octave first, and then the lower. Because the *sarod* has a metal fingerboard and no frets, its great strength as a solo instrument is that it allows continuous slides between pitches. Instead of separately plucking many of the pitches, the player deftly slides his fingernail to them after the initial pluck, sometimes stopping at several notes after a single pluck.

Because we do not have room here for the entire twenty-one-minute performance, we include two excerpts, the first from the *alap* and the beginning of the *gat* or metered section, and the second from the very end of the piece.

VOCAL MUSIC IN INDIA

Because of the legacy in the United States and Europe of legendary performers such as Ravi Shankar and Ali Akbar Khan, it is easy to form the impression that most Indian music is instrumental. However, the voice is traditionally the most important instrument in India because it is the only instrument that can convey text. Writers from the *Natyasastra* to the present day have traced this primacy of song back to the *Vedic* hymns, which they consider to be the source of many fundamental concepts of Indian music, including the cyclic philosophy now reflected in the concept of *tala*, the concept of melodic types now codified as raga, ornamentation practices (*gamak*), and the idea that music for any purpose is fundamentally devotional and spiritual in nature.

Because most vocal forms rely on a preexisting text, the structure of improvisation in vocal performances has to be carefully controlled. The singer can elaborate on phrases of an existing song, extending notes, interpolating tones, and adding ornamentation according to the rules of the raga. At other times, the singer may improvise without the restriction of having to set a text. Just as

CD 2:1 & 2:2. Raga _Khamaj. Sarod_, Ali Akbar Khan; _tabla_, Pandit Mahapurush Misra.

Alap: sthai section.

The _tambura_ softly strums scale tones one and five (_sa_ and _pa_), the most common drone pitches, but also adds the third scale step (_ga_), the _samvadi_ in this raga.

Sarod plays drone strings (_chikari_) throughout the performance, especially in between major melodic phrases.

0:10

The _sarod_ quickly ascends to the high tonic (_sa_) and then alternates, with elaboration, between _sa_ and _ni_, the semitone just below—an alternation characteristic of raga _Khamaj_. The alternation introduces us to the _vadi_, _ni_, and its role as a stressed note in this raga.

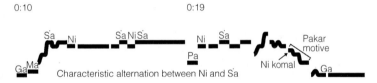

0:22

The _sarod_ descends the scale to _ga_, the _samvadi_. Listen for the lower scale tone seven (_ni-komal_) used in the descending scale. This descent with _ni-komal_, often with a slide, becomes a central motive, or _pakar_, for this performance.

0:35

With the melody settled on _ga_, the _sarod_ elaborates on a characteristic oscillation between the third and fourth scale steps, _ga_ and _ma_. The phrase ends on the lower tonic (_sa_), completing the exposition of the entire octave below our starting point.

0:47

The first half of the *alap* (the *sthai*) ends with a statement of the entire ascending scale. Note that the second scale step, *re,* is missing in the ascending scale of raga *Khamaj.* The melody comes down again with the *pakar* motive and cadences on the *samvadi, ga.*

Alap: antara section.

0:55

The *pakar* motive again, but this time in the lower octave. *Sarod* explores and re-traces some of the important *Khamaj* motives but now in a lower octave and with increasing motion and diversity. Once again, *sarod* emphasizes the alternation between *ni* and *sa,* at times dramatically lingering on *ni* to create a sense of yearning for resolution to the tonic, *sa.*

1:32

Another statement of the *pakar* brings us down to the bottom of the scale and another exploration of the *ga-ma* semitone.

2:36

One more statement of the *pakar* precedes our ascent back to the central tonic and a short ending section emphasizing *ni-sa* and a final cadence on upper *ga,* the *samvadi* again.

Gat (metered section).

2:56

After a short roll on the *tabla, Sarod* and *tabla* both land on the first beat, *sam.* This *tala* is *chachar,* a metrical pattern of 3 4 3 4, for a total of fourteen beats per cycle. The eighth beat (the beginning of the second half) is *khali* or the unstressed beat. *Sarod* expresses these two halves of the cycle by landing on the fifth scale step (*pa*) at the beginning and the third scale step (*ga, the samvadi*) at the halfway point, often anticipating or delaying their appearance. These phrases are variations of the theme (*gat*) of the first part of the metered section.

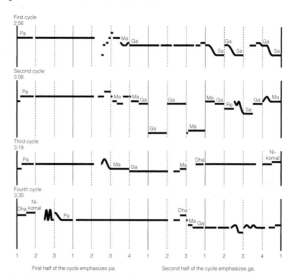

Saval-Javab (question-answer) section CD 2:2.

`0:00`

The tempo has become much faster; typically, instrumental performances get gradually faster. For the second half of the metered section, the *tala* has changed to *tintal*, a sixteen-beat pattern of 4 + 4 + 4 + 4.

The melodic soloist improvises a phrase, and the drummer spontaneously imitates the phrase's rhythm and melodic contour. It is an exciting game of question-answer that increases in tension as the phrases become more complex and then more compressed.

Jhala section.

`2:03`

The *sarod* launches the climactic final section.

Fast repeating notes alternate between melody tones and strokes on the *chikari* (drone) strings—a technique called *jhala*. This technique allows a speed suitable to the finale and emphasizes rhythm.

`3:17`

As the tempo speeds up yet again, *sarod* uses the *jhala* technique of *thok jhala*. *Thok* literally means "hit," and refers to the fact that three successive down plucks ("hits") on the melody string follow a stroke on the *chikari* drone string. Other variations follow as the strokes become faster and more virtuosic. The *sarod* recapitulates several important melodies, including the *gat* theme from the beginning of the metered section and the *pakar* motive.

`5:30`

By unspoken agreement, Khan on *sarod* and Misra on *tabla* arrive at the very last *tala* cycle with a dramatic unison rhythm, without *jhala*, that recapitulates the important alternation between the seventh scale step (*ni*) and the high tonic (*sa*) that began the performance.

| **Listening Exercise 6** | **CD 2:1 & 2.2. Raga _Khamaj_** |

1. At 1:57 in the first excerpt, the soloist plays
   a. the descending *pakar* motive.
   b. the back-and-forth *ga* to *ma* semitone.
   c. a slide down to *sa* (the tonic).

2. At 4:17 in the first excerpt, the soloist plays
   a. the descending *pakar* motive.
   b. the back-and-forth *ga* to *ma semitone*.
   c. a slide down to *sa* (the tonic).

3. At the beginning of the second excerpt, the *sarod* and the *tabla* trade solos every
   a. three beats.
   b. four beats.
   c. six beats.
   d. eight beats.

4. The rhythms of the performers at 5:04 in the second excerpt
   a. are suddenly nonpulsatile.
   b. temporarily overlay a polyrhythm on the *tala* cycle.
   c. switch to half tempo.

You can take this Listening Exercise online and receive feedback or e-mail answers to your instructor at the World Music Resource Center.

jazz vocalists improvise using so-called scat syllables, Indian singers may sing neutral syllables such as *ah*, solfege syllables (*sa, re, ga, ma, pa, dha,* and *ni*), or the rhythmic patterns of syllables used by the drummer (*theka*).

NORTH INDIAN VOCAL MUSIC

From the time of the Vedas through the Middle Ages, the primary source for song texts was devotional religious poetry, first in Sanskrit and later in regional languages. As patronage in North India shifted to the Islamic courts, the song texts sometimes, although not always, shifted from praise of gods to praise of kings and sultans and romantic subjects.

Despite this general rule, one important type of religious song emerged from the **Qawal**, wandering Sufi mystics who sang devotional Islamic songs known as **qawwali**. Today, the *Qawal* are generally professional musicians who give concerts that are still primarily devotional and religious. Before his death in 1997, Nusrat Fateh Ali Khan did much to popularize this art form in the West (Figure 9.4). *Qawwali* share some Indian concepts of raga and *tala*, but they also show characteristics of Middle Eastern vocal music such as florid melismas. A *qawwali* ensemble may include one or more harmoniums,

© Kapoor Baldev/Sygma/CORBIS

FIGURE 9.4

Nusrat Fateh Ali Khan (left) performing *qawwali*. Among the instruments accompanying him are two harmoniums in the foreground.

a **dholak** (small hand-held drum), and instruments such as the *bansuri*, *tabla*, and *tambura*.

From at least the fifteenth century until their decline in the early twentieth century, the Hindustani courts provided the primary patronage for classical music in the North. With the support of a ruler, a musician could devote himself to music full time, and apprentices could learn their craft over years without having to worry about earning a living. Recitals were intimate and only for the educated elite. In this context, composers could develop long and sophisticated musical forms without having to worry about appealing to large audiences or arranging concert schedules.

The primary musical form associated with this period is the grand but austere vocal form called **dhrupad**. The majestic *dhrupad* is the musical equivalent of that other famous icon of the Mughal period—the monument known as the Taj Mahal. A performance of *dhrupad* is a vocal tour de force that can last up to three hours and include accompaniment by the *bin*, *tampura*, and the **pakhavaj**, the ancient double-headed drum (instead of the modern *tabla*). Although rarely performed today, the *dhrupad* was an important influence on many subsequent forms, including instrumental performances.

The *dhrupad* begins with an unmeasured *alap* sung on neutral syllables derived from mantra chants, moving into a quasi-pulsatile section called the *jor*. When the drummer enters, the audience hears the precomposed song that is the basis for the performance, followed by elaborate improvisations on sections of the song. Although the song may be either devotional or secular, it is always serious and profound. In keeping with the reverence and austerity of the form, the performance is only lightly ornamented, and self-indulgent displays of virtuosity are definitely out of place.

Today, the **khyal** is the most prominent vocal genre in Hindustani concerts. Some writers credit the invention of the *khyal* to the influence of the florid and melismatic *qawwali* on *dhrupad* singers of the Mughal courts. Highly ornamented in comparison to the relatively unadorned lines of the *dhrupad*, *khyal* creates elegant and ornate lines suited to the lighter and often romantic texts. Men most often sing *khyal*, accompanied by the *tabla* and *tampura*, or sometimes with an added melodic instrument such as the *sarangi* or harmonium. Unlike Hindustani instrumental performances, in *khyal* performances, the tempo does not gradually increase, but the *tala* cycle may be suddenly halved at some point, in effect doubling the tempo. Adding to the excitement toward the end of the performance are fast scalar runs, called **tans**, or sometimes fast sections derived from a related form known as **tarana**.

Thumri is the most important light classical Hindustani vocal genre; these are lyrical songs of love or lost romance. Unlike the virtuosic *khyal*, the focus is not on the virtuosity of the singer but on the poignancy of the text. Thus, the raga and *tala* are usually relatively simple, and *thumri* are especially popular as short closing pieces for concerts.

SOUTH INDIAN VOCAL MUSIC

Kriti are the most popular of the major vocal forms of South Indian performances. Although their length can be variable, they are often, like the Hindustani *khyal*, the long centerpiece of a concert. Both men and women may sing *kriti*, most often accompanied by a single melody instrument, usually a violin, in addition to the *tambura* and *mrdangam* (drum). The form of the song on which a *kriti* is based is similar to the verse/refrain form of many Western songs; the refrain is called the ***pallavi***, and the verse is called the ***caranam***. A contrasting section known as the ***anupallavi*** is also common. The singer may repeat each section several times, with different elaborations and ornamentation.

Improvisational sections may follow the song or may be inserted between each *pallavi-caranam* or *pallavi-anupallavi* pair. In addition to free elaborations on preceding phrases of the song, there are a number of standard improvisation types, including *svara kalpana*, improvisation using solfege syllables, and *niraval*, improvisation that retains the text of the *kriti*. An opportunity for the drummer to take a solo usually arises.

The ***ragam-tanam-pallavi*** is a long and virtuosic form associated with court patronage, much like the northern *dhrupad*. Rather than featuring elaborations on fixed devotional song, the *ragam-tanam-pallavi* is nearly entirely free improvisation with very little text. The *ragam* of the title refers to the first part of the performance, consisting of an *alapana* section performed by the singer and the violinist (or other instrumentalist) in turn. The quasi-pulsatile *tanam* section follows the *ragam*, then metered improvisations on the *pallavi*, or fixed text.

Relatively fixed songs are popular everywhere in Indian musical culture. ***Bhajan***, for example, are well-known popular devotional songs that frequently close a South Indian concert. ***Tillana***, a form used to accompany dance, consists entirely of *bols* (drum syllables); the Hindustani equivalent is *tarana*. ***Kirtana*** are songs that include improvisation and form an intermediate step for the student singer between nonimprovised forms and long virtuoso forms such as *kriti*. *Kirtana* are nevertheless popular concert works, although generally shorter and less elaborate than *kriti*.

PERFORMANCE OF THE *KRITI* "NINNADA NELA"

Tyagaraja (1767–1847) is probably South India's most famous composer. To the people of this region, he represents much more than a composer of songs or a great poet in the Telugu language, although he was both of these. He is remembered as a holy person for whom music was a means of devotion and spiritual enlightenment. Tyagaraja was a devotee of the god Rama, whom his lyrics address in a startlingly personal and emotional tone, often expressing the disappointments and failures of the composer's own life—as they do in our audio selection.

The form Tyagaraja chose for most of his compositions was the *kriti*. The performer on our recording sings the melody of the *kriti* substantially as Tyagaraja composed it (as far as we know) but with extensive ornamental variations and extemporaneous repeats. The *kriti* itself may be introduced with an unmetered *alapana* and followed by more improvisatory sections, but this performance consists of only the *kriti* proper—the *pallavi, anupallavi,* and *caranam*. The singer's variations of the melody are extremely ornate and recall the elaborations of some traditions of *Sama-veda* chant. Such fluid lines are characteristic of much South Indian vocal music, especially when compared to similar forms in the North. Given this ornamentation, it is surprising that most of the time, the violinist follows the singer very closely, but the violinist is as familiar with the composition as the singer and listens very closely so he can anticipate the singer.

CD 2:5. *"Ninnada Nela"* ("Why Should I Blame You?"),[1] Tyagaraja. Singer, Ramnad Krishnan; violin, V. Thyagarajan; *mrdangam*, T. Ranganathan; *kanjira*, V. Nagarajan.

Pallavi **section.**

| 0:00 | *Tambura* drone enters (some preliminary tuning). |

| 0:15 | *Pallavi* begins. The first phrase of the *pallavi*, on the words *"Ninnada nela"* ("Why should I blame you?"), lasts one cycle of *adi tala*, which has a form of 4 + 2 + 2. However, the sung phrase begins and ends somewhat before *sam* (the first beat of the cycle). |

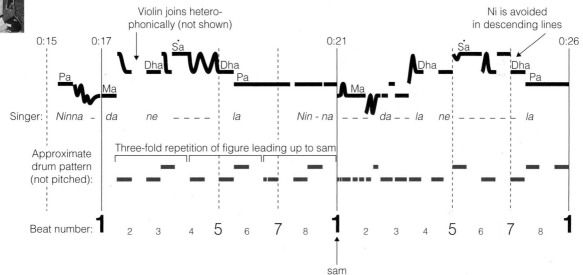

Ornate vocal variations on the melody, with violinist following closely. Florid exploration of the tetrachord (four notes) below *sa* (the tonic).

Try to match the actual vocal performance with the graphic representation of the ascending and descending scale (Graphic 9.4). The singer sings this phrase six times in different variations, increasing the range toward the end.

| 0:46 | The next phrase of the *pallavi nirajaksha Sri Rama* ("Lord Rama") makes it clear that the poet is addressing the god Rama in a personal, nearly blasphemous tone that leads the listener to wonder, "Why does the singer blame the benevolent god Rama?" |

[1]Translation adapted from C. Ramanujachari, *The Spiritual Heritage of Tyagaraja* (Madras: The Ramakrishna Mission Students' Home, 1957); 261. 1:54

1:06	A sudden emptying of the texture through an unspoken coordination among the singer, violinist, and drummer leads to a short ending section that wraps up the *pallavi*.
	The drummer twice interpolates a new threefold repeat that finally lands on the first beat of the next section, the *anupallavi*.

Anupallavi section.

1:17	The vocalist's next phrase, *kannavari paini kaka seya nela?* ("Is it fair for a child to be angry with his parents?"), offers, if not a justification, a way to consider this most human reaction to despair.
	The *anupallavi's* long notes centering around *sa* (the tonic) provide dramatic contrast to the florid character of the *pallavi*.
	The vocalist repeats the first half of the *anupallavi* a total of seven times, each with more elaborate deviations from *sa* and opening up the register above *sa*.
1:54	The vocalist begins the *anupallavi's* second half—the dramatic centerpiece of the *kriti*—with a melody that now extends in striking sweeps.
	A *kanjira* (a kind of tambourine) joins the ensemble, doubles the *mrdangam* (drum) part.

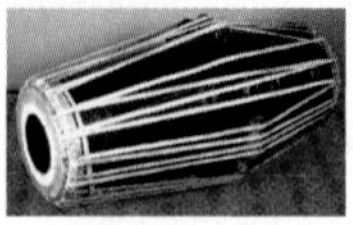

Tyagaraja wrote a total of three *caranam* sections, the balance of which would normally follow the last refrain on our recording, but this is an abbreviated performance. Singers may perform several such short *kriti* before a concert's centerpiece of a full performance with *alapana* and improvisation. Tyagaraja composed "*Ninnada Nela*" in raga *Kannada*. The *arohana/avarohana* shows how in this raga, pitch *ri* (the second scale degree) is avoided in ascent and *ni* (seventh scale degree) is avoided in descent. There is also a characteristic turn around pitch *ma* (fourth scale degree) in both ascent and descent.

GRAPHIC 9.4

Arohana/avarohana of raga Kannada

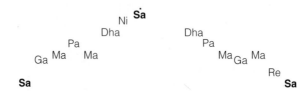

Pallavi refrain.

`2:04`

The *pallavi* returns as a refrain to round out the first large section of the *kriti*.

Caranam section.

`2:25`

The poetry of this section answers the questions previously posed: *Sattva rupa ninnu sannuti jesi tattvamu telisina tyagarajuniki* ("Tyagaraja [the composer] has learned the secret of success in spiritual fulfillment comes only at a cost"). He resigns himself to the uselessness of anger in the face of *dharma* (fate) and accepts the spiritual truth that comes through devotion.

The *mrdangam* takes a more active part that culminates in . . .

Tense series of high subdivisions of the beat during the ending part of this line.

`2:55`

The second line of the *caranam*, now joined by the *kanjira*.

Pallavi refrain.

`3:30`

The violinist joins the singer once again for the final coda.

Three powerful strokes on the *mrdangam* and *kanjira* end the performance.

Hear and see the traditional instruments of *"Ninnada Nela"* in your downloadable **ACTIVE LISTENING TOOLS**, available at the World Music Resource Center.

FOLK SONG IN INDIA

Despite the prominence of its large cities, the vast majority of India's population lives in rural villages. The ethnic diversity of the subcontinent is reflected in the many different styles and instruments of folk music. Some versions of the instruments have found their way into the classical tradition, although, as exemplified by the *sarangi* fiddle and the *shahnai* double reed, they are now built in much more finely crafted and standardized forms.

Although prerecorded cassettes and movies have replaced some of the traditional roles of folk music, traditional performances are still common, especially for festivals, weddings, and performances for tourists, where you can still find the so-called snake charmer. Folk traditions are especially well known in the northwestern state of Rajasthan, where a special caste of Muslim folk musicians known as *Langa* play for festivals and celebrations and in restaurants. Among the many folk ensembles in the south is the **cinna melm** instrumental ensemble of

Listening Exercise 7 | **CD 2:5 "Ninnada Nela"**

1. The final cadence of the *pallavi* section at 1:12 is on what pitch?
   a. Both the violinist and vocalist cadence on *sa* (tonic).
   b. The vocalist cadences on *sa*, but the violinist cadences on the *vadi* pitch (five steps up).
   c. Both the violinist and the vocalist delay resolution at the cadence by singing the pitch above *sa*.

2. The repetition of the *pallavi* section at 2:04 now includes the *kanjira* (tambourine).
   a. True
   b. False

3. How many times does the singer repeat the phrase of the second half of the *anupallavi* section (1:54 to 2:04)?
   a. The phrase is sung once.
   b. The phrase is sung twice.
   c. The phrase is sung four times.

4. How many *tala* cycles are there in the *caranam* section (2:25 to 2:55)? Remember that each cycle of *adi tala* has 4 + 2 + 2 beats.
   a. Four cycles
   b. Six cycles
   c. Eight cycles

 You can take this Listening Exercise online and receive feedback or e-mail answers to your instructor at the World Music Resource Center.

FIGURE 9.5

A Baul singer (center) in Kenduli, India, accompanies himself with a *khamak*, a drum with a string attached to the head. The musician on the left plays a *khol*, a double-headed drum with a clay body; the musician on the right plays a *dotara* lute.

© Chris Lisle/CORBIS

the Kerala state, who accompany certain ritual dances with the powerful sound of massed barrel-shaped drums, double reeds or flutes, and drones. One of the most famous folk traditions, however, comes from the culture of the Bauls of Bengal.

BAUL MUSIC

One very distinctive folk tradition is the music of the Bauls, a minority religious sect in Bengal, a state in Eastern India, and Bangladesh. The Bauls are a distinct cultural group whose unique blend of mystical Hinduism and Islam emphasizes simplicity and social equality; they often come from the poorest segments of society. Although their songs are not usually explicitly religious, their texts usually consist of religious or moral allegories, the meanings of which are often obscure.

On the streets of Bengal, in celebrations and festivals, the Baul singer is often a one-person band who plays, for example, a drone chordophone in one hand and a small drum in the other and jingles ankle bells to movements of a dance, all while singing. A distinctive instrument of the tradition is the string-drum known as the **khamak**. A drum membrane resonates a long string that can generate swooping sounds as the player varies the string tension by squeezing two flexible pieces of wood forming the neck to which the string is attached. In professional concerts or radio broadcasts, other musicians may join in the accompaniment, playing flutes, plucked lutes, or other drums, but the focus is still on the singer (Figure 9.5).

The singing style is full, expressive, and open-throated. Recognizing its surprising similarities to American blues singing, the Paul Butterfield Blues Band presented a Baul ensemble as an intermission feature during their 1969 tour. Charles Capwell, whose book *The Music of the Bauls of Bengal* is the best study of this music, relates an interesting anecdote about this relationship.

> By chance, Laksman [a famous Baul singer] once heard a recording of Janis Joplin when he was visiting an American friend at her hotel in Calcutta. Listening with surprising intentness, he occasionally murmured a word of approval. After the song was over, he inquired about the meaning of the text, and when he learned that the text concerned a woman's desire that her lover [actually God] buy her a Mercedes-Benz automobile, he asked, slightly puzzled, if there were not mention of yoga or some other spiritual-physical discipline; he was incredulous to think that such emotional energy as Joplin put into her performance could be expended on such a trivial matter as the desire for a car.[2]

FILMI POPULAR MUSIC

One of the most common sights accompanying a drive through any of India's busy urban centers is certainly the profusion of colorful movie posters. As important as classical art music is to the culture of India, a person's everyday experience of music is most likely to originate not from raga improvisations nor even Western pop music, but from songs originating in popular films, music known as *filmi*. India today produces more than 1,000 commercial films every year, more than any other country. The historical center of this industry is the city of Mumbai, formerly known as Bombay, which has therefore earned the nickname "Bollywood." Unlike movies from elsewhere in the world, however, nearly all Bollywood films include at least five songs performed on screen as in a musical. These songs are so popular that, in many cases, the films serve merely as vehicles for the music, which is as likely to be heard over shop and car radios as in the movie theater.

Since India's first sound picture in 1931, music has been an integral part of this ubiquitous entertainment. The orchestra and singing is recorded before filming. During the actual production, the recorded music is played back on the set so that the actors can sing along and, in some cases, play along, if there are any instrumentalists on screen, although no sound is recorded on the set. This process allows the music to be recorded in a studio but appear synchronized when later combined. This process also allows the singer to be a different person than the actor who appears on screen, so that the studios could hire the most popular singers, even though they may not be actors themselves.

These singers are known as "playback artists" because their recordings are played back on the set for synchronization, and they have often achieved fame quite independent of the actors who lip-sync their songs. Two of the most famous of India's playback artists are the sisters Lata Mangeshkar and

[2]Charles Capwell, *The Music of the Bauls of Bengal* (Kent, OH: Kent State University Press, 1986); 48–49.

SAJJAD HUSSAIN/AFP/Getty Images

FIGURE 9.6

Over six decades, the enduringly popular Asha Bhosle has been a playback singer for nearly one thousand Bollywood films.

Asha Bhosle (Figure 9.6), each of whom has recorded literally thousands of songs. The era of about 1950–1980 is sometimes spoken of as the "golden age" of Indian film music, although *filmi* remains popular today, and these songs can be heard not only on the streets of South Asia but also in the Middle East and elsewhere in Asia.

The style of the music itself may vary widely, depending on the nature of the film. Disco, jazz, rock, hip-hop, and techno sounds are found just as frequently as more traditional style melodies, although certain characteristics are distinctive to most *filmi*. First, the prominent vocal part has a somewhat reedy timbre in comparison to that of American singers and is often recorded with a generous amount of electronic reverberation. The vocal lines will also feature much more melisma and ornamentation (*gamaka*) than in the West, even in styles directly derived from American genres. The orchestra accompanying film songs will sometimes include a mixture of Western instruments—such as instruments of the violin family, vibraphones, harps, guitars, and drum sets—and traditional Indian instruments—such as *tabla*, *sitar*, or *sarangi*.

In contrast to classical art music performances, multiple *sitars* or *tablas* may accompany songs, playing fixed melodies rather than improvisations. Even the most traditional-sounding film songs usually include Western harmonies. As a result, the use of classical ragas as a basis of composition is sometimes limited or somewhat flexible because ragas are fundamentally melodic constructs not necessarily compatible with Western harmonies.

PERFORMANCE OF "*DIL CHEEZ KYA HAI*"

The 1981 film *Umrao Jaan* tells the story of a girl who is kidnapped and sold to become a courtesan in the nineteenth-century city of Lucknow. The girl, now named Umrao Jaan, grows up to become a famous poet, singer, and dancer but is tragically unable to find love or escape her fate. The composer of the film songs was the well-known Mohammed Zahur "Khayyam" Hashmi, and the playback artist was Asha Bhosle, one of the most famous playback singers of all time. The song *"Dil Cheez Kya Hai"* ("What Is a Heart?") occurs toward the beginning of the film when Umrao Jaan entertains a nobleman. Nineteenth-century Lucknow was the center of *thumri*, the vocal form sung by women entertainers and accompanied by *sarangi* and *tabla*. Khayyam intended for this song to evoke the old *thumri* form, although it uses the Western harmonies, string instruments of the violin family, and refrains typical of *filmi* songs. In the film, the actress Rekha sings and performs a dance that similarly evokes classical *kathakali* style with an entrancing smile, although the lyrics (by Shahryar) reflect the courtesan poet's inner sadness and yearning for love.

CD 2:6. *"Dil Cheez Kya Hai"* ("What Is a Heart?"), Khayyam. Singer, Asha Bhosle.

Alap section.

0:00

Like a classical *thumri* song, this one begins with a nonpulsatile introduction, or *alap*, introduced by the standard melodic accompanist to *thumri* songs, the *sarangi*. However, rather than just drone pitches from traditional instruments, the background is mainly formed by instruments of the violin family and a vibraphone (an American metallophone) playing a Western triad (a conventional European harmony—see Chapter 14).

0:13

As in a traditional *alap*, Bhosle sings her elaborately ornamented line on the neutral syllable "ah," and the sarangi fills in short imitations between her phrases. The melody suggests the raga *Bihag*, although not as strictly as in a classical performance. This raga uses a scale here rendered as a Western major scale but with a *ma tivra* (raised fourth degree) in descent, which we do not hear yet.

0:24

Bhosle introduces a free, still nonpulsatile version of the refrain melody with the lyrics:

Dil cheez kya hai aap meri jaan lijiye.	What is a heart? Take my life.
Bas ek baar mera kaha...	But just once, listen ...

(Each line is sung twice.) With this, the character (Umrao Jaan) says to her lover that if he will just once give her what she asks, he will have her heart and her very life.

First refrain.

1:02

As the previous line ends, a *tabla* and *kanjira* (tambourine) enter, establishing the beat in *tintal tala* (sixteen-beat cycle). The Western instruments now accompany the singer, playing a sequence of three different triads (chords), which divide up the *tala* cycle into 4 + 4 + 8 beats. The lyrics continue:

maan lijiye,	listen to what I say,
Bas ek baar mera kaha maan lijiye.	But just once, listen to what I say.
Dil cheez kya hai aap meri jaan lijiye.	What is a heart? Take my life.

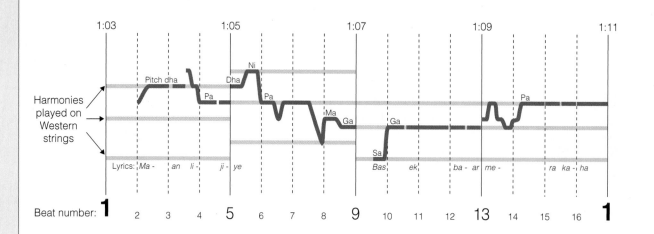

Harmonies played on Western strings

Lyrics: *Ma -* | *an li -* | *ji -* | *ye* | | | | *Bas* | *ek* | | *ba - ar me -* | | *ra ka - ha*

Pitch dha · Dha · Ni · Pa · Pa · Ma · Ga · Sa · Ga · Pa

Beat number: **1** 2 3 4 **5** 6 7 8 **9** 10 11 12 **13** 14 15 16 **1**

Time markers: 1:03 · 1:05 · 1:07 · 1:09 · 1:11

1:23

Sitars and other Indian instruments now play an interlude in unison and octaves without harmony. The syncopated rhythms correspond to choreographic movements in the film.

1:33

The *sarangi* and Western string instruments answer in a contrasting phrase of the interlude, followed by the *sitars* again.

First verse.

1:56

This first verse is again accompanied by Western harmonies.

2:06

In a bridge between repetitions of the first lines of the verse, Bhosle inserts a melisma that dips down for the first time to *ma-tivra* (raised fourth scale degree) characteristic of raga *Bihag*. She then completes the verse:

Is anjuman mein aap ko	In this place
aana hai baar baar	where you come time and again
Deevaar-o-dar ko gaur se,	contemplate the walls and doors,

Umrao Jaan may be telling her lover to remember carefully the place where they meet, but she may also be reminding him in a symbolic way of his familiarity with her own body (this place).

Second refrain.

2:41

The last line leads into a repetition of the refrain:

pehchaan lijiye,	Take this recognition,
Deevaar-o-dar ko gaur se.	contemplate the walls and doors.
Dil cheez kya hai aap meri jaan lijiye.	What is a heart? Take my life.

2:59

Another interlude section featuring Indian instruments, as at 1:23, but now with a new melody played by the *sitars* alternating with a solo on the *sarangi*.

Second verse.

3:22

The second verse follows the format of the first (1:56) but with variations on the melody. The character sings:

Maana ke doston ko nahin	I know that friends don't
dosti ka paas,	supervise each other,
Lekin yeh kya ke gair ka...	But is it so that from a stranger ...

Third refrain.

`3:56`

The refrain melody completes the thought:

ehsaan lijiye?	You would take favors?

`0:51`

Lekin yeh kya ke gair ka	Is it so that from a stranger
ehsaan lijiye?	You would take favors?
Dil cheez kya hai aap meri jaan lijiye.	What is a heart? Take my life.

Now the sad situation narrated by Umrao Jaan seems clearer. She suggests that her lover has betrayed her trust and sought comfort from a stranger.

`4:14`

The next transition section is in the form of a *tabla* solo, followed by a melody on the *sarangi* (with violins), and finally a new unison *sitar* melody.

After the end of our excerpt, the final verse is a variation at a higher pitch, as if the character's emotions are breaking through:

Kahiye to aasmaan ko,	If you say so,
zameen par utaar laaye.	I will bring the sky to the ground.
Mushkil nahin hai kuch bhi agar,	Nothing is difficult,

Followed by the last refrain and an ending section:

thaan lijiye.	If you persevere.
Mushkil nahin hai kuch bhi agar,	Nothing is difficult,
thaan lijiye.	If you persevere.
Dil cheez kya hai aap meri jaan lijiye.	What is a heart? Take my life.
Bas ek baar, bas ek baar	Just one time, just one time
Bas ek baar mera kaha maan lijiye.	Just one time, listen to what I say.
Maan lijiye, maan lijiye.	Listen to what I say.

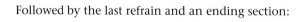

In 1967, at the height of the counterculture movement, the Indian sitarist Ravi Shankar (see Instrument Gallery) electrified the audience at the Monterey Pop Festival with his performance of the afternoon raga *Bhimpalasi*, introducing Indian classical music to Western popular audiences. In many ways, Shankar's unique career made him the ideal musical emissary. The son of a Bengali Brahmin (high-caste) family, Shankar was educated in both India and Europe and spent his teenage years participating in an innovative dance troupe organized by his older brother Uday. Uday's new choreography and music fused European and Indian influences, but Shankar was drawn to the resurgence of Indian nationalism, then at the height of its resistance to British colonial rule.

At age eighteen, he apprenticed himself to the famous Alauddin Khan, whose eclectic musical background included study within the *gharana* of Tansen, the famous Mughal-period composer. During Shankar's seven years of intensive study, he befriended a fellow student, Alauddin Khan's son, Ali Akbar Khan (see Instrument Gallery), who specialized in the *sarod*. While retaining great respect for and command of the classical traditions, Shankar also composed film scores using combinations of Western and Indian instruments. He toured Europe and America extensively in the 1950s, and by the 1960s, his recordings brought him to the attention of jazz musicians and, most famously, George Harrison of the Beatles.

Certainly many Western writers had expressed respect for and interest in Indian classical music through the colonial period and saw in it correspondences to the European classical tradition. Both are sophisticated traditions performed by professionals dedicated to the subtleties of emotional expression. At the same time, the two seemed very far apart. Indian music is largely improvised and was not deemed compatible with Western harmonic progressions and modulations.

Those limitations were less of an issue with Harrison, whose "Within You Without You" used a *sitar*, melismas, and slow changes in harmony to imitate surface elements of an Indian performance. Although the Beatles were later disillusioned with their study with a spiritual guru on a trip to India, Harrison befriended Shankar, who gave him some lessons on the *sitar*. The Monterey Pop Festival and other large concerts followed. Although Shankar respected Harrison and other Western musicians he met, he was ambivalent about some of the concert venues, believing that many of the young people in these audiences did not properly respect the music or its spiritual basis.

The melodic and improvisational basis of Indian classical music was an inspiration rather than a limitation for many jazz musicians, especially with the popularity of so-called modal jazz in the 1960s. In these works, performers such as John Coltrane and Miles Davis, like Indian musicians, focused mainly on the resources of the scale as a basis for improvisation, rather than the usual harmonic progression. Davis's guitarist John McLaughlin studied Indian music, and some Indian-influenced pieces appeared on Davis's album *Big Fun* from 1969. McLaughlin went on to produce a number of solo albums with Indian collaborators, and formed the group Shakti in the 1970s with South Indian violinist L. Shankar and percussionists Zakir Hussain and T. H. Vinayakram. Other groups who adopted Indian influences in the 1970s included the Paul

FIGURE 9.7

Terry Riley in performance at Intermedia '68. Riley used tape loops to create drones and ostinati over which he improvised raga-like melodies on this soprano saxophone.

Winter Consort and Oregon, a jazz ensemble devoted to Indian fusion.

Indian music's deep meditations on the worlds within the sounds of the raga also impressed some musicians of the classical avant-garde. The American composer La Monte Young was especially impressed with the modal improvisations of Coltrane and recordings of Ali Akbar Khan. In the mid-1960s, he began studying with North Indian vocalist Pandit Pran Nath. Among the elements of Indian music that influenced Young were its tuning systems, the drone, the exploration of a single scale, and improvisation. Because these elements could be left unchanged literally for hours, Young became one of the first composers associated with the label **minimalism**, a style in which composers experimented with a minimum of means.

Another composer known as a minimalist was Young's friend Terry Riley (Figure 9.7), who also studied with Pran Nath. In the 1970s, he performed improvisations based on his own raga-like scales and melodic formulations for hours. He also used Eastern drums, Indian-style singing, and other South Asian elements. Unlike some of the less successful jazz and rock fusion pieces, there is nothing about these works that suggest mere exoticism or a superficial imitation of Indian elements.

Many Indian musicians have also written compositions involving both Western and Indian instruments and concepts. Both Ravi Shankar and Ali Akbar Khan opened music schools in California to which they brought the ideals of devotion, discipline, and spiritual peace through music to new generations of dedicated students from many countries.

REFERENCES

DISCOGRAPHY

NORTH INDIA   Khan, Ali Akbar. *Signature Series* (4 vol.). San Anselmo, CA: AMMP CD 9001–9004, 1968–73/1990–94.

Narayan, Ram. *North India: Pandit Ram Narayan, sarangi.* Paris: Ocora C 559060, 1989.

Shankar, Ravi. *The Sounds of India.* New York: Columbia CK 9296, 1966/1989.

Shankar, Ravi. *Three* Ragas. New York: Angel CD 67310, 1956/2000.

SOUTH INDIA   Balachander. *Veena Virtuoso.* Tokyo: King Record Co. KICC 5199, 1982.

Ramnad Krishnan, Vidwan. *Music of South India: Songs of the Carnatic Tradition.* New York/Los Angeles: Elektra/Nonesuch 9 72023-2, 1968/1988.

Subramaniam, L. *Le violon de l'Inde du sud.* Paris: Ocora C559029, 1980/1988.

Khan, Nusrat Fateh Ali. *Shahen-Shah*. Beverly Hills, CA: RealWorld, 1989.

Purna Chandra Das Baul. *The Bengal Minstrel: Music of the Bauls*. New York: Nonesuch 72068, 1975.

Shakti. *Handful of Beauty*. New York: Sony SRCS 7015, 1977/1999.

OTHER TRADITIONS

 BOOK COMPANION WEBSITE

You will find flashcards, a glossary, and tutorial quizzes, as well as other materials that will help you succeed in this course, at the *Music of the Peoples of the World, 2nd Edition,* Companion Website at www.cengage.com/music/alves/world2e.

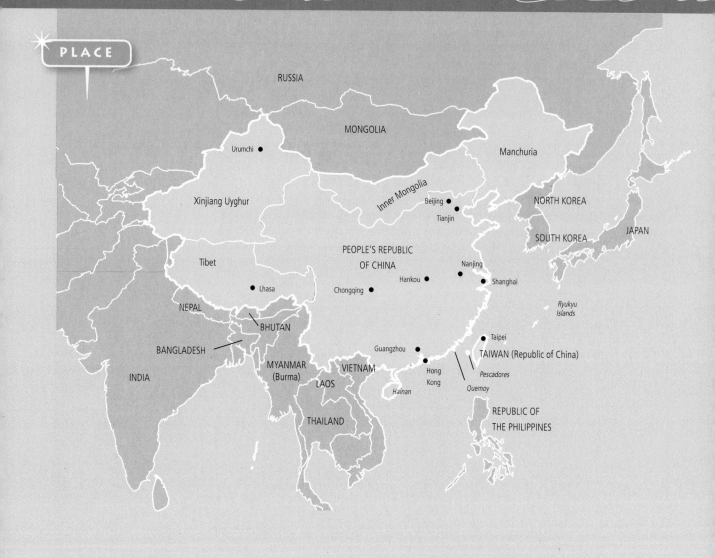

c. 2205–c. 1766 BCE	c. 1766–c. 1030 BCE	c. 1030–256 BCE	221–207 BCE
Xia Dynasty. According to legend, Huang Di ("Yellow Emperor") ordered court entertainer Ling Lun to create a standard system for music. Ling Lun traveled until he found suitable bamboo for fashioning a pipe. He fixed the pitch according to the song of the phoenix bird, and this pitch, called the Yellow Bell, *huang zhong*, became the basis for the Chinese musical system.	Shang Dynasty. First surviving musical instruments include bone whistles, bronze bells (*zhong*), globular flutes (*xun*), and stone chimes (*qing*). Pitch measurements of extant instruments have been inconclusive, although it is clear that the pentatonic system of Chinese music was established at a very early date.	Zhou Dynasty. Period of Lao Zi (604–517 BCE), founder of Daoism and Kong Fuzi "Confucius" (551–479 BCE), founder of Confucianism. Confucius is especially associated with introspective music of the *guqin* zither.	Qin Dynasty. To fight influence of Confucians, Emperor Shi Huangdi orders destruction of all books, including music books. This means loss of most music theory and notation from earlier periods. Much Confucianist music and theory from later periods is based on attempts to recover this ancient heritage.

CHINA

Although they are rare in today's People's Republic, one hundred years ago, the homes of the intellectual class were found by idyllic streams and mountainsides in China, their seclusion symbolizing the scholar's withdrawal from the human world and closeness to nature. It might be more accurate to say that they viewed themselves as a part of nature, ideally in harmony with it. The sparse furnishings of their dwellings would have included such emblems of the intelligentsia as a brush and ink, a carefully crafted arrangement of flowers, and a number of books. Foremost among these items would be the ancient Chinese zither known as the **guqin** (pronounced goo-chin) as shown in Figure 10.1.

 CD 2:7

"Ping sha lo yen" ("Wild Geese Descending onto the Sandbank"), Li Xiang-Ting

The *guqin* has seven strings, traditionally made of silk, but no frets (Figure 10.2, page 178). It is a curved board about four feet long set on a low table and plucked. The sound is very soft. When a scholar played the instrument, he would play for a few friends in his home or perhaps out in the woods for his own pleasure.

202 BCE–220 CE	c. 64 CE	221–581	581–906	
Han Dynasty. Period of rebuilding and Confucian influence, including development of tuning systems, musical symbolism, and codification of court rituals. Establishment of imperial music bureau.	Buddhism brings new philosophies of music, rituals, and Central Asian and Indian influences. Buddhist rituals, including chant, established in great monasteries that become meccas for Buddhist monks and scholars from throughout China and other countries.	Period of Three Kingdoms and Southern and Northern Dynasties. Influence of Central Asian kingdoms and Silk Road (trade route to Europe) leads to importation of musical styles and instruments, including *pipa* lute. By end of period, northern imperial music bureau records ten separate court music groups from different regions. Tradition of court orchestral music retained in Korea and Japan but not China.	Sui and Tang Dynasties. Era representing greatest extent of internationalism and cultural interchange, later seen as a classical period for music, poetry, and other arts. Chinese music greatly influences music in Korea and Japan.	

FIGURE 10.1

This *guqin* player figurine is from the later Han dynasty (c. 25–220 CE), a time of reaffirmation of Confucian values.

Such a performance would be an extraordinary experience. The delicate, floating tones are played very slowly, even reverently, so that one's attention focuses not so much on the melody but on each sound as an individual event. The contemplative attitude of the performer gives little hint of the extremely complicated and difficult performance technique the instrument requires. Each tone requires a precise method of plucking, holding, touching, moving, or otherwise manipulating the string with both hands. As the sounds of the instrument drift across the quiet surroundings of bamboo and flowers, they are meant to evoke beautiful images of nature and transport listeners through a kind of mystic journey.

Because of its refinement and sophistication, *guqin* music is cultivated by relatively few. The panorama of styles in this large country includes exciting, fast, earthy, and dramatic traditional music, and, in many ways, *guqin* music is not as representative as some repertories of Chinese traditional music. Yet in many ways, the *guqin* represents ideals not only of Chinese classical music and art but also of a way of life. The ideas of spiritual connection with nature, beauty in simplicity, and art as inward contemplation are all closely associated with the mystic Chinese religion of Daoism. The tones of the *guqin* are sometimes described as "the sound of emptiness," referring to the Daoist goal of freeing one's mind through the contemplation of nothingness, a goal it shares with Buddhism. But most of all, the *guqin* is associated with the Confucian religion and its social class of literati who cultivate the ideals of balance, harmony, and moderation. *Guqin* texts often point out that in Chinese, a homonym of *qin* (zither) is the word meaning "restraint."

For the most part, class distinctions and their various emblems, such as the library in the cottage by the stream, have not survived the social leveling of communism, especially the attack on intellectuals during the Cultural Revolution (1966–1976), but the *guqin* is enjoying a modest resurgence of interest in recent times. And although the trappings of class distinction are no longer a prerequisite for the study of the *guqin*, its historical association with devotion and contemplation, harmony, and balance remain a crucial part of its legacy.

China today is the world's most populous country, with well over 1 billion people, of whom 94 percent are of the Han ethnic group. This vast population has a great variety of languages and customs, as well as music. Mandarin Chinese is the language of the People's Republic of China, and major regional

▶ | 960–1279 | 1260–1368 | 1368–1644 | 1644–1911 |
|---|---|---|---|
| Song Dynasty. Period of more nationalistic and isolationist character. Theatrical schools established. | Yuan (Mongol) Dynasty. Period of rule by Genghis Khan and his Mongolian successors. | Ming Dynasty. Development of dramatic forms, including *kunqu*, *gaoqiang*, and *banziqiang*. These become basis for *jingxi* or Beijing (Peking) opera and other regional theatrical forms. | Qing (Manchu) Dynasty. As in Yuan period, northern invaders, this time from Manchuria, take control of China. Period of isolationism and struggles with European imperialists. |

dialects, such as Cantonese, are largely unintelligible to people of other regions. The system of writing, however, using classical Chinese ideographic characters, is understood throughout the country and has always allowed the Chinese to transmit laws, rituals, and philosophy, forging a unity across thousands of miles. This section will primarily cover the music of the Han people.

ELEMENTS OF TRADITIONAL CHINESE MUSIC

Composers and performers emphasize the melodic aspects of composition, in which balance and harmonious proportions are especially important.

- **Monophonic, heterophonic textures.** Much of the traditional art music of China was written for a single instrument; when more than one instrument plays, heterophony enriches the texture while still emphasizing the original melody.

- **Importance of ornamentation.** Ornamentation is highly developed, as might be expected in a melodic tradition, and much of an instrument's performance technique rests on knowing the appropriate use of ornaments.

- **Timbre as a compositional element.** Variations in timbre, effected through subtle distinctions in performance technique or changes in singing style, can be as important as melodic ornamentation to the character of a melody.

- **Variation form.** The forms of many pieces, from folk songs to *guqin* performances, are based on a series of elaborate variations of a basic melody.

RELIGION AND MUSIC IN CHINA

Despite the official support of atheism in the People's Republic, the three historical religions of China—Daoism, Confucianism, and Buddhism—have occupied an important position in the culture and music of China. Although not necessarily mutually exclusive, each religion emphasizes different ideas.

Late 19th C	1911–1949	1931–1945	1945–1949
Christian missionaries teach European music in some regions; military music and political songs with European harmonies also become popular.	Republic. Period of warlords followed by government under Nationalist party. Ancient court rituals and music associated with them near extinction. Western popular songs are common in urban areas, and Songs for the Masses are composed on Western models.	Japenese take Manchuria and later invade most of China.	After defeat of Japanese at end of World War II, Mao Zedong leads communist revolution. Republican government flees to Taiwan.

Founded by Lao Zi in the sixth century BCE, Daoism, or Taoism, is the first major religion of China. It is essentially a mystical and inward-looking philosophy overlaid by a variety of later rituals. Music is used in its rituals, but Daoism in its pure form has no use for stimulation of the senses. As suggested by the following passage from Lao Zi, music for entertainment is looked upon with suspicion.

The five colors blind our eyes.
The five tones deafen our ears.
The five flavors confuse our taste.
Racing and hunting madden our minds.
Possessing rare treasures brings about harmful behavior.
Therefore the sage regards his center, and not his eyes.[1]

Nevertheless, the influence of Daoism is clear in the contemplative nature of much Chinese music, its emphasis on simplicity, and its connection with the natural world.

The sixth-century BCE philosopher Kong Fuzi, known to the West as Confucius, established the second great Chinese religion. Because Confucius was especially concerned with establishing strict norms of moral behavior, social classes, theories of government, and ritual traditions, Confucianism is especially associated with the intellectual class. Like his near-contemporary Plato, Confucius saw music's capability to influence behavior as a powerful tool that should be controlled by the state. He encouraged the cultivation of music that inspired noble sentiments and other emotions useful to society, and he advocated state censorship for music for entertainment or music that inspired harmful emotions.

Books about and attributed to Confucius are full of references to the power of music and its proper place in society. In particular, music had an important place in ritual and in the personal expression of ideals of goodness and propriety. Confucius himself was said to have been a player of the *guqin*, sometimes moving people to tears with the emotions his playing could express. The playing of the *guqin* and the *se* (another ancient zither) becomes a metaphor in this poem attributed to Confucius:

[1]Translation by Charles Muller. Reprinted by permission of Barnes & Noble Publishing, Inc.

1949

People's Republic. The communist government of Mao Zedong institutes socialist realism, censorship in arts, and surveys of folk music. Western musical influence appears in workers' songs, political songs, and orchestras of traditional instruments.

1966–1976

Cultural Revolution sends many musicians, composers, and intellectuals to labor camps and begins strict censorship of arts. Chinese opera theaters closed or allowed to present only approved operas in style of socialist realism.

1976

After death of Mao Zedong, foreign contact resumes and censorship relaxes. By the 1980s, religious music and popular music are tolerated.

When one has a loving wife,
It's like the playing of *guqin* and *se*,
When there is congeniality between brothers,
It resembles the beautiful music that gathers.

—Translation by Hsu Wen-Ying

Since the time of Confucius, Chinese music has maintained a clear demarcation between the refined and elegant art music of the court and rituals, known as **yayue**, and common entertainment and folk music, known as **suyue**. An elaborate layer of metaphysics and cosmology was later added to Confucian thought, which continued to control many aspects of court life and court decisions until the end of dynastic China in 1911. Each of the twelve pitches in the Chinese tuning system was associated with one of the twelve months of the year and one of the twelve hours into which the Chinese traditionally divide both the day and the night. The five pitches of the pentatonic modes were related to five metals, five planets, and so on. Intimate knowledge of these associations helped composers craft music to heal, to instill warlike feelings, to inspire noble behavior, and so on.

The third main religion of China is Buddhism, which entered China through its trade with South and Central Asia in the first century of the Current Era. By the third and fourth centuries, Buddhism had brought not only new philosophies and metaphysics but also new instruments, rituals, and music.

Like Daoism, Buddhism emphasizes meditation and inner knowledge. Because much traditional Chinese art music is intended for a single instrument, playing it is similar to meditation. The presence of an audience is incidental. It is the relationship of the performer to the sound that is important.

Although Buddhism and Daoism were not outlawed under the communist government, religious practice, including music, was suspect, and temples were sometimes closed, and even plundered. Since the 1980s, the government's attitude towards religion has grown more tolerant, temples have reopened, and many traditional religious practices are allowed without interference.

TRADITIONAL MUSIC THEORY IN CHINA

In many musical cultures, music theorists are writers who attempt to articulate and elucidate the often unspoken and complex processes underlying musical composition and performance. Although there may always be a gap between practice and theory, the goal of theory is to codify what musicians do and why. In China, however, the purpose of music theory has been to find music's philosophical basis and its relationship to the cosmos. If musical practice does not completely agree with music theory, then those performances are considered vulgar, ill informed, or out of balance.

A document from the third century BCE describes a tuning system in which successive pitch ratios of 3:2 derive a scale of twelve pitches per octave. This method was probably known long before that time in many ancient societies, including Europe, where it became known as Pythagorean tuning. Chinese theorists, like later musicians in Europe, extended this tuning system to derive a twelve-tone scale. Each of the twelve pitches is known as **lü**. Traditional zithers, such as the *guqin*, are still tuned this way, although most modern versions of Chinese instruments adopt the compromise of twelve-tone equal temperament so that, like their European counterparts, they can easily transpose and be grouped into larger orchestras.

From this theoretical set of twelve pitches, theorists next derived various heptatonic (seven-pitch) scales that are basically the same as the diatonic scales of Europe. However, as far as we know, most traditional Chinese music was pentatonic, not heptatonic; the two extra notes, called ***bianyin*** (changing tones), were sometimes used as auxiliary pitches. These pentatonic scales left out the semitones (small intervals) of the heptatonic scales. Thus the pentatonic scales are sometimes called **anhemitonic** (without semitones) scales. The black keys of the piano keyboard approximate these scales.

There are five possible anhemitonic pentatonic modes, or ***diao***, one for each possible tonic or home pitch. Musicologists often name these pentatonic scales by numbering them within the heptatonic system, leaving out those numbers corresponding to the two absent notes. The pitches are numbered so that 1 always represents the tonic. Therefore the five possible pentatonic modes are the following:

gongdiao	1	2	3	–	5	6	–
shangdiao	1	2	–	4	5	–	7
juediao	1	–	3	4	–	6	7
zidiao	1	2	–	4	5	6	–
yudiao	1	–	3	4	5	–	7

Gongdiao and *zidiao* are the most common modes in use. As listed in Table 10.1, a great deal of classical writing in Chinese music theory was devoted to the cosmological significance of such musical components as these modes. Clearly, the tonic pitch affects the symbolism of a piece as well as its relationship to the other pitches.

In Chinese opera, many different aspects of a performance may characterize a mode apart from its scale—the sequence of pitches that end phrases (cadential pitches), the music's relative range, and even the instruments. The character of

---

Table 10.1   TABLE OF THE NOTES OF THE CHINESE MUSICAL SCALES AND THEIR SYMBOLIC CONNECTIONS

Musical Notes	Gong	Shang	Jue	Zi	Yu
Cardinal Points	center	west	east	south	north
Political Structure	king	minister	people	national affairs	natural world
Virtues	faith	righteousness	benevolence	respect	knowledge
Colors	yellow	white	blue	red	black
Elements	earth	metal	wood	fire	water
Heavenly Bodies	constellations	earth	stars	sun	moon
Planets	Saturn	Venus	Jupiter	Mars	Mercury
Flavors	sweet	pungent	sour	bitter	salty
Emotions	desire	melancholy	anger	joy	fear
Sounds	song	weeping	shouting	laughter	mourning

the mode makes it most appropriate to the rhythms and meters, the degree of ornamentation or melisma, and the characters in the opera.

TRADITIONAL CHINESE INSTRUMENTS

CHORDOPHONES

Despite the historical existence of orchestras and chamber music (small groups of musicians), China's musical traditions have emphasized the role of the solitary performer. Each classical instrument has developed its own tradition, idiomatic techniques, and sometimes, notation. Each instrument is often associated with a particular social class, context for performance, and character of piece. For example, the ancient and revered *guqin* is associated with Confucian rituals and the literati class, whereas another curved board zither, the **zheng** (see Instrument Gallery), was associated historically with the household and romantic songs. On a *guqin,* the player plays different pitches by pressing the string down to the resonator, whereas the *zheng* has a different string for each pitch, although pitches can also be bent by pressing down behind the bridge after plucking.

During the period of the Northern and Southern dynasties (265–581 CE), China engaged in considerable contact with Central Asian cultures. Orchestras from several of these cultures were installed in Northern courts, and many of their invigorating styles and instruments were quite popular. Among the instruments the Chinese adopted was the pear-shaped lute now known as the **pipa** (see Instrument Gallery). Because of its origins, the *pipa* does not have the same place in the Chinese tradition as the *guqin,* but respect for its evocative power is clear from the famous poem "Song of the Pipa Player" by Bai Juyi (772–846):

> Strong and loud, the thick string sounded like a sudden shower;
> Weak and soft, the thin string whispered in your ear.
> When strong and weak, loud and soft sounds were mixed,
> They were like big and tiny pearls falling on a jade plate.[2]

The *pipa* has traditionally been associated with banquet music and storytelling. The style of its music is much more extroverted and dynamic than traditional Confucian music. Although the tradition of epic narratives for banquets has all but died out, much of the *pipa*'s repertory still consists of pieces intended to represent historical or mythological scenes. The pictorial nature of its performance technique is much more explicit than the *guqin*'s or the *zheng*'s. For example, the player may hit the instrument body to effect sounds representing battle. A string may be plucked so hard that it ricochets against the sound body and produces a loud snap. A galloping horse may be evoked by accelerating strums, and so on. Descriptive solo pieces are the specialty of Northern *pipa* players today, whereas the Southern school concentrates on *pipa* ensemble music.

Hu or **huqin** has become a generic name for traditional bowed lutes in China, although it originally meant "foreign" because the bowed fiddle was introduced from Central Asia. Mentioned as early as the twelfth century, bowed

[2]From T. C. Lai and Robert Mok, *Jade: The Story of Chinese Music,* © 1985 Schocken Books

INSTRUMENT GALLERY

TRADITIONAL CHINESE INSTRUMENTS

Courtesy Minnesota Chinese Music Ensemble

ZHENG

The **zheng** is a curved board zither with approximately twenty-one metal or nylon strings. The strings are supported by intermediate bridges that can be moved to tune the strings to the desired mode. Plectra are taped to three fingers of the player's right hand, and the left hand effects pitch bends and vibratos by pressing down on the string behind the bridge.

Courtesy Danlee Mitchell

PIPA

The **pipa** is a four-string pear-shaped fretted lute held nearly upright. The sound body is solid, not hollow, and hewn from a single piece of wood. This gives the *pipa* a bright and dry timbre. The frets are raised high above the fingerboard so that it is possible to obtain both fixed pitches (by placing the finger directly on the fret) and sizable pitch bends (by placing the finger on the string behind the fret). Plectra (picks) were used when the instrument first appeared in China; today players use artificial fingernails.

Courtesy Danlee Mitchell

ERHU

The **erhu** is a two-string bowed spike fiddle with a cylindrical or hexagonal resonator covered with snakeskin or hide. Like the Islamic spike fiddle (*rabab*, Chapter 7), the *erhu* has a cylindrical neck but no fingerboard. The player stops the string with pressure from the fingers of the left hand, which do not press the string all the way down to the neck, thus facilitating pitch slides and bends. An unusual feature is that the hair of the bow is threaded between the strings. The hair is loose, so that the player holds it taut against one of the strings with a right-hand finger.

Courtesy Minnesota Chinese Music Ensemble

RUAN

The **ruan** is a four-string fretted lute with a large circular resonator. The resonator is hollow and covered with thin wood.

Courtesy Minnesota Chinese Music Ensemble

YANGQIN

The **yangqin** is a trapezoidal hammered box-zither. It was adapted from the Middle Eastern *santur* (see Chapter 7) brought by traders to China's southern coast in the seventeenth century. As with the *santur*, each string is stretched over an intermediate bridge, but the strings alternate on the right and left side. The strings are struck with light and thin bamboo sticks or "hammers." It is a relatively soft instrument used primarily for solo pieces and to accompany songs.

Courtesy Gilbert Blount

PAIXIAO, DIZI, XUN

The **paixiao** is a set of end-blown bamboo panpipes. The **dizi** is a transverse bamboo flute with six fingerholes. In addition, this flute has a hole covered with a thin rice paper membrane that buzzes when the flute is played, giving it a distinctively rich, reedy timbre. It is a common solo and small ensemble instrument and is the principal carrier of the melody in *kunqu* (classical opera). The **xun** is a globular flute made of clay.

Courtesy Minnesota Chinese Music Ensemble

XIAO

The *xiao* bamboo notch flute has six finger holes and comes in different sizes; this one is relatively long.

© Michael S. Yamashita/CORBIS

SUONA (LABA)

The **suona** or **laba** is a loud double reed with a conical bore and a trumpet-like flared bell. The player places the reeds in his mouth, not between the lips. It is derived from the Middle Eastern *zurna* (Chapter 7) through Central Asia and is usually associated with outdoor processions and folk music.

INSTRUMENT GALLERY

TRADITIONAL CHINESE INSTRUMENTS

Courtesy Danlee Mitchell

SHENG

The **sheng** has multiple pipes, each with a single reed connected to an air chamber. The player both blows into and sucks air from the mouthpiece, like a harmonica, and allows air into the various pipes by uncovering holes. Unlike the Japanese counterpart, the *sho*, the *sheng* plays single melodies, not chords, although the melodies are usually played in parallel fourths or fifths, thickening the texture.

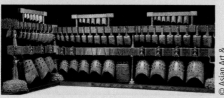

© Asian Art & Archaeology, Inc./CORBIS

BIANZHONG

The **bianzhong** is a collection of bronze bells suspended from a wooden stand. The bells do not use clappers and have a distinctive shape—cylindrical or elliptical. The most famous set was recovered from the tomb of the Marquis of Zeng (433 BCE). This replica of that set is played at the Wuban Music Academy in China.

Hear and see traditional Chinese instruments in your **ACTIVE LISTENING TOOLS**, available at the World Music Resource Center.

fiddles are especially associated with the Mongols who ruled China during the Yuan dynasty (1260–1368). Bowed fiddles are common throughout Islamic countries and in Central Asia, where they are held vertically.

The most important *hu* type is the **erhu** (see Instrument Gallery), which is primarily a solo instrument, although it is also featured in the *sizhu* ensemble (discussed later). Although the *erhu* may sometimes be used in opera performances, the lead instrument in Beijing opera (*jingxi*) is the **jinghu**, a fiddle pitched an octave higher. Other variants are used in other regional opera forms. In the 1950s, larger *hu* were invented to function like the viola, cello, and bass of the Western symphony orchestra. They are used in modern orchestras of traditional instruments, and the larger versions have four strings and fingerboards like their Western counterparts.

The **sanxian** is a lute with a very long fretless fingerboard and a shallow box resonator covered in snakeskin. Its three strings can be tuned to suit the range of a singer. It is used in opera (usually the smaller *sanxian*) and to accompany musical storytelling and epic narratives (usually the larger *sanxian*). Although associated with the Yuan (Mongol) dynasty (1260–1368), its earlier history is obscure, probably because it was a folk instrument.

Another plucked lute is the **yueqin**, also known as the "moon lute" because of its distinctive circular resonator. Like the *sanxian*, it also comes in different sizes and is used in regional opera and storytelling genres. According to traditional history, the earliest version of this instrument, the **ruan** (see Instrument Gallery), was invented in the third century.

WIND INSTRUMENTS

The legendary creator of music, Ling Lun, established the *huang zhong* (Yellow Bell) pitch by blowing over a piece of bamboo. Such a simple instrument is common wherever bamboo grows. A piece of bamboo is stopped at one end and blown over at the other, like a bottle. In China, as elsewhere, several bamboo tubes of different pitch were tied together to form the **paixiao** (see Instrument Gallery), bamboo pipes arranged to resemble the wings of the phoenix bird, Ling Lun's inspiration.

Related to this instrument is the bamboo vertical flute, the **xiao,** which, of course, is basically a single tube of the *paixiao* with fingerholes and an open end. The mouth end is mostly covered, except for a small notch carved into the side into which the player blows. Although the *paixiao* is no longer commonly used, the *xiao* is frequently found as a solo instrument or in chamber ensembles. The most common of the several types of Chinese transverse flutes is the **dizi**. The *dizi* has a higher range than the *xiao* and a much brighter timbre.

There are two varieties of traditional double-reed instruments: the **guan** is a short, cylindrical double reed, and the **suona** or **laba** is a loud outdoor instrument. The **sheng** is a multiple pipe instrument, like the *paixiao*, but with single reeds and an air chamber.

PERCUSSION

Expert bronze casting was already practiced in southern China in the second millennium BCE. Among the artifacts surviving from this period are bronze bells, some very large, and bronze drums. Bronze drums are actually idiophones, not membranophones, because the head is made of metal. Similar instruments in Vietnam, Burma, and Indonesia possibly developed into gongs. Gongs, **luo**, in China are often used in folk bands and Chinese opera. Although they don't generally have a definite pitch like those of Southeast Asia and Indonesia, Chinese gongs are often built so that the pitch swoops up or down when the gong is hit. A collection of dish-shaped gongs on a stand, sometimes used in theater music, is called **yunluo**.

Bronze bells have been recovered from many imperial graves dating back to 1500 BCE. Traditionally, sixteen or more of these bells are collected in a set called a **bianzhong**. Sixty-five bronze bells dating from 433 BCE were part of the spectacular discovery of the tomb of the Marquis of Zeng in Suixian, Hubei province (see Instrument Gallery), proving that sets of such bells were associated with imperial courts from the time of Confucius; they are still found in Confucian temples.

Another very early instrument found in Suixian and elsewhere is the **qing**, a stone chime that gives a mellow, dry sound when tapped by hammers. Sets of these L-shaped carved stones, called **bianqing**, were also associated with imperial courts and Confucianist rituals.

Although drums are not often used in modern Chinese classical music, there were apparently many different kinds in ancient times. A large, barrel-shaped drum with riveted heads, the **dagu**, is commonly used in folk music, religious music, and some repertories of court music. It is set horizontally in a stand in front of the player, who plays with two sticks. Drums of a wide variety are used in folk music, and drumming ensembles can be found in folk processionals. The player of the **xiaogu**, a small horizontal drum on a stand, serves as the conductor in many forms of Chinese opera and in *sizhu* chamber ensembles. He also sets tempos with an idiophone called a **ban**, a set of small wooden slats tied together on a string. With a flick of the wrist, the conductor can make the slats come together in a powerful "pak!"

GUQIN MUSIC

The **guqin**, or simply **qin**, the Chinese zither (see Figure 10.2), is the most revered instrument in China. An ancient instrument known in the time before Confucius, the earliest surviving *guqin* are from the Han dynasty (202 BCE–220 CE). Since then, the *guqin* has been associated with the Confucianist social class and represents the epitome of the Chinese ideal of music as meditation. Formerly used in Confucian ritual orchestras and to accompany songs, the *guqin* is primarily an extremely sophisticated solo instrument.

Solo *guqin* music is almost always peaceful, serene, and balanced; the meter is relatively free and slow. Typically, a free and expressive introduction is followed by a series of variations based on a traditional melody or series of melodies. Books of *guqin* notation sometimes give the player a scene or idea to contemplate as he plays each variation: "The autumn river is glossy like silk" or "Ascending into pure emptiness."[3]

Even though *guqin* pieces are often slow, the *guqin* is one of the most difficult Chinese instruments to master because of the huge number of ways in which a tone can be generated. The pitch of a note can be bent up or down by sliding the finger of the left hand. No fewer than thirty-three types of vibrato are codified. In addition, a note can be played with the fleshy part of the finger, with the fingernail, as a **harmonic**, as an open string, or as a stopped (fingered) note. When all of these possibilities are combined, there can be more than a hundred different ways of playing a single pitch. Much of the interest in a *guqin* performance comes from the artistic exploitation of these tiny nuances.

The invention of a notation system that specifies the string to be plucked, the manner of the plucking, and the action of the left hand for each note helped to codify these subtle complexities. This notation system was in place by about 1200, although earlier pieces that have been handed down, perhaps by earlier notation systems, date back to the year 589.

Courtesy Minnesota Chinese Music Ensemble

FIGURE 10.2

The *guqin* has seven strings, traditionally made of silk but today generally made of steel-wound nylon. The body of the *guqin* is a long curved board with bridges on either end over which the strings are stretched. Unlike most other East Asian zithers (see the photo of the *zheng* on page 170), however, the *guqin* has no frets or movable bridges. The performer changes pitch by pressing the finger of the left hand to the soundboard; small dots of inlaid mother-of-pearl called **hui** along the table of the instrument serve as a guide. This difficult performance technique makes possible a wide variety of ornaments and nuances.

[3]These examples are from translations by R. H. van Gulik, *The Lore of the Chinese Lute* (Tokyo: Sophia University, 1940); 89, 92.

A *GUQIN* PERFORMANCE

The composition of the famous *guqin* classic *"Ping sha lo yen"* ("Wild Geese Descending onto the Sandbank") is attributed to Prince Ning Xian (d. 1448), although the earliest surviving publication is from 1634. Geese in Chinese poetry have a number of symbolic connotations, including devotion. Geese mate for life, and even the death of one will not cause its mate to seek another. Thus the image of a lonely flying goose may be symbolic of the loss of a loved one, as in the following poem by Li Ching-tsao (1080–?), who lost her husband during the collapse of the Northern Sung Dynasty.

Slow Sound
Seeking, searching,
Icy, sparkling,
Aching sadness deepen,
Time of mild warmth and lingering cold,
Is the hardest to hold
Scanty wine two, three cups bit by bit,
Fierce wind blowing at night, how can I stand it?
Wild geese fly by fast,
Oh, miserable heart!
A reminiscence of the past.
Petals of yellow flowers are piling,
Freshness fading,
Who will care picking?
By the window I harden,
Solitarily waiting till the day does darken.
Leaves of *wu-tung* and misty rain,
At dusk dripping and dropping,
As it is,
How can I put the word, "grief," in restraint?

—Li Ching-tsao[4]

An early *guqin* publication suggested various pictorial descriptions to be associated with each section of the piece. For example, the writer suggests that during the first section, the player contemplate the following image (translation by Liang Mingyue): "Autumn wild geese in flight crossing the river; as the first goose alights on the sandy shore, the other geese—singly, in pairs, and more—follow suit."

Like many classical *guqin* works, the performance on our audio selection opens with a playing technique known as **fan yin** (harmonics). In this technique, the left hand lightly touches the vibrating string at certain points (marked by inlaid dots on the soundboard) but does not completely stop the vibration. *Fan yin* allows only certain vibrations in the string and creates a crystalline timbre that, depending on where the left hand touches the string, can sound at least an octave higher than the open string.

[4]Translated by Hsu Wen-Ying, *The Ku-Ch'in* (Pasadena, CA: Wen Ying Studio, 1978); 427–28.

CD 2:7. *"Ping sha lo yen"* (excerpt) ("Wild Geese Descending onto the Sandbank"), Li Xiang-Ting

Introduction

0:00	Opens with high, pure sounds symbolic of the heavens, the sky, and geese flying before they alight on a sandbank (*fan yin* performance technique).
	The introduction introduces the mode, which, in this performance, seems to imply the scale of 1 – 3 4 5 – 7 (*yudiao*), although sources differ on the mode of this piece.

Variation 1

0:45	Just the skeletal core tones of the theme are stated, beginning with a characteristic ornament of a scoop up in pitch, which can be heard throughout the performance. Notice how the tone of the string subtly changes through left-hand manipulations after it has been plucked. The focus is not on a continuous melody but on the delicate ornamentation of single notes.
1:06	Listen for the technique in which the right hand plucks a string and the left hand moves while the string is still vibrating, so that several notes of the melody sound without the right hand replucking the string. This technique will become common in the rest of the performance.

Variation 2

2:07	As the melody becomes more elaborate, it begins to expose the key melodic motives of the piece.

Ending section

3:14	New material emphasizing pitch 3 replaces the familiar tune and builds to a climax in this first part of the closing section.
3:33	A dramatic damped strum marks the emotional climax of the piece and leaves us hanging, expecting a return to the tonic (pitch 1). Fragments of familiar motives—as if the poet's thoughts are now wandering back to the peaceful scene of the geese.
4:05	The *fan yin* (harmonics) return, the tonality of the opening returns, and we end on the opening pitch with a sense of closure. Although ending with harmonics is a common device in *guqin* pieces, here you can imagine it representing the geese flying like a departed loved one up into the heavens.

Hear and see the instruments of *"Ping sha lo yen"* in your **ACTIVE LISTENING TOOLS**, available at the World Music Resource Center.

After this introduction, this piece presents a series of variations. The first of these includes only the fundamental core tones that define the melody. Each subsequent variation fills in many more notes around those core tones, like the intricate designs of jade carvings. Graphic 10.1 illustrates this process by overlaying a schematic representation of the first statement of the core tones (blue) with the following variation (red). The numbers refer to the pitches in the scale (here transcribed as a 1 – 3 4 5 – 7 mode).

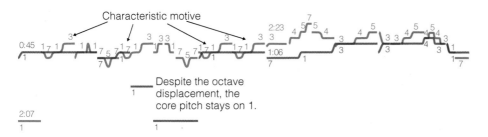

GRAPHIC 10.1

Two different variations from *Ping sha lo yen* superimposed.

The rhythm and meter of *guqin* pieces are known mainly from oral tradition and may vary from one performance to the next. The rhythm is not as crucial to the variation as the melody and ornamentation.

FOLK AND CONTEMPORARY MUSIC

Although the classical traditions of solo instrumental performance, opera, and orchestras are the best known of China's music, by far the most extensive repertories here, as elsewhere, are found in the folk music tradition. Aside from the many work songs, entertainment songs, lullabies, and other typical folk songs, instrumental ensembles play an important role in traditional Chinese life, especially in rural areas.

INSTRUMENTAL FOLK ENSEMBLES

Outside of the urban centers, major life events and holidays are nearly always accompanied by music, especially as performed by instrumental ensembles. Although the instrumentation varies in different regions, these bands usually provide music for ceremony and music for processions. At its simplest, such an ensemble includes one or more riveted-head barrel drums (*dagu*), gongs (*luo*), and *small cymbals* (**bo**). Such gong-and-drum ensembles (**luogu**) are very common in rural areas.

If two *suona* double reeds are added, the ensemble is called **guchui**, and the loud *suona* carry the melody. More instruments can be added, but the *suona* still tend to dominate. The pieces these ensembles play are usually improvised variations of familiar tunes, sometimes folk songs or traditional instrumental pieces and sometimes pieces borrowed from historical operas.

SIZHU

In teahouses and people's homes, ensemble music of a more subdued and refined sort was played for entertainment. These ensembles, traditionally known as **sizhu**, silk-and-bamboo ensembles (Figure 10.3), generally feature a *dizi, sanxian, erhu*, and perhaps other soft instruments such as the *xiao, sheng, yueqin*, or *yangqin*. These ensembles play traditional tunes in an elaborate heterophonic tapestry with a soft drum or clappers (*ban*) to keep the beat.

Sizhu pieces, like classical works, are frequently based on a sequence of variations of a core tune. Sometimes musicians create new versions of a piece by lengthening the time between the core tones to allow for denser elaborations. This process, poetically known as "slowing and adding flowers," is similar to the process found in Javanese gamelan music (see Chapter 12) and elsewhere. Although the repertories, techniques, and level of refinement of these ensembles overlap with those of the classical traditions, and the players who cultivated the silk-and-bamboo tradition tended to be from the upper intellectual class, this is music by amateurs for everyday entertainment. The popularity of *sizhu* has declined, but informal *sizhu* clubs still regularly meet at teahouses, especially in southern regions around Shanghai.

FIGURE 10.3

This historical photograph of a traditional chamber ensemble includes, from left to right, *xiaogu* (played with the right hand), *ban* (in the player's left hand), *sanxian, yangqin, sihu* (four-string fiddle), and *pipa*.

© Roger Viollet/Topham/The Image Works

A *SIZHU* PERFORMANCE:
FAN INSTEAD OF GONG

Like many pieces in the *sizhu* repertory, *Fan Instead of Gong* is a variation of an older "parent" tune and exists in several variants, which themselves may eventually become descendants of this one. Unlike many Chinese pieces, *sizhu* pieces generally have rather abstract and technical titles, rather than evocative or programmatic ones. This title refers to the fact that one way in which this piece differs from its parent tune is that the third scale degree (here called *gong*) has been replaced with the fourth diatonic scale degree (*fan*). Therefore, the mode has been altered from a 1 2 3 - 5 6 - scale to a 1 2 - 4 5 6 - scale. Pitch 7 is used occasionally as a *bianyin* or "changing note"—an ornamental tone outside of the mode—as, for example, at 1:30.

A *sizhu* performance typically involves several instruments playing in heterophony, which some Chinese musicologists compare to a river branching and coming back together. The ethnomusicologist J. Lawrence Witzleben has pointed out that musicians frequently use water imagery to describe *sizhu*, as its gently rippling sounds evoke the many rivers and lakes of the countryside around Shanghai.[5] Although certain instruments are more typical or appropriate for this music, the instrumentation is never fixed. The following performance includes a *yangqin, erhu, pipa, ruan*, and two *xiao*.

[5]J. Lawrence Fitzleben, *"Silk and Bamboo" Music in Shanghai* (Kent OH: Kent State University Press, 1995): 106, 119.

LISTENING GUIDE

CD 2:8. *Fan Instead of Gong* (excerpt), Shanghai Traditional Music Society

0:00 	The piece begins with five introductory tones. Here you can more easily hear typical ornaments for some of the instruments. On the third note, for example, the *xiao* play a short trill (quick alternation between adjacent notes, called a *chanyin*).
0:15	The first section (which we will call A) of the piece begins slowly, with some instruments already introducing melodic variations from one another.
0:21 	At this first cadence, you can hear not only the *xiao* playing *chanyin* (trills) but also the pipa playing an extended tremolo (fast repeating notes, called *lunzhi*). Listen for short examples of *lunzhi,* which the pipa often uses at the beginnings of extended notes throughout the piece.
1:01	The next section of the piece (which we will call B) follows. Note how the tempo has increased slightly, like a gentle brook flowing down a mountainside.
1:34	Now the A section repeats but with new and livelier variations. The graphic shows how the instruments combine their variations heterophonically.

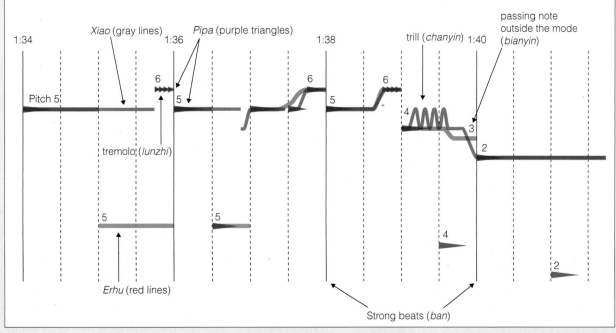

179

CD 2:8. *Fan Instead of Gong* (excerpt), Shanghai Traditional Music Society *(continued)*

2:09	A new section (C) forms the large middle of the overall structure of the piece. In this section, the instruments play variations on a simple alternation between the pitches 5 and 1. This simple alternation creates a period of static repose, as if the stream has flowed into a still mountain lake. The alternation is first every 16 beats, then every 12, then 8, and finally 4.
3:16	The B section returns but now rather faster and with more energy.
3:38	The A section returns.
4:00	Section B returns but now the tempo has doubled, or, as the musicians view it, the melody has become twice as compressed. Instead of four beats for every *ban* or "strong beat," there are now two.
4:15	Section A returns in compressed form.

Hear and see the instruments of *Fan Instead of Gong* in your **ACTIVE LISTENING TOOLS**, available at the World Music Resource Center.

Listening Exercise 8 | **CD 2:8 *Fan Instead of Gong***

1. The long cadence tone at 0:49 is broken up halfway through by
   a. the *erhu* playing the pitch an octave higher.
   b. the *pipa* or *ruan* plucking the pitch an octave lower.
   c. the *xiao* playing a trill (*chanyin*).

2. At 1:28
   a. the *xiao* plays a trill (*chanyin*).
   b. the *erhu* plays a sliding pitch.
   c. the *pipa* plays a tremolo (*luzhin*).

3. The meter of this piece is
   a. simple duple.
   b. simple triple.
   c. compound duple.

4. At 2:09, the main melody note is immediately preceded by
   a. a quick slide up on the *erhu*.
   b. a tap on the body of the *pipa*.
   c. a short tremolo (*luzhin*) on the *pipa*.

You can take this Listening Exercise online and receive feedback or e-mail answers to your instructor at the World Music Resource Center.

REFORM MUSIC

In the late nineteenth century, European missionaries in many regions of China taught Christian music with group singing and Western harmonies. Because of the compatibility of European and Chinese tuning systems, harmonization of Chinese songs was a straightforward process and was often adopted to create new "modern" school and military songs. After the fall of the empire (1911) and the subsequent rejection of old Confucian values, reformers created "Songs for the Masses" with European modes and harmonies, often based on models from the Soviet Union. At the same time, Western popular music could be heard in many urban areas. As reformers condemned traditional music associated with the court and the old intellectual class, many of the old practices neared extinction.

When Mao Zedong and the communists assumed power in 1949, they adopted a policy of socialist realism in the arts—that is, all art should serve the state and be a genuine expression of the masses rather than entertainment for the elite. The government supported the collection of traditional folk songs and other ethnomusicological research, and, at state-sponsored music conservatories, some of the traditional practices, such as solo instrument repertories, were refined and notated. At the same time, the government suppressed religious music, music of shamanism, and other traditions that were contrary to official atheism.

Possibly the most visible innovation during this period was the establishment of orchestras modeled on European orchestras but with Chinese instruments. The creation of these Chinese orchestras required the standardization of instruments to conform to a single tuning based on twelve-tone equal temperament and the invention of some new instruments, such as large versions of the *hu* bowed lutes that were the counterparts of the European cello and double bass. Professional composers often adapted traditional melodies to Western harmonies but without the experimentation or intensely personal expression that has characterized much Western orchestral music. This music is very familiar in modern China through concerts, film scores, and radio broadcasts.

During the Cultural Revolution of 1966–1976, conservatories were closed, most musical institutions disbanded, and many composers and performers were sent to rural re-education camps. This was a time of great hardship for these artists, but many returned with a greater understanding and appreciation of the folk music they encountered. After 1980, a liberalization of artistic expression was accompanied by a reduction in state sponsorship of music conservatories and other institutions.

CHINESE DRAMATIC MUSIC

NARRATIVE SONG AND FOLK DRAMAS

By the tenth century, Central Asians brought to China a love of epic storytelling with musical accompaniment. Over a period of months, professional storytellers, accompanied on the *pipa* or *sanxian*, depending on the region, would narrate their stories in one- or two-hour episodes of nightly entertainment. Many of these regional genres of epic storytelling have died out since the Cultural Revolution.

A shorter type of sung narrative is **guqu**, the "drum song" so named because the singer accompanies himself or herself with a clapper and wooden frame drum (*dagu*). An ensemble may also accompany songs and play interludes. Each presentation of *guqu* lasts about fifteen to twenty minutes, and performances may be strung together for an evening's entertainment or placed in between acts of another drama or variety show.

Although court entertainments have a long history in China, the center of theatrical activity moved to the public stage after the fall of the Tang dynasty (960).

As is common throughout East Asia, the actors in Chinese folk dramas do not use a script but instead improvise the dialogue from their intimate knowledge of the story and certain standardized ways of speaking for each character type. The music usually consists of well-known folk songs adapted for use in a particular drama.

REGIONAL OPERA

By the thirteenth century, dramas in the Song and Mongol courts developed into sophisticated forms with precomposed songs and lyrics. These and later types of Chinese musical drama have been called operas by Western writers, even though they differ in many ways from Western opera. In Chinese opera, spoken dialogue, mime, and acrobatics combine with singing to produce a unique synthesis. The staging often lacks the elaborate and realistic sets and props found in the West.

Many of the elements in these forms have become conventionalized and are well known to the cognoscenti. Actors learn elaborate codified movements and expressions to indicate the emotions of a particular character type, and actors tend to specialize in only one sort of character—old men, for example, or military heroes. Most stories derive from episodes contained within a handful of medieval novels and traditional tales, usually classified either as military (heroic historical tales) or civilian (typically romantic stories), although most stories include elements of both.

As in folk drama, these sophisticated genres are highly regionalized, so that today one hears references to Canton opera, Sichuan opera, Shanghai opera, and so on. Each of these forms shares many fundamental concepts but differs in dialect and conventions such as gestures, costumes, acrobatics, singing styles, melody types, modes, and instruments. One of the oldest of these genres that still exists is ***kunqu***, which appeared in the sixteenth century. Like contemporary Shakespearean drama, *kunqu* is today considered a classical dramatic form known for its ornate sophistication.

JINGXI—BEIJING OPERA

Those who could afford the best tickets to an opera performance in 1920s Beijing sat at one of the tables that surrounded the stage on three sides and were served tea and snacks. Others sat or stood on the surrounding balconies. The stage, a large wooden platform with corner columns supporting a sloping roof, was bare, except for a small table and two chairs in front of a large elaborate curtain. A small orchestra sat off to one side. Audiences were noisy, conversing during lulls in the action or enthusiastically applauding and shouting after an actor's featured solo. These connoisseurs often found the greatest beauty in the graceful curves expressed in every theatrical detail from an actor's gestures and walk to his speech and melodies.

Rather than a complete drama full of conflict and resolution, an evening's entertainment might consist of a series of unconnected episodes from various operas and culminate in an acrobatic battle scene late in the evening. Troupes were normally all male, and some of the most famous actors were those who cultivated a high falsetto and sang female roles. Some character types had faces painted with striking symbolic patterns, and the elaborate nature of the costumes more than made up for the sparse sets.

This was ***jingxi*** theater, better known in the West as **Beijing Opera** or Peking Opera, the most popular of the regional opera styles. Its origins reflect the cosmopolitan nature of the capital at the end of the eighteenth century, when the city's opera drew upon *kunqu* and elements from other folk and regional opera styles. Within a hundred years, its increasing popularity and imperial patronage made it into a national theater, and *jingxi* theaters could be found in many cities outside of the capital.

The Japanese occupation of World War II and the subsequent communist revolution created drastic changes in *jingxi*. Women now performed, and theaters began to use realistic staging and proscenium stages. In the People's Republic, *jingxi* was adapted to socialist realism, and Mao's wife Jiang Qing, a former singer, led a movement during the Cultural Revolution (1966–1976) to completely reform Chinese theater. All traditional and modern opera companies were shut down. In their place, Jiang commissioned eight new "model dramas" based partly on Western dramatic conventions and harmonies but with Chinese instruments. Only these model dramas were allowed during this period.

After Mao's death and the fall of Jiang Qing, *jingxi* returned but without its former popularity and some of its conventions. New experimentation has resulted in more elaborate staging and newly composed stories, some, for example, based on Shakespeare. Today, Beijing has four *jingxi* companies catering mostly to audiences of connoisseurs and tourists, and you can also see performances on television and video (Figure 10.4).

A *jingxi* play is divided into dialogue, songs, dances, pantomimes, and musical interludes. About ten standard rhythmic types (**ban**) classify *jingxi* songs not just by meter but also tempo, rhythmic density (notes per beat), and the relationship of the poetry to the meter. At one end of the spectrum are songs in *manban*, slow beat, an expansive and highly melismatic style appropriate for a character's expressive introspection, and often an emotional high point in the opera. *Yuanban*, primary beat, is a moderate tempo that accompanies simple narration or description. *Liushuiban*, flowing water beat, is a fast tempo often used for exciting scenes and sung with little or no melisma.

In much Chinese opera, there is a distinctive terminology and complex theory of modes, and *jingxi* operas are based entirely on two modes, *xipi* and *erhuang*. **Xipi** is similar to *gongdiao* (page 168) in that it uses a 1 2 3 – 5 6 – mode, but mode includes many other concepts in addition to the scale. For example, the setting of a couplet of text typically traverses a certain series of internal cadence pitches. Further *xipi* subtypes are characterized by typical melodic contours, the text's relationship to the rhythm, and the rhythmic types appropriate for the mode, although these characteristics are further adjusted depending on the gender of the character. Whereas *xipi* is considered bright and happy, **erhuang**, a 1 2 – 4 5 – 7 mode, is usually more serious and introspective.

The instrumentation of the *jingxi* orchestra (Figure 10.5) varies according to the troupe and the

© Dean Conger/CORBIS

FIGURE 10.4

A performance of *The Monkey King*, a favorite *jingxi* play, takes place in Beijing, 1981, shortly after Chinese opera resumed following the death of Mao. Unlike more traditional staging, this one uses a proscenium with a projected background.

© Dean Conger/CORBIS

FIGURE 10.5

In this orchestra practicing for a *jingxi* performance, the front row instruments include (left to right) the *ruan*, *yueqin*, *sheng*, and two *dizi*. Just visible behind the *yueqin* is a *hu* player. In the back, stand three percussionists.

needs of a particular drama, but the core instruments of the ensemble include *jinghu* (high fiddle), *erhu* (lower fiddle), *yueqin* (moon lute), *ban* (wooden clappers), *xiaogu* (a small drum), *luo* (gongs), and *naobo* (cymbals). The conductor of the ensemble, a percussionist playing the *ban* with the left hand and the *xiaogu* with the right, plays important cues, starts the group, and establishes tempos. As the most prominent melodic instrument, the *jinghu* forms a nearly constant heterophonic accompaniment of the voice. In the classical opera form of *kunqu*, and whenever the *jingxi* orchestra adopts *kunqu* melodies, the *dizi* flute takes on the vocal accompaniment role.

Other instruments may be added for specific occasions, such as a *suona* double reed to accompany processions or to imitate horses, large drums for military scenes, and so on. In addition to articulating the rhythmic structure of the songs, the percussion also provides many sound effects during both songs and stage action not otherwise accompanied by music. The characteristic swooping pitch of the *luo* gongs is a nearly constant accompaniment to blows in battle scenes and other important dramatic actions.

A JINGXI PERFORMANCE: THE DRUNKEN CONCUBINE

Probably the most famous *jingxi* performer of all time was Mei Lanfang (1894–1961), a man known for his refinement and innovation playing leading female roles (**_dan_**). One of his signature roles was the title character in the short opera *The Drunken Concubine (Guifei zui jiu)*.

The play opens with the emperor's favorite concubine, Yang Guifei, and her attendants processing through the imperial gardens to a grand pavilion, where she has ordered a great feast for herself and the emperor. As she sits and the wine is poured for two, word comes that the emperor will not attend. He is spending the night with another woman.

Crushed and furious but too proud to display these emotions in front of her attendants, Yang Guifei drinks both glasses of wine. As the glasses are refilled, anger and jealousy give way to bitterness and abandon, expressed largely through a series of remarkable dances. Finally, her sorrow breaks through her pride, and she expresses her loneliness and grief in a poignant series of songs. Accepting her fate, she and her entourage leave the banquet hall without having seen the emperor.

The Drunken Concubine is entirely in the *erhuang* mode, as befits its serious and thoughtful subject. Different rhythmic types (*ban*) and subtypes of *erhuang* provide the contrast among the opera's musical pieces. The play opens in the primary rhythmic type (*yuanban*), with the leader of the orchestra sounding the clappers every two beats. The first series of songs is in the subtype of the *erhuang* mode known as *sipingdiao*, which, in company with the primary rhythmic type, expresses an atmosphere of dignity and confidence that appropriately establishes Yang Guifei's pride and power.

In the first song, as she anticipates her dinner with the emperor, Yang Guifei's poetic descriptions of the imperial gardens evoke her emotional state of optimism, satisfaction, and pride. Most *jingxi* text is in couplets, and the musical phrases reflect the unsettled end of the first line resolving in the second line. *Sipingdiao* sets a conventional sequence of core tones at important metrical points, although these may not be immediately obvious in the song's elaborate melodies, especially as ornamented by a singer such as Mei Lanfang.

CD 2:9. "An Island in the Sea," *The Drunken Concubine*, **Mei Lanfang with the National Opera of China**

0:00 	Instrumental music (excerpted here) for the *jinghu* fiddle, the *erhu* (low fiddle), *yueqin* (moon lute), *ban* (wooden clappers), and *xiaogu* (a small drum) opens the play.
0:01 & **0:08**	The *luo* gong punctuates the gestures of the concubine, Yang Guifei, as the actor (Mei Lanfang) enters. Graceful movement of his sleeves was a highly regarded part of Mei Lanfang's artistry.
0:16	Yang Guifei sings: "An island in the sea," to an important motive, which we will call motive *a*, consisting of pitches 7, up to 1, and then down to 6, 5, and 4 (sometimes they are numbered differently). Pitch 6 is a *bianyin*, an alternate pitch outside the basic pentatonic scale. Motives such as this help unify this extensive melody. Listen to how the *jinghu* closely shadows the voice and the *ban* clappers help establish the dignified walking tempo of *yuanban* (primary rhythmic type) as the characters progress through the garden.
0:35	"The water wheel begins to turn and rise," is sung to another important motive, which we will call *b*. Motive *a* then returns, like the water wheel coming around. Beginning with the third line, the melody follows the same core tones as the first two, as is appropriate for *sipingdiao*, a subtype of the *erhuang* mode.
0:51	Yang Guifei sings: "See the scared rabbit."
1:04	*The rabbit again turns east and leaps.* *The water wheel leaves the island in the sea.* Motive *b* is again followed by motive *a*. Musically and textually, this resolves the first three lines.
1:28	*All heaven and earth shine brilliantly, The bright moon is in the middle of the sky.* Motive *a* returns to accompany this lyric.

1:59	*It looks just like Chang-E going to the moon palace.*
	This concubine is like Chang-E going to the moon palace.
	The melody of 0:51 repeats.
	One level of meaning in the lyric now becomes apparent. Chang-E is the legendary goddess who drank the elixir of immortality and flew to the moon, where her companion is a rabbit. The moon, like an island in the sea of night, brilliantly illuminates the Emperor's garden. By comparing herself to this goddess and symbol of the female principle, Yang Guifei not only metaphorically expresses her pride but also foreshadows her isolation and downfall.
	The song ends on pitch 5, cadence pitch for *sipingdiao*.
2:37	Prominent strikes on the *xiaogu* drum set a new tempo as the percussionist-conductor leads the orchestra directly into an interlude.
2:57	Stylized dialogue. The *sheng*, Yang Guifei's male attendant, and the *chou*, the clown attendant, introduce themselves in speech and bow to their lady. She answers in the stylized speaking voice of a *dan* (female role), which, like her gestures, consists of graceful sweeps of pitch with no sharp points. (The continuation of their dialogue after the end of the interlude is not included in this recording. There follows a reprise of the previous song, also not included here.)
3:25 	*Ban* clappers signal the beginning of the next piece
	In the limitless sky, a wild goose.
	The rhythm suddenly changes to a nonpulsatile rhythmic type known as *sanban* ("dispersed rhythm"), as if Yang Guifei's breath is taken away by the unexpected sight of the wild goose, a good omen. The instruments, primarily the *jinghu* and *erhu*, play the core tones heterophonically with the voice, ornamenting the long tones with periodic quick slides from the scale tone below.
3:47	Accelerating strikes from the *ban* clappers and a strike from the *luo* gong end the section and then introduce the next song:
	A wild goose flies.
	Oh! The wild goose is scared.
	Although this section is again metered in *yuanban* (primary rhythmic type), the tempo is somewhat faster than before, reflecting Yang Guifei's building excitement.

4:14	*The wild goose also flies up.*
4:17	*Hearing me, then falls in the shade of the willow tree.*
	The repeat of motives *b* and *a* here connect the previous mention of the scared rabbit with the wild goose. The image of rise and descent in the lyric foreshadows Yang Guifei's own downfall.
4:31	*This scenery is almost intoxicating.*
	A more obvious foreshadowing of Yang Guifei's own intoxication.
4:38	A shout from the attendant signals that they have reached the Hundred-Flower Pavilion where the banquet will be served. Woken from her musings, Yang Guifei also remarks that they have arrived.
	The melody of the phrase emphasizes the core tone of pitch 5, which ends the melody on a more serious but not yet settled tone.
4:47	The tempo increases yet again in a brief orchestral postlude as Yang Guifei sits at the banquet table to await the emperor.

Hear and see the instruments of *The Drunken Concubine* in your **ACTIVE LISTENING TOOLS**, available at the World Music Resource Center.

POPULAR MUSIC

On May 10, 1986, the singer Cui Jian (Figure 10.6) walked onto the stage of the Beijing Worker's Stadium, wearing ruffled, out-of-date fatigues from the People's Liberation Army and a guitar slung over his back. After a succession of pretty female performers singing pale, romantic ballads at the "One Hundred Pop Stars" concert, the sight of Cui was astonishing. At the time, even what Westerners would consider unremarkable love songs in the West were controversial in a culture in which the state had controlled all public musical expression for nearly forty years. During the period of Mao, the songs people heard on radio and television, even broadcast over loudspeakers in city streets, unceasingly praised socialism, patriotism, optimism, and faith in the Communist Party. Just a few years before the "One Hundred Pop Stars" concert, songs of personal, individual expression, even in the form of an innocent love song were suspect or even banned.

Then Cui Jian plugged in his electric guitar and in his crying, gravelly voice sang:

I've asked tirelessly, when will you go with me?
But you just always laugh at my having nothing.

© MIKEA FIALA/AFP/Getty Images

FIGURE 10.6

Cui Jian performs his song "A Piece of Red Cloth" while wearing a red blindfold, a protest against the Communist Party's control of the people, in 1992. After a performance of this song, the Chinese government cancelled his tour.

I've given you my dreams, given you my freedom
But you just always laugh at my having nothing.[6]

By the end of the song, Cui was singing over and over to the stunned audience, "I have nothing," and young people in the audience of over 20,000 were cheering and dancing. However, Party officials were infuriated. What may have seemed to an outsider a simple song about a poor boy trying to win the affection of a rich girl instead was to them a clear denunciation of the government and a mocking reference to the communist anthem the "Internationale" (which every Chinese schoolchild knew by heart):

Slaves rise up, rise up,
We cannot say that we have nothing
We will be masters of all under heaven.[7]

Cui would not be allowed to perform at a major concert venue again for three years.

Western-influenced popular songs of the pre-revolutionary period had never disappeared from Hong Kong (then under British control) or from Taiwan. With the new opening of China to foreign trade and influences in 1978, Taiwanese romantic ballads, now called *tongsu*, became greatly popular in the mainland through the new audiocassette technology. Most of the singers of the "One Hundred Pop Stars" concert were mainland imitators of the genre.

In the Communist system, to earn a salary, use recording studios, or perform at a legal venue, all musicians had to be employed by state-sanctioned work units. Before he formed his own band, Cui Jian had played trumpet in the Beijing Philharmonic Orchestra, for example. Gradually state work units employed *tongsu* singers and their songwriters, but no such opportunities existed for those young people who were inspired by the appearance of another type of music on cassettes: Western rock and roll.

After Cui Jian's appearance first gave a voice to youthful feelings of alienation and frustration, many more rock bands began to appear in urban areas in the late 1980s, as part of a growing youth movement. The climax of this movement would come with the tragic events of the spring of 1989, when semi-illicit Chinese rock bands formed the soundtrack to the thousands protesting in Beijing's Tiananmen Square and elsewhere. After soldiers took back the square, killing hundreds of protesters, the government banned rock music from public performance.

Nevertheless, popular music continued to circulate through cassettes, and gradually musicians such as Cui Jian have been allowed to perform again. Many of these groups have tried to distinguish their music from that of Western popular music and to impart distinctiveness and authenticity through, for example, the use of pentatonic melodies (although still accompanied by Western diatonic harmonies) and

[6]Translation from Andrew F. Jones: *Like a Knife: Ideology and Genre in Contemporary Chinese Popular Music* (Ithaca NY: Cornell University East Asia Program, 1992): 134.

[7]There are several versions of the lyrics of the "Internationale." These come from the translation of the Chinese version given by Jones 1992, 137.

occasionally traditional Chinese instruments—some songs of Cui have included *zheng* and *suona*, for example. Still, any hint of social protest in music is viewed very seriously by the Chinese authorities, and the days of music as a vehicle for social activism may have passed.

Traditional elements have also been used to create an exotic export in the new capitalist model of popular music in China. In 2001, the music producer Wang Xiao-Jing decided to update the Chinese orchestral tradition in the light of the popularity of the Irish *Riverdance* stage show and other "world music" and pop instrumental albums. He recruited young women from traditional music conservatories and orchestras, each an accomplished performer on instruments such as the *erhu, pipa, dizi, yangqin,* and *zheng*. The resulting Twelve Girls Band (Figure 10.7) has been a great international success. The composer Jianfeng Liang arranges synthesizer and drum backings for their frequently pentatonically tinged melodies, always with simple diatonic harmonies of similar pop genres, creating a gentle hybridizing of Chinese tradition with Western pop.

FIGURE 10.7

Members of the Twelve Girls Band perform on the *erhu, yangqin,* and *pipa.* A keyboard synthesizer accompanies them in the background.

REFERENCES

DISCOGRAPHY

Chinese Orchestra of Shanghai Music Conservatory, et al. *Sword Dance: Chinese Plucked String Music.* Hong Kong: Hugo HRP 724-2, 1988.

Cui Jian. *The Best of Cui Jian 1986-1996.* Hong Kong: EMI CD ISRC CN-C07-96-358-00/A-J6, 2004.

Lanfang, Mei, and others. *Guifei Zui Jiu [The Drunken Concubine].* Video CD, Beijing Audio-Visual Production Ltd ISRC CN-A08-99-0114-0/V.J8, 1999.

Li, Xiangting. *Soul of China: Guqin Recital.* Voyager CD SV 1337, 1993.

Twelve Girls Band. *Eastern Energy.* Los Angeles: Platia Entertainment 72438-64515-0-7, 2004.

Various artists. *China: Classical Music.* Paris: Ocora C 559039, 2001.

Various artists. *China: Music of the First Moon: Shawms from Northeast China.* Paris: Buda Musique 92612-2, 1994.

Wu Man. *Pipa: Chinese Traditional and Contemporary Music.* Wyastone Leys, Monmouth, UK: Nimbus Records NI 5368, 1993.

 BOOK COMPANION WEBSITE

You will find flashcards, a glossary, and tutorial quizzes, as well as other materials that will help you succeed in this course, at the *Music of the Peoples of the World, 2nd Edition,* Companion Website at www.cengage.com/music/alves/world2e.

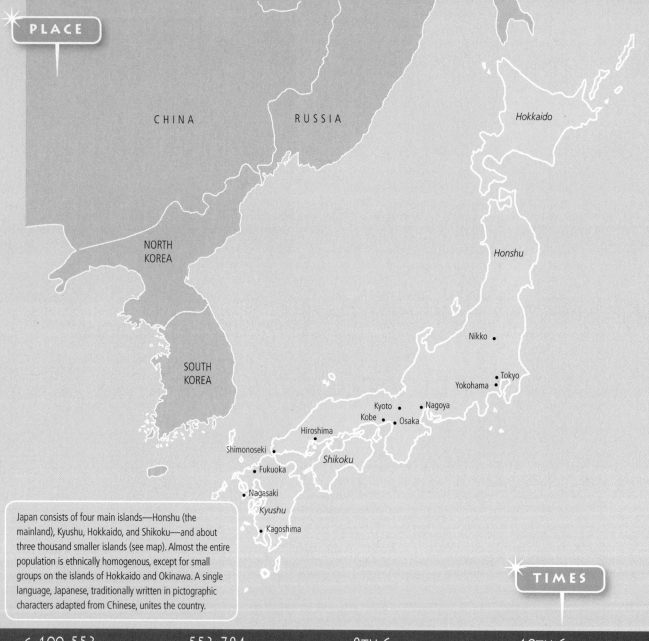

CHINA

RUSSIA

Hokkaido

NORTH
KOREA

Honshu

SOUTH
KOREA

Nikko •

• Tokyo
Yokohama •

Kyoto • • Nagoya
Kobe • • Osaka
Hiroshima •

Shimonoseki • *Shikoku*

• Fukuoka

• Nagasaki

Kyushu

• Kagoshima

Japan consists of four main islands—Honshu (the
mainland), Kyushu, Hokkaido, and Shikoku—and about
three thousand smaller islands (see map). Almost the entire
population is ethnically homogenous, except for small
groups on the islands of Hokkaido and Okinawa. A single
language, Japanese, traditionally written in pictographic
characters adapted from Chinese, unites the country.

TIMES

c. 100–553	553–794	9TH C	10TH C
Yamato period: Japanese courts adopt pictographic characters and other Chinese ideas by fifth and sixth centuries. Introduction of Buddhism inspires Japanese monks to travel to China and India, bringing back musical instruments and other influences.	Nara period. Beginnings of *gagaku* (Japanese court orchestral music). First extant native literature from the eighth century shows that court musicians at this time were Chinese or trained in Confucian *yayue* court music tradition of China.	Heian period (794–1185). *Koto* zither is adapted from Chinese *zheng*.	Tradition of blind priests singing and playing *biwa* (*moso-biwa*).

JAPAN

SETTING

Watching and listening to a performance on the **shakuhachi**, the traditional vertical bamboo flute of Japan (Figure 11.1), one notices the transported state of the musician as much as the sound of the instrument. The music quietly and slowly enfolds you in this contemplative state, one in which time seems nearly suspended. The music of the *shakuhachi* is often compared to the sound of a breeze blowing through a bamboo forest, and, although such an explicit connection with nature is common in the contemplative music of China as well, here this music has at once a spacious and melancholy quality that is distinctively Japanese.

SOUNDS

CD 2:10

Daiwa gaku, Jin Nyodo (1891–1966); *shakuhachi*, Bill Shozan Shultz

This quality of necessary emptiness within a space is an integral part of traditional Japanese art, a principle known as ***ma***. In much traditional Japanese art, the composition does not fill the canvas to the edges of the frame. Instead, the subtle but strategic placement of a few isolated elements serves to suggest the space through their very sparseness. The same principle appears in room decoration, architecture, and music; the music is often very slow, with suggestive pauses that let the sounds breathe.

11TH–12TH C	12TH–13TH C	1300s	C. 1370 ▶▶▶
Rise of samurai warrior. Courts of this period tend to be isolated from the world and extremely refined. The most respected pursuits for aristocracy are arts and contemplation of beauty through music, poetry, calligraphy, painting, moon-viewing, and other pastimes.	Kamakura period (1185–1333). Rise to dominance of Zen Buddhism and Shogun as ruler of Japan.	Beginning of *komuso*, wandering Zen priest *shakuhachi* players, who use *shakuhachi* as meditation aid.	Muromachi period (1333–1615). Creation of Noh drama (based on earlier forms), which becomes a refined theatrical form largely influenced by Zen.

Courtesy of Bill Shozan Schultz

FIGURE 11.1

The *shakuhachi* is the traditional vertical bamboo flute of Japan. Its melancholy, almost otherworldly sound and the controlled breathing required by its performance seem perfectly suited to attaining the meditative state sought by Buddhist monks who made it their own. (See also Figure 11.7.)

Scholars of Zen, the distinctive sect of Buddhism that is the major religion of Japan, often speak similarly of emptiness, the void achieved when meditation takes one beyond sensory experience to a deeper, wordless truth. Zen Buddhist monks sometimes use the disciplined breathing required to play the *shakuhachi* as an aid to this meditation. The other major Japanese religion is Shinto, a tradition of prayer and ritual associated with an ancient body of music also connected with Buddhism.

Just as Shinto, the indigenous religion of Japan, and Buddhism, a religion of foreign origin, represent two sides of spiritual practice for the Japanese, many other aspects of Japanese culture demonstrate the enthusiastic adaptation of foreign ideas that coexist with native elements in a unique synthesis. Historically, alternating periods of isolationism and the embrace of foreign ideas, including music, have shaped Japan's national identity.

Even as video game music and pop fill Japan's airwaves, the introspective and serene tones of the *shakuhachi* still represent qualities that are as essential to the Japanese character now as they were in centuries past.

ELEMENTS OF JAPANESE MUSIC

Despite the impressive musical diversity of Japan, highly refined and often remarkably consistent traditions in the classical arts have evolved from the country's ethnic homogeneity and occasional historical isolation. Common elements that are distinctively Japanese and help distinguish their arts from those of China or Korea include the following:

◆ **Scales with semitones.** Many of the most prominent genres of classical music in Japan use scales that include relatively large as well as very small

1500s	1603	1614–1685	1638
Establishment of first *koto* school (Tsukushi) and introduction of *shamisen* from China. Both largely associated with rise of mercantile class.	Traditional date for invention of *Kabuki* theater.	Lifetime of composer Yatsuhashi Kengyo, composer who nearly single-handedly invented solo school of *koto* playing, including a new and decidedly un-Chinese scale with semitones, known as *in*.	All foreigners expelled at beginning of period of isolationism that characterized the Edo, or Tokugawa, period (1615–1868).

intervals called semitones, although their tuning may vary somewhat. Like Chinese scales, Japanese scales are pentatonic (five pitches per octave), but they sound very different because of the presence of semitones.

◆ **Slow tempos.** Some prominent genres of traditional Japanese music have tempos so slow they may at first seem nonpulsatile. Other genres are in fact nonpulsatile but also unfold at a very slow pace.

◆ **Sense of space.** Sometimes the temporal space between notes is cultivated as much as the notes themselves. This space is known as *ma*. These spaces help create a musical architecture of understated simplicity and balance.

◆ **Prominent classical solo repertories.** Despite the importance of orchestral court and dramatic music, some of the most prominent traditions in Japanese classical music have developed within schools of solo instrumental performance, each with its own repertory and style, and frequently its own notation and terminology.

KAGURA: SHINTO MUSIC

The rituals and music that are a part of the Shinto religion have their roots in the purification rites, pantheism, and ancestor worship of prehistoric Japan. Shinto music is generically known as **kagura**. Today the most visible form of *kagura* takes place in the colorful folk festivals held for various occasions, especially in the harvest season. These festival performances are called **satokagura** and are especially popular in rural areas. A festival may consist of several parts, including a procession to the shrine, purification ceremonies, and so on, but dances are performed at seemingly impromptu times. They become part of the celebratory atmosphere.

A popular *satokagura* dance is the lion dance (**shishi-mai**). Like the dragon costumes in festivals in China and elsewhere in East Asia, the lion costume covers one or several people inside the lion's body and a carved wooden head with jaws that clack together ferociously. The lion through the village and visits stores and homes, bringing good luck to the inhabitants and to the dancers theselves.

The dances are accompanied by a small folk ensemble known as **hayashi**. It may include one or more transverse flutes, usually known as **takebue**; one

c. 1690	1700s	1800s	1868–1912
Establishment of Gidayu school of *bunraku* puppetry.	Development of *shamisen* repertory and styles of playing.	Establishment of classical chamber music known as *sankyoku*.	Meiji period. Constitutional monarchy established, ending feudalism and isolationism; opening to Western trade and cultural influences. Imported musical influences include European harmonies and scales, especially through popular music. Music conservatories established that teach both Western and Japanese classical music.

or more small, shallow drums called **taiko**; a very large barrel drum with riveted heads called **o-daiko**; and small cymbals or gongs. The flute plays a high, piercing melody with abundant ornaments between the extended notes, but the real interest is in the lively drum parts. While the *o-daiko* keeps a steady rhythm, the *taiko* plays fast, elaborate rhythms against it. Quite frequently these, rhythms are syncopated—that is, metric stress shifts away from the expected beat—as are many of the rhythms of Japan's distinctive folk songs.

More recently, these rhythms have served as an inspiration for a new type of drum ensemble. In 1971, musician Den Tagayasu formed such an ensemble, not only to revitalize Japanese folk traditions but also to return to Shinto's spiritual asceticism. Living on a remote island, his performers meditated, trained athletically, and rehearsed drumming. The group became known as Kodo and has toured widely throughout the world. Since their popularity, many other groups have imitated their instrumentation and playing style, now known as **taiko drumming**, which includes precise choreography of the drummers' movements. Even though it lacks the polyrhythms of Africa and the complex improvisations of India, *taiko* drumming is overwhelming in its sheer power and precision.

Another form of Shinto music is **mikagura**, the ancient music for imperial court rituals (distinct from the *gagaku* court orchestra music that we will discuss later). The music of *mikagura* is very different in instrumentation and style from the music of Shinto folk celebrations. Like most court music, it is very reserved and refined. Three or four instrumentalists often accompany a chorus and traditionally perform for special court rituals or prior to an emperor's pronouncements.

SHOMYO: BUDDHIST CHANTS

In Japan, Buddhism and Shintoism are not considered mutually exclusive. In fact, it is often difficult to separate the Buddhist and Shinto elements in some festivals and rituals. However, the main musical expression of Japanese Buddhism is found in the chants sung by various schools of monks. These

1920s	1931–1945	1950s–PRESENT
Contemporary Japan (c. 1912–present). Beginnings of *shinkyoku* (new music) style through innovations of composer Miyagi Michio (1894–1956).	Manchuria, later China and Southeast Asia, invaded and annexed. After Japan's loss in World War II, Allies impose government that becomes a constitutional democracy.	Remarkable economic growth makes Japan world economic superpower. Western jazz, rock, pop, and techno music have tremendous impact and provide overwhelming majority of music heard in everyday Japan. Distinctively Japanese styles of popular music—j-pop and video game music—become popular in West. Some Japanese composers in Western classical tradition, such as Toru Takemitsu (1930–1996), seek to merge influences of Japanese traditional music and Western classical music.

chants called **shomyo**, were imported from China and Korea in the early eighth century, or perhaps even earlier (Figure 11.2).

A service is announced by the ringing of a giant cylindrical bell called a **densho** (refer to Figure 2.2 in Chapter 2, page 10). It has no clapper but is rung with a hammer or a log suspended perpendicular to the bell. The music is performed responsorially—that is, a lead singer intones a part and is answered by the rest of the monks. At certain times, small ceremonial bells may be rung. The music is often nonpulsatile, but the impression is that it is very slow. The starting pitch may be left up to each monk, resulting in tone clusters similar to those heard in some Tibetan Buddhist chants.

Despite the apparent flexibility of tuning, *shomyo* is the source of classical Japanese modal theory, and ancient Buddhist texts discuss music theory in some detail. The modes of *shomyo* were eventually adopted in *gagaku* court music and other genres; these modes are distinct from the indigenous modes found in folk music and solo instrumental music.

© Michael S. Yamashita/CORBIS

FIGURE 11.2

In a Tokyo monastery, a Japanese Buddhist monk of the Fuke sect chants *shomyo*, very slow, repetitive, nonpulsatile recitations of sacred texts. The monks behind him play *shakuhachi* (flutes) to foster disciplined breathing and meditation. In front of them are the traditional baskets the monks wear on their heads. In the left foreground are two *mokugyo* (large woodblocks carved in the shape of fish) whose sounds accompany chants and call the monks to prayer.

MODES IN JAPANESE MUSIC

Buddhist chant brought Chinese music theory to Japan, and, although this theory was later modified, Japanese *modes* called **choshi** are modeled on Chinese modes lacking semitones (see page 168). The pentatonic modes the Japanese eventually adopted are the **ryo** 1 2 3 – 5 6–scale and the **ritsu** 1 2 – 4 5 6 – (see Graphic 11.1). Each mode consists of five pitches in the octave with two gaps where auxiliary pitches called **hennon** are occasionally inserted; in our graphic, the auxiliary pitch names are shown in parentheses. The three scales differ most clearly in the placement of these gaps. *Ryo* and *ritsu* may be transposed into different keys. But each transposition may vary the traditional melodies and result in different treatments on various instruments with limited ranges. *Choshi* modes, then, are distinguished not only by the basic scale but also by range, tones emphasized, and melodic contours. *Ryo* and *ritsu* still form the basis for *gagaku* court music and Buddhist music traditions. Another pentatonic mode, **yo**, is associated with folk music rather than the classical *choshi*.

GRAPHIC 11.1

Schematic diagram of various Japanese scales

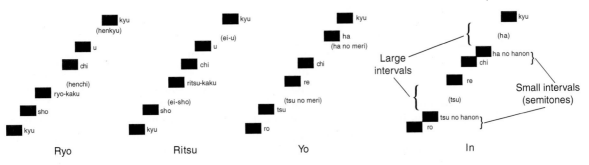

Ryo	Ritsu	Yo	In
kyu (henkyu)	kyu	kyu	kyu
u	(ei-u) u	ha (ha no meri)	(ha)
chi	chi	chi	ha no hanon chi
(henchi) ryo-kaku	ritsu-kaku	re	re
sho	(ei-sho) sho	(tsu no meri) tsu	(tsu)
kyu	kyu	ro	tsu no hanon ro

Large intervals

Small intervals (semitones)

The most distinctive of Japanese modes—and the one that clearly distinguishes most Japanese classical music from Chinese music—is the **in** mode (see Graphic 11.1). Unlike Japan's other pentatonic modes, the *in* mode has a distinctive scale that includes two semitones balanced by larger intervals. The invention of the *in* mode, which is associated with music outside the court tradition, is attributed to the famous seventeenth-century composer Yatsuhashi Kengyo, who first established it as a tuning for the *koto*, discussed later in this chapter. The *in* mode has also become associated with music for the *shamisen* and *shakuhachi*.

The names of the pitches in the scales differ from one instrument or tradition to another—those given in Graphic 11.1 for *yo* and *in* come from *shakuhachi* (flute) terminology. The exact tuning of each of these pitches may vary, even within the same performance, and some pitches may be substituted or left out of the scale. For example, some songs use pitch 5 (*chi*) in the *yo* mode so infrequently that it is considered another auxiliary tone. Often, pitch 7 (*ha*) of the *in* scale is used in ascending melodies, and pitch 6 (*ha no hanon*) in descending.

The indigenous population of Okinawa, one of the few groups ethnically distinct from the majority of Japanese, uses another pentatonic mode known as **ryukyu**. Although different from *in*, this distinctive mode also includes semitones and resembles some modes found in Southeast Asia.

 CD 2:11 Japanese scales (*ryo, ritsu, yo, in, ryukyu*) and demonstrations of *shakuhachi* ornamentation and playing techniques

GAGAKU: ANCIENT COURT ORCHESTRAL MUSIC

The ancient court orchestras of China found their way to Korea, where they still exist, and on to Japan, where, beginning in the sixth century, the art of **gagaku**, the ancient orchestral court music of Japan, took root. With the introduction of Indian Buddhist melodies and indigenous Japanese compositions, the repertory of Chinese and Korean melodies expanded into two basic genres: **togaku** ("music of the left," or old melodies), a repertory that includes Chinese and Indian influences, and **komagaku** ("music of the right"), a repertory that includes Korean, Manchurian, and indigenous melodies. The distinctive choreography and costumes for **bugaku**, the graceful and controlled dances that sometimes accompany *gagaku*, also distinguish the two repertories. Probably the oldest continuous tradition of orchestral art music in the world, *gagaku* has survived apparently with little change for more than a thousand years. Many of the musicians of today's imperial *gagaku* orchestra in Tokyo (Figure 11.3 on page 204) can trace their ancestry back through hundreds of years' membership in *gagaku* orchestras.

The *gagaku* orchestra divides its instruments into three main groups—wind instruments, string instruments, and percussion—as shown in the Instrument Gallery. The wind instruments include three *ryuteki* flutes and three *hichiriki* double reeds, all of which have the responsibility of carrying the melody. Players of both of these instruments can bend their pitches substantially. Carefully coordinated scoops up to a pitch and slides between pitches are characteristic of their performance style. Another aerophone, the *sho*, is a mouth organ that

INSTRUMENT GALLERY

INSTRUMENTS OF THE *GAGAKU* ORCHESTRA

Kenneth Hamm/Photo Japan

SHO, HICHIRIKI, RYUTEKI

The **sho** (left) is a collection of seventeen single-reed pipes connected to an air chamber. The player manipulates fingerholes to allow air into the pipes, usually creating chords consisting of up to seven notes. Like a harmonica, the *sho* can be played by both inhaling and exhaling, enabling it to sustain chords for a long time. It is the Japanese counterpart to the Chinese *sheng* (Chapter 10's Instrument Gallery). The **hichiriki** (second from left) is a small cylindrical-bore double reed similar to the Chinese *guan* but much louder. The **ryuteki** (third from left) is a transverse bamboo flute used in *gagaku*. In some repertories, it may be replaced with the slightly smaller *koma-bue*.

Courtesy of Bill Shozan Shultz

BIWA

The **biwa** is a four-string, fretted, pear-shaped lute. Although similar in form to the Chinese *pipa* (Figure 10.2), it is held horizontally and constructed so that the relatively loose strings rattle against the neck. It has long been used to accompany narrative songs and play melodies associated with a group of blind priests. However, the version of the instrument pictured here, the *gaku-biwa*, is used exclusively in *gagaku*. Periodically, the player forcefully plucks the strings with a very large plectrum, resulting in a loud, dry tone. The black leather strap extending across the resonator protects the wood of the body from these powerful hits.

Courtesy of Gilbert Blount

KAKKO

The player of the **kakko**, *a small double-headed cylindrical drum*, is the conductor of the *gagaku* orchestra. The drummer plays the *kakko* with two mallets, one for each side, and the drum rests on a stand in front of the drummer, who sits cross-legged in front of it. By playing accelerating rolls and carefully timed taps, the *kakko* player controls the tempo and coordinates the performance. In some repertories, a slightly larger hourglass-shaped drum called the *san-no-tsuzumi* replaces the *kakko*.

Courtesy of Gilbert Blount

TSURI-DAIKO

The **tsuri-daiko** is a large vertically suspended bass drum with an elaborately painted drum head. Some *gagaku* repertories use other sizes of hanging drums, which regularly interpunctuate the melody.

Courtesy of Gilbert Blount

SHOKO

The **shoko** is a small metal disc hung vertically from a stand. The player strikes the *shoko* on the concave side (the side opposite that showing in this picture) with two metal-tipped mallets, one slightly ahead of the other. Its high, dry sound punctuates the melody just after the beginning of every four-beat metrical unit.

Hear and see the instruments of the *gagaku* orchestra in your downloadable **ACTIVE LISTENING TOOLS,** available at the World Music Resource Center.

© Mitsuru Kanamori/HAGA/The Image Works

FIGURE 11.3

In the *gagaku* court orchestra, the front row includes (left to right) the *shoko*, the *tsuri-daiko*, and the *kakko*. Behind them are the string players, two *gaku-so* (a version of the *koto* zither) on the left and two *gaku-biwa* on the right. In the back row are the aerophones, including (left to right) *ryuteki* (three), *hichiriki* (usually three, but only one is visible here), and *sho* (usually three, but two are visible here).

plays constant background chords. The bottom notes of these chords form a skeletal version of the melody. The string instruments consist of two each of special forms of the *biwa* and *koto*, which interpolate short fragments between phrases of the melody. The percussion instruments include the large *tsuri-daiko* hanging drum and the small *shoko* gong, both of which divide the melodic phrases at regular points. Another drummer who plays the *kakko*, an hourglass drum, sets the tempo.

A *gagaku* piece, which may last from five to twenty or more minutes, is generally performed in three large sections, a tripartite division common in Japanese arts. Different melodic phrases, rather than dramatic changes in texture, distinguish the three sections. These sections are called **jo** (*introduction*), **ha** (*exposition*), and **kyu** (*ending*), and each section repeats. *Gagaku* music unfolds so slowly that it may at first seem nonpulsatile, but when you becomes attuned to its extremely slow tempos, it can envelop the listener, producing an experience of weightless refinement, balance, and serenity.

A *GAGAKU* PERFORMANCE

The work *Etenraku, Nokorigaku Sanben* is one of the oldest and best-known pieces in the *gagaku* repertory. It is especially associated with New Year celebrations and other symbols of new beginnings, and Shinto rituals also use its tune. Despite its composition in *hyojo*, a *ritsu* mode with no semitones, the *hichiriki* and *ryuteki* parts have gravitated over the years toward alternate pitches that allow the occasional semitones so characteristic of Japanese music outside the *gagaku* court tradition. *Etenraku* is a *togaku* piece from the old repertory "of the left." A short prelude, known as a **netori**, not heard on our recording, sometimes precedes a *gagaku* performance.

In Graphic 11.2, we show the texture of *Etenraku* in a diagram of the first half of section A. In this opening section, as each instrument enters, the texture builds. The diagram shows the beats as vertical lines; the beginning of each four-beat metric unit is a solid line. Although carefully controlled, the exact timings of these beats are somewhat flexible, and not all instruments line up as precisely as shown here. The *ryuteki* flute and *hichiriki* double reed (in red) carry the melody; the strings (green horizontal lines) interject short notes and patterns at the beginning of each four-beat unit; the *shoko* gong (light blue) plays just after the beginning of each four-beat unit; and the *kakko* drum (medium blue) controls the timing with an accelerating roll around the middle of the phrase and a constant roll at the end of the phrase. The *sho*

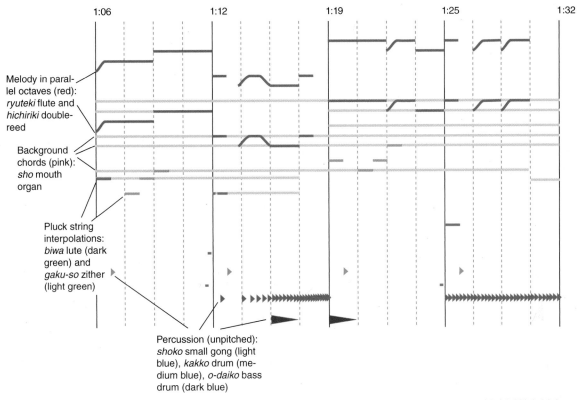

Melody in paral-
lel octaves (red):
ryuteki flute and
hichiriki double-
reed

Background
chords (pink):
sho mouth
organ

Pluck string
interpolations:
biwa lute (dark
green) and
gaku-so zither
(light green)

Percussion (unpitched):
shoko small gong (light
blue), *kakko* drum (me-
dium blue), *o-daiko* bass
drum (dark blue)

GRAPHIC 11.2

Texture of *Etenraku*

mouth organ (pink) provides a constant chordal background throughout with complex movements from one chord to another, indicated only generally in the graphic.

JAPANESE INSTRUMENTAL MUSIC

MUSIC FOR THE *SHAMISEN*

The **shamisen** is a fretless long-necked lute (Figure 11.4) similar to the Chinese *sanxian*, although thought to have been brought to mainland Japan via the island of Okinawa in 1562. Priest-musicians who had previously accompa-nied their songs with the *biwa* lute were the first to take up the *shamisen*. Thus narrative songs, **katarimono**, similar to those from the *biwa* tradition, make up a large portion of the *shamisen* repertory. *Shamisen* music plays an important part in *kabuki* theater music, but the most famous *shamisen* songs are the narratives that accompany **bunraku**, puppet theater. In *bunraku*, a master puppeteer and two assistants dressed in black, each manipulating a single large puppet, create complicated and stunningly graceful movements that make the puppets appear uncannily human. A single *shamisen* player and

CD 2:12. *Etenraku, Nokorigaku Sanben* (excerpt), Imperial Court Ensemble of Tokyo.

A section

0:00

The *ryuteki* flute establishes the extremely slow tempo and carries the first melody, **A**.

0:07

The *kakko* (lead drum and conductor) and *shoko* (small metal gong) enter with sudden strikes. Despite an extremely slow and elastic tempo, the *kakko* conductor keeps the ensemble tightly integrated throughout the piece. The *shoko* continues striking just slightly after each of the strong beats.

0:09

The *kakko* accelerates the beat, still within the meter, as the *ryuteki* continues the melody.

0:12

The *tsuri-daiko* hanging bass drum strikes with a resonant thud halfway through the acceleration.

0:16

Just in advance of the next melodic phrase, the *sho* mouth organ enters with an enveloping chord that forms a background throughout the piece. The *sho* changes to certain standard chords, called *aitake*, throughout the piece, generally chosen so that the lowest tone corresponds to the main pitch of the melody at that point.

Hichiriki double reeds enter to carry the melody with the *ryuteki*. In this mode and style, they always play a characteristic scoop up in pitch when the melodic phrase begins on the tonic.

Tsuri-daiko bass drum strikes mark the quarter and three-quarter points of the section.

| 0:43 | The *gaku-biwa* (plucked lute) enters with a forceful plunk. The *gaku-biwa* plays a short gesture every eight beats. The long pauses between its notes represent *ma*, the Japanese aesthetic principle of space. |

| 0:52 | The *gaku-so* zither enters—the last instrument to join—played at this point by just one performer. During melodic gaps, the *gaku-so* plays one of two standard melodic fragments every eight slow beats. |

| 1:06 | The full orchestra now plays the melody. Note that the tempo has become slightly faster, although the acceleration has been so gradual we were hardly aware of it. |

B section

| 1:55 | The *ryuteki* and *hichiriki* play the first half of contrasting melody, **B**, in their lower range and the second half in their upper range. |

| 2:37 | **B** melody repeats. |

| 3:07 | The percussion drops out of the texture as the **B** melody comes to a close. From this point to the end, the texture thins as other instruments gradually drop out. |

C section

| 3:16 | A new melody, **C**, enters and repeats. Unlike the previous melodies, **C** ends with a prolonged note but not the tonic. From this point to the end (not heard in our excerpt), instruments depart one by one: the *sho*, *ryuteki*, and *hichiriki*, finally leaving only the skeletal fragments played by the string instruments to suggest the form. As in much Japanese music, the absence of sound can carry as much impact as the sound itself. |

Hear and see the instruments of *Etenraku, Nokorigaku Sanben,* in your downloadable **ACTIVE LISTENING TOOLS,** available at the World Music Resource Center.

Listening Exercise 9	CD 2:12. *Etenraku*

1. At the very beginning, the *ryuteki* flute plays
   a. a slight scoop up in pitch.
   b. short ornamental notes ("grace notes") before the main note.
   c. a trill (quick alternation between two adjacent pitches).

2. At 1:38, the *kakko* leads the orchestra to the next emphasized beat by playing
   a. a steady series of short notes (roll).
   b. an accelerating series of notes.
   c. a single note on each of the beats.

3. The beat at 2:30 is emphasized by a forceful note on the
   a. *gaku-so (koto)*.
   b. *biwa.*
   c. *shakuhachi.*

4. After 3:08, what instruments have dropped out?
   a. The *ryuteki* and the *koto*
   b. The *hichiriki* and the *biwa*
   c. The percussion instruments

You can take this Listening Exercise online and receive feedback or e-mail answers to your instructor at the World Music Resource Center.

Courtesy of Gilbert Blount

FIGURE 11.4

The *shamisen* is a fretless, long-necked lute played with a very large plectrum, borrowed from the *biwa* lute, and has a somewhat louder tone than the *biwa*. The resonator of the *shamisen* is box-shaped and covered with cat skin. Its three strings, traditionally made of silk but today commonly nylon, are stretched over a long, thin fingerboard.

© Michael S. Yamashita/CORBIS

FIGURE 11.5

The *gidayu* (narrator) and *shamisen* player perform in *bunraku* puppet theater.

a separate narrator, known as a *gidayu* (Figure 11.5), usually accompany these plays. The *gidayu* sings and speaks the narration and characters' dialogue with great force and melodrama.

The *shamisen* lute also accompanies lyrical songs, called **utaimono** or **jiuta**. As this music became more refined and entered the classical repertory in the eighteenth century, it became the basis for songs in **sankyoku**, a chamber ensemble made up of *shamisen*, *koto*, and *shakuhachi* (Figure 11.6). In keeping with the *jiuta* tradition, the *shamisen* player in these ensembles is also the singer.

FIGURE 11.6

In the *sankyoku* ensemble, the *koto* (left) plays the basic melody while the *shamisen* (center) and the *shakuhachi* (right) overlay more elaborate heterophonic variations. *Sankyoku* performances consist of suites of songs, sung by the *shamisen* player, and instrumental interludes. These interludes may feature responsorial forms in which the focus shifts to each of the instruments in turn.

MUSIC FOR THE *SHAKUHACHI*

The **shakuhachi** is a vertical bamboo flute (Figure 11.7). When originally introduced from China, the *shakuhachi* was associated with court music. In the Kamakura period, however, Buddhist monks of the Fuke sect, often displaced samurai, took up *shakuhachi* performance as an aid to meditation. Early monks blew repeating patterns of one or two pitches that occasionally grew into longer melodic fragments that monks, playing in unison, adopted as a classical repertory for the *shakuhachi*, known as **honkyoku**. The breathing cycles that are part of meditation establish a very slow, nonpulsatile rhythm that, rather than follow a fixed meter, arises out of these long phrases.

The *in* mode gives most *shakuhachi* music a melancholy character, and the breathy tone evokes the lonely wind. Although the tone is relatively soft, loud bursts and expressive changes in dynamics are common. A single note may slowly grow louder from near silence, or it may begin with a startling chiff, the short puff of noise at the beginning of a tone. Overblowing can cause sudden high notes to precede the main note, and shaking the head while playing can create vibrato (wavering pitch).

Before the nineteenth century, *shakuhachi* instruction was offered only to Buddhist monks known as *komuso*. Later, two new schools of *shakuhachi* performance, Kinko and Tozan, began accepting lay students. Even today these organizations expect years of commitment and impose rigorous examinations on their students. New compositions

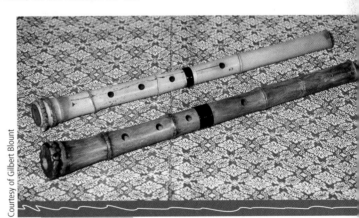

FIGURE 11.7

The player of the **shakuhachi**, a *vertical bamboo flute*, blows over a notch carved into the side of one end. A small piece of ivory or buffalo horn is inserted in the notch to keep the edge sharp. The player plays a tone by tightly focusing an air stream over this notch, a very difficult technique. However, this rather unwieldy nature is the *shakuhachi's* greatest strength because it allows skilled players to attain a wide dynamic range and effects not possible on some other flutes—pitch bends, vibratos, microtones, tremolos (fast variations in loudness), and so on. Unlike its Chinese counterpart, the *xiao* (see Chapter 10's Instrument Gallery), the *shakuhachi* is carved from the root of the bamboo tree, making it relatively thick and heavy.

Courtesy of Bill Shozan Schultz

FIGURE 11.8

The *koto* consists of thirteen silk or nylon strings stretched over a curved board resonator. Large bridges shaped like an inverted V that lift the strings above the resonator can be moved to tune the strings. The player plucks the strings with plectra attached to rings on the first three fingers of the right hand. The left hand bends pitches by pressing down on the string behind the bridge. The wide pitch bends affected by this technique are a distinctive ornament associated with the *koto*. It is related to the Chinese *zheng* (See Chapter 10's Instrument Gallery).

for the *shakuhachi*, called **shinkyoku**, began to proliferate in the twentieth century. These new works often introduced new scales and nontraditional techniques often borrowed from Western flute music.

A *SHAKUHACHI* PERFORMANCE

The *shakuhachi* master Jin Nyodo composed *Daiwa gaku* in 1941, although he humbly credited himself only as the "facilitator" of its creation. Nyodo began in the Kinko *shakuhachi* school but was inspired to seek out the origins of *shakuhachi* playing. He traveled to the few remaining Zen temples that still used the instrument as an aid to meditation, a technique known as *suizen* or "blowing zen," and carefully transcribed the pieces he discovered. His elaborately detailed and calligraphic scores reinvigorated the practice of *honkyoku*, or traditional style *shakuhachi*. Nyodo composed *Daiwa gaku* in this style.

In his notation for this composition, Nyodo included characters to suggest that this composition represents a cycle: a day, a year, or a lifetime, depending on one's perspective.[1] The title *Daiwa gaku* literally translates as "music of great harmony," perhaps referring to the harmony in one's spiritual life as well as, in Nyodo's words, music as the "harmony of heaven." In addition, the characters can be read as "Yamato music." Yamato was the medieval capital of Japan and the mythical center of the universe. This double meaning implies a reverence for ancient tradition found in *honkyoku* and in the monastic *shakuhachi* traditions that Nyodo studied.

MUSIC FOR THE *KOTO*

The *wagon*, an ancient zither, is apparently indigenous to Japan, but the far more widely used **koto** zither (Figure 11.8), related to the Chinese *zheng* and

[1]Thanks to Bill Shozan Schultz for his translation and interpretation of Nyodo's score.

CD 2:10. *Daiwa gaku* by Jin Nyodo; Bill Shozan Schultz, *shakuhachi*

0:00

Daiwa gaku begins with two notes suggesting *suizen*. Players call this deceptively difficult technique *sasabuki* or "bamboo leaf" because the shape of this leaf describes the note's soft-louder-soft envelope. In between the two notes, there is an extended silence. This is *ma*, or the empty space, which is such an important aesthetic principle in Japanese traditional arts. Like most *honkyoku* pieces, this one is nonpulsatile, with each phrase's length determined by the player's breath and *ma* between each phrase. Next to the notation for the first note, on the pitch *re*, Nyodo wrote the character for "father," and next to the second note, the pitch *ro*, he wrote the character for "mother," a first hint of the symbolism of the piece (see graphic).

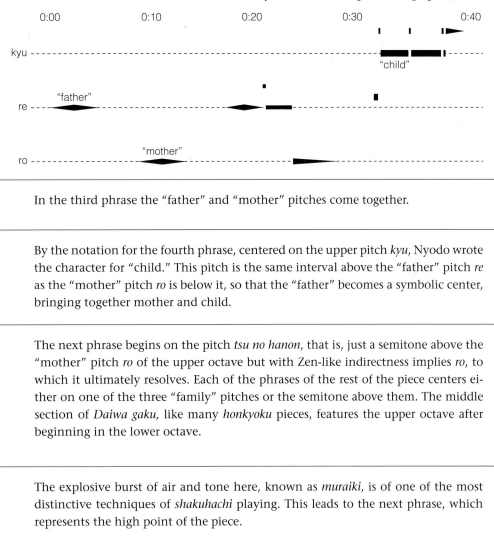

0:17

In the third phrase the "father" and "mother" pitches come together.

0:31

By the notation for the fourth phrase, centered on the upper pitch *kyu*, Nyodo wrote the character for "child." This pitch is the same interval above the "father" pitch *re* as the "mother" pitch *ro* is below it, so that the "father" becomes a symbolic center, bringing together mother and child.

0:41

The next phrase begins on the pitch *tsu no hanon*, that is, just a semitone above the "mother" pitch *ro* of the upper octave but with Zen-like indirectness implies *ro*, to which it ultimately resolves. Each of the phrases of the rest of the piece centers either on one of the three "family" pitches or the semitone above them. The middle section of *Daiwa gaku,* like many *honkyoku* pieces, features the upper octave after beginning in the lower octave.

1:12

The explosive burst of air and tone here, known as *muraiki*, is of one of the most distinctive techniques of *shakuhachi* playing. This leads to the next phrase, which represents the high point of the piece.

1:41

At this point in the score, Nyodo writes the characters for 10 o'clock and for "young adult," clues about where we are in the symbolic cycles of a day and of a lifetime.

| 2:24 | At this point, Nyodo writes the characters for "getting old" and "evening." |

| 2:40 | Now Nyodo writes the characters for "death" and then "autumn." After a gradual descent of the pitch contour, the melody has returned to the lower octave. Some musicians compare the contour of this and similar *honkyoku* pieces to the shape of a mountain. Nyodo wrote that the techniques included in this piece are as important for beginners as experts, a statement that recalls the spiritual journey of Zen, up the mountain of enlightenment, and back to earth. |

Hear and see the instruments of *Daiwa gaku* in your downloadable **ACTIVE LISTENING TOOLS**, available at the World Music Resource Center.

Dan 1 (1:44)

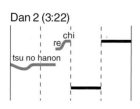

Dan 2 (3:22)

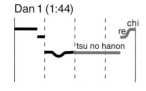

Dan 4

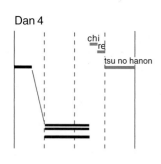

Dan 5

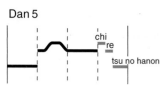

GRAPHIC 11.3

The variation of one four-beat metrical unit in *Rokudan no shirabe*

the Korean *kayagum*, was imported from China as part of the *gagaku* court orchestra. Although it has been a part of court music since medieval times, the *koto* became better known when it moved to the homes of the emerging middle class beginning in the seventeenth century. This movement was the result of the work of composer Yatsuhashi Kengyo (1614–1685), who established the use of the *in* mode, created new playing techniques, and composed much of the early repertory for the *koto*. We will hear a *koto* composition by Yatsuhashi Kengyo as our audio selection.

The *koto* sometimes accompanies a woman singing a cycle of songs known as **kumiuta**. The meter of the original sixteenth-century *kumiuta* poems defined a constant phrase length, called a **dan**, that varied from 64 to 120 beats. This form was carried over into purely instrumental compositions, creating slow but regular phrases that distinguish solo *koto* music from nonpulsatile *shakuhachi* music, for example. Each *dan* usually represents a variation of a basic melody, although unrelated interludes may be interpolated for the sake of variety.

A *KOTO* PERFORMANCE

Yatsuhashi Kengyo's *Rokudan no shirabe* is one of the most famous classical pieces for the *koto*. *Rokudan* means "six *dan*" (although we will hear only the first three *dan* in our excerpt), and each *dan* is a variation of the first. Except for the four-beat introduction, each *dan* has exactly twenty-six metrical units of four beats, divided evenly into two halves.

You can see how the variation process works by comparing corresponding four-beat units in each *dan* variation. Using a characteristic motive—the notes *tsu no hanon*, *re*, and *chi*—Graphic 11.3 shows a particular four-beat segment as it appears in each *dan*. In the first *dan*, the motive occurs at the end of this four-beat unit, but in the second *dan*, the motive moves to the beginning of the unit.

CD 2:13. *Rokudan no shirabe* (excerpt), Yatsuhashi Kengyo; Nakanoshima Kin'ichi, *koto*.

0:00	First four beats on the *koto* announce central motive in simple, introductory form.
	This motive persistently reappears, sometimes in different octaves, in short form, elongated form, and so on.

First *dan*.

0:07	Pungently dissonant repeated two-note chords also serve as a recurring landmark.
	Not all notes begin with a pluck. Listen to how the left hand presses down on the string behind the bridge to cause the pitch to slide to the next note. The player's left hand also creates some vibrato or slight bending of pitch on nearly every note.
1:31	A startling appearance of a pitch outside the scale, *hennon,* characteristically withheld for just such striking occasions.

Second *dan*.

2:04	The tempo is slightly faster.
2:36	An example of an ornament called ***waren***, a quick strumming across the strings.

Third *dan*.

3:40	Another important ornament called ***sa-rarin***, a fluttering tremolo on a single string followed by a sweep down the strings. Tempo has increased noticeably. Variation and ornamentation are somewhat sparer because of the faster tempo.

Hear and see the instruments of *Rokudan no shirabe* in your downloadable **ACTIVE LISTENING TOOLS,** available at the World Music Resource Center.

f

In *dan* 4 and 5, the same motive is reversed. Furthermore, the increased speed of the *dan* requires that the player separately pluck *chi* and *re* rather than slide between them. Transformations of these sorts occur throughout the variations that make up a classical *koto* composition. The use of small motives holds this piece together and creates a unified performance in the midst of a serene and floating sound quality.

MUSIC OF THE JAPANESE THEATER

NOH CLASSICAL THEATER

Noh is the classical theater of Japan. Like much Japanese fine art, it is highly refined, stylized, and reserved; to those unfamiliar with its conventions, it may seem inaccessible. Props and settings, reflecting the sparsity of the *ma* principle, are represented only symbolically, if at all. Similarly, the slow, weightless movements of the actors create spaces during which only the hollow sound of the *nohkan* flute pierces the silence. However, like the weightless mountains of Japanese landscape paintings, the experience of *noh* can surround the audience with a floating timelessness.

FIGURE 11.9

The **hayashi,** the musical ensemble that accompanies noh dramas, includes (from left to right) a *taiko* cylindrical drum, the *o-tsuzumi* drum held in the lap, the small *ko-tsuzumi* drum held on the shoulder, and the *nohkan* transverse bamboo flute. The *taiko* is the same drum found in folk ensembles and *taiko* drumming groups. The *o-tsuzumi* and *ko-tsuzumi* are similar to but smaller than the double-headed cylindrical drums of *gagaku*.

© Toshiro Morita/HAGA/The Image Works

Despite this stylization, *noh*'s roots lie in folk dramas full of acrobatics, pantomime, and comic interludes that moved into the courts in the late fourteenth and early fifteenth centuries. During this period of political upheaval, *noh* served as an emblem of ruling-class status and sophistication as well as a reflection of its Buddhist and traditional values. In the past hundred years, the patronage of *noh* has shifted to include the middle class, and today *noh* is appreciated by educated connoisseurs.

Nearly everything about the *noh* play is standardized, from the musical ensemble to the structure of the play and the stage itself. Actors use stylized gestures that represent the expression of particular emotions to the audience familiar with these conventions. The actors often wear masks painted with graceful, understated elegance, which seem to come to life in the enveloping atmosphere of the play. *Noh* stories are usually drawn from mythology or ancient narratives, and because they are infused with the spirit of Zen, cause and effect and logical chronology are not as important as atmosphere and mood. Traditional *noh* performances were all-day events of five full *noh* plays with comic interludes known as *kyogen*. Today, it is common for a single *noh* play to be performed as an evening's entertainment.

Two or three principal actors perform in the *noh* drama, accompanied by a small male chorus and a small musical ensemble made up of a single flute and drums. The standardized stories and stylized speech and action are so well known to the expert performers that *noh* plays are not rehearsed. The musicians, too, know the order and placement of pieces that accompany the action of the play, and there is considerable give-and-take between the actors and the musicians. Most of the music in a *noh* drama is nonpulsatile, which frees the actors' expression as well as the audience's sense of time.

The musical ensemble that accompanies *noh* is called **hayashi** (Figure 11.9), and it is made up of four instruments: the *nohkan* bamboo flute and three small drums. A surprising variety of sounds can come from this spare ensemble. As the only melodic instrument aside from the singing voice, the *nohkan* leads the ensemble in all instrumental pieces and provides expressive counterpoint to dialogue and songs. Most *nohkan* music consists of a large number of short, stereotyped melodies—motives appropriate to certain moods—that the performer varies and extemporaneously orders to fit the sections of the play.

Unlike other flutes, the *nohkan* has a smaller cylinder inserted between the mouthpiece and the fingerholes. Normally, when a flute player increases air pressure beyond a certain point, called overblowing, the instrument produces a tone an octave higher, but because of the *nohkan*'s unique construction, the tone produced is somewhat lower than an octave. This lack of emphasis on the octave tends to obscure the tonal sense, and it is not unusual for songs to start and end on different tonal centers. The resulting sense of suspended tonality is appropriate for the floating, dreamlike meditation of the *noh* theater.

The *ko-tsuzumi* is the smallest but most important drum in the *noh* ensemble. The ropes that are laced through the heads are held in the player's left hand and allow the player to control the drum's pitch by squeezing or loosening the ropes. The player also uses small pieces of paper attached to the inside of the back head to control the tone. Also important to these ensembles are the shouts and exclamations from the drummers, called **kakegoe**.

Noh drumming consists of certain standard patterns strung together and varied by each drummer. Different drummers may play different patterns at the same time, not necessarily synchronized, and this layered effect is one of the distinctive characteristics of *noh*. Nevertheless, the drummers are listening to one another. If anything, the freedom of the rhythm necessitates even closer attention than in more pulsatile music.

The singing style of *noh* is most closely related to *shomyo*, Buddhist chant. It is mostly free in rhythm, the pitch that the actor begins on is not necessarily important (unless he or she is singing with the chorus), and the vocal quality is rather tense. There are two types of singing: a kind of free recitative in a heightened speech-song called **kotoba** and song melodies called **fushi**.

KABUKI CLASSICAL THEATER

By the late sixteenth century, *noh* theater had already become highly conventionalized and largely patronized by the samurai upper class. The emerging middle class turned to a variety of other entertainments, including *bunraku* puppet theater, folk dramas, acrobatics, and so on. According to tradition, in 1603, a famous female performer brought a Buddhist dance, along with other dances and pantomimes, into the secular setting of a *noh* theater. The performance was called **kabuki**, a word which then meant strange or out of balance but which has since come to be associated with this genre of theater (Figure 11.10).

Kabuki became wildly popular in the eighteenth and nineteenth centuries, and star actors were national celebrities. Over time, *kabuki* became conventionalized, but the genre has never been as rigid or as unchanging as *noh*.

FIGURE 11.10

In the *kabuki* drama *Musume Dojoji,* a woman atop a sacred bell reveals herself to be a demon. Behind her are the onstage *kabuki* musicians. In the front row are musicians of the *shitakata* ensemble, including *o-tsuzumi* (shoulder drums, left) and *nohkan* (flutes, right). In the back row is the *debayashi* ensemble, which includes multiple *shamisen* players (right) and singer-narrators (left).

Today, *kabuki* is a form of classical theater rather than popular entertainment, although it continues to be supported by and popular among the middle and upper classes. Although most *kabuki* plays come from a standard repertory, some troupes experiment with new plays and forms of staging.

Kabuki borrowed heavily from *noh, bunraku*, and other genres. The musical ensembles from these genres were incorporated wholesale, with no attempt to merge the groups. Thus, the most distinctive musical aspect of *kabuki* is its use of not one but up to four different ensembles, each of which performs largely independently of the others. Although the instrumentation and placement of these groups may vary depending on the play performed, a standard complement consists of four ensembles.

♦ **Debayashi.** The core of *kabuki* music, the *debayashi* ensemble was borrowed from the tradition of lyric songs accompanied by the *shamisen*. Made up of four to eight *shamisen* players and a chorus of male singers, the group sits on a platform onstage, usually in the center in the back, just in front of the backdrop.

♦ **Shitakata.** Sitting on a lower platform in front of the *debayashi*, the *shitakata* group uses the standard *noh* ensemble of *nohkan* (flute), *o-tsuzumi*, *ko-tsuzumi*, and *taiko* drums. *Debayashi singers* take the place of the *noh* chorus, and a second flute, the *takebue* or *shinobue*, occasionally joins the ensemble.

♦ **Gidayu.** This is the narrator-*shamisen* pair from *bunraku*, sometimes multiplied so that there are three or four of each. The *gidayu* narrates the play and comments on the action, much like a Greek chorus. The *gidayu* is usually placed either on a platform at one corner of the stage or behind a bamboo curtain to the side of the stage.

◆ ***Geza.*** Hidden from the audience, the *geza* is a group of musicians who provide stylized sound effects and music that set or accompany the scene. Clappers may accentuate footsteps, cymbals and gongs represent the sound of thunder, and so on. The instrumentation of the *geza* is not fixed but generally contains four or more musicians playing a *shamisen, nohkan*, and a large, diverse battery of percussion.

Kabuki scores are often drawn from existing pieces that are appropriate to a given situation and character. However, they may also be newly composed. It is not uncommon to have a different composer (or arranger) for the onstage and offstage ensembles. Many of the musical styles of *kabuki* have been adapted from the same sources as the instrumental groups. *Kabuki* also adapted some *noh* forms of movement, story structures and types, and so on. Nevertheless, *noh* and *kabuki* are clearly different.

Noh is a small theater form—there are just four instrumentalists and only a few actors—whereas *kabuki* is large in scale, employing a large number of musicians and actors and a large set. Movements and gestures in *noh* are subtle, a kind of code that audiences learn and understand. Although gestures in *kabuki* can also be stylized, they are much more flamboyantly theatrical. Sets and props in *noh* are extremely simple and sparse, whereas sets in *kabuki* can be quite elaborate and may feature complicated changes executed in full view of the audience.

In its emphasis on musical diversity and grand spectacle, *kabuki* stands in strong contrast to the spare, contemplative atmosphere of *noh*, and yet both represent different sides of Japanese cultural ideals. Whereas *noh* exemplifies the radiance of spiritual emptiness, the *kabuki* stories of great passion and violence exist inside a carefully controlled, strict discipline of dramatic form, acting, movement, and music.

POPULAR MUSIC AND INFLUENCES FROM THE WEST

When Japan opened its borders in 1868, it embraced cultural influences from Europe and America much as it had Chinese influences more than a thousand years before. Eager to reform education on Western models, Japanese bureaucrats visited the United States and Europe and hired specialists from abroad to help establish a music education program for Japanese classrooms. These Western musicians brought European harmony and diatonic melodies, and a young generation of Japanese composers began to apply these innovations to Japanese melodies. For example, Rentaro Taki's (1879–1903) song "Moon Over the Castle Ruins" is in European minor mode and harmonized with European triads (see Chapter 14), but the melody emphasizes the pitches of the *in* mode. Generations of Japanese schoolchildren memorized school songs such as this, called ***shoka***. European musical influences also found their way into society through military bands, political songs, and recordings.

Japanese composers trained in Western techniques applied their skills to symphonic film scores, notably Toru Takemitsu (1930–1996), who wrote scores for the director Akira Kurosawa as well as concert works for orchestra. Some of Takemitsu's works use traditional instruments and playing styles, such as *November Steps* for European orchestra, *shakuhachi*, and *biwa*. Other of his works reflect distinctively Japanese aesthetics in their very slow pace, their evocative atmospheres, and their use of *ma* (space).

American jazz and related genres have long been popular in Japan, especially since the nine years of American occupation following World War II. During this time, **enka**, a new type of sentimental song generally about lost love or nostalgia, became popular. Although these songs might be compared to the songs of American "crooners" such as Frank Sinatra of the 1940s and 1950s, *enka* often had distinctively Japanese elements, such as the use of the *in* or other pentatonic modes. New generations in the 1960s and 1970s, however, preferred singing to the more energetic sounds of Western pop genres. **J-pop**, as it came to be known in Japan, still focused on star singers, often in television talent shows, but lost the melancholic flavor that *enka* borrowed from traditional genres. Rock bands and other popular groups, while common, were rarely distinguishable from their Western counterparts, apart from the difference in language.

By the end of the 1970s, Japan was the world center of the synthesizer and electronic music industry. The use of these instruments therefore came naturally to such composers as Ryuichi Sakamoto of the Yellow Magic Orchestra and Kitaro, who were among the pioneers of popular synthesizer bands. Both composers have sometimes incorporated traditional Japanese elements in their work. In the 1980s to the present, Japan has been a world center for techno and other electronic genres, notably so-called noise or **noise-core** music. Noise-core bands layer thick textures of highly distorted electric guitars and percussion, sometimes with recordings of industrial noise. Some critics called such sounds an angry reflection of the crowded urban culture of modern Japan, seemingly distant from the contemplative sonorities of the *shakuhachi*.

Even so, the ancient attributes of traditional Japanese culture often lie just beneath the surface of its modern society. In its music as well as many other arts and aspects of modern life, one can still recognize a Zen-inspired spontaneity, an appreciation for emptiness and space, and an introspective quest for serenity.

REFERENCES

DISCOGRAPHY

Ensemble Nipponia. *Japan: Traditional Vocal and Instrumental Music.* New York: Elektra/Nonesuch 9-72072-2, 1976.

Imperial Court Gagaku Ensemble. *Gagaku: Ancient Japanese Court and Dance Music.* Pismo Beach, CA: Legacy International CD 402, n.d.

Kodo. *Kodo: Heartbeat Drummers of Japan.* Santa Barbara, CA: Sheffield Lab CD-KODO, 1985.

Kyoto Nohgaku Kai. *Japanese Noh Music.* New York: Lyrichord 7137, 1964.

Miki, Minoru. *Selected Works*. Takuo Tanura cond. Pro Musica Nipponia. Tokyo: Camerata 30CM-55, 1982/1994.

Takemitsu, Toru. *Compositions of Toru Takemitsu*. Hiroyuki Iwaki cond. NHK Symphony. Tokyo: CBS Sony 58DC 282–58DC 283, 1984.

Various artists. *Japan: Semiclassical and Folk Music*. Paris: Auvidis/Unesco D-8016, 1974/1989.

Various artists. *Japanese Masterpieces for the Shakuhachi*. New York: Lyrichord 7176, 1980/1993.

Various artists. *Japon: Musique du Kabuki et du Jiuta-mai*. Paris: Auvidis B 6809, 1994.

Various artists. *Music of Japanese Festivals*. Tokyo: King Records KICH 2028, 1991.

Various artists. *Music of Okinawa*. Tokyo: King Records KICH 2025, 1991.

 # BOOK COMPANION WEBSITE

You will find flashcards, a glossary, and tutorial quizzes, as well as other materials that will help you succeed in this course, at the *Music of the Peoples of the World, 2nd Edition,* Companion Website at www.cengage.com/music/alves/world2e.

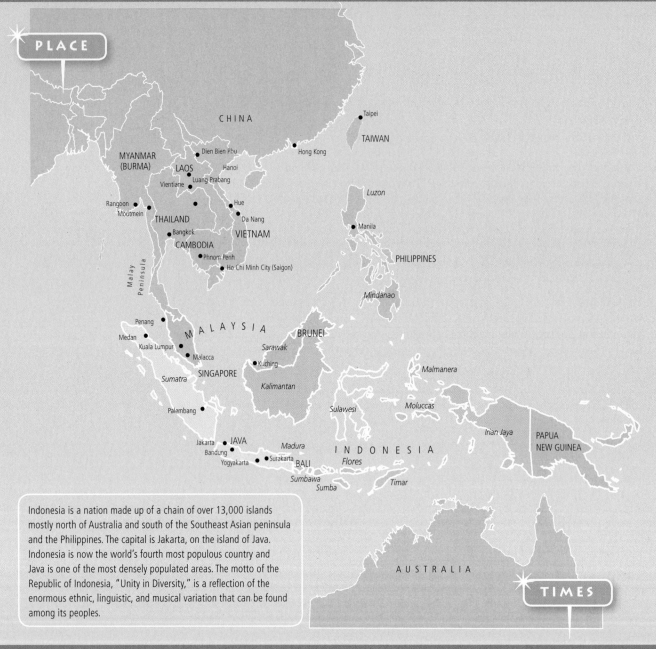

Indonesia is a nation made up of a chain of over 13,000 islands mostly north of Australia and south of the Southeast Asian peninsula and the Philippines. The capital is Jakarta, on the island of Java. Indonesia is now the world's fourth most populous country and Java is one of the most densely populated areas. The motto of the Republic of Indonesia, "Unity in Diversity," is a reflection of the enormous ethnic, linguistic, and musical variation that can be found among its peoples.

TIMES

c. 200	5TH C	8TH–9TH C	14TH–15TH C
Bronze working imported from China. Some artifacts from this period include large bronze drums (actually idiophones), which may have developed into gongs.	Hinduism and Buddhism arrive in Java from India.	Central Javanese kingdoms build great stone monuments depicting Indian musical instruments and a few indigenous instruments. Some literary evidence of masked dances, possibly *wayang* puppet dramas.	Height of East Javanese Majapahit empire, whose influence possibly extends as far as Philippines. Bronze gongs and similar instruments, possibly a result of these cultural connections, are found throughout Southeast Asia.

INDONESIA

SETTING

It may seem unlikely that the most venerated and renowned art of the art-saturated Indonesian islands of Java and Bali is a shadow puppet show, but the ***wayang kulit*** (Figure 12.1) is not just an entertainment for children. Each play—narrated by a single virtuoso puppeteer, the ***dalang***, and accompanied by an orchestra of mainly bronze instruments known as the ***gamelan***—is an all-night epic that recounts the never-ending battles of the forces of light and dark, good and evil. Witnessing such a performance is like glimpsing the ghostly echoes of the world of the gods and demons, of ancient kings and princes.

SOUNDS

CD 3:1

Ladrang Pangkur, Gamelan Paguyuban "Suko Raras"

The puppets are flat and carved with lace-like features projected onto a large screen by the light of an oil lamp (traditionally) or an electric bulb (more commonly) so that their images flicker evanescently before the audience (Figure 12.2). Just as the intricately carved patterns of each puppet are supported by a buffalo horn center stick, so the ornate melodies of many gamelan instruments weave around a central core melody.

The stories of the *wayang kulit* typically come from the Hindu epics, the *Mahabharata* and the *Ramayana*, which recall this region's ancient Hindu kingdoms. Just as the equilibrium of heaven and earth, of good

15TH C	16TH C	1602	18TH C	▶▶▶
Islam established in parts of Java, eventually bringing musical influences. However, devotion to Hindu-based art forms, in particular stories of *wayang*, remains strong.	Majapahit empire falls. Some courts flee to Bali, which remains Hindu even as Islam is gradually accepted throughout Java and elsewhere in Indonesia. The Portuguese are the first to colonize parts of Java and Sumatra.	Dutch East Indies Companies chartered, beginning period of Dutch colonization and expanding European influence.	Central Javanese Kingdoms in Yogyakarta and Surakarta develop gamelan music and associated dance forms.	

FIGURE 12.1

From the audience's perspective, we see the shadow puppets of the *wayang kulit*. Behind the screen and light source, a single puppeteer manipulates the flat leather puppets. And behind the puppeteer sits the gamelan orchestra that accompanies the play.

FIGURE 12.2

In this view of the *wayang* screen as seen from the *dalang*'s (puppeteer's) side, the puppets are stuck in a banana tree log set horizontally below the screen, with the forces of evil on the left and the forces of good on the right. The *dalang* will sit cross-legged in the center, his head just behind the lamp.

and evil, is fundamental to Hindu cosmology, so too is the performance space divided by a screen that creates two different realities. The same dualism is everywhere in the musical tradition as well—in the two different tuning systems, in the binary meters and forms, in the contrasting sections of loud and soft, fast and slow, vocal and instrumental.

It is not unusual for audience members to come and go during these nine-hour performances, eat snacks, and watch from both sides of the screen. Many

▶ 1906   1948

Dutch take control of Bali, eliminating most courts and their associated music. New popular styles emerge, notably the dynamic *kebyar* style, which remains the most popular and important genre in Bali.

Independence from Dutch; Republic of Indonesia founded.

come in anticipation of their favorite scenes, especially those that include the popular clown characters, whose improvised vernacular speech offers the *dalang* occasion for topical humor, even political jokes. What is important is not so much the specifics of the story with its gradual unfolding of heroic conflicts, but the mood and ritual-like atmosphere, the confirmation of the eternally revolving wheels of days, years, lives, and civilizations.

The Hindu cycles of life also form the foundation of the music as articulated by the periodic tolling of gongs in the gamelan. Today, gamelan is one of the most famous music traditions in the world. The quiet complexities of the Javanese gamelan and the dynamic intricacies of the Balinese variety have entranced listeners around the world for more than a century. In this chapter, we will look primarily at the rich traditions from cultures on the neighboring islands of Java and Bali and, in particular, at the composition and performance of gamelan music.

ELEMENTS OF GAMELAN MUSIC

It would be hard to mistake the gamelan orchestras of Java and Bali for one another. The gently floating tones of the Javanese gamelan invite serene contemplation, "like flowing water," to quote a common metaphor, whereas the brilliant Balinese gamelan can be fast and dynamic. Nevertheless, beneath the surface, these neighboring islands share important elements in their history and culture that allow us to generalize about aesthetic features that they share.

- ◆ **Orchestras featuring bronze instruments.** In these cultures that emphasize the importance of community, the orchestra rather than the solo performer represents the classical ideal. These large ensembles feature a number of drums, winds, and string instruments, but dominating the instrumentation are the famous bronze instruments, generally of two types: **metallophones** (metal-keyed xylophones) and tuned gongs, hanging vertically or suspended horizontally on taut cords.

- ◆ **Compositions guided by a core melody.** A skeletal melody, the **balungan** in Java and **pokok** in Bali, directs the intricate parts of gamelan texture. Despite its very simple rhythm, the *balungan* is an artful combination of various contour types and melodic motives appropriate to the mode. For example, one tone of the five in the melody may be intentionally saved for an important point of change. The pattern of notes may be offset from the meter so that when it finally arrives on a strong beat, the event is marked with a satisfying gong stroke. By methods such as these, the *balungan* directs a constant flow of contrasts and resolutions.

- ◆ **Polyphonic texture.** The *balungan* is only one of a rich fabric of melodies in gamelan music. Like the elaborate, lace-like carving of the *wayang kulit* puppet, various levels of faster melodies form filigrees that weave around the *balungan* core. These melodies are not guided by principles of harmony but instead follow the *balungan*, periodically diverging and then returning to the *balungan* tones at important points.

- ◆ **Colotomic structure.** The regular punctuation by gongs in gamelan music articulates the metrical cycle and creates what musicologists call a colotomic structure. Depending on the form of a gamelan composition, a player tolls the largest gong every 8, 16, 32, 64 or more beats. The other gongs reflect this regularity on a smaller level, dividing the periods between the large gong strokes by 2, 4, 8, and so on. Thus, these gongs build a cyclic hierarchical structure that serves as the foundation for the piece.

◆ **Paired families of tuning systems.** Gamelan compositions are nominally in one of two tuning systems, *pelog* or *slendro*. **Pelog** is a tuning system of seven pitches per octave with some adjacent intervals significantly larger than others. **Slendro** is a tuning system of five pitches per octave with the adjacent intervals close to the same size. However, each gamelan's version of *pelog* and *slendro* is slightly different from that of every other gamelan, giving each set of instruments a unique sound.

◆ **Stress at the end of metrical cycles.** Most musical cultures number their beats from the start of a metrical unit so that beat one (the "downbeat") receives the most stress. However, beats in gamelan music are numbered so that the stress comes at the *end* of every metrical unit instead of the beginning (Graphic 12.1). The fact that the Javanese hear the gong as the culmination of the cycle rather than its beginning has important consequences. Melodies often anticipate the tones of the *balungan*, for example.

GRAPHIC 12.1

The stress on beats in gamelan music

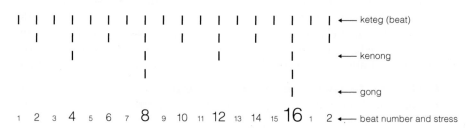

JAVA, ITS GAMELAN AND INSTRUMENTS

About half of the 130 million inhabitants of Indonesia live on the island of Java, historically the most politically and culturally influential island of the Indonesian archipelago. The most famous gamelan traditions come from Central Java, specifically the cities of Yogyakarta (also called Yogya) and Surakarta (also called Solo). Although separated by only 60 kilometers, they have had rival courts and traditions for the past 200 years (Figure 12.3).

JAVANESE CULTURE

Many Javanese follow a form of Islam that blends traditional Islam with belief in a spirit world and other remnants of Java's Hindu and pre-Hindu past. Hindu stories are still common in dramas and gamelan performances even if they have lost much of their religious, if not cultural, significance. Like many aspects of Javanese tradition, spirituality balances the light and dark sides. In such Javanese dramas as the *wayang kulit* shadow puppet play, the forces of good and evil are in constant contention. Such opposites exist even in a single character, and the best characters are those who keep these opposing forces in balance. Certain acts such as prostration, meditation, or good deeds strengthen one's personal spirit and influence one's daily life as well as religious status. Commissioning or taking part in a good musical performance may give a person spiritual strength. A sense of spirituality surrounds musical instruments and certain other inanimate objects, which are treated with respect.

The Javanese, especially the Central Javanese, highly prize **alus**, a characteristic sometimes translated as "refined." This quality is reflected above all in the heroes of their dramas, especially the *wayang kulit*, who have balanced the spiritual forces within themselves and fulfilled their destinies. The counterbalancing side from *alus* is frequently given as **kasar**, usually translated as "coarse." Even gamelans are sometimes classified by one of these qualities.

To the Javanese, *alus* includes indirectness in social intercourse. A Javanese asking a favor is not likely to ask directly but instead expects the listener to determine the unspoken meaning of the conversation and comply, thus preserving the pride of both asker and answerer. The qualities of indirectness and ambiguity pervade Javanese arts. The audience at the *wayang* sees only the shadows of the puppets. Performers in a drama may present social commentary veiled by elaborate symbolism and historical references. Song lyrics may present a proverb hidden within the poem.

FIGURE 12.3

The Sultan's *kraton* (palace), seen above, is in Yogyakarta, Java. The Sultan remains an important and respected cultural and political force in the region.

THE JAVANESE GAMELAN

The music of the Javanese gamelan (Figure 12.4) is refined and often moderate and contemplative in temperament. A piece is likely to start with an instrument such as the *bonang* kettle-gongs or *rebab* fiddle playing in a seemingly offhand manner, as if just tuning up. However, this short introduction, the **buka**, actually leads the listener into the world of the gamelan and, more specifically, the mode and character of the piece to be played. Toward the end of the *buka*, the drummer, who functions as the conductor, enters to set the tempo. The end of the *buka* is marked by a stroke on the great gong, and everyone joins in.

Just as dramatic stories contrast the forces of light and darkness, gamelan performances feature sections in which the softer instruments bring their ornate melodies to the foreground and other sections in which the louder instruments dominate. The drummer subtly leads the ensemble through changes in tempo and character that suggest new perspectives on repeated melodies and the ways in which they together weave the sonic fabric.

A typical Javanese gamelan piece may last from three minutes to thirty, but about fifteen minutes is common. The drummer plays a loud cue to slow down and signals the approach of the ending. The great gong dramatically sounds its final note alone, followed by the rest of the gamelan.

FIGURE 12.4

This gamelan is one of those in the royal collection at the court of Surakarta.

JAVANESE GAMELAN INSTRUMENTS

The Javanese term *gamelan* is now used to describe ensembles throughout the archipelago but especially the classical orchestras of mostly bronze instruments in

INSTRUMENT GALLERY

INSTRUMENTS OF A TYPICAL CENTRAL JAVANESE GAMELAN

William Alves

SARON

The **saron** is a thick-keyed metallophone with a box resonator played with a single hard wooden or horn mallet in the right hand, while the left simultaneously damps the key previously hit. The *saron* are constructed in three different sizes, each size playing an octave apart. The *saron demung* is the lowest, the *saron barung* (shown here) an octave higher, and the *saron panerus* or *peking* an octave higher than that.

William Alves

SLENTEM

The **slentem** is the bass member of the *gendér* family. Unlike its higher-pitched relatives, it is played with a single large padded mallet.

William Alves

GENDÉR

The *gendér* (pronounced with a hard G) is a family of thin-keyed metallophones with tube resonators. Mallets with disc-shaped heads covered in felt strike the instrument with a soft, mellow tone. The *gendér barung* is the larger and lower-pitched of the two sizes of *gendér*; the *gendér panerus* is pitched an octave higher. A mallet is held in each hand and keys are damped with the palms or sides of the hands.

William Alves

BONANG

The **bonang** family comprises horizontal bronze kettle-gong instruments, of which there are two or three sets, each set tuned to a different octave: *bonang panembung* (lowest), *bonang barung* (middle), and *bonang panerus* (highest, shown above left). The gongs are laid across strings and set in a frame (shown below). Players hold a stick mallet in each hand, and the mallets are softened with cord wrapped around the end.

William Alves

William Alves

REBAB

A two-string vertical spike fiddle, the **rebab** is played by the melodic leader of the orchestra. The *rebab*'s thin, singing tone leads the melodic instruments of the Javanese gamelan.

William Alves

GAMBANG

The **gambang** is a wooden xylophone with a box resonator. Played in parallel octaves with two flexible mallets, their disc-shaped ends wrapped in felt, the *gambang* has a soft and delicate sound.

William Alves

CELEMPUNG

The **celempung** (sometimes replaced by the smaller *siter*) is a large zither plucked with the fingernails. The ornate carving and feet of the instrument were influenced by European furniture of the colonial period.

William Alves

SULING

The **suling** is an end-blown bamboo duct flute.

William Alves

KENONG

The **kenong**, a set of large horizontal kettle-gongs, seem similar to the *bonang*, but the *kenong* gongs have much taller, sloping faces and perform a different function.

INSTRUMENT GALLERY

INSTRUMENTS OF A TYPICAL CENTRAL JAVANESE GAMELAN

Courtesy of Danlee Mitchell

KEMPUL

The **kempul** are small hanging gongs.

William Alves

GONG AGENG

The **gong ageng**, or simply *gong*, is the largest vertical gong, shown here next to the slightly smaller *gong suwukan*. These extremely low gongs dramatically end the metrical cycle of gamelan music.

William Alves

William Alves

KENDANG

In the Javanese gamelan, a single drummer usually plays two double-headed drums, **kendang**, set before him. The *ketipung* (left) is the smaller of the two and the *kendang gending* (below) is the larger. Other drums are sometimes used for dance or ritual pieces.

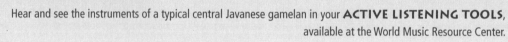

Hear and see the instruments of a typical central Javanese gamelan in your **ACTIVE LISTENING TOOLS**, available at the World Music Resource Center.

Java and Bali. Although the instrumentation of the gamelan may vary considerably depending on the region, function, and context, the most characteristic and obvious instruments are usually metallophones and gongs. Other instruments may include drums, wooden xylophones, zithers, fiddles, and bamboo flutes.

The most impressive instruments in the gamelan are the large, low-sounding, vertically hanging gongs. Gamelan gongs are carefully shaped to sound a definite pitch as well as a throbbing "wah-wah" effect. Unlike orchestras elsewhere in the world, which are usually defined by their personnel, gamelans are defined by a set of instruments, no matter who plays them. The instruments within one ensemble share a particular tuning system which is likely unique. For this reason, it is practically impossible to bring an instrument from one gamelan to another and play in tune.

Gongsmiths (instrument makers) build their instruments in pairs, so that there is one of each instrument for *pelog* and *slendro*. The instruments in one tuning system are set at right angles to their counterparts in the other tuning system so that the players can shift from one to the other by simply changing their sitting positions. Instruments from the two tuning systems are never played at the same time.

JAVANESE COMPOSITION

Although the *balungan*, the core melody played by the *saron* metallophones, often dominates the texture of Javanese gamelan compositions, musicians do not consider it the central melody of the piece. Instead, they refer to a more ornate melody, the **lagu**, even though this melody is never explicitly heard—it exists only in the minds of the musicians. This underlying melody subtly guides the delicate filigree of the higher instruments and the lyrical counter-melodies of the strings and singers into an elaborate polyphonic fabric. The *lagu*, like the shadow puppet, may be hidden from the audience, but we are always aware of its shadows from the ways the other instruments artfully suggest its presence.

THE *BALUNGAN*

The *balungan*, then, is a simplified version of the *lagu*, boiled down to its essential tones within a simple rhythm and limited range. The *balungan* is prominent not because it is the most important melody, but because it forms a middle ground between the slowly sounding gongs and the faster melodic instruments. When contemporary musicians want to notate or teach a composition, it is the *balungan* that they write down. A Javanese gamelan made up of experienced performers can perform a piece given only the *balungan*, the form, and some details of a style. The *saron* and *slentem* metallophones play the *balungan*, although the melody has to be restricted to their limited range. Skilled players can infer the rest of the instrumental parts in a manner appropriate to the style.

Melodic motives are very important to a *balungan*. They not only distinguish its identity, but they also help establish the mode and character of the piece. These motives, which are familiar to the Javanese music lover, may signal a return to home territory or embarkation to a new section.

THE *KEMBANGAN*

Some writers have called the melodies with more notes per beat than the *balungan* "elaborating melodies," but the Javanese often refer to them as the **kembangan**, literally the "flowering" of the music. Although guided by the same mode, contour, and other melodic forces that shape the *balungan*, they are hardly inessential decoration but the heart of Javanese gamelan performance.

Often these elaborating instruments play variations on certain known patterns, called **cengkok**, that ultimately coincide with the *balungan* at the ends of phrases. A player chooses a particular *cengkok* based on the important tones in the *balungan*, the mode, the tempo, and so on. Some cadences, that is, phrase endings, have less finality and others sound more final and coincide with the sounding of the gongs. Thus the polyphony of a Javanese gamelan consists of many melodies, diverging and coming back together, the degree of agreement often depending on this elaborate hierarchical architecture.

The *rebab* player leads the melodic instruments, even though the drummer is the rhythmic conductor. The other elaborating instruments listen to the *rebab* for cues about when to move on to a new section or when to emphasize a certain register (range of pitches). The *rebab* plays a lyrical, almost singing line that often shadows the *balungan* and, more than any other instrument, brings to light the relationship between the simple *balungan* melody and the *lagu*.

PATET (MODE)

The guiding structure of melody in the *pelog* and *slendro* tuning systems is called **patet**, a term often translated as "mode" but that includes a hierarchy of stressed and unstressed tones and characteristic motives. These small fragments of melodies soon become familiar to one who has listened to the music for some time. These patterns are most prominent (and most studied) in the *balungan*, although they permeate all the melodies of the gamelan. Because all *slendro patet* share the same five nearly equidistant pitches, these motives may be the most identifiable features of the patet. *Pelog patet* use five-tone subsets of the seven-tone tuning system, so that all gamelan compositions are basically pentatonic. Each *patet* has certain emotional associations, which sometimes connect with their use in the *wayang kulit*. The three acts of the *wayang kulit*, each lasting nearly three hours, are themselves called *patet* because all the music of each act is restricted to a single mode.

COLOTOMIC STRUCTURE

Colotomic structure refers to the pattern of regular punctuation of the composition by certain gong strokes; this structure is fixed and repeating for a particular type of compositional form. The large gong marks the slowest, or primary, punctuation. One gong note sounds every 8, 16, 32, 64, 128, or even 256 beats, depending on the colotomic pattern for that particular composition. A **gongan** is the large phrase defined by the duration between successive gong notes.

At the second level of punctuation, usually playing two or four times faster than the gong, is the *kenong*. The *kempul* plays at the same level of frequency but in between the *kenong* strokes. The first *kempul* beat within a cycle may be left *silent*, or **wela**, in the Central Javanese style. The *ketuk* plays the next highest level of punctuation (in between the *kempul* and *kenong* beats), and the optional fastest level is played by the *kempyang*.

Because of the Javanese love of bilateral symmetry, reflecting the dualism of Hindu cosmology, almost all colotomic structures are based on powers of two. *Gongan* are usually 8, 16, 32, or 64 beats in length, and the other punctuations are based on successive halving of these large cycles. The sense is of an ever-turning cycle and cycles within cycles rather than an edifice of hierarchical progressions.

Thus the Javanese often classify forms not only by the number of beats between each gong type, but, more importantly, by their relative relationships. Because the *kempul*, when present, always plays in between the *kenong* notes, the number of *kenong* strokes per gong and the number of *ketuk* strokes per *kenong* define most Javanese forms.

For example, any form that has only two *kenong* strokes per gong is called a *ketawang*. In Solonese terminology, the word *kerep* ("often") or *arep* ("sparse")

GRAPHIC 12.2

Examples of colotomic forms
shown schematically

Ladrang—32 beats, a common
form

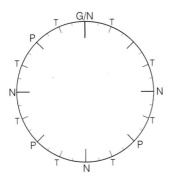

Ketawang—16 beats with fewer
Kenong subdivisions

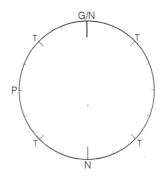

Merong Ketuk 2 Kerep or *Candra*—
64 beats with 2 *ketuks* per
kenong

Merong Ketuk 4 Kerep or
Candra Dawah—64 beats
with 4 *ketuks* per *kenong*

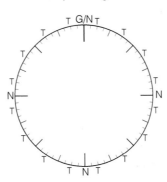

in the name of the form indicates the number of *ketuk* strokes per *kenong* stroke, such as "*merong ketuk* 4 *kerep*." These forms can be shown as a cycle, as in Graphic 12.2.

In these diagrams, each hash mark represents a beat, and time moves clockwise. The abbreviations are G for gong, N for *kenong*, P for *kempul*, and T for *ketuk*. Note that longer forms don't necessarily use the *kempul*, and the shorter forms may contain silence (*wela*) during the cycle's first beat when the *kempul* would otherwise play. Despite the differences between the forms, there are important similarities made clear by this representation—the *kenongs* always divide the cycle into four or two, for example, and the *kempul/wela*, when present, divides the *kenong* phrase into two.

IRAMA AND STRATIFICATION OF RHYTHM

Probably the most immediately striking aspect of the rhythmic structure of a Javanese performance is that, generally speaking, the higher an instrument's pitch, the more notes it plays per beat—that is, the higher its **rhythmic density**. The stratified rhythmic texture of Javanese gamelan music may include ten or more levels of rhythmic activity. The ratio of rhythmic density between each level of activity is two, or powers of two in a given colotomic form. For example, Table 12.1 shows the typical relationships for a *ladrang* (32-beat form). One of these levels is the beat and is usually, although not always, the rate at which the *saron demung*, *saron barung*, and *slentem* play the *balungan* notes.

The word **irama** refers to these relationships between the rhythmic densities of various instruments to the beat. Frequently, a piece undergoes several changes in *irama*. To signal these changes, the drummer loudly plays a pattern that slows or speeds up the tempo. If the drummer slows the tempo, for example, when the tempo becomes so slow that it is half the original speed, the fast melodic instruments (i.e., the two *gendér*, the two *bonang*, the *gambang*, and the *peking*) shift up a level, and play twice as many notes per beat as they played previously. Because the tempo, or beats per second, has been halved, the number of notes per second of these instruments remains the same, but an important shift in relationships has occurred. Were the tempo of *irama* I (Table 12.1) to change in this way, it would result in the relationships shown in Table 12.2.

Table 12.1

Irama I The typical relationships between rhythmic densities (notes per beat) of instrument parts in a *ladrang* (32-beat form) in *irama* I in the Central Javanese gamelan. The *rebab*, voices, and *suling* are too free in their rhythm to fit easily into this table.

Level	Instruments	Typical Rhythmic Density
8	*bonang panerus, gendér panerus, gambang*	4 notes per beat
7	*bonang barung, gendér barung, peking*	2 notes per beat
6	*saron demung, saron barung, slentem*	1 note per beat
5	*bonang panembung, kempyang* (when present)	1 note per 2 beats
4	*ketuk*	1 note per 4 beats
3	*kenong, kempul*	1 note per 8 beats
2	(no instruments)	1 note per 16 beats
1	gong	1 note per 32 beats

Table 12.2

Irama II The relationships of instruments after shifting from *Irama* I (Table 12.1) to *Irama* II. Although the tempo of the beat is twice as slow in this configuration, the instruments of the first two rows in this table play twice as many notes per beat and therefore about the same number of notes per second as in *Irama* I.

Level	Instruments	Typical Rhythmic Density
9	*bonang panerus, gendér panerus, gambang*	8 notes per beat
8	*bonang barung, gendér barung, peking*	4 notes per beat
7	(no instruments)	2 notes per beat
6	*saron demung, saron barung, slentem*	1 note per beat
5	*bonang panembung, kempyang* (when present)	1 note per 2 beats
4	*ketuk*	1 note per 4 beats
3	*kenong, kempul*	1 note per 8 beats
2	(no instruments)	1 note per 16 beats
1	gong	1 note per 32 beats

In this example, the instruments playing faster than the *balungan* (one note per beat) have shifted from level 7 to level 8 or from level 8 to level 9, creating a new level. Changes to a faster beat (that is, *irama* shifting down) is effected the same way—the drummer loudly signals a new tempo, and the musicians follow. When the speed has doubled, the higher-pitched instruments shift to half as many notes per beat.

A JAVANESE GAMELAN PERFORMANCE

Pangkur is a well-known classical piece in the Central Javanese repertoire, and versions of this piece exist in several *patet*. This example is in *patet manyura* in the *slendro* tuning system. *Pangkur* is in the form of a *ladrang*—that is, a 32-beat gong cycle divided into 4 by *kenong* strokes. Each of the phrases articulated by the *kenong* are divided again by the *kempul*, except for the first, in which the *kempul* is *wela* (silent).

Modern Javanese musicians notate *balungan* melodies using **kepatihan**, or cipher notation, in which numbers represent pitches. In the *slendro* tuning system, the pitches are numbered 1, 2, 3, 5, and 6 with dots above or below to indicate octave displacements. Graphic 12.3 shows the *balungan* melody for *Pangkur* and clearly illustrates the way *patet manyura* stresses pitch 6, coming as it does at the most important point to coincide with the gong. For the colotomic notes, N stands for *kenong* (which actually sounds an octave higher), P for *kempul*, T for *ketuk* (shown without its pitch, which may vary among gamelans), and G for large gong (also shown without its pitch, which is very low). Note how the *kempul* and *kenong* together outline a simple melody that nevertheless retains the important movement that occurs on the stressed beats. The relative stress of the beats is shown by the font size of the beat numbers.

Certain motives also characterize *patet manyura*, especially the pattern 3–2–1–6 that ends the section. Javanese hear this motive as the equivalent of a continual step down, even though the pitch 6 is higher than pitch 1 when played by the *saron*. However, the musicians are listening not so much to the *saron* melody itself as to the *lagu*, the inner melody that the *saron* melody represents. In the *lagu*, unrestricted by the range of the *saron*,

GRAPHIC 12.3

Black rectangles mark *Pangkur's balungan* melody. Rectangles with letters indicate the colotomic notes.

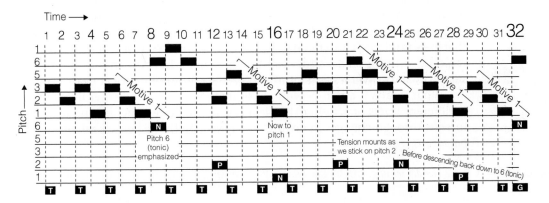

pitch 6 is in the lower octave, and therefore one step *down* from pitch 1. The melody of *Pangkur* repeatedly uses this stepping-down motive (motive 1) to establish different important tones, and thereby a journey to different tonal regions.

The *balungan* establishes this journey on many different levels. For example, if we look at every other note of the melody, that is, just those that land on the even-numbered or stressed beats, another melody is formed (in Yogyanese style, the *bonang panembung* may play this melody) that retains the basic outline of the important *balungan* tones as well as interest on its own right. We can continue this process of distillation further by looking at just the *kenong* and *kempul* strokes, which makes clear the journey from pitch 6 and back again.

A well-composed *balungan* sounds good at a variety of levels in the context of the colotomic form and *patet*. This *kembangan*, or flowering, of the basic tones continues at levels of rhythmic activity even faster than the *balungan*. For example, the *bonang* in this piece plays a kind of elaboration known as **pipilan**, in which *a new melody is created mostly by alternating between pairs of* balungan *tones*, as shown in Graphic 12.4. The gray rectangles represent the

GRAPHIC 12.4

In this section of *Pangkur*, red rectangles mark the *bonang barung* part. Black and gray rectangles mark the original *balungan* notes.

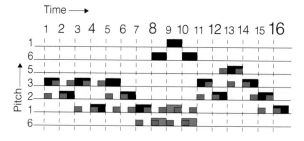

same balungan pitches in the lower octave to make clear the melody's relationship to the *bonang* part. Note that the *bonang* part creates a simple "flowering" or elaboration consisting of alternations between pairs of notes that follow the *balungan* pitches. The *bonang panerus* (the highest instrument of the family) plays the same patterns but at twice the rhythmic density, thus alternating back and forth twice for every single alternation in this part.

At a level of greater rhythmic density, other instruments, including the *gendér barung*, *gendér panerus*, *gambang*, and *celempung*, weave more elaborate melodies around the *balungan*, coinciding at metrically important points, generally every four *balungan* notes. The section of the *gendér* part shown in Graphic 12.5 is a variation of a *cengkok* (a stock melodic outline) known as *tumurun*, which the player has chosen because it is appropriate for a *patet manyura balungan* phrase that goes from pitch 1 to pitch 6, as in this example. Note how the melody corresponds with the *balungan* at beats four and eight. In between these beats, this supple melody diverges and returns to partial correspondence at beats 5 and 6.

GRAPHIC 12.5

In this single phrase from *Pangkur*, red rectangles mark the *gendér barung* part and show its more complex "flowering" of the *balungan*, marked by black and gray rectangles.

What results is a rich polyphony of melodies that fit together like fractals, at different levels of activity. The players give the piece structure and maintain interest through changes in texture and *irama* (rhythmic density relative to the *balungan*).

 Pangkur examples: CD 3:2 *Gendér barung*, CD 3:3 *Rebab*, CD 3:4 *Gambang*, CD 3:5 *Kendang*, CD 3:6 *Bonang barung*

CD 3:1. *Ladrang Pangkur,* Gamelan Paguyuban "Suko Raras." Djarwo Saminto, director

---

The *buka*—introduction.

0:00

Gendér barung plays short solo.

Kendang drum enters, establishes the tempo, and cues the orchestra's entrance.

Part I—loud style, *irama I.*

0:06

Large gong signals the end of the *buka,* and the whole orchestra enters.

Orchestra plays first phrase (beats 1 to 8), ending with the descending motive 3 2 1 6 and *kenong* stroke.

The gamelan establishes *patet manyura* by ending on pitch 6 and avoiding pitch 5.

0:11

The second phrase (beats 9 to 16), ends with the motive 5 3 2 1.

This motive, a transposition of the characteristic *manyura* motive 3 2 1 6, now lands on pitch 1. Because of this new emphasis on pitch 1, the melody seems to take us to new territory.

0:16

The third phrase (beats 17 to 24) builds tension by emphasizing pitch 2.

The third phrase introduces yet another transposition of the characteristic motive, this time to 6 5 3 2.

0:21

The drummer suddenly plays more loudly to indicate a change in texture for the second gong cycle (*gongan*).

The fourth and final phrase of the melody (beats 25 to 32) repeats the descending motive in successively lower transpositions.

Now the 6 5 3 2 on which the previous phrase ended is followed by 5 3 2 1 and finally 3 2 1 6 that brings us back to the feeling of *patet manyura*.

The gong indicates the end of the melody.

Part II—soft style, *irama I*

0:28

The *celempung* zither, *suling* flute, and *rebab* fiddle play intricate melodies elaborating on the *balungan;* the *gambang* xylophone and *gendér* metallophones are also playing.

Their intricate melodies shadow the *balungan*, weave around it, and always come back.

4:03

The drummer loudly signals a change in *irama* (rhythmic density).

4:12

The tempo slows dramatically to about half the previous tempo.

4:24

The faster instruments shift rhythmic density to play twice as many notes per *balungan* tone.

Although there are just as many notes per second, the fact that the melodic lines weaving around the *balungan* now have twice as far to go between each point of correspondence creates a new perspective, as if we are zooming in on the same melody. That shifting point of view is the essence of a change in *irama*, often used to give structure and variety to Javanese gamelan performances.

Part III—soft style, *irama II.*

4:48

New gong cycle, slow melody.

6:28

A sharp drum cue silences all but the *slentem, rebab*, and *suling*, suddenly opening up the texture for the gong to shine through.

Part IV—alternating textures, *irama II.*

6:32

The *slentem, rebab*, and *suling* (the very soft instruments) and the colotomic gongs create a lyrical perspective of the melody.

| 7:01 | The other instruments return, but only briefly at the midpoint of the melody. |

| 7:28 | The drum cues the return of the full orchestra in time for the gong. |

Part V—new countermelody, *irama II*.

8:15	A drum cue again opens up the texture to the *slentem, rebab,* and *suling.*
	The *saron* play a new countermelody, shadowed by the rebab.
	This new melody (composed, not improvised) still corresponds to the *balungan* tones at important points.

| 9:07 | The rest of the orchestra reappears on a subtle drum cue in time for the gong. |

| 9:57 | A drum cue opens the texture once again. |
| | A solo *rebab* plays the countermelody; brief orchestral interruptions as before. |

| 10:52 | New *gongan* with the whole orchestra. |

| 11:14 | The drum signals a gradual increase in tempo at this midpoint in the cycle. |

Part VI—return of loud style, *irama I*

| 11:28 | Gong sounds. |
| | The tempo has doubled, the melodic instruments shift to the original *irama,* and the texture returns to the opening loud statement of the melody. |

| 11:42 | The drum signals the gradual slowing down of tempo to prepare for the ending. |

| 11:58 | The final tone of the melody is dramatically withheld until after the last gong has sounded. |

Listening Exercise 10

CD 3:1. *Ladrang Pangkur*

1. The *buka* (introduction) is played by the
   a. *bonang panerus.*
   b. *gambang.*
   c. *gendér barung.*
   d. *rebab.*

2. How many times is the melody played before the section in which the *irama* changes (at 4:08)?
   a. Six times
   b. Nine times
   c. Twelve times
   d. Sixteen times

3. At 6:48, a single stroke from a colotomic instrument punctuates the soft trio of *slentem*, *rebab*, and *suling*. This instrument is the
   a. *kenong.*
   b. *kempul.*
   c. *gong.*
   d. *gendér barung.*

4. Which instruments drop out when the melody returns to *irama I* at 11:28?
   a. *Saron* family
   b. *Bonang* family
   c. *Suling* and *celempung*

You can take this Listening Exercise online and receive feedback or e-mail answers to your instructor at the World Music Resource Center.

BALI, ITS GAMELAN AND INSTRUMENTS

Since the 1930s, when Western anthropologists, artists, and ethnomusicologists first explored its lush volcanic hillsides, the island of Bali has been justly famous in the West for its unique culture and embarrassment of riches in the arts. Today, these hills echo with the sounds of motorcycles and tour buses, but arts and rituals are as much a part of daily life for the Balinese as they were in previous centuries. In Balinese communities, virtually everyone is an artist—a rice farmer may also be a poet, a housewife a dancer, a taxi driver a sculptor, or a construction worker a gamelan player. Professional musicians exist, of course, but are mainly associated with the modern music conservatories. Art is a natural part of community life for nearly everyone.

The complex web of social obligations to one's local community, or *banjar*, is a crucial part of life for the Balinese, and represents the Hindu virtue of *dharma*, fulfilling one's place in society and harmony with the world. Cooperation within one's community and society as a whole is

William Alves

FIGURE 12.5

An audience at a Balinese village watches dances during one of the frequent gamelan performances. Villages may commission a performance for an important ritual, such as the anniversary of the founding of a temple. In such a case, the most important audience may be gods.

deeply ingrained and reflected in aspects of social life from the distribution of irrigation water, which is controlled by certain priests, to the formation of neighborhood music and dance clubs that play for local rituals, competitions, spiritual fulfillment, or for enjoyment.

Unlike its neighbor Java, which converted to Islam hundreds of years ago, Bali remains a primarily Hindu region in which rituals form a nearly constant part of daily life. These ceremonies often require elaborately decorated offerings of fruit and flowers to the gods as well as an offering of music. Rituals, artistic performances, even concerts for tourists and the most mundane of everyday events can be spiritually charged and connected to the supernatural (Figure 12.5).

CHARACTERISTICS OF THE BALINESE GAMELAN

The Balinese gamelan, although outwardly similar to the Javanese version, plays a thrilling, dynamic music apt to create a flood of sensory impressions (Figure 12.6). All the gamelan parts interconnect, not through controlled individual elaborations, as in Java, but through memorization of set parts, sometimes composed communally, so that each of the parts cooperates precisely with the others.

One of the most famous and characteristic techniques of the Balinese gamelan is the creation of a melody through the combination of two or more extremely fast and rhythmically intricate interlocking parts. Interlocking means that when one of the two melodies is playing, the other may be resting, and vice versa, so that, heard together, they form a single unbroken line. As in other aspects of Balinese life, the split-second timing of such techniques requires absolute cooperation.

Another remarkable facet of Balinese performance, especially in the style called **kebyar**, is the ability of the entire orchestra to stop and start on a dime and to play seemingly nonmetrical rhapsodic sections as if they were a single instrument. There is no esoteric secret behind such ability—just hours and hours of rehearsal.

Another distinctive characteristic of the Balinese gamelan is the fact that the instruments are *deliberately detuned* from one another, producing a jarring effect that the Balinese cultivate. The detuning is not haphazard but precisely calibrated to give a constant "wah-wah" effect, a kind of sparkle to the sound that one can hear especially as the sound decays.

William Alves

FIGURE 12.6

A Balinese gamelan plays at a ceremony.

Table 12.3

A Comparison of Generalizations About Balinese and Central Javanese Characteristics in Gamelan Music

Balinese	Central Javanese
dynamic, extreme contrasts	generally sedate, "like flowing water"
fast interlocking rhythms	moderate, simple rhythms
bright, exciting	refined, gentle
distinct gamelan ensembles	standardized set of gamelan instruments
pairs of instruments clearly detuned to give a jarring effect and characteristic shimmering sound	octaves slightly detuned to give a very subtle life to the sound
slow core melody in background	slow *balungan* melody often dominates texture
instrumental compositions common	vocal music with gamelan common
dance often fast and exciting	dance often extremely graceful and stylized
sudden stops and starts in *kebyar* style	tempo mostly constant except for *irama* shifts and slowing down at end
little or no improvisation	improvised variations of *cengkok* patterns
highly precise	ambiguous
competitive	nonconfrontational, indirect

The Balinese gamelan shares some of the characteristics of the Javanese gamelan: colotomic structure (the periodic punctuation by gongs), a tempo conducted by drummers, compositions made up of repeated sections, and of course the similar instruments—Table 12.3 compares the two varieties. Nevertheless, it is unlikely that one would mistake the loud and brilliant sound of the Balinese gamelan for the often sedate, meditative music of its neighbor. Both traditions have points of correspondence that converged, especially during the period of the great East Javanese kingdoms 500 years ago, but the directions they have taken reflect their different cultures.

THE *GAMELAN GONG KEBYAR*

On humid summer nights on the streets of Bali's largest city and capital, Denpasar, one can hear the nearly constant echoes of gamelans even above the motorbikes and shouts from street food stalls. This is the time of the *Pesta Kesenian Bali*, or Bali Arts Festival, an enormous annual competition and showcase for everything from temple offerings to mask-making to fashion, and, of course, different types of gamelan.

Unlike the ensembles of Java, where the classical gamelan has become a more or less standardized set of instruments that plays for many different repertories, styles, dances, and dramas, Bali has many distinct types of gamelan, some common and others rare, each with its own repertory and often performance contexts. But the most popular type of gamelan by far is the **gamelan gong kebyar** (also called *kebyar* and *gong kebyar*), whose brilliant sounds seem to be nearly everywhere.

This large ensemble not only plays for the dance after which it was named but also accompanies other dances, ceremonial and occasional music, and unaccompanied instrumental performances. The word *kebyar* literally means to flare up like the lighting of a match and that is an apt description for the explosive nonpulsatile introductions found in many *kebyar* pieces. The main body of a *kebyar* composition consists of a series of repeated sections in which core melodies serve as foundations for amazingly fast and virtuosic figurations. Unlike other traditional repertories, *kebyar* compositions are not necessarily associated with a dramatic form or dance that tells a story.

Competitions at the Bali Arts Festival are not small affairs for connoisseurs but elaborate, exciting events attended by thousands of spectators from all over the island. The rivalry is fierce, and the audience merciless. A wrong note may result in a chorus of boos, and a dazzling passage may inspire spontaneous applause and yells of encouragement.

The rise of such pan-Balinese festivals in the past century and especially the past thirty years or so brought some important changes to performance practice, and nowhere are these changes more evident than in *kebyar*. The style has become faster and more virtuosic, with greater precision. Performances are also often visually flashy—the **ugal** (lead metallophone player) may spin his mallet, for example, and dull facial expressions can lead to deductions of points.

There are several different stories about the birth of *kebyar*, but most agree that it was a style that emerged around 1915, at the same time as the decline of the courts following the Dutch takeover of the island in 1906. *Kebyar*'s spectacular, dynamic style appealed to the common people who dominated the organization of gamelans in the absence of the courts, and the *kebyar* style quickly spread throughout the island. Many old court gamelans were recast into *kebyar* instruments, so that today the earlier gamelan types are relatively rare. Whereas the more ancient instruments often include all seven pitches of the *pelog* scale, the instruments of the gong *kebyar* are usually tuned to a five-tone subset of *pelog* known as **selisir**.

THE *KEBYAR* INSTRUMENTS

The *kebyar* orchestra contains two families of metallophones. Softer single-octave instruments play the slow-moving **pokok** or core melody, and bright two-octave instruments mainly play the very fast figuration. All of these metallophones typically have thin keys suspended over individual tube resonators. Players of the *pokok* metallophones use padded mallets, giving the section a soft, mellow tone that creates a resonant underpinning for the rest of the orchestra.

The metallophones that play fast figuration are collectively referred to as the **gangsa** and include (from low to high) **ugal** (also called *giying*), **pemade**, and **kantilan**. Each of the metallophone instruments, with the possible exception of the *ugal*, has a partner with which it is precisely detuned. There are usually four players on each of the *pemade* and *kantilan* so that each detuned pair can play interlocking parts with another pair. The **reyong** is a set of twelve kettle-gongs mounted horizontally in a frame. Unlike the similar Javanese *bonang*, four players share the single row of kettle-gongs, often playing virtuosic interlocking figuration. The *suling* is a vertical flute that plays an elaborate

INSTRUMENT GALLERY

INSTRUMENTS OF A TYPICAL BALINESE *GAMELAN GONG KEBYAR*

William Alves

GONGS AND *POKOK* METALLOPHONES

Shown here are the gongs and *pokok* metallophones of a Balinese gamelan. In the back row are two **jegogan**, the lowest metallophones of this group, which play every other or every fourth note of the *pokok*. In the middle row are a *gendér* (not part of this section) and two **calung** or *jublag* metallophones, which play the *pokok* an octave higher than the *jegogan*. In the front row are the two **penyacah**, optional metallophones tuned an octave higher than the *jublag*.

Courtesy instrument collection of the Music Department of Pomona College

GANGSA

The **gangsa**, shown here, is the collective name for the metallophones that play fast figurations elaborating the core melody. Those in the back row are the **kantilan** (generally four in the ensemble) that are struck with a single wooden mallet in the right hand while the left hand damps the sound. The metallophone on the left is a **pemade** (generally four in an ensemble) that plays the same figuration as the *kantilan* but an octave lower. In the foreground is the **ugal**, or *giying* (generally one or two in the ensemble), a low-octave metallophone that plays the main melody with elaborations and leads the *gangsa* section. In the background are the **gong** (the largest hanging gong), the **kempur** (a medium-sized hanging gong), and the high-pitched hanging *gong* **kentong** or *kemong*, which often divides the cycle into two. In front of the *gangsa* is the **kempli** or *kajar*, the single kettle-gong that keeps the beat.

William Alves

REYONG

The **reyong** is a single set of twelve kettle-gongs mounted horizontally in a frame and shared by four players.

William Alves

CENG-CENG

The **ceng-ceng** *cymbals* (one or two performers) reinforce drum patterns. The bottoms of these small cymbals are always mounted on the back of a carving of a turtle, representing the animal that holds up the world in Hindu mythology.

Hear and see the instruments of a typical Balinese *gamelan gong kebyar* in your **ACTIVE LISTENING TOOLS,** available at the World Music Resource Center.

form of the melody in soft sections. Often, several (two to four) play together heterophonically.

The *kendang* (drums) lead the orchestra. Usually played by two players, the *kendang* control the tempo and dynamic level and signal repeat or dance cues. Like the other paired instruments, the two drummers often create interlocking patterns of their own. **Ceng-ceng** are cymbals that reinforce the drum patterns. The colotomic underpinning is provided by a single player who plays up to three types of gongs, along with the important **kempli** player, who helps synchronize the fast parts by playing a metronomic beat on this single kettle-gong.

BALINESE COMPOSITION AND PERFORMANCE

TOPENG (MASK DANCE) AND *KEBYAR*

In Bali, dances can be dynamic and exciting with rapid angular motions suddenly and effortlessly changing to slow, fluid movements. One traditional dance commonly in the repertoire of the *gamelan gong kebyar* is the mask dance or **topeng**, in which the solo dancer represents the character depicted in the mask (Figure 12.7).

The dance begins with a brief solo by the *ugal*, the large metallophone that leads the *gangsa* (melody elaboration) section. The drummer joins to set the tempo, and then the entire gamelan answers with an explosive chord and begins to play. At this time, the dancer enters. The music for *topeng* dances consists of a series of **tabuh**, or short repeated melodies (ostinatos), played in their most complete form by the *ugal*. The *penyacah*, if present, plays a simplified version of the same melody, one note per beat; the *jublag* plays every other note of the *penyacah* melody or one note every two beats; and the lowest *jegogan* plays every other note of the *penyacah* melody or every four beats. After the ostinato has been established, the players of the *reyong* kettle-gongs enter, playing fast interlocking figuration.

The musicians, like the dancer, seem quiescent but alert, softly playing this repeating pattern. Suddenly, the dancer makes a bold movement. This movement, called an **angsel**, is a cue to the drummer, who in turn loudly cues the rest of the gamelan. At the drummer's signal, the gamelan moves out of the ostinato and plays a loud cadence (ending) phrase. This new phrase (itself called an *angsel*) may serve as a signal to move on to the next section, depending on the subsequent cue from the drummer. Thus the drummer, in cooperation with the dancer, signals via audible cues what sections to play when and how many times. The *angsel* breaks form an important structural element not just in dances but in many types of gamelan pieces and may signal complicated variations, alternate melodies, or sectional changes.

William Alves

FIGURE 12.7

Topeng is the masked dance-drama of Bali.

Most Balinese dances are based on this system of repeating melodies interrupted by *angsel*. In dances such as those of the *topeng* genres, the exact placement of the *angsel* is left up to the dancer, but in ensemble temple dances, for example, the *angsels* come at set points in every performance. Gamelan pieces not based on dances may still rely on repeated melodies, but the melodies can at times be very long and elaborate, especially in slow ritual repertories.

KECAK

Around a flickering fire late at night, a group of bare-chested men sit in concentric circles to perform one of Bali's most famous forms of music called *cak* or **kecak** (pronounced "chak" and "kechak"). This music does not use instruments at all. Rather, the roles of the instruments are taken over by the shouts, chants, and songs of the men, so that they themselves become the gamelan. Invented in the 1930s as a form of dance drama often representing stories from the *Ramayana* epic, the origins of the music go much further back to a now rare ritual for communicating with dead ancestors.

The performance may include a narrator who sings and speaks the story in the manner of the *dalang* puppeteer in the *wayang* shadow puppet play, and sometimes dancers. Several men take on the roles of the colotomic instruments of the orchestra, including the *kempli* (imitated with the syllable "pung!"), the *kentong* (a small hanging gong imitated with the syllable "tong!"), and the large gong (whose low wavering sound is imitated with a rolled "sirrr!").

Suddenly a shout goes up from the leader of the chorus, and the men begin shouting the syllable "chak!" in different interlocking patterns, so that the result is electrifying polyrhythmic shouting that sounds something like "chakachakachakachaka . . .." Graphic 12.6 illustrates these interlocking patterns. When sounded together, these rhythms evoke the terrifying monkey army of King Rama in the *Ramayana* story.

GRAPHIC 12.6

The interlocking rhythms of *kecak*

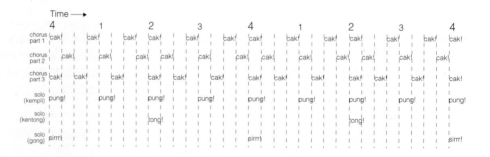

INTERLOCKING PATTERNS

Whereas the more rhythmically dense melodies of the Javanese gamelan create a dense polyphonic tapestry from the combination of all the individual instrument lines, Balinese figuration is characteristically based on the precise cooperation of rhythms and melodies that interlock like puzzle pieces. Cymbal players in processional gamelans, known as **belaganjur**, and other forms use the same rhythms as in *kecak* to create these exciting patterns.

When pitched instruments such as metallophones or kettle-gongs play such figuration, the interlocking patterns have to be carefully coordinated not only to each other but also to correspond to important pitches of the *pokok*, or core melody. This lightning-fast figuration thus creates one more level of melody in the *gamelan* texture. A composer carefully works out these precise interlocking melodies before the performance. There is no room for improvisation.

KOTEKAN

Possibly the most dazzling technique of the *kebyar* style is the type of figuration known as **kotekan**. In *kotekan*, the players of the *pemade* and *kantilan* metallophones or *reyong* divide into two parts, known as the *polos* and the *sangsih*, each of which consists of fast, complex syncopations, which when played together form a very fast composite melody, precisely interlocking the two parts. In Graphic 12.7, half the *pemade* metallophones play the notes represented by the light blue rectangles (the part called the *polos*), while the other half plays the notes represented by the pink rectangles (the *sangsih*). When they overlap, it is always on a unison pitch (colored purple here), and the two parts combine to make a single unbroken and very fast melody. This melody corresponds at important times to the notes of the core melody, or *pokok*, played by the softer *calung* and *jegogan* metallophones in different octaves. This particular subset of the seven-tone *pelog* tuning system uses only pitches 1, 2, 3, 5, and 6, and the irregularly spaced grid lines roughly represent the gapped intervals between the steps of this scale.

GRAPHIC 12.7

Kotekan

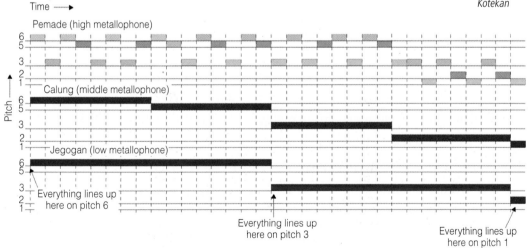

A BALINESE GAMELAN PERFORMANCE

Gending Pengalang or *Bebarongan* is used to accompany the famous **barong** dance of Bali. The *barong* is a mythical dragon-like animal that is the holy

CD 3:7. *Gending Pengalang Bebarongan, Gamelan Punia Bhakti,* I Nyoman Wenten, director

Kawitan section—introduction.

0:00

The *ugal* metallophone plays a short introduction.

The drummer follows and sets the tempo.

0:03

The balance of the orchestra enters.

The *calung* plays the *pokok* core melody.

The *jegogan* plays a slower abstraction (every fourth note) of the *calung* melody.

The *gangsa* (*ugal, pemade,* and *kantilan* metallophones) play a simple elaboration of the melody in unison.

The *ceng-ceng* cymbals and *kendang* drums add noisy life to this introduction as . . .

The *barong* (dancers) enter.

The *calung* and *jegogan* players use padded beaters that give the piece a resonant foundation that nevertheless remains in the background.

0:21

The *ugal* and *suling* flutes (in heterophonic accompaniment) play an interlude.

0:26

The *gangsa* respond with *kotekan* (interlocking parts) to end the section.

Pengawak section—main body (a more expansive melody than in either first or last sections).

0:29

Transition again features *ugal* and *suling.*

0:41

A flurry of *kotekan* follows.

0:47

The *gangsa* interrupt with three short notes created by hitting the bar while holding it with the other hand.

The *gangsa* repeat the phrase and introduce a more expansive section.

0:55	The *gangsa* with the *kotekan* accompany an extended melody.
	Notice that *kotekan* figuration does not have to be loud; in fact, the preference is to play it lightly, cleanly, and softly. Every note is clearly heard, even though the melody is split between the two parts.
1:28	The melody repeats.

Pengecet section—fast ending.

2:42	The colotomic structure suddenly contracts as the dance picks up energy.
	The gong alternates with the *kentong* (a high-pitched gong) every two beats.
	The melodic instruments repeat a simple pattern while the drummer and dancers improvise an exciting interlude.
2:55	*Angsel*—the *barong* dancer suddenly leaps and the drummer responds with three loud strokes—a signal to the orchestra to move on to the main body of the *pengecet* section.
2:58	The orchestra plays the exciting body of the *pengecet* section.
	The *gangsa* play ever faster *kotekan* in an electric finale.
3:16	The drummer loudly signals an *angsel* responding once again to a signal from the *barong* dancers.
	Although the dancers have some freedom in the placement of the *angsel*, it must always occur at the proper place in the colotomic structure and often, as in this case, in the melody.
	The *gangsa* instruments interrupt their otherwise continuous figuration.
4:01	Another *angsel*.
4:44	Final *angsel* signals a break.
4:49	Short repeated pattern (ostinato) until the *barong* dancers exit.
5:02	The drum signals a slowing tempo to anticipate the end of the piece.

Hear and see the instruments of *Gending Pengalang Bebarongan* in your **ACTIVE LISTENING TOOLS**, available at the World Music Resource Center.

 CD 3:8 Balinese gamelan examples

Listening Exercise 11 | CD 3:7. *Gending Pengalang Bebarongan*

1. How many beats are between the *gong* at 0:28 and the *gong* at 0:44?
   a. 8
   b. 16
   c. 24
   d. 64

2. Which colotomic instrument plays at 1:10?
   a. *Kentong* (high hanging gong)
   b. *Kempur* (medium hanging gong)
   c. *Gong* (lowest hanging gong)

3. Which instruments temporarily stop playing in response to the *angsel* at 3:18?
   a. *Gangsa* and *ceng-ceng*
   b. *Suling*
   c. *Pokok* (core melody) instruments
   d. Colotomic instruments

You can take this Listening Exercise online and receive feedback or e-mail answers to your instructor at the World Music Resource Center.

FIGURE 12.8

Beneath the costume for the *barong*, the mythical dragon that protects Balinese villages, are two dancers; the one in front controls the jaws of the beast.

William Alves

protector of a village (Figure 12.8). In a dance-drama acted out for certain ceremonies (and, today, for tourists), two men dress up in an elaborate *barong* costume and dance together, generally accompanied by a *kebyar*-style orchestra.

In this drama, Rangda, an evil witch, challenges the *barong*. Sometimes the man who plays Rangda goes into a trance in which he is possessed by her spirit. Other men of the village also go into trances and try to attack Rangda with ceremonial daggers called *kris*. However, Rangda's magic is too strong, and she forces the *kris* back against her attackers. Under her spell, each of these men tries mightily to stab himself, but is protected by the *barong*, so that no matter how hard they push, the *kris* never draw blood. In the end, the *barong* defeats Rangda and saves the village.

Like many Balinese pieces, *Gending Pengalang* is in three large parts, which the Balinese sometimes refer to as the "head," "body," and "feet" of the composition. More formally, they are called the *kawitan*, *pengawak*, and *pengecet*.

POPULAR MUSIC IN INDONESIA

While the courts of Central Java were looking inward to develop highly refined and sophisticated gamelan music and other arts, other areas of what is now Indonesia absorbed popular and folk music from many other regions. This was especially true of the areas around the key shipping lanes through the Straits of Malaka, that is, the coastal areas of Sumatra, Malaysia, and northwest Java. Arabic traders with instruments from the Middle East were followed by Portuguese colonists, Chinese immigrants, and finally the Dutch, who brought their own instruments, popular songs, and musical theater.

By the twentieth century, a new popular genre called *kroncong* emerged from this mixture, although its roots lie in the plucked string ensembles of Portuguese sailors. The origin of the name remains unclear, although it could refer to the sound of the gritty strums on the small guitar-like instrument of the ensemble, also called *kroncong*. A *kroncong* ensemble may also include a standard guitar, a plucked cello or double bass (low instruments of the European violin family), and perhaps a bowed violin or other melodic instrument along with a singer.

Kroncong songs have adopted the simple harmonies of European popular songs, strummed by the *kroncong* lute and guitar in characteristic rhythms that often emphasize off-beat syncopations (i.e., stressing divisions of the beat that would not ordinarily be given metrical stress). These rhythms seem to reflect *kroncong*'s Iberian heritage, like the light and graceful syncopations of many Brazilian popular songs. (Brazil was also a sixteenth-century Portuguese colony.)

Despite occasional bans or suppression of Western popular music during the period 1942–1965, the influence of American pop music was widespread. Just as important, however, was popular music from Latin America and film music from India. By the 1960s, a new popular form emerged from these disparate influences known as *dangdut*.

Dangdut bands use the same sorts of instruments found in pop music bands elsewhere in the world—electric guitars, synthesizers, drum sets, and so on—but are characterized by rhythms that emphasize beats one and four of a four-beat metrical unit. This distinctive beat is probably the origin of the name: dang - DUT - two - three - dang - DUT - two - three, and so on. *Dangdut* singers often mix American pop styles with the same reedy vocal timbres and melismas as in film music from India. Unlike sentimental *kroncong* songs, *dangdut* lyrics address a variety of topics, including social protest, and the iconic *dangdut* singer Rhoma Irama has written songs commenting on poverty and domestic violence.

An interest in the development of recognizably indigenous elements in regional music has led to wonderfully hybrid genres. *Gambang kromong* is a style from West Java that integrates the *gambang* xylophone, gongs (also known as *kromong*), *kendang* drums, *rebab* fiddle, and a double-reed aerophone (similar to the Chinese *suona* or Middle Eastern *zurna*), with Western instruments such as flutes, trumpets, and electric bass, sometimes with exuberant clashes of tuning systems. Another West Javanese style called *jaipongan* originally included only gamelan instruments such as the *saron*, *bonang*, *kendang*, and *rebab*, with a female singer. Unlike other popular genres, *jaipongan* used cyclic gong forms and gamelan tuning systems. However, more recently, some groups have adopted *jaipongan*'s rhythms and sensuous song styles to more conventional pop bands using Western tuning and harmonies.

Another musician who has combined traditional gamelan with modern popular forms is the Balinese electric guitarist I Wayan Balawan. American jazz-rock fusion styles have inspired Balawan, but he sometimes also includes Balinese drumming, interlocking cymbals from *belaganjur* ensembles, and metallophone figuration in his band. To match the tuning of the metallophone with the fixed Western tuning of his guitars, his musicians play their interlocking patterns on American vibraphone bars instead of the traditional keys of the Balinese *gangsa* metallophone.

NEW GAMELAN MUSIC

Although popular music now dominates the public experience of music in Indonesia, gamelan is still a vital and evolving art. Gamelan composers, especially those associated with the arts academies and universities, have experimented with new meters, forms, instruments, and textures. They have sometimes even borrowed from popular music, as in the 1950s when the *kroncong* hit "Gambang Suling" was adapted for Javanese gamelan and then became the basis for a Balinese *kebyar* piece. Over his long life, the famous Javanese composer Ki K. P. H. Wasitodiningrat wrote new and widely popular gamelan compositions that borrowed Latin American rhythms and European polyphony while at the same time confronting contemporary issues such as poverty, government corruption, and environmental damage. Many of the most innovative compositions have come from Bali, where the mainstream press regularly debates new forms, techniques, and provocative experiments presented at arts festivals.

The gamelan has also been a medium of new musical developments outside of Indonesia. In 1955, ethnomusicologist Mantle Hood brought a Javanese gamelan to the University of California, Los Angeles, with the then unusual idea that American students could best learn about Javanese musical culture by playing gamelan music under instruction from a Javanese master. Many colleges throughout the world, especially in the United States, have since followed this example, so that today many non-Indonesians play in hundreds of these ensembles outside of Indonesia.

Inspired by this tradition, in 1970, the American experimentalist composer Lou Harrison (1917–2003), along with instrument builder William Colvig, constructed an "American gamelan" out of aluminum tubes, bars, and plates. He immediately began composing for the ensemble he and Colvig built and was soon building others and studying with Wasitodiningrat (who was by then teaching in the United States). Harrison composed dozens of works for gamelan, often in combination with Western instruments, believing that, just as some Indonesian composers write for the Western orchestra, there is nothing wrong with Western composers returning the compliment.

Betty Freeman

FIGURE 12.9

Lou Harrison plays a *suling* flute.

REFERENCES

DISCOGRAPHY

JAVANESE GAMELAN MUSIC

Gamelan Pura Paku Alaman, Yogyakarta. *Javanese Court Gamelan*, rereleased as *Java: Court Gamelan*. New York/Los Angeles: Elektra/Nonesuch 9 72044-2, 1971/2003.

Gamelan Sekar Tunjung. *The Music of K.R.T. Wasitodiningrat*. New York: CMP Records CD 3007, 1992.

Pawiyatan Kraton Surakarta. *Court Music of Kraton Surakarta*. Tokyo: King Record Co. Ltd. KICC 5151, 1992.

Sarasehan Krawitan Surakarta. *Chamber Music of Central Java*. Tokyo: King Record Co. Ltd. KICC 5152, 1992.

Various artists. *Java: Palais Royal de Yogyakarta* (4 CDs). Paris: Ocora C 560067-70, 1973/1995.

BALINESE GAMELAN MUSIC

Gamelan Semar Pegulingan, Kamasan, Bali. *The Heavenly Orchestra of Bali*. New York: CMP Records CD 3008, 1991.

Gamelan STSI. *Music of the Gamelan Gong Kebyar*. El Cerrito, CA: Vital Records 401, 1996.

Various artists. *Bali: Gamelan and Kecak*. New York/Los Angeles: Elektra/Nonesuch 9 79204-2, 1989.

OTHER TRADITIONS

Harrison, Lou. *Gamelan Music*. Ocean, NJ: MusicMasters 01612-67091-2, 1992.

Various artists. *Indonesian Popular Music: Kroncong, Dangdut, and Langgam Jawa*. Washington DC: Smithsonian Folkways SFW40056, 1991.

 BOOK COMPANION WEBSITE

You will find flashcards, a glossary, and tutorial quizzes, as well as other materials that will help you succeed in this course, at the *Music of the Peoples of the World, 2nd Edition,* Companion Website at www.cengage.com/music/alves/world2e.

PLACE

NORWAY

SWEDEN

• Stockholm

Baltic Sea

FINLAND

Helsinki •

• Tallinn

ESTONIA

• Riga

LATVIA

RUSSIA

Moscow •

DENMARK

• Copenhagen

LITHUANIA

Vilnius •

• Minsk

BELARUS

NETH.

Berlin •

POLAND

• Warsaw

• Kiev

BELG.

GERMANY

LUX.

• Prague

CZECH REP.

SLOVAKIA

UKRAINE

Vienna •

• Bratislava

MOLDOVA

SWITZERLAND

AUSTRIA

• Budapest

HUNGARY

Ljubljana •

• Kishinev

FRANCE

SLO.

Zagreb •

ROMANIA

ITALY

CROATIA

Sarajevo •

• Belgrade

• Bucharest

BOSNIA

YUGOSLAVIA

Black Sea

• Sofia

Skopje •

BULGARIA

• Rome

Tirana •

MACEDONIA

ALBANIA

• Ankara

GREECE

Sicily

Athens •

TURKEY

Eastern Europe here includes the Baltic states, Poland, the Czech Republic, Slovakia, Hungary, Romania, Bulgaria, Albania, the states of the former Yugoslavia, Greece, and the parts of the former Soviet Union that are ethnically Slavic, including Moldova, Belarus, and Ukraine. This chapter will concentrate on Hungary, Bulgaria, and Russia. Because of Russian expansion and settlements, Russian culture extends into vast parts of Central Asia. The Central Asian republics of the former Soviet Union have sizable ethnic Russian minorities, and thus two (or more) distinct musical traditions coexist in them.

TIMES

c. 700–143 BCE	1ST–5TH C CE	5TH–9TH C	9TH–10TH C
Classical Greek civilization, crucial source of much European and Arabic music theory and philosophy. Singing of epic songs, traditional in this region, perhaps dates back to Homeric bards.	Period of Roman Empire. In 395, empire breaks up into Eastern (Byzantine) and Western halves, precipitating important cultural, religious, and musical schism that helps distinguish Eastern from Western Europe.	Magyars arrive in Hungary from Central Asia, bringing distinctive musical characteristics.	First Russian state established amid Byzantine influence from modern Turkey. Russian conversion to Eastern Christianity and adoption of Eastern liturgical chant distinct from less elaborate Western ("Gregorian") chant. Other regions, including Poland, Hungary, Slovakia, and Czech Republic, adopt Roman Catholicism.

EASTERN EUROPE

SETTING

Although listeners familiar with Western European choral music will recognize some of the elements in the song *Dilmano, Dilbero*—a diatonic scale and harmonies—the brash singing style and unfamiliar meter exhibit a very different and in some ways ancient aesthetic. In 1904, the young Hungarian composer Béla Bartók had a similar listening experience that would change the path of his career. Vacationing in the resort town Gerlicepuszta (now Ratkó in Slovakia), he heard a young nursemaid (Lidi Dósa) sing a haunting, simple tune. It was Bartók's first glimpse of the authentic folk heritage of his country.

SOUNDS

CD 3:10

Dilmano, Dilbero

It may seem strange that Bartók was unfamiliar with the musical traditions of his own country, but he was raised in an upper-middle class, urban culture that rarely mixed with the peasantry. He knew only the sentimental parlor songs and the earthy, flamboyant dances of the urban dance bands popular in Hungary at that time. The overly expressive, somewhat exotic sound of these bands had inspired Hungarian Romantic composers such

1240	14TH–15TH C	1345–1913	18TH C	
Mongol invasion and establishment of Mongol Empire throughout Central Asia bring Asian influences.	Turkish and Russian dominance. The Roma, known to Europeans as "Gypsies," migrate from Asia to Europe and settle especially in southeastern and central Europe but also in Italy, France, and Spain.	Ottoman Turks control much of Greece, Balkans, Bulgaria, Romania, Hungary, and Albania, where they introduce Islamic musical and cultural influences that remain strong in many areas today.	Russia, a growing international power, seeks closer ties with the West and establishes Western European–style court music. Russia still relies on serfdom, and, as in many areas of Eastern Europe, agricultural economy influences a rich heritage of folk song.	

as Ferenc (Franz) Liszt, whose *Hungarian Rhapsodies* (1852 and 1880) captured the sentimental, often patronizing, view of the hearty peasant.

To Bartók, the sentimental "slop" (as he called it) of popular music did not represent the authentic voice of the Magyars (indigenous Hungarians). Hungary was then under the rule of the Austrians, as it had been under the Hapsburgs and Turks at various times since the Middle Ages, and Bartók was devoted to the nationalist cause then sweeping many areas of Eastern Europe. At the same time, however, modernist innovations in music were just beginning in Europe, and Bartók found himself torn trying to reconcile his own creative voice with nationalist elements in his music.

All that changed when he heard Dósa's song, a song completely unlike either the syrupy popular violin tunes or Western European folk songs. Bartók immediately wrote down the song and later wrote to his sister that this revelation had inspired him to "collect the finest examples of Hungarian folk music and raise them to the level of works of art." Within two years, Bartók and his friend Zoltán Kodály were traveling from village to village, writing down all the folk music they could find.

Although the collection of folk songs was not a new idea—folk-song societies of Britain, for example, had inspired the nationalist composer Ralph Vaughan Williams—never before Béla Bartók had this study been so comprehensive, systematic, and scientific (Figure 13.1). In adopting such a scholarly approach, Bartók went beyond styles that romanticized superficial aspects of peasant culture to discover the true nature of his cultural heritage.

Furthermore, Bartók did not stop his investigations with the Magyars but followed lines of influence to the Slovaks, the Serbs, the Romanians, the Bulgarians, the Croatians, the Macedonians, the Turks, and even into North Africa. Bartók was a respected ethnomusicologist before he was known as one of the century's most famous composers.

Bartók heard in this peasant music a truly original voice of astonishing beauty, one that resonated with his own expression as a composer. Transcending the superficial quotation of peasant melodies, Bartók wove folk influences deeply into his compositions.

From the mind-bendingly complex meters and spicy dissonances of the Balkans to the epic singing traditions that likely date back to Homer, Eastern European folk music has a stark and unique beauty. As a crossroads of the many cultures of Asia, the Middle East, and Europe, Eastern Europe forged truly distinctive traditions in its diverse cultures.

▶ 19TH C	1906	1917	1932
Breakup of Hapsburg control in Eastern Europe leads to nationalist movements in art and music; composers sometimes collect folk songs and spark interest in their countries' folk music heritage.	Béla Bartók (1881–1945) and Zoltán Kodály (1882–1967) begin collecting and studying Eastern European folk songs.	Soviet Revolution leads to state sponsorship of national and folk music.	Soviet Union begins policy of socialist realism in arts and censors or withdraws support for music not explicitly in service of state. Industrialization, collective farming, suppression of religious practices, and censorship bring great changes to folk and popular music.

© CORBIS

FIGURE 13.1

Bartók recording folk songs on a cylinder recorder in 1907 in Daraz, now Drazovce, Slovakia.

ELEMENTS OF EASTERN EUROPEAN FOLK MUSIC

Historically, the dominance of peasant culture in Eastern Europe coincides with the importance of folk song. The subjects and functions of these songs were closely tied to peasant life and included harvesting songs, other work songs, and songs for village occasions such as holidays and weddings. However, during the communist period, industrialization, collective farming, and censorship caused many of these songs (the ones Bartók collected, for example) to disappear, at least from their original context.

Still, the forms and spirit of these folk songs remain in many modern environments. Weddings, for example, are still very important events in these regions and may consist of several days of rituals and celebrations, each day having

1946–1989

1985

Cold War. Communist states in Eastern Europe create professional "folk" ensembles and control and refine their expression.

Gorbachev introduces policy of *glasnost* (openness), effectively ending strict government control over media and arts, and accelerating introduction of Western popular music styles. New freedom in arts reinvigorate national heritages and folk music, sometimes now in new hybrid popular forms.

FIGURE 13.2

The sort of Hungarian band that plays at weddings. In this case, the band includes a violin, tenor saxophone, accordion, and, in the right foreground, a *cimbalom*, a trapezoidal hammered dulcimer with multiple courses (several strings per pitch) made of metal. The hammers are covered with cotton to soften the timbre.

its own songs and dances. Today, these songs and dances may be accompanied by amplified bands with a mixture of indigenous and popular instruments (Figure 13.2). Songs for other occasions, such as Christmas and other holidays, are also popular.

Here are some of the distinctive characteristics of the songs and other music of this region that help distinguish Eastern European folk music from that of Western Europe.

◆ **Nonpulsatile songs.** In many areas of Eastern Europe, some genres of song have no fixed beat and often have expressive, florid ornamentation. Some of these elaborate and emotional song types show evidence of Middle Eastern influence.

◆ **Asymmetrical meters.** Areas of the Balkans, especially Bulgaria, are known for their complex meters with beats that quickly change duration.

◆ **Repetitive dance rhythms.** Many dances of these regions are known as much by their characteristic propulsive rhythms as their meter. In some areas, these short rhythms repeat even as the melody notes change, a technique known as **isorhythm.**

◆ **Bright timbres.** In many regions of Eastern Europe, singers, especially women, commonly cultivate rich and brassy timbres.

◆ **Epic songs.** An important tradition in this region, although less common today, these hours-long songs of heroic tales are sung by a single bard.

◆ **Socialist realism.** An aesthetic style during the communist period in which the arts served the state, socialist realism enforced to greater or lesser degrees professional composition and so-called folk ensembles.

EPIC SONGS

Homer, the legendary southeast European author of the *Iliad* and *Odyssey*, did not read or recite his famous epics but, like generations of bards before and after him, sang them. Such epic singing can still be found in Eastern Europe as well as Turkey, Central Asia, China, and even Southeast Asia. Epic singing traditions also existed in Western Europe, notably in Ireland, but generally died out after the Middle Ages.

Specially trained in this art form, the singers are usually men, professionals or semi-professionals who have memorized poems often of several thousand lines. Some epic performances, split over successive nights, are several days long. The performer memorizes a certain number of stock melodies and applies them to fit the poetic meter and mood of the text. Improvised ornamentation is always important, and these variations give life to what would otherwise be literally repeating melodies.

The epic singers usually sing without accompaniment, or they accompany themselves on an instrument such as a fiddle or plucked string instrument. In only a few traditions do other musicians accompany the epic singer. In part, this is a practical decision because it is very difficult for accompanying musicians to follow a singer in a partly improvised, perhaps nonpulsatile song. When the singer accompanies himself, he is able to imitate, anticipate, and play along with his improvisations in a way that would be difficult or impossible for a separate accompanist.

Today, many epic traditions have died out or are endangered. The last singers of Russian epics, called **bylini** or **starini**, sang about wars against the Tartars during the late Middle Ages, epics that died out in the early twentieth century. The art is still lost, despite attempts during the Soviet period to reinvigorate the tradition with socialist realist stories.

In Finland, the epic tradition is drawn from the *Kalevala*, the story of the legendary Finn leader, Väinemöinen. The *Kalevala* songs are traditionally accompanied on the **kantele**, a plucked zither. Ukrainian songs from about the same period are called **dumy**. The songs of the Serbians recall their resistance to Turkish occupation during the thirteenth to seventeenth centuries, but there are also new compositions. Serbian epic singers, like the Croats, Montenegrins, Bulgarians, Romanians, and other people from the same region, accompany themselves on a pear-shaped fiddle.

ASYMMETRICAL METERS

Some cultures use not only beats that can be divided into two (simple meter) and beats that can be divided into three (compound meter) but also meters that mix the two kinds of beats, called **asymmetrical meters**. Asymmetric meters are especially popular in Greece, Bulgaria, and some other Balkan regions. For example, a group of two pulses and another of three may alternate to create a larger metrical group of five, as shown in Graphic 13.1. Another possibility would be to group them as 3 + 2. In either case, the groups are of unequal sizes and hence asymmetrical. At a slow tempo, we could hear each pulse as a beat grouped into these patterns.

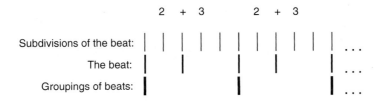

GRAPHIC 13.1

Example of asymmetrical meter

In most cases, however, the pulses go by so fast (at times, 320 per minute) that one hears the beat as occurring on the next metrical level. In those cases, we say that *the beat changes length*. First it is three, then two subdivisions in length. These shifting beats often reflect particular dance steps, some of which take more or less time to complete.

Apparently, such asymmetrical meters were common in ancient Greece, where the language indicated accents in words by making the syllable twice as long, rather than giving it more stress, as in English. Although the Greek language has changed, it is possible that the attraction to these meters has remained in the music.

SOCIALIST REALISM

A period of astonishing avant-garde artistic activity in the Soviet Union of the 1920s came to an abrupt end when Stalin instituted the policy known as socialist realism. This doctrine, named by the writer Maxim Gorky, was in part a reaction to a perceived elitism and bourgeois self-absorption in the arts. Socialist realism held that all art should exist to serve the state, and through it, the people. In the early years of the Soviet Union, the state established professional so-called folk music groups, and many composers self-consciously created didactic and patriotic works.

In the 1930s, Stalin made socialist realism a part of his cult of personality, a path that was emulated in Maoist China. Avant-garde experiments were bitterly attacked, and some artists were imprisoned or even executed. The famous Russian composer Igor Stravinsky, who had used folk elements in his earlier works, left Russia in 1917; Dmitri Shostakovich and Sergei Prokofiev lived in the Soviet Union and endured periodic censure from the government. Even folk musicians, whom the government could not always control as directly, were denied access to audiences and media. The disruption of traditional ways of life through collectivization, mass movements of workers to urban factories, and the homogenization of language and culture also caused the decline of many folk art traditions.

When the Eastern European states came into the Soviet orbit after World War II, they too instituted socialist realism to varying degrees. Some states, notably Poland, did not see modernism as necessarily inconsistent with socialism, although works glorifying the state and the people's cultural heritage were still encouraged. Since the social liberalization movement known as *glasnost* ("openness") and the breakup of the Soviet state, socialist realism as a state policy exists in only a handful of countries, such as North Korea.

PROFESSIONAL FOLK ENSEMBLES

In their search for genuine artistic expression rooted in popular traditions and compatible with the interests of the state, some communist governments formed ensembles of folk musicians who had sufficient training to play arrangements written by conservatory-trained composers. These works included such musical innovations as triad-based harmony (see Chapter 14) that had been absent from peasant folk music prior to World War II.

To effect these innovations, musicians had to read conventional music notation. Notation enabled large orchestras of traditional instruments to play harmony, but the folk arts of improvisation and ornamentation disappeared or were greatly modified. Professional arrangers often created more refined structures and censored bawdy or political lyrics. Unlike traditional folk musicians, these professional groups enjoyed access to state record labels, radio, and television, and were presented to the world as the authentic musical expression of the country. Although the sources of the music remained for the most part folk songs and dances collected from the countryside, the refinements that professional groups introduced, as well as performance contexts so different from the traditions of the countryside, clearly distinguish these performances from other folk music.

To support these efforts, ethnomusicology in general enjoyed a good deal of state support in the Soviet Union and other communist states. Thanks to this support, collections and detailed studies of literally hundreds of thousands of folk songs now exist in Hungary, Russia, and other regions.

In 1973, the Russian musician Dmitri Pokrovsky formed a new group that applied these ethnomusicological studies to create a new sort of folk ensemble that recovered regional singing and improvisational styles. Because this approach threatened the authenticity of official folklore groups and because he revived religious and other censored lyrics, the Pokrovsky Ensemble found it difficult to perform and record its music. Nevertheless, Pokrovsky sparked a revival movement in folk music that accelerated after the policy of *glasnost* (openness) began in 1985 (see listening guide on p. 265).

HUNGARIAN FOLK MUSIC

HISTORICAL BACKGROUND

The Magyars, the major ethnic group of Hungary, settled there between the fifth and ninth centuries. The Magyars are most closely related to the Finns and certain small ethnic groups in Russia, and the Magyar language and culture are quite distinct from those of the surrounding Slavic groups. As in many areas of Eastern Europe, for centuries, the peasantry made up the largest portion of the population and created a musical heritage built on folk songs and dances.

Christianity came to Hungary in the tenth century and for centuries was the main patron of what art music there was. During the sixteenth century, when Hungary was under Ottoman Turkish rule, Turkish instruments and other musical influences entered Hungarian culture. Around the same time, the first Romani people had also settled in the region and brought their own distinctive musical culture. This ethnic group became known as "Gypsies" because of a mistaken notion that they originated in Egypt. Many Romani ethnic groups, each with distinct dialects and musical traditions, are scattered throughout Europe.

Romani instrumentalists became particularly sought after in the eighteenth century as an attraction at military recruiting fairs. Thereafter, Romani bands were associated with the word for "recruiting," **verbunkos**, even in other contexts. These bands originally featured violins and bagpipes, but the bagpipes were soon replaced with the **cimbalom**, the hammered zither that probably came into Hungary from Turkey. The other *verbunkos* instruments were usually two violins (one playing the melody and the other a countermelody) and a string bass (Figure 13.3).

By the mid-nineteenth century, *verbunkos* bands had become famous throughout Europe as popular urban entertainment. Despite the fact that their

(2) © Barry Lewis/CORBIS

FIGURE 13.3

This band led by Zsolt Boni plays outside a restaurant in Budapest; it includes two violins, a bass, and a *cimbalom*. This *cimbalom* (close-up image on the right), unlike the simpler form in Figure 13.2, uses string dampers controlled by a pedal mechanism like that used on a piano. Here, too, the ends of the mallets are covered in cotton to soften the tone.

repertory was unrelated to actual Romani folk music, the sound of the Gypsy violin remains famous even in present-day Budapest, the capital of Hungary. The popular tunes played by *verbunkos* bands often featured nondiatonic modes probably descended from Turkish influence but sometimes known as Gypsy scales.

As Bartók and other researchers showed, *verbunkos* music is not the music of the Magyar peasants. Indeed, with its distinctive scales, ornamentation, and frequent use of *rubato* (expressive changes or stretching of tempo), this music was very different from either the indigenous Magyar peasant music or the Romani folk music tradition. These qualities in turn influenced nineteenth-century sentimental parlor songs known as **magyarnota**. The *verbunkos* dances also influenced the development of the **csárdás**, a distinctive dance of contrasting fast and slow tempos in simple duple meter, now the national dance of Hungary.

THE CHARACTERISTICS OF HUNGARIAN FOLK SONG

By carefully studying and comparing music of neighboring regions and the Magyar's ethnic cousins in Russia, Bartók and Kodály were able to isolate at least two historical strata of folk song characteristics. The earliest folk songs show many Central Asian characteristics, including the **anhemitonic pentatonic scale**—a scale of five pitches per octave with no semitones—the type of scale used in China, Mongolia, and elsewhere in Central Asia. Later songs show European influence, including the use of diatonic scales.

What is most characteristic of these old songs, however, are their patterns of repetition and transposition (repetition at another pitch). Old Hungarian folk songs typically repeat a phrase transposed by the interval of five scale steps. Hungarian folk songs also show distinctive rhythmic characteristics. Bartók named the most prominent rhythmic types **parlando-rubato** (an Italian term meaning "free speech rhythm") and **tempo giusto** (an Italian term meaning "strict tempo"). Nonpulsatile, heavily ornamented *parlando-rubato* songs are common in many areas of Eastern Europe and often emphasize emotional expression and the meaning of the text, whereas *tempo giusto* songs emphasize repetitive dance rhythms. Sometimes songs of both types alternate or are paired for contrast.

© Barry Lewis/CORBIS

FIGURE 13.4

The Hungarian *citera* is a plucked zither with frets. The melody is played on one or two strings while two other strings provide a drone.

REPRESENTATIVE HUNGARIAN INSTRUMENTS

Hungarian musical instruments reflect the diverse influences of this crossroads nation. Related to the *santur* of the Middle East and probably introduced during the period of Turkish rule, the *cimbalom* hammered zither (refer to Figures 13.2 and 13.3) has become a highly cultivated instrument and often rivals the piano as a standard instrument in urban homes. The **citera** (Figure 13.4) is a plucked zither with frets. It is related to the Austrian *diskantzither* (Figure 14.6 in Chapter 14) as well as the mountain dulcimer from the United States (see first Instrument Gallery in Chapter 16). The Hungarian **furulya** (Figure 13.5) is a shepherd's vertical duct flute. Versions of this instrument reach up to a meter in length, and performers on this low flute sometimes murmur and hum while playing, creating a distinctive timbre.

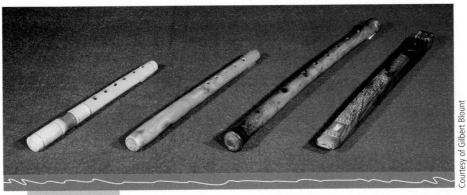

Courtesy of Gilbert Blount

FIGURE 13.5

The *furulya* is a duct flute found in Hungary and surrounding countries. Pictured here are versions from different regions.

DANCE HOUSE MUSIC

Under the communist folk revival movement of the 1950s and 1960s, the Hungarian government established several professional folk music and dance groups. Dissatisfied with the refinements of these state-sponsored groups, in the 1970s, two young folk dancers, Béla Halmos and Ferenc Sebö, like Bartók and Kodály before them, set out to collect folk music, primarily dances, from the countryside. Rather than present musicological museum pieces, however, Halmos and Sebö sought to incorporate the spirit of the music in a rousing new repertory played on amplified violins and bass in dance clubs. These clubs are known as **tanchaz** (dance houses), after the traditional village music hall.

During the 1970s and 1980s, the growth in popularity of *tanchaz* music presented a challenge to the state-sponsored control of the arts and the definition of authenticity. *Tanchaz* musicians in neighboring Romania sometimes traveled secretly, without official permission, to ethnic Hungarian villages in Transylvania to collect folk music. Since the fall of communism, *tanchaz* has become state-supported, and musicians such as Márta Sebestyén and Muzsikás are internationally famous (Figure 13.6). Today, dance music may include gypsy bands and various electric instruments. As in other areas of Eastern Europe, wedding music bands are popular and may include clarinets, synthesizers, and drums.

© Béla Kása

FIGURE 13.6

Márta Sebestyén and the Hungarian music group Muzsikás play *tanchaz*, the now state-supported repertory that incorporates the spirit of folk dances on amplified violins and bass in dance clubs.

ROMANI FOLK SONG

Although urban popular music bands defined Gypsy music in most people's minds, the Roma, or "Gypsy," ethnic minority has its own folk traditions unrelated to the popular songs of the *verbunkos* bands. Many Romani groups arrived in Hungary after the establishment of the *verbunkos* bands. Although Romani folk music

CD 3:9. *Téglaporos a kalapom.* Vocal, Mihály Váradi with István Balázs, Pál Balogh, Sándor Kardelás, and Ferenc Lakatos.

0:00	The lead solo male singer, using the syllable "la," improvises a brief variation of the song tune to follow.

This style of improvisation is called *pergetés* ("rolling") and, in this case, is highly syncopated (metrical stress is shifted away from our expectations). The mode is diatonic, although not major or minor, and the tuning of certain tones is flexible.

0:06	Two more members join, one clapping, the other creating half-sung percussive sounds—*szájbögö*, or mouth bass—both providing a strong rhythmic framework for syncopated rolling melody.

The vertical lines indicate the beats, and the solid lines indicate the beginning of four-beat metrical units.

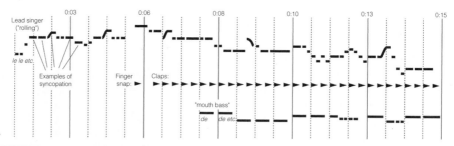

0:18	The lead singer launches main tune; the humorous lyrics describe the worker's life.

Several exclamatory (but otherwise meaningless) syllables (shown in parentheses) enter the lyric merely for rhythmic effect.

Téglaporos a kalapom,	My hat is covered with brick dust,
Mer' a téglagyárban lakom;	Since I live in the brick factory

shares some of the diatonic modes found in Magyar folk music as well as their four-phrase form, the distinctively Magyar repetition at the interval of a fifth is rare.

Even more surprising is the absence of instrumental music, even for dances, among the Vlach and Romungre ethnic groups. To accompany dances, they sing a repertory of highly rhythmic songs that include fragmentary texts, vocables (nonsense syllables), and mouth sounds to create a kind of vocal percussion known as **szájbögö** (mouth bass). The dancers also use shouts, finger snaps, and claps to enliven the songs, as their Roma cousins in Spain do for the flamenco dance (see Chapter 14).

In addition to the dance songs, the Roma have a repertoire of *parlando-rubato* (nonpulsatile) songs that are typically slow and emotionally intense. The Romungres

(hej de) Onnét tudják, hogy ott lakom:	(hey de!) They know that I live there because
(mer') Téglaporos a kalapom.	(mer!) My hat is covered with brick dust.[1]

0:33	The lead singer uses vocables for more elaborate rolling improvisation.
	More participants join, thickening the rhythmic accompaniment with more mouth bass and finger snaps.

0:48	Another verse from the lead singer, this time sending encouragement to the dancers between rolled syllables.
	The mouth bass emphasizes the offbeat (the second of every beat division).

1:02	Next verse; the singer doubles the rhythmic density of his syllables still within the main tune's framework.

1:16	The lead singer sings a variation of first verse.
	The players add the sound of spoons on the tabletop.

1:30	Several verses follow. The singer inserts improvised syllables to encourage the dancers.
	The mouth bass participants also shout their encouragement as the texture grows thicker and more exciting, and the tempo quickens.

[1]Lyrics with English translation by Rudolf Vig of the song *Téglaporos a kalapom* from the CD *Gypsy Folk Songs from Hungary*. Hungaroton HCD 18028-29 (1976). (Vocal, Mihály Váradi with István Balázs, Pál Balogh, Sándor Kardelás, and Ferenc Lakatos.) Reprinted by permission.

Hear and see the instruments of *Téglaporos a kalapom* in your downloadable **ACTIVE LISTENING TOOLS**, available at the World Music Resource Center.

sometimes sing in improvised parallel thirds (two melodies two scale steps apart), and other groups at times improvise heterophony or simple polyphony.

A PERFORMANCE OF A ROMANI SZÁJBÖGÖ—MOUTH BASS SONG

Téglaporos a kalapom is an example of a Romani *szájbögö* or mouth bass dance. The percussive accompaniment for these dances is created entirely by the impromptu rhythmic syllables, mouth sounds, and claps of the singers; there are no other instruments. Although many *szájbögö* dances are entirely without words, the lyrics of those that do have words are often light-hearted, humorous, nonsensical, and repetitive. Singers, dancers, and onlookers may offer shouts of encouragement or teasing.

BULGARIAN FOLK MUSIC

HISTORICAL BACKGROUND

Bulgaria has several rich and distinctive folk music traditions that trace back to the mythological Greek musician Orpheus, who came from the region of Thrace. The ethnic group known as the Bulgars came to this region in the seventh century and by the ninth century had adopted Christianity along with a form of Byzantine chant. Despite the close association with Byzantine culture, Bulgarian Christianity has preserved a distinctive blend of Christian and pagan customs and thought. Ostensible Christmas songs are thinly disguised harvest and fertility ritual songs, and Easter songs are tied to spring rituals such as the turning of bundles of straw. Peasant women, not allowed to sing in church, became the main carriers of the secular folk song tradition.

The Ottoman Turks ruled Bulgaria for almost 500 years, until 1878. Turkish attempts at converting the Bulgarians to Islam were not generally successful, and pagan elements were further entrenched in the religion of the people. Only after Bulgarian independence did secular art music begin to develop. In 1944, the country underwent a socialist revolution and became part of the Soviet bloc. The government formed and supported professional folk ensembles in preference to traditional folk music.

Filip Kutev (1903–1982) was a pioneering composer and choral director who organized the Bulgarian State Radio and Television Female Vocal Choir. He harmonized and arranged many folk songs while retaining many of their distinctive characteristics. This choir was later recorded by the American Nonesuch label and, in the 1980s, became very popular through those recordings and subsequent tours. In 1992, Bulgaria became a multiparty democracy, and, in the liberalization that followed, many types of music suppressed under communism flourished, including Western popular music. One of the most popular genres is the dance music played at weddings, which has now evolved from small folk dance ensembles to elaborate amplified bands that now feature less traditional instruments such as the clarinet and accordion.

BULGARIAN FOLK SONGS

Folk songs can be divided according to function, and often each has its own distinctive musical characteristics. Harvesting songs, for example, are generally sustained and nonpulsatile (*parlando-rubato*), with a narrow range and an ornament called **provikvaniyo**—a type of sudden yell upward at the ends of phrases. Many songs are associated with holidays and other seasonal activities, although the actual subjects of the songs may be unrelated to the season. Nevertheless, common themes, such as stories of resistance against Turkish rule and songs of courtship and marriage, prevail. Pagan references survive in songs begging for rain and in fertility rituals during the winter. Many of these songs and the annual traditions with which they were associated have changed or disappeared since the communist era.

Some of the most elaborate folk rituals, as elsewhere in Eastern Europe, surround weddings. There are many types of wedding songs, one for each part of a ceremony that can last up to three days. Some of these songs are sung *antiphonally* (by alternating groups). Today, weddings commonly feature bands playing amplified instruments, perhaps in combination with traditional instruments; accordions, clarinets, and electric guitars may join *gaida* bagpipes or a *kaval* flute.

Bulgarian folk music often has a narrow range; the *provikvaniyo* yell is an exception. Modes are most often made up of five or fewer pitches per octave. Diatonic modes dominate, but nondiatonic modes, some including microtones, can also be found, perhaps because of Turkish or Romani influence.

Folk polyphony is found in many regions of Bulgaria. Melodies with a drone are common to some areas, and singers occasionally use spicy parallel seconds. In the Pirin mountain region, heterophonic textures are common. Sometimes polyphony results when a slow and a fast song are sung simultaneously.

BULGARIAN RHYTHM

One of the most distinctive and well-known attributes of Bulgarian folk music is its use of complex asymmetrical meters. These meters are generally made up of beats of two different sizes, the longer beat half again as long as the short beat. When broken down to a common denominator, the long beats are represented as made up of three fast pulses, and the short beats two.

As one might expect in a culture in which community and cooperation have been important in the rural areas, folk dances, such as line dances or circle dances (**horo**), tend to be lively and energetic communal activities. Some of these folk dance types are listed here:

- **Paidushko.** Round dance in two beats alternating two and three subdivisions, which we write as 2 + 3.

- **Ruchenitsa.** Wedding round dance in 2 + 2 + 3.

- **Daichovo.** Dance in 2 + 2 + 2 + 3.

- **Grancharski horo.** Potters' dance in 2 + 3 + 2 + 2.

- **Krivo horo.** Dance in 2 + 2 + 3 + 2 + 2.

- **Khoro eleno mome.** Dance in 2 + 2 + 2 + 2 + 2 + 3.

- **Buchimish.** Round dance in 2 + 2 + 2 + 2 + 3 + 2 + 2.

Because these beat subdivisions usually go by far too fast to be counted individually, it really makes more sense to feel the beat as a constantly shifting duration. The sequence of different beats may be related to the amount of time a particular dance step takes. Not all Bulgarian songs and dances are in asymmetrical meters; regular meters and nonpulsatile songs are also common.

REPRESENTATIVE BULGARIAN INSTRUMENTS AND THEIR PERFORMANCE

The **kaval** (Figure 13.7) is a rim-blown flute held at an angle in front of the player. It is related to the Middle Eastern *nay* flute. The **gudulka** is a

Courtesy of Kovács László and Flótás

FIGURE 13.7

The *kaval* is a rim-blown flute found in Bulgaria and surrounding regions, related to the *nay* of Turkey and the Middle East. This version is from Hungary.

© Adam Woolfitt/CORBIS

FIGURE 13.8

The Bulgarian *gudulka* is a pear-shaped vertical bowed fiddle with three gut (sometimes metal) strings. Like Indian chordophones, this one has several sympathetic strings tied to the shorter pegs.

© Hideo Haga/HAGA/The Image Works

FIGURE 13.9

A performer holds the *gaida* (bagpipe) at a festival in Bulgaria.

pear-shaped vertical bowed fiddle with three strings (Figure 13.8), occasionally having sympathetic strings as well. The **gaida** is a bagpipe with a drone pipe and a melody pipe (Figure 13.9). Well known for its distinctive virtuosic ornamentation, the *gaida* is a popular instrument for weddings and outdoor celebrations. The **tambura** is a long-necked fretted lute with four strings or double courses. Originally a melody instrument (unlike its Indian namesake) with drone strings, it now more commonly plays strummed chords. The **tupan** is a large cylindrical bass drum, slung across the body, and played with two sticks (Figure 5.27 in Chapter 5).

Bulgarian instrumental playing styles are known for their especially florid ornamentation. On instruments such as the *gaida* and *kaval*, long notes are automatically decorated with trills or other ornaments, and players often interpolate short grace notes produced by flips of the players' fingers between main melody notes. Singers of nonpulsatile (*parlando-rubato*) folk songs often ornament those melodies in similar ways.

A PERFORMANCE OF A BULGARIAN FOLK SONG

This short, lively tune, *Dilmano, Dilbero*, demonstrates a complex sequence of meters. Filip Kutev, the most famous arranger of traditional works for professional folk ensembles, arranged this song, originally from the Shopski region, for folk ensemble and women's choir. The text is humorous with its obscure double entendres between a flirting couple, but it also betrays an ancient connection between reproduction and agricultural fertility.

LISTENING GUIDE

CD 3:10. *Dilmano, Dilbero.* Filip Kutev National Folk Ensemble.

0:00

The instrumental ensemble introduces the melody.

The *gaida* plays with elaborate ornamentation accompanied by the *tupan* drum.

0:06

The choir enters with a fast 2 + 3 + 3 meter.

> Filip Kutev carefully composed and notated the choral harmony. Despite occasional folk polyphony, such harmonies would not be found in traditional folk performances. While keeping the original folk melody clear and harmonizing it within the narrow and low Bulgarian folk song range, Kutev emphasized drone pitches as they might be played on the *gaida*. This schematic of the first phrase shows how the melody aligns with the distinctive asymmetric meter.

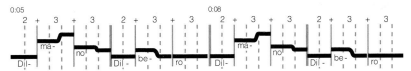

0:12

The meter changes strikingly in the second phrase of the melody.

In the lyric, Dilbero (young man) has asked Dilmano (young woman) how to plant peppers.

The musical phrases and lyric repeat.

> The asymmetrical meter shifts to add an extra beat of three subdivisions in the pattern 2 + 3 + 3 + 3 before returning to 2 + 3 + 3. This variation could indicate an extra dance step.

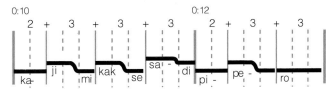

0:27

Dilbero continues: "To bloom and ripen"—in a contrasting musical phrase.

The *gaida* returns with its thrilling ornamentation. It had rested during the first phrases to allow the singers the spotlight.

CD 3:10. *Dilmano, Dilbero.* Filip Kutev National Folk Ensemble. *(continued)*	

0:32	The meter returns to the changing pattern. Dilbero: "To gather, gather, gather/As much as you want." Lyric playfully emphasizes "*beresh*" (gather) on each of the long beats.
0:42	The *gaida* and *tupan* repeat the introduction.
0:47	Dilmano answers: "Push here, poke there/Just like that, you plant peppers!"

Hear and see the instruments of *Dilmano, Dilbero* in your downloadable **ACTIVE LISTENING TOOLS**, available at the World Music Resource Center.

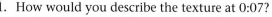

Listening Exercise 12	**CD 3:10. *Dilmano, Dilbero***

1. How would you describe the texture at 0:07?
   a. Monophonic with drum
   b. Homophonic with drum
   c. Polyphonic with drum

2. How would you describe the texture at 0:27?
   a. Heterophonic melody with accompanying harmony and drum
   b. Polyphonic with drum
   c. Monophonic (voices and *gaida*) and drum

3. In the phrase (sung twice) from 1:06 to 1:11, what does the drum play?
   a. Every strong beat in the asymmetrical meter
   b. Two beats at the end of each phrase repetition
   c. The drum doesn't play

 You can take this Listening Exercise online and receive feedback or e-mail answers to your instructor at the World Music Resource Center.

RUSSIAN FOLK MUSIC

FOLK SONGS AND GENRES

Although many folk songs disappeared during the communist period, some genres, notably wedding songs, are still popular in rural areas. Other traditional Russian folk song genres include work songs, short work calls (***pripevki***) similar to the holler of the United States, and calendar songs—that is, songs for a particular holiday or season (Figure 13.10).

Calendar songs, wedding songs, and laments share several features, despite the significant differences among regions in this large country. Scales often have only two to five pitches per octave and melodies may be limited in range. Semitones are common in these scales, unlike Central Asian pentatonic scales, and contribute to the particularly poignant character of laments. Melodies are frequently made up of combinations of simple repetitive motives.

Calendar songs also have distinctive rhythms that they share with many dance genres. Their rhythms are driving combinations of single pulses and divisions into two. These rhythmic motives often repeat many times, even while the notes of the melody change. This distinctive practice is called **isorhythm**. Occasionally, polyrhythm results when a song accompanies a dance in a different meter; most dances include singing.

Russian folk songs are often sung by choruses that are sometimes segregated by gender. Russian men's choruses in particular have become famous for their booming chest voices and extremely low ranges. Women singers often cultivate a rich, brassy tone quality. Responsorial and antiphonal singing is common in many repertories.

Heterophony and improvised polyphony is found in certain regions, particularly in lyric songs, such as those sung at traditional weddings. In South Russia, some singers improvise a higher part, often following the original melody in parallel thirds or fourths, a technique known as **vtora**.

Folk polyphony is even further developed in the neighboring country of Georgia where **table songs**, sung traditionally around a table at a party or banquet, include improvised polyphony of up to four parts. These parts are formed around a center melody by singing in parallel thirds and fourths, with ostinatos (repeating melodies) and bass drones. These Georgian and South Russian improvisations often lead to spicy, surprising dissonances.

© Wolfgang Kaehler/CORBIS

FIGURE 13.10

This Russian folk band includes a *bayan* (button accordion, rear left), a *zhaleyka* (single-reed horn), and a *domra* (long-necked lute on the right).

© Dave G. Houser/CORBIS

FIGURE 13.11

The *balalaika* is known for its distinctive triangular body. Here, a member of the folk music ensemble Kizh plays the bass member of the *balalaika* family. Originally a folk instrument, in the late nineteenth century, it was made into a chromatic (i.e., twelve pitches per octave) instrument in different sizes. In this form, groups of *balalaikas* formed popular entertainment bands and sometimes even large orchestras.

RUSSIAN INSTRUMENTS

The **balalaika** (Figure 13.11) is an instrument of the lute type with frets and a distinctive triangular sound body. Similar to the *balalaika*, the **domra** (refer to Figure 13.10) is a lute with a round sound body, usually used to strum chords. A plucked zither described as having a wing shape, the **gusli** (Figure 13.12) is thought to have come originally from Byzantium in the Middle Ages and is indeed similar to the *kanun* of present-day Turkey. The **bayan** is a button accordion (refer to Figure 13.10), a popular instrument since the nineteenth century, now found in many folk bands. The **zhaleyka** (refer to Figure 13.10) is a small

Courtesy of the Ossipov National Academic Folk Orchestra of Russia

FIGURE 13.12

The *gusli* is a Russian zither that often has this distinctive "winged" shape. In this form, it is held upright and plucked or strummed in the player's lap. Like the Turkish *kanun*, to which it is related, a series of small levers is sometimes used to change the tunings of the metal strings.

single-reed shepherd's pipe. In southern regions, it appears in a version with double pipes, similar to the double-pipe, single-reed instruments found in the former Yugoslavia, Greece, and Egypt.

A PERFORMANCE OF A RUSSIAN FOLK SONG

Traditional Russian weddings are long and elaborate affairs, even today, and nearly every part of the ritual and celebration has particular music associated with it. Guests of the bride arrive at her family's house on the morning of the wedding. As bridesmaids dress the bride, she sings a series of laments called **prichitaniya** (which are also sung at funerals) to express her sorrow at leaving her family. The guests will also sing, sometimes at the same time, songs of both celebration and sadness, such as the following example, "Play, *Skomoroshek*."

The *skomorokh* was a medieval entertainer often hired to perform at weddings. Although their association with bawdy behavior, political topics, and perhaps a pagan past caused them to be outlawed in the seventeenth century, wedding entertainers never disappeared from traditional life. Russian Jews had their own such jester-musicians known as *badhkones*, who were sometimes hired to perform at Christian weddings as well.

While the bride dresses and sings her laments, the groom and his friends have to gain entrance to her house in the face of resistance from the young men of the bride's family. The groom must use bribes of money, vodka, and song to eventually gain entrance (all the more challenging if the bride lives in a large Soviet-era apartment building). If the wedding ceremony itself is held in a Christian church, it may be accompanied by sacred chant, although civil ceremonies are more common since the communist period. A celebration sometimes lasting two days will follow, filled with game songs, drinking songs, teasing songs, dancing songs, and so on.

These songs are participatory, often sung responsorially with a song leader. Many consist of short phrases repeated over and over with different lines of lyrics. These so-called **formula songs** have driving, sometimes isorhythmic patterns.

CD 3:11. "Play, *Skomoroshek.*" The Dmitri Pokrovsky Ensemble.[2]

0:00	The song leader, known as the *golosnik*, begins the song with a bright timbre and loud voice, singing, "Play, play *skomoroshek*, from village to village."
0:06	As the *golosnik* continues to sing a drone pitch, the first group of singers joins her, singing the vocables (syllables without literal meaning) *"Okh eliolo, ah leh ley lioli."* After the first note, they diverge into two different polyphonic melodies.

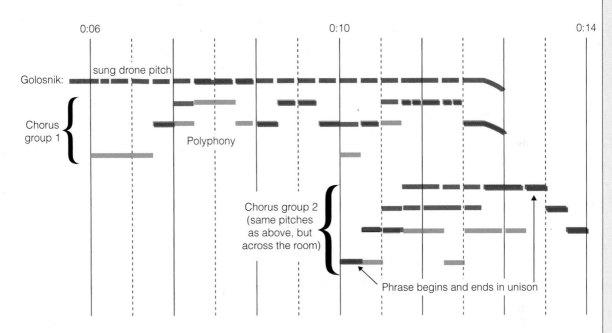

0:10	Toward the end of the phrase, a second group of singers answers antiphonally (alternating groups). Note that all singers, men and women, sing this polyphony in the same close range, not octaves apart.
0:13	Overlapping with the end of the second group, the first group begins again, singing the second line of text, "So our Marenushka [the bride] would be happy," to the same "formula" or basic melodic phrase.
0:17	The second group answers again. Each phrase starts on unison, diverges to polyphony, and comes back again to unison. The scale for this song has only four notes, a subset of an anhemitonic pentatonic scale.

[2]Translation of lyrics by Theodore Levin and Dmitri Pokrovsky, from insert notes to Pokrovsky Ensemble, *Les Noces and Russian Village Songs* (New York/Los Angeles: Elektra/Nonesuch 9 79335-2, 1994).

0:21

The formula continues this way to the end of the song. The lyrics continue as follows, each line corresponding to one musical phrase exchanged between the two antiphonal groups:

All winter and summer a pine tree was green,

On Friday Marenushka was merry,

On Saturday she combed her hair,

On Sunday she went to the coronation [wedding] and cried,

She said to her own father:

You're not kind to me,

You give me away young to marry,

Three gardens are left without me,

Three green gardens are blooming

They bloom with scarlet flowers,

You will always wake up early dear father,

And water three gardens,

By early morning dawn,

With your bitter tears.

Hear and see the instruments of "Play, *Skomoroshek*" in your downloadable **ACTIVE LISTENING TOOLS,** available at the World Music Resource Center.

Especially in certain regions, some songs are polyphonic, heterophonic, or include a sung drone. The example above is from the Belgorod region in southern Russia, where polyphonic singing is common.

In 1923, the famous Russian composer Igor Stravinsky (1882–1971) completed his own commemoration of this tradition, his ballet *Svadebka* (*The Wedding*) for choir and percussion. Stravinsky was never an ethnomusicologist like Bartók, but several of his early works present loving, if detached, evocations of Russian folk traditions. Stravinsky created a montage of sonic images in *Svadebka*, combining fragments of wedding folk songs (including "Play, *Skomoroshek*"), the ostinati of formula songs, the exuberant dissonances of folk polyphony, and the overlapping of songs within the wonderful chaos of the wedding celebration.

REFERENCES

DISCOGRAPHY

Bartók, Béla. *Bartók for Orchestra*. Adam Fischer cond. the Hungarian State Symphony Orchestra. Waystone Leys, Monmouth, UK: Nimbus Records NI 1771, 1992.

Muzsikás and Márta Sebestyén. *Morning Star*. Salem MA: Hannibal/Ryko HNCD 1401, 1997.

Various artists. *Gypsy Folksongs from Hungary*. Budapest: Hungaraton HCD 18028-29, 1995.

Various artists. *Tánchász-Népzene: Hungarian Dance-House Folk Music*. Budapest: Hagyományok Háza HHCD0102, 2003.

HUNGARY

Bulgarskoto radio i televiziia, Zheni khor. *Le mystère des voix bulgares*. New York: Elektra/Nonesuch 9 79165-2, 1987.

Philip Koutev National Folk Ensemble. *Bulgarian Polyphony I*. Tokyo: JVC VICG 5001–2, 1990.

Various artists. *Village and Folk Music of Bulgaria*. New York: Elektra/Nonesuch 79195, 1965/1990.

BULGARIA

Dmitri Pokrovsky Ensemble. *Les Noces and Russian Village Songs*. New York/Los Angeles: Elektra/Nonesuch 9 79335-2, 1994.

Dmitri Pokrovsky Ensemble. *Wild Field*. New York: RealWorld 62316, 1993.

Pesen Zemli. *Russia: Polyphonic Wedding Songs*. Geneva: AIMP VDE 837, 1995.

RUSSIA

The Rustavi Choir. *Georgian Voices*. New York/Los Angeles: Elektra/Nonesuch 9 79224-2, 1989.

Various artists. *Village Music of Yugoslavia*. New York/Los Angeles: Elektra/Nonesuch 9 72042-2, 1971/1995.

OTHER REGIONS

 ## BOOK COMPANION WEBSITE

You will find flashcards, a glossary, and tutorial quizzes, as well as other materials that will help you succeed in this course, at the *Music of the Peoples of the World, 2nd Edition*, Companion Website at www.cengage.com/music/alves/world2e.

PLACE

TIMES

c. 700–143 BCE

Classical Greece is credited with much of the cultural and philosophical basis for Western European civilization, including music theory.

1ST–5TH CENTURIES

Government, law, and perhaps musical attributes such as the predominance of diatonic scales are some of the legacies of the Roman Empire. However, some of the oldest European folk songs show characteristics such as anhemitonic pentatonic scales, which may have originated in non-Roman tribes.

C. 4TH CENTURY

Rise of the Western Christian Church (the Roman Catholic Church) and its acceptance by Roman emperors. The Church becomes the crucial source of patronage and scholarship of music in Western Europe for centuries.

711–1492

Islamic forces rule Spain and Portugal, bringing Arabic influences, ancient musical texts, and instruments into Europe.

WESTERN EUROPE

About a century ago, a new dance called the **waltz** scandalized polite society in Vienna, a city in many ways at the center of Europe. One particularly outraged writer said of a violinist leading a waltz orchestra, "his own limbs no longer belong to him when the thunderstorm of his waltz is let loose; his fiddle-bow dances with his arms...the tempo animates his feet; the melody waves champagne glasses in his face and the devil is abroad."[1] The loose-limbed violinist in question was the composer Johann Strauss Jr. (1825-1899), who, unlike many composers of earlier generations, was able to make a living selling tickets to performances of his compositions and selling printed notation of his works, which were wildly popular despite the protests of such conservatives.

[1] Laube, *Reisenovellen*, vol. 3 from *Gesammelte Werke* vol. 6, ed. H. H. Houben, Leipzig, 1908, 22ff. Quoted and translated in Henry Schnitzler "Gay Vienna—Myth and Reality," *Journal of the History of Ideas*, 15/1 (Jan., 1954), 112.

SOUNDS

CD 3:12

"*Die lustige Bäurin*" ("The Merry Farmer's Wife"), Hamot Trio

C. 9TH CENTURY	15TH CENTURY	16TH CENTURY	C. 1600–1750
Musical notation gradually develops as one tool for the political and religious unification of Europe. The practice of polyphonic singing aided by notation also begins, eventually evolving into modern harmony.	The period known as the Renaissance emphasized individuality (individual composers become known for distinctive styles) and a rebirth of classical humanism (musical scholarship is advanced independently of the Church).	The Reformation splits Western Christianity into Roman Catholic and Protestant sects. Music printing leads to greater music literacy and a wide dissemination of compositions. The discovery of the Americas leads to the period of European colonialism and the spread of Western European musical influences to the Americas, Australia, Africa, and elsewhere. The violin family, including also the viola, cello, and double bass, becomes one of the most characteristic family of instruments of Western Europe, and the guitar develops in Spain.	During the Baroque Period, the rise of the aristocracy supports the creation of art music institutions such as opera and orchestras. Baroque art music composers included Johann Sebastian Bach (1685–1750).

KT/Alamy

FIGURE 14.1

The Vienna Philharmonic Orchestra is a well-known example of the European orchestra, sometimes also known as a **symphony orchestra**, an ensemble of fifty or more players reading from notated music. Most orchestra musicians play instruments of the violin family (violin, viola, cello, double bass), but aerophones in the orchestra may include, depending on the piece, the flute, oboe (double reed), clarinet (single reed), bassoon (double reed), and buzzed-lip or "brass" instruments: French horn, trumpet, trombone, and tuba. Some pieces also call for membranophones and idiophones, but these represent a relatively small part of the total. Orchestras are led by a single conductor, who does not otherwise play but whose motions synchronize the many players and communicate expressive goals.

Dance or "light classical" orchestras such as this often entertained patrons of outdoor restaurants and coffee houses, where intellectuals such as psychologist Sigmund Freud or philosopher Ludwig Wittgenstein gathered. But in this city perhaps more famous for its music at the time than any other in Europe, you could also hear military bands, amateur choirs, small ensembles of string instruments, or perhaps an accordion player. For the price of a ticket, you could also see large orchestras of up to a hundred players (Figure 14.1) performing or accompanying **opera**, an elaborately staged dramatic work in which the characters sing all their lines. By 1907, Vienna had three resident orchestras and several opera theaters, although unlike the orchestras of Johann Strauss, these large art music or "classical music" institutions could not make a profit from ticket sales alone. They depended in part on funds from the Austrian government or wealthy patrons (such as Wittgenstein's family), and they still do.

But whether the music you heard came from a small coffee house ensemble playing popular dance tunes or a huge orchestra playing long and complex compositions, an amateur community choir or a military band, all of this music would share certain important characteristics. First of all, this music was usually written down. That is, unlike traditional music in most of the rest of the world, all of the musicians in these ensembles would read their part from a carefully prescribed notation, allowing little if any improvisation or other extemporaneous variation.

The detailed notation developed in Europe allowed for the precise coordination of many musicians and singers in any combination, permitting the use of harmonies and other complex structures that would be difficult or impossible to achieve any other way. This system implies the existence of a trained professional— the composer—to create the notated parts the other musicians play. Although some composers, such as Johann Strauss, might also perform their own works, this separation of functions is very different from many other traditions in the

▶ | **C. 1750–1810** | **C. 1810–1910** | **20TH CENTURY** |

This period of the so-called Enlightenment (also known as the "Classical" era in music) saw the rise of the middle class, democracy, and industrialism. The piano became a popular instrument, and the modern symphony orchestra developed. Music began to reach a larger public as old patronage systems declined. Classical era composers included Wolfgang Amadeus Mozart (1756–1791) and Ludwig van Beethoven (1770–1827).

In art music, this period was associated with Romanticism, which emphasized the idea of art as a profound, personal expression of a unique individual. Romantic composers included Richard Wagner (1813–1883) and Johannes Brahms (1833–1897). At the same time, this period saw the rise of popular music aimed at a mass audience and the early collection and study of folk music.

In art music, the term Modernism denotes this period's group of styles that emphasized sometimes radical innovation and originality. Composers included Igor Stravinsky (1885–1974) and Arnold Schoenberg (1874–1951). However, the immense rise of popular music, especially through recordings and other new technologies, largely overshadowed innovations in art music. Colonialism and modern media spread European styles and especially popular music throughout the world.

world. It also enables the composer to articulate a personal style independent of different performers, an expression of individuality distinctive in a culture known for its emphasis on the individual, at least since the time of the Renaissance of the fifteenth century.

Despite the prominence of music notated by professionals in our experience of early twentieth-century Vienna, perhaps most of the music was not created that way at all. In homes, mothers still sang lullabies learned from their mothers, and the patrons of beer halls still sang along with folk songs. Even though many musicians who played along with these informal songs might never have learned to read notation, at times they could add harmony through chordal instruments such as the piano (Figure 14.2), the Austrian harp-zither (Figure 14.5), or, elsewhere in Europe, the guitar.

Although it is often convenient to divide European music into folk, popular, and art music, music in Vienna as elsewhere was a panorama of overlapping styles and social functions. Thus amateur choirs might sing for small community gatherings, for church functions, or as part of a performance with a professional orchestra. The composer Gustav Mahler (1860–1911), who was at that time the conductor of the Imperial Opera in Vienna, conducted Johann Strauss's waltzes and drew upon Austrian folk songs even as he created works of enormous length and complexity. Mahler was a celebrity in the city, recognized and loved by common people who had never set foot inside a concert hall, and newspapers devoted front-page space to debates of his performances.

This legacy continues today in Vienna, where one can still find classical orchestras, opera, waltz orchestras (now playing mostly for tourists), community choirs, and lullabies. However, a direct lineage exists between the tickets that paid for Strauss's concerts and those that support electronic dance music in Vienna's many night clubs. This chapter will explore some of these diverse musical traditions and cultures, although concentrating on certain folk traditions and leaving most of the intricacies of art music history and theory to other sources.

© Design Pics Inc./Alamy

FIGURE 14.2

In the eighteenth century, the piano developed from earlier keyboard instruments such as the organ and the harpsichord. Its distinctive characteristic, however, is that pressing keys causes a felt hammer to strike a string, allowing gradations of loudness (hence its name, short for *pianoforte*, Italian for "soft-loud"). Like many European instruments, pianos are standardized and constructed in factories. Because of the piano's capability to play harmony and multiple simultaneous melodies, it became popular as an instrument in the home as well as the concert hall.

ELEMENTS OF WESTERN EUROPEAN MUSIC

◆ **Use of harmony.** Since its invention in Western European art music, harmony based on standard chords (a collection of simultaneous pitches) accompanying a melody in a homophonic texture has become pervasive in many genres. Harmony may be formed by combining the melodies of monophonic instruments or voices or by playing chords on instruments such as the guitar or piano.

◆ **Use of notation.** Western European art music (or "classical" music) since the late Middle Ages has relied on a standardized notational system for all instruments, which has enabled the creation of complex combinations of pitches, a wide dissemination of compositions, and the reliable preservation of earlier compositions. Thus, musicians often read a carefully prescribed part while performing rather than extemporaneously creating their own as in some other traditions. Folk and popular music may not use notation for performance but may still be written down for preservation.

◆ **Use of standard tuning system.** So that instruments can be combined into variable ensembles, all instruments now use a standard tuning system of twelve pitches per octave, called *equal temperament*.

◆ **Use of diatonic modes.** Most Western European music uses diatonic modes, usually the two known as *major* and *minor*. Although these modes lack the associated motives and ornamentation that help define modes in other cultures, their use is usually closely connected with harmony.

◆ **Goal-directed phrases.** Unlike the cyclic forms of some cultures, European forms often emphasize a progression toward the phrase ending, and these phrases may be hierarchically combined to form larger structures.

◆ **Regular phrase lengths.** Phrases are very often made up of four groups of four beats or four groups of three beats. Unlike music of the Middle East and Eastern Europe, the great majority of Western European music is metric and pulsatile.

◆ **Strophic folk songs.** Folk songs usually consist of a repeating melody with different words on each repetition, a form described as **strophic**. Even though art music is not usually strophic, it too relies on repeating structures such as recurring themes.

EUROPEAN HARMONY AND NOTATION

In the most general sense, harmony means the simultaneous sounding of two or more pitches, and in this sense, harmony can be found in many of the world's traditions—certainly in Africa and Indonesia, for example. However, the type of harmony that has developed in Europe was unique in the way that it required the very specific coordination of different simultaneous melodies, so that the relationships between the pitches could be carefully worked out. In contrast, the simultaneous pitches of Javanese gamelan music, for example, mostly arise incidentally as each melody finds its own way around the core melody, and melodic players may have some freedom to vary their individual melodies.

Early composers of European harmony classified each and every interval (two pitches) produced by simultaneous melodies as a **consonance** or a **dissonance**. Although theorists described consonances as "pleasant" and dissonances as "unpleasant," this did not mean that they avoided all dissonances, any more than a cook would prepare a dish with no spices or a playwright a drama with no conflict. Just as the ancient philosopher Aristotle would prescribe stories with tension and resolution, so composers carefully followed each dissonance with a consonance, a kind of musical resolution.

Creating independent melodies that nevertheless work together to control consonance and dissonance in this fashion is like solving a musical crossword puzzle, and this craft is known as **counterpoint**. Counterpoint is not easily created through group improvisation. Instead, this type of harmony came to require two elements: a specialist composer and a standard system of musical notation in which the composer could work out this musical structure and communicate it to the performers. European musical notation began to develop around the ninth century for a very different purpose, the standardization of Roman Catholic Christian worship services (Figure 14.3). Once developed, though, it served as a way to create resonant harmonies, impressive musical structures appropriate for the architecture of the age of the great cathedrals.

By at least the seventeenth century, the most common sets of consonant intervals (or "chords") had become standard three-pitch structures known as **triads** (Graphic 14.1). Although other notes and intervening dissonances could be added to harmonies, triads have remained the basis for most European harmonies to the present day.

Just as important is the particular sequence of triads, known as the **harmonic progression** or chord progression. This sequence of chords works together with melody and phrases to create a sense of forward motion toward the resolution at the end of the phrase or collection of phrases. These harmonic progressions can be relatively simple, such as in the standard harmonic progression that defines blues music in the United States, or very complex, as in a symphony, an elaborate art music form played by an orchestra.

Especially important is the tonic triad (represented by the Roman numeral I) because, like a melody that ends on the tonic, a harmonic progression that ends on the tonic triad sounds complete or resolved. European composers have frequently used harmony to accompany a melody and thus create a homophonic texture. Melodies would consist mostly of pitches contained in the harmony sounding at that time, though not always. Melodic pitches not coinciding with the harmony formed dissonances with it, and these dissonances had to be carefully resolved.

Even as harmony developed in art music, folk and popular music continued for centuries, much as before, with monophonic textures, as the intricacies of composing harmonically remained the specialty of trained composers. However, it is easy to overstate the resulting gap between art music and folk

William Alves

FIGURE 14.3

Over the centuries, European music notation evolved from simple mnemonic aids to very complex and detailed descriptions of sound. These are examples of European notation (from top to bottom) from c. 900, c. 1200, c. 1500, c. 1700, and c. 1900.

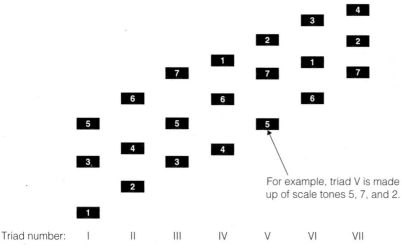

For example, triad V is made up of scale tones 5, 7, and 2.

Triad number: I   II   III   IV   V   VI   VII

Triads are identified by Roman numerals to avoid confusion with the numbering of scale steps.

GRAPHIC 14.1

Triads, groups of three notes each two scale tones apart, are the basis of traditional European harmony. Because one may build a triad beginning on any pitch in the diatonic scale, there are seven possible diatonic triads, shown here numbered by the lowest pitch in this arrangement (the **root**). The triads come in distinct types depending on the specific intervals involved, each with its own sound quality. The most common types are those called **major** and **minor**. In practice, chords would still be called triads and be treated the same if the pitches were rearranged, duplicated, or in different octaves, as long as the three basic notes remained.

FIGURE 14.4

This broadside from Scotland c. 1870 would have been sung by street entertainers. Although it does not include music notation, the poetry is in a standard form to fit well-known tunes the ballad singer could choose from. This ballad commemorates the tragic love of the Scottish poet Robert Burns for Mary Campbell.

music. With the invention of music printing, folk musicians had access to the techniques of harmony, and art music composers could draw upon and adapt folk dance forms and folk song melodies.

With instruments such as the guitar, a single player could produce harmonies without having to depend on notation for multiple singers or players of monophonic instruments. Thus, a folk guitarist could strum a standard harmonic progression without having to work out the intricacies of counterpoint. In this way, by the nineteenth and twentieth centuries, harmony and homophonic textures became just as commonly a part of folk and popular music as they were of art music. Harmonic progressions influenced folk and popular melodies, even when musicians performed those melodies without harmonies. This implication of harmonic progressions gives Western European folk and popular melodies of the most recent centuries a distinctive character not found elsewhere or in earlier times.

FOLK MUSIC

Although musicologists often find it useful to distinguish notated music created by professionals from music of the oral tradition, or between music of the Christian Church and music of everyday life, such distinctions can be overemphasized. The status and training of musicians in the Middle Ages, for example, ranged across a spectrum from aristocratic troubadours and Church music professionals to town trumpeters and wandering entertainers.

But for centuries, the heart of musical culture in most people's everyday lives was singing. As in most agricultural and peasant societies, many songs were naturally tied to the agricultural calendar and life events. Musicologists consider these some of the oldest songs of the Western European tradition, and they often have a narrow range, are short and strophic, and may use fewer than the full seven pitches of the diatonic scale. Some old European songs use anhemitonic pentatonic scales, which they have in common, perhaps since ancient times, with the music of Central Asia and China. Folk songs, often sung in family and small community gatherings, were often associated with women, whereas men usually played purely instrumental works. Unlike many traditions in the world, Europeans often kept the playing of instruments distinct from sung music.

Many later types of folk songs also used strophic forms, most famously the **ballad**. Ballads often had four-line stanzas that corresponded to regular musical phrases, as well as a repeating refrain. Most important, ballads tell a story within the confines of this repeating poetic structure, often a tragic story of lovers, but also regional legends, ghost stories, and exploits of famous outlaws such as Robin Hood. Wandering ballad singers were entertainers at town fairs and often carriers of news and history. Later, these stories were printed up in large sheets called **broadsides**, a kind of musical newspaper sold by the street singer (Figure 14.4). Many broadsides and other ballads remain beloved traditional songs in Europe, Australia, and North America, including "Barbara Allen," "Greensleeves," and "Scarborough Fair."

Like other later Western European songs, ballads were most often based on diatonic modes. Because the diatonic pitch set is heptatonic, there are seven possible diatonic modes (Graphic 14.2). However, the development of harmony and goal-directed harmonic progressions led to an increasing preference for only two of these modes, now known as **major** and **minor**, and later songs composed under the influence of harmony nearly always used these two modes.

GRAPHIC 14.2

Diatonic modes: Because any of the seven pitches in a diatonic set can be made the tonic, there are seven possible diatonic modes. Therefore, the characteristic placement of small intervals known as semitones in the scale is different for each one. Later theorists named these modes after ancient Greek scales (although the actual Greek scales were different).

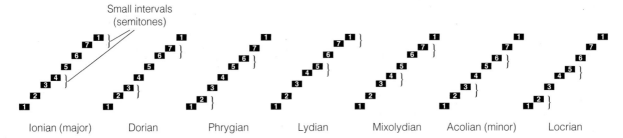

Ionian (major) Dorian Phrygian Lydian Mixolydian Aeolian (minor) Locrian

By the twentieth century, folk musicians frequently added harmony to their songs, often through instruments capable of playing chords, such as the accordion and the guitar. The rise of popular music during this time led to a professionalization of some folk music performance, that is, the development of professional bands who would perform traditional music often with harmony, electronic amplification, and sometimes nontraditional instruments.

THE RISE OF POPULAR MUSIC

The distinction between folk and art music that developed in Western Europe also mirrored the economic history of the continent. For centuries, the concentration of wealth in the Christian church and among the aristocracy supported specialist composers and performing musicians, whereas the great majority of people enjoyed access only to the oral traditions of nonspecialist folk musicians. However, the rise of the middle class, modern capitalism, and industrial economies in the eighteenth and nineteenth centuries created a new model for the support of music not only in Western Europe but also in areas colonized by Europeans, including the Americas and Australia. Musicians could now sell concert tickets and printed music to the public, and so music itself could be a commodity to be sold.

Although this model continued to support art music somewhat, the expense and narrow appeal of art music usually necessitated the financial support of governments, philanthropists, and universities. Instead, this modern economy gave rise to popular music: music specifically created to have mass appeal in the marketplace. With the invention of music recordings and radio in the early twentieth century, popular music came to dominate the public experience of music.

Although there were many genres of Western popular music, nearly all of them retained some of the most distinctive characteristics of Western European music, including harmonic progressions, relatively simple rhythms, phrases based on metrical units of four groups of four or three, and the use of European instruments. However, the harmonic progressions remained relatively simple compared to those used in art music and were typically realized without counterpoint on instruments such as the guitar or piano.

The availability of recordings, along with the wide dissemination of Western European culture beginning with the period of colonialism through radio, television, and the Internet, helped spread Western popular music throughout the world. Today, there is hardly a culture on the planet that has not been touched by this music and with it triadic harmonies and harmonic progressions.

Although some people have feared that the easy accessibility of Western popular music (like other forms of popular entertainment) could overwhelm and eventually drown out traditional musical cultures, engaging hybrids have emerged in many places in the world. We have already seen, for example, how Western harmony and song structures have been merged with cyclic forms and indigenous rhythms to create new and unique music in Sub-Saharan Africa. Often the process then continued in reverse, with Western popular music absorbing influences from other traditions throughout the world. Characteristics originating in the music of African slaves have greatly influenced nearly all forms of popular music of the Americas.

MUSIC IN AUSTRIA

The invention of printing and music notation in Europe has made possible the preservation of music history with specificity and comprehensiveness nearly unique in the world. Nowhere is this reverence more visible than in Austria, where monuments to its famous composers look out with the same projection of permanence as the facades of its old palaces and theaters. By the Middle Ages, Vienna had developed into a powerful capital at the strategic crossroads of central Europe, absorbing influences from across the continent and even the Ottoman Empire in Turkey.

As the Austrian Empire and its wealth grew, the center of professional music-making moved from churches to the courts, which spent lavishly on the arts, subsidizing composers, orchestras, and opera among other activities. However, the richness of this musical culture permeated many levels of society beyond the aristocracy, through Church music, education, and, eventually, public ticket sales to performances. Therefore, whereas many of the folk music traditions of other European countries have retained monophonic or heterophonic textures, harmony from a very early time greatly influenced Austrian folk music.

Folk dances include the **ländler**, like the waltz, a triple-meter couple dance, but sometimes faster. These dances were often played on instruments that could supply some harmony, including the **diskantzither** (Figure 14.5) and the **hackbrett** (a dulcimer or zither with strings struck with hammers, like the Hungarian *cimbalom* (see Figure 13.3 in Chapter 13). The first **accordion** (at least so named) was invented in Vienna in 1829, and versions of it became a very popular folk and dance instrument in Austria and many other countries of Europe (Figure 14.7). These rustic dances found their way into art music of the eighteenth century, and even famous composers, such as Wolfgang Amadeus Mozart and Ludwig van Beethoven, wrote these forms for the Austrian court and aristocratic balls.

© JTB Photo Communications, Inc./Alamy

FIGURE 14.5

The *diskantzither* is an Austrian zither developed in the nineteenth century that has some melody strings over a fretted fingerboard (like that of a guitar) and other unstopped strings used for bass and harmony pitches.

FIGURE 14.6

In the Alpine region, herdsmen and farmers since ancient times have crafted large buzzed-lip horns of wood, known as **alphorns**, to signal over the expansive alpine river valleys (rather like the horns used in similar valleys of Tibet, see Figure 8.3). Although the alphorn has no keys, slides, or valves, players can play from a set of pitches known as the harmonic series (like a bugle). The distinctive tuning of these pitches is sometimes imitated in singing in the Alps region.

FIGURE 14.7

The *Schrammelgitare* or harp-guitar (right) is a guitar with two necks invented in Austria toward the end of the nineteenth century. The lower fingerboard has the frets of a conventional guitar, while the upper neck has bass strings, enabling the player to alternate bass pitches and chords on a single instrument. The accordion (left) consists of an air reservoir that the player can push or pull to suck or push air through a series of reeds controlled by keys and buttons. In a modern instrument like this one, the keyboard on the player's right can be used to play melodies, and the buttons on the player's left create standard chords.

Around the end of the eighteenth century, researchers and other intellectuals developed a further interest in folk songs and dances because of both nationalist inclinations and a belief that folk songs were somehow representative of a purer, more unaffected expression of a culture. (German intellectuals from this period coined the term *volksmusik*, or "music of the people," to refer to traditional music, from which we get the English term "folk music.") Not content to leave folk songs as such, however, composers added harmonies to monophonic ballads and "cleaned up" rustic improvised polyphony.

In this form, rural folk music became popular in urban settings, such as with amateur choirs, bands, and other ensembles often reading from written music. Near the end of the nineteenth century, two brothers, Johann and Joseph Schrammel, organized such an ensemble consisting of two violins, accordion or sometimes clarinet, and harp-guitar (Figure 14.7). The **Schrammel ensemble** became so popular that it lent its name to what became a whole genre of music for this ensemble. Recently, guitarist and composer Roland Neuwirth has brought influences from jazz, blues, and rock to his band Extremschrammeln.

Like Neuwirth, other musicians have taken traditions in new directions, deriding *lederhosenmusik*, old popular folk styles so named for the traditional dress musicians put on for tourists. Christof Dienz and the ensemble Knödel took the band music (*blasmusik*) associated with lederhosen and gave it sophisticated harmonies, complex rhythms, and unusual orchestrations. The band Attwenger (Markus Binder and Hans-Peter Falkner) brought punk rock distortion and hip-hop rhythms to folk instruments of the Alpine region.

CD 3:12. *"Die lustige Bäurin"* ("The Merry Farmer's Wife"), Hamot Trio, Purgstall, Austria

In the region of the Alps mountains south and west of Vienna, much of the singing has an open-throated tone that may be associated with calling over river valleys, as well as the distinctive technique, heard clearly here, of yodeling. **Yodeling** is a technique of quickly switching between vocal registers (also found in Africa, the Pacific, the United States, and some other regions). Because of the long influence of harmony throughout the culture, Austria still has a strong tradition of polyphonic folksinging. This song is made polyphonic not by a composer's working out the harmonies on paper and asking the players to read notation, as in art music, but by developing over time a repertory of nonwritten techniques that tend to result in triadic harmonies.

0:00

The singer sings **vocables**, syllables without linguistic meaning, here and throughout the selection. Ornamentation throughout the piece consists of slight slides up or down to pitches as a part of the yodel.

0:05

Two singers join the first singer. The harmony here is based on the tonic (I) triad. The three singers, two men and a woman, interlace their yodels quite closely (shown as differently colored lines in the following graphic), so that all pitches of the tonic triad are always present.

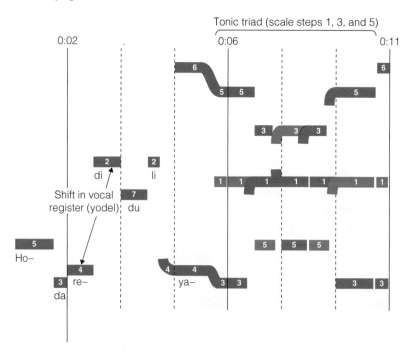

0:10   Listen to how the harmony now changes, in this case to the V triad, before creating a dissonance.

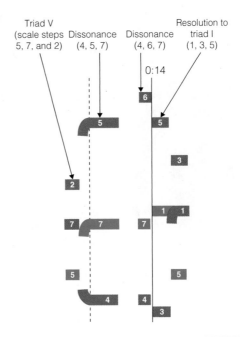

0:14   The dissonance resolves to the tonic triad.

0:18   For contrast, the texture changes to just two voices and new harmonies, before returning again to the tonic triad.

0:26   Dissonance is again introduced to create tension before resolution in the final chord of the section.

0:33   The song is repeated, but this time, all the pitches are shifted up by a fixed amount, a technique called a **key change** or **modulation**.

1:04   The song is repeated once again at a yet higher pitch.

Hear and see the instruments of "*Die lustige Bäurin*" in your downloadable **ACTIVE LISTENING TOOLS,** available at the World Music Resource Center.

TRADITIONAL MUSIC OF IRELAND

At the end of a cul-de-sac in Sligo, a town on Ireland's northwest coast, is an unassuming pub. Amid the crowded tables is an area in one corner, which by common consent, remains empty until around 9:00 P.M., when several men bring pints (beers) and musical instruments over to these tables. This is a night of a "session," a meeting of players of traditional Irish music (Figure 14.8). The musicians are not paid entertainers, although the rest of the customers are free to listen and perhaps buy the musicians a drink. The pub does not advertise their performance, though it may let it be known that sessions are open on certain nights.

FIGURE 14.8

This session in County Kerry, Ireland, features fiddle, *uilleann* pipes, guitar, and tin whistle.

The musicians chat, but none plays until the oldest of them finally arrives and slowly takes a fiddle (another name for a violin) out of its case. He sits down on the corner stool. After some casual tuning and perhaps a few draughts, he begins unassumingly playing a **reel**, a duple-meter dance. There are no others playing, and the performance is monophonic. With each repeat of the tune, he finds a new perspective, new ornamental possibilities in the seemingly simple melody, and just as the sound becomes louder and more direct, he switches to a new reel melody, and the tempo climbs up a notch or two. Just as the second reel finds its height, the fiddler launches into a third, and the room has taken notice. Despite the quick tempo, an increasingly supple flurry of notes emerges between each of the long notes of the melody, like the intricate twists of ancient Celtic art.

Conversation has stopped, and many customers in addition to the musicians find themselves smiling and tapping along, although the player does not outwardly show any emotion or acknowledge the occasional murmurs of approval or encouragement. At last, the piece comes to a stop amid warm applause.

The night continues with other musicians young and old taking their turns or joining in. When more than one musician is playing, the texture is usually heterophonic, with every musician playing his or her own ornamented version of the melody. In recent years, however, guitarists have become common in sessions, providing harmony rather than another melody. Although the musicians play dance music nearly exclusively, as the session gets going patrons often scarcely have room to sit at a table, much less dance.

Irish music has become possibly the most popular traditional music from Europe in recent years, with dance companies incorporating large productions with synthesizers and other nontraditional innovations. Yet Irish music still betrays a conservative core, a love of tradition, and is as at ease in the informal surroundings of a local pub or restaurant now as it might have been two centuries ago. Here a cab driver, college student, or farmer might unpretentiously summon a performance of great artistry.

HISTORICAL BACKGROUND

Ireland is perhaps the only country whose national symbol is a musical instrument—the **Irish harp** (or *cruit* in Gaelic, the native language of Ireland) can be found on the Irish flag and coins. A **bard**—a person who was a combination poet, composer, and musician—was an indispensable member of the inner circle of every ancient Irish king's court. More than mere entertainers, they were keepers of history and genealogies, symbols of royal status, and respected custodians of the art and culture of their land.

During this early period, the harp music of the bards amounted to an art music of professionals. Beginning in the twelfth century, the English invaded and gradually replaced the Irish kingdoms with English rule. English language began to replace Gaelic (nearly completely today), and English culture and music had a great influence.

The English considered the bard such a powerful symbol of the Irish culture and royalty it had suppressed that by the sixteenth century, membership in the profession carried a death penalty. The last remnants of this proud tradition survived as itinerant entertainers into the eighteenth century, the most famous of whom was the blind harpist Turlough O'Carolan (1670–1738). O'Carolan drew upon folk tunes of various regions as easily as he did the art music of continental Europe, leaving a legacy of some of the earliest notated Irish music.

Just as O'Carolan made use of notation, folk song collectors began to write down the songs and dances of ordinary people for the first time. By the early twentieth century, thousands of tunes had been published, preserving an invaluable legacy for future musicians. Yet the art of Irish music comes not so much from the tunes themselves, which are relatively simple, but instead from the ornamentation, phrasing, and other elements that can only be reliably transmitted orally, or, to some extent now, from recordings.

Still, musicologists are able to discern that most of the melodies that modern Irish players draw upon were created in the past two or three centuries, although the extensive variations and borrowings of one melody from another have created complex family trees of gradually evolving and changing tunes, a process that continues today.

The Irish have often expressed their political resistance to British rule in Ireland musically. In the 1890s, a group of intellectuals created a nationalist organization known as the Gaelic League, which supported the development of traditional folk music as a distinctive Irish cultural treasure, through competitions, concerts, and *ceili*, or traditional social gatherings. However, the League cultivated a refined form of the music sometimes at odds with folk practices in rural areas. Notated harmonies written for piano, already found in publications, became a central feature of so-called **ceili bands**, which largely replaced solo or small group heterophonic performances in the 1930s and 1940s.

Concerned that the traditional music of the people was dying out, some musicians formed schools and **fleadh**, or festivals, supporting more traditional playing and singing. The classically trained composer Seán Ó Riada (1931–1971) led a reform movement in the 1960s that reinvigorated *sean nós* (a traditional song form) and regional styles, and created a new form of ensemble playing that shunned Romantic-style playing and instruments such as the piano. However, he did not give up harmony but often created sophisticated arrangements with subtle harmonizing parts (bringing to mind the seventeenth-century harmonies of O'Carolan) that left room for traditional ornamentation and improvisation.

The ensemble Ó Riada created for this purpose in 1960 featured some of the best-known and most knowledgeable musicians of the traditional styles who nevertheless were a new breed of professionals often associated with specialized schools and *fleadh*. In 1962, the piper of Ó Riada's ensemble, Paddy Moloney,

Barry McCall/Courtesy of The Chieftains

FIGURE 14.9

The Chieftains have brought traditional Irish music to the world stage for more than forty-five years. The core group currently consists of (left to right) Sean Keane (fiddle), Paddy Moloney (uilleann pipes), Kevin Conneff (bodhran), and Matt Molloy (flute).

Abhann Productions/Courtesy of Riverdance

FIGURE 14.10

The success of the stage show *Riverdance* created a surge in popular interest in modern Celtic music. *Riverdance* was composed by Bill Whelan, produced by Moya Doherty, and directed by John McColgan.

reconstituted the group as the Chieftains (Figure 14.9). The Chieftains would go on to perform around the world and create many albums and film scores, leading a renewed interest in Irish traditional music both within and outside of Ireland.

In the 1970s and later, others went further with innovations, bringing guitars and amplification into traditional music or traditional instruments and styles into pop and rock bands. Among the best-known groups are Altan and De Dannan, and bands such as The Pogues even married punk rock influence with Irish tunes. The term *Celtic music* is often used today to express the wider range of traditions on which some of these bands draw. The Celts are an ethnic group that arrived in Ireland during the Bronze Age but who also include other groups in the other British islands, Northern France, and Spain. The popularity of the Celtic sound has influenced hybrids with techno, blues, and rock, and has influenced the Irish rock singer Van Morrison and the group U2.

In 1994, composer Bill Whelan and choreographers Michael Flatley and Jean Butler created a stage show to feature professional Irish dancers. Whelan updated traditional dance forms to include the rhythms and synthesized timbres of this more international Celtic sound, and the choreographers transformed informal solo dances into virtuosic group dances in perfect synchronization (Figure 14.10). The immense success of the result led to a full-length touring show known as *Riverdance*, followed by Flatley's *Lord of the Dance* in 1996. Although these shows are largely responsible for the current popularity of Irish music, they also included international hybrids, such as rock, Spanish flamenco, and Eastern European folk dance.

IRISH GENRES

Although most people know Irish music today through the infectious meters of instrumental dance music, the Irish, unusually for Europe, also have a long history of nonpulsatile or quasi-pulsatile forms. The elasticity of rhythm in these pieces allows for great emotional expression and elaborate ornamentation. However, even this expressivity is typically subdued and introverted, without histrionic effects. This desire to let the art speak for itself can be found in the often impassive faces of dancers and musicians, even as their songs may tell stories of great tragedy.

SINGING

The oldest form of nonpulsatile singing may be in songs of laments, or **keening**, sung at funerals even in the times of the bards. Today, the genre known as **sean nós** (pronounced "shawn nose" translating to "old style") represents this type of unaccompanied, typically nonpulsatile singing. Seán Ó Riada and others brought this rare form to public attention by recording different regional styles, which may differ greatly in their ornamentation, rhythm, and range. Since then, even the Irish pop star Sinead O'Connor has recorded songs influenced by *sean nós*. Although *sean nós* were traditionally sung in the Gaelic language, many *sean nós* singers have adapted English songs for their repertoire as well.

INSTRUMENT GALLERY

IRISH MUSICAL INSTRUMENTS

Boltin Picture Library/The Bridgeman Art Library

IRISH HARP

The Irish harp or *cruit* is smaller than the modern European concert harp and is tuned diatonically. Players today normally string Irish harps with nylon, giving them a smooth and sweet timbre. The ancient *cruit*, however, were strung with bright-sounding brass wire and plucked with specially trimmed fingernails. The harpists had to master the difficult technique of dampening some strings while plucking others, rather than simply letting the tones ring indefinitely. This fifteenth-century instrument is one of the earliest surviving examples of the *cruit*.

Lebrecht Music and Arts Photo Library/Alamy

UILLEANN PIPES

Bagpipes are found in many European countries and most often consist of a bag air reservoir filled by blowing through a valve, a reed pipe with holes known as the "chanter" to play melodies, and one or more other reed pipes without holes to play drones. Bagpipes in this form are famous in the highlands of neighboring Scotland and were found in Ireland before the eighteenth century. Around that time, a distinctively Irish form of the instrument was invented that replaced the mouth pipe for filling the bag with a bellows operated by the player's left elbow (*uilleann*, pronounced "WEE-uhn," means "elbow"). Played sitting, it has a much softer sound than the Scottish pipes and is suitable for indoor playing. In addition to a chanter with keys and a wide range, it has three drone pipes and a set of "regulator" keys, which provide standard chords to accompany the melody.

TravelStockCollection—Homer Sykes/Alamy

TIN WHISTLE

With the Industrial Revolution of the nineteenth century, musical instrument makers in England found that a version of the recorder, a type of duct flute, could be fashioned very cheaply from a metal body, so cheaply that these six-holed flutes were often called *pennywhistles*. Their affordability and ease of playing made them a favorite of Irish amateur musicians, although it has won respect among professionals as well. Irish bands also sometimes feature a transverse wooden flute (refer to Figure 14.9, right).

David Lyons/Alamy

BODHRAN

Until relatively recently, percussion seems to have been mostly absent from Irish traditional music. The *bodhran* (pronounced "BOW-rahn") is a medium-size circular frame drum whose original function may have been as a kitchen tray occasionally beaten for certain religious rituals. The *fleadh* (festivals) and especially the innovations of Seán Ó Riada in the 1960s made this drum a common sight in Irish bands. The player holds it upright on the lap and may find different tones with the fingers on the skin or play with a stick on the rim. Other common Irish percussion instruments include bones (two animal knucklebones clacked together in the player's hand) and spoons (two spoons hit against the hand and knee).

Hear and see the instruments of Ireland in your downloadable **ACTIVE LISTENING TOOLS**, available at the World Music Resource Center.

DANCE MUSIC

Dance music in Ireland is related to the repeating structure found in strophic forms. Nearly all dance tunes are in two-part, or binary form, the second half forming a contrast to the first. Each half is usually played twice (making the form AABB) with the whole dance repeated an indeterminate number of times. The endings, or cadences, of the A and B sections usually vary, so that the first time through, the melody feels unfinished, usually by ending on a nontonic pitch. The second time through, the melody finds its way to the tonic, signaling a satisfying resolution. This pattern of relatively unresolved (or "open") and resolved (or "closed") cadences is repeated in smaller form in the interior phrases of each section, creating a hierarchy common in European music. Each phrase is usually four metrical units long and makes up exactly half of the section.

In performance, three or so dances are usually strung together, one immediately following another of the same type, to create a **medley**, a long piece made up of shorter compositions. Because many tunes share the same tonic pitch, they flow easily from one to another, although some musicians may have preferences for which pieces are appropriate to play together.

The most common dance types in traditional Irish music, called **step dances** (Figure 14.11), include the following:

FIGURE 14.11

Irish reels, jigs, and hornpipes are example of step dances, so called because the upper part of the body remains mostly motionless while the feet execute complicated steps.

scenicireland.com/Christopher Hill Photographic/Alamy

- **Reel.**   This quick simple duple meter dance is the most common of Irish dance forms.

- **Jig.**   This dance is also very popular and often serves as a contrast to reels because it is in a compound duple meter. Musicians often distinguish a single jig, which has a characteristic rhythm of long-short, long-short, with a double jig, whose rhythm is a mostly constant short-short-short, short-short-short.

- **Slide.**   This form is a variant of the jig performed at a faster tempo but with twice as many beats per section. Therefore, most musicians feel it as a quadruple rather than duple meter.

- **Slip jig.**   This dance has a distinctive compound triple meter.

- **Hornpipe.**   This was originally a sailor's dance, presumably played on reed instruments with a horn on the end, as are found in some Mediterranean countries. Although it is also a simple duple meter dance like the reel, it is slower and characterized by heavy dance steps and different rhythms.

The jig, reel, and hornpipe were brought to Ireland around the seventeenth and eighteenth centuries and have since been adapted to their present distinctively Irish forms.

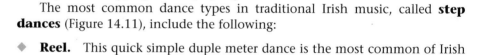

AN IRISH INSTRUMENTAL PERFORMANCE

Nonpulsatile or slow instrumental pieces are called **slow airs**, and their intricate and expressive ornamentation makes them the instrumental counterpart to *sean nós* singing. Like many slow airs, this one originates in a *sean nós* song called

"Bean An Fhir Rua/O'Farrell's Welcome to Limerick" ("The Red-Haired Man's Wife"), the Chieftains. *The Chieftains 2*, Claddagh Records, CC7CD, tracks 3-4. May be downloaded at MP3fiesta.com.

0:00	In this first phrase, nearly every note of the core melody is extensively decorated with very short notes, what European musicians sometimes call "grace notes." Moloney ornaments each of the long notes with vibrato, a quick fluctuation of pitch effected on the pipes with quick fluttering of the fingers over certain keys.

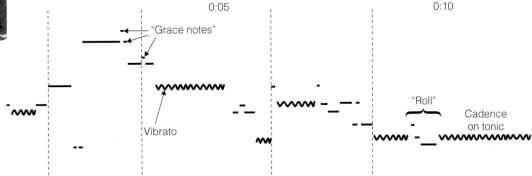

0:09	The first phrase ends with a cadence on the tonic. The player uses a special ornament, known as a "roll," which consists of a quick alternation between the note above, the tonic, the note below, and back to the tonic.
0:22	The second phrase ends. The player then repeats the second phrase but with different ornaments and timings.
0:37	The climax comes at the beginning of the fourth phrase, when the melody includes a singular and poignant deviation from the mode—the 7th scale step is lowered.
0:48	After the final cadence of the melody, the pipes player for the first time adds pitches from the drone pipes. For the second repetition of the melody, a fiddle (violin) joins the *uilleann* pipes. Both play the melody with individual ornaments, creating a heterophonic texture above the drone pitches.
1:47	For the final repetition of the melody, the fiddle and pipes are joined by a tin whistle, which adds another layer of heterophonic variation.

2:43 	For the final cadence of this slow air, the *uilleann* pipes player for the first time uses the regulator pipes to create a full triad.
0:00 	Now the slip jig dance begins, with the same three instruments, *uilleann* pipes, fiddle, and tin whistle playing the melody heterophonically, and the regulator pipes accompany the melody with drone pitches. Although it is difficult to hear at this point in this recording, *bodhran* (frame drum) now joins the other instruments.
0:10 	Just before the cadence of this phrase, the pipe player changes his drone pitches to a triad on the fifth scale degree before returning to the original pitches. The player will follow this pattern of changing to this triad just before each cadence of the rest of the piece. Although the most traditional of Irish performances lack harmony, chords such as these are commonly used on the *uilleann* pipes. Like most Irish dances, after four metrical groupings (twelve beats, in this case), the first section, known as the ***fonn*** or A section, repeats.
0:18	The second section, known as the ***casadh*** ("turn") or B section begins. Note how it contrasts the first section by emphasizing the upper register. One of the most common ornaments used in this dance can be heard in the second beat of this

"*Bean An Fhir Rua*" or "The Red-Haired Man's Wife," the emotional lament of a man who has fallen in love with another man's wife and who has ceased to care about the society's sanctions that his passion may bring. Chieftains *uilleann* piper Paddy Moloney introduces this major mode melody with perhaps just a vestige of a triple meter though most listeners would probably hear it as nonpulsatile. Slow airs give instrumentalists the opportunity to explore elaborate and expressive ornamentation, and the *uilleann* pipes are known for their especially extensive ornamentation techniques.

Very often, musicians will follow a performance of a slow air with a dance, in this case, "O'Farrell's Welcome to Limerick," named after a famous measure—when two notes of a melody skip a tone in the scale, the players will often fill in the missing scale tone. The notes of the new three-note pattern, called a "triplet," are shortened to fit in the same time duration. The players also repeat this twelve-beat section, as they do all the sections.

0:32 Although most Irish dances have just two sections (*fonn* and *casadh*, played AABB), this one now has a third section (C), which is a variation on the first section. The second half of this section is the same as the first half of the A section.

0:46 The next section (D) is another variation of the A section.

1:00 The melody now returns to the *casadh* (B) section.

1:13 The players repeat the entire jig. Try to hear where each section and repetition begins.

2:21 For a welcome contrast on the final repetition of the melody, the *uilleann* pipes player shuts off the drone pitches. It is now easier to hear the *bodhran* providing an exciting beat to end the dance.

3:28 To end the piece, the *uilleann* pipes player plays a triad on the tonic pitch.

piper. This tune is a slip jig, that is, a dance in compound triple meter, and is in the Mixolydian mode. Like most Western European folk music, the modes of Irish traditional music are usually diatonic, although the older melodies are more likely to be in modes other than major and minor. Although the ornamentation in a quick dance like this is not as elaborate as in a slow air, the execution of certain ornaments, often different for each instrument, is standard practice. Because the pipe player in particular is not able to articulate a separate beginning of each note like the tin whistle player (by interrupting the air with his tongue) or the fiddle player (by changing direction of the bow), he often articulates notes by inserting quick ornaments in between.

SPAIN

The Iberian peninsula juts out into the ocean with faces toward the Atlantic and the Mediterranean, Europe and Africa. Its people also form cultural border-lands that still retain the imprint of the many groups who have settled there: the Greeks, the Romans, the Carthaginians, and the Visigoths. Spain's rugged mountain ranges separate its provinces, which often still retain distinctive tra-ditions and even languages. The population of the east speaks Catalan, and in the north, the Basque minority retain distinct traditions and language.

In the year 711, Arabs invaded from North Africa, and most of the peninsula would remain Islam's foothold in Western Europe for nearly eight centuries. The influence of Islam and Arabic culture was profound, although Christians and Jews were shown tolerance under Islamic rule. Under Arabic rule, Spain became a center for arts and scholarship, absorbing influences from throughout the Islamic world. Several important instruments emerged during this period, including the lute and the guitar.

In the middle of the fifteenth century, a new group settled in southern Spain, today known as the Roma (see Chapter 13), often known as "gypsies" to other Europeans, and known in Spain as ***gitanos***. By the end of that cen-tury, the Christian reconquest of Spain was complete, but tolerance for other religions ended. Jews and Muslims were forced to convert or be expelled from the country. Many resettled in other parts of the Mediterranean region (see Chapter 7), while others converted. However, some of those who converted secretly kept not only their religion but also their traditions, especially in the southernmost region of Spain. In this area, known as Andalucía, a vast under-class formed of nominally converted Muslims and Jews together with *gitanos*. Their music forged by this upheaval sang of experiences as minority outcasts, who endured repression, prison, and other tragedies.

The same year that Christian forces conquered the last Islamic center in Spain, 1492, Christopher Columbus claimed the Americas for this newly unified country. The riches brought by colonialism made Spain both a political power and a center for art music. The newly rich elite heard grand polyphonic religious music in their churches and ***zarzuelas***, a kind of opera, in their theaters.

However, it was the colorful folk traditions that captured the imagination of much of Europe in the nineteenth and twentieth centuries. Many art music com-posers, from the Russian Piotr Tchaikovsky to the Frenchman Claude Debussy, evoked the unusual modes and invigorating rhythms of the regions in their work, as did Spain's native composers, such as Manuel de Falla (1876–1946).

SPAIN'S FOLK TRADITIONS

The diversity and historical isolation of Spain's regions makes it difficult to generalize about its folk music. For example, although diatonic modes are common here as they are throughout Europe, Spanish songs are more likely to use diatonic modes other than major or minor, especially Phrygian, with its characteristic semitone (small) step above the tonic. When harmonized with the guitar (Figure 14.12), these qualities led to the "dark" and distinctive alternation of major and minor triads, qualities imitated by nineteenth-century art music composers all the way up to modern film composers who use these now well-known harmonic progressions to set a scene in Spain.

These harmonic progressions frequently occur in repeating patterns, like the poetic forms of the songs themselves. Stanzas in folk songs are known as **coplas**, a term that originally meant couplet. The musical structure of stanzas often retains the binary form this term implies, as in the frequently back-and-forth or repeating cycles of harmonic progressions played on guitars. Contrasting refrains are called **estribillos**. Although the text setting is often syllabic (one note per syllable, as in most of Western Europe), the ends of phrases are frequently decorated with short melismatic (multiple notes per syllable) flourishes, a characteristically Spanish device perhaps derived from Arabic influence. Similar embellishments are characteristic of the famous trumpet fanfares that introduce bull fights.

One of the most common of Spanish folk songs is the **ronda**, the song of the roving bands of musicians known as **rondallas** or *tuna* that serenade the inhabitants of towns throughout Spain (Figure 14.13). In earlier times, these clubs were formed as a way for young men to romance young women, although they also led to good-natured competitions between groups. Today, *rondallas* may sing for tourists in bars as well as for young women from street corners.

One of the forms *rondallas* play is the **jota**, a couple dance in a quick triple meter often accompanied by song. It is based on regular phrases of four groups of three beats, a form tied to the *copla*. The harmonic progression conventionally used in this form also reflects the pairing of lines in the *copla*, alternating between triads that place the tonic triad resolution at the ends of the pairs.

The *jota*, like many Spanish dances, often has a heavy rhythmic emphasis provided in part by strumming guitars, but more particularly by percussion sounds made by the dancers themselves. Dancers often use **castanets**, small pairs of wooden idiophones clacked together in the palm of the dancer's hand. Images of dancers using such hand-held clappers go back to ancient Roman times. Dancers also create their own percussion by the rhythmic stamping of their feet, known in Spain as **zapateado**. Neither the use of castanets nor *zapateado* is completely free; they must adhere to prescribed rhythms associated with the dance like any other musical instrument.

AA World Travel Library/Alamy

FIGURE 14.12

The guitar is one of the world's most popular instruments today, as guitarists can provide harmony and articulate rhythm through strumming and melody through plucking. Today the typical instrument consists of six double or single courses over a fretted fingerboard and its distinctive, inward curved resonator. While plucked chordophones have a long history in the Middle East, North Africa, and Europe, this distinctive form began to appear in Europe toward the end of the Middle Ages. Musicologists still debate whether the instrument originated in Europe or in North Africa, but by the time of the Renaissance, when Spain was again under Christian control, it was already widely popular there. Like its cousin the lute, which did originate as an adaptation of the Arabic *'ud*, the guitar enjoyed a period of popularity in the rest of Western Europe. However, unlike the lute, which was normally plucked, the guitar was from this early period already a strummed instrument, at least among folk musicians. Although the guitar's place as a classical instrument declined somewhat after the Renaissance, it became essentially Spain's national instrument through its popularity accompanying flamenco singers and in other folk music. Spanish colonists brought the instrument to the Americas, where its portability made it very popular among settlers from Argentina to North America.

FLAMENCO

The famous Spanish poet Federico García Lorca (1898-1936) wrote of the artistic quality the Spanish call *duende*—literally "demon"—but implying the authentic spirit of artistic expression, even bordering on spiritual possession. A connoisseur of traditional Spanish song, he described the famous Spanish singer Pastora

FIGURE 14.13

A *rondalla* ensemble serenades a house in Madrid. The singers accompany themselves on guitars and *bandurrias* (a plucked chordophone cousin of the guitar).

Paul Almasy/CORBIS

Pavón, popularly known as *La Niña de los Peines* or "The Girl with the Combs":

> As though crazy, torn like a medieval mourner, *La Niña de los Peines* leaped to her feet, tossed off a big glass of burning liquor, and began to sing with a scorched throat: without voice, without breath or color, but with *duende*. She was able to kill all the scaffolding of the song and leave way for a furious, enslaving *duende*, friend of sand winds. . . . *La Niña de los Peines* had to tear her voice because she knew she had an exquisite audience, one which demanded not forms but the marrow of forms, pure music, with a body lean enough to stay in the air. She had to rob herself of skill and security, send away her muse and become helpless, that her *duende* might come and deign to fight her hand-to-hand. And how she sang! Her voice was no longer playing. It was a jet of blood worthy of her pain and her sincerity, and it opened like a ten-fingered hand around the nailed but stormy feet of a Christ by Juan de Juni.[2]

García Lorca himself together with the composer Manuel de Falla organized a festival of traditional song in 1922 to reinvigorate this type of song, known as **cante hondo** or "deep song." *Cante hondo* is the most traditional category of songs of the Andalucían region, the southern area of Spain where an oppressed underclass largely of *gitanos* (Roma or "gypsies") absorbed the imprint of Arabic and Jewish cultures and sang of profound feelings and deep sorrow. But *cante hondo* is also a way of singing, what García Lorca called a "gored, Dionysian cry" of raspy timbre, elaborate ornamentation, use of melismas (many notes to a syllable), but above all, a passionate ferocity.

FIGURE 14.14

The American painter John Singer Sargent famously captured the emotional intensity of *gitano* flamenco performers in his painting *El Jaleo* (1880).

Isabella Stewart Gardner Museum/The Bridgeman Art Library

Cante hondo were the core repertory of what by the end of the eighteenth century became known as **flamenco** (Figures 14.14 and 14.15). Many people know flamenco through its expression as a dramatic and passionate dance, but flamenco is at its core an art of song, sung by both men and women. Some of the oldest flamenco repertoires are unaccompanied, but most commonly a single guitarist accompanies flamenco song. Flamenco demands a very specialized form of guitar playing that follows the singer's melodic contour, pauses, ornamentation, forceful phrase endings, and, above all, expression. Flamenco guitarists use specialized techniques, such as **rasgueado** (Figure 14.16).

As important as the guitar in accompanying flamenco song is the practice of **palmas**, or rhythmic hand clapping. This practice does not simply mean any audience participation in clapping along but rather clapping of specific and complicated rhythms, known as **compás**, often by a single specialist. Another important element is the cries of the audience, known as **jaleo**, including the well-known *¡olé!*, a shout equivalent to "bravo!" but probably originating in the Arabic *wa-Allah!* or "by God!"

Flamenco style became a well-known entertainment in Andalucían bars in the nineteenth century, so popular that singers incorporated other song forms into this style. Today, flamenco includes many types of song forms, or **palos**, many associated with particular cities or regions of Andalucía. Nineteenth-century cafés and fiestas (celebrations) were also the places where flamenco

[2]Federico García Lorca, "The Play and Theory of the Duende," in *Deep Song and Other Prose*, trans. Christopher Maurer (New York: New Directions, 1975): 45–46.

FIGURE 14.15

A performance of flamenco traditionally includes a single guitarist, a singer, and perhaps another performer of *palmas* (clapping). Dance is often but not necessarily part of the performance.

FIGURE 14.16

In the guitar technique known as *rasgueado*, the fingers unfold as the wrist moves down, creating a rolling, extended strum.

dance developed, with its expressive sweeping of the arms and use of *zapateado* to emphasize the *compás* of the music. These café performances became so popular with nongitano patrons and tourists that by the end of the century flamenco performers were appearing on the stage in operettas. Purists such as García Lorca decried this commercialization, and he and others sought to revive a more authentic form of this traditional art.

Thanks to the efforts of the supporters of this form, flamenco enjoyed a period of resurgence in the 1950s and 1960s. In the 1970s, the singer José Monge Cruz (better known by his nickname El Camarón de la Isla) added an electric bass and other innovations in his very successful performances and albums, often in collaboration with the innovative guitarist Paco de Lucía. Together they inaugurated a style of experimental hybrids known as **Nuevo Flamenco**. In the 1980s and after, groups such as Ketama and Pata Negra added influences from rock, blues, and Latin American popular music. In the *peñas* (clubs) and festivals of Andalucía, though, one can still hear the *duende* of traditional singing.

A FLAMENCO PERFORMANCE

A **soleá** is one of the oldest forms of flamenco song, often danced by women and sung by a man with guitar accompaniment. Each of these phrases has a certain pattern of emphasized beats within the meter called the **compás**. These patterns are one of the main characteristics that distinguish one flamenco song form from another. The *compás* for the *soleá* usually emphasizes beats 3, 6, 8, and 10 within a twelve-beat phrase in simple triple meter. The guitarist accompanies each twelve-beat phrase with variations on standard patterns, called *falsetas*, appropriate for the form and *compás*. The composer of this *soleá* is the *gitano* poet Francisco Moreno Galván (1925–1999), who became well known for revitalizing old forms such as this. The mode is complex, sometimes suggesting Mixolydian, other times Phrygian diatonic modes, but most characteristic of the sound is the very small interval, a semitone, just above the tonic.

CD 3:13. *Fuente de Piyaya (The Fountain of Piyaya),* José Menese with Melchor de Marchena, guitar

0:00	
	The guitar introduces the song first with a series of strong strummed tonic chords, and then you will hear a percussive knock—this is a *golpe*, a rapping of the guitarist's fingers on the body of the instrument. Although traditional flamenco does not include percussion instruments, percussive sounds such as this and the *zapateado* of the dancer (not heard here) are crucial additions to prominent beats.

0:04	The guitarist begins the first of a series of introductory phrases known as *falsetas*, here played with typical complexity and virtuosity, alternating between very fast patterns up and down the scale, strummed chords, or chord tones played one at a time (called **arpeggios**). Listen, too, for the first of many cries of *jaleo*.

0:11	The next phrase begins. In this phrase, you will hear a strong chord on beats 3 and two more strong chords emphasizing the cadence on beats 9 and 10. The phrase ends with a *golpe*.

0:16	The singer enters just before beat 3 of the next phrase, singing vocables ("le le le…"), a typical way to introduce a flamenco song known as ***glosolalia***. The high tessitura and ornamented melody ends with a cadence on the tonic pitch.

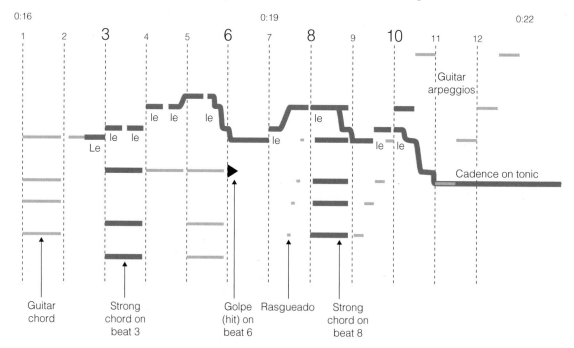

0:22 In the next *falseta* (guitar interlude), you can easily hear the *compás* start with three big chords on beats 1, 2, and 3, and then strong strums culminating on beats 8 and 10.

0:26 Another *glosolalia*.

0:47 **Palmas**, or clapping, now joins the guitar *falseta* to outline the *compás*.

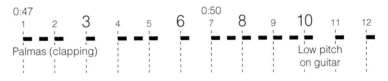

0:57 The singer begins the first *copla*, or stanza of the song.

Fuente de Piyaya	Piyaya fountain
si poquito se bebía	it would dry up
conpoquito se secaba.[3]	with just a sip.[3]

Piyaya is a street in the Andalucían town of La Puebla de Cazalla, the home of Moreno Galván. Oblique, personal, and ruminating lyrics such as these match the intensely personal expression of the flamenco singing style. The significance of this suggestion of the fragility of life may become clearer in the subsequent *coplas*. The singer repeats each of these lines, each time varying the intricate melodies, especially the melismas on words ending each line.

1:37 The guitar *falseta* is a variation on the one at 0:47.

[3]Francisco Moreno Galván, *Letras Flamencas* (Madrid: Universidad Autónoma de Madrid, 1993): 38. Translation by Isabel Balseiro, used by permission.

1:46

The next copla now tells us that the song is about a woman, the narrator's love whom he glimpses walking in the distance:

M'enteré como venía	I found out she was on her way
y yo no quiero sabé de dónde,	from where, I don't wanna know
puñalito pa matarme	a small dagger ready to kill me
y el poquito pan que come.	yet skinny as a rail.

The last lines indicate that even this slight woman has the power to metaphorically stab the narrator fatally in the heart.

2:42

The guitarist plays another variation on the *falseta* from 0:47 and 1:37.

2:56

The next copla expresses the lover's fury at her presumed infidelity:

No eres tú gachi de bien,	You're no good,
eres moneíta falsa,	counterfeit coin,
mala puñala te den.	one day they'll cut you up.

Many of the phrases have a descending melodic contour, reflecting the lover's emotional cry.

3:37

Another *falseta,* and the guitarist increases the tempo and tension.

3:50

The final copla returns to the narrator's description as he watches his lover disappear:

Pasó por la Puerta Ronda	She was passing by Ronda Gate
como tallo se movía,	swaying as a stalk,
la conocí por el aire,	I recognized her ways,
la cara no le veía.	for I could not see her face.

The Ronda Gate is a large, stone medieval portal to the Andalucían city of Ronda. The expressive ferocity of this copla makes it the climax of the song.

4:57

A final and emphatic phrase from the guitar with *palmas* closes the song.

Hear and see the instruments of *Fuente de Piyaya,* in your downloadable **ACTIVE LISTENING TOOLS,** available at the World Music Resource Center.

Listening Exercise 13	CD 3:13. *Fuente de Piyaya*

1. At 1:02, the first three beats of the next cycle are emphasized by
   a. powerful strums.
   b. *rasgueado.*
   c. *golpe.*

2. At 1:24, what technique does the singer employ on the word *bebía*?
   a. falsetto singing
   b. melisma
   c. yodeling

3. At 3:48, the *palmas* divides the beats into
   a. twos.
   b. threes.
   c. fours.

 You can take this Listening Exercise online and receive feedback or e-mail answers to your instructor at the World Music Resource Center.

REFERENCES

DISCOGRAPHY

Camarón de la Isla, with Tomatito. *La leyenda del tiempo*. MSI Music, 1979/2006. [Nuevo Flamenco]

Ceoltóirí Cualann. *Ó Riada sa Gaiety*. Dublin, Ireland: Gael-Linn CEF CD 027, 1988. [Irish traditional music]

The Chieftains. *The Chieftains 2*. Dublin, Ireland: Claddagh Records 83322-2, 1969/2000. [Irish traditional music]

Menese, José. *Cantes Flamencos Basicos*. Madrid, Spain: RCA/BMG Music, Spain 74321 55159 2, 1967/1997. [Flamenco]

Various artists. *Atlante di musica tradizionale*. San Germano, Italy: Robi Droli RDC 5020/5042, 1997. [Italian folk music]

Various artists. *Classic Ballads of Britain and Ireland*. Recorded by Alan Lomax. Cambridge MA: Rounder Records CD 1775-76, 2000.

Various artists. *Meisterspel*. Oslo, Norway: Grappa musikforlag HCD 7132, 1997. [Norwegian folk music]

Various artists. *Musiques en France*. Genéne, France: Auvidis B 6852, 1997. [French folk music]

Various artists. *Portugal: The Story of Fado*. Los Angeles: Blue Note Records 7243 8 55647 2 7, 1997. [Portuguese folk music]

Various artists. *Tondokumente zur volksmusik in Österreich*. Vienna: Institut für Volksmusikforschung, RST Records 91558, 1993. [Austrian folk music]

BOOK COMPANION WEBSITE

You will find flashcards, a glossary, and tutorial quizzes, as well as other materials that will help you succeed in this course, at the *Music of the Peoples of the World, 2nd Edition*, Companion Website at www.cengage.com/music/alves/world2e.

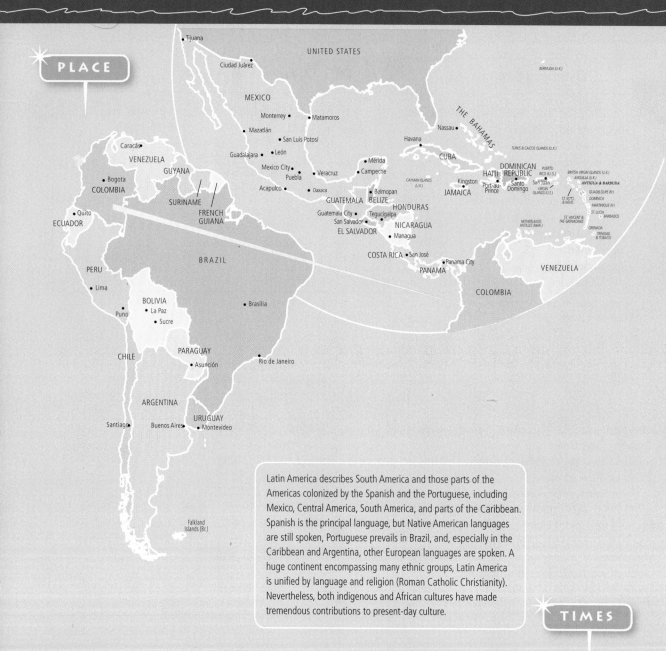

UNITED STATES

BERMUDA (U.K.)

Tijuana

Ciudad Juárez

MEXICO

Monterrey • Matamoros

Mazatlán

San Luis Potosí

Guadalajara • León

Nassau

THE BAHAMAS

TURKS & CAICOS ISLANDS (U.K.)

Havana

CUBA

Caracás

VENEZUELA

GUYANA

Bogotá

COLOMBIA

SURINAME

FRENCH GUIANA

Mexico City

Puebla

Acapulco

Veracruz

Oaxaca

Mérida

Campeche

Belmopan

BELIZE

GUATEMALA

Guatemala City

San Salvador

EL SALVADOR

Tegucigalpa

HONDURAS

NICARAGUA

Managua

CAYMAN ISLANDS (U.K.)

JAMAICA

Kingston

HAITI

Port-au-Prince

DOMINICAN REPUBLIC

Santo Domingo

PUERTO RICO (U.S.)

San Juan

VIRGIN ISLANDS (U.S.)

BRITISH VIRGIN ISLANDS (U.K.)

ANGUILLA (U.K.)

ANTIGUA & BARBUDA

ST. KITTS & NEVIS

GUADELOUPE (Fr.)

DOMINICA

MARTINIQUE (Fr.)

ST. LUCIA

BARBADOS

ST. VINCENT & THE GRENADINES

NETHERLANDS ANTILLES (Neth.)

GRENADA

TRINIDAD & TOBAGO

COSTA RICA • San José

PANAMA

Panama City

VENEZUELA

COLOMBIA

Quito

ECUADOR

PERU

Lima

BRAZIL

Brasília

BOLIVIA

La Paz

Sucre

Puno

PARAGUAY

Asunción

Río de Janeiro

CHILE

ARGENTINA

Santiago

Buenos Aires

URUGUAY

Montevideo

Falkland Islands (Br.)

Latin America describes South America and those parts of the Americas colonized by the Spanish and the Portuguese, including Mexico, Central America, South America, and parts of the Caribbean. Spanish is the principal language, but Native American languages are still spoken, Portuguese prevails in Brazil, and, especially in the Caribbean and Argentina, other European languages are spoken. A huge continent encompassing many ethnic groups, Latin America is unified by language and religion (Roman Catholic Christianity). Nevertheless, both indigenous and African cultures have made tremendous contributions to present-day culture.

c. 1150 BCE–1533 CE

A series of powerful and complex empires dominates central Mexico, including Olmec, Zapotec, Toltec, and Aztec civilizations. Aztec rituals apparently included complex drumming patterns on the *teponatzli* (wooden slit drum) and the *huehuetl* (large footed drum). Other instruments included flutes, whistles, and trumpets. Mayan civilization dominates Central America; Incan civilization is located in the Andes.

1492

Christopher Columbus lands in Hispañola, opening Americas up to European colonization. In 1521, Europeans take capital of the Aztecs, which becomes Mexico City. By 1533, Spanish defeat Inca Empire.

1527

Spanish priests begin to teach European sacred music to indigenous people. Sixteenth-century forms include sacred songs and dramas called *autos*.

1538

First African slaves arrive in Brazil. Slave trade continues until nineteenth century, bringing African influences to many regions, especially Caribbean and along Atlantic coasts of South America.

LATIN AMERICA

SETTING

On a humid evening in Salvador, a large city on the coast of Brazil, in a simple building that serves as a *terreiro* (meeting place) for members of the Candomblé religion, three drummers and an iron bell player create an intricate polyrhythmic accompaniment to a call-and-response song led by the *terreiro's Pai de Santo* (father of saint). The participants, mostly Afro-Brazilians from the poor neighborhood that surrounds the *terreiro*, are on their feet, moving to the hypnotic, energetic beat (Figure 15.1). Although the music resembles that of Brazil's famous **carnaval** percussion bands, this ritual is very serious, and the music is spiritually charged. The song is a call to Oxossi (one of the Candomblé deities of African origin), a plea to come down and speak to those assembled. Suddenly, a woman in the crowd stops her dance, adopts an entirely different stance and manner, and everyone knows that Oxossi has descended.

The woman is in a trance; that is, Oxossi has taken control of her body and, speaking quietly to the *Pai de Santo*, answers questions and responds

SOUNDS

CD 3:15

Ritmo, Nelsinho e Sua Orquestra

18TH C	19TH C	1816–1825	C. 1840–1920	▶▶▶
Touring theatrical groups perform popular songs and dances. Among those are Brazilian *lundus*, Mexican *sones*, and Andean *huaynos*.	Italian opera dominates theatrical music among *criollos* or European descendents, although Spanish *zarzuela* is also popular.	Most of Latin America gains independence from Spain and Portugal in aftermath of Napoleonic wars.	Nationalistic musicians compose salon piano pieces and other works using distinctive forms of folk songs and dances. This period is the height of popularity of European ballroom dances—polka (*polca*), waltz (*vals*), two-step (*paso doble*)—that become basis for many popular forms, including Mexican *conjunto*.	

© Stephanie Maze/CORBIS

FIGURE 15.1

An ensemble of three drummers plays a large repertory of polyrhythmic patterns to accompany rituals in the Candomblé religion.

to requests for earthly interventions. Immediately, the drummers change their cadence to a song welcoming the spirit. In the view of Candomblé devotees, spirits inhabit many planes of existence beyond our own, and music is one way to reach beyond the realm of ordinary experience. These spirits may be indigenous, African, or even Catholic saints—in some traditions St. Sebastian is associated with Oxossi.

About 5,000 miles to the northwest is the Mexican city of San Luis Potosí. Here sacred dances also honor the same St. Sebastian but with the very different sounds of the **huasteca**, an ensemble that features the sweet falsetto tones of a male singer accompanied by two guitars (in different sizes) and a lively violin. As penance for their sins, indigenous groups, perhaps inspired by medieval Spanish liturgical dances, may perform dances on the steps of the San Sebastián cathedral.

These two very different examples demonstrate not only the great diversity of Latin American music but also the rich artistic hybrids that result from **syncretism**—the fusion of cultures that takes place when different ethnic groups meet. Anthropologists believe that at such times, similarities between the cultures are reinforced, and their differences disappear or remain distinct. Thus, musical traditions that had some common ground with those of the European invaders were preserved, albeit in hybrid forms. This combining of traditions is evident in the conflation of Catholic saints with African deities; in the mixture of African, European, and indigenous musical instruments; and also the cultural attitudes that continue to drive artistic creativity in this huge region.

ELEMENTS OF TRADITIONAL LATIN AMERICAN MUSIC

Influences from European, African, and indigenous sources have shaped the characteristics of Latin American music. In areas where large-scale political structures existed at the time of the European invasion—principally the Aztec region of Central Mexico and the Inca empire in the Andes—indigenous culture and

▶ 1890s–1920s	1910s–1920s	1930s	1930s–1950s
Carnival festivals in Brazil begin dance competitions. Music of Brazilian *choros* folk bands eventually blends with African-influenced dances to create samba.	Argentinean *tango* becomes first Latin American dance to become widely popular in Europe and North America.	Adaptation of *mariachi* ensemble to suit urban needs, including addition of trumpets. In this form, the ensemble is popularized through films and recordings.	Height of Latin big band popularity; many Latin dances introduced to North America in commercialized forms.

religion were especially influential, despite European attempts at suppression. African influence was especially focused in the Caribbean and other coastal regions. European musical characteristics are associated with the elite urban dwellers, known as **criollos**, and the **mestizos**, Latin Americans of mixed race. These terms have also come to refer to the different strata of music in these cultures, from the art music and theater of the *criollos* to the hybrid *mestizo* forms. The following are some of the distinctive characteristics forged from this rich synthesis:

◆ **Use of harmony.** Folk and popular music throughout Latin America adopted European harmonic techniques and harmonic progressions, often heard in the guitar strumming.

◆ **Parallel thirds.** Singers and instrumentalists thicken textures by adding a parallel melody two scale steps away that creates a consonant succession of intervals called thirds.

◆ **Paired phrases.** Song texts are often written in paired lines, **coplas**, with pauses between lines. The first line of the pair ends with an unsettled feeling, which the second line resolves.

◆ **Distinctive dance rhythms.** Characteristic rhythms often derived from the *habañera* and *sesquialtera* largely define Latin American dances.

◆ **Rhythm guitar.** Vigorous harmonic strumming of the guitars, as well as percussion, emphasize dance rhythms.

LATIN AMERICAN DANCE RHYTHMS

Latin American cultures are justly famous for their many dance forms, although the folk versions of some of these forms are quite different from their ballroom or popular namesakes. Although most dances have strong national ties (the **samba** with Brazil, the **rumba** with Cuba, the **tango** with Argentina, and so on), some characteristics are common throughout Latin America (see Table 15.1).

In many cases, it is possible to trace the origins of a dance back to a European model. Specific Iberian traits still found in some dances include foot stomping, finger snapping, and dancers contributing to the sound of the music in general. The contradance, a popular European dance of the eighteenth century, became, under Afro-Cuban influence in the nineteenth century, the **habañera**, made famous in the French opera *Carmen* by Georges Bizet.

1960s–1980s

Sequences of military dictatorships in many Latin American countries, sometimes together with censors, parallel explosion of youth culture and popular music: *MPB* in Brazil, *nueva canción* in Chile and Argentina, *chicha* in Andean countries, and *salsa* in Puerto Rico and the United States.

| Table 15.1 | MAJOR DANCE FORMS OF LATIN AMERICA | |

Dance	Country of Origin	Description
Bambuco	Colombia	Moderate *sesquialtera* courtship dance associated with the highlands of Colombia
Bossa nova	Brazil	Relaxed modern samba influenced by cool jazz
Cueca	Chile	Fast *sesquialtera* couple dance
Cumbia	Colombia	African-influenced fast duple meter dance
Jarabe	Mexico	Moderate *sesquialtera* dance
Joropo	Venezuela	Fast *sesquialtera* couples dance
Malambo	Argentina	Fast *sesquialtera* competition dance of *gauchos* (cowboys)
Merengué	Dominican Republic	Fast African-influenced dance with a distinctive simple duple rhythm
Rumba	Cuba	Highly syncopated simple duple rural dance, later known in a ballroom version
Samba	Brazil	Simple duple syncopated dance now known in many rural, urban, and ballroom types
Tango	Argentina	Slow urban couple dance with pronounced downbeats

GRAPHIC 15.1

The basic *habañera* rhythm can be varied in many ways. Some of these syncopated variations correspond to rhythms characteristic of African music. Variation 1 is characteristic of many Latin American forms and is known as the *tresillo* rhythm in Cuba. Variation 2 is characteristic of the Dominican *merengué*.

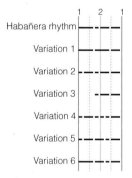

The core rhythmic motive of the *habañera* (see Graphic 15.1) became widely influential throughout Latin America and is still heard in this form in the Argentine tango, for example. Typically syncopated variations of this rhythm often correspond with rhythms of African origin, rhythms often found in such dances as the Cuban *danza*, the Brazilian *samba*, and the Dominican *merengué*. Other popular European dances, such as the waltz, the polka, the quadrille, and the two-step have also left important legacies, particularly in Mexico.

One of the most distinctive characteristics of many Latin American dances is the alternation between simple triple and compound duple meters—that is, between three groups of two and two groups of three. In some forms, the two meters may be played simultaneously, creating polyrhythm. This characteristic metrical type is called **sesquialtera** and is characteristic of the Colombian *bambuco*, the Cuban *cueca*, the Argentinean *gato* and *malambo*, and the Mexican *jarabe*.

Although the name and rhythm of the *sesquialtera* probably derives from Arabic influences in Spain, its place in many dances originates in African versions of the same polyrhythms. Many Latin American dances, including the Colombian *cumbia*, the Cuban rumba, and the Dominican *merengué,* clearly have their origins in or were influenced by African sources. The Brazilian samba derived from earlier Afro-Brazilian dances such as the *batuque* and the *lundu*.

In the 1930s and 1940s, films and recordings popularized Latin American dances in North America and elsewhere, and the big bands of the swing era refined the traditional rhythms to create ballroom forms often far different from their original models. Some of the forms often associated with jazz from the 1930s through the 1960s include the *mambo*, the *bossa nova*, the *conga*, and the *chachachá*.

HARMONY

One of the most distinctive influences of European music in Latin America is the use of harmony (see Chapter 14). Strumming chords has become a common technique in Latin American music and became the basis for guitar playing in much popular music in North America as well. Although strumming does not easily permit the polyphonic textures of the classical guitar tradition, it does allow the guitarist to create strong rhythmic emphasis through the patterns and loudness of the strums. In blues and rock music, this role is called rhythm guitar, but the technique originated in Spanish and Latin American folk and popular music.

Harmony has long been one of the central European elements in Latin American folk and popular music. Musicians even added harmony to monophonic indigenous melodies, provided the melodies used something close to a diatonic scale. Particular harmonic progressions characterize many popular dances and song forms as much as their rhythms or melodic characteristics. The use of harmony based on triads is also related to the characteristically Latin American practice of singing or playing in parallel thirds—that is, two simultaneous melodies that are the same but separated by the interval of two scale steps. Although probably related to folk practices from Europe, parallel thirds are also found in certain African regions.

LATIN AMERICAN MUSICAL INSTRUMENTS

Musicologists often categorize Latin American musical instruments through their origins—indigenous, African, or European—even though many of them represent hybrids or local variations of an existing model. Various types of vertical flutes, drums, and rattles are among the most widespread survivors of pre-Columbian (meaning, before Columbus) indigenous instruments. The simple bow was the only chordophone on the continent before the Europeans, and European string instruments have made a large impact. Instruments of the violin family are now common, sometimes in folk versions made with improvised materials. Jesuit missionaries originally introduced the harp, which then became widespread in a form that often includes a distinctively large resonator.

The European chordophone that has had the greatest influence, however, is the guitar, which exists in almost uncountable forms throughout the region—with two to twelve strings, from very large bass instruments to tiny treble ones, played with vigorous strumming or by plucking single notes. European wind instruments, including trumpets, clarinets, accordions, and saxophones, are very common, as are European-style bands and classical orchestras.

African instruments are widespread in areas associated with the slave trade, especially the Caribbean and eastern South America. These instruments include many types of drums and idiophones as well as the musical bow. Refined versions of these instruments are now standard additions to orchestras and dance bands—congas, bongos, claves, and timbales all come from Africa via Cuba—and the marimba is still played in its original form in Central America (Figure 15.2).

© Lindsay Hebberd/CORBIS

FIGURE 15.2

Although originally from Africa, the marimba has become the center of a distinctive tradition of southern Mexico and Central America. Often multiple players play on a single instrument. It may be either chromatic (twelve pitches per octave like a piano) or diatonic (white keys only), with or without tube resonators. The marimba also became associated with Latin dance bands and then North American jazz bands.

MUSIC IN MEXICO

FIGURE 15.3

Every year around December 12th in Mexico, special groups of musicians and dancers called *concheros* (after the armadillo shells used in their lutes) lead processions to honor the Virgin of Guadalupe. Aspects of the rituals, such as the costumes, are derived from pre-Columbian Aztec models.

At the time of the European invasion, the highlands of central Mexico were a part of the large and advanced Aztec empire. Many sources indicate that music was an integral part of the Aztec religious rituals. The Aztecs associated elaborate drumming patterns and perhaps flute melodies with particular rituals and days of the year, but the Europeans destroyed all traces of Aztec religion (and hence religious music) that they could find.

In a few short years, a cathedral was built, and missionaries began to teach music to the Aztecs. These priests were astonished at the musical aptitude of the Aztecs, who readily adopted Spanish church and folk music. By 1540, one of the indigenous people had already written a mass in the European style. Even so, many elements of pre-Columbian music presumably survive and color some qualities of modern Mexican music. Syncretism can be found in many folk religious practices, including processionals and folk religious dramas called **autos**, in which music still plays an important part (Figure 15.3).

THE *SON* AND OTHER *MESTIZO* FORMS

FIGURE 15.4

Although the *mariachi* ensemble has become a national symbol of Mexico, it was originally associated with the *rancheros* of the Jalisco region, and *mariachis* still wear traditional *ranchero* costumes.

The *mariachi* band has become the popular image of folk music in Mexico (Figure 15.4), but it is only one of a rich variety of distinct types of folk bands, each associated, like food and dress, with different regions within the country. Spanish writers noted this regionalization of Mexican *mestizo* music as early as the eighteenth century, especially through the form known as the **son**. Although the *son* has come to refer to a wide variety of different song and dance types, all usually use the *sesquialtera* (juxtaposition of simple triple and compound duple meters), strumming guitars, and a fast stamping couple dance known as the *zapateado*.

The song lyrics are typically in pairs of lines, known as **coplas**. Each line usually corresponds to a musical phrase of regular length, with a pause between each line during which time the instruments (or shouts from the musicians) fill in. The first of a pair of phrases often ends (cadence) in an unsettled harmony and melodic tone, and the second resolves both the harmony and the idea expressed in the text. Many Mexican *sones*, as well as other forms, such as the northern *conjunto*, therefore have a kind of gentle back-and-forth motion between phrases and a regularity of phrases and harmony set atop vigorous rhythms and lively tempos.

FOLK BANDS IN MEXICO

Although *conjunto* is a generic term for folk band in Mexico, the term has become mostly associated with popular bands of northern Mexico and the southwest United States. Other regions are known for their own types of bands, each with its own music, singing style, instrumentation, and traditional dress:

FIGURE 15.5

With its very large resonator, the **guitarrón** is the distinctive bass instrument of the *mariachi* ensemble and is much more suited to strolling bands than the large harps and double basses used in other types of bands. It is played by plucking with the fingers, not strumming.

◆ **Chilena.** This type originated in Acapulco on the Pacific coast of Mexico, supposedly from Chilean sailors during the nineteenth-century gold rush, and it does show the influence of the South American *cueca*. The group usually includes a guitar, another small guitar called a *requinto*, and sometimes wind instruments and a string bass.

◆ **Huapango.** From the rural regions around Mexico City in central Mexico, this ensemble includes a medium-sized guitar known as a **jarana** and a special large guitar, the **huapanguera**. However, its most distinctive instrument is the violin, which plays fast-running figures rather than the slow countermelodies of the *mariachi*.

◆ **Mariachi.** Although this form originated in the ranches around Guadalajara, by the mid-twentieth century, ensembles in their traditional *charro* costumes made their way to Mexico City street corners. Bands replaced the traditional harp with the more portable large bass guitar known as the **guitarrón** (Figure 15.5), and a pair of trumpets (more suitable for a noisy urban setting) replaced or supplemented the violins. In this form, the *mariachi* band and its repertory of *ranchera* songs became famous through film and recordings, so that today it is a fixture throughout Mexico and in the United States. Its songs are typically love ballads, often sung in parallel thirds echoed by the trumpets and violins during instrumental breaks.

◆ **Jarocho.** This band from the Veracruz region (Figure 15.6) is known for its fast lively dances and songs such as the famous *La Bamba*.

A PERFORMANCE OF A *SON JAROCHO*

The Mexican state of Veracruz stretches from tropical Gulf Coast beaches to fertile volcanic mountainsides. For many years, amateur musicians dressed in traditional white shirts and hats periodically gathered for large celebrations called *fandangos*, at the center of which was a raised wooden platform to amplify the **zapateados**—stamping, boot-tapping dances that would go on perhaps until dawn. The *fandango* today is more likely to be a festival of invited musical groups, and the musicians are more likely to be professionals who play at restaurants and weddings. Even so, the exciting, rustic spirit of the music and dances of the *fandango* remain a vital part of Veracruz culture.

© Studio Federico Patellani/CORBIS

FIGURE 15.6

A *jarocho* ensemble plays near the docks of Veracruz. The **arpa** (left) is a diatonic harp with a very large wooden resonator. This distinctive form of the harp is important throughout Latin America, especially in South American countries such as Paraguay, where it is the "national instrument." Sizes may vary from small versions that rest on the player's lap to very large harps carried by two people. It is often played in very rhythmic and even polyrhythmic plucking, and sometimes the resonator may be hit as well. Because these harps do not use the system of pedals for chromatic tuning that was added to the European concert harp, traditional harp music is limited to one diatonic key without retuning. The **jarana** (second from left) is a medium-sized strummed guitar. The **requinto** (second from right) is a very small guitar with four or five strings. It is played melodically in *sones jarocho*, although small guitars in other traditions may be strummed.

Although often overshadowed by the ever-popular *mariachi* style, the traditional music of the Veracruz *fandango* is the *son jarocho*. The core *jarocho* ensemble is made up of three instruments: the **jarana**, a five-course guitar slightly smaller than the Spanish guitar; the **requinto**, a small guitar; and the **arpa**, *a* diatonically tuned harp (Figure 15.6). Other instruments may be added, especially a guitar, but the ensemble usually lacks the characteristic trumpets of the *mariachi* and the violin of the *huasteca* ensemble of neighboring regions.

Although the *son jarocho* usually lacks percussion instruments, the rhythmic and percussive use of the instruments of the ensemble more than makes up for it. The *jarana* and guitar players create these rhythms by alternating patterns of up and down strums called **maniqueos** or **rasgueado**. *Rasgueado* also refers to one of the most distinctive of these strokes in which the fingers unfold over the strings as the wrist moves down, creating a long emphasized strum that can be heard in this excerpt just as the guitar and *jarana* enter (refer to Figure 14.16). This technique is also a characteristic of Spanish flamenco guitar and other styles in Latin America.

Like the more famous *jarocho* song *La Bamba, Siquisirí* (the name has no translation) is a traditional song, although the date of its origin is uncertain. Because of its greeting text, it is often the first song in a performance. However, only part of the text is fixed, and traditionally the lead singer improvises some of the lines. The lead singer is usually the guitarist or other instrumentalist, and the remaining instrumentalists form the chorus. The texts of *sones jarochos*, like many Latin American songs, are based on Spanish poetic forms called *coplas*, or lines in pairs. The text of *Siquisirí* is in the form of a *sextilla*, in which the verses have six lines, although lines may be repeated, as in this case.

CONJUNTO

European ballroom dances were very popular in nineteenth-century Latin America, and hundreds appeared in salon arrangements for piano, including waltzes, two-steps, and, most importantly in Mexico, the polka. Many of these dance forms became especially popular in this region among the working-class people in newly settled northern Mexico and Texas.

At the same time, the diatonic button accordion was introduced in the north and, along with the **bajo sexto** guitar (Figure 15.7), became the foundation for dance bands that became very popular on both sides of the border. Many of these forms were made into songs, such as the revolutionary period **canciones revolucionarias**. By the 1920s, these dance forms and songs had moved from the salon to the popular bands of the region, now known as **conjunto norteña**, or simply **conjunto**.

In the 1930s, with the arrival of commercial recording companies in the southwest United States, *conjunto* (Figure 15.8) became very popular within Mexican immigrant communities. The instrumentation was now more or less standardized as accordion, guitar, string bass, and singer. Of these instruments, the accordion is the most distinctive sound of the ensemble, and it became a leading melody instrument when modern keyed varieties replaced the old button types.

While sharing the same kinds of harmonic patterns and song types with other bands, such as the *mariachi*, this ensemble also introduced innovations

CD 3:14. *Siquisirí,* Los Pregoneros del Puerto (José Gutiérrez, Gonzalo Mata, Oliverio Lara, Valente Reyes).

0:00

Although performances of *Siquisirí* may vary among groups, it normally begins with a harp solo. The main harp melody consists of various arpeggios (sequential sounding of notes in a chord) outlining a harmonic progression that alternates between two basic chords. The notes are grouped at times into twos and other times into threes. This pervasive alternation and overlapping of two meters, known as *sesquialtera,* helps define the distinctively propulsive rhythm of many *son jarocho* songs and dances.

0:07

At this point, the other instruments enter—in this recording, the *requinto,* the *jarana,* and a six-course Spanish guitar. The players powerfully strum the *jarana* and guitar, alternating between the same two chords as in the introduction while emphasizing a *sesquialtera* rhythm. Meanwhile, the *requinto* and the right hand of the harpist play quick melodies, and the left hand of the harpist plays the bass line.

0:25

After the instrumental introduction, the lead singer begins the song with the *verso,* a fixed text that bids a good evening to the listeners (the text can be modified depending on the time of day and the audience).

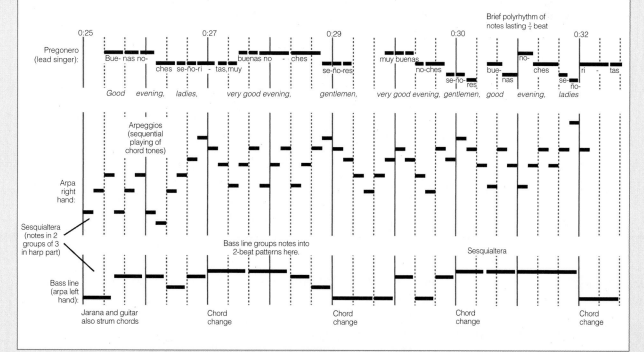

Especially helpful for the Listening Guide was Daniel Sheehy's *The Son Jarocho: History, Style, and Repertory of a Changing Mexican Musical Tradition.* PhD diss. UCLA, 1979.

CD 3:14. *Siquisirí,* Los Pregoneros del Puerto (José Gutiérrez, Gonzalo Mata, Oliverio Lara, Valente Reyes).[1] *(continued)*

0:32

The chorus (the rest of the instrumentalists) sings the remaining lines of the fixed *verso*:

A todas las florecitas	All the little flowers
de rostros cautivadores	With the captivating faces
van las trovas más bonitas	We dedicate this beautiful verse
de estos pobres cantadores.	From these poor singers.

0:39

In the next contrasting verse, called the *estribillo*, the lead singer improvises verses for the occasion, usually standard lines introducing himself and the band, expressing appreciation for being there, or perhaps humorous teasing of members of the audience. Again, the six-line form of the *sextilla* is broken up, this time by interpolated lines in which the chorus answers each line or two with stock responses.

(Chorus: *Ay! Que sí, que sí, que no*	Ay! And yes, and yes, and no)
Leader: *Que traigo un pulido deseo . . .*	I have a nice wish . . .
(Chorus: *Ay! Que sí, que sí, que no*	Ay! And yes, and yes, and no)
Leader: *de decirte la verdad . . .*	to tell you the truth . . .
(Chorus: *Ahora sí, mañana no*	Now yes, tomorrow no)
Leader: *porque cuando yo te veo . . .*	because when I see you . . .
(Chorus: *Con la grande sí, con la chica no*	With the big one, yes, with the girl, no)
Leader: *volteas la cara pa' atrás.*	you turn your head away.
¡Si lo haces porque soy feo	If you do it because I am ugly,
reclámale a mi mamá!	complain to my mother!

0:56

This instrumental break is derived from the introduction but now played by all the instruments. Throughout the *versos* and *estribillos*, the instruments continue their basic patterns, alternating between chords while emphasizing the *sesquialtera* rhythms.

1:20

The lead singer repeats the first two lines of the second *verso*, followed by the chorus singing last four lines.

[1]Translations by Daniel Sheehy.

1:33

The second *estribillo*. The following translation leaves out the responses from the chorus, which are the same as in the preceding translation:

Que ni la tan en su apogeo	Not the moon at its apogee
ni el sol tan capacitado	nor the sun is able
satisfacen los deseos	to fulfill one's desires . . .
como él que llega a Alvarado	like he who arrives in Alvarado,
y el arpa suena el trineo	and the harp sounds the high melody
del "Siquisirí" afamado.	of the famed "Siquisirí."

1:50

The instruments suddenly drop out except for the harp, which now plays a rhythmically intricate solo.

2:30

The harp continues, but now it is the *requinto* player's turn for a solo. Unlike many small guitars in Latin America, the *requinto* of the *jarocho* ensemble is nearly always a melodic and not a strummed instrument.

2:48

The rest of the band joins in as the *requinto* and harp interlock their *sesquialtera* melodies.

3:05

A final *estribillo* ends the piece.

Que no hay muchacha que sea fea	There is no girl who is ugly
cuando viste de jarocha	when she dresses like a *jarocha*
y más cuando zapatea	and more so when she dances the *zapateado*
con tu gracia de morocha	with your grace of a dark woman
la tarima se cimbrea	the dance platform sways
y ésta es mi tierra jarocha. ¡Ay, ay!	and this is my *jarocho* land. Ay ay!

Listening Exercise 14 | CD 3:14. *Siquisirí*

1. What is the texture at 0:25?
   a. heterophony
   b. homophony
   c. polyphony

2. What is the tessitura of the lead singer?
   a. low
   b. high
   c. varying over a wide range

3. From 1:43 to 1:54, how does the harp player's right hand divide the meter?
   a. into twos
   b. into threes
   c. irregularly

4. The final pitch the players sing (at 3:23) is
   a. pitch 1 of the scale (the tonic).
   b. pitch 2 of the scale.
   c. pitch 5 of the scale.

You can take this Listening Exercise online and receive feedback or e-mail answers to your instructor at the World Music Resource Center.

© Kit Kittle/CORBIS

FIGURE 15.7

The **bajo sexto** (left) is a bass guitar with six double courses tuned an octave lower than a traditional Spanish guitar.

© Bob Daemmrich/The Image Works

FIGURE 15.8

A *conjunto* festival in Austin, Texas, spotlighting the characteristic accordion.

such as electric instruments and influences from North American rock. Today, *conjunto* is one of the most popular types of Mexican music, not only in Mexico but especially in the southwest United States.

ART MUSIC IN MEXICO

Mexico has one of the richest legacies of art music from the colonial period in Latin America. Important cathedrals and music schools were established at Mexico City, Puebla, Morelia, and elsewhere. Secular theater developed in the eighteenth century with the production of Spanish **zarzuelas**, a type of operetta. As elsewhere in Latin America, native-born composers of the nineteenth century wrote mainly salon piano music. The importance of this music lay mostly in the growing interest in nationalism, under the influence of nationalistic trends in Europe. The first important nationalistic composer in Mexico was Manuel Ponce (1882–1948), who wrote piano suites and symphonic tone poems meant to evoke Mexican dances and folk tunes.

After the Mexican revolution, a revival of interest in indigenous culture influenced many artists, including the muralist school of Mexican painters, such as Diego Rivera and José Clemente Orozco. This so-called Aztec renaissance found its foremost musical expression in the compositions of Carlos Chávez (1899–1978). In his famous *Sinfonia India* [*Indian Symphony*], Chávez used indigenous (Indian) folk songs and percussion instruments to evoke his ancient Mexican heritage. Chávez was also instrumental in the support of the National Conservatory of Music in Mexico City and served as conductor of the *Orquesta Sinfónica de Mexico* for many years.

Silvestre Revueltas (1899–1940), a contemporary and friend of Chávez, also wrote pieces representing Mexico's pre-Columbian past, but he is best known for his brash and dynamic representations of contemporary *mariachis* and other folk groups. In some of these, he evokes the lively competitions of *mariachi* groups playing at the same time on the streets of Mexico City. These simultaneous sounds produce dissonant clashes, polyrhythms, and polytonalities (use of two or more keys at the same time).

MUSIC IN BRAZIL

Every year around February, the streets of Brazilian cities give way to an invasion of tourists, sidewalk food and beer stalls, seas of neighborhood dancers following trucks blasting out dance music like electric pied pipers, and the thunderous sounds of the most famous of Brazil's many musical traditions—the **carnaval**. In the days preceding Lenten abstinence, months of rehearsal come to a close for the **samba schools**, which parade through the streets, competing for the recognition of judges, street revelers, and millions who watch the spectacle on television. Each "school" consists of hundreds of elaborately costumed dancers on top of and beside lavish floats and a hundred or more percussionists who make up the **bateria**, or samba percussion band. Although the samba is most famous in this modern mass media form, its roots reach deep into the African and *mestizo* heritage of this country's vibrant musical heritage.

THE AFRO-BRAZILIAN HERITAGE

Brazil is the largest country in Latin America and the only one to have been colonized primarily by the Portuguese rather than the Spanish, although there is a large indigenous population, and African slaves were first brought there in 1538. On plantations sometimes far from the influence of the church authorities and the European *criollos* of the urban areas, many of these slaves retained African languages and cultural elements of African ethnic groups such as the Yoruba (from present-day Nigeria), Ewe (Ghana), and Fon (Benin). As is clear from the onomatopoeic name of one of their earliest characteristic dances, the **batuque**, the slaves also brought percussive ensembles, including drums, from Africa. As in West Africa, participants formed a circle, and pairs took turns dancing in the

FIGURE 15.9

Of the folk festivals of Brazil, the most widespread is the *Bumba meu boi*, which involves the magical resurrection of a bull who saves the life of a slave. Many different varieties of music accompany folk dramas such as this, depending on the region.

FIGURE 15.10

Three *berimbau* players (sitting against the back wall) accompany *capoiera*. Part dance, part game, and part martial art, *capoiera* may have arisen as a way to train fighters for the resistance to slavery. The *berimbau* is derived from the musical bow of Africa (refer to Figure 6.6 in Chapter 6).

middle, often including the touching of navels, a practice (which scandalized church authorities) known as *semba*, probably the origin of the word "*samba*."

Missionaries brought to these plantations the Iberian traditions of religious processions, dances, and didactic religious dramas. African people also appropriated these forms, sometimes to represent veiled satires of their masters or express an African identity (Figure 15.9). Like samba processions, these dramas are communal and to an extent participatory. The music may therefore involve many different types of instruments, although drums are usually prominent.

Another symbol of resistance to slavery is a **capoiera**, a stylized martial art dance. The musical instrument most associated with *capoiera* is the **berimbau**, a musical bow tapped with a stick and equipped with a half-gourd resonator placed against the chest (Figure 15.10). The player can effect slight changes in pitch by varying the tension or by holding a coin as a bridge against the string, but the *berimbau* is mainly a rhythmic instrument, not a melodic or harmonic one. A tall drum called an **atabaque**, along with a tambourine and **agogô** (double iron bell) may also join in the accompaniment. *Capoiera* remains very popular today not only in Brazil but also in *capoiera* clubs in the United States, Europe, and elsewhere.

After the emancipation of the slaves in 1888, many African-Americans emigrated to urban areas, especially those on the northern and eastern coasts, such as in the state of Bahia. In addition to bringing their music and instruments, they also brought their spiritual practices, which became distinct religions such as Candomblé and Umbanda. Music in these religions plays the crucial role of calling and welcoming various deities who take over the bodies of participants. Typically, an *agogô* and a set of three conical or barrel-shaped drums called, from smallest to largest, **le**, **rumpi**, and **rum**, accompany a complex repertory of songs, each unique to a particular spirit, with intense polyrhythms clearly related to the African and *batuque* precursors of the style (Figure 15.11).

THE SAMBA

Of the several popular Afro-Brazilian dances such as the *batuque*, the **lundu** was the one that filtered into urban salons as early as the eighteenth century. Still, the division between the music of the urban elite and the poor slum dwellers

© Ricardo Azoury/CORBIS

FIGURE 15.11

The *rum*, or largest drum of the *atabaques* ensemble, accompanies folk dances and religious rituals, such as this ceremony of the Umbanda religion.

© Genevieve Naylor/CORBIS

FIGURE 15.12

The ***repenique*** (left) is a medium-sized deep cylindrical drum. The virtuoso leader of the samba band plays this drum with one stick and one free hand, producing a variety of tones. The ***cuíca*** (middle) is a friction drum—a small stick is attached to the inside of a drum head, and the player rubs his fingers down the stick. The stick's vibration is resonated by the drum head, producing a quick, sliding tone. A skilled player can make this instrument sound like human speech or laughter. The ***caixa*** (right) is a cylindrical drum with snares—small wires that rattle against the head. Although there are different sizes, *caixas* are usually shallower than the *repenique* and have a less-defined pitch. Although these drums are commercially produced today, with modern tuning screws, plastic drum heads, and metal bodies, homemade versions are also common in villages.

remained strong. The hillside slums, or *favelas*, were known for their bands of street musicians, called ***choros***, who played versions of popular dances like the *lundu*, the polka, or the ***maxixe***, a highly syncopated Brazilian dance from the early twentieth century. Such dances probably all fed into the vibrant parades that began accompanying pre-Lenten *carnaval* in Rio de Janeiro around the turn of the twentieth century and became the famous samba (Figure 15.12).

By the 1920s and 1930s, neighborhood samba groups first formalized themselves as "schools" that local governments recognized, organized into competitions, and even used for political purposes. The samba became internationally famous, largely through the recordings and film performances of singer Carmen Miranda. The samba of professional big bands, often accompanying songs known as *samba canção*, produced a more relaxed and refined version of the dance. Today, both forms of the samba coexist: smooth samba songs dominated by guitars and percussive samba bands made famous by their use in *carnaval* festivities. The latter type is sometimes known as ***batucada***.

Although the *batucada* bands of today's *carnaval* are professionally produced and highly rehearsed, they are still largely made up of amateur percussionists ensembles from working-class neighborhoods. Since the end of the military dictatorship in 1985, parades have even included themes of social protest. In the 1970s and 1980s, musical clubs known as ***blocos afro*** championed a reintroduction of self-consciously African elements into their bands as a way to reestablish African traditions and an ethnic identity (Figure 15.13). Apart from the *carnaval*, the rhythms of the samba continue to form a dominant influence throughout Brazilian popular music.

© Jeremy Horner/CORBIS

FIGURE 15.13

Blocos afro, such as this group from Bahia, are community percussion groups that have developed music inspired by African roots.

A PERFORMANCE OF A SAMBA *BATUCADA*

In February in Rio de Janeiro, the *cariocas* (local inhabitants) greet each other with a warm "*Bom carnaval!*" The famous festival is here, and the narrow streets of Rio's neighborhoods are filled at night with a colorful chaos of lights, food stalls, and the sounds of samba. Nearly every neighborhood has its own *bloco*, or samba club, whose working class members often rehearse well into the early morning hours on these humid summer nights. They are not to be confused with the samba "schools"—the twenty or so organizations of several thousand percussionists, dancers, and others whose parade of elaborate floats and costumes into the giant Sambadrome coliseum is the climax of Rio's *carnaval*.

The *blocos* instead play for neighborhood street parties filled with irreverent costumes and dances of joyous abandonment. Although a decorated truck with amplified singers and guitarists may lead the *bloco*, no one doubts that the spirit of the samba lies with the *bateria*, the very large group of percussionists whose densely layered polyrhythms are at once clearly African in origin and yet unmistakably Brazilian. The *bateria* of a samba school may have well over a hundred players, who have been practicing late at night for months prior to the final competition. *Blocos* are generally more informal and stylistically diverse, sometimes experimenting with elements of rock and hip-hop, but always over the core samba rhythm of the *bateria*. The following recording, although made in a studio, demonstrates the role of some of the most prominent *bateria* instruments.

CD 3:15. *Ritmo,* Nelsinho e Sua Orquestra.

This performance consists of variations of polyrhythmic ostinatos, periodically interrupted for instrumental solos. The graphic below shows two examples of how each instrument may vary its ostinato pattern.

`0:00`

Listen at first for the two *surdo* bass drums. They alternate, with the higher pitch or *primeira* ("first") drum on beats one and three and the lower pitched or *marcação* ("marker") drum on beats two and four of a four beat cycle, although they may fill in variations between those beats. The *bateria* is normally led by the smaller *repenique* drum.

Photo Credit: Courtesy of Luen Instruments

`0:10`

The band stops for a solo from the *pandeiro*, a frame drum with small cymbals (also known as a tambourine). The player is able to create a wide variety of tones by hitting the drum head and cymbals in different places with fingers. This typical samba rhythm emphasizes a grouping of 4 + 4 + 3 + 3 + 2 (see graphic). This recording pans the *pandeiro* from left to right to simulate the dynamic movement of the samba parade.

Photo Credit: Courtesy of Luen Instruments

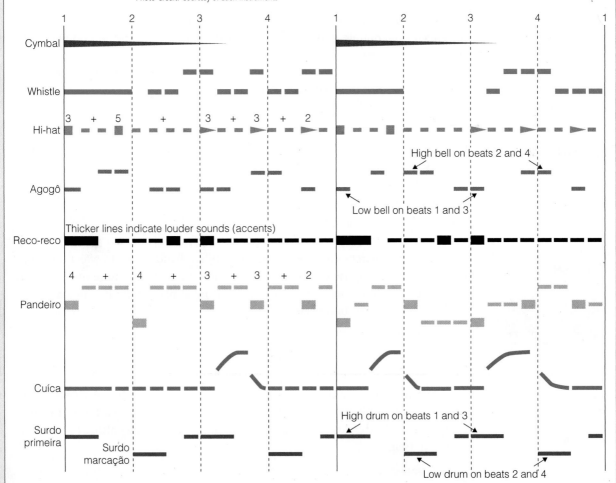

0:18	With a deep hit from the *surdo marcação*, the rest of the *bateria* enters again. Try to hear the *pandeiro* in the texture.
0:31 	The next solo is for a hi-hat cymbal and finger cymbals (the high bell-like tone). Although the hi-hat is not a traditional samba instrument, it plays a samba rhythm similar to that of the *pandeiro*: 3 + 5 + 3 + 3 + 2. *Photo Credit:* iStockphoto
0:54	The next solo is for the *reco-reco*, a scraper today made of metal springs stretched above a hand-held metal resonator. The first rhythm of its solo is 3 + 3 + 3 + 2 + 2 + 3, but it more typically plays 6 + 2 + 6 + 2 or 4 + 4 + 4 + 4. *Photo Credit:* Courtesy of Luen Instruments
1:16	The next solo features the *agogô,* two metal bells joined by a flexible U-shaped bar, descended from double iron bells of West Africa (refer to the *gankogui* on page 56). The player can squeeze the bells together to dampen them. The *agogô* plays highly syncopated variations of an alternation between the low bell (on beats one and three) and high bell (on beats two and four). *Photo Credit:* Courtesy of Luen Instruments
1:42	The next somewhat longer break features the *cuíca* friction drum, which can make a variety of sliding pitches. Try to listen to its rhythms in the section following the break. Although there are many variations, a high note usually comes just after the first and third beats of the cycle. *Photo Credit:* Courtesy of Luen Instruments
2:32 	The next player marches with a cymbal in each hand and is able to effect different rhythms by bringing the cymbals together firmly to damp the tone or by letting them ring. During the ostinato sections, the cymbal player simply articulates the first beat of every four-beat cycle. *Photo Credit:* iStockphoto
2:59 	Another familiar samba instrument is a whistle of the type used in sports or by police. It is often blown by the *repenique* player as a way to signal the rest of the *bateria* in the noisy chaos of a parade. However, the whistle may also, as here, play a rhythm itself. *Photo Credit:* iStockphoto

Hear and see the instruments of *Ritmo* in your downloadable **ACTIVE LISTENING TOOLS,**
available at the World Music Resource Center.

MPB—MÚSICA POPULAR BRASILEIRA

In 1959, Antônio Carlos Jobim and João Gilberto produced an album called *Chega de Saudade*, which referred to a new sound, called *"bossa nova"* in the liner notes, meaning "new skill or knack." Unlike the commercial big-band sambas, these intimate songs featured sophisticated harmonies and rhythms and emphasized the poetry of the lyrics. In place of the large percussion section of samba jazz was a smooth and refined rhythm driven by intricate syncopations on a single guitar, called *violão gago* ("stammering guitar").

Although the *bossa nova* also became a familiar ballroom dance, its original form was very influential for the next generation of Brazilian popular songwriters, whose music became known in general as **música popular brasileira** or **MPB**. The composers Caetano Veloso and Gilberto Gil brought electric instruments and rock influence into the mix, and others, such as Milton Nascimento and Jorge Ben, introduced African elements. After the 1964 military coup, their cheerful sounds, irresistible rhythms, and oblique lyrics often masked dark social and political protests. In response, the government censored many songs, imprisoned some songwriters, and forced others into exile.

Still, MPB remained widely popular through the end of the military dictatorship in 1985. As newer composers introduce further innovations, the echo of the samba rhythm usually remains, as does the often poignant juxtaposition of samba's festivity and optimism with references to continuing social problems.

ART MUSIC IN BRAZIL

As in most of Latin America, professional music directors at the large Catholic cathedrals wrote the first art music in Brazil. By the middle of the nineteenth century, the theater replaced the church as the primary patron of art music. Pianos became popular instruments in the salons of the urban *criollo* class, and a vibrant music publishing industry followed. Some professional pianist-composers began to arrange traditional genres such as the **modhina**, whose smooth lyricism can still be heard in Brazilian melody.

The most famous of Brazil's composers to explore this cultural heritage was Heitor Villa-Lobos (1887–1959). Although he was the son of amateur classical musicians and learned cello and clarinet at an early age, he was just as at home with the folk and popular musicians of his day. At eighteen, instead of studying European classical music at the conservatory in Rio de Janeiro, he traveled around Brazil, collecting folk songs and performing as an itinerant musician.

His largely intuitive style is full of life and energy, but he was aware of the contemporary modernist movement in the arts in Europe. His dissonant, "primitivist" adaptations of folk and popular styles made him a controversial figure when he went to Paris in the 1920s. Upon his return, he became a pedagogue, lobbying the Brazilian government for reforms and funding of music education throughout the country.

Villa-Lobos's two most famous series of pieces are his sixteen *Choros* and his nine *Bachianas Brasilieras*. As suggested by the title, the *Choros* are an homage to the vitality of the roving popular street bands that Villa-Lobos participated in as a young man. The *Bachianas Brasilieras* are a seemingly unlikely marriage of the unity and classicism of the works of the great eighteenth-century composer Johann Sebastian Bach and the vibrancy of the folk and popular music of Brazil. The *Bachianas Brasilieras* include movements evocative of *modhinas*, *choros*, and Brazilian dances but often using eighteenth-century European forms.

MUSIC IN ANDEAN COUNTRIES

FIGURE 15.14

Aymara people from Bolivia play *sikus* and *bombo* drums at a festival in Puno, Peru. *Siku* bands like this one create melodies through alternation playing.

Every February, the impressive sounds of bands of fifty or more pan-pipe (*siku*) players echo down the streets of the Peruvian city of Puno on the shores of Lake Titicaca, as they, together with dance troupes and pilgrims, celebrate the festival of the *Virgen de la Candelaria*. Although ostensibly a feast of the Roman Catholic Christian church, this lively celebration has elements that reach far back into the pre-Columbian past of this Andean region. Early European writers noted monthly festivals tied to agricultural cycles among the Incas, and although Christian feast days absorbed these events, villages and cities throughout the Andes still host thousands of syncretic festivals every year.

The Aymara-speaking people of this region associate Mary, the mother of Jesus, with Pachamama, the Incan earth goddess whose benevolence allows crops to grow in the cold, dry air at this great altitude (some 3,800 meters or 12,500 feet). While priests celebrate mass in the churches and cathedrals, in other parts of the city, celebrants make offerings of wine and seeds wrapped in coca leaves, accompanied by special ritual melodies, to ensure a bountiful harvest from Pachamama/the Virgin for the coming year. Other festivals and musical instruments are associated with Pachatata, the father god of the mountains.

The performances of the *siku* (panpipes) bands also represent a male/female duality (Figure 15.14). Because the technique of blowing puffs of air over the tops of the tubes of panpipes makes smooth or fast melodies difficult, *siku* bands create melodies through alternation playing. By splitting up the notes between two groups of players (the "male" and "female," although they are usually all men), the players can also avoid getting dizzy constantly blowing over the pipes in the thin mountain air. Large *siku* bands in this area have several different sizes of *sikus*, playing in parallel octaves or other intervals (Figure 15.15). The choreography these bands accompany (little of this music exists without dance) represents this dualism through couple dances or dances of parallel lines. Wild improvising dancers dressed as devils or wild men likewise contrast with the holy rituals going on inside the churches.

Aside from the people who speak Aymara around Lake Titicaca, most of the indigenous people of the Andes mountains ranging from Ecuador to Chile speak Quechua, the modern version of the language of the Incas. Even so, and despite many similarities, their music is highly regionalized. Some villages emphasize the music of the **kena** notch flute and **bomba** drum (Figure 15.16), whereas in others, Spanish instruments such as the harp and violin

Courtesy Danlee Mitchell

FIGURE 15.15

Panpipes, known as *siku* (Aymara language), *antara* (Quechua), or *zampoña* (Spanish), are common throughout the Andes and high Amazon regions. They consist of stopped narrow tubes of bamboo of varying lengths tied together in one or two rows. The player directs an air stream over the edge of these stopped pipes the way one plays a soda bottle. *Siku* come in many different sizes, from tiny soprano versions to very large bass ones such as this. Players often create melodies through alternation playing, although in some regions, bands of *siku* play together in parallel intervals.

(2) Courtesy of Carlos Quinche

FIGURE 15.16

An Andean musician plays the **kena** (notch flute) on the left and the **bombo** (bass drum) on the right. This musical tradition goes back to the European Middle Ages.

Charango player courtesy of Danlee Mitchell; *Charango* back courtesy of Gilbert Blount

FIGURE 15.17

The **charango** (shown here in performance and displaying the back shell) is a small guitar-like lute with five double courses of nylon or metal. Traditionally, the resonator is made from an armadillo shell. Today, the endangered armadillo is protected in many regions, so that *charangos* are often made from wood. It may be strummed or played melodically.

predominate. The **charango** (Figure 15.17) is a small guitar popular in many regions.

The most popular dance form throughout the Andes is the **huayno**, a lively duple meter dance with a characteristic long-short-short rhythm, often played on a *bomba* (Figure 15.14). Above this constant foundation is a highly syncopated, often lilting melody. Traditionally, couples with scarves dance the *huayno*, sometimes with *zapateado* (foot stamping), especially during the fast final section, known as the *fuga* (meaning escape or running).

Until the mid-twentieth century, the music of the Andean countries was largely segregated like the people, isolating the indigenous peoples of the mountains and their culture from the urban *criollos* of the coastal regions who cultivated music and instruments more directly related to European models. Following liberalizing reforms and economic changes that brought many mountain dwellers to the cities, new musical styles were forged, and the music of the *campesinos* (mountain peasants) became the basis for a pan-Andean popular music sound.

Because of the ethnic mixtures they represented, these forms were known as *mestizo* music. *Mestizo* bands combined *charangos* and guitars, harps and mandolins, *sikus* and synthesizers, and added harmonies to Andean melodies. One of the most popular of these hybrid sounds is ***chicha***, a style combining the Colombian *cumbia*, Cuban percussion, and North American rock with the local *huayno*. The styles developed by descendents of African slaves in some coastal areas represent yet another distinctive hybrid, an important element of which is the percussiveness of the ***cajón***, an open wooden box that a drummer sits on and plays with his or her hands.

This dense swirl of cultural influences—indigenous, European, and African—coalesces into unique expressions in different regions and villages, often each with its own type of ensemble. Even with European harmonies and instruments, the echoes of the area's ancient past resonate within the music of the festivals and street corners, here as elsewhere among the rich traditions of Latin America.

R E F E R E N C E S

DISCOGRAPHY

MUSIC OF MEXICO

Chávez, Carlos. *The Complete Symphonies*. Eduardo Mata cond. London Symphony Orchestra. Englewood Cliffs, NJ: Vox Box CDX5061, 1992.

Gutiérrez, José, Felipe Ochoa, and Marcos Ochoa. *La Bamba: Sones Jarochos from Veracruz*. Washington DC: Smithsonian-Folkways SF 40505, 2003.

Pregoneros del Puerto, Los. *Music of Veracruz*. Cambridge, MA: Rounder Records 5048, 1990.

Revueltas, Silvestre. *Hommage à Silvestre Revueltas*. Fernando Lozano cond. Orchestre Philharmonique. Paris: Forlane UCD 16614, 1990.

Various artists. *Anthology of Mexican Sones*, 3 vol. Mexico: Corason CO-101-103, 1993.

Various artists. *Conjunto! Texas-Mexican Border Music*, 6 vol. Cambridge, MA: Rounder Records 6034, 1988–94.

MUSIC OF BRAZIL

Various artists. *Beleza Tropical: Brazil Classics 1*. Fly/Sire Records 25805-1, 1989.

Various artists. *Bresil: Les Eaux d'Oxalá — Candomblé*. Paris: Buda Records 92576-2, n.d.

Various artists. *Brazil Roots Samba*. Cambridge, MA: Rounder Records RDR-5045, 1989.

Villa-Lobos, Heitor. *Bachianas Brasilieras No. 5-2-1, etc.* Lazare Gozman cond. Leningrad Chamber Orchestra. Paris: Le Chant du Monde/Melodia 278 644, 1978.

Inti-Illimani. *Andadas*. Danbury, CT: Green Linnet Records GLCD 4009, 1993.

Various artists. *Mountain Music of Peru*, 2 vol. Washington DC: Smithsonian-Folkways
   SF 40020/40406, 1994.

**MUSIC OF
THE ANDES**

Various artists. *Caribbean Island Music*. New York: Elektra/Nonesuch 9 72047-2,
   1972/1998.

Various artists. *Cuba: Afroamérica. Afro-Cuban Songs and Rhythms*. Geneva: AIMP LIII/
   VDE 959, 1997.

**OTHER LATIN
AMERICAN MUSIC**

 BOOK COMPANION WEBSITE

You will find flashcards, a glossary, and tutorial quizzes, as well as other materials that
will help you succeed in this course, at the *Music of the Peoples of the World, 2nd Edition,*
Companion Website at www.cengage.com/music/alves/world2e.

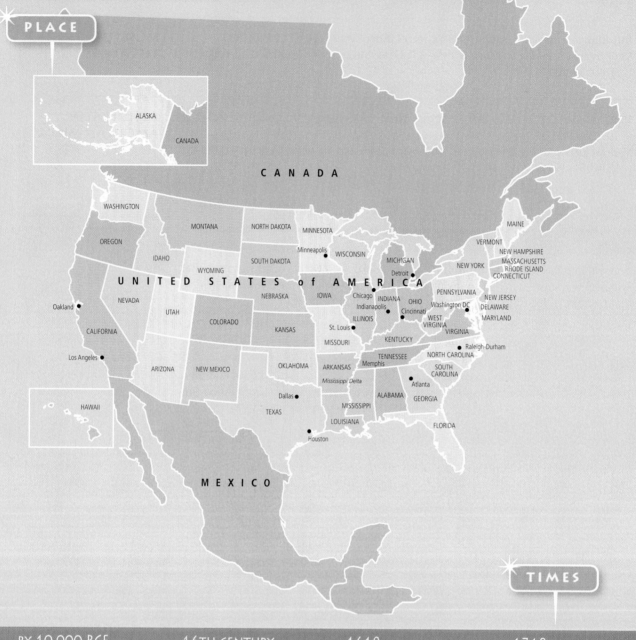

PLACE

ALASKA

CANADA

CANADA

WASHINGTON

MONTANA

NORTH DAKOTA

MINNESOTA

MAINE

OREGON

IDAHO

SOUTH DAKOTA

WYOMING

Minneapolis

WISCONSIN

MICHIGAN

VERMONT

NEW HAMPSHIRE
MASSACHUSETTS
RHODE ISLAND
CONNECTICUT

NEW YORK

Detroit

U N I T E D   S T A T E S   of   A M E R I C A

NEVADA

UTAH

NEBRASKA

IOWA

Chicago

INDIANA

OHIO

PENNSYLVANIA

NEW JERSEY
DELAWARE

Oakland

COLORADO

KANSAS

Indianapolis

ILLINOIS

Cincinnati

Washington DC

WEST
VIRGINIA

MARYLAND

CALIFORNIA

St. Louis

MISSOURI

KENTUCKY

VIRGINIA

Los Angeles

ARIZONA

NEW MEXICO

OKLAHOMA

ARKANSAS

Memphis

TENNESSEE

NORTH CAROLINA

Raleigh-Durham

SOUTH
CAROLINA

HAWAII

Mississippi Delta

Dallas

TEXAS

MISSISSIPPI

ALABAMA

Atlanta

GEORGIA

LOUISIANA

FLORIDA

Houston

M E X I C O

TIMES

BY 10,000 BCE	16TH CENTURY	1619	1718
Human beings first migrate from Asia to Americas, forming indigenous culture groups now referred to as First Nations Peoples, Native Americans, or American Indians.	Explorers from France, Netherlands, Spain, and England claim North American territories. By eighteenth century, introduced disease and warfare decimate population of indigenous peoples and cause huge internal migrations.	The first African slaves brought to North America arrive in Virginia. By the time the slave trade to North America ends in 1808, about 10 million Africans have been transported.	French establish New Orleans, and French cultural influence remains strong in the region.

NORTH AMERICA

SETTING

On a warm and humid morning in a small town in eastern Georgia, a sign is stretched across trees in front of a small wooden church reading "Sacred Harp Singing." Before long, cars begin to arrive with men and women, sometimes children, carrying covered dishes of food and a copy of *The Sacred Harp*, a songbook that uses a peculiar form of musical notation known as "shape note." By 10:00 A.M., the benches in the church have been rearranged so that all the rows face inward, forming a square. This is not music for an audience nor for a worship service. Occasionally, someone will come to find a seat just to listen, but everyone else, young and old, novice or expert, experiences this music as a participant.

After placing their dishes of food on a series of long tables to the side, the men and women take their places. Each side of the square consists of rows of singers of a particular vocal range: high women (treble), low women (alto), high men (tenor or lead), and low men (bass). Unlike conventional choirs in European and American churches, schools, and classical concerts—which would feature a single specialist conductor who

SOUNDS

CD 3:16

"Weeping Mary," The Southern Traditional Singers led by Hugh McGraw

1775–1781	1826–1864	c. 1830–1910	1861–1865	▶▶▶
The United States establishes independence from England after a revolutionary war.	Lifetime of Stephen Foster. His popular songs in a folk-like style become widely successful when sold as printed sheet music, helping establish the industry of commercial popular music.	Stage performances known as minstrel shows, in which performers portray African Americans, often in degrading ways, tour the United States. These shows help make elements of African-American music and dance popular among white audiences; cultural influences of minstrelsy extend well into the 1950s.	U.S. Civil War ends slavery.	

Courtesy of Paul Figura

FIGURE 16.1

Shape note singings are still a popular activity in many regions of the United States.

teaches, rehearses, and leads performances—**shape note singings** such as this have a conductor whose only job is to stand in the middle of the square and beat time (Figure 16.1). The post of the shape note singing conductor is a rotating one, at which nearly everyone will have a turn before the day is over, in a musical equivalent of town hall democracy.

After the greetings of friends and good-natured chatter dies down, the first leader steps up and calls out the number of a particular tune in the songbook. Next, one of the participants, selected by committee, sings out a pitch (which does not necessarily match the one notated in the book) to serve as the reference tonic for the singers. While holding the songbook in his left hand, the leader raises his right and signals a great torrent of sound.

Shape note historian Buell Cobb wrote about the experience: "Settling back to the severity of their wooden benches, [the singers] whip their voices up to a volume that billows and almost deafens, ringing off the dusty pine walls. Foot-stamping is impulsive and irresistible, and the arms of the singers swing up and down, keeping rigorous hold on the rhythm."[1] The singers sing everything at top volume, creating a sound as raw and direct as the spiritual feelings they express. They make no pretensions to the purity of classical choirs. As Cobb put it, this is not the music of angels but of proud people of this earth.

European ancestors of these singers immigrated to North America for a variety of reasons: to escape religious persecution, to seek their fortunes, to find a new beginning outside the restrictive social opportunities they left behind. In doing so, they abandoned not only social restrictions but also cultural institutions built up over centuries. Large orchestras, opera companies, music education traditions, and other art music institutions were slow to develop in the United States and Canada, and professional artists were unlikely to be among the early immigrants.

---

[1] Buell E. Cobb Jr. *The Sacred Harp: A Tradition and Its Music* (Athens: University of Georgia Press, 1978): 2.

▶ **c. 1880–1930**

Heyday of "Tin Pan Alley," area in New York City known for its commercial music publishers. Their competition helps establish a distinctive sound for American popular songs that would find its way into musicals and recordings.

c. 1895–1920

Ragtime music becomes popular through performances and publications.

c. 1900

Presumed beginnings of jazz and blues as distinct genres.

c. 1904

The distinctively American musical—popular theater with spoken word and popular songs—is established in New York.

This new continent was in some ways a blank slate for these immigrants, who had the opportunity to develop entirely new styles and genres unburdened by the weight of hoary traditions. At first, these new sounds developed as folk music and popular music that frequently drew upon the rich influences brought by African Americans, although North American art music also reflected this high value put on freedom and innovation.

Of course the Europeans and Africans did not encounter a completely free and open land—indigenous people had already lived in North America for many thousands of years, developing their own cultural traditions and music. However, the music of the indigenous Americans did not have the same influence on European Americans as did that of the African Americans.

Unlike African slaves, who lived in constant contact with Europeans, indigenous Americans usually lived in areas well separated from European American communities. Although Africans and Europeans shared many fundamental musical instrument types and song structures that made an exchange of musical influences relatively easy, indigenous music for the most part had only drums and idiophones accompanying songs that made little sense outside their contexts in the lives of indigenous Americans. For these reasons and others, traditional indigenous American music has remained apart from the best-known alloys of American traditions forged from European and African influences.

In addition to indigenous Americans and African Americans, the United States and Canada have felt the musical influence of immigrants from nearly every corner of the planet. Especially prominent were successive waves of immigration from Ireland, of Jewish people, from Italy, and from Eastern Europe. The French settled many regions, including Louisiana and Quebec. In some regions, immigrants from Scandinavia, Germany, or Russia predominated. The importation of laborers from China brought the first major immigration from East Asia in the nineteenth century, and others followed from Japan, Southeast Asia, and elsewhere, chiefly to the west coast of the continent.

In the face of such diversity, this chapter focuses primarily on the folk music of Anglo-Americans (here meaning immigrants from Britain and Ireland and their descendants) and African Americans, and the ways in which they have created the foundation for the popular styles of country, jazz, and blues.

1917–1920	1930s	c. 1945	1950s	▶▶▶
First recordings of jazz and blues make the styles famous worldwide.	Big band and swing jazz become popular. Country genres such as western swing and cowboy vocal groups are also widespread.	A new and sophisticated small-ensemble jazz, known as bebop, is established. String band country music known as bluegrass also develops.	White performers adopt the largely African-American genre of rhythm and blues, and the distinctive instruments of electric guitar, bass guitar, and drum set, to create rock and roll. Rock and roll, or rock, goes on to great commercial success within many subgenres.	

Indigenous American music will be considered separately. We will not have the space to devote to art music of the region.

ELEMENTS OF EUROPEAN AND AFRICAN MUSICAL TRADITIONS IN NORTH AMERICA

Although the most identifiable characteristics of European-American music—the use of harmony, notation, diatonic modes, a twelve-tone tuning system, and so on—are the same as in Europe, influences from Africa and elsewhere as well as native developments have created distinctive elements in the music of North America. We will discuss some specific qualities that distinguish the many different North American genres from styles in Europe and elsewhere. Nevertheless, here are some distinctively North American characteristics found in many types of music:

- ◆ **Rhythmic vitality.** The famous American composer Aaron Copland wrote, "[T]here seems to me no doubt that if we are to lay claim to thinking inventively in the music of the Americas our principal stake must be a rhythmic one."[2] This characteristic is most clear in the wide use of syncopation not only in clearly African-American genres but also in many folk and popular styles.

- ◆ **"Blue" notes.** These pitch inflections, often microtonal (smaller than a semitone), are also of African origin and have influenced many genres, from blues to jazz, country, and rock and roll.

- ◆ **Alternating improvisations in ensemble music.** This characteristic may ultimately derive from African responsorial forms, and, although it is most identifiable in jazz, it is also common in genres such as rhythm and blues, bluegrass, and rock and roll.

[2]Aaron Copland, *Music and Imagination* (Cambridge MA: Harvard University Press, 1952): 83.

▶ 1960s	1970s	1980s	1990s-PRESENT
The Folk Music Revival, paralleling the American civil rights movement, introduces new generations to traditional American music and influences popular music and culture. Rock music introduces many innovations and becomes associated with youth culture not only in North America but also around the world.	Diversification of popular music scene to include hard rock, progressive rock, and funk, followed by hip-hop, rap, and disco.	The new technologies of digital recording, MIDI, and the personal computer revolutionize music production, which now often includes sampling, drum machines, digital synthesizers, and loop-based computer music editors. These tools are especially influential in electronic dance music, or electronica, which, like most popular music now, is no longer an exclusively North American style.	The Internet allows free exchange of music throughout the world and its appropriation in computer mixes and "mash-ups." The availability of international influences leads to new hybrids sometimes called "worldbeat" or "global pop."

EARLY EUROPEAN AMERICAN MUSIC

In 1770, William Billings, perhaps the first white composer in what became the United States, wrote his own musical declaration of independence: "Nature is the best dictator, for not all the hard, dry, studied rules that ever was prescribed, will not enable any person to form an air. . . . For my own part, . . . I don't think myself confined to any rules of composition, laid down by any that went before me." The touch of cantankerous pride in his proclamation of disregard for tradition was early evidence of what was to become a theme in music of nonindigenous North Americans—a sense of freedom from the expectations of tradition and a willingness to experiment.

Early European immigrants to North America tended to be members of persecuted religious sects, farmers, merchants (Billings himself was a tanner by trade), and anyone searching for a new beginning. They brought with them their ballads and other folk songs, religious songs, and folk dances, but they did not bring the large arts institutions, music schools, and patronage systems that supported art music in Europe. Until then, professional musicians were in short supply, so churches depended on congregational monophonic singing of psalms. The first book printed in British North America was the *Bay Psalm Book* in 1640, whose strict translations showed the immigrants' lack of concern with poetic elegance or refined musical meters.

Congregations often sang these psalms through a process called **lining out**, in which the minister would sing a line that was then repeated by the congregation, who might not otherwise be able to read either the music or the words. Some conservative churches, which might not even allow instrumental accompaniment, retained the practice of lining out well into the twentieth century, creating a slow, nearly nonpulsatile and hypnotic heterophony that influenced later country singers.

Men like Billings found this state of affairs deplorable and set out to create a new and vibrant musical tradition for American churches. For a fee, Billings and other "singing school masters," would visit a church and teach amateurs how to sing in harmony. The songs they created were less like the slow psalms of the old European churches and more like the people's beloved folk songs. To simplify the learning of these new songs, called **hymns, anthems**, or **spirituals**, they would teach them using **solfege**, a system in which each pitch in the scale is associated with a particular syllable, as in the familiar do, re, mi, fa, sol, la, ti. By the early nineteenth century, another simplification appeared in publications, the printing of notes in different shapes for each solfege syllable. Thus, a triangle might represent fa, a circle sol, and a square la, for example, even though the rest of the notation was unchanged (Figure 16.2). With this innovation, trained singers could quickly read a hymn without having to worry about being able to read keys or notes in staff notation.

The pieces Billings and his successors wrote demonstrated their determination not to be "confined to any rules of composition." These musicians replaced the complex methods European professional composers spent years learning to produce the refined harmonies of art music with simplified conventions. These new conventions often resulted in incomplete triads and other austere sounds that suggested an aesthetic preference for puritan

FIGURE 16.2

In this notation for the hymn "Weeping Mary" from the 1855 collection *The Social Harp*, the pattern of intervals is represented by just four shapes: a diamond for "mi," a triangle for "fa," an oval for "sol," and a square for "la." The color (white or black) and other parts of the note indicate the rhythmic duration, although these symbols are unchanged from conventional European notation.

INSTRUMENTS OF NORTH AMERICA

No instruments used in the folk traditions of European Americans and African Americans originated entirely in North America, although several have acquired distinctive characteristics only after having been developed there.

Michael Ochs Archives/Getty Images

BANJO

The **banjo** (played here by folk singer Pete Seeger) became possibly the most identifiable North American instrument after slaves and white minstrels developed it. This long-neck lute probably originated in northwest Africa and was a favorite among Spanish and Portuguese sailors, among whom it was known as the *bandore*. Although soon forgotten in Europe, it became a popular instrument of American slaves, often homemade with gourd resonators. By the 1840s, white minstrel performers popularized the instrument and standardized its construction. Perhaps because of these racist associations, the instrument became less popular with African Americans in the twentieth century but was retained in rural white folk music, especially in the southeastern United States. The modern banjo has five single metal strings stretched over a long fretted fingerboard. The resonator is circular with a parchment-like head stretched over it, rather like a frame drum. The banjo's dry and bright timbre, so unlike the guitar's, is suited to quick arpeggiations (successive soundings of notes in a chord) and interpolations of drone pitches in between melody notes. Players often wear metal plectra (picks) on their fingers and thumb to pluck the strings in quick succession.

Redferns Music Picture Library/Alamy

GUITAR

Like the banjo, the **guitar** was popular with Spanish sailors and slave-traders and, probably through them, both slave owners and slaves in America. The Spanish introduced it independently in the Southwest, where its portability made it an iconic companion to the cowboy. As with folk traditions in Spain, the guitar was usually strummed, providing both a rhythmic and a chordal accompaniment to song. Among African Americans, however, a more complex combination of melodic plucking and strumming emerged that made the guitar one of the most common accompaniments to blues singing by the 1930s. Because the guitar is fretted and therefore normally restricted to a fixed scale, it would seem at a disadvantage when playing blues, a type of music known for its subtle slides and inflections of pitch outside the standard tuning system. Blues guitarists solved this problem by placing a broken-off neck of a glass soft drink bottle (later a specially made tube) over the left forefinger (see the photo at left). Pressing the smooth glass neck to the fingerboard allows the player to slide it smoothly to create continuous changes in pitch.

PEDAL STEEL GUITAR

Like blues guitarists, Hawaiians independently developed sliding pitches on a guitar (introduced by European sailors) but instead held it horizontally on the player's lap. By tuning the strings to pitches of a single triad (called "slack key" tuning), players of the **Hawaiian guitar** could slide whole chords up and down. This distinctive sound became widely popular in the United States in the 1920s and 1930s, inspiring many variations to that instrument, such as the **pedal steel guitar** (left), an electronically amplified instrument played without a resonator. The strings and fingerboard are set horizontally on a stand in front of the sitting player. The pitch of the strings can be altered through a system of foot pedals in addition to sliding a metal bar along the fingerboard. In this configuration, the instrument resembles a zither rather than a lute, although the amplification is entirely electronic. Although the Hawaiian guitar is no longer common, the distinctive sound of the pedal steel guitar is found in many forms of country music in the United States.

Ohad Shahar/Alamy

MOUNTAIN DULCIMER

The **mountain dulcimer** (left) is a plucked or strummed zither with frets over a distinctive curved hourglass-shaped resonator. It originated from similar instruments brought by German and perhaps Scandinavian immigrants (see Figure 14.5 in Chapter 14). Despite its name, the mountain dulcimer is not the same instrument as the **hammered dulcimer**, a trapezoidal zither that is essentially the same instrument as the Eastern European *cimbalom* (see Figure 13.3 in Chapter 13), although without the pedal damper mechanism sometimes found there. Unlike the mountain dulcimer, the hammered dulcimer is played with mallets called hammers and is not fingered.

William Alves

Eric Schaal/Time Life Pictures/Getty Images

AUTOHARP

A new variation of the European zither called the **autoharp** (pictured at the bottom of the photograph of the Carter Family on the left) was invented in Germany toward the end of the nineteenth century. On this instrument, pressing down different buttons will result in dampers (felt weights) being raised from certain combinations of strings, so that when the player strums all of the strings, a chord will sound. Although it did not achieve wide popularity in its country of origin, the autoharp became a popular folk instrument in the United States, like many other instruments, because of its availability through mail order sources such as the Sears Roebuck catalog. The autoharp's mechanism makes it very easy for untrained amateurs to create harmonic accompaniments to songs, although some players have created specialized techniques combining plucking with strumming.

Hear and see the instruments of North America in your downloadable **ACTIVE LISTENING TOOLS**, available at the World Music Resource Center.

simplicity and directness also found in the "carpenter's gothic" architecture of rural protestant churches. Also, instead of the highest women's voices singing the primary melody or tune, the highest male singers sang it, a practice going back to the Middle Ages.

Such shape note hymnbooks as *The Sacred Harp* and *The Southern Harmony* became some of the most popular publications of the time and could be found on many a farmer's shelf next to the Bible and little else. As urban churches modernized, however, most turned to hymns with conventional European harmonies and the melody in the highest voice, classically trained choirs, and professional music directors. Although some African Americans adopted shape note singing, many segregated black churches developed their own styles of spirituals and gospel songs. Shape note singing lived on, however, in some rural communities, especially in the southern United States.

In these communities, the tradition of shape note singing developed into a pastime often independent of church worship services. Since a mid-twentieth-century revival of shape note singing, this distinctively American participatory art has become more popular than ever through regional conventions and workshops, rather than in churches. In a shape note "singing" today, each leader has the opportunity to call up two or three songs, known as a "lesson" for the "class" or choir, terms dating back to the time of the singing school masters.

Each song lasts just a minute or two, and, even allowing time for a bit of conversation and joking between selections, the singers get through several dozen before it's time to break for a pot-luck lunch and some fellowship. After lunch, the singing will continue until two or three in the afternoon and require more than a little stamina. Although these Christian hymns may give the same sense of spirituality to these singers as they did to their great-great-grandparents, this is not a religious service, and many of the participants may come from different sects and churches. The singers sing for the sheer joy of joining their voices in this enthusiastic and welcoming community.

A SHAPE NOTE HYMN PERFORMANCE

John McCurry was a farmer in rural Georgia in the 1850s who earned money on the side as a singing master, teaching shape note singing to churches of this region. He composed a number of songs himself, including that on the next page, and also collected songs from others in the area. A frequent venue for these tunes was the revival meeting, an all-day or sometimes several-day gathering not in a church but in the countryside. African-American congregations might hold their own meeting nearby, their songs frequently intermingling with those of the whites. In 1855, McCurry found a publisher for his collection, called *The Social Harp*, all in the "old" style of three (instead of four) individual parts, and four (instead of seven) shapes corresponding to four solfege syllables (mi, fa, sol, and la). "Weeping Mary" is classified as a "set piece," that is, a song of irregular poetic meter not based on Biblical text, used for various occasions and not a specific place in a worship service.

CD 3:16. "Weeping Mary," The Southern Traditional Singers led by Hugh McGraw.

0:00  Courtesy of Paul Figura	Shape note singers traditionally sing the hymn once through using solfege syllables rather than the lyrics. Three different melodies make up the polyphonic texture, and the middle melody (the tenor) is the primary tune. However, some men sing the women's (treble) melody an octave lower, while some women sing the tenor an octave higher, thickening the texture. Although this practice somewhat obscures the melodic contours of the individual melodies, this is music for the singers themselves rather than an audience listening for the tune.
0:09	The prominent syncopation here may be evidence of African-American influence.
0:12	The A section (known as the verse and refrain) repeats. This diatonic mode is Aeolian or minor (see Graphic 14.2 in Chapter 14) but without the semitone adjustments normally found in European minor mode music since the seventeenth century.
0:23	The B section (known as the chorus).
0:31	The B section repeats.
0:40	Listen to the last chord at this point. Those familiar with conventional European harmony sometimes describe this as an "empty" sound because the chord is an incomplete triad, consisting of just the tonic and the fifth scale degree. This austere sonority is characteristic of shape note harmony.
0:44	The singers now repeat the entire hymn with the lyrics, which begin: *Are there anybody here like Mary a'weeping?* This line refers to the story in the Christian Bible (John Chapter 20) when Jesus' follower Mary Magdalene weeps after his death, not realizing that he has come back to life and is standing next to her. The next line (the refrain) offers advice to such doubters:

0:49

Call to my Jesus, and he'll draw nigh.

On the key word *call*, the notation indicates a *fermata*, that is, a sign that that note is to be held for a longer, indeterminate duration, briefly interrupting the meter as if the singers themselves are calling Jesus.

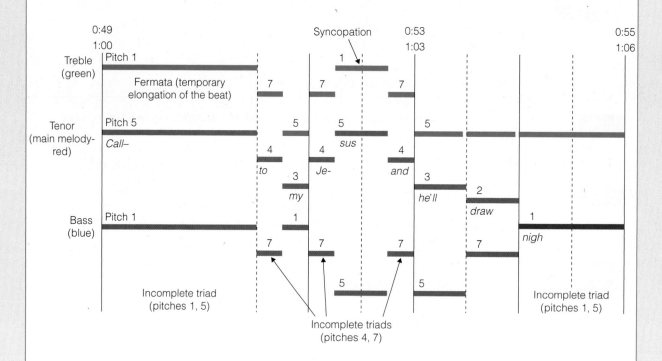

0:55

The verse repeats with new words:

Are there anybody here like Peter a'sinking?

This line refers to another Biblical story (Matthew Chapter 14) in which the fisherman Peter is caught in his boat in a storm. Jesus asks Peter to walk on the water toward him. He does, but when his faith wavers, he begins to sink and is caught by Jesus.

1:06

In the chorus section, the choir sings:

Glory, glory, glory, glory,

Glory be to my God on high.

ANGLO-AMERICAN FOLK MUSIC

In 1916, in part to escape the ravages of the war in Europe, English folk song researcher Cecil Sharp sailed for the United States. There, he thought, he might find some vestiges of British ballads and other songs he so loved. For two years, he trudged up and down the dirt wagon roads of the Appalachian mountains, finding to his astonishment a tradition of folk singing far more vital than the one he had left, a living tradition as yet untouched by urban entertainments and other influences (Figure 16.3). He wrote down these songs and lectured on them, exhorting Americans to appreciate the richness of their own tradition. When someone asked if the preservation of old British ballads in the American mountains was a case of "arrested development" of the music, he replied that he rather preferred to call it a case of "arrested degeneration."[3]

Yet Sharp recognized that these songs were not frozen in the form in which they had arrived in the eighteenth century but rather developed in their own distinctively American way. Sharp described Americans' singing as more free and unselfconscious, and he speculated that this style might be a reflection of the fact that, unlike British peasants, these Americans owned their own lands for generations. The inhabitants of these isolated hamlets sang ballads not as market entertainments nor even for community participation but only for self expression. "The genuine folk-singer," Sharp wrote, "is never conscious of his audience—indeed, as often as not, he has none—and he never, therefore, strives after effect, nor endeavours in this or in any other way to attract the attention, much less the admiration of his hearers."[4]

The expressiveness of the singers was therefore quite personal, introverted, and unaffected. American singers had the distinctive habit of dwelling on a particular note in the melody for expressive purposes, extending the note sometimes several beats beyond its normal duration. Singers carefully, but never ostentatiously, ornamented melodies, often with a rather tense throat and reedy vocal timbre.

The collections of Sharp and others also show a difference in subject matter preference between the ballad singers of Britain and the United States. The anonymous narrator of English ballads in America becomes an individual, often dwelling on the plight of the common person and the rootless wanderer. American ballad singers were often women, whose hard lives were reflected in a preference for stories of women caught in tragic romantic situations and an unforgiving society. For example, in the ballad "The Elfin Knight" (made famous by the 1960s duo Simon and Garfunkel as "Scarborough Fair"), a demonic elf threatens to abduct a young woman unless she can perform a series of impossible tasks. In the more modern "Frankie and Johnny," a wronged woman shoots down her husband with a .44 pistol.

Through the nineteenth century, musicians usually reserved instruments for accompanying dances rather than songs, often in a faster, more rhythmically complex manner than instrumental dances in England or Ireland. English and Irish reels became **hoedowns** and **breakdowns**, vigorous group dances

English Folk Dance & Song Society

FIGURE 16.3

Cecil Sharp (left) and his assistant Maud Karpeles (right) record folk songs sung by Mrs. Doc Pratt of Hindman, Kentucky in September 1917.

[3]Maud Karpeles, *Cecil Sharp: His Life and Work* (Chicago: University of Chicago Press, 1967): 146.

[4]Cecil Sharp, *English Folk Songs from the Southern Appalachians* ed. Maud Karpeles (London: Oxford University Press, 1932): vol. 1, xxvii.

featuring elaborate instrumental figurations. Seemingly every small region had its own style of "picking" the banjo, using two or three fingers to interpolate drone pitches and successive chord pitches between the melody notes, creating a rhythmically propulsive dance dense with notes. In contrast to fiddlers from England and Ireland, American fiddlers often used open strings (i.e., the strings without the player's fingers on them) to thicken the texture and quick back-and-forth bow strokes to accentuate rhythms. Fiddlers from Texas were especially known for their elaborate style.

COUNTRY MUSIC

Even in his time, Sharp worried that modernization would soon doom this beautiful tradition, and in some ways, his concern was justified. In just a few years, roads and radio would reach nearly every corner of these mountains, bringing new influences and the commercialization of music. The guitar followed new roads and electrical lines, and in just a few years, old songs acquired chordal accompaniments. The ancient hexatonic and pentatonic modes that Sharp notated suddenly disappeared to accommodate the diatonic major mode harmonies of the strummed folk guitar.

At the same time, traditions adapted to the new ways, and musicians exploited radio and recordings to spread their sounds to new audiences. Anglo-American rural communities offered a huge new market for recordings, and the proliferation of recordings and radio programs allowed for the cross-pollination of regional styles. For example, the guitarist and singer Maybelle Carter drew on techniques from Anglo-American and African-American musicians to create a unique and highly influential style of playing the melody on the low strings with the thumb while interspersing chords with the other fingers on the upper strings. Maybelle was a member of the famous **Carter Family**, who between 1927 and 1943 recorded over 300 songs and sold millions of recordings (see the photo of the Carter Family, with autoharp, in the Instrument Gallery).

Recording companies then labeled this sound "hillbilly music," but by the 1940s, it was known as "country music," a category that, by then, included many genres:

- **String bands** consisting of banjo, guitar, fiddle, and, later, bass (European double bass of the violin family) and playing traditional dance tunes and accompanied singers

- **Singing cowboys,** who were popular in recordings and Hollywood movies, often in small vocal ensembles like those of gospel groups

- **Western swing,** a fusion of country and big band jazz originating in Texas

- **Honky-tonk,** another genre from Texas that featured the electric slide steel guitar

Kentuckian **Bill Monroe** created one of the most enduring country music genres when he put together a string band that focused on quick tempos and instrumental virtuosity. Known as the Bluegrass Boys, after the nickname of Monroe's home state, the group's many imitators soon came to call the style itself **bluegrass**. The players trade solos, much like jazz performers, and often developed remarkably innovative instrumental techniques, as did, for example, the banjo player **Earl Scruggs** (Figure 16.4).

THE FOLK MUSIC REVIVAL

In 1931, efforts to unionize the coal miners of Harlan County, Kentucky, had provoked violence. One day, deputized thugs ransacked the home of Florence Reece, searching for her husband, Sam, a labor organizer. She was so outraged that, after they left, she tore a page off a wall calendar and did what many Americans have when faced with social injustice: she wrote a song. The song, "Which Side Are You On?" became an anthem for working people during the Great Depression.

As commercial country music established itself as a large industry in the 1930s, the folk music of the common people did not disappear. Especially in rural areas, singers in the old styles could still be found, although new topics became more relevant: stories of unemployment, civil rights, and corruption replaced old English legends. A tradition of social protest runs through American folk songs from nineteenth-century abolitionist songs to ballads protesting the wars in Vietnam and Iraq.

Such examples raise the question of whether these songs should be called "folk music" at all because they were written by living professional composers, among them **Woody Guthrie**, composer of "This Land is Your Land," and **Pete Seeger**, composer of "If I Had a Hammer" (Seeger is pictured with his banjo in the Instrument Gallery). Their music is usually distinguished from other popular music because it draws directly on folk song traditions, often in the same style as earlier folk songs, or even, as with "Which Side Are You On?" written to an existing folk tune.

In the 1950s, Seeger, Guthrie, and others brought these old songs and old-style folk songs to new popular audiences, establishing what is now known as the Folk Music Revival movement. By the 1960s, these singers inspired many young musicians to take up the acoustic guitar and songs of their grandparents. The Folk Music Revival directly influenced many well-known popular musicians, including Bob Dylan, Joan Baez, and Paul Simon. The varieties of American folk music are still popular in conventions, workshops, and coffee houses throughout the United States and Canada.

Frank Driggs Collection/Hulton Archives/Getty images

FIGURE 16.4

One of the most famous bluegrass bands was the Foggy Mountain Boys led by Lester Flatt, guitar, and Earl Scruggs, banjo. Also shown in this photograph from the 1950s is a double bass at the far left and a fiddle at the far right.

MUSIC OF INDIGENOUS AMERICANS

In 1872, Black Elk (Figure 16.5), a nine-year-old boy of the Lakota people, known to whites as the Sioux Indians, became seriously ill. As he lay bedridden, he saw men descend from the clouds and tell him, "Hurry! Come! Your Grandfathers are calling you!" Black Elk followed them into the spirit world, where he met the six sacred Grandfathers. The Grandfathers began to teach him the powers of their world, and they sang to him. The Second Grandfather, the Grandfather of the North, sang[5]:

They are appearing, may you behold!
They are appearing, may you behold!
The thunder nation is appearing, behold!

[5]John G. Neihardt, *Black Elk Speaks* (Lincoln NE: University of Nebraska Press, 3rd ed., 1972): 21–32.

FIGURE 16.5

Black Elk (1863–1950) photographed in the 1880s, shortly before the Wounded Knee massacre.

Hulton Archives/Getty Images

Later in the vision, a great black stallion, the chief of all horses sang to him:

My horses, prancing they are coming.
My horses, neighing they are coming;
Prancing they are coming.
All over the universe they come.
They will dance, may you behold them.
They will dance, may you behold them.

When Black Elk awoke from what to his parents appeared to be a twelve-day coma, he was forever changed by this vision of the spirit world, and he was now destined for a life as a Lakota holy man. Throughout his famous career, these songs, given to him by the spirits, remained his personal connection to their world. He would sing them at special sacred ceremonies or at other times when he wanted to call upon the beings he met in his vision.

The quest for visions of the spirit world is common to nearly all indigenous American groups. Sometimes, as in Black Elk's case, they come unbidden, but other times, people will seek them through fasting in isolation in the wilderness. In many traditions, one of the most important gifts from this profound experience will be a song bestowed by a spirit. This song will thereafter become that individual's personal property, his or her own connection to the spirit world. The Ute of nineteenth-century Colorado received all their songs in this way.

More commonly, however, vision songs represented just a fraction of the musical life of indigenous Americans, which also included lullabies, game songs, social songs, war chants, and so on. Nevertheless, Black Elk's songs demonstrate several important aspects of indigenous American musical traditions that continue to exert an influence even today.

Indigenous Americans across the continent saw themselves as one strand amid a web of relationships in the natural and spiritual worlds, and even the most mundane song was often an expression of those relationships or communication across worlds. European writers have therefore emphasized the religious nature of nearly all indigenous American music, sometimes without further adding that one's spiritual life was never separate from one's everyday existence and interactions with the natural world. Thus the tones of a song—even those of gambling songs, work songs, and humble lullabies—were an aspect of existence that reached from this plane of existence to another.

ELEMENTS OF INDIGENOUS AMERICAN TRADITIONAL MUSIC

◆ **Short monophonic songs.** Like Black Elk's songs, nearly all traditional Native American songs are relatively short, sung by a single singer, and frequently include repetitive lyrics, often in strophic forms.

◆ **Use of vocables.** Songs very frequently include vocables, that is, syllables without literal meaning, such as "heya-ya" or "le-le-le." Some songs have no other words.

◆ **Limited use of instruments.** The use of instruments in traditional music is almost always restricted to drums and idiophones playing constant beats as accompaniment to singing. However, traditions of solo flute playing, although relatively uncommon a century ago, have expanded greatly among many performers in the past few decades.

◆ **Rhythm often follows words, rather than the other way around.**
Therefore, traditional songs may have fairly complex changing meters or
may consist of strings of durations that are difficult to classify in a meter
at all. This characteristic gives most traditional music an asymmetry quite
different from the phrase structure of most European music.

◆ **Functional music**. Virtually all traditional music has a practical role to
play in society. Even game songs or party songs had their place in cementing

INSTRUMENT GALLERY

Indigenous American Musical Instruments

William Alves

RATTLES

Idiophones are the most common instruments among indigenous Americans, nearly always used to accompany dance. **Rattles** are made from gourds, sewn hides, or baskets with seeds or pebbles inside. After Europeans introduced metals, metal rattles ("sleigh bells") were often attached to the clothing of dancers. Shown here are (left to right) a deer-hoof rattle (Maidu), gourd rattle (Cahuilla), and moth cocoon rattle (Pomo).

William Alves

DRUMS

Drums are used throughout the continent to accompany singing, sometimes in the form of frame drums and other times with deeper resonators. Today, a circle of drummers plays a single large double-headed drum at powwow ceremonies. In some areas, drums had small bones or teeth attached to them to rattle as snares. Shown here is a decorated frame drum of the Makah people of the Northwest Coast.

Canyon Records

FLUTE

Although not common, the duct flute was found throughout the Plains areas and some other regions in the nineteenth century, where it was a personal (rather than ritual) instrument, often associated with young men courting women. Today, a more or less standardized version of this instrument, the Native American flute, has become popular. It is unusual in that it has an obstruction partially blocking the tube between the mouthpiece and the six fingerholes. This splitting of the resonator creates a uniquely soft and "breathy" timbral quality.

Hear and see indigenous American musical instruments in your downloadable **ACTIVE LISTENING TOOLS,**
available at the World Music Resource Center.

community bonds. The concept of music as a nonproductive entertainment found its way into indigenous societies only through the influence of European-American music in the twentieth century.

◆ **Commonality in mode types.** With the exception of some songs of the Northwest Coast area, the great majority of indigenous songs are diatonic, anhemitonic pentatonic, or a diatonic or pentatonic subset.

INDIGENOUS AMERICAN REGIONS

ARCTIC NORTH AMERICA

The people of the north coast of North America, sometimes known as Eskimo or Inuit, have adapted to life in this forbidding climate over thousands of years. Long and dark winter months offer many opportunities for indoor social games and rituals in which music plays a key role, including gambling and other game songs, songs for juggling, courting dances, and the important ritual known as the drum dance. To many indigenous Americans, singing, rather than being

This map is a simplified depiction of the distribution of the related indigenous American musical styles in the nineteenth century. Naturally, the distinctions between neighboring styles are never as absolute as depicted here, and the groupings of styles to some degree reflect the subjective judgments of musicologists.

an activity distinct from speech, is a heightened form of it. To the indigenous people of the Arctic, conventional songs lie at one end of a spectrum of vocal expression, which also includes speech, dog sled calls, and chant. Songs often take the form of prose, where repetition may be varied to accommodate a text or may be absent altogether. Rhythms often follow the flow of the prose, creating songs of great rhythmic complexity and subtlety.

NORTHWEST COAST

As with Arctic groups, the winter is a time of important social interactions among the indigenous groups living in the narrow region of the northwestern United States and far west Canada between the coastal mountain range and the Pacific Ocean. Central among these rituals is the potlatch, an extended time of feasting, dance, and music given by an individual to gain prestige or to celebrate important life events. The ceremonial songs, unusually for indigenous Americans, are sometimes nondiatonic and often have a jagged, descending contour, in which the early researcher Natalie Curtis heard the cry of a seagull.[6] Unlike most other indigenous Americans, the drumbeats may have a complex relationship to the songs they accompany; for example, a drumming pattern in quintuple meter may accompany a duple meter melody. In other cases, the beats may not coincide with the melody at all. Curtis compared the rhythms of the Kwakiutl to the unbroken but irregular sound of ocean waves crashing against the rocky shores of the Pacific Northwest.

CALIFORNIA AND THE GREAT BASIN

A distinctive characteristic of the indigenous people of the California coast is a melodic contour known to musicologists as the Rise. Most songs will have a contrasting second or middle phrase that suddenly moves the range of the melody up, sometimes by as much as an octave, other times by smaller intervals. Unlike the singing of the Plains and Southwest, the vocal timbre is relaxed and nonpulsating throughout both California and the Great Basin. The songs are relatively simple, with those of the Great Basin area characterized by repeated phrases.

SOUTHWEST

Like the steep canyons of the Southwestern deserts, the traditional songs of the Navajo (pronounced Navaho) have jagged, disjunct contours and high, wide ranges. These complex contours contrast with relatively simple rhythms and constant drum beats. Traditional music among the Navajo is often greatly spiritually charged and so powerful that it may not be casually used.

PUEBLO

Although surrounded by Navajo and other groups, the Hopi, Zuni, and other people of the Pueblos—villages of adobe and stone—maintained distinct agriculture-based societies in an unforgiving region. At special ceremonies tied to the agricultural cycles, dancers wearing masks representing *kachinas*,

[6] Natalie Curtis Burlin, *The Indians Book* (Harper, 1923, rpt. New York: Dover, 1968): 298.

or spiritual manifestations of natural and cosmic forces, mediate between the worlds of peoples and of the spirits to bring rain and good fortune. The songs accompanying these rituals are among the most complex of the indigenous traditions of North America. They have wide-ranging melodies that might mix different scales and rhythm that flows like water, one duration after another, defying any attempt to confine it to a meter. The participants sing in unison and repeat these complex melodies with absolute precision.

PLAINS AND SUBARCTIC

The Plains region (here including the northern Rocky Mountains and other subarctic areas) represents the largest and most identifiable stylistic region of indigenous music. As with the songs of Black Elk, traditional music was often a spiritual gift, a connection to one's soul, and therefore a very personal expression. Phrases are often initiated with a cry-like rapid ascent, followed by a gradually sloping descent in pitch sung with a tense, nasal vocal timbre. Extended notes are often sung with a pulsation, that is, a rhythmic variation in loudness. Nearly all songs have rhythmic accompaniment, although the drum beats, while constant, are subtly just ahead or behind the sung beats.

EASTERN

One of the most distinctive characteristics of the people of the Eastern hills and woodlands is responsorial and antiphonal (two groups alternating) forms. The rhythms could be complex alternations of twos and threes, although with a constant beat accompaniment. The voice is not as tense as in the Plains style though with some pulsation and shouts at the beginning and end of a song.

PAN-INDIAN MUSIC

In the hard winter of 1890, United States soldiers had rounded up Black Elk with other Lakota Sioux in the hills of South Dakota. Because of broken treaties and the decimation of buffalo herds, the people were starving. Then they heard a rumor about a Paiute holy man named Wovoka who had been given a vision of singing and dance. This music connected the dancers to the spirit world where they could meet their ancestors. The ancestors gave a hopeful prophecy to these desperate people, that the earth would be renewed to its state before the coming of the white people, that the buffalo would return, and the white people disappear. Wovoka taught these songs and dances to his people, but now, at a time when the indigenous Americans were gathered on reservations facing a common enemy, their hopeful message spread throughout the indigenous groups of the United States.

Because Wovoka predicted that this dance would bring back Native American ancestors, the white people named it the **Ghost Dance**. The Ghost Dance was a mass participation dance, rather than a ritual performed by a few. Like many Paiute songs, most Ghost Dance songs had no other accompaniment than the stamping of the feet of the dancers. Even distant indigenous groups retained the Paiute characteristics of the songs, such as a relaxed nonpulsating vocal timbre, creating a Pan-Indian identity through music. As described by some witnesses, the dances would continue for hours, and many participants would fall into trance as they, too, visited the ancestors in the spirit world. The

Ghost Dance gave Black Elk a vision of a newly youthful earth and people, and he described his vision to his people in song.

However, many white Americans viewed the Ghost Dance with suspicion or outright alarm, interpreting its message as a call to rebellion. That winter, soldiers came to stop the Ghost Dance and escort Black Elk's group to a reservation. Amid the high tensions near Wounded Knee creek, gunfire broke out and the soldiers began to shoot indiscriminately, ultimately killing more than 150 men, women, and children, though Black Elk survived.

Although the Wounded Knee Massacre effectively ended the Ghost Dance movement, the Ghost Dance helped create a shared cultural identity among disparate indigenous peoples and helped spread certain musical characteristics across the continent. Intertribal meetings known as **powwows** evolved into popular events where people from many different groups gathered for music, dance, and celebration (Figure 16.6).

Another expression of Pan-Indian identity is the Native American Church, a religion established near the beginning of the twentieth century, which combines elements of Christianity with indigenous practices. Native American Church members consume peyote, a hallucinogenic cactus as a sacrament in all-night ceremonies accompanied by music. Indigenous groups in Mexico and the Southwest knew of the powers of peyote for centuries, but a holy man from the Ute people of the Great Basin is said to have introduced it to the Native American Church. As a result, the songs specifically associated with the peyote ceremony resemble those of the Great Basin and Plains regions but also have distinct characteristics (Figure 16.7).

CONTEMPORARY INDIGENOUS AMERICAN MUSIC

Because the Native American flute was found among many indigenous groups of the Plains, the Great Basin, and the southeast, it became a popular instrument in intertribal powwows and experienced a revival in the 1960s. No one has popularized the instrument more than R. Carlos Nakai (shown in the Instrument Gallery). Nakai's recordings often place the flute's distinctive timbre and ornamentation on a bed of synthesized or soft instrumental tones. The flute is often recorded with a generous amount of reverberation, which is meant to evoke the canyons of the Southwest. (Nakai is of Ute and Navajo heritage.)

The work of Nakai and others marrying the Native American flute with other contemporary sounds is only one example of how indigenous musicians continue to bring their own traditions to a variety of genres. Every fall in the United States, Native American Music Awards (nicknamed the Nammies) are given in categories of Native American jazz, country, church music, New Age, pop, and rock. Although the traditional songs described previously may no longer be an important part of the daily life of indigenous people in North America, indigenous musicians continue to reflect their ancient traditions in new genres.

Lee Foster/Alamy

FIGURE 16.6

The music at a modern powwow is provided by a group of singers who beat on a single large shared drum. The drum is double sided with a rawhide membrane and mounted horizontally between the group (also known as a drum) who sit in a circle around it. Although the beats are constant and evenly separated, they are grouped into patterns through the loudness of the strokes. The predominant singing style at these events derives from that of the Plains peoples, although many different regions might be represented.

Carl Iwasaki/Time & Life Pictures/Getty Images

FIGURE 16.7

The peyote ceremony of the Native American Church is an all-night ritual that involves the singing of special songs by each of the participants in turn. These songs resemble those of the Plains but are quicker with rhythms that flow with only two durational values. The participant sitting next to the singer accompanies him with quick constant beats on a small ceremonial drum.

AFRICAN-AMERICAN MUSIC

In the 1850s, a white music scholar named Lucy McKim visited the islands off the coast of South Carolina, intent on studying the music of a slave culture there that had developed largely in isolation. One humid night, she found herself in a large meeting house where the slaves were performing a **ring shout**. Beneath the flickering lamp flames, the barefoot slaves danced for hours in a circle accompanied only by their own forceful and elaborate singing. Sometimes the repetitive song and dance would help send a participant into trance. A loud and expressive solo singer led the others in what McKim recognized as religious songs, or **spirituals**. But these songs were quite unlike the versions McKim might have heard in the segregated churches of whites. In particular, she wrote of "the curious rhythmic effect produced by single voices chiming in at different irregular intervals, seem almost as impossible to place on the score as the singing of birds. . . ."[7]

The forms of the songs lent themselves to repetition by the dancers, as well as a group of back-up singers known as "basers," who would respond to and heterophonically accompany the lead singer. The pitches used also seemed quite distinctive, and early writers noted their inability to accurately notate the supple inflections of intonation in African-American singing that deviated distinctively from the fixed pitches of the European diatonic scale. These expressive, small (microtonal) changes and slides lowered the pitches of certain scale steps relative to the European diatonic scale, and these notes would much later become known as **blue notes**. Although usually smaller than a semitone, these changes in pitch would have to be approximated by semitone changes on instruments with a fixed tuning system, such as the banjo or piano.

Each of these characteristics—distinctive rhythms, responsorial forms, microtonal pitch inflections—are clearly related to African music. In fact, the perceived proximity of the ring shout to its African origins particularly alarmed some whites and led to it being banned in many areas. Slaves brought a rich diversity of African music to North America, but unlike some slaves in the Caribbean and South America, their cultures and languages were deliberately suppressed and intermixed.

By 1800, black populations outnumbered white in some states in the southern United States, and some white masters, always fearful of slave rebellions, outlawed large gatherings (perhaps excepting church services) and some musical instruments, especially drums, which could be used as signaling devices. The complex polyrhythmic layering of large drum ensembles found in Africa was therefore generally not possible in the oppressive environment of slavery. Although written reports show the continuing existence of African instruments such as drums, mbiras, and bows in some areas, Africans were instead encouraged to take up European instruments such as the fiddle (violin) to play for white dances. It was only natural for slaves to transfer African elements to the new instruments, at least when playing for each other.

The most common instruments available to African Americans, apart from the voice, were the violin, guitar, and banjo, and these instruments often

---

[7]Lucy McKim, letter in *Dwights Journal of Music*, Nov. 8, 1862. Quoted in William Francis Allen, Charles Pickard Ware, and Lucy Kim, *Slave Songs of the United States* (New York: A. Simpson, 1867): vi.

combined to form a **string band**, an ensemble also popular with rural whites. Perhaps the effect of "collapsing" the distinctively African polyrhythmic layers onto a single line instrument produced the characteristic syncopation that became most associated with African-American music. In any case, white performers were imitating this characteristic rhythmic style as early as the 1840s.

Minstrel shows, popular theater that combined music and skits imitating blacks often in degrading stereotypes, first became widespread in this period. They nevertheless became one of the principal platforms for the popularization of new songs and dances by such composers as **Stephen Foster** (1826–1864), whose minstrel songs "Oh Susanna" and "Old Folks at Home" went on to become icons of Americana. These performances eventually fused Anglo-American ballads and fiddle tunes with the syncopations, instruments, and responsorial forms of African-American music to create new sounds as distinct from European songs as a New Yorker's dialect was from a Londoner's. The sales of sheet music from these and other popular songs of the period helped establish the industry of popular music in North America. The minstrel shows also served to introduce shadows of African-American elements into popular white culture, and, in doing so, helped establish distinctly American musical idioms.

WIND BANDS AND RAGTIME

The famous 1893 World's Columbian Exposition in Chicago was a hugely extravagant demonstration of the United States' new central spot on the world stage in art and culture, industry and commercialism. Representing high culture musically at the fair was the conductor Theodore Thomas (1835–1905), who led performances of European orchestral music beneath imposing neoclassical facades lit with a dazzling array of electric lights. More popular, however, was the wind band of **John Philip Sousa** (1854–1932), which played in a nearby open air pavilion (Figure 16.8).

Although European in origin, an orchestra made up primarily of aerophones, known as a **wind band**, brass band (if only buzzed-lip instruments), or simply band, had become a widely popular fixture in hundreds of American communities in the period following the Civil War. Unlike the European symphony orchestra, the band was suitable for outdoor concerts and parades. In addition to military marches, composers such as Sousa adapted popular songs, art music, and ballroom dances to the distinctive instrumentation. These marches and dances consisted of a strictly fixed form in which each section consisted of sections called **strains** of four phrases, each phrase being four measures (metrical groupings) of two, three, or four beats each. A complete piece would consist of four repeated strains, perhaps with a one-phrase introduction and a one-phrase transition section (or **bridge**) between the strains. The texture was mostly homophonic, with accompaniment typically consisting of alternating bass notes and triads (the so-called oom-pah pattern).

United States Marine Band

FIGURE 16.8

In this photograph from 1893, the same year as the Columbian Exposition, band leader and composer John Philip Sousa poses with his band, which includes clarinets (left side), flutes (second row far left), cornets (a buzzed-lip conical bore instrument, front row right), saxophones (various sizes, second row right), French horns (third row far right), trombones (fourth row right), a Sousaphone (a variation of the tuba made more portable, rear right), and drums, including two timpani drums in the foreground. The popularity of the Sousa band helped establish the wind band as a common ensemble in American schools.

Michael Ochs Archives/Getty Images

FIGURE 16.9

Scott Joplin (1867?–1917) was the foremost composer of ragtime.

In this form, these dances were popular in arrangements for piano as well as for ensembles ranging from mandolin orchestras to string bands of violins and banjos, many of whom also played at the many musical venues at the Chicago Exposition. However, probably the most startling innovation of this form at the Exposition came from the unlikely pavilion of the country of Haiti. When the Exposition's organizers chose to exclude African-American performers, the famous African-American abolitionist and writer Frederick Douglass accepted the offer of the delegation from Haiti to organize performances at their pavilion. Among the performers he invited was a pianist and cornet player from Texas named **Scott Joplin** (Figure 16.9).

Joplin grew up among the pervasive syncopations of African-American banjo and other instrumental music of former slaves so often imitated in minstrel shows. Although conventional venues were often closed to blacks, pianists like Joplin could find work playing popular songs and dances in bars and brothels, where they could introduce syncopated variations, that is, make the rhythm or timing "ragged." They could also adapt African-American dances, particularly the **cakewalk**, a strutting dance with a cake prize, presumably originating in blacks' comic parody of white formal dances.

African-American developers of this new style of extremely syncopated but lilting melodies over oom-pah accompaniments converged on the Haitian pavilion in Chicago, bringing together regional styles developed around the Midwest and Southern United States. Within three or four years, these compositions found their way into print in versions for piano called **ragtime**. Joplin became the most famous composer of this widely influential style, and although he was known for the four-strain form familiar from band marches, he also (like Sousa) composed songs and operas. Ragtime is chiefly remembered today as a piano genre because that was the most commercially viable way to publish these compositions.

However, the ragtime style was just as popular with small ensembles, such as the one Joplin took to Chicago; with vocal groups, which Joplin also performed in; and, later, with larger groups, sometimes called "syncopated orchestras." The area in New York City where the popular music publishers were concentrated, known as Tin Pan Alley, quickly adopted ragtime's syncopations in popular songs as well. Even pieces not written as rags could be extemporaneously "ragged," or played in improvised syncopated variations, eventually leading to a new style: jazz.

EARLY JAZZ

In 1917, a reviewer for the *New York Sunday Sun* wrote, "The musical riot that breaks forth from clarinet, trombone, cornet, piano, drum, and variants of tin pan instruments resembles nothing so much as a chorus of hunting hounds on the scent with an occasional explosion in the subway thrown in for good measure."[8] Despite the alarm sounded by such critics, this musical riot was already the rage in New York, Chicago, and Los Angeles. They were calling it **jazz** after a black slang word referring to its lively and "hot" energy (often in the context of sex, to the further outrage of critics), so different from the genteel and graceful syncopations of ragtime.

The syncopations remained but now in a seemingly unruly improvised polyphony, which, when finally recorded in 1917, sold hundreds of thousands of

[8]Quoted in Alyn Shipton, *A New History of Jazz* (New York: Continuum, 2001): 104.

records in that year alone. The well-mannered tunes of popular ragtime melodies were replaced with complex runs of notes idiomatic to "lead" instruments such as the trumpet, cornet (similar to a trumpet but with a different bore), trombone, clarinet, and saxophone. The notes growled, they bent, they slid, they enthusiastically collided. Buzzed-lip instrumentalists used a wide variety of mutes—devices that covered the end, or bell, of the instrument in different ways—to create novel timbres. Musicians would much later claim contradictory dates for the invention of this style, some going back to the 1890s, but most agreed that the new sound flowed, like water down a delta, from one source: New Orleans.

New Orleans at the turn of the twentieth century was a spicy mélange of cultures and music. Whites maintained the legacy of French culture at society dances where orchestras played ballroom music and popular songs; elsewhere, wind bands played outdoor concerts, and opera was popular. On the other side of Canal Street, African Americans had their own wind bands, ragtime pianists, and vaudeville (popular variety theater) singers. At least for a time, mixed-race, or creole, musicians navigated both worlds and brought their education in reading and composing music "downtown" to the segregated black neighborhoods.

For instrumentalists who did not read notated music, some amount of improvisation was a necessity as well as an aesthetic choice. However, the nature of improvisation in such a context is frequently misunderstood. To create a part that fits with all the others in this polyphonic context, follows the harmonic progression, and still allows room for the player's expression and artistry requires careful rehearsal and a knowledge of the theory of harmony. What resulted in the best of these bands was hardly the riotous sound early critics complained about but instead a careful polyphony with nuanced phrasing and rhythm. This was the New Orleans style, later known as **Dixieland**, that wowed audiences as its masters toured the United States and Europe in the 1920s (Figure 16.10).

The melody instruments or "front line"—often a trumpet or cornet, clarinet or saxophone, and trombone—would weave this polyphony around the so-called **rhythm section**: the harmonic oom-pah of ragtime piano, double bass or tuba, drums, and perhaps banjo. Instead of the contrasting strains of ragtime, jazz compositions were usually based on popular song forms of stanza and refrain, often in a series of improvised variations. The development of this art of improvisation led to a shift of emphasis away from "front line" polyphony and toward the instrumental **solo**, a repetition of the tune featuring only a single instrumentalist with rhythm section accompaniment, as the focus of jazz creativity. By the late 1920s, the standard jazz structure of alternating solos after an initial statement of the tune (the **head**) was already established, and no other musician did more for the development of the jazz solo than the extraordinary New Orleans trumpet player **Louis Armstrong** (1901–1971).

Michael Ochs Archives/Getty Images

FIGURE 16.10

Joe "King" Oliver and his Creole Jazz Band (here shown c. 1923) was one of the most famous of the early New Orleans jazz bands. It included (left to right) Honore Dutrey on trombone; Baby Dodds, drums; Oliver, shown here playing a slide trumpet with his cornet on the ground; Louis Armstrong in the rear on cornet with a mute; Lil Hardin, later to be Armstrong's wife, piano; Bill Johnson, banjo; and Johnny Dodds, clarinet.

In the hands of musicians like Armstrong, jazz became one of the most lasting and distinctive artistic contributions to emerge from North America. The 1920s in the United States was known as the Jazz Age.

BLUES

Along the Mississippi River docks at the turn of the twentieth century, stevedores still sang out wordless melodies known as **hollers**, that preserved African yodels as well as blue note inflections also found in the church spirituals and work songs. Black "songsters" throughout the southern United States applied these mournful styles to existing ballads and other songs, and by the beginning of the twentieth century this style coalesced as the **blues**, after a long-standing slang for depression. Although they shared many influences, especially in New Orleans, jazz and the blues were parallel developments with distinct characteristics.

The first of these differences was the form of the songs. Rather than the familiar strains of 16 metrical units (measures) standard in ragtime and other popular songs, blues songs most frequently had a distinctive pattern of 12-measure sections. Spirituals and other songster lyrics also had fixed forms with repeated lines, but sometimes quite different from popular tunes. Lucy McKim and her collaborators notated this spiritual in the years around the Civil War:

> My army cross over,
> My army cross over,
> Pharaoh's army drowned.

This AAB structure sometimes results in a form with six or twelve metrical units instead of the usual four or eight found in jazz and other popular songs. On the guitar, African-American singers could accompany these lines with slow back and forth harmonies which developed into a standard pattern known as the **12-bar blues** (Graphic 16.1). These harmonies offered a conventionalized framework on which singers could hang their expressive melodic ornamentation derived from old hollers and work songs.

GRAPHIC 16.1

The form of the twelve-bar blues is commonly used not just in blues but also in jazz, gospel, soul, and rock and roll. It is defined by a standardized sequence of triads, or harmonic progression, although many variations to this basic pattern are possible. Triads are represented by the roman numeral of their root pitch (see Graphic 14.1). A bar or measure is a metrical unit usually consisting of four beats.

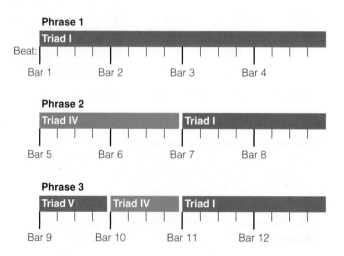

The early style of blues, sometimes known as **country blues** or folk blues, is primarily associated with male singer-guitarists from the Mississippi Delta region such as **Robert Johnson** (1911–1938) and **Edward "Son" House** (1902–1988). Country blues guitarists often used bottleneck slides (see the Instrument Gallery) to create the expressive melodic slides so crucial to the blues.

However, the blues were a more general style of singing as well, and by 1914 jazz band leaders such as W. C. Handy were already performing and publishing works with "blues" in the title. These "urban blues" songs from cities such as Memphis and Chicago often used the 12-bar harmonic patterns and above all the characteristic blue note ornaments but now arranged for a larger ensemble accompanying women singers. Early masters of blues singing included **Bessie Smith** (Figure 16.11).

Unlike Anglo-American ballad singers, who were known for their modest, introspective style, blues singers growled and shouted, whispered and sighed soul-rending gales of sound. Their expressive blue notes and other emotional expressions found their way into popular songs, jazz, gospel, country, and rock and roll, to become part of the shared vocabulary of American vernacular music.

Frank Driggs Collection/Hulton Archives/Getty Images

FIGURE 16.11

Bessie Smith (1894–1937) of Tennessee became the most popular of a series of female blues singers in the 1920s and 30s, selling millions of recordings and collaborating with jazz musicians such as Louis Armstrong.

GOSPEL MUSIC

The shape note and lining-out traditions of American church music reflected the puritan and Calvinist religious heritage of many of the original English colonies. Their belief in unvarnished simplicity, even to the exclusion of musical instruments, created the musical equivalent of their hard-backed wooden pews. In the song lyrics, images of terrifying hell alternate with ecstatic visions of union with God. In some regions, folk song collectors like Cecil Sharp and Alan Lomax were told that all secular songs were sinful.

In the period following the Civil War, many churches adopted new songs with messages of consolation and optimism, focusing on the gospel books (that is, those books about the lifetime of Jesus) of the Christian Bible. This new gospel music also distanced itself from the austere harmonies of the shape note singing masters. Mid-nineteenth-century musical reformers led by the composer Lowell Mason sought to replace shape note and other folk practices with full and sweet European harmonies. Among the tunes arranged in this way were African-American spirituals sung by trained choirs, including the Fisk Jubilee Singers, who raised money for the incipient Fisk University in Tennessee, a college for newly freed slaves.

Many African-American preachers declaimed their sermons in a half speaking, half chanting manner, often answered in similar quasi-musical responses from the congregation, a practice recalling the close connection between music and language in Africa (see Chapter 6). When many African-American churches adopted the new gospel songs (often replacing the older spirituals), they adapted them with "ragged" (syncopated) rhythms, blue-note inflections, and responsorial forms. While the older spirituals emphasized community through group singing, gospel songs allowed the leader in responsorial forms to create much more elaborate and expressive solos. These new sounds were popular outside the church as well as within.

At the turn of the twentieth century, small professional vocal ensembles entertained in a variety of genres, including ragtime, jazz, and popular tunes (later known as **barbershop** singing). Scott Joplin, as we have seen, led such a group. By the 1920s, quartets singing gospel songs inflected with blues styles became so

FIGURE 16.12

In African-American church gospel singing, congregational swaying movements, stamping, claps, and shouts may accompany the singing, suggesting an unbroken connection to the ring shouts of slaves—as depicted in this scene from the 1980 film *The Blues Brothers.*

popular that conservative religious leaders railed against it. In 1921, a Dr. H. M. Poteat thundered, "Jazz, waltzes, 'blues,' ragtime, slushy sentimentality have become the musical expression of so many people *outside* the church, that the same sort of thing, with a poor, thin veneer of religion, is demanded *in* the church."[9]

Even so, new religious movements such as Pentecostalism welcomed the use of instruments and popular style singing in white churches, and country singers often recorded gospel songs alongside secular tunes. White gospel songs, though, frequently borrowed the blue-note inflections and other idioms from African-American traditions. Singers in black churches might alternate a slow or non-pulsatile, heavily ornamented blues style with fast rhythmically driving, even ecstatic singing. Early performances were accompanied by whatever instruments were available, but by the 1950s, the electronic organ, drum set, and electric guitar became inescapably associated with the black gospel sound (Figure 16.12). The earlier style of small, unaccompanied vocal ensembles also remained popular in the 1950s and early 1960s in the secular form known as **doo-wop**.

BIG BAND TO BEBOP

As the popularity of jazz exploded in the United States, many composers and ensembles began adopting its characteristic rhythms and forms. The Tin Pan Alley songwriter **George Gershwin** (1898–1937) sought to adapt the new style to hybrid art music forms, including his famous *Rhapsody in Blue*, a work for piano with an ensemble in the form of a European classical orchestra. Writing an extended form for such a large group generally precludes the use of the improvisation so central to jazz, however, and Gershwin wrote down all the parts for this and his other works.

FIGURE 16.13

Duke Ellington's orchestra from 1942 shows a typical instrumentation for a jazz big band, including five saxophones of different sizes (left), double bass (back row far left), guitar (back row left), drum set (back center), three trombones (right) and three trumpets (front row right, one not visible). Ellington led the band from the piano, shown here in front.

While other ensembles did not have the same ambitions to bring jazz into art music, they faced the same problem of incorporating improvisation into a group larger than Dixieland bands. Such **big bands** might have multiple wind instruments of a single type, so each one would have to have a written-out part in order to harmonize with the others. Composers such as **Edward Kennedy "Duke" Ellington** (1899–1974) created works that left sections open for single players to improvise solos, while all other parts were more or less prescribed (Figure 16.13). Big bands could have louder sounds, more varied textures, and more complex arrangements than Dixieland groups.

By the 1930s, big bands represented the standard jazz ensemble. They would typically include three or four each of saxophones (the saxophones could be of different sizes), trumpets, and trombones, plus a rhythm section of piano, double bass, drum set, and perhaps guitar. They were popular both in concert and as accompanists to social dances, especially the new style known as **swing**. With the introduction of microphones and electronic amplification, big bands could also accompany popular singers.

[9]Hubert M. Poteat, *Practical Hymnology* (Boston: R. G. Badger, 1921): 62.

However, the increasing size of big bands and their association with popular songs led to a reaction from critics complaining that these ensembles had softened jazz's original energy, blurred its sound in thick textures, and deemphasized the centrality of the soloist as creative focus. After World War II, new smaller ensembles emerged, preferring intimate night clubs to large dance halls, and intricate solos to elaborate orchestrations, creating a new style known as **bebop**.

While retaining the form of a lead followed by alternating solos, the bebop style emphasized great speed and virtuosity. Bebop compositions often used relatively complex harmonies and rhythms that were often difficult for many people to follow, much less dance to. With this change jazz became more of an art music than a popular music, which came to appeal to a relatively select group of connoisseurs rather than a mass audience. Performers such as **Charlie Parker** (1920–1955) created a sophisticated and "cool" art appropriate for the age (Figure 16.14). In the 1960s and '70s, jazz musicians such as **Miles Davis** (1926–1991) continued to innovate, adopting influences from rock and traditional music from other cultures, improvisation free of harmonic progressions, and electronic instruments.

Michael Ochs Archives/Getty Images

FIGURE 16.14

Charlie Parker (left) on saxophone and Dizzy Gillespie (right) on trumpet were friends who often played in small ensembles (combos) together. In the 1940s they helped invent the new style of elaborate solos, harmonic complexity, and fast, complex rhythms known as bebop.

A BEBOP PERFORMANCE: "KOKO" BY CHARLIE PARKER

In 1951, the American writer Jack Kerouac famously captured the free, ecstatic spirit of bebop improvisation in his novel *On the Road*, as in this passage in which the character Dean cheers on a tenor saxophone soloist (tenorman): "Uproars of music and the tenorman *had it* and everybody knew he had it. Dean was clutching his head in the crowd, and it was a mad crowd. They were all urging that tenorman to hold it and keep it with cries and wild eyes, and he was raising himself from a crouch and going down again with his horn, looping it up in a clear cry above the furor."[10] Like a bebop solo, Kerouac's prose hardly pauses for a breath, and Kerouac credited one person in particular for the musical inspiration in his work: Charlie Parker.

Charlie "Bird" Parker was born in Kansas City but moved to New York City, the center of the jazz world, when he was a young man. There he made a living playing in big bands, but his real love came after hours, when he and like-minded friends would play in small ensembles in Manhattan's late night clubs. There, unconstrained by the tempos and rhythms necessary to accompany dancers, Parker and his friends could explore the limits of the art of jazz solo improvisations. One night, when playing Ray Noble's big band tune "Cherokee," Parker related how he discovered how he could make the melody "come alive" by adding more and more complex pitches to the basic triads of the harmony.[11] Equally innovative were the breakneck tempos, which called for a new way of drumming.

On November 26, 1945, Parker joined his friend trumpeter John "Dizzy" Gillespie, bassist Curly Russell, and drummer Max Roach to create what many felt was the first recording of the new bebop style. The following piece, "Koko,"

[10]Jack Kerouac, *On the Road* (New York: Viking Press, 1955): 162 in the Signet edition.

[11]Nat Shapiro and Nat Hentoff, *Hear Me Talkin' to Ya* (New York: Rinehart, 1955): 354.

CD 3:17. "Koko," Charlie Parker, alto saxophone; Dizzy Gillespie, trumpet and piano; Curly Russell, bass; and Max Roach, drums

Section 1: The head

0:00

The trumpet (Gillespie) and saxophone (Parker) play the precomposed melody, called the **head**, in unison. The trumpet uses a mute, a cone-shaped device stuck in the bell of the trumpet to change the timbre. Although the meter is simple duple, it is obscured by the pervasive and quick syncopations. The drummer, Max Roach, recalled that even he at first found it difficult to hear the meter.

0:06

Unlike many heads, this one has short improvised sections. The trumpet takes the first solo. Although it may be difficult to hear at this tempo, the fast notes are always in a rhythm of long-short, long-short, instead of all equal durations. This pattern is known as **swing rhythm** and is the default playing style in many jazz genres.

0:12

After the trumpet plays one phrase, the saxophone takes over and plays another improvised solo. In typical bebop fashion, the drummer mostly keeps a fast but steady swing rhythm with metal brushes on the hi-hat cymbal, while the bass player plays plucked notes at a constant rate, forming a stable backdrop for the soloist.

0:19

The improvised section of the head ends, and the trumpet returns to play a precomposed melody in parallel with the saxophone. The two play the complex tune exactly two scale steps apart (the interval of a third), and then shift to unison to conclude the head.

Section 2: The chorus (first time)

0:25

The next section of the piece, called the chorus, has no precomposed melody but does have a progression of chords that serve as the basis for improvisation. Gillespie at this point has set down his trumpet and now plays those chords on the piano. The drummer switches from soft brushes to louder sticks, and Parker's solo begins.

0:28

Parker's solo artfully contrasts quick streams of notes with successions of variations on particular motives, such as this one. Note how in the third and fourth repetition of the motive, one of the pitches changes to accommodate the change in harmony.

0:32

The following graphic shows how Parker's solo corresponds to the harmony. Although these chords are much more complex than those in much classical European art music of the eighteenth and nineteenth centuries, a good jazz improviser will still follow the same careful succession of consonance and dissonance, so that melodic pitches not in the harmony are followed by (resolve to) harmonic pitches.

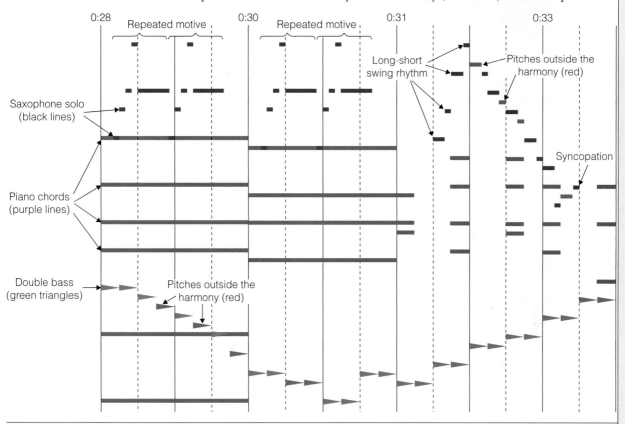

0:40

Parker brings back the melody he improvised at the beginning of the chorus. A good jazz improviser often uses repetition to create unity in the improvisation.

Section 3: The chorus (second time)

1:16

The succession of chords that define the chorus repeat now, but with a newly improvised solo over them. Although it is nearly obscured by the fast tempo, Parker here plays a fragment from another piece, "High Society," an old Dixieland tune.[12] Quotations such as this can be inside jokes for the musicians and attentive listeners, and also demonstrate the improviser's skill in extemporaneously combining the fragment with the current piece's harmonic progression.

[12]Carl Woideck points out this quotation in *Charlie Parker: His Music and Life* (Ann Arbor MI: University of Michigan Press, 1996: 116.

CD 3:17. "Koko," Charlie Parker, alto saxophone; Dizzy Gillespie, trumpet and piano; Curly Russell, bass; and Max Roach, drums *(continued)*

| 1:54 | Parker again returns to a variation of the melody he used to open the improvisation. |

Section 4: Drum solo

| 2:07 | Now the drummer Roach, who had been providing a steady backbone to the complex rhythms, plays a solo in which the rhythms are so pervasively syncopated that our impression of the beat may disappear. The complex polyrhythms Roach plays, with typical bebop bravura against an unheard reference beat, leave us floating, unsure where the beat will fall. |

iStockphoto

Section 5: Head

| 2:30 | The beat comes back dramatically as Gillespie and Parker play the opening head in unison. |

| 2:36 | The improvised trumpet solo phrase of the head. |

| 2:43 | The improvised saxophone solo phrase of the head. |

| 2:49 | The final composed phrase in parallel thirds. |

Listening Exercise 15	CD 3:17 "Koko"

1. What is the texture of the first part of the head (0:00 to 0:18)?
   a. monophony with drums and cymbals
   b. heterophony with drums and cymbals
   c. polyphony with drums and cymbals
   d. homophony with drums and cymbals

2. What is the texture of the chorus (0:25 to 2:07)?
   a. monophony with drums and cymbals
   b. heterophony with drums and cymbals
   c. polyphony with drums and cymbals
   d. homophony with drums and cymbals

3. Which of the following best describes the piano part beginning at 0:25?
   a. arpeggiations (notes of the chords played one at a time)
   b. background chords, sometimes short, sometimes sustained
   c. single-line counter-melody accompaniment

4. Which instrument of the drum set does Max Roach not play during his solo (2:07 to 2:30)?
   a. snare drum
   b. bass drum
   c. hi-hat cymbal

You can take this Listening Exercise online and receive feedback or e-mail answers to your instructor at the World Music Resource Center.

is Parker's own composition, although it is based on the chord progressions from "Cherokee." Because this recording was intended for 10-inch 78 records, which had a very short capacity, the performance is less than three minutes long. In a live performance, however, this same piece could last much longer, with each musician given a turn to play longer solos.

In the next few years, Parker's performances would electrify the jazz world. By the 1950s, however, Parker's addictions to heroin and alcohol were devastating his music and his health. He died in 1955 at the age of thirty-four.

POPULAR MUSIC IN AMERICA

ROCK AND ROLL

On a summer night in 1954 in Memphis, Tennessee, popular music producer Sam Phillips was trying out a new singer and guitarist in his recording studio, a nineteen-year-old truck driver named Elvis Presley (Figure 16.15). Phillips had arranged for another guitarist and bass player from a local country band to back up Presley, but their performances of old country ballads sounded awkward and uninspiring to Phillips. Frustrated, Phillips told them to take a break.

During the break, Presley began fooling around with an upbeat blues tune, "That's Alright Mama" by Arthur Crudup. Since at least the 1940s, blues notes, prominent bass patterns, and blues harmonic progressions had been used not just in the traditional slow soulful songs that gave blues their name but also in danceable, up-tempo tunes sometimes called jump blues or **rhythm and blues**. The lead guitarist joined Presley, backing up his enthusiastic voice with

FIGURE 16.15

Elvis Presley (left) singing and playing rhythm guitar with Scotty Moore, guitar, and Bill Black, double bass. A drum set is in the background.

licks from the tradition of African-American blues guitarists. The double bass player plucked the strings hard enough so that they rebounded against the fingerboard, a percussive technique known as "slap bass."

The infectious combination caught the ear of Phillips from the recording booth. "What's that you're doing?" he asked. "Oh, nothing," they replied. Phillips told them to hang on a second while he rewound the tape machine and to start again. When they finished recording, the bass player, Bill Black, said, "Damn. Get that on the radio and they'll run us out of town." Black's joke referred to the fact that, at the time, most radio stations, especially those in the southern United States, were racially segregated, and the major record companies released the music of African Americans on separate labels targeted only to those communities. But getting "That's All Right Mama" on white radio stations was exactly what Phillips intended, and soon the song became the first in a remarkable series of hit tunes recorded by Presley.

Phillips saw that America's post-war prosperity had created a lucrative new market—teenagers with disposable income—that had no interest in crooning cowboys or sophisticated jazz. Young people were not spending money at jazz clubs but instead on new inexpensive and high-quality recording formats—"singles" and LPs—of fun, danceable tunes. Phillips was not the first producer to get white country musicians to record rhythm and blues, but Presley was the first to become internationally famous as a singer of what was being called a new genre: **rock and roll**, or, later, simply rock.

Although early rock and roll was mostly a new name for white musicians performing what had been an African-American style, by the 1960s, the genre had developed the distinctive characteristics that would define it up to the present day:

◆ **The prominent use of electric guitar.** North American instrument makers since the 1920s had experimented with ways to enable the normally quiet tone of the guitar to compete in big bands and noisy dance halls. By the late 1940s, instrument makers had perfected the modern electric guitar, in which the vibrations of the strings are converted to changes in electrical voltages, amplified, and sent to a loudspeaker. Because hollow acoustic resonators no longer performed this amplification function, in the 1960s, they were often replaced with the solid bodies of the familiar rock guitar. At that time, rock guitarists such as Jimi Hendrix combined virtuosic technique with electronic distortion (changing the timbre by deliberately pushing an audio signal past the amplification limit), feedback (creating tones through the recirculation of sounds from the loudspeaker back into the guitar microphones or "pickups"), and extreme loudness.

◆ **Small ensembles.** Like many country and bluegrass groups but unlike jazz big bands, rock bands usually consist of only three to six players, who often both sing and play instruments. In addition to the electric guitar, modern rock groups normally include a drum set (as in jazz) and an electric bass guitar. Some bands also include keyboard instruments, but, after the 1950s, wind instruments such as the saxophone were less common.

◆ **Emphasis on singing.** Unlike jazz pieces, rock compositions are nearly always sung, and the lead singer frequently projects a marketable personality in dress, hair style, and attitude.

- **Strong beats within a four-beat cycle.** The rhythms of rock are usually not as complex or as syncopated as those of jazz. Instead, the rhythmic propulsion is focused on the drum set, which generally emphasizes beats two and four of a four-beat cycle, articulated on the snare drum, while the bass drum plays on beats one and three.

- **Creative use of technology.** Whereas record companies had previously sought to record musicians who had already become popular as live performers and to capture the sound of a live performance, Sam Phillips wanted to create a particular, marketable sound directly in the recording studio. Since that time, rock groups have often put their creative efforts first into studio recordings and taken advantage of techniques unavailable in live performance, such as multitrack recording (the ability to layer multiple separate recordings).

- **Emotional, powerful styles.** As in blues, rock singers cultivate an extroverted, emotional singing style but, unlike blues singers, often emphasize power and rebellious excitement. The common use of extremely loud volumes and "grungy" timbres is also a reflection of rock's emphasis on primal energy.

- **Simplified harmonic progressions.** Rock and roll songs from the 1950s used only a small number of standard harmonic progressions, such as the twelve-bar blues. Although rock songs since then have used many other progressions, including some outside of traditional major and minor modes, the harmonies are relatively simple and change rather slowly compared to those in modern jazz.

After the prosperous and conservative 1950s had passed, America's youth confronted issues of civil rights and the war in Vietnam, and rock music led this cultural rebellion. The complex poetry and tradition of social protest in the Folk Music Revival made its way into rock when folksinger **Bob Dylan** "went electric"—that is, adopted the electric guitar and other idioms of rock—in 1965 (Figure 16.16). However, the group that most famously represented this transition to innovative anthems of cultural revolution was the Beatles.

The Beatles were at the forefront of the so-called British Invasion, bands from the United Kingdom who came to dominate much of rock music in the United States, and so represented the newly international scope of popular music genres. From the time of their first hits in 1963 to their breakup in 1970, the Beatles' early simple love songs evolved into complex works making use of classical and unconventional instruments, special electronic and studio recording effects, and oblique and surreal lyrics, sometimes in reference to or inspired by psychedelic drugs. They influenced many other **progressive rock** bands, which in the 1970s, emulated this seriousness of purpose, experimentation, and influences from art music.

However, as the popular music industry greatly expanded in the 1970s, it tended to discourage experimentation and social protest in favor of powerful sounds to accompany theatrical performances in large venues. **Hard rock** and, later, **heavy metal** came to represent these forms and their self-conscious distance from smoother, more inoffensive pop songs. The perceived pretentiousness of these bands and hypocrisy of rebellious individualism preached from the platform of corporate conformity led to the

Michael Ochs Archives/Getty Images

FIGURE 16.16

Folk-rock musician Bob Dylan performs for the first time on electric guitar at the Newport Folk Festival in July 1965.

backlash known as **punk rock** (for example, the Sex Pistols) in the late 1970s and the calculated irony of **new wave** (the Talking Heads) in the early 1980s. These are just a few of the many subgenres that have proliferated in rock music to the present, including punk descendants such as **thrash metal** and neo-hard rock bands known as **grunge**.

FROM SOUL TO RAP

Although rock and roll took its heritage of rhythm and blues down a particular path, the roots of this music continued to be a vital force in the often segregated African-American musical communities. The expressive, melismatic, nearly ecstatic singing in gospel music became an important fixture of secular rhythm and blues in the 1950s, and the responsorial singing between a soloist and church choir became exchanges between a lead singer and "backup" singers. Unlike the small, tight ensembles of rock and roll and bluegrass, rhythm and blues bands grew to include not only backup singers but also a big-band-like ensemble of wind instruments that often played a responsorial role similar to that of the backup singers. Bands would also include electric guitars, an electric bass, drum set, and a "horn" section of trumpets, trombones, and saxophones, creating a dense texture of sound.

In the 1960s, the term **soul music** came to replace rhythm and blues as the genre evolved, and this sound also was associated with particular African-American record labels. Singers such as **Aretha Franklin** matched the expressive power and popularity of rock and roll bands during this period and often reflected concerns of the African-American community. If rock and roll simplified the harmonic progressions of jazz, soul music took this process even further. Often a song would teeter back and forth between just two chords, focusing attention instead on the repetitive "groove" within its dense textures.

In the 1970s, **James Brown**'s emphasis on texture and rhythm would sometimes halt the flow of harmonic progression completely, creating the new style known as **funk**. These layered textures would include a prominent slap bass line, and wind instruments (saxophones, trumpets, and trombones) would stab punctuations in the music, as would Brown's intermittent whoops, yells, grunts, and screams (Figure 16.17).

The funk of Brown and others was ever popular at dance parties in urban black neighborhoods in cities such as New York, Detroit, and Chicago, where the creative focus was not on a live band but rather an MC (master of ceremonies) or DJ (disc jockey) who would creatively juxtapose songs using multiple LP turntables. The dancers especially liked the purely instrumental sections or **breaks**, which were originally used for transition or contrast but which were perfect for dancing.

DJs such as **Grandmaster Flash**, often from black Caribbean immigrant communities, learned how to cue up break sections on a second turntable so they could seamlessly stitch together breaks from multiple recordings. Sometimes DJs would add to the beat themselves through rhythmically moving the record back and forth, or **scratching**, creating distinctive electronic whoops as the turntable needle

Michael Ochs Archives/Getty Images

FIGURE 16.17

James Brown and his band performing on the television show Soul Train in 1973.

passed quickly over the record. Such innovations essentially made the turntable into a musical instrument, and this art became known as **turntablism**.

As DJs presided over these block parties, some would also speak, or "rap," rhythmic rhymes to the dancers. This style, which had antecedents in the Jamaican and African-American communities from street preachers to the boastful rhymes of boxer Muhammad Ali, became known as **rap music**. The term **hip-hop** has since been used as a general term for African-American styles with these elements. In the early 1980s, the Los Angeles group **NWA** and others turned hip-hop's previous focus on dance and braggadocio to the concerns of inner-city blacks. This so-called **gangsta rap** was criticized for its perceived misogyny and condoning of violence, but others opened up hip-hop subjects to more positive treatments of social concerns.

Technology was an important factor in hip-hop's innovations. Whereas DJs of the 1970s used turntables to splice together prerecorded breaks, hip-hop musicians in the 1980s made use of digital **sampling** technology, that is, the ability to digitally record and easily play back any sound source. Musicians often used **drum machines**, an application of this technology that allowed the digital creation of drum parts without a live drummer. Therefore, hip-hop performances might include no live musical instruments at all.

ELECTRONICA

Copyright laws prevented DJs from releasing commercial recordings of the breaks put together from other recordings, but many musicians in the 1970s created their own breaks for dance clubs, aided by the availability of inexpensive recording technology and electronic **synthesizers**. Bands such as **Tangerine Dream** demonstrated how synthesizers could create rhythmic textures in addition to or even instead of drums. Dance music of the late 1970s discarded rock's insistent emphasis of beats two and four and instead planted a powerful bass drum on every beat (sometimes called "four on the floor"). This music became known as **disco**, a shortened version of *discotheque*, a European term for dance club.

A refined form of disco music with more conventional song structures soon gained great popularity outside of African-American dance clubs. Their thick, studio-produced textures would often include synthesizers, funk bass, strings of the violin family, and other orchestral instruments. Although disco in this form died out in the 1980s, musicians and DJs in the United States and Europe continued to experiment with danceable drum machine and synthesizer textures.

Aided by the technology of **MIDI sequencers**, which allowed them to program all the notes played by synthesizers and drum machines in repetitive **loops**, these composers stripped disco of its empty lyrics, its lyrical strings, most of its harmonic progressions, and its verse and refrain song forms. What remained was an insistent electronic beat, frequently a constant rapid-fire hi-hat cymbal, 16-beat phrases, novel (often sampled) timbres, and variety created by sudden changes in the texture or "breaks." The result was sometimes known as **techno** because of its sometimes unrelentingly mechanistic aesthetic but has since become more generally known as **electronica** or simply electronic dance music.

Since the wide availability of personal computers in the 1980s, electronica composers have been able to create their works entirely independently of bands, singers, and expensive recording studios. Major record labels in the United States have largely shunned electronica because of its lack of lead singers and live bands to market, although electronica styles are popular in commercials and film and television scores. This neglect and the sharing of this music over the Internet have allowed composers the independence to experiment, often resulting in a bewildering proliferation of subgenres and styles. (Some of the most prominent include trance, industrial, drum and bass, hardcore, ambient, and acid jazz.)

THE SHRINKING MUSICAL PLANET

In 1992, French composers Michel Sanchez and Erik Mouquet released *Deep Forest*, an album in which they layered samples from various ethnomusicological field recordings from Africa and the Solomon islands on top of moderate tempo techno beats, synthesized strings, and gentle chord progressions (often adding Western harmonies to the original recording). To Sanchez's and Mouquet's many admirers, their music represented a warm expression of global harmony. More cynical critics, however, questioned the ethics and legality of several of these instances of sampling, which was done without the knowledge of the original musicians.

The "world music" label of the 1970s and 1980s gave way to "worldbeat" and "global pop" and a new set of musical questions. The age of the Internet has opened up an unprecedented opportunity to exchange information, including music, throughout the planet. Genres such as electronica cannot be called North American music anymore, and composers can easily draw upon an expanding universe of both influences and actual sounds.

Software such as Apple's GarageBand and the free exchange of loops on the Internet and commercial CDs allows users to participate in this new compositional medium, sometimes called meta-music or mash-ups, that is, new music composed through the creative combination of other precomposed building blocks. The use of loops and samples without their creator's permission has been a contentious issue, leading some to call for a revision or elimination of copyright laws and others for sensitivity for cultural and composer rights.

The ease with which composers can use samples and loops originating in other cultures has led in some cases to a renewal of the aesthetic of exoticism discussed in Chapter 1. But new global access to information can also lead us to consider more carefully how to respect music and its makers as we are conscious of its cultural and social context.

REFERENCES

DISCOGRAPHY

Nakai, R. Carlos. *Canyon Trilogy: Native American Flute Music*. Phoenix AZ: Canyon Records CD CR-610, 1989.

Southern Traditional Singers. *The Social Harp: Early American Shape-Note Songs*. Rounder CD 0094, 1994.

Various artists. *Anthology of American Folk Music*, 5 vols. ed. Harry Smith. Washington DC: Smithsonian Folkways CD SFW40090, 1952/1997.

Various artists. *Classic African American Ballads from Smithsonian Folkways*. Washington DC: Smithsonian Folkways CD SFW40191, 2006.

Various artists. *Classic African American Gospel from Smithsonian Folkways*. Washington DC: Smithsonian Folkways CD SFW40194, 2008.

Various artists. *Classic Bluegrass from Smithsonian Folkways*. Washington DC: Smithsonian Folkways CD SFW40092, 2002.

Various artists. *Classic Blues from Smithsonian Folkways*. Washington DC: Smithsonian Folkways CD SFW40134, 2003.

Various artists. *Classic Canadian Songs from Smithsonian Folkways*. Washington DC: Smithsonian Folkways CD SFW40539, 2006.

Various artists. *Classic Southern Gospel from Smithsonian Folkways*. Washington DC: Smithsonian Folkways CD SFW40137, 2005.

Various artists. *Creation's Journey: Native American Music*. Washington DC: Smithsonian Folkways CD SF40410, 1994.

Various artists. *Mountain Music of Kentucky*. Washington DC: Smithsonian Folkways CD SFW 40077, 1994.

Various artists. *The Smithsonian Collection of Classic Jazz*. 5 vols. Washington DC: Smithsonian CD RD 033, 1973/1987.

 ## BOOK COMPANION WEBSITE

You will find flashcards, a glossary, and tutorial quizzes, as well as other materials that will help you succeed in this course, at the *Music of the Peoples of the World, 2nd Edition,* Companion Website at www.cengage.com/music/alves/world2e.

BIBLIOGRAPHY

GENERAL

Broughton, Simon, et al., ed. *World Music: The Rough Guide* (2 vols). London: The Rough Guides, 2000.

Sadie, Stanley, ed. *The New Grove Dictionary of Music and Musicians*, 2nd ed. London: Macmillan, 2001.

Porter, James, and Timothy Rice, eds. *The Garland Encyclopedia of World Music*. New York: Garland, 1998.

CHAPTER 6

Arom, Simha. *African Polyphony and Polyrhythm: Musical Structure and Methodology*. Translated by Martin Thom, Barbara Tuckett, and Raymond Boyd. Cambridge: Cambridge University Press, 1991.

Barz, Gregory. *Music in East Africa*. Oxford: Oxford University Press, 2004.

Bebey, Francis. *African Music: A People's Art*. New York: L. Hill, 1975.

Berliner, Paul. *The Soul of Mbira: Music and Traditions of the Shona People of Zimbabwe*. Berkeley: University of California Press, 1978.

Charry, Eric. *Mande Music: Traditional and Modern Music of the Maninka and Mandinka of Western Africa*. Chicago: University of Chicago Press, 2000.

Chernoff, John Miller. *African Rhythm and African Sensibility: Aesthetics and Social Action in African Musical Idioms*. Chicago: University of Chicago Press, 1979.

Floyd, Malcolm, ed. *Composing the Music of Africa: Composition, Interpretation, and Realisation*. Brookfield, VT: Ashgate, 1999.

Graham, Ronnie. *The Da Capo Guide to Contemporary African Music*. New York: Da Capo Press, 1988.

Jones, A. M. *Studies in African Music*. London: Oxford University Press, 1959.

Merriam, Alan P. *African Music in Perspective*. New York: Garland, 1982.

Nketia, J. H. Kwabena. *The Music of Africa*. New York: W. W. Norton, 1974.

Stone, Ruth. *Music in West Africa*. Oxford: Oxford University Press, 2004.

CHAPTER 7

Cohen, Dalia. *Palestinian Arab Music: A Maqam Tradition in Practice*. Chicago: University of Chicago Press, 2006.

Danielson, Virginia. *The Voice of Egypt: Umm Kulthum, Arabic Song, and Egyptian Society in the Twentieth Century*. Chicago: University of Chicago Press, 1997.

During, Jean, and Zia Mirabdolbaghi. *The Art of Persian Music*. Washington DC: Mage, 1991.

Farmer, Henry George. *A History of Arabian Music to the XIIIth Century*. London: Luzac, 1929.

Idelsohn, Abraham Z. *Jewish Music: In Its Historical Development*. 1929. Reprint, New York: Schocken, 1967.

Marcus, Scott Lloyd. *Music in Egypt*. Oxford: Oxford University Press, 2007.

Racy, Ali Jihad. *Making Music in the Arab World: The Culture and Artistry of Tarab*. Cambridge: Cambridge University Press, 2003.

Rothmüller, Aron Marko. *The Music of the Jews: An Historical Appreciation, rev. ed.* Cranbury, NJ: A. S. Barnes & Company, 1975.

Sapoznik, Henry. *Klezmer!: Jewish Music from Old World to Our World*. New York: Schirmer, 1999.

Shiloah, Amnon. *Music in the World of Islam: A Sociocultural Study*. Detroit: Wayne State University Press, 1995.

Signell, Karl L. *Makam: Modal Practice in Turkish Art Music*. Seattle: Asian Music Publications, 1977.

Stokes, Martin. *The Arabesk Debate: Music and Musicians in Modern Turkey*. Oxford: Oxford University Press, 1992.

Touma, Habib. *The Music of the Arabs*. Portland, OR: Amadeus Press, 1996.

Zonis, Ella. *Classical Persian Music: An Introduction*. Cambridge, MA: Harvard University Press, 1973.

CHAPTER 8

Haslund-Christensen, Henning. *The Music of the Mongols: Eastern Mongolia*. New York: Da Capo Press, 1971.

Levin, Theodore. *The Hundred Thousand Fools of God.* Bloomington, IN: Indiana University Press, 1996.

_____. *Where Rivers and Mountains Sing: Sound, Music, and Nomadism in Tuva and Beyond.* Bloomington, IN: Indiana University Press, 2006.

Norbu, Jamyang, ed. *Zlos-gar: Performing Traditions of Tibet.* Dharamsala, H.P., India: Library of Tibetan Works & Archives, 1986.

Pegg, Carole. *Mongolian Music, Dance, and Oral Narrative.* Seattle: University of Washington Press, 2001.

Sakata, Hiromi Lorraine. *Music in the Mind: The Concepts of Music and Musician in Afghanistan.* Kent, OH: Kent State University Press, 1983.

Slobin, Mark. *Music in the Culture of Northern Afghanistan.* Tucson: University of Arizona Press, 1976.

CHAPTER 9

Bor, Joep, ed. *The Raga Guide: A Survey of 74 Hindustani Ragas.* Netherlands: Nimbus Records, 1999.

Capwell, Charles. *The Music of the Bauls of Bengal.* Kent, OH: Kent State University Press, 1986.

Jairazbhoy, Nazir. *The Ragas of North Indian Music: Their Structure and Evolution.* Middletown, CT: Wesleyan University Press, 1971.

Neuman, Daniel M. *The Life of Music in North India: The Organization of an Artistic Tradition.* Detroit: Wayne State University Press, 1980.

Pesch, Ludwig. *The Illustrated Companion to South Indian Classical Music.* Delhi: Oxford University Press, 1999.

Ruckert, George E. *Music in North India.* Oxford: Oxford University Press, 2004.

Shankar, Ravi. *My Music, My Life.* New York: Simon and Schuster, 1968.

Sorrell, Neil. *Indian Music in Performance: A Practical Introduction.* New York: New York University Press, 1980.

Viswanathan, T., and Matthew Harp Allen. *Music in South India.* Oxford: Oxford University Press, 2004.

Wade, Bonnie C. *Music in India: The Classical Traditions.* Englewood Cliffs, NJ: Prentice-Hall, 1979.

CHAPTER 10

Baranovitch, Nimrod. *China's New Voices: Popular Music, Ethnicity, Gender and Politics, 1978-1997.* Los Angeles: University of California Press, 2003.

Gulik, Robert Hans van. *The Lore of the Chinese Lute: An Essay in Ch'in Ideology.* Tokyo: Sophia University, 1940.

Hsu, Wen-Ying. *The Guqin: A Chinese Stringed Instrument, Its History and Theory.* Los Angeles: Wen Ying Studies, 1978.

Jones, Stephen. *Folk Music of China: Living Instrumental Traditions.* Oxford: Clarendon Press; 1995.

Lai, T. C. *Jade Flute: The Story of Chinese Music.* New York: Schocken Books, 1981.

Mingyueh, Liang. *Music of the Billion: An Introduction to Chinese Musical Culture.* New York: Heinrichshofen Edition, 1985.

Wiant, Bliss. *The Music of China.* Hong Kong: Chung Chi Publications, Chung Chi College, Chinese University of Hong Kong, 1965.

Wichmann, Elizabeth. *Listening to Theatre: The Aural Dimension of Beijing Opera.* Honolulu: University of Hawaii Press, 1991.

Witzleben, J. Lawrence. *"Silk and Bamboo" Music in Shanghai.* Kent OH: Kent State University Press, 1995.

Yung, Bell, ed. *Celestial Airs of Antiquity: Music of the Seven-String Zither of China.* Madison, WI: A-R Editions, 1997.

CHAPTER 11

Harich-Schneider, Eta. *A History of Japanese Music.* London: Oxford University Press, 1973.

Isaku, Patia R. *Mountain Storm, Pine Breeze: Folk Song in Japan.* Tucson, AZ: University of Arizona Press, 1981.

Kishibe, Shigeo. *The Traditional Music of Japan.* Tokyo: Kokusai Bunka Shinkokai, 1969.

Malm, William P. *Japanese Music and Musical Instruments.* Tokyo and Rutland, VT: C. E. Tuttle Co., 1959.

_____. *Six Hidden Views of Japanese Music.* Berkeley: University of California Press, 1986.

Tanabe, Hisao. *Japanese Music*, 2nd ed. Tokyo: Kokusai Bunka Shinkokai, 1959.

Wade, Bonnie C. *Music in Japan.* Oxford: Oxford University Press, 2005.

CHAPTER 12

Brinner, Benjamin. *Music in Central Java.* New York: Oxford University Press, 2008.

Gold, Lisa. *Music in Bali*. New York: Oxford University Press, 2005.

Hood, Mantle. *The Evolution of the Javanese Gamelan* (3 vols). Wilhelmshaven, Netherlands: Heinrichshofen, 1980.

Kunst, Jaap. *Music in Java: Its History, Its Theory and Its Technique*, 3rd ed. The Hague: Nijhoff, 1973.

McPhee, Colin. *Music in Bali*. New Haven, CT: Yale University Press, 1966.

Pickvance, Richard. *A Gamelan Manual: A Player's Guide to the Central Javanese Gamelan*. London: Jaman Mas Books, 2005.

Sorrell, Neil. *A Guide to the Gamelan*. London, Boston: Faber and Faber, 1990.

Sumarsam. *Gamelan: Cultural Interaction and Musical Development in Central Java*. Chicago: University of Chicago Press, 1995.

Tenzer, Michael. *Balinese Music*. Berkeley: Periplus Editions, 1991.

_____. *Gamelan Gong Kebyar: The Art of Twentieth-Century Balinese Music*. Chicago: University of Chicago Press, 2000.

CHAPTER 13

Bartók, Béla. *Hungarian Folk Music*. London: Oxford University Press, H. Milford, 1931.

_____. *Rumanian Folk Music*. The Hague: Martinus Nijhoff, 1967.

_____. *Yugoslav Folk Music*. Albany, NY: State University of New York Press, 1978.

Czekanowska, Anna. *Polish Folk Music: Slavonic Heritage, Polish Tradition, Contemporary Trends*. Cambridge: Cambridge University Press, 1990.

Kodály, Zoltán. *Folk Music of Hungary*. New York: Da Capo Press, 1987.

Krustev, Venelin Georgiev. *Bulgarian Music*. Sofia: Sofia-Press, 1978.

Olson, Laura J. *Performing Russia: Folk Revival and Russian Identity*. New York: Routledge, 2004.

Prokhorov, Vadim. *Russian Folk Songs: Musical Genres and History*. Lanham, MD: Scarecrow Press, 2002.

Rice, Timothy. *May It Fill Your Soul: Experiencing Bulgarian Music*. Chicago: University of Chicago Press, 1994.

_____. *Music in Bulgaria*. New York: Oxford University Press, 2004.

Sárosi, Bálint. *Gypsy Music*. Translated by Fred Macnicol. Budapest: Corvina Press, 1978.

Warner, Elizabeth. *Russian Traditional Folk Song*. Hull, UK: Hull University Press, 1990.

CHAPTER 14

Duckworth, William. *A Creative Approach to Music Fundamentals*. New York: Cengage, 2009.

Grout, Donald J., Claude V. Palisca, and J. Peter Burkholder. *A History of Western Music*, 7th ed. New York: W. W. Norton, 2005.

Hast, Dorothea E. *Music in Ireland*. London: Oxford University Press, 2004.

Karpeles, Maud. *An Introduction to English Folk Song*. London: Oxford University.

Ling, Jan. *A History of European Folk Music*. Translated by Linda and Robert Schenk. Rochester, NY: University of Rochester Press, 1997.

Nettl, Bruno. *Folk and Traditional Music of the Western Continents*, 3rd ed. Englewood Cliffs, NJ: Prentice Hall, 1990.

Ó Riada, Seán. *Our Musical Heritage*. Mountrath, Ireland: Dolmen Press, 1982.

Totton, Robin. *Song of the Outcasts: An Introduction to Flamenco*. Portland, OR: Amadeus, 2003.

CHAPTER 15

Appleby, David P. *The Music of Brazil*. Austin: University of Texas Press, 1983.

Béhague, Gerard. *Music in Latin America: An Introduction*. Englewood Cliffs, NJ: Prentice-Hall, 1979.

Clark, Walter Aaron, ed. *From Tejano to Tango: Latin American Popular Music*. New York: Routledge, 2002.

Feldman, Carolyn. *Black Rhythms of Peru: Reviving African Musical Heritage in the Black Pacific*. Middletown, CT: Wesleyan University Press, 2006.

Geijerstam, Claes af. *Popular Music in Mexico*. Albuquerque: University of New Mexico Press, 1976.

Otter, Elisabeth den. *Music and Dance of Indians and Mestizos in an Andean Valley of Peru*. Delft, The Netherlands: Eburon, 1985.

Schechter, John M., ed. *Music in Latin American Culture: Regional Traditions*. New York: Schirmer Books, 1999.

Schreiner, Claus. *Música Brasileira: A History of Popular Music and the People of Brazil*. Translated by Mark Weinstein. New York: Marion Boyars, 1993.

Sheehy, Daniel. *Mariachi Music in America*. New York: Oxford University Press, 2006.

Stevenson, Robert M. *Music in Mexico, A Historical Survey*. New York: Crowell, 1952.

CHAPTER 16

Bierhorst, John. *A Cry From the Earth: Music of the North American Indians*. Santa Fe, NM: Ancient City Press, 1979.

Butler, Mark J. *Unlocking the Groove: Rhythm, Meter, and Musical Design in Electronic Dance Music*. Bloomington, IN: Indiana University Press, 2006.

Cobb, Buell E. *The Sacred Harp: A Tradition and Its Music*. Athens, GA: University of Georgia Press, 1978.

Cohen, Norm. *Folk Music: A Regional Exploration*. Westport, CT: Greenwood Press, 2005.

Curtis, Natalie. *The Indians' Book: Songs and Legends of the American Indians*. 1923. Reprint, New York: Dover, 1968.

Davis, Ronald L. *A History of Music in American Life*, 3 vols. Malabar, FL: R. Krieger, 1980.

Gioia, Ted. *The History of Jazz*. New York: Oxford University Press, 1997.

Herndon, Marcia. *Native American Music*. Norwood, PA: Norwood Editions, 1980.

Hitchcock, H. Wiley. *Music in the United States: A Historical Introduction*, 3rd ed. Englewood Cliffs, NJ: Prentice Hall, 1988.

Lomax, Alan. *The Folksongs of North America*. Garden City, NY: Doubleday, 1960.

Malone, Bill C. *Country music U.S.A.: A Fifty-Year History*. Austin, TX: University of Texas Press, 1968.

Nettl, Bruno. *North American Indian Musical Styles*. Philadelphia, PA: American Folklore Society, 1954.

_____. *Blackfoot Musical Thought: Comparative Perspectives*. Kent, OH: Kent State University Press, 1989.

_____. *Folk and Traditional Music of the Western Continents*. Englewood Cliffs, NJ: Prentice-Hall, 1973.

Shapiro, Peter. *The Rough Guide to Hip Hop*. London: Rough Guides, 2001.

Shipton, Alyn. *A New History of Jazz*. New York: Continuum, 2001.

Southern, Eileen. *The Music of Black Americans: A History*. New York: Norton, 1971.

Ward, Ed, Geoffrey Stokes, and Ken Tucker. *Rock of Ages: The Rolling Stone History of Rock & Roll*. New York: Rolling Stone Press, 1986.

Weissman, Dick. *Which Side Are You On?: An Inside History of the Folk Music Revival in America*. New York: Continuum, 2005.

INDEX AND GLOSSARY

This index also serves as a brief glossary. Short definitions of terms appear in italics after the terms, and further details about the terms can be found in the pages cited.

A

a cappella (*choral music without instruments*), 69
accelerando (*gradual increase in tempo*), 19
accent (*loud or sharp attack*), 22, 48, 88, 100, 313
accidental (*note outside the scale*), 86, 98
accordion (*reed aerophone with keys and hand-pumped bellows*), 94, 100, 102, 250, 258, 259, 263, 270, 275, 276, 277, 301, 304, 308
acid jazz (*genre of electronic dance music*), 356
Ade, King Sunny (*West African popular musician*), 74
adhan (*Islamic call to prayer*), 81
adungu (*bow harp from Uganda*), 52
aerophone (*wind instrument*), 31, 32, 36–38, 50–51, *see also* individual instruments
Afghanistan, 80, 106, 122
Africa, 5, 44–75; Arabic influence, 44, 45, 51; British influence, 69; Christian influence, 55; Cuban influence, 68; dance, 2, 47, 53–59, 64, 68–69; European influence, 69, 269, 276; family relationships, 45–46; geography, 44, 54; history, 44–46; Indonesian influence, 44; influence of India, 44; influence of United States, 67–70; influence on Latin America, 54, 296, 298–301, 309–315; influence on United States, 321–323, 345; Islamic influence, 45, 49, 50, 55, 60; language and music, 46–48, 50, 57–58; meter, 46–48, 57–59, 62, 65–66; musical form, 16, 47, 57–59, 68; musical instruments, 47–53; nationalism, 46, 68; participatory arts, 47; popular music, 46, 60–61, 64, 67–73, 75; texture, 272; *see also* individual countries
African Americans 3, 67, 296–298, 309–312, 321–324, 328, 329, 340–352, 354–355
Afrika Shrine, 67–68
Afro-Beat (*African popular music style*), 68
agogô (*double metal bell in Brazilian samba band*), 54, 310, 313–314
air column (*aerophone vibrating space*), 36
aitake (*sho chord transitions*), 200

alap (*non-pulsatile melodic introduction in Indian music*), 134, 141–144, 147, 148, 155
alapana, *see* alap
Albania, 247
Algeria, 94
Alhambra, Spain, 90
Ali, Muhammad (*American boxer*), 355
al-jil (*Middle Eastern popular music style*), 94
alphorn (*large Central European buzzed-lip aerophone*), 277
Altan (*Irish popular music band*), 282
alternation playing (*performance of a single melody by multiple players alternating notes*), 51, 313, 316, 317, *see also* interlocking patterns
alus (*Javanese characteristic of refinement*), 219
amplification, electronic, 93, 250, 255, 259, 282, 312, 327, 346, 352
amplitude (*sound wave height/loudness*), 17
Andalucía, Spain, 288, 290, 294
Andean countries, 296–299, 316–318
anga (*beat grouping in South Indian meter*), 139
angle harp, *see* harp, angle
angsel (*break phrase or cue in Balinese music*), 237, 241
anhemitonic pentatonic modes (*five-tone modes without semitones*), 168, 254, 265, 268, 274, 336
Anloga, Ghana, 46
antara (*Andean panpipe*), *see* siku
antara (*second half in Indian alap form*), 142, 144
anthem (*European-American religious choral form*), 325
antiphonal form (*alternation between groups*), 85, 97, 263, 265–266, 338
anupallavi (*contrasting section in South Indian vocal forms*), 148, 150
apala (*West African drum*), 68
apartheid, 3, 46, 69
Arabic music, 76–94; and dance, 94; folk music 93–94; influence of India, 94; influence on Central Asia, 106; influence on Iran, 95–96; influence on Jewish music, 100, 104; influence on Indonesia, 242–243; influence on Spain, 77, 82, 268, 288–290, 300; language and music, 85, 88; mode 85–88, 102; musical form, 89–90; music theory, 85–89, 246; popular music, 93–94; rhythm and meter, 88
Arabic poetry, 88, 90
Argentina, 298, 299, 300

arghul (*Middle Eastern single reed instrument*), 84
Aristotle (*ancient Greek philosopher*), 272
Armenia, 77, 79, 82, 83
Armstrong, Lil, *see* Hardin, Lil
Armstrong, Louis (*American jazz musician*), 343–344, 345
arohana/avarohana (*ascending/descending scale in India*), 135–137, 150
arpa (*Latin American harp*), 35, 304–305, 307 See also harp
arpeggio (*sequential sounding of chord notes*), 292, 305, 326
art music (*music created by professionals for an elite audience*), 5; in Arabic countries, 77, 78, 82, 85; in Central Asia, 106, 113, 116; in India, 125–151, 153, 154; in China, 167; in Japan, 196, 212; in Eastern Europe, 247–248, 251–252, 253, 258; in Western Europe, 269–276, 281, 288–289, 297, 325, 349; in Latin America, 299, 308, 315–316; in North America, 322–325, 341, 346, 347, 353
Ashanti (*ethnic group in West Africa*), 40, 53
Ashkenazim (*Jewish people from Central and Eastern Europe*), 99–100
asymmetrical meter (*meter not divisible into equal parts*), 250–251, 259, 261
atabatque (*Afro-Brazilian drum*), 310, 311
atoke (*iron idiophone from Ghana*), 54–57
atonality (*music without a sense of tonic*), 9–10
atsimewu (*large drum from Ghana*), 55, 57–59
Attwenger (*Austrian popular music band*), 277
Austin, Texas, United States, 307
Australia, 269, 274, 275
Austria, 248, 254, 269–271, 274, 276–279, 295
auto (*Latin American religious folk dramas*), 296, 302
autoharp (*European-American zither with dampers that create chords*), 327, 332
avant garde, European, *see* modernism
avarta (*tala cycle in North Indian meter*), 139
Avicenna *see* Sina, Abu Ali Ibn
avritti (*tala cycle in South Indian meter*), 139
axatse (*bead rattle from Ghana*), 54, 57–59
Ayinde, Sikiru (*West African popular musician*), 74
Aymara (*Andean ethnic group/language*), 316–317
Azerbaijan, 38
Aztec civilization (*empire in Central Mexico*), 296, 298, 302, 309
Aztec renaissance (*arts trend in 1930s Mexico*), 309

B

Bach, Johann Sebastian (*Baroque period German composer*), 3, 269, 316

Bachianas Brasilieras (*set of compositions by Heitor Villa-Lobos*), 315–316, 318

badhkones (*Jewish wedding entertainers*), 264

Baez, Joan (*American folk/popular singer*), 333

Baghdad, Iraq, 77, 85

baglama (*long-neck lute from Turkey*), 82

bagpipe (*reed instrument with bag air reservoir*), 253, 259, 260, 283

Bahia, Brazil, 310, 312

Bahrain, 87

Bai Juyi (*Chinese poet*), 169

bajo sexto (*Mexican bass guitar*), 304, 307

bala, *see* balafon

Balachander (*South Indian vina player*), 160

balafon (*West African xylophone*), 50, 61

balalaika (*Russian lute with triangular resonator*), 263

Balawan, I Wayan (*Balinese guitarist/composer*), 243

Bali Arts Festival, *see* Pesta Kesenian Bali

Bali, Indonesia, 9, 31, 215, 216, 217, 232–242

ballad (*European folk song form*), 101, 274, 277, 295, 325, 331, 333, 341, 344, 345, 357

ballad (*slow tempo popular song*), 187–188, 351

balungan (*core melody in Javanese gamelan*), 217, 218, 223, 227–228, 230, 231, 234

bambuco (*Colombian dance*), 300

ban (*Chinese opera rhythm types*), 180, 183, 184–187

ban (*Chinese wooden clappers*), 174, 178, 184, 185–187

band, *see* wind band

bandish (*short composed songs in North India*), 128

bandurria (*Spanish lute-type chordophone*), 290

Bangladesh, 127, 152

banjar (*Balinese community*), 232

banjo (*American lute with circular resonator*), 326, 332–333, 340, 342, 343

bansi (*Indonesian transverse flute*), 37

bansuri (*Indian transverse bamboo flute*), 129, 131, 147

Banyumas, Indonesia, 38

banziqiang (*Chinese opera form*), 164

Baqli, Ruzbihan (*Sufi writer*), 81

bar (*metrical group in European music*), 344

barbershop singing (*small American a cappella vocal ensemble music*), 345

bard (*professional epic singer/poet/composer*), 109, 118, 246, 250, 280–282

barong (*Balinese mythical animal*), 239–242

Baroque period (*period in European arts in 17th, 18th centuries*), 269

Bartók, Béla (*Hungarian ethnomusicologist/composer*), 247–249, 254, 255, 266, 267

bashraf (*Middle Eastern instrumental form*), 90–91

Basques (*Western European ethnic group*), 288

bass drum (*low-pitched drum*), 353

bass guitar, electric (*low-pitch electronically amplified chordophone*), 70, 243, 323, 352, 354

bassoon (*European low double-reed aerophone*), 270

bateria (*percussion section in Brazilian samba*), 309, 312–314

batucada (*form of Brazilian samba dominated by percussion*), 311–314

batuque (*Afro-Brazilian dance*), 300, 309

Baul (*religion/ethnic group in Bengal and Bangladesh*), 152–153, 161

Bay Psalm Book (*first book printed in North America*), 325

baya (*metal drum of North Indian tabla*), 132

bayan (*Russian accordion*), 263

beat, 18–22, *see also* meter

Beatles, The (*English rock group*), 159, 353

bebop (*jazz genre*), 323, 346–350

bedug (*large Indonesian drum*), 39

Beethoven, Ludwig van (*Classical-period German composer*), 3, 270, 276

Beijing opera, *see* jingxi

Beijing Philharmonic Orchestra (*European-style orchestra in China*), 188

belaganjur (*Balinese processional gamelan*), 239, 243

Belarus, 246

bell (*category of idiophone*), 7, 8, 41, 46, 47, 50, 53, 54, 56–59, 60, 74, 152, 162, 172, 173, 195, 297, 310, 313–314

Ben, Jorge (*Brazilian singer/songwriter*), 315

bendir (*Middle Eastern frame drum*), 84

Bengal, India, 152–153, 159, 161

Benin, 44, 309

berimbau (*Brazilian musical bow*), 310

Berliner, Paul (*American ethnomusicologist*), 64

bhajan (*composed South Indian devotional songs*), 148

Bhatkhande, Vishnu Narayan (*North Indian music theorist*), 127, 135–137

Bhosle, Asha (*Indian playback singer*), 154–158

Bhutan, 109, 110

bianqing (*Chinese collection of stone chimes*), 173

bianyin (*alternate pitches outside a Chinese pentatonic mode*), 168, 178–179, 185

bianzhong (*Chinese collection of bronze bells*), 172, 173

Bible (*Jewish or Christian sacred text*), 85, 99, 328–330, 345

big band (*large ensemble jazz music*), 298, 300, 311, 315, 323, 332, 346, 347, 352, 354

Big Fun (*Miles Davis album*), 159

Billings, William (*early United States composer*), 325

bin (*North Indian classical stick zither*), 129, 130, 147

Binder, Markus (*Austrian musician*), 277

bira (*ritual in Zimbabwe*), 64, 66

birimintingo (*contrasting phrases in kora music*), 60, 62–63

biwa (*Japanese pear-shaped lute*), 190, 197–199, 201, 202, 212

Bizet, Georges (*French composer*), 299

Black Elk (*indigenous American spiritual leader*), 333–334, 338, 339

Black Panthers, 67

Black, Bill (*early rock-and-roll bass player*), 352

blasmusik (*Austrian/German wind band music*), 277

bloco (*Brazilian community*), 312

blocos Afro (*Afro-Brazilian community/percussion group*), 311, 312

blue notes (*pitch inflection in blues, jazz*), 324, 340, 344, 345, 346, 351

bluegrass (*string band genre in United States*), 323, 324, 332–333, 352, 354, 357

Bluegrass Boys (*bluegrass band*), 332

blues (*American popular music style*), 3, 33, 153, 273, 277, 282, 291, 301, 322–324, 326, 327, 344–346, 353, 357

Blues Brothers, The (*film*), 346

blues guitar (*playing styles associated with the blues*), 33, 326, 345

bo (*Chinese cymbals*), 177

boba (*drum from Ghana*), 55

bodhran (*Irish frame drum*), 281, 283, 286

bogino duu (*Mongolian metered songs*), 117–118

bol (*Indian drumming syllable*), 141, 148

Bolivia, 37, 316

Bollywood (*nickname for Indian film industry*), 153

bomba (*Andean bass drum*), 316–317

Bombay, *see* Mumbai, India

Bön (*Tibetan indigenous religion*), 110

bonang (*Javanese set of kettle-gongs*), 219, 220, 226, 228, 235, 243

bonang barung (*middle range Javanese bonang*), 220, 226

bonang panembung (*low range Javanese bonang*), 220, 226

bonang panerus (*high range Javanese bonang*), 220, 226

bones (*American/Irish idiophone made from animal bones*), 283

bongos (*pair of Cuban hand drums*), 301

bore (*aerophone tube shape*), 36, 38

bossa nova (*Brazilian popular song/dance type*), 300, 315

bow harp, see harp, bow

box zither, *see* zither, box

Brahmin (*priest caste in India*), 124

Brahms, Johannes (*German composer*), 270

brass instrument, *see* buzzed-lip instrument

Brazil, 22, 243, 296–300, 309–316, 318; African influence, 54, 309–315; art music, 315–316; dance, 297–298, 300, 301, 310–312, 315, 316; dramatic music, 310; history, 310–311; influence of United States, 312, 315; musical instruments, 54, 310–311; popular music, 315; religious music, 310; Western European influence 309, 316

brdung (*pattern of percussion strikes in Tibetan ritual music*), 112, 113, 114–115

break (*instrumental section in popular song*), 354

breakdown (*Anglo-American instrumental dance music form*), 331

bridge (*piece of chordophones that lifts up strings*), 32, 33

bridge (*transition section*), 341

British Invasion (*period of popularity of British rock bands in United States*), 353

broadside ballad (*narrative folk song published on large sheets*), 274

Brown, James (*rhythm and blues musician*), 68, 70, 354

buchimish (*Bulgarian round dance*), 259

Budapest, Hungary, 253, 254

Buddhism, 106–117, 122, 124, 163–165, 167, 190–192, 194–195, 203, 208, 209, 214

bugaku (*Japanese dance accompanied by gagaku*), 196

bugle (*European buzzed-lip aerophone with no valves or keys*), 277

buka (*short introduction to Javanese gamelan piece*), 219

bulgar (*Jewish dance form*), 103

Bulgaria, 14, 246, 248, 258–262, 267; dance, 259; history, 247, 258; meter, 250, 251, 259, 260–262; mode, 259; musical instruments, 40, 82, 83, 259–260; Romani influence, 259; song types, 251, 258–259; Turkish influence, 247, 258, 259; wedding music, 258–259

Bulgarian State Radio and Television Female Vocal Choir, 258, 267

Bulgars (*Eastern European ethnic group*), 258

Bulgarskoto radio i televiziia, Zheni khor, *see* Bulgarian State Radio and Television Female Vocal Choir

Bumba meu boi (*Brazilian folk drama*), 309

bunraku (*Japanese puppetry form*), 193, 199, 202, 209

Burma, 173

Bustan Abraham (*Israeli band*), 104

Butler, Jean (*Irish choreographer*), 282

buzuki (*Greek long-neck lute*), 82

buzuq (*Syrian/Iraqi long-neck lute*), 82

buzzed-lip instrument (*category of aerophone*), 36, 38, 51, 72, *see also individual instruments*

bylini (*Russian epic songs*), 251

Byrne, David (*American popular musician*), 4

Byzantine Empire, 76, 246; chant, 258; mode, 76, 85–86, 100; influence on Bulgaria, 258; influence on Russia, 263

C

cadence (*phrase ending*), 13–15, 121, 137, 138, 144, 152, 179, 180, 183, 186, 223, 237, 284–286, 292, 298, 302

Cahuilla (*indigenous American ethnic group*), 335

caixa (*shallow snare drum in Brazilian samba*), 311

cajón (*Afro-Peruvian drum box*), 318

cak, *see* kecak

cakewalk (*African American dance*), 342

calendar songs (*Eastern European folk songs associated with certain times of the year*), 263

California, United States, 160, 337

call-and-response, *see* responsorial form

calligraphy, 78, 87, 191, 205

calung (*Balinese metallophone*), 236, 239, 240

Camarón de la Isla, El, *see* Monge Cruz, José

Canada, 322–323, 333, 336, 337, 357

canciones revolucionarias (*Mexican folk songs from the revolutionary period*), 304

Candomblé (*South American religion*), 297–298, 310, 318

candra (*Javanese gamelan form*), 225

canon (*form in imitative polyphony*), 25

cante hondo (*traditional Spanish flamenco forms*), 290

cantillation (*method of chanting Biblical texts*), 99

Canton (Guangzhou), China, 165, 182

cantor (*music leader in Jewish religious services*), 76, 99, 100, 102

Capetown, South Africa, 45

capoiera (*Brazilian martial arts dance*), 310

caranam (*section in South Indian vocal forms*), 148

Caribbean, 68, 296, 301, 319, 354

Carmen (*opera by Georges Bizet*), 299

carnaval (*Brazilian festival*), 297, 298, 309, 311–312

Carter family (*early country music ensemble*), 327, 332

Carter, Maybelle (*country music guitarist/ singer*), 327, 332

casadh (*section in Irish dance forms*), 286–287

castanet (*hand-held clacking idiophone*), 289

caste (*hereditary social class*), 45, 59, 97, 124, 129, 151, 155

Caucasus, 84

ceili band (*Irish dance music ensemble*), 281

celempung (*Javanese plucked zither*), 221, 228, 230

cello (*low-pitch European bowed lute*), 29, 30, 35, 81, 172, 181, 243, 269, 270, 315

Celtic music (*modern music associated with Celt European ethnic group*), 282

ceng-ceng (*Balinese cymbals*), 236, 237, 240

cengkok (*standard patterns for Javanese melodic elaborations*), 223, 228, 234

censorship, 118, 166, 243, 248, 252, 299, 315

Central Asia, 80, 106–121, 250; Arabic influence, 106; dance, 113, 116; geography, 106; history, 106–108; influence on China, 106, 163, 169, 181; influence on Eastern Europe, 246–247, 254, 263, influence on Hungary, 254, influence on Russia, 263; Iranian influence, 106; Middle Eastern influence, 106; musical instruments, 110–112, 119; ritual music, 109–116; Russian influence, 107; song types, 116, 117–119; *see also individual countries*

chachachá (*Latin American ballroom dance*), 300

chahar mezzrab (*metered section in Iranian classical music*), 95–98

Chaikovsky, Piotr See Tchaikovsky, Piotr

chalan (*melodic synopsis of raga*), 137, 138, 142

chalumeau (*medieval European single-reed aerophone*), 84

'cham, 113, 116

Chang-E (*Chinese goddess*), 186

chant (*monophonic religious song*), Buddhist 163, 194–195, 209, Byzantine 258, Christian 76, 246, Gregorian 246, indigenous American 337, Islamic 80–81, 84, Jewish 76, 100, Russian 246, 264, Tibetan 107, 108–113, 115, 122, Vedic 126–127, 139, 148

chanyin (*Chinese flute trill ornament*), 179

charango (*Andean small guitar*), 317–318

Chavéz, Carlos (*Mexican composer*), 309, 318

Chenggis Khan, *see* Genghis Khan

Chicago, United States, 341–342, 345, 354

chicha (*Andean popular music style*), 299, 318

Chieftains, The (*Irish ensemble*), 281, 285–287, 295

chikari (*drone strings on Indian chordophones*), 130, 143, 145

Chile, 299, 300, 316

chilena (*Mexican popular music genre*), 303

China, 48, 106, 108, 109, 116, 162–189, 250, 323; Central Asian influence, 106, 163, 169, 181; court music, 163, 173; dance, 183, 184, 193, 196, 209; dramatic music, 164, 168–169, 171, 172, 173, 177, 181–187; European influence, 165, 180–181, 183; folk music, 171, 173, 174, 177–181; influence of India, 163; influence on Indonesia, 214, 242; influence on Japan, 163, 172, 190, 192, 195, 196, 203, 211; influence on Korea, 163; influence on Mongolia, 117, 120; influence on Tibet, 106, 110, 113, 116; internationalism, 106, 163; isolationism, 164; Middle Eastern influence, 81, 171; mode, 168–169, 178–179, 181, 183–186; Mongolian influence, 109, 118, 119, 172; musical form, 16, 174–177, 178–180; musical instruments, 83, 169–174, 183–184; music theory, 10, 167–169; popular music, 165, 166, 186–189; reform music, 180–181; religion and music, 165–167, 181; Soviet influence, 252; Western influence, 188–189; tuning systems, 86, 163, 167, 180, 181

Ching-tsao, Li (*Chinese poet*), 175

choirs and choral singing, 2, 5, 23, 25, 56–57, 60, 69, 71, 74, 81, 85, 89, 208–210, 238, 247, 258, 260, 261, 263, 265, 266, 267, 270, 271, 277, 304, 306–307, 321–322, 328–330, 345, 354

chord progression, *see* harmonic progression

chordophone (*string instrument*), 31–35, 51–53, 81–82, 133, 169, 260, *see also individual instruments*

choros (*Brazilian folk band*), 298, 311, 315–316

Choros (*series of compositions by Heitor Villa Lobos*), 315

chorus (*repeating section*), 348–350, See also refrain

chorus (*synonym for choir*), *see* choirs and choral singing

choshi (*Japanese modes*), 195

chou (*clown character in Chinese opera*), 186

Christian music, 15–16, 76, 180, 246, 264, 272, 274, 276, 296–298, 328, 345–346

Christianity, 76, 79, 165, 180, 246, 253, 258, 264, 268, 269, 272, 274, 275, 276, 288–289, 296–297, 315–316, 328, 329, 339, 345–346

chromatic scale (*sequential set of all pitches in a twelve-tone tuning system*), 263, 301, 304

cimbalom (*Eastern European trapezoidal hammered zither*), 33, 100, 250, 253–254, 276, 327

cinna melm (*folk ensemble from Kerala, India*), 151–152

cipher notation, *see* kepatihan notation

circular breathing (*aerophone playing technique*), 85

citera (*Hungarian fretted zither*), 254

Civil War, United States, 321, 341, 344, 345

clarinet (*European single-reed aerophone*), 36, 81, 84, 100, 102–104, 255, 258, 259, 270, 277, 301, 315, 341, 342, 343

Classical Period (*artistic period in 18th-century Europe*), 270

claves (*Cuban wood stick idiophones*), 301

Cobb, Buell (*shape-note singing writer*), 322

Cokro, Pak, *see* Wasitodiningrat, Ki K. P. H.

Colombia, 300, 318

colonialism (*establishment of one country's sovereignty over another*), 45–46, 68, 78, 126, 129, 155, 164, 215, 269, 270, 276, 288, 296

Colorado, United States, 334

colotomic structure (*regular interpunctuation of metrical cycles*), 217, 234, 241, 243

Coltrane, John (*American jazz musician*), 159, 160

Columbus, Christopher (*Italian explorer*), 288, 296, 301

Colvig, William (*American instrument maker*), 244

communism (*economic/political system*), 107, 110, 118, 164–167, 181, 183, 187–188, 249–250, 252, 255, 259, 262, 264

compás (*rhythmic types in flamenco*), 290–294

compound meter (*meter with beats divisible by three*), 20–21, 47–48, 97, 251, 284, 287, 300, 302

conchero (*Mexican lute-type chordophone and musicians who play them*), 302

conductor (*leader of musical ensemble*), 54, 58, 174, 184, 186, 197, 200, 219, 223, 234, 270–271, 309, 321–322, 341

Confucian music (*ritual music of Confucianism*), 162, 173, 190

Confucianism (*Chinese religion*), 162, 163–167, 173, 181, 190

Confucius (*Chinese philosopher*), 162, 166, 167, 173

conga (*Afro-Cuban drum*), 70, 74, 300, 301

Congo, 53

conjunct motion (*type of melodic motion*), 13

conjunto (*popular music from northern Mexico and southwestern United States*), 297, 303, 304, 318

conjunto norteña, *see* conjunto

Conneff, Kevin (*Irish musician*), 281

consonance (*type of interval sonority*), 272, 273, 279, 299, 349

Constantinople, *see* Istanbul

contour, melodic (*characterization of melody*), 12–13, 66, 91, 121, 138, 145, 183, 195, 205, 217, 223, 290, 294, 329, 337

contrabass, *see* double bass

copla (*Spanish/Latin American poetic form*), 289, 293, 299, 302, 304

Copland, Aaron (*American composer*), 324

cornet (*European buzzed-lip aerophone*), 102, 341, 342, 343

counterpoint (*art of combining simultaneous melodies*), 209, 272, 274–275

country blues (*style of blues in United States*), 345

country music (*American popular musical genre*), 323, 324, 325, 327, 332–333, 339, 345, 351, 352

course (*set of strings associated with one pitch*), 33

cowboy singers (*American popular music style*), 323, 332, 352

Cowell, Henry (*American composer*), xii, xv, 3

Creole Jazz Band (*early jazz ensemble*), 343

crescendo (*to get gradually louder*), 22

criollo (*Latin American people of European descent*), 297, 299, 315, 317

Croatia, 248, 251

Crudup, Arthur (*American songwriter/musician*), 351

cruit, *see* Irish harp

crusades (*Western European invasion of Palestine*), 77

csárdás (*Hungarian dance*), 254

Cuba, 68, 299, 300, 301, 318, 319

cueca (*Cuban dance*), 300, 303

cuíca (*friction drum in Brazilian samba*), 311, 313–314

Cultural Revolution (*period of social upheaval in China*), 110, 116, 164, 166, 181, 183

cumbia (*Colombian dance*), 300, 318

Curtis, Natalie (*researcher of indigenous American music*), 337

curved board zither, *see* zither, curved

cymbal (*unpitched metal disc idiophone*), 7, 39, 41, 50, 103, 108, 111–116, 120, 177, 184, 194, 211, 236–237, 239, 240, 243, 313–314, 348, 355

Czech Republic, 246

D

daff (*Middle Eastern frame drum*), 81, 84

dagu (*Chinese drum*), 173, 177, 181

daichovo (*Bulgarian dance*), 259

Dalai Lama, *see* Gyatso, Dalai Lama Tenzin

dalang (*Indonesian puppeteer*), 215–217, 238

dan (*leading female role in Chinese opera*), 184

dan (*sections in Japanese music, poetry*), 206–207

dance and dance music, in Africa, 2, 47, 53–59, 64, 68–69; in Andean countries, 316–318; in Argentina, 300; in Austria, 269–271, 274, 276, 277; in Brazil, 297–298, 300, 301, 310–312, 315, 316; in Bulgaria, 258–259, 261; in Caribbean, 68; in Chile, 300; in China, 183, 184, 193, 196, 209; in Colombia, 300; in Cuba, 299, 300; in Dominican Republic, 300; in Eastern Europe, 247, 250–259, 261, 263; in Hungary, 253–257; in India, 124, 148, 152, 154, 155; in Indonesia, 214, 215, 222, 234–235, 237–242; in Ireland, 21, 280–282, 284, 286–287; in Latin America, 21, 297–304, 309–312, 315–317; in Mexico, 298, 300, 302–305, 309; in Middle East, 80, 81, 84, 85, 88, 94, 96; in North America, 298, 300, 321, 324, 325, 331–335, 337–343, 346–347, 351, 352, 354–355; in Russia, 263; in Spain, 289–292; in Tibet, 113, 116; in Western Europe, 269–271, 274, 276–277, 280–282, 284, 286–287, 289–292, 297, 299, 300; Jewish, 100, 103

dance house, *see* tancház

dangdut (*popular music genre in Indonesia*), 243, 245

Danielou, Alain (*French ethnomusicologist*), 130

danza (*Cuban dance*),300

Daoism (*Chinese religion*),162, 164–167

darabukka (*Middle Eastern goblet drum*), 84, 88, 94, 104

darbuka (*Turkish goblet drum*), 84

dastgah (*basis for Iranian classical improvisation*), 76, 95–98

Davis, Miles (*American jazz musician*), 159

daya (*wooden cylindrical drum of North Indian tabla*), 132

dbyangs (*Tibetan tone-contour melody chants*), 110, 111, 115, 118

De Dannan (*Irish band*), 282

debayashi (*ensemble used in Japanese kabuki drama*), 210

Debussy, Claude (*French composer*), 288

decrescendo (*to get gradually softer*), 22

Deep Forest (*world music album*), 356

def, *see* daff

definability of pitch, 41–42

demung, *see* saron demung

Denpasar, Bali, Indonesia, 234

densho (*large Japanese temple bell*), 8, 195

dervish (*member of Mevlevi Sufis*), 81

Detroit, United States, 354

detuning (*deliberate slight difference in pitch of instruments*), 233–235

Dharamsala, India, 109, 116

dharma (*Hindu religious concept*), 232

dhikr (*Sufi ritual of remembrance*), 81

dholak (*folk hand drum in India*),147

dhrupad (*long classical North Indian vocal form*), 130, 147, 148

diao (*Chinese pentatoic mode*), 168,176

diaspora (*ethnic scattering*), of Jews 76, 79, 96, 100, 323, of Africans 68

diatonic set (*a heptatonic pitch set*), 10, 62, 86, 100, 102, 168, 188–189, 211, 247, 254, 256, 268, 272–275, 283, 287, 288, 291, 301, 304, 324, 329, 332, 336, 337, 340

Dienz, Christoph (*Austrian musician*), 277

digital technology, 324, 355

dilruba (*Indian plucked lute*), 32

Din, Safi al- (*medieval Islamic scholar*), 77

disco (*popular music genre*), 154, 324, 355

disjunct motion (*melody with large intervals*), 13, 337

diskantzither (*Austrian fretted zither*), 254, 271, 276

dissonance (*type of interval sonority*), 133, 207, 248, 263, 266, 272, 273, 279, 309, 315, 349

Dixieland (*name for style of early jazz*), 343, 346, 349

dizi (*Chinese bamboo transverse flute*), 171, 173, 178, 184, 189

DJ (*disc jockey, performer playing turntables*), 354–355

Dodds, Baby (*American jazz musician*), 343

Dodds, Johnny (*American jazz musician*), 343

Doherty, Moya (*stage producer*), 282

doina (*Jewish form*), 102–103

Dominican Republic, 300

domra (*Russian lute chordophone*), 263

'don (*repetitive Tibetan chants of heightened recitation*), 111

donno (*hourglass drum from Ghana*), 39, 40

doo-wop (*United States popular a cappella style*), 69, 346

Dósa, Lidi, 247–248

dotar (*Central Asian lute*),122

dotara (*Indian two-string lute*), 152

double bass (*large European chordophone*), 25, 81, 100, 102, 103, 243, 253, 255, 269, 270, 303–304, 332, 333, 343, 346, 348–349, 352

double reed (*category of aerophone*), 36, 38, *see also individual instruments*

Douglass, Frederick (*African American leader*), 342

doumbak (*North African goblet drum*), 39

downbeat (*beginning of metrical cycle*), 46

doyna, *see* doina

dozal (*Kurdish single-reed aerophone*), 84

Drazovce, Slovakia, 249

drone (*long, unchanging tone*), 26, 81–82, 84, 91, 96–98, 120–121, 125, 128–129, 130–131, 133, 143, 145, 149, 152, 156, 160, 254, 259, 260, 261, 263, 265–266, 283, 285–287, 326, 332

drum and bass (*genre of electronic dance music*), 356

drum machine (*electronic device for automatically playing drum sounds*), 324, 355

drum polyphony (*texture of drumming ensemble*), 27, 56–59

drum set (*group of drums played by a single player*), 70, 94, 102–103, 154, 189, 243, 255, 323, 343, 346, 348–350, 351–354

drum song, *see* guqu

drums and drumming, 7, 32, 38–40; among indigenous Americans, 323, 334, 335, 337, 338–339; and texture, 25–27; in Africa, 44–48, 49–50, 53–60, 64, 68, 70; in Bulgaria, 260–262; in Brazil, 297–298, 309, 310, 311, 313–314; in China, 173, 174, 177–178, 181, 184, 185–186; in India, 125, 126, 128, 129, 132–133, 140–142, 144–146, 147, 148, 149–151, 152; in Indonesia, 217, 219, 222, 223, 226, 227–231, 234, 236, 237, 240–241, 243; in Ireland, 283, 286; in Japan, 194, 197, 198–201, 208–210; in Latin America, 296–298, 301–302, 316–317; in Mexico, 296, 302; in Middle East, 84, 88–89, 94, 96, 99; in Peru, 316, 317; in Tibet, 111, 112, 114–115, 116; in United States, 160, 340, 341; resonators, 39–41; *see also* drum set

duct flute, *see* flute, duct

duende, 289–291

dukar-tikar (*Indian hemispherical drum*), 40

dulab (*Middle Eastern instrumental form*), 90, 92

dulcimer (*trapezoidal hammered box zither*), 83, 95, 100, 116, 117, 250, 254, 276, 327, *see also* cimbalom, hackbrett, santur, santuri, yangqin, yoochin

dulcimer, mountain, *see* mountain dulcimer

dumbuk (*Iraqi goblet drum*), 84

dumy (*Ukrainian epic songs*), 251

dung-chen (*large Tibetan buzzed-lip aerophones*), 110, 112, 114–115

Dunstable, John (*medieval English composer*), 25

duple meter (*meter with beats grouped in twos*), 20, 22, 47–48, 96–98, 103, 254, 280, 284, 300, 302, 317, 337, 348

Dutch East Indies Company, 215

Dutrey, Honore (*American jazz musician*), 343

duzele (*single reed aerophone from Azerbaijan*), 38

Dylan, Bob (*American folk/rock musician*), 333, 353

dynamics (*changes of loudness in music*), 22

E

Eastern Europe, 246–267; art music, 247–248, 251–252, 266, 288; Central Asian influence, 246–247, 254, 263; dance, 247, 250–259, 261, 263; folk music, 247–266; geography, 246; history, 246–249, 253–254, 258; Middle Eastern influence, 247–248, 250, 253–254, 258, 259; meter, 250, 251, 259, 260–262; mode, 254, 259, 263; musical form, 254, 256–257, 263, 264–266; musical instruments, 253–255, 259–260, 263–264; popular music, 248–249; Turkish influence, 247–248, 253–254, 258, 259; wedding music, 249, 250, 258–259, 263–267; Western influence, 247–248, 249, 253–254, 258, 259; *see also individual countries*

echoi (*modes of Byzantine chant*), 76, 85

Ecuador, 316

Egypt, 52, 76, 78, 79, 80, 84, 88, 89, 90, 92, 93, 94, 104, 264

elbow stick (*curved or bent African drumstick*), 49

electric guitar (*electronically amplified chordophone*), 33, 69, 70, 116, 212, 187, 243, 259, 323, 346, 352–354

electronic dance music (*genre of synthesized music*), 4, 154, 194, 212, 271, 324, 355–356

electronica, *see* electronic dance music

electrophone (*category of instruments which use loudspeakers*), 32

Ellingson, Ter (*American ethnomusicologist*), 111–112

Ellington, Edward Kennedy "Duke" (*American jazz musician*), 346

endere (*flute from Uganda*), 51

endongo (*lyre from Uganda*), 52

England, U. K., 25, 281, 282, 283, 320, 321, 331, 332, 333, *see also* Great Britain, United Kingdom

enka 212

Enlightenment (*period in European history*), 270

ensemble, heterogeneous (*group of dissimilar instruments*), 29

ensemble, homogeneous (*group of instruments of the same family*), 29–30

epic singing (*extended performances of historical/mythical narratives*), 67, 99, 107, 109, 116, 118, 119, 124, 169, 172, 181, 215, 246, 248, 250–251

equal temperament (*category of tuning systems*), 272, *see also* tuning system, twelve-tone equal temperament

erhu (*Chinese bowed spike fiddle*), 170, 172, 178, 184, 185, 189

erhuang (*Chinese opera mode*), 183–185

Eskimo (*name for arctic ethnic group*), 336

estribillo (*section of Latin American folk song*), 289, 306–307

Ethiopia, 34, 79

ethnocentrism (*judging culture by relation to one's own*), 4

ethnomusicology (*study of music in culture*), xii, 4, 5, 31, 181, 248, 252, 356

Europe, 4, 8, 9; Arabic influence, 82–84; influence on China, 165, 180–181, 183; influence on Indonesia, 215, 221, 242–244; influence on Iran, 95–96; influence on Jewish music, 100; musical instruments, 82–84; tuning system, 9, 86, 272; *see also* Western Europe, Eastern Europe

Ewe (*West African ethnic group*), 46, 53–59, 309

exoticism (*interest in culture for the sake of novelty*), 4, 160, 189, 356

extramusical association (*musical symbolism of non-musical things*), 119, 134, 138–139, 167–168, 174–176, 178, *see also* programmaticism

Extremschrammeln (*Austrian band*), 277

F

Falkner, Hans-Peter (*Austrian musician*), 277

Falla, Manuel de (*Spanish composer*), 288

falseta (*pattern of flamenco guitar performance*), 292–294

falsetto (*high-pitch mode of vocal cords in male singing*), 117, 182, 298

fan yin (*technique of guqin performance*), 174–176

fandango (*Mexican music and dance festival*), 303–304

Farabi, Abu Nasr al- (*medieval Islamic scholar*), 77, 85–86

fasil (*Turkish/Syrian classical music suite*), 89

fermata (*held note in European/American music*), 330

fiddle, *see* violin

film music, 5, 282, 289, 298, 300, 303, 356; in China, 181; in India, 94, 116, 125, 126, 127, 153–158, 243; in Japan, 212; Middle East, 93–94

filmi, *see* film music, India

finger cymbals (*small idiophone*), 314

fingerboard (*flat neck on lute*), 34, 82, 83, 130, 142, 170, 172, 202, 276, 277, 289, 326, 327, 352

fingerboard lute, *see* lute, fingerboard 34

Finland 251, 253

fipple (*sharp ramp on a duct flute*), 36

firqa (*Egyptian orchestra*), 93

First Nations peoples, *see* indigenous Americans

Fisk Jubilee Singers (*African-American choir*), 345

Fisk University, 345

flamenco (*genre of Spanish music and dance*), 256, 282, 289–295, 304

flat (*notation to lower scale step by a semitone*), 86, 135

Flatley, Michael (*Irish choreographer*), 282

Flatt, Lester (*American bluegrass musician*), 333

fleadh (*Irish traditional music festival*), 281, 283

flute (*category of aerophones*), 36–37; duct, 36–37, 221, 254, 255, 283, 335; European, 270, 341; globular, 36–37, 162, 171; in Africa 47, 48, 51; in China 162, 171, 173, 184; in Eastern Europe 254, 255, 259, 260; in India 120, 129, 131, 152; in Indonesia 221, 222, 230, 235, 243–244; in Japan 191–198, 200, 202–204, 208–210; in Latin America 296, 301, 302, 316, 317; in Middle East 81, 83, 89, 94, 95, 259; in Mongolia 117; indigenous American 334, 335, 339; Irish 281, 283; notch 36–37, 83, 171, 173, 203, 316–317; transverse 36–37, 117, 120, 129, 131, 171, 193, 197, 208, 283

flute, Native American, *see* Native American flute

Foggy Mountain Boys (*American bluegrass band*), 333

folk blues, *see* country blues

folk music (*music created by amateurs for community enjoyment*), defined, 5; origin of term 277

Folk Music Revival (*movement in North American music*), 324, 333, 353

Fon (*West African ethnic group*), 309

fonn (*section in Irish music*), 286–287

form, see musical form

formula song (*Eastern European folk song form*), 264–266

Foster, Stephen (*American songwriter*), 321, 341

frame drum (*shallow drum without resonator*), 39, 41, 49, 81, 84, 283, 286, 313, 326, 335

France, 247, 282, 288, 295, 299, 320, 323, 343

Franklin, Aretha (*American soul singer*), 354

French horn (*European buzzed-lip aerophone*), 36, 270, 341

frequency (*measurement of sound waves*), 7, 11, 31, 36

fret (*raised part of chordophone fingerboard*), 33–35

Freud, Sigmund (*Austrian psychologist*), 270
freylekhs (*quick Jewish dance*), 103
fuji (*West African popular music style*), 68, 75
Fuke (*Japanese monastic sect and shakuhachi school*), 195
funk (*American popular music style*), 68, 70, 72, 324, 354, 355
furulya (*Eastern European duct flute*), 254–255
fushi (*noh drama songs*), 209

G

Gabriel, Peter (*English popular musician*), 2
gadulka (*Bulgarian bowed lute*), 83, 259–260
Gaelic League (*society promoting Irish national art*), 281
gagaku (*Japanese court orchestral music*), 15, 29, 190, 195–202, 206, 208, 212
gaida (*Bulgarian bagpipe*), 259, 260, 261
gaita (*North African double reed instrument*), 84, *see also* zurna
gaku-biwa (*Japanese lute used in gagaku*), 197–199, 201, *see also* biwa
gaku-so (*Japanese zither used in gagaku*), 198–199, 201, *see also* koto
gamak (*characteristic ornamentation in Indian raga performance*), 134, 138, 141, 142, 154
gamaka See gamak
gambang (*Javanese wooden xylophone*), 221, 226, 228, 230, 243
gambang kromong (*Indonesian popular music style*), 243
Gambia, 59, 62, 63
gamelan (*Indonesian orchestra*), 9, 15, 17, 25, 178, 215–245, 272
gamelan gong kebyar, *see* kebyar
gamelan selonding (*Balinese ritual orchestra*), 9
gamelan semar pegulingan (*Balinese court orchestra*), 245
Ganges river, 126, 127
gangsa (*family of Balinese metallophones*), 235, 236, 237, 240–241, 243
gangsta rap (*American popular music style*), 355
gankogui (*double iron bell from Ghana*), 54, 56–59, 314
Gao, Mali, 45
gaoqiang (*Chinese opera form*), 164
GarageBand (*music composition software*), 356
Garfunkel, Art (*American popular musician*), 331
gaspah (*Algerian end-blown flute*), 94
gat (*metered part of North Indian instrumental performance*), 138, 142–145
gato (*Argentinian dance*), 300
Gautama Siddhartha (*founder of Buddhism*), 124
gendér (*Indonesian metallophone*), 30, 31, 220, 226, 228, 229, 230, 236

gendér barung (middle octave gendér), 220, 226, 228, 229
gendér panerus (higher octave gendér), 220, 226
gendér wayang (Balinese metallophone for accompanying shadow puppet play), 31
Genghis Khan (*Mongolian leader*), 164
Georgia, 263
Georgia, United States, 321
ger (*traditional Mongolian dwelling*), 116, 117
Germany, 277, 323, 327
Gershwin, George (American composer), 3, 346
Gesar (*Tibetan epic*), 116, 118
geza (*ensemble used in Japanese kabuki drama*), 211
Ghana, 44–46, 49, 50, 53–59, 68, 74, 309
gharana (*music teaching tradition in India*), 125, 129, 159
ghawazi (*Middle Eastern women music entertainers*), 80
Ghost Dance (*indigenous American ritual*), 338–339
gidayu (*Japanese singer/narrator and ensemble*), 193, 202, 210–211
gijak (*Central Asian bowed lute*), 82
Gil, Gilberto (*Brazilian popular musician*), 315
Gilberto, João (*Brazilian popular musician*), 315
Gillespie, John "Dizzy" (*American jazz musician*), 347–351
gitam (*short composed songs in South India*), 128
gitano (*term for Romani people in Spain*), 247, 288, 290 See also Roma
giying, *see* ugal
glasnost (*Soviet policy of openness*), 249, 252
Glass, Philip (*American composer*), 61
glissando (*sliding pitch*), 33, 66, 83, 91
global pop (*popular music label*), 324, 356
globular flute, *see* flute, globular
glosolalia (*use of vocables in Spanish flamenco singing*), 292–293
golosnik (*lead singer in south Russian folk song*), 265
golpe (*technique of guitarist striking instrument body*), 292
gong (*circular metal idiophone*), 29, 38, 41, 42, 173, 177, 184–186, 194, 198–200, 211, 214, 217–227, 229–231, 234, 235–239, 241, 243
gong ageng (*large Indonesian idiophone*), 222, 224–225, 226, 229, 231, 236
gong bambu (*Indonesian buzzed-lip instrument*), 38
gong cina (*Indonesian idiophone*), 42
gong suwukan (*Javanese idiophone*), 222
gongan (*Indonesian section delineated by gong stroke*), 224, 229, 231

Gorbachev, Mikail (*Soviet premier*), 249
Gorky, Maxim (*Russian writer*), 251
gospel music (*American popular religious music*), 328, 344–346, 354, 357
grace notes (*quick ornamental tones*), 202, 260, 285
Graceland (*Paul Simon album*), 2–4, 69
Granada, Spain, 90
grancharski horo (*Bulgarian dance*), 259
Grandmaster Flash (*Caribbean-American hip-hop musician*), 354
Great Britain, 45, 69, 126, 127, 129, 131, 155, 188, 281, 282, 323, 331, 353, *see also* United Kingdom
Greece, 82, 246, 247, 251, 264; ancient, 10, 77, 85–86, 95, 100, 246, 251, 258, 268, 275, 288
griot (*term for West African musician*), 59, *see also* jali
groaner (*singer in South African popular choral music*), 69
grunge rock (*genre of popular music*), 354
guan (*Chinese small cylindrical double-reed aerophone*), 173, 197
guchui (*Chinese folk double-reed and drum ensemble*), 177
guellal (*Algerian pipe drum*), 94
guitar (*European lute chordophone*), 23, 25, 32, 33; in Africa, 64, 67–68; in China, 187; in Europe, 269, 271, 274, 275, 276, 277, 280, 282, 288, 290–294; in Indonesia, 243; in Latin America, 298, 299, 300, 301, 302–308, 311, 312, 315, 317, 318; in Middle East, 94, 101, 154, 155; in North America, 326–327, 332–333, 340, 344, 345, 351, 352; *see also* electric guitar, guitarrón, Hawaiian guitar, pedal steel guitar, slide guitar
guitarrón (*large Mexican bass guitar*), 303
gumboot (*South African popular music/dance style*), 2–3, 69
guqin (*Chinese curved-board zither*), 14, 162–167, 169, 174–177
guqu (*Chinese narrative "drum song"*), 118, 181
guru (*traditional teacher in India*), 128, 129
gusheh (*melodic basis of classical Iranian improvisation*), 95, 97–98
gusli (*Russian zither*), 263–264
Guthrie, Woody (*American folk songwriter*), 333
Gyatso, Dalai Lama Tenzin (*Tibetan spiritual leader*), 110
gypsy, *see* Roma

H

habañera (*Spanish/Latin American dance rhythm*), 103, 299, 300
hackbrett (*Central European zither*), 276
Hafiz, Shams al-Din Muhammad (*Iranian poet*), 77–78, 80

Haiti, 342

Hakim (*Egyptian popular musician*), 94, 104

Halmos, Béla (*Hungarian folk musician*), 255

hammered dulcimer, *see* dulcimer

Hancock, Herbie (*American popular musician*), 61

Handy, W. C. (*American jazz musician*), 345

Hapsburgs (*family of European rulers*), 248

hard rock (*popular music style*), 324, 353, 354

hardcore (*genre of electronic dance music*), 356

Hardin, Lil (*American jazz musician*), 343

Harlan County, Kentucky, United States, 333

harmonic (*chordophone playing technique*), 174–176

harmonic (*type of overtone*), 36, 52, 60

harmonic progression (*sequence of chords*), 66, 70, 155, 273–276, 289, 299, 301, 304–305, 344, 347–349, 351, 353–356

harmonic series (*frequency series found in wind, string instruments*), 36, 277

harmonium (*portable reed organ*), 126, 131, 132, 134, 138, 146, 147

harmony (*technique of combining multiple simultaneous pitches*), 4, 7, 13, 15, 23–26, 128; and Africa, 66–67, 68–70; and China, 165, 180, 181, 183, 188–189; and Eastern Europe, 252, 258, 261–262; and India, 154–157; and Indonesia, 243, 247; and Japan, 193, 211; and Jewish music, 99, 100, 102, 103; and Latin America, 299, 300–301, 302–305, 315; and Middle East, 78, 94; and North America, 324, 325, 327–329, 332, 343–349; and Western Europe, 269, 270–281, 286, 288, 289, 292; *see also* harmonic progression, triad

harp (*category of chordophones*), 35, 47, 48, 52, 81, 99, 154, 280–281, 283, 301, 303, 304–305, 307–308, 316, 318, angle 35, 52, bow 35, 52

harp-guitar, *see* Schrammelgitare

harpsichord (*European plucked string keyboard*), 271

harp-zither, *see* diskantzither

Harrison, George (*English popular musician*), 159

Harrison, Lou (*American composer*), xv, 3, 244–245

Hashmi, Mohammed Zahur (*Indian film composer*), 154–158

Hasidim (*Jewish religious group*), 100

hatsiatsia (*genre of pieces from Ghana*), 54–56

Hawaiian guitar (*lute chordophone*), 327

hayashi (*Japanese ensemble*), 193, 208

hazzanut (*Jewish sung prayer form*), 100

head (*beginning tune in jazz*),343, 348–350

head (*stretched membrane of a drum*),38–39, 45, 49, 50, 55, 58, 89, 112, 132, 147, 152, 173, 177, 194, 197, 208, 209, 222, 311, 313, 335

heavy metal (*popular music style*), 353

Hendrix, Jimi (*American popular musician*), 352

hennon (*auxiliary tones outside Japanese mode*), 195

heptatonic mode (*mode of seven tones per octave*), 10, 61, 95, 113, 135, 168, 274

hertz (*unit of frequency measurement*), 7

heterophony (*texture of simultaneous variations*), 25–26, 79, 89–93, 96, 116–118, 120, 165, 184, 186, 203, 237, 240, 257, 259, 263, 266, 276, 280, 281, 285, 286, 325, 340

hexatonic mode (*mode of six tones per octave*), 10, 332

hichiriki (*Japanese cylindrical double reed aerophone*), 196–201

highlife (*West African popular music style*), 67, 74

hi-hat cymbal (*double idiophone struck or operated with foot pedal*), 313–314, 348, 355

hil huur, *see* morin huur

hillbilly music, *see* country music

Hinduism, 124–127, 139, 152, 214–215, 216–218, 224, 232–233, 236

Hindustani music (*tradition of North Indian music*), 125, 127, 135, 147, 148

hip-hop (*American popular music style*), 154, 312, 324, 355

Hispañola, 296

Ho, Ghana, 49, 50

hoedown (*American folk dance*), 331

holler (*African American singing style*), 263, 344

Homer (*ancient Greek bard*), 246, 248, 250

homophony (*texture of melody and harmonic accompaniment*), 24–27, 271, 273, 341

Hong Kong, China 188

honkyoku (*classical repertory of shakuhachi music*), 203, 204

honky-tonk (*genre of American country music*), 332

Hood, Mantle (*American ethnomusicologist*), xvi, 244

höömii (*Mongolian multiphonic singing*), 118–120, 122

Hopi (*indigenous American ethnic group*), 337

horn (*buzzed-lip aerophone*), 47, 51, 72, 99, 277, See also French horn

horn section (*aerophone group in jazz, rhythm and blues*), 68, 354

Hornbostel, Erich von (*Austrian ethnomusicologist*), 31

hornpipe (*European dance*), 284

horo (*Bulgarian round dance*), 259

hosho (*rattle from Zimbabwe*), 64–66

House, Edward "Son" (*American blues musician*), 345

Howard University, 3

hu (*family of Chinese bowed lutes*), 117, 120, 169–170, 172, 181, *see also* erhu, jinghu, sihu

huang zhong (*"yellow bell" ancient Chinese pitch standard*), 162, 173

huapango (*type of Mexican folk dance/band*), 303

huapanguera (*Mexican guitar used in huapango*), 303

huasteca (*Mexican folk music style*), 298, 304

huayno (*Andean folk dance*), 297, 317, 318

huehuetl (*Aztec large footed drum*), 296

hui (*inlaid dots on guqin*), 174

Hungary, 33, 246, 247, 252, 253–258, 276; art music, 247–248; history, 253–254; Turkish influence, 253–254; musical instruments, 253–255; dance, 254–258; Central Asian influence, 246, 254; Western European influence, 254; mode, 254; musical form, 16, 254, 256–257

huqin, *see* hu

huro (*singing style in Zimbabwe*), 66

Hussain, Zakir (*Indian drummer*), 159

hymn (*European religious song*), 15–16, 325, 328–330

I

idiophone (*category of instruments which vibrate as a whole*), 32, 39, 41–42, 48, 50, 56, 173, 214, 270, 323, 334, 335, See also individual instruments

imitation (*repetition of melody in different instruments/sung parts*), 25

imitative polyphony (*texture that includes imitation*), 25

improvisation (*extemporaneous decisions in musical performance*), 5, 26, 47; in Africa, 62, 64, 66, 69; in Arabic music, 85, 87, 92, 94; in Austria, 277; in China, 177; in Eastern Europe, 250, 252; in Hungary, 256–257; in India, 126–129, 133, 134, 137, 141, 142, 143–145, 147, 148–150, 153, 155; in Indonesia, 234; in Iran, 77–78, 95–97; in Ireland, 281; in jazz, 155, 160, 342, 343, 346, 347–350; in Jewish music, 100, 102; in Middle East, 77–80; in Mongolia, 118; in North America, 324; in Russia 263; in United States, 160, 342, 343, 346, 347–350

in (*Japanese mode with semitones*), 192, 195–196, 203, 206, 211

inanga (*zither from Uganda*), 53

Inca (*Andean civilization*), 296, 298, 316
India, 3, 8, 10, 11, 32, 38, 40, 83, 94, 108, 124–160; British influence, 126, 129, 131; dance, 124, 148, 152, 154, 155; film music, 94, 116, 125, 126, 127, 153–158, 243; folk music, 152–153; geography, 124; history, 124–127; influence from Iran, 125; influence on Africa, 44; influence on Arabic music, 94; influence on China, 163; influence on Indonesia, 214, 243; influence on Iran, 125; influence on Japan, 190, 196; influence on Middle East, 94; influence on Tibet, 106, 110, 113, 116; Islamic influence, 77; music theory, 21, 134–141; musical education, 128–129; musical instruments, 129–133; patronage, 126, 147; popular music, 125, 153–158; scales, 134; texture, 25, 26, 149–150; tuning system, 86, 134–135; vocal music, 142, 146–159; wedding music, 125, 126, 131
Indians, American, *see* indigenous Americans
indigenous Americans, 296, 298–299, 301, 309, 320,323, 333–339, 357; musical instruments 334–335; musical form 334–335
Indonesia, 9, 31, 34, 37, 38, 39, 42, 124, 173, 214–245; Arabic influence, 242–243; Chinese influence, 214, 242; dance, 214, 215, 222, 234–235, 237–242; dramatic music, 214–217, 238, 239–242; Dutch influence, 242; European influence, 215, 221, 242–244; geography, 214; history, 214–216; influence of India, 214, 243; influence of Latin America, 243, 244; influence of United States, 243; influence on Southeast Asia, 214; influence on United States, 244; Islamic influence, 215, 218; mode, 224; music theory, 223–231; musical form, 223–231; musical instruments, 219–222, 235–237; popular music, 242–244, 245; Portuguese influence, 242; tuning systems, 9–10, 216, 218, 222, 224, 227, 239, 243
instrumentation (*list of instruments*), 29
interlocking patterns (*separate instruments combining to make a single melody*), 233, 238, 239, 240–241, 243
Internet, 276, 324
interval (*difference in pitch*), 8
Inuit (*Arctic ethnic group*), 336
iqa' (*Arabic rhythmic forms*), 88–91
irama (*Javanese relationships of rhythmic density*), 225–227, 228, 230
Irama, Rhoma (*Indonesian dangdut musician*), 243

Iran, 33, 35, 36, 41, 76–80, 82–84, 94–96, 104; Arabic influence, 95–96; dance, 96; European influence, 95–96; influence on Central Asia, 106, 113; influence on India, 125; musical form, 96; musical instruments, 82–84; poetry, 96; popular music, 96; revolution, 79, 96
Iraq, 82, 83, 84, 89, 333
Ireland, 21, 250, 280–287, 323, 331; history, 280–282; English influence, 281; dance, 21, 280–282, 284, 286–287; musical instruments, 280–281, 283; musical form, 284, 285–287; popular music 282
Irish harp (*diatonic chordophone*), 280–281, 283
iscathamiya (*popular music style in South Africa*), 2
isicathulo (*popular music style in South Africa*), 69
Islam and music, 80–81, 146
Islam, 45, 55, 77–81, 94, 106, 125, 127, 146, 151–152, 215, 218, 233, 247, 258, 268, 288
Islamic music, 60, 68, 84, 94, 146, 247
isorhythm (*repeating rhythm with changing melody*), 250, 263, 264
Israel, 78, 79, 100–101, 104
Istanbul, Turkey, 76
Italy, 247, 295, 297, 323

J

jaipongan (*Indonesian popular music genre*), 243
Jakarta, Java, Indonesia, 214
jaleo (*shouts at flamenco performance*), 290, 292
jali (*West African hereditary musician caste*), 45, 50, 52, 56–64, 74
Jamaica, 355
Jammu and Kashmir, India, 40
Japan, 8, 15, 29, 165, 190–213, 323; Chinese influence, 163, 172, 190, 192, 195, 196, 203, 211; court music, 190, 194, 195–202; dance, 209; dramatic music, 199, 208–211; festivals, 193–194, 213; folk music, 193–195; influence from India, 190, 196; influence of United States, 211–212; isolationism, 192, 193; mode, 192–193, 211; Korean influence, 195, 196; mode, 195–196, 203, 206; musical form, 198, 200–201, 204–205, 206–207; musical instruments, 29, 197, 199, 202–207; popular music, 211–212; religion, 190–195; rhythm, 19, 194, 203, 209; texture, 26, 198–199, 201; Western influence, 193, 194, 204, 211–212
jarabe (*Mexican folk song/dance type*), 300

jarana (*medium Mexican guitar*), 303–305
jarocho (*type of Mexican folk band*), 303–305, 318
Java, Indonesia, 3, 9, 10, 13, 15, 17, 21, 25, 34, 39, 42, 178, 214–231, 233, 234, 238, 242–245, 272
jaw's harp (*mouth-resonated, plucked idiophone*), 52, 119
jazz (*American music style*), 2, 3, 21, 92, 146, 322–324, 339, 342–354, 357; bebop, 323, 346–350; big band, 298, 300, 311, 315, 332, 346–347, 352; Dixieland, 342–344, 346, 349; Indian influence, 159–160; influence on African music, 67, 69; influence on India, 154–155; influence on Indonesia, 243; influence on Japan, 194, 212; influence on Jewish music, 100–101; influence on Latin America, 300; Latin American influence, 298, 300–301, 311; modal, 159; swing, 68, 300, 323, 346
jegogan (*large Balinese metallophone*), 236, 239, 240
jeli, *see* jali
Jerusalem, Israel, 76, 77
Jesuits (*Roman Catholic monastic order*), 301
Jesus (*spiritual leader and deity to Christians*), 76, 79, 316, 329–330, 345
Jewish music 96, 99–104, 264; and dance, 100, 103; and mode, 100, 102; Arabic influence, 100, 104; folk, 99, 100; European influence, 96, 99, 100; influence on Christian music, 76; influence on Europe, 288, 290; influence on Russia, 264; popular, 100–104; religious, 76, 99–100; Turkish influence, 102–103, 104; United States influence, 100–101
Jewish people, 288, 290, 323
Jew's harp, *see* jaw's harp
jhala (*Indian technique of interpolating drone pitches between melody notes*), 142, 145
Jian, Cui (*Chinese popular musician*), 187–189
Jiang Qing (*Chinese leader*), 183
jifti (*Persian Gulf region single-reed aerophone*), 84
jig (*Irish/British dance*), 284
jin (*scale fragments in Arabic music*), 86
jinghu (*Chinese high bowed spike fiddle*), 172, 184, 185
jingles (*small cymbals or metal rattles*), 50, 61, 152
jingxi (*Beijing opera, Chinese dramatic form*), 164, 172, 182–187
jiuta, *see* utaimono
Jobim, Antônio Carlos (*Brazilian popular musician*), 315
jo-ha-kyu (*Japanese form*), 198
Johnson, Bill (*American jazz musician*), 343

Johnson, Robert (*American blues musician*), 345

Joplin, Janis (*American rock singer*), 153

Joplin, Scott (*American ragtime composer*), 342, 345

jor (*quasi-pulsatile section in North Indian performance*), 142

joropo (*Venezuelan folk dance*), 300

jota (*Spanish folk dance*), 289

joza (*bowed lute in Iraq*), 82

j-pop (*Japanese popular music*), 194, 212

jublag, *see* calung

Judaism, 76, 78, 79, 96, 99–100, 264, 288, 290

juju (*West African popular music style*), 67–68, 74

jump blues, *see* rhythm and blues

K

kabuki (*Japanese classical theater form*), 192, 199, 209–211, 213

kachina (*Hopi spirit*), 337–338

kaganu (*small drum from Ghana*), 55, 58–59

kagura (*Japanese Shinto music*), 193

Kagyu (*tradition of Tibetan Buddhism*), 113

kajar, *see* kempli

kakegoe (*Japanese shouts from musicians*), 209

kakko (*Japanese cylindrical drum*), 197–200

Kalevala (*Finnish epic*), 251

k'aman (*Armenian bowed lute*), 83

kaman (*violin in Middle East*), 81 *see also* violin

kamanche (*Arabic bowed chordophone*), 83

kamancheh (*Iranian bowed chordophone*), 82, *see also* rabab

kanjira (*South Indian tambourine*), 149–150, 151, 155

Kanté, Mory (*Senegalese popular musician*), 61

kantele (*Finnish zither*), 251

kantilan (*Balinese metallophone*), 236, 239, 240

kanun (*Turkish plucked zither*), 83, 263, 264, *see also* qanun

Karnatic music (*tradition of South Indian music*), 125, 127, 129, 147–151

Karpeles, Maud (*English ethnomusicologist*), 331

kasar (*Javanese characteristic of coarseness*), 219

Kashmir, *see* Jammu and Kashmir

katarimono (*Japanese narrative song*), 199

kathakali (*Indian classical dance*), 154

kaval (*Eastern European vertical notch flute*), 259–260

kawitan (*introduction in Balinese form*), 240, 242

kayagum (*Korean curved board zither*), 33, 206

Kazakhstan, 106

Keane, Sean (*Irish musician*), 281

kebyar (*style of Balinese gamelan*), 216, 233, 234–238, 244, 245

kecak (*Balinese chorus of interlocking shouts*), 238, 245

kecapi (*Indonesian box zither*), 34

keening (*Irish sung lament*), 282

kembangan (*Indonesian process of elaboration*), 223–224, 228

kemençe (*Turkish bowed chordophone*), 83, *see also* kamanche

kemong, *see* kentong

kempli (*Balinese time-keeper gong*), 236, 237

kempul (*Javanese small hanging gong*), 222, 224–227

kempur (*Balinese medium hanging gong*), 236

kempyang (*small Javanese gong*), 224, 226

kena (*Andean notch flute*), 316

kendang (*Indonesian drum*), 222, 229, 237, 243

Kenduli, India 152

kenong (*Javanese large kettle gong*), 221, 224–227, 229

kentong (*Balinese small hanging gong*), 236, 241

Kentucky, United States, 331, 332, 333, 357

Kenya, 7, 74

kepatihan (*Indonesian number notation*), 227

Kerala, India, 152

kerep (*relative density of ketuk in Javanese forms*), 224–225

Ketama (*Spanish Nuevo Flamenco group*), 291

ketawang (*Javanese gamelan form*), 225

ketipung (*Javanese drum*), 222

ketuk (*Javanese small kettle-gong*), 225, 226

key (*mode and tonic*), 11, 16, 195, 279

key center, *see* tonic

key change (*shift in tonic*), 279

khali (*deemphasized beat in Indian tala cycle*), 140, 144

khamak (*Baul string drum*), 152

Khan, Alauddin (*Indian classical musician*), 159

Khan, Ali Akbar (*Indian classical musician*), 130, 141–145, 159, 160

Khan, Nusrat Fateh Ali (*Pakistani qawal singer*), 146, 161

khana (*phrases in Arabic bashraf*), 91

Khayyam, *see* Hashmi, Mohammed Zahur

Khoikhoin (*African ethnic group*), 44

khol (*double-headed clay Indian folk drum*), 152

Khomeini, Ruhollah (*Iranian spiritual leader*), 80

khomuz (*Mongolian jaw's harp*), 119

khoro eleno mome (*Bulgarian dance*), 259

khyal (*North Indian vocal form*),147

kidi (*drum from Ghana*), 55, 58–59

Kiganda (*ethnic group in Uganda*), 51

Kindi, Abu Yusuf Ya'qub ibn Ishaq al- (*medieval Islamic scholar*), 77

Kinko (*tradition of shakuhachi instruction*), 203

kirtana (*South Indian vocal form*), 148

Kitaro (*Japanese popular music composer*), 212

Klezmatics (*American klezmer band*), 100–101

klezmer (*Jewish popular music ensemble*), 99, 100–104

Knight, Roderick (*American ethnomusicologist*), xvi, 62

Knödel (*Austrian band*), 277

Kodály, Zoltan (*Hungarian composer/ ethnomusicologist*), 248, 255

Kodo (*Japanese taiko ensemble*), 194, 212

koma-bue (*Japanese transverse bamboo flute*), 197

komagaku (*repertory of gagaku*), 196

komal (*lowered Indian scale step*), 135

komuso (*Japanese wandering Zen priest players of shakuhachi*), 191, 203

Kong Fuzi, *see* Confucius

kora (*West African harp-lute*), 52, 60–63, 74

Korea, 26, 31, 33, 83, 110, 162, 163, 192, 195, 196, 206, 252

Korea, North 252

Koryak (*Russian ethnic group*), 41

kotekan (*Balinese interlocking technique*), 239, 240–241

koto (*Japanese curved board zither*), 33, 190, 192, 196, 198, 202, 203, 206–207

kotoba (*heightened speech-song from noh drama*), 209

ko-tsuzumi (*Japanese small shoulder drum*), 208–209

kris (*Indonesian ritual dagger*), 242

Krishna (*Hindu deity*), 131

Krishnan, Vidwan Ramnad (*South Indian singer*), 149–150, 160

kriti (*South Indian vocal form*), 147–151

krivo horo (*Bulgarian dance*), 259

kroncong (*Indonesian popular music genre*), 243, 245

Kulthum, Umm (*Egyptian singer*), 93–94, 104

kumbengo (*ostinato basis in kora music*), 60, 62–63

kumiuta (*Japanese classical songs accompanied by koto*), 206

kungling (*Tibetan buzzed-lip instrument*), 108, 112, 114

kunqu (*classical Chinese opera form*), 164, 171, 182, 184

Kurds (*Middle Eastern ethnic group*), 84

Kurosawa, Akira (*Japanese film director*), 212

Kutev, Filip (*Bulgarian folk song arranger*), 258, 260–262, 267

Kuti, Fela Anikulapo (*Nigerian popular musician*), 67–68, 70–74

Kuti, Femi (*Nigerian popular musician*), 68

kuuchir (*Mongolian bowed spike fiddle*), 117

Kwakiutl (*indigenous North American ethnic group*), 337

kwela (*popular music style in South Africa*), 69

k'yamancha (*Armenian bowed lute*), 82, *see also* rebab

kyogen (*Japanese comic plays*), 208

Kyrgystan, 106

L

La Puebla de Cazalla, Spain, 293

laba, *see* suona

Ladino (*language of Sephardic Jews*), 101

ladrang (*Javanese gamelan form*), 225, 226, 227, 229

Ladysmith Black Mambazo (*South African popular music choral group*), 69, 74

Ladzekpo, Alfred (*musician from Ghana*), xvi, 55

Ladzekpo, C. K. (*musician from Ghana*), 45

Ladzekpo, Kobla (*musician from Ghana*), xvi, 45, 53, 57–59

Lagos, Nigeria, 67, 68

lagu (*inner melody of Javanese gamelan*), 223, 227

Lake Titicaca 316

Lakota 333–334, 338

lament (*song of sorrow*), 263–264, 282, 286

ländler (*Austrian dance*), 276

Langa (*caste of Rajasthani musicians*), 151

langgam Jawa (*Javanese popular song*), 245

language and music, 46–48, 50, 57–58, 85, 88, 345

Lao Zi (*founder of Daoism*), 162, 166

Latin America 243, 296–319; African influence, 54, 296, 298–301, 309–315; art music, 297, 308–309, 315–316; dance, 21, 297–304, 309–312, 315–317; dramatic music, 296, 297, 302, 308; European influence, 296–302, 309, 316–318; geography, 296; history, 296–299, 302, 310–311, influence of United States 300, 308, 312, 315, influence on Europe 298; influence on Indonesia, 243, 244; influence on North America, 298–299, 301, 318; influence on Spain, 291; Middle Eastern influence 81; music theory, 300–301; musical form, 299–300, 302–303; musical instruments, 301, 302–304, 316–318; popular music, 297–301, 304, 308, 315, 318; religious music, 296–298, 302, 310, 316; Spanish influence, 296–298, 301, 304

layali (*Arabic vocal form*), 87, 90, 93

le (*Afro-Brazilian drum*), 310

lead instruments (*main melodic instruments in jazz ensemble*), 343

Lebanon, 23–24, 79

Levites (*ancient Jewish musician-priests*), 76, 99

lhamo (*Tibetan folk theater*), 116

Liang, Jianfeng (*Chinese popular music composer*), 189

limba (*Mongolian transverse flute*), 117, 120

Linda, Solomon (*South African songwriter*), 69

Ling Lun (*legendary Chinese inventor of music*), 162, 173

lining out (*American method of religious singing*), 325, 345

Liszt, Ferenc (Franz),(*Hungarian composer*), 248

Lomax, Alan (*American ethnomusicologist*), 345

long songs, *see* urtyn duu

loops (*electronically repeating sections*), 355–356

Lorca, Federico García (*Spanish writer*), 289–291

Lord of the Dance (*Irish dance stage show*), 282

Los Angeles, United States, 96, 342, 355

loudness in music, 15, 17, 18, 22

Louisiana, United States, 320, 323, 343–344

LP (*recording format*), 352

lü (*pitch of Chinese tuning system*), 167

Lucía, Paco de (*Spanish flamenco guitarist*), 291

lullaby (*song for child's sleep*), 177, 271, 334

lundu (*Afro-Brazilian dance*), 297, 300, 310

lung (*Buddhist winds of inner spirit*), 110

lunzhi (*tremolo ornament on Chinese chordophone*), 179

luo (*Chinese gongs*), 173, 177, 184, 185

luogu (*Chinese folk drum and gong ensembles*), 177

lute (*category of chordophone*), defined, 34; *see also individual instruments*

lute (*Renaissance-period European chordophone*), 82, 288–289

lute, spike (*category of chordophone*), 34, 82, 117, 170, 221

lyre (*category of chordophone*), 35, 47, 48, 52, 81, 99

M

ma (*Japanese aesthetic principle*), 191–192, 193, 201, 204, 208, 212

Maal, Baaba (*Senegalese popular musician*), 74

Macedonia, 248

Madagascar, 34

magruna (*North African single-reed instrument*), 84

Magyar (*Hungarian ethnic group*), 246, 248, 253–254, 256

magyarnota (*Hungarian parlor songs*), 254

Mahabharata (*ancient Hindu epic*), 124, 215

Mahakala (*Buddhist deity*), 113, 114

Mahler, Gustav (*Austrian composer*), 271

mahon'era (*Zimbabwe singing style*), 66

Maidu (*indigenous American ethnic group*), 335

Majapahit (*ancient Javanese kingdom*), 214–215

major mode (*Western diatonic mode*), 10, 62, 96, 156, 256, 272–274, 286–288, 332, 353

Makah (*indigenous American ethnic group*), 335

malambo (*Argentinian dance*), 300

Mali, 44, 60

mambo (*Latin American ballroom dance*), 300

Manchuria, China, 194, 196

mandala (*symbolic symmetrical spiritual art*), 107, 108, 111, 112–113

Mande (*West African ethnic group*), 58–59, 62

Mandingo Griot Society (*American-African fusion music band*), 61

mandolin (*European plucked lute*), 33, 318, 342

Mangashkar, Lata (*Indian playback singer*), 153–154

maniqueos (*Mexican guitar strumming patterns*), 304

mantra (*repeated spiritual textual formula*), 107, 126, 127,139, 147

Mao Zedong (*Chinese leader*), 165, 166, 181, 183, 187

Mapfumo, Thomas (*African popular musician*), 75

maqam (*Arabic mode/melodic basis*), 76, 83, 85–92, 95, 100

maracas (*Latin American rattles*), 54, 70

march (*European instrumental form*), 341–342

Marchena, Melchor de (*Spanish guitarist*), 292–294

mariachi (*Mexican popular band style*), 302, 303, 304, 309

marimba (*Latin America-African xylophone*), 30, 42, 50, 301

Marquis of Zeng, 172, 173

Masai (*East African ethnic group*), 7

mash-ups (*electronic remixes of recordings*), 324, 356

masingo (*Ethiopian bowed lute*), 34

Mason, Lowell (*American religious music composer*), 345

mawwal (*Arabic song form*), 90, 94

maxixe (*syncopated Brazilian dance*), 22, 311

Maya (*Central American civilization*), 296

maye (*Iranian scale type*), 95

mbalax (*West African popular music style*), 69

mbaqanga (*South African popular music style*), 2, 69

mbira (*African plucked idiophone*), 47, 50, 61, 64–67, 74, 340

mbira dzavadzimu (*large mbira of Zimbabwe*), 64

mbira pop (*Zimbabwe popular music genre*), 64

mbube (*South African popular music style*), 69

McColgan, John (*stage director*), 282

McCurry, John (*American shape-note composer*), 328

McKim, Lucy (*American ethnomusicologist*), 340, 344

McLaughlin, John (*English-American guitarist*), 159

measure (*European metrical grouping*), 341, 344

Mecca, Saudi Arabia, 79

meditation and music, 5, 108, 111, 126, 167, 174, 191–192, 195, 203–204

medley (*piece made up of a juxtaposition of several other pieces*), 284

Mei Lanfang (*Chinese opera performer*), 184, 189

melakarta (*South Indian scale system*), 125, 135

melisma (*many notes to one syllable*), 79, 81, 85, 87, 94, 113, 117, 146, 147, 154, 155, 158, 169, 183, 243, 289, 290, 293, 354

melodic contour, *see* contour, melodic

melodic motion, 13

melody (*variation in pitch with rhythm*), 7, 11–16

membranophone (*instruments with vibrating membrane*), 32, 38–41, 49–50, *see also* drums and drumming

Memphis, Tennessee, United States, 345, 351

Menese, José (*Spanish flamenco singer*), 292–295

merengué (*Dominican dance/song type*), 300

merong (*Javanese gamelan form*), 225

mestizo (*Latin American people or music of mixed heritage*), 299, 302, 309, 318

metallophone (*metal idiophone with bars or keys*), 156, 217, 220, 223, 230, 235–237, 239, 240, 243

meta-music (*music made up of remixing existing compositions*), 356

meter (*patterns of beat groupings*),19–22; in Africa, 46–48, 58, 62, 65; in Central Asia, 117; in China, 169, 174, 183, 186; in Eastern Europe, 247–248, 250–251, 254, 259–263; in India, 126, 128, 133, 139–142, 144–147, 156; in Indonesia, 216–217, 244; in Jewish music, 99–100; in Japan, 200, 203, 206; in Latin America, 300, 302, 305, 317; in Middle East, 79, 88–89, 91–93, 96–98; in North America, 325, 330, 335, 337–338, 348; in Western Europe, 20, 21, 276, 280, 284, 286, 287, 289, 291

metrical stress (*feeling of beat emphasis*), 21–22, 48, 140, 194, 218, 224, 227, 228, 243, 256

Mevlevi (*order of Turkish Sufis*), 81

Mexico, 296–298, 300, 301, 302–309, 318, 339; art music, 308–309; dance, 298, 300, 302–305, 309; history, 296–298, 302; influence from North America, 308; influence from South America, 303; influence from Spain, 304; musical form, 302–303; musical instruments, 35, 37, 42, 302–304; popular music, 304, 308; religious music, 296, 302; texture, 24

Mexico City, Mexico, 296, 303, 309

Michio, Miyagi (*Japanese composer*), 194

microtone (*interval smaller than a semitone*), 79, 134, 203, 259, 324, 340

Middle East, 76–105; dance, 80, 81, 84, 85, 88, 94, 96; European influence, 78, 93–94; folk music, 80, 88, 93–94; influence of India, 94; influence on Central Asia, 106; influence on China, 171; influence on Eastern Europe, 247–248, 250, 253–254, 258, 259; language and music, 85, 88; mode, 85–88; music theory, 85–89; musical form, 89–90, 91–92; musical instruments, 81–84; nationalism, 78; poetry, 88, 90; popular music, 78, 93–94; religious music, 80–81, 84

MIDI (*protocol for digital communication of musical information*), 324, 355

mijwiz (*Middle Eastern single-reed aerophone*), 84

mikagura (*Japanese Shinto ritual music*), 194

Miki, Minoru (*Japanese composer*), 212

military band, 211

minimalism (*Western experimental music style*), 160

minor mode (*Western diatonic mode*), 10, 11, 211, 256, 272–275, 287, 288, 329, 353

minstrels, United States (*entertainers imitating African-American music styles*), 321, 326, 341

Miranda, Carmen (*Brazilian singer*), 311

Misra, Pandit Mahapurush (*Indian tabla player*), 143–145

Mississippi River, United States, 344, 345

mizmar (*Egyptian double reed instrument*), 84

mnemonic aids and music, 89, 141, 273

mode (*melodic/pitch basis of musical piece*), 10–11, 16; in Africa, 62, 70; in China, 167–169, 176–179, 181, 182, 183–187; in Eastern Europe, 254, 256, 259; in Japan, 195–196, 198, 200, 203, 206, 211, 212, 217; in Jewish music, 99, 100, 102; in India, 125, 126, 134–139; in Indonesia, 219, 223, 224, 227–229; in Middle East, 76, 79, 85–88, 96; in North America, 324, 329, 332, 336–337, 353; in Tibet, 113, 117; in Western Europe, 272, 274–275, 285–288, 291

model operas (*Chinese socialist realist dramas*), 183

modernism (*style in twentieth-century art music*), 248, 251–252, 270

modhina (*Brazilian traditional lyrical song*), 315, 316

modulation (*temporary change in mode or tonic*), 16, 87, 88, 89, 95, 98, 135, 155, 279

mokugyo (*Japanese woodblocks used in Buddhist rituals*), 195

Moldova, 246

Molloy, Matt (*Irish musician*), 281

Moloney, Paddy (*Irish musician*), 281, 285–287

monasticism and music, 107–115, 163, 190–192, 194–195, 203–205

Monge Cruz, José (*Spanish flamenco singer*), 291, 295

Mongol (*Central Asian ethnic group*), 85, 106–107, 109, 172

Mongolia, 106, 107, 109, 113, 116–122; epic singing, 116, 118; influence of China, 117, 120; influence of nature, 119, 121; influence of Tibet 111; influence on China, 109, 118, 119; musical instruments, 119–120

Mongolian Empire 85, 106, 164, 172, 182, 247

monophony (*texture of a single melody*), 23–24, 26, 81, 93, 131, 165, 271, 273, 276, 277, 280, 325, 334

Monroe, Bill (*American bluegrass musician*), 332

Montenegro, 251

Monterey Pop Festival, 159

Moore, Scotty (*American rock-and-roll musician*), 352

Morelia, Mexico, 308

Moreno Galván, Francisco (*Spanish poet*), 291–294

morin huur (*Mongolian bowed "horsehead" lute*), 117, 118, 119, 120

Morocco, 79, 82, 89, 104

Morrison, Van (*Irish popular musician*), 282

moso-biwa (*Japanese priest singers and players of biwa*), 190, 197

motive (*melodic fragment*), 10, 11, 14, 15; in Africa, 62, 63; in China, 176–177, 185–187; in India, 125, 126, 128, 134, 138, 141–146; in Indonesia, 217, 223–224, 227–229; in Japan, 206–207, 209; in Jewish music, 100; in Middle East, 77; in Russia, 263; in United States, 348–349; in Western Europe, 272

motive, cadential (*short melody associated with phrase endings*), 13–14

motreb (*Iranian light classical musicians*), 96

mountain dulcimer (*American fretted zither*), 254, 327

Mouquet, Erik (*French popular music composer*), 356

mouth bass, *see* szajbögö

movement (*discrete section of composition*), 15, 92, 96

Mozart, Wolfgang Amadeus (*classical-period Austrian composer*), 270, 276

MPB (*Brazilian popular music*), 299, 315

mpuunyi (*conical drum from Uganda*), 40

Mrad, Nidaa Abou (*Lebanese musician*), 90, 92

mrdangam (*double-headed cylindrical drum of South India*), 132, 147, 149–150, 151

mu'adhdhin (*Islamic singers of call to prayer*), 81

mudra (*Buddhist symbolic hand positions*), 113

Mughal (*period of Islamic empire in India*),125, 147, 159

Muhammad (*founder of Islam*), 77

multiphonic singing (*single singer producing more than one identifiable pitch simultaneously*), 108, 109, 111, 115, 118

multitrack recording (*technique of electronically overlaying sounds from multiple recordings*), 353

Mumbai, India, 153

murali (*classical Indian transverse flute*), 131

muraiki (*shakuhachi playing technique*), 204

music and language, *see* language and music

music printing, 95, 269, 274–276, 281, 315, 321–322, 325, 328, 341, 342, 345

music theory (*analysis of music and musical systems*), xii, 4, 10, 21, 22, 77–78, 80, 85–89, 125, 127, 129, 134–141, 167–169, 183, 195, 223–231, 246, 268, 270–274, 343

Música Popular Brasileira, *see* MPB

musical (*American popular theater form*), 100, 322

musical bow (*single string chordophone*), 51–52, 301, 340

musical form (*structure of musical compositions*), 15–16, 23; in Africa, 16, 47, 57–59, 68; in Arabic music, 89–90; in China, 16, 174–177, 178–180; in Hungary, 16, 254, 256–257; in indigenous American music, 334–335; in Indonesia, 223–231; in Iran, 96; in Ireland, 284, 285–287; in Japan, 198, 200–201, 204–205, 206–207; in Latin America, 299–300, 302–303; in Mexico, 302–303; in Russia, 263, 264–266; in Spain, 290; in United States, 334–335, 343–344; in Western Europe, 272, 284, 285–287, 290

musical instruments, 29, 30–42; in Africa, 47–53; in Andean countries, 316–318; in Austria, 276–277; in Brazil, 310–311; in Bulgaria, 259–260; in China, 169–174, 183–184; in Hungary, 253–255; in India, 129–133; in Indonesia, 219–222, 235–237; in Ireland, 280–281, 283; in Japan, 197, 199, 202–207; in Latin America, 301, 302–304, 310–311, 316–318; in Middle East, 81–84; in Mongolia, 119–120; in Russia, 263–264; in North America, 326–327, 334–335; in Tibet, 110–113; of indigenous Americans, 334–335

musical style (*combination of elements that describe or categorize music*), 41, 43

musicology (*study of music history*), xii, 4, 23, 44, 168, 274, 281, 289, 301, 336, 337

mute (*device to change or soften instrument timbre*), 343, 348

muwashshah (*Arabic song form*), 90, 92

Muzsikás (*Hungarian band*), 255, 267

Myanmar, *see* Burma

N

nagasvaram (*South Indian double-reed instrument*), 131

nair (*Mongolian celebration*), 116, 118

Nakai, R. Carlos (*Native American flute player*), 339, 356

Nammies, *see* Native American Music Awards

nangma (*Tibetan folk and popular music*), 116, 122

naobo (*Chinese opera cymbals*), 184

Napolean Bonaparte (*French monarch*), 78

Napoleonic Wars, 45, 297

Narayan, Ram (*Indian sarangi player*), 160

Nascimento, Milton (*Brazilian popular musician*), 315

nashid (*Islamic popular music*), 94

Nath, Pandit Pran (*Indian musician*), 160

nationalism (*expression of national heritage in art*), 46, 68, 78, 164, 248, 277, 297, 309

Native American Church, 339

Native American flute (*indigenous American aerophone*), 335, 339

Native American Music Awards, 339

Native Americans, *see* indigenous Americans

natural (*notation to play unaltered scale step*), 135

Natyasastra (*ancient Indian text of music and drama theory*), 125, 134, 138, 142

Navajo (*indigenous American ethnic group*), 337, 339

nawbah (*North African classical suite*), 89

nay (*Middle Eastern notch flute*), 81, 83, 89, 259

Nepal, 109, 110, 124, 127

Netherlands, 45, 215, 216, 235, 242, 320

netori (*gagaku prelude*), 198

Neuwirth, Roland (*Austrian musician*), 277

New Age music (*popular music style*), 2, 339

New Orleans, United States, 320, 343, 344

new wave (*popular music style*), 354

New York City, United States, 322, 342, 354

Newport Folk Festival, 353

nga chin (*large Tibetan double-headed drum*), 112, 114–115

ngoma (*drum from Zimbabwe*), 64

Nigeria, 67, 68, 70, 309

nigun (*Hasidic Jewish song form*), 100

Niña de los Peines, La, *see* Pavón, Pastora

niraval (*South Indian vocal improvisation style*), 148

Noble, Ray (*American jazz musician*), 347

Noces, Les, see Svadebka

noh (*Japanese classical theater form*), 191, 208–209, 210, 211

nohkan (*Japanese transverse bamboo flute*), 208–209, 210, 211

noise-core (*popular music style*), 212

non-pulsatile rhythm (*music without a perceptible beat*), 18–19

North America, 320–357; African influence, 321–323, 345; art music, 323, 341, 346, 352; Caribbean influence, 354–355; dance, 298, 300, 321, 324, 325, 331–335, 337–343, 346–347, 351, 352, 354–355; dramatic music, 321–322; European influence, 269, 323, 325; folk music, 331–333, 357; French influence, 343; geography, 320, 336; history, 320–324; mode, 336–337; musical form, 334–335, 343–344; musical instruments, 326–327, 334–335; popular music, 321–324, 332–333, 339, 341–347, 351–356; religious music, 325, 328–330, 333–334, 337–339, 345–346; Spanish influence, 326; *see also* Canada, United States

North Korea See Korea, North

Norway 295

notation, musical (*symbolic written representation of music*), xiv–xv, 14, 22; Chinese, 162, 169, 174, 181; in India, 124, 127, 140–141; in Middle East, 93, 95, 97, 99; Indonesian, 223, 227; Japanese, 193, 204–205; shape-note, 321–322, 325, 330; Tibetan, 111; Western 8, 252, 261, 269–274, 276, 281, 324–325, 340, 343, 346

notch flute, *see* flute, notch

note (*individual sonic event in music*), 18

nuba (*Moroccan classical suite*), 89

nueva canción (*South American popular music form*), 299

nuevo flamenco (*Spanish popular music form*), 291

NWA (*American rap group*), 355

Nyodo, Jin (*Japanese shakuhachi musician/ composer*), 191, 204–205

O

Ó Riada, Seán (*Irish musician*), 281, 282, 283

oboe (*European double reed instrument*), 84, 270

ocarina (*globular flute instrument*), 37

O'Carolan, Turlough (*Irish harpist*), 281

O'Connor, Sinead (*Irish popular music singer*), 282

octave (*fundamental musical interval*), 8

o-daiko (*Japanese hanging bass drum*), 194, 199

Oequesta Sinfónica de Mexico, 309

Okinawa, 190, 196, 199, 213

Oliver, Joe "King" (*American jazz musician*), 343

Olmec (*ancient Mexican civilization*), 296

opera (*sung dramatic form*), Chinese 13, 164, 168–169, 171–173, 177, 182–187; European 4, 13, 269, 270, 271, 276, 288, 297, 299, 322, 342, 343

operetta (*music theater form*), 291, 308

orchestra (*large music ensemble*), 29; African, 55–58; balalaika, 263; Chinese, 163, 166, 168, 172, 174, 181, 183–184, 186, 189; Egyptian, 93; European, 31, 55, 93, 172, 181, 188, 212, 252, 269–271, 273, 276, 301, 322, 341; Korean, 31; in India, 129, 153; mandolin, 342, Mongolian ,119; jazz ,342, 346

orchestra, Indonesian, *see* gamelan

orchestra, Japanese, *see* gagaku

orchestration (*art of combining timbres*), 29, 277, 347

Oregon (*American jazz ensemble*), 160

organ (*European aerophone keyboard*), 271; electric, 346; *see also* harmonium

Original Evening Birds (*South African singing group*), 69

ornamentation (*method of elaborating melody*), 10, 11, 14, 16, 25–26; in Africa, 66; in Arabic music, 85, 90–93; in Austria, 278; in Bulgaria, 258, 260, 261; in China, 165, 169, 174, 176, 177–179, 184, 186; in Eastern Europe, 250, 252, 254, 258; in Hungary, 254; in India, 126, 128, 129, 133, 134, 138, 141, 142, 147, 148, 154, 156; in Iran, 77; in Ireland, 280, 281–282, 284–287; in Japan, 194, 196, 206, 207; in Jewish music, 102; in Mongolian music, 117, 120–121; in Spain, 290, 292; in Tibet, 107, 112; in United States, 331, 339, 344, 345, 346

Orozco, José Clemente (*Mexican muralist*), 309

ostinato (*short repeating melody*), 47, 51, 57–60, 62, 64, 68–70, 96, 237–238, 241, 263, 266, 314

o-tsuzumi (*Japanese cylindrical drum*), 208, 210

Ottoman Empire, 85, 102–103, 247, 253, 258, 276, *see also* Turkey

oud, *see* 'ud

overblowing (*aerophone playing technique*), 36, 209

overtone, *see* partial

P

paidushko (*Bulgarian round dance*), 259

Paiute (*indigenous American ethnic group*), 338

paixiao (*Chinese bamboo panpipes*), 171, 173

pakar (*characteristic motive in Indian raga*), 138, 143–145

pakhavaj (*double-headed cylindrical classical drum of North India*), 132, 147

Pakistan, 124, 127

Palestine, 76, 77

pallavi (*South Indian vocal refrain*), 148, 149–150

palmas (*clapping patterns in flamenco*), 290–291, 293–294

palm-wine music (*popular music style in West Africa*), 68

palos (*flamenco song forms*), 290

pandeiro (*Brazilian tambourine*), 313–314

Pan-Indian music, 338

panpipes (*collection of end-blown flutes*), 37, 171, 316, 317

Paraguay, 304

parallel octaves (*melody played with itself transposed by an octave*), 8, 24, 221, 316

Parker, Charlie (*American jazz musician*), 347–351

parlando-rubato (*Eastern European non-pulsatile style*), 254, 256, 258, 260

partial (*sine wave component of a timbre*), 109, 115, 118, 119 See also harmonic

paso doble, *see* two-step

Pata Negra (*Spanish popular music group*), 291

patet (*Javanese concept of mode, melodic basis*), 224, 227–229

patronage (*system of economic support for arts*), in Africa, 44, 59, 60–61, 63; in Central Asia, 106; in China, 183; in Eastern Europe, 253; in India, 125, 146–148; in Japan, 208–209; in Latin America, 315; in Middle East, 77, 80, 89, 93; in North America, 325; in Western Europe, 268, 270, 275–276

Paul Winter Consort (*American ensemble*), 160

Paul Butterfield Blues Band (*American ensemble*), 153

Pavón, Pastora (*Spanish flamenco singer*), 289–290

pedal steel guitar (*electronically amplified chordophone*), 327, 332

peking, *see* saron panerus

Peking opera, *see* jingxi

pelog (*Indonesian seven-tone tuning system*), 218, 222, 224, 235, 239

pemade (*Balinese metallophone*), 235, 236, 239, 240

pengawak (*main body of Balinese composition*), 240, 242

pengecet (*fast ending section in Balinese composition*), 241–242

pennywhistle jive, *see* kwela

pennywhistle, *see* tin whistle

pentatonic mode (*mode of five tones per octave*), xii, 10–11, 116–118, 120–121, 162, 167–168, 185, 188, 193, 195–196, 212, 254, 263, 265, 268, 274, 332, 336

Pentecostalism, 346

penyacah (*Balinese metallophone*), 236

pergetés (*Hungarian Romani "rolling" vocal improvisation*), 256–257

Persia, *see* Iran

Peru, 319

Pesta Kesenian Bali (Bali Arts Festival), 234–235

petia (*West African drum*), 40

Philippines, 214

Phillips, Sam (*American music producer*), 351–352

phrase (*section of melody*), 13, 15

piano (*European struck zither with keyboard*), 8–9, 10, 17, 30, 32, 33, 73, 79, 168, 253, 254, 270–271, 275, 281, 297, 301, 304, 308–309, 315, 340, 342–343, 346, 348–351

pick, *see* plectrum

pipa (*Chinese pear–shaped lute*), 163, 169, 170, 178–181, 189, 197

pipilan (*elaborating pattern for bonang*), 228

Pirin Mountains, Bulgaria, 259

pishdaramad (*Iranian instrumental form*), 96

pitch (*characteristic of sound associated with frequency*), 7, 11; definability 7–8

Plato (*ancient Greek philosopher*), 10, 166

plectrum (*device used to pluck strings*), 82, 113, 130, 197, 202, 326

poetry and music 47, 67, 80, 85, 87, 88, 96, 139, 146, 151, 163, 175, 183, 191, 274, 353

Pogues, The (*Irish band*), 282

pokok (*core melody in Balinese gamelan*), 217, 235, 239, 240

Pokrovsky, Dmitri (*Russian musician*), 252, 267

Poland, 246, 252

polca, *see* polka

polka (*European dance*), 297, 300, 304, 311

politics and music, *see* censorship, social protest music

Polo, Marco (*European explorer*), 106

polos (*one part in Balinese kotekan*), 239

polyphony (*texture of simultaneous independent melodies*), 24, 25–27, 46, 69, 122, 217, 223, 228, 238, 244, 257, 259, 261, 263, 265–267, 269, 277, 288, 301, 329, 343; imitative, 25; non-imitative, 25

polyrhythm (*multiple simultaneous meters*), 27; in Africa, 46–48, 51, 57–60, 62–65, 73, 194; in Middle East, 98; in India, 146, 238, 263, 297–298, 300, 304, 305, 310, 312, 340, 341, 350

polytonality (*multiple simultaneous tonal centers*), 309

Pomo (*indigenous American ethnic group*), 335

Ponce, Manuel (*Mexican composer*), 309

popular music (*music created by professionals for a mass audience*), 5, 10, 24, 26; form, 16; in Africa, 46, 60–61, 64, 67–73, 75; in China, 165, 166, 181, 186–189; in Eastern Europe, 248–249, 253–255; in Hungary, 253–255; in India, 127, 153–158; in Indonesia, 242–243, 245; in Japan, 193–194, 211–212; in Middle East, 78, 93–94, 96; in Tibet, 116; in Western Europe, 270, 271, 273–277, 282, 291, 297–301, 304, 308, 315, 318, 321–324, 332–333, 341–347, 351–356; Jewish, 100–104; tempo, 19; texture, 24–26

portamento (*continuous sliding pitch*),102, *see also* glissando

Portugal, 99, 242–243, 297, 309, 326

potlatch (*indigenous northwest American ritual festival*), 337

powwow (*indigenous American meeting and ritual*), 339

praise singing, 44, 59–60, 62–64

pregonero (*lead singer in Mexican band*), 305

Presley, Elvis (*American rock and roll singer*), 351–352

prichitaniya (*Russian lament song*), 264

primitivism (*artistic style*), 315

printing, music, *see* music printing

pripevki (*Russian sung work calls*), 262

professional folk ensembles (*professional performers of music in the style of folk music*), 107, 249, 251–252, 255, 258, 333

programmaticism (*music which evokes a scene or tells a story*), 119, *see also* extramusical associations

progressive rock (*popular music style*), 324, 353

Prokofiev, Sergei (*Russian composer*), 252

provikvaniyo (*Bulgarian sung ornament*), 258, 259

psalm (*Biblical poetic praise song*), 99, 325

psaltery (*medieval European zither*), 83

Puebla, Mexico, 308

pueblo (*indigenous American dwelling*), 337

Puerto Rico, 299

puja (*Tibetan Buddhist prayer ritual*), 113–114

punk rock (*popular music style*), 277, 282, 354

Puno, Peru, 316

Pygmy (*Central African ethnic group*), 50, 74

Pythagoras (*ancient Greek philosopher*), 167

Q

qanun (*Middle Eastern plucked zither*), 83, 89, 92, 104

qasidah (*Arabic song form*), 90, 93

qawal (*Sufi mystics and singers of Islamic songs*),146

qawwali (*tradition of Islamic songs from Pakistan*), 146–147

qin, *see* guqin

qing (*Chinese stone chime*), 162, 173

qira'ah (*Islamic chant*), 80–81

quadrille (*European dance*), 300

quarter-tone (*very small pitch interval*), 79, 86, 93, 95, 97

Quechua (*Andean ethnic group/language*), 316

quotation (*brief incorporation of existing music into composition*), 349

Qur'an (*sacred book of Islam*), 78, 80

R

R&B, *see* rhythm and blues

rabab (*Middle Eastern bowed chordophone*), 45, 82, 94, 170

radif (*collection of Iranian dastgah*), 95, 97

radio, 2, 5, 81, 93, 94, 126, 139, 152, 153, 181, 187, 252, 275–276, 332, 352

raft zither, *see* zither, raft

raga (*basis of melodic improvisation in India*), 11, 128, 133, 134–139, 141–144, 147, 153–155, 156, 158, 160; extramusical associations, 138–139; motives, 138, 141, 143–145; ornamentation, 138, 141–142; scales, 135–137, 150; time associations, 139

ragamala (*collection of paintings symbolically illustrating Indian raga*), 11, 139, 141

ragam-tanam-pallavi (*long South Indian vocal form*),148

ragtime (*American popular music form*), 322, 341–343, 345, 346

raï (*Algerian popular music form*), 94

Rajasthan, India, 151

rallentando, *see* ritardando

Ramayana (*ancient Hindu epic*), 215, 238

Rangda (*Balinese mythical witch*), 242

range (*interval between highest and lowest melodic pitch*), 10, 11, 13, 121

rap (*popular music style*), 324

rasa (*Indian aesthetic emotion*),138

rasgueado (*guitar playing technique*), 290–291, 304

Ratkó, Slovakia, 247

rattle (*category of shaken idiophone*), 42, 47, 50, 53, 54, 57–58, 64, 301, 335

rebab (*Indonesian spike fiddle*), 219, 221, 223, 230, 231, 243

recorder (*European duct flute*), 283

recording technology, 2, 61, 68, 93, 129, 133, 139, 154–155, 188, 211, 212, 249, 258, 275–276, 281, 298, 300, 303, 304, 311, 322, 323, 324, 332, 339, 345, 347, 351–353, 354–356

reco-reco (*Brazilian metal spring scraper*), 313–314

Reece, Florence (*American songwriter*), 333

reed (*small piece of wood used in aerophone mouthpieces*), 36, *see also* double reed, single reed

reel (*Irish dance*), 284, 331

Reformation (*period of religious division in Europe*), 269

refrain (*section with repeated words and music*), 15–16, 90, 92, 94, 117, 148–151, 154–159, 274, 289, 329, 343, 355

reggae (*Caribbean popular music style*), 68

Renaissance (*period of European history*), 269, 271

reng (*Iranian instrumental form*), 96

repenique (*cylindrical drum in Brazilian samba*), 311, 313–314

repetition and musical form, 14–16

requinto (*small Mexican guitar*), 303, 304, 305, 307

resonance (*amplification by acoustic reinforcement*), 30, 36, 39

responsorial form (*alternation between group, soloist*), 47, 57, 60, 68, 70, 85, 99, 195, 203, 263, 264, 297, 306–307, 324, 338, 340–341, 345, 354

Revueltas, Silvestre (*Mexican composer*), 309, 318

reyong (*Balinese set of kettle-gongs*), 235, 236

rgya-gling (*Tibetan conical double-reed instruments*), 112

Rhapsody in Blue (*composition by George Gershwin*), 346

rhythm and music, 17–22

rhythm and blues (*American popular music style*), 3, 67–68, 69, 70, 323, 351–352, 354

rhythm guitar (*guitar in role of emphasizing rhythm by strumming*), 299, 301

rhythm section (*section in jazz band*), 343, 346

rhythmic density (*notes per beat*),16, 183, 226, 228, 230, 257

Rig-Veda (*ancient Hindu book of prayers*), 124

Riley, Terry (*American composer*),160

ring shout (*early African-American participatory music*), 340, 346

Rio de Janeiro, Brazil, 311, 312, 315

riqq (*Middle Eastern tambourine*), 84, 88, 89, 90, 91

Rise (*section in indigenous American song*), 337

ritardando (*gradual slowing of tempo*), 19

ritsu (*Japanese mode*),198

Rivera, Diego (*Mexican muralist*), 309

Riverdance (*stage show of Irish dance*),189, 282

Roach, Max (*American jazz drummer*), 347–350

rock and roll (*popular music genre*), 2, 4, 61, 154, 160, 188, 194, 212, 243, 277, 282, 291, 301, 308, 312, 315, 318, 323–324, 339, 344, 345, 347, 351–354, 355

rock, *see* rock and roll

roll (*Irish ornament*), 285

rolling, *see* pergetés

Roma (*Eurasian ethnic group*),105, 247, 253, 255–258, 259, 267, 288

Roman Catholic Church (*Christian denomination*), 246, 268, 269, 272, 296, 298, 315, 316, See also Christianity

Roman Empire, 76, 99, 246, 268, 288, 289

romance, *see* romancero

romancero (*Sephardic Jewish song form*), 101

Romania, 14, 102, 246, 247, 248, 251, 255

Romanticism (*European artistic period/style*), 248, 270

Romungre (*Hungarian ethnic group*), 256

ronda (*Spanish folk song*), 289

Ronda, Spain, 294

rondalla (*Spanish street singers*), 289–290

root (*fundamental pitch in triad*), 273

round (*form of imitative polyphony*), 25

rta (*Tibetan chants*), 111

ruan (*Chinese lute with circular resonator*), 170, 172

rubato (*flexible tempo*), 254

ruchenitsa (*Bulgarian round dance*), 259

rudra vina, *see* bin

rul-mo (*Tibetan cymbals*), 111, 112, 113–115

rul-mo (*Tibetan ritual instrumental music*), 112, 113–115

rum (*Afro-Brazilian drum*), 310, 311

rumba (*dance form in Cuba*), 299, 300

Rumi, Jalal al-Din (*Iranian poet*), 81, 95

rumpi (*Afro-Brazilian drum*), 310

Russell, Curly (*American jazz musician*), 347–348

Russia, 106, 109, 246, 252, 253, 262–267, 323; art music, 251–252, 266, 288; Byzantine influence, 246, 263; Central Asian influence, 263; influence on Central Asia,107; Jewish music in, 96, 100, 264; mode, 263; musical form, 263, 264–266; musical instruments, 41, 263–264; song types, 262–263; wedding music, 263–267; *see also* Union of Soviet Socialist Republics

ryo (*Japanese mode*), 195–196

ryuku (*mode from Okinawa, Japan*), 196

ryuteki (*Japanese transverse bamboo flute*), 196–201

S

Sachs, Curt, 31

Sacred Harp, The 321, 328, *see also* shape-note singing

Saddler, Joseph, *see* Grandmaster Flash

Sakamoto, Ryuichi (*Japanese popular music composer*), 212

salsa (*Latin American popular music form*), 299

Salvador, Brazil, 297

sam (*first beat of Indian tala cycle*), 140

sama'i (*Arabic instrumental form*), 90

Samarkand, Uzbekistan, 107

Sama-Veda (*ancient collection of Hindu chants*), 124, 126, 148

samba (*Brazilian dance*), 54, 298, 299, 300, 309–315, 318

samba cancão (*sung version of samba*), 311

samba schools (*large associations of samba musicians/dancers*), 309, 311, 312

sampling (*use of digital recording playback in music*), 324, 355–356

samurai (*class of Japanese warrior-leaders*),191

samvadi (*secondary stressed pitch in Indian raga*), 137, 142, 143, 144

San (*southern African ethnic group*), 44

San Luis Potosí, Mexico, 298

Sanchez, Michael (*French popular music composer*), 356

sangsih (*one part in Balinese kotekan*), 239

sankyoku (*Japanese classical chamber music*), 193, 202, 203

san-no-tsuzumi (*Japanese cylindrical drum*), 197

santur (*Middle Eastern hammered zither*), 33, 83, 95, 171, 254

santuri (*Indian hammered zither*), 138

sanxian (*Chinese long neck fretless lute*), 172, 178, 181, 199

sarangi (*Indian bowed lute*), 129, 131, 132, 147, 151, 154–158

sa-rarin (*koto ornament*), 207

Sargent, John Singer (*American painter*), 290

sarod (*plucked lute in India*), 33, 126, 129, 130, 132,142–145, 159

saron (*Javanese metallophone*), 220, 223, 227, 231, 243

saron barung (*middle octave member of saron family*), 220

saron demung (*low octave member of saron family*), 220, 226

saron panerus (*high octave member of saron family*),220, 226

sasabuki (*shakuhachi playing technique*), 204

satokagura (*Japanese folk festival performances*), 193

Saudi Arabia, 77, 85

saval-javab (*question-answer section in Indian improvisation*), 145

sax jive, *see* mbaqanga

saxophone (*European single-reed aerophone*), 37, 67, 69, 72, 94, 102, 160, 250, 301, 341, 343, 346, 347–350, 352, 354

sayr (*basis for Arabic maqam improvisation*), 87, 92

saz (*Turkish long neck lute*), 82

scale (*available pitches in order starting on tonic for one octave*), 10–11; in Africa, 62; in Arabic music, 76, 79, 85–88, 91–92, 93; in China, 167–168, 176–178, 183, 185–186; in Eastern Europe, 247, 254, 263, 265; in India, 124, 125, 133, 134–138, 141–145, 149–150, 155, 156, 158; in Indonesia, 235, 239; in Iran, 95–98; in Japan, 193, 195–196, 204, 207; in Jewish music, 100, 102, 103; in Latin America, 301; in Mongolia, 120–121; in Tibet, 113; in United States, 160, 325–326, 338, 340; in Western Europe, 268, 273–275, 278–279, 287; *see also* mode, tuning system

Scandinavia, 323, 327

scat (*sung improvised syllables in jazz*), 146

Schoenberg, Arnold (*Austrian composer*), 270

Schrammel, Johann (*Austrian musician*), 277

Schrammel, Joseph (*Austrian musician*), 277

Schrammelgitare (*Austrian double-neck harp-guitar*), 277

Scotland, 274, 283, *see also* United Kingdom, Great Britain

scratching (*use of turntable as a musical instrument*), 354–355

Scruggs, Earl (*American bluegrass musician*), 332–333

se (*ancient Chinese zither*), 166–167

sean nós (*traditional Irish non-pulsatile song form*), 281, 282, 284

Sebestyén, Marta (*Hungarian singer*), 255, 267

Sebö, Ferenc (*Hungarian musician*), 255

Seeger, Charles (*American ethnomusicologist*), xvi

Seeger, Pete (*American folk singer*), 326, 333

sehtar (*Iranian long neck lute*), 35, 82, 95

selisir (*Balinese subset of pelog*), 235

Senegal, 59, 61, 69

Sephardim (*Jewish people from Mediterranean region*), 99, 101, 104

sequence (*melody repeated at successive transpositions*), 98

Serbia, 248, 251

seron (*lyre from Uganda*), 35

sesquialtera (*Latin American dance rhythm*), 299, 300, 302, 305–307

session (*informal Irish gathering for music*), 280

Sex Pistols (*punk rock band*), 354

sextilla (*Spanish poetic form*), 304, 306

sgra-snyan (*Tibetan plucked fretless long-neck lute*), 113

sha'bi (*Egyptian popular music style*), 93

shahed (*stressed pitch in Iranian dastgah*), 98

shahnai (*double reed instrument in India*), 38, 40, 131, 132, 151

Shahryar (*Indian lyricist*), 154

Shakespeare, William (*English writer*), 182, 183

Shakti (*fusion Western-Indian band*), 159, 161

shakuhachi (*Japanese vertical bamboo notch flute*), 191–192, 195, 196, 202, 203–205, 212, 213

shamanism (*traditional religious practice*), 110, 117, 181

shamisen (*Japanese fretless long-neck lute*), 192, 193, 196, 199, 202–203, 210, 211

Shanghai, China, 178, 182

Shanghai opera (*regional Chinese opera*), 182

Shankar, Lakshminarayanan (*South Indian violinist*), 159

Shankar, Ravi (*Indian sitarist*), 130, 142, 159, 160

Shankar, Uday (*Indian choreographer*), 159

shape-note singing (*tradition of American amateur choral music*), 321–322, 328–330, 345, 356

sharp (*notation to raise scale step by a semitone*), 86, 135

Sharp, Cecil (*English ethnomusicologist*), 331–332, 345

shawm (*medieval European double reed instrument*), 84

Sheehy, Daniel (*American ethnomusicologist*), 305

sheng (*Chinese single reed mouth organ*), 172, 173, 178, 197

Shi Huangdi (*Chinese emperor*), 162

shinkyoku (*Japanese new compositions for traditional instruments*), 194, 204

shinobue (*Japanese transverse bamboo flute*), 210

Shinto (*traditional Japanese religion*), 192, 193–194, 198

shishi-mai (*Japanese folk lion dance*), 193

shitakata (*ensemble used in kabuki drama*), 210

sho (*Japanese single reed mouth organ*), 29, 196–201

shofar (*Jewish ram's horn trumpet*), 99

shoka (*modern Japanese school songs*), 211

shoko (*Japanese small metal gong*), 197–200

shomyo (*Japanese Zen Buddhist chant*), 194–195, 209

Shona (*Southern African ethnic group*), 64

short songs, *see* bogino duu

Shostakovich, Dmitri (*Russian composer*), 252

shteygers (*modes in Jewish cantoral singing*), 100

shuddh (*Indian scale step which is neither raised nor lowered*), 135

Siberia, Russia, 110

Sichuan opera (*regional Chinese opera*), 182

Sierra Leone, 74

sihu (*Chinese four-string fiddle*), 178

siku (*Andean panpipes*), 37, 316–318

Silk Road (*Asian trade route*), 106, 163

silk-and-bamboo music, *see* sizhu

Simon, Paul (*American popular musician*), 2–3, 69, 331, 333

simple meter (*meter with beats divisible by two*), 20, 47–48, 88, 98, 251, 256, 284, 291, 300, 302, 348

Sina, Abu Ali Ibn (*medieval Islamic scholar*), 77

single reed (*category of aerophones*), 36–38, *see also individual instruments*

Sioux (*indigenous American ethnic group*), 333–334, 338

sitar (*plucked lute from India*), 8, 31, 33, 126, 129, 130, 132, 154–158, 159

siter (*Javanese small box zither*), 221

sizhu (*Chinese silk and bamboo chamber music*), 174, 178–180

skiffle (*English popular music style*), 69

skomorokh (*Russian wedding entertainer*), 264–266

slack key tuning (*method for tuning guitar strings*), 327

slap bass (*double bass played with rebounding strings*), 352, 354

slavery, 45, 50, 276, 296, 301, 309–310, 320, 323, 326

slendro (*Indonesian five-tone tuning system*), 218, 222

slentem (*Javanese metallophone*), 220, 223, 230, 231

slide (*device for changing pitch on an aerophone*), 36, 343

slide (*Irish dance*), 284

slide guitar (*chordophone allowing continuous pitch slides*), 33, 326–327, 345, *see also* pedal steel guitar, Hawaiian guitar

slide trumpet (*European buzzed-lip aerophone with slide*), 343

Sligo, Ireland, 280

slip jig (*Irish dance*), 21, 284, 286–287

Slovakia, 246, 248, 249

slow air (*Irish instrumental form*), 284

Smith, Bessie (*American blues singer*), 345

snare (*device for creating rattling sound on drums*), 39, 335

snare drum (*type of membranophone*), 39, 311, 353

Social Harp, The (*shape-note publication or singing from it*), 325, 356, See also shape-note singing

social protest in music, 67–68, 70–73, 94, 118, 187–189, 243, 244, 311, 315, 333, 353, 355

socialist realism (*policy in which art should serve the state*), 166, 181, 183, 248, 250, 251–252

sogo (*low drum from Ghana*), 55, 58–59

sokattu (*pattern of South Indian drumming syllables*), 141

soleá (*traditional flamenco song form*), 291

solfege (*syllables used to indicate scale steps*), 135, 146, 148, 325, 328–329

Solo, *see* Surakarta

solo, jazz (*section featuring single performer improvisation in jazz*), 343, 345–351

Solomon Islands, 356

son (*Mexican instrumental music*), 297, 302–307, 318

Songhai, 44

Songs for the Masses (*Chinese political song form*), 165, 181

songsters (*early African-American singers*), 344

sornay (*Iranian double reed instrument*), 84, *see also* zurna

soul (*African-American popular music genre*), 68, 344, 354

Soul Train (*music television show*), 354

Sousa, John Philip (*American wind band composer*), 341, 342

sousaphone (*low buzzed-lip aerophone invented as portable tuba*), 341

South Africa, 2–3, 69

South Carolina, United States, 340

South Dakota, United States, 338–339

Southern Harmony, The (*publication of shape-note music*), 328

Soviet Union, *see* Union of Soviet Socialist Republics

Spain, 80, 269, 282, 288–295, 296–297, 320; Arabic influence, 77, 82, 90, 268, 288–290, 300; folk music, 288–295; influence of Latin America, 291; influence of United States, 291; influence on Latin America, 296–298, 301, 304, 308, 316; influence on United States, 326; history, 288; Jewish people in, 99, 101, 288, 290; musical form, 290; musical instruments, 82,

289–290, 326; popular music, 291; Romani people in, 247, 256, 291–294

spike fiddle (*category of chordophones*), 34, 82, 117, 170, 221, *see also* lute

spiritual (*type of American religious song*), 325, 328, 340, 344, 345

spoons (*used as musical instrument*), 257, 283

Sri Lanka, 124

sruti (*microtone or step in Indian tuning system*), 134

sruti box (*South Indian reed organ used as drone*), 133

Stalin, Josef (*Soviet leader*), 251, 252

stanza (*section of song*), 15–16, 274, 289, 293, 343, *see also* verse

starini (*Russian epic songs*), 251

step dance (*dance style in which upper body remains mostly still*), 284

sthai (*first half of Indian form*), 142, 143–144

stick zither, *see* zither, stick

strain (*section of European/American march or dance*), 341

Strauss Jr., Johann (*Austrian composer*), 269–270, 271

Stravinsky, Igor (*Russian composer*), 252, 266, 270

string band (*American popular ensemble of chordophones*), 332, 340–341, 342

string bass, *see* double bass

string instrument, *see* chordophone

string quartet (*European ensemble of violin family instruments*), 29, 30

strophic form (*form with repeating melody and changing lyrics*), 15, 92, 118, 272, 284, 334

structure, *see* musical form

Subramaniam, Lakshminarayanan (*South Indian violinist*), 160

Sufism, 81, 84, 90, 105

suite (*collection of pieces performed together*), 89, 90

Suixian, Hubei, China, 173

suizen (*meditation practice aided by shakuhachi*), 204

Sulawesi, Indonesia, 37

suling (*Indonesian bamboo duct flute*), 37, 221, 230, 231, 235, 240

Sumatra, Indonesia, 215

suona (*Chinese double reed instrument*), 171, 173, 177, 184, 189, 243

Surakarta, Java, Indonesia, 215, 218, 219, 224–225, 244

surdo (*Brazilian bass drum*), 313

surnay (*double reed from Central Asia*), 84, *see also* zurna

Suso, Foday Musa (*Gambian musician*), 61

Suso, Nyama (*Gambian musician*), 62–64

suyue (*Chinese term for folk music*), 167

Svadebka (*cantata by Igor Stravinsky*), 266

svara (*scale steps in Indian music*), 135

svara kalpana (*South Indian vocal improvisation on solfege*), 148

swing (*style of jazz music, dance*), 68, 300, 323, 346

swing rhythm (*style of performing beat divisions unequally in jazz*), 348–349

symbolism, musical 167–168, *see also* extramusical associations

sympathetic vibration (*acoustical phenomenon of transferred vibration*), 31, 39, 130, 131, 133, 260

symphony (*large composition for European orchestra*), 273, 309

symphony orchestra, *see* orchestra, European

synagogue (*Jewish place of worship*), 76, 99, 102

syncopated orchestra (*American popular music ensemble*), 342

syncopation (*shifting of expected metrical stress*), 21–22, 100, 157, 194, 239, 243, 256, 300, 311, 314, 315, 317, 324, 329–330, 341–342, 345, 348–349, 350, 353

syncretism (*anthropological phenomenon between meeting cultures*), 298, 302, 316

synthesizer (*electrophone which electronically synthesizes tones*), 94, 189, 212, 243, 255, 280, 282, 318, 324, 339, 355–356

Syria, 89

szajbögö (*Romani "mouth bass" sung dance music*), 256–258

T

ta'amim (*signs to indicate Jewish cantillation formulas*), 99

tabla (*pair of Indian hand drums*), 126, 132, 144–145, 147, 154, 155

table song (*Georgian song with improvised sung polyphony*), 263

tabuh (*Balinese melodic pattern*), 237–238

Tagayasu, Den (*Japanese musician*), 194

tahmilah (*Arabic form with alternating solos*), 90

taiko (*Japanese cylindrical drum*), 194, 208, 210

taiko drumming ensemble (*Japanese drum ensemble*), 194, 212

Taiwan, 165, 188

Taj Mahal (*Indian architectural landmark*), 147

Tajikstan, 106

takebue (*Japanese transverse bamboo flute*), 193, 210

Takemitsu, Toru (*Japanese composer*), 194, 212, 213

takht (*Arabic classical ensemble*), 89, 90

Taki, Rentaro (*Japanese composer*), 211

taksim, *see* taqsim

tala (*Indian metrical system*), 128, 139–141, 142–145, 147, 149, 155

Talking Heads (*American new wave band*), 354

tambourine (*frame drum with small cymbals*), 39, 84, 88–89, 91–93, 150, 156, 310, 313

tambura (*Bulgarian long-neck lute*), 260

tambura (*fretless lute for playing drones in India*), 82, 128, 131, 133, 143, 147, 149

tampura, *see* tambura

tanbur (*Arabic long neck lute*), 81, 82

tancház (*type of Hungarian popular music*), 255, 267

Tang dynasty (*period in Chinese history*), 106, 163

Tangerine Dream (*German electronic music group*), 355

tango (*Argentinian dance*), 298, 299, 300

tanka (*Buddhist religious painting*), 108, 113

tanpura, *see* tambura

tans (*fast scalar passages in North Indian performances*), 147

Tansen, Miyam (*North Indian musician*), 125, 159

tantra (*esoteric Buddhist teachings*), 110, 122

Tanzania, 74

Taoism, *see* Daoism

taqsim (*Arabic solo improvisation*), 87, 90, 92, 95, 100, 102

tar (*Iranian plucked lute*), 82, 95, 97–98

tar (*Middle Eastern frame drum*), 84

tarab (*Arabic ecstasy in musical performance*), 85, 89, 94

taraf (*Indian sympathetic strings*), 130, 133

tarana (*North Indian vocal form*), 147, 148

taslim (*recurring phrase in Arabic musical form*), 91

tasnif (*Iranian classical song*), 96

Tchaikovsky, Piotr (*Russian composer*), 288

techno, *see* electronic dance music

television and music, 81, 94, 183, 187, 212, 252, 276, 309, 354, 356

tempo (*speed of music*), 15, 16, 19, 54, 146–147, 179–180, 183, 193, 198, 219, 223, 230–231, 237, 254, 284, 347–348, 356

tempo giusto (*Eastern European metered style*), 254

Tennessee, United States, 345, 351

teponatzli (*Aztec wooden slit drum*), 296

terkish (*Jewish dance*), 103

tessitura (*pitch of melody relative to instrument/vocal range*), 13

tetrachord (*scale of four notes*), 85, 88

Texas, United States, 304, 318, 332

texture (*relative distribution and role of melodies*), 16, 23–27, See also heterophony, homophony, monophony, polyphony

Thailand, 9, 25

that (*North Indian scale*), 135–137

theka (*pattern of North Indian drumming syllables*), 141, 146

theme (*whole recognizable, recurring melody*), 15

theme and variations form (*structure consisting of repeating, varied melody*), 16, 60, 66, 165, 174, 176–177, 178–180, 206–207

theory, *see* music theory

thrash metal (*genre of rock music*), 354

throat singing, *see* multiphonic singing

thumri (*North Indian light classical romantic songs*), 147, 154–155

Tibet, 13, 106–118, 195, 277; art music, 116; dance, 113, 116; folk music, 113; Chinese influence, 106, 110, 113, 116; influence of India, 106, 110, 113, 116; influence on Mongolia, 111; mode, 113; musical instruments, 111–113; popular music, 116; ritual music, 110–115, 122; Western influence, 116

Tibetan Institute of Performing Arts (*Tibetan expatriate arts institution*), 116, 112

tilawah (*Islamic chant*), 80–81

tillana (*South Indian vocal form to accompany dance*), 148

timbales (*Cuban drums*), 301

timbre (*tone color*), 29, 165, 250

Timbuktu, Mali, 45

timpani (*large European hemispherical drums*), 49, 341

Timur (*Central Asian emperor*), 107

Tin Pan Alley (*New York area of popular music publishers and their style*), 322, 342, 346

tin whistle (*European metal duct flute*), 69, 283, 285–286

tivra (*raised Indian scale step*), 135

togaku (*repertory of gagaku*), 196

Togbui Adeladza II (*Ewe king*), 46

Tokyo, Japan, 196

Toltec (*Central American civilization*), 296

tombak (*Iranian goblet drum*), 41, 84, *see also* darrabukka

tomoraba (*West African tuning system*), 62

tonal center see tonic

tonality (*sense of attraction to one pitch in scale*), 9–10, 62, 128, 176, 209

tone poem (*European programmatic form*), 309

tone-contour melody (*Tibetan chant with slow continuous variations in pitch, timbre, and loudness*), 109, 115

tongsu (*Chinese popular songs*), 188

tonic (*pitch in scale which gives sense of finality to melody*), 9–11, 16, 66, 82, 86, 91, 92, 96–98, 103, 120–121,

128, 132, 133–137, 142–146, 149–150, 168, 176, 200–201, 227, 273, 278–279, 284–285, 287–288, 291–292, 322, 329

topeng (*Indonesian masked dance*), 214, 237–238

topshuur (*Mongolian plucked unfretted lute*), 119

töshe (*Tibetan instrumental art music*), 116, 122

totombito (*raft zither from the Congo*), 53

Touré, Ali Farka (*popular musician from Mali*), 74

township jive, *see* mbaqanga

Tozan (*tradition of shakuhachi instruction*), 204

trance (*genre of electronic dance music*), 356

trance and music, 64, 242, 297, 333–334, 338–339, 340

transposition (*moving all pitches in a melody by a fixed amount*), 16, 86, 168, 195, 229, 254, 256

transverse flute, *see* flute, transverse

Transylvania, Romania, 255

tremolo (*rapid oscillation in loudness of note*), 82, 83, 91, 179, 203, 207

tresillo (*Cuban rhythm*), 300

triad (*type of chord in European harmony*), 156, 211, 252, 273, 276, 278–279, 286–287, 288–289, 301, 325, 327, 329–330, 341, 344, 347

triangle (*metal idiophone*), 7

triangular harp, *see* angle harp

trill (*ornament consisting of rapid alternation between two adjacent pitches*), 14, 179, 260

triple meter (*beat groupings into threes*), 20–21, 47–48, 92, 96, 276, 284, 286, 287, 289, 291, 300, 301

trombone (*European buzzed-lip instrument*), 36, 102, 126, 270, 341, 342, 343, 346, 354

troubadour (*European medieval poet/ composer*), 274

trough zither, *see* zither, trough

trumpet (*category of buzzed-lip aerophones*), 48, 51, 72, 99, 108, 110–112, 114–115

trumpet (*European buzzed-lip aerophone*), 36, 67, 72, 126, 188, 243, 270, 274, 289, 301, 303, 304, 343, 346–348, 350, 354

trumpet, slide (*European buzzed-lip aerophone*), 343

tshig rnga (*percussion interjections in Tibetan ritual music*), 115

Tsukushi (*tradition of koto instruction*), 192

tsuri-daiko (*Japanese hanging bass drum*), 197–200

tuba (*European low buzzed-lip instrument*), 126, 270, 341, 343

tube zither, *see* zither, tube

Tumbash ensemble (*Mongolian traditional music ensemble*), 117

tuna, *see* rondalla

tuning system (*selection of pitches to be represented on an instrument or in a musical system*), 8–11, 62, 85–86, 97, 128, 134–135, 160, 163, 167, 180, 181, 196, 216, 218, 222, 224, 227, 239, 243, 272, 277, 324, 326, 340

tupan (*Bulgarian bass drum*), 40, 260, 261–262

Turkey, 85, 89, 90, 102–103, 105, 246–248, 250, 251; influence on Bulgaria, 258, 259; influence on Eastern Europe, 247–248, 253–254, 258, 259; influence on Hungary, 253–254; musical instruments, 82–84; religious music, 81; *see also* Byzantine Empire, Ottoman Empire

Turkmenistan, 106

turntablism (*use of turntable as a musical instrument*), 354–355

tuul' (*Mongolian epic songs*), 118

Tuva, Russia, 109, 122

Twelve Girls Band (*Chinese ensemble*), 189

twelve-bar blues (*harmonic progression found in blues and other genres*), 344, 353

twelve-tone equal temperament (*standard Western tuning system*), 8–9, 167–168, 181, 272, 324

two-step (*European dance*), 297, 300, 304

ty ba (*fretted plucked lute from Vietnam*), 32

Tyagaraja (*Indian poet, composer*), 126, 148–150, 151

U

U2 (*Irish popular music band*), 282

'ud (*Middle Eastern lute*), 10, 81, 82, 89, 91, 94

ugal (*Balinese metallophone*), 235, 236, 237, 240–241

Uganda, 35, 40, 51–53

uilleann pipes (*form of Irish bagpipes*), 281, 283, 285–287

Ukraine, 102, 251

Umbanda (*South American religion*), 310, 311

Umrao Jaan (*Indian film*), 154–158

Union of Soviet Socialist Republics, 107, 181, 246, 248, 251–252, 258; *see also* Armenia, Azerbaijan, Belarus, Georgia, Kazakhstan, Kyrgystan, Moldova, Russia, Tajikstan, Turkmenistan, Ukraine, Uzbekistan

United Kingdom, 45, 127, 155, 188, 320, 321, 353; influence on Africa, 69; influence on India, 126, 129, 131; influence on Ireland, 281–283; influence on United States, 323, 331–333, 353